The Essential St. John of the Cross

The Essential St. John of the Cross
by Saint John of the Cross

Ascent of Mount Carmel
Dark Night of the Soul
A Spiritual Canticle of the Soul
and the Bridegroom Christ
Twenty Poems by St. John of the Cross

©2008 Wilder Publications

Wilder Publications, LLC.
PO Box 3005
Radford VA 24143-3005

ISBN 10: 1-60459-284-2
ISBN 13: 978-1-60459-284-9

Ascent of Mount Carmel

Translated by E. Allison Peers

Table of Contents

BOOK I

BOOK II

BOOK III

Translator's Preface to the First Edition

For at least twenty years, a new translation of the works of St. John of the Cross has been an urgent necessity. The translations of the individual prose works now in general use go back in their original form to the eighteen-sixties, and, though the later editions of some of them have been submitted to a certain degree of revision, nothing but a complete retranslation of the works from their original Spanish could be satisfactory. For this there are two reasons.

First, the existing translations were never very exact renderings of the original Spanish text even in the form which held the field when they were first published. Their great merit was extreme readableness: many a disciple of the Spanish mystics, who is unacquainted with the language in which they wrote, owes to these translations the comparative ease with which he has mastered the main lines of St. John of the Cross's teaching. Thus for the general reader they were of great utility; for the student, on the other hand, they have never been entirely adequate. They paraphrase difficult expressions, omit or add to parts of individual sentences in order (as it seems) to facilitate comprehension of the general drift of the passages in which these occur, and frequently retranslate from the Vulgate the Saint's Spanish quotations from Holy Scripture instead of turning into English the quotations themselves, using the text actually before them.

A second and more important reason for a new translation, however, is the discovery of fresh manuscripts and the consequent improvements which have been made in the Spanish text of the works of St. John of the Cross, during the present century. Seventy years ago, the text chiefly used was that of the collection known as the Biblioteca de Autores Espanoles (1853), which itself was based, as we shall later see, upon an edition going back as far as 1703, published before modern methods of editing were so much as imagined. Both the text of the B.A.E. edition and the unimportant commentary which accompanied it were highly unsatisfactory, yet until the beginning of the present century nothing appreciably better was attempted.

In the last twenty years, however, we have had two new editions, each based upon a close study of the extant manuscripts and each representing a great advance upon the editions preceding it. The three-volume Toledo edition of P. Gerardo de San Juan de la Cruz, C.D. (1912-14), was the first attempt made to produce an accurate text by modern critical methods. Its execution was perhaps less laudable than its conception, and faults were pointed out in it from the time of its appearance, but it served as a new starting-point for Spanish scholars and stimulated them to a new interest in St. John of the Cross's writings. Then, seventeen years later, came the magnificent five-volume edition of P. Silverio de Santa Teresa, C.D. (Burgos, 1929-31), which forms the basis of this present translation. So superior is it, even on the most casual examination, to all its predecessors that to eulogize it in detail is superfluous. It is founded upon a larger number of texts than has previously been known and it collates them with greater skill than that of any earlier editor. It can hardly fail to be the standard edition of the works of St. John of the Cross for generations.

Thanks to the labours of these Carmelite scholars and of others whose findings they have incorporated in their editions, Spanish students can now approach the work of the great Doctor with the reasonable belief that they are reading, as nearly as may be, what he actually wrote. English-reading students, however, who are unable to master sixteenth-century Spanish, have hitherto had no grounds for such a belief. They cannot tell whether, in any particular passage, they are face to face with the Saint's own words, with a translator's free paraphrase of them or with a gloss made by some later copyist or early editor in the supposed interests of orthodoxy. Indeed, they cannot be sure that some whole paragraph is not one of the numerous interpolations which has its rise in an early printed edition — i.e., the timorous qualifications of statements which have seemed to the interpolator over-bold. Even some of the most distinguished writers in English on St. John of the Cross have been misled in this way and it has been impossible for any but those who read Spanish with ease to make a systematic and reliable study of such an important question as the alleged dependence of Spanish quietists upon the Saint, while his teaching on the mystical life has quite unwittingly been distorted by persons who would least wish to misrepresent it in any particular.

It was when writing the chapter on St. John of the Cross in the first volume of my Studies of the Spanish Mystics (in which, as it was published in 1927, I had not the advantage of using P. Silverio's edition) that I first realized the extent of the harm caused by the lack of an accurate and modern translation. Making my own versions of all the passages quoted, I had sometimes occasion to compare them with those of other translators, which at their worst were almost unrecognizable as versions of the same originals. Then and there I resolved that, when time allowed, I would make a fresh translation of the works of a saint to whom I have long had great devotion — to whom, indeed, I owe more than to any other writer outside the Scriptures. Just at that time I happened to visit the Discalced Carmelites at Burgos, where I first met P. Silverio, and found, to my gratification, that his edition of St. John of the Cross was much nearer publication than I had imagined. Arrangements for sole permission to translate the new edition were quickly made and work on the early volumes was begun even before the last volume was published.

II

These preliminary notes will explain why my chief preoccupation throughout the performance of this task has been to present as accurate and reliable a version of St. John of the Cross's works as it is possible to obtain. To keep the translation, line by line, au pied de la lettre, is, of course, impracticable: and such constantly occurring Spanish habits as the use of abstract nouns in the plural and the verbal construction 'ir + present participle' introduce shades of meaning which cannot always be reproduced. Yet wherever, for stylistic or other reasons, I have departed from the Spanish in any way that could conceivably cause a misunderstanding, I have scrupulously indicated this in a footnote. Further, I have translated, not only the text, but the variant readings as given by P. Silverio, except where they are due merely to slips of the copyist's pen or where they differ so slightly from the readings of the text that it is impossible to render the differences in English. I beg students not to think that some of the smaller changes noted are of no importance; closer examination will often show that, however slight they may seem, they are, in relation to their context, or to some particular aspect of the Saint's teaching, of real interest; in other places they help to give the reader an idea, which may be useful to him in some crucial passage, of the general characteristics of the manuscript or edition in question. The editor's notes on the manuscripts and early editions which he has collated will also be found, for the same reason, to be summarized in the introduction to each work; in consulting the variants, the English-reading student has the maximum aid to a judgment of the reliability of his authorities.

Concentration upon the aim of obtaining the most precise possible rendering of the text has led me to sacrifice stylistic elegance to exactness where the two have been in conflict; it has sometimes been difficult to bring oneself to reproduce the Saint's often ungainly, though often forceful, repetitions of words or his long, cumbrous parentheses, but the temptation to take refuge in graceful paraphrases has been steadily resisted. In the same interest, and also in that of space, I have made certain omissions from, and abbreviations of, other parts of the edition than the text. Two of P. Silverio's five volumes are entirely filled with commentaries and documents. I have selected from the documents those of outstanding interest to readers with no detailed knowledge of Spanish religious history and have been content to summarize the editor's introductions to the individual works, as well as his longer footnotes to the text, and to omit such parts as would interest only specialists, who are able, or at least should be obliged, to study them in the original Spanish.

The decision to summarize in these places has been made the less reluctantly because of the frequent unsuitability of P. Silverio's style to English readers. Like that of many Spaniards, it is so discursive, and at times so baroque in its wealth of epithet and its profusion of imagery, that a literal translation, for many pages together, would seldom have been acceptable. The same criticism would have been applicable to any literal translation of P. Silverio's biography of St. John of the Cross which stands at the head of his edition (Vol. I, pp. 7-130). There was a further reason for omitting these biographical chapters. The long and fully documented biography by the French Carmelite, P. Bruno de Jesús-Marie, C.D., written from the same standpoint as P. Silverio's, has recently been translated into English, and any attempt to rival this in so short a space would be foredoomed to failure. I have thought, however, that a brief outline of the principal events in St. John of the Cross's life would be a useful preliminary to this edition; this has therefore been substituted for the biographical sketch referred to.

In language, I have tried to reproduce the atmosphere of a sixteenth-century text as far as is consistent with clarity. Though following the paragraph divisions of my original, I have not scrupled, where this has seemed to facilitate understanding, to divide into shorter sentences the long and sometimes straggling periods in which the Saint so frequently indulged. Some attempt has been made to show the contrast between the highly adorned, poetical language of much of the commentary on the 'Spiritual Canticle' and the more closely shorn and eminently practical, though always somewhat discursive style of the Ascent and Dark Night. That the Living Flame occupies an intermediate position in this respect should also be clear from the style of the translation.

Quotations, whether from the Scriptures or from other sources, have been left strictly as St. John of the Cross made them. Where he quotes in Latin, the Latin has been reproduced; only his quotations in Spanish have been turned into English. The footnote references are to the Vulgate, of which the Douai Version is a direct translation; if the Authorized Version differs, as in the Psalms, the variation has been shown in square brackets for the convenience of those who use it.

A word may not be out of place regarding the translations of the poems as they appear in the prose commentaries. Obviously, it would have been impossible to use the comparatively free verse renderings which appear in Volume II of this translation, since the commentaries discuss each line and often each word of the poems. A literal version of the poems in their original verse-lines, however, struck me as being inartistic, if not repellent, and as inviting continual comparison with the more polished verse renderings which, in spirit, come far nearer to the poet's aim.

My first intention was to translate the poems, for the purpose of the commentaries, into prose. But later I hit upon the long and metrically unfettered verse-line, suggestive of Biblical poetry in its English dress, which I have employed throughout. I believe that, although the renderings often suffer artistically from their necessary literalness, they are from the artistic standpoint at least tolerable.

III

The debts I have to acknowledge, though few, are very large ones. My gratitude to P. Silverio de Santa Teresa for telling me so much about his edition before its publication, granting my publishers the sole translation rights and discussing with me a number of crucial passages cannot be disjoined from the many kindnesses I have received during my work on the Spanish mystics, which is still proceeding, from himself and from his fellow-Carmelites in the province of Castile. In dedicating this translation to them, I think particularly of P. Silverio in Burgos, of P. Florencio del Ni–o Jesús in Madrid, and of P. Cris—gono de Jesús Sacramentado, together with the Fathers of the 'Convento de la Santa' in Avila.

The long and weary process of revising the manuscript and proofs of this translation has been greatly lightened by the co-operation and companionship of P. Edmund Gurdon, Prior of the Cartuja de Miraflores, near Burgos, with whom I have freely discussed all kinds of difficulties, both of substance and style, and who has been good enough to read part of my proofs. From the quiet library of his monastery, as well as from his gracious companionship, I have drawn not only knowledge, but strength, patience and perseverance. And when at length, after each of my visits, we have had to part, we have continued our labours by correspondence, shaking hands, as it were, 'over a vast' and embracing 'from the ends of opposed winds.'

Finally, I owe a real debt to my publishers for allowing me to do this work without imposing any such limitations of time as often accompany literary undertakings. This and other considerations which I have received from them have made that part of the work which has been done outside the study unusually pleasant and I am correspondingly grateful.

E. Allison Peers.
University of Liverpool.
Feast of St. John of the Cross,

Translator's Preface to the Second Edition

During the sixteen years which have elapsed since the publication of the first edition, several reprints have been issued, and the demand is now such as to justify a complete resetting. I have taken advantage of this opportunity to revise the text throughout, and hope that in some of the more difficult passages I may have come nearer than before to the Saint's mind. Recent researches have necessitated a considerable amplification of introductions and footnotes and greatly increased the length of the bibliography.

The only modification which has been made consistently throughout the three volumes relates to St. John of the Cross's quotations from Scripture. In translating these I still follow him exactly, even where he himself is inexact, but I have used the Douai Version (instead of the Authorized, as in the first edition) as a basis for all Scriptural quotations, as well as in the footnote references and the Scriptural index in Vol. III.

Far more is now known of the life and times of St. John of the Cross than when this translation of the Complete Works was first published, thanks principally to the Historia del Carmen Descalzo of P. Silverio de Santa Teresa, C.D, now General of his Order, and to the admirably documented Life of the Saint written by P. Cris—gono de Jesus Sacramentado, C.D., and published (in Vida y Obras de San Juan de la Cruz) in the year after his untimely death. This increased knowledge is reflected in many additional notes, and also in the 'Outline of the Life of St. John of the Cross' (Vol. I, pp. xxv-xxviii), which, for this edition, has been entirely recast. References are given to my Handbook to the Life and Times of St. Teresa and St. John of the Cross, which provides much background too full to be reproduced in footnotes and too complicated to be compressed. The Handbook also contains numerous references to contemporary events, omitted from the 'Outline' as being too remote from the main theme to justify inclusion in a summary necessarily so condensed.

My thanks for help in revision are due to kindly correspondents, too numerous to name, from many parts of the world, who have made suggestions for the improvement of the first edition; to the Rev. Professor David Knowles, of Cambridge University, for whose continuous practical interest in this translation I cannot be too grateful; to Miss I.L. McClelland, of Glasgow University, who has read a large part of this edition in proof; to Dom Philippe Chevallier, for material which I have been able to incorporate in it; to P. José Antonio de Sobrino, S.J., for allowing me to quote freely from his recently published Estudios; and, most of all, to M.R.P. Silverio de Santa Teresa, C.D., and the Fathers of the International

Carmelite College at Rome, whose learning and experience, are, I hope, faintly reflected in this new edition.

E.A.P.

June 30, 1941.

Principal Abbreviations

A.V.— Authorized Version of the Bible (1611).

D.V.— Douai Version of the Bible (1609).

C.W.S.T.J.— The Complete Works of Saint Teresa of Jesus, translated and edited by E. Allison Peers from the critical edition of P. Silverio de Santa Teresa, C.D. London, Sheed and Ward, 1946. 3 vols.

H.—E. Allison Peers: Handbook to the Life and Times of St. Teresa and St. John of the Cross. London, Burns Oates and Washbourne, 1953.

LL.— The Letters of Saint Teresa of Jesus, translated and edited by E. Allison Peers from the critical edition of P. Silverio de Santa Teresa, C.D. London, Burns Oates and Washburne, 1951. 2 vols.

N.L.M.— National Library of Spain (Biblioteca Nacional), Madrid.

Obras (P. Silv.)— Obras de San Juan de la Cruz, Doctor de la Iglesia, editadas y anotadas pot el P. Silverio de Santa Teresa, C.D. Burgos, 1929-31. 5 vols.

S.S.M.— E. Allison Peers: Studies of the Spanish Mystics. Vol. I, London, Sheldon Press, 1927; 2nd ed., London, S.P.C.K., 1951. Vol. II, London, Sheldon Press, 1930.

Sobrino.-Jose Antonio de Sobrino, S.J.: Estudios sobre San Juan de la Cruz y nuevos textos de su obra. Madrid, 1950.

An Outline of the Life of St. John of the Cross

1542. Birth of Juan de Yepes at Fontiveros (Hontiveros), near Avila.

The day generally ascribed to this event is June 24 (St. John Baptist's Day). No documentary evidence for it, however, exists, the parish registers having been destroyed by a fire in 1544. The chief evidence is an inscription, dated 1689, on the font of the parish church at Fontiveros.

1543. Death of Juan's father. 'After some years' the mother removes, with her family, to Arivalo, and later to Medina del Campo.

1552-6. Juan goes to school at the Colegio de los Ninos de la Doctrina, Medina.

1556-7. Don Antonio Alvarez de Toledo takes him into a Hospital to which he has retired, with the idea of his (Juan's) training for Holy Orders under his patronage.

1559-63. Juan attends the College of the Society of Jesus at Medina.

1562. Leaves the Hospital and the patronage of Alvarez de Toledo.

1563. Takes the Carmelite habit at St. Anne's, Medina del Campo, as Juan de San Mat'as (Santo Mat'a). The day is frequently assumed (without any foundation) to have been the feast of St. Matthias (February 24), but P. Silverio postulates a day in August or September.

1564. Makes his profession in the same priory — probably in August or September and certainly not earlier than May 21 and not later than October.

1564 (November). Enters the University of Salamanca as an artista. Takes a three-year course in Arts (1564-7).

1565 (January 6). Matriculates at the University of Salamanca.

1567. Receives priest's orders (probably in the summer).

1567 (? September). Meets St. Teresa at Medina del Campo. Juan is thinking of transferring to the Carthusian Order. St. Teresa asks him to join her Discalced Reform and the projected first foundation for friars. He agrees to do so, provided the foundation is soon made.

1567 (November). Returns to the University of Salamanca, where he takes a year's course in theology.

1568. Spends part of the Long Vacation at Medina del Campo. On August 10, accompanies St. Teresa to Valladolid. In September, returns to Medina and later goes to Avila and Duruelo.

1568 (November 28). Takes the vows of the Reform Duruelo as St. John of the Cross, together with Antonio de Heredia (Antonio de Jesus), Prior of the Calced Carmelites at Medina, and José de Cristo, another Carmelite from Medina.

1570 (June 11). Moves, with the Duruelo community, to Mancera de Abajo.

1570 (October, or possibly February 1571). Stays for about a month at Pastrana, returning thence to Mancera.

1571 (? January 25). Visits Alba de Tormes for the inauguration of a new convent there.

1571 (? April). Goes to Alcala de Henares as Rector of the College of the Reform and directs the Carmelite nuns.

1572 (shortly after April 23). Recalled to Pastrana to correct the rigours of the new novice-master, Angel de San Gabriel.

1572 (between May and September). Goes to Avila as confessor to the Convent of the Incarnation. Remains there till 1577.

1574 (March). Accompanies St. Teresa from Avila to Segovia, arriving on March 18. Returns to Avila about the end of the month.

1575-6 (Winter of: before February 1576). Kidnapped by the Calced and imprisoned at Medina del Campo. Freed by the intervention of the Papal Nuncio, Ormaneto.

1577 (December 2 or 3). Kidnapped by the Calced and carried off to the Calced Carmelite priory at Toledo as a prisoner.

1577-8. Composes in prison 17 (or perhaps 30) stanzas of the 'Spiritual Canticle' (i.e., as far as the stanza: 'Daughters of Jewry'); the poem with the refrain 'Although 'tis night'; and the stanzas beginning 'In principio erat verbum.' He may also have composed the paraphrase of the psalm Super flumina and the poem 'Dark Night.'

1578 (August 16 or shortly afterwards). Escapes to the convent of the Carmelite nuns in Toledo, and is thence taken to his house by D. Pedro Gonzalez de Mendoza, Canon of Toledo.

1578 (October 9). Attends a meeting of the Discalced superiors at Almodevar. Is sent to El Calvario as Vicar, in the absence in Rome of the Prior.

1578 (end of October). Stays for 'a few days' at Beas de Segura, near El Calvario. Confesses the nuns at the Carmelite Convent of Beas.

1578 (November). Arrives at El Calvario.

1578-9 (November-June). Remains at El Calvario as Vicar. For a part of this time (probably from the beginning of 1579), goes weekly to the convent of Beas to hear confessions. During this period, begins his commentaries entitled The Ascent of Mount Carmel and Spiritual Canticle .

1579 (June 14). Founds a college of the Reform at Baeza. 1579-82. Resides at Baeza as Rector of the Carmelite college. Visits the Beas convent occasionally. Writes more of the prose works begun at El Calvario and the rest of the stanzas of the 'Spiritual Canticle' except the last five, possibly with the commentaries to the stanzas.

1580. Death of his mother.

1581 (March 3). Attends the Alcala Chapter of the Reform. Appointed Third Definitor and Prior of the Granada house of Los Mertires. Takes up the latter office only on or about the time of his election by the community in March 1582.

1581 (November 28). Last meeting with St. Teresa, at Avila. On the next day, sets out with two nuns for Beas (December 8-January 15) and Granada.

1582 (January 20). Arrives at Los Mertires.

1582-8. Mainly at Granada. Re-elected (or confirmed) as Prior of Los Mertires by the Chapter of Almodevar, 1583. Resides at Los Mertires more or less continuously till 1584 and intermittently afterwards. Visits the Beas convent occasionally. Writes the last five stanzas of the 'Spiritual Canticle' during one of these visits. At Los Mertires, finishes the Ascent of Mount Carmel and composes his remaining prose treatises. Writes Living Flame of Love about 1585, in fifteen days.

1585 (May). Lisbon Chapter appoints him Second Definitor and (till 1587) Vicar-Provincial of Andalusia.

1587 (April). Chapter of Valladolid re-appoints him Prior of Los Mertires. He ceases to be Definitor and Vicar-Provincial.

1588 (June 19). Attends the first Chapter-General of the Reform in Madrid. Is elected First Definitor and a consiliario.

1588 (August 10). Becomes Prior of Segovia, the central house of the Reform and the headquarters of the Consulta. Acts as deputy for the Vicar-General, P. Doria, during the latter's absences.

1590 (June 10). Re-elected First Definitor and a consiliario at the Chapter-General Extraordinary, Madrid.

1591 (June 1). The Madrid Chapter-General deprives him of his offices and resolves to send him to Mexico. (This latter decision was later revoked.)

1591 (August 10). Arrives at La Peouela.

1591 (September 12). Attacked by fever. (September Leaves La Peouela for òbeda. (December 14) Dies at òbeda.

January 25, 1675. Beatified by Clement X.

December 26, 1726. Canonized by Benedict XIII.

August 24, 1926. Declared Doctor of the Church Universal by Pius XI.

General Introduction to the Works of St. John of the Cross

I: Dates and Methods of Composition — General Characteristics

With regard to the times and places at which the works of St. John of the Cross were written, and also with regard to the number of these works, there have existed, from a very early date, considerable differences of opinion. Of internal evidence from the Saint's own writings there is practically none, and such external testimony as can be found in contemporary documents needs very careful examination.

There was no period in the life of St. John of the Cross in which he devoted himself entirely to writing. He does not, in fact, appear to have felt any inclination to do so: his books were written in response to the insistent and repeated demands of his spiritual children. He was very much addicted, on the other hand, to the composition of apothegms or maxims for the use of his penitents and this custom he probably began as early as the days in which he was confessor to the Convent of the Incarnation at Avila, though his biographers have no record of any maxims but those written at Beas.

One of his best beloved daughters however, Ana Mar'a de Jesús, of the Convent of the Incarnation, declared in her deposition, during the process of the Saint's canonization, that he was accustomed to 'comfort those with whom he had to do, both by his words and by his letters, of which this witness received a number, and also by certain papers concerning holy things which this witness would greatly value if she still had them.'

Considering, the number of nuns to whom the Saint was director at Avila, it is to be presumed that M. Ana Mar'a was not the only person whom he favoured. We may safely conclude, indeed, that there were many others who shared the same privileges, and that, had we all these 'papers,' they would comprise a large volume, instead of the few pages reproduced elsewhere in this translation.

There is a well-known story, preserved in the documents of the canonization process, of how, on a December night of 1577, St. John, of the Cross was kidnapped by the Calced Carmelites of Avila and carried off from the Incarnation to their priory. Realizing that he had left behind him some important papers, he contrived, on the next morning, to escape, and returned to the Incarnation to destroy them while there was time to do so. He was missed almost immediately and he had hardly gained his cell when his pursuers were on his heels. In the few moments that remained to him he had time to tear up these papers and swallow some of the most compromising. As the original assault had not been unexpected, though the time of it was uncertain, they would not have been very numerous. It is generally supposed that they concerned the business of the infant Reform, of which the survival was at that time in grave doubt. But it seems at least equally likely that some of them might have been these spiritual maxims, or some more extensive instructions which might be misinterpreted by any who found them. It is remarkable, at any rate, that we have none of the Saint's writings belonging to this period whatever.

All his biographers tell us that he wrote some of the stanzas of the 'Spiritual Canticle,' together with a few other poems, while he was imprisoned at Toledo. 'When he left the prison,' says M. Magdalena del Esp'ritu Santo, 'he took with him a little book in which he had written, while there, some verses based upon the Gospel In principio erat Verbum, together with some couplets which begin: "How well I know the fount that freely flows, Although 'tis night," and the stanzas or liras that begin "Whither has vanished?" as far as the stanzas beginning "Daughters of Jewry." The remainder of them the Saint composed later when he was Rector of the College at Baeza. Some of the expositions were written at Beas, as answers to questions put to him by the nuns; others at Granada. This little book, in which the Saint wrote while in prison, he left in the Convent of Beas and on various occasions I was commanded to copy it. Then someone took it from my cell — who, I never knew. The freshness of the words in this book, together with their beauty and subtlety, caused me great wonder, and one day I asked the Saint if God gave him those words which were so comprehensive and so lovely. And he answered: "Daughter, sometimes God gave them to me and at other times I sought them."'

M. Isabel de Jesús Mar'a, who was a novice at Toledo when the Saint escaped from his imprisonment there, wrote thus from Cuerva on November 2, 1614. 'I remember, too, that, at the time we had him hidden in the church, he recited to us some lines which he had composed and kept in his mind, and that one of the nuns wrote them down as he repeated them. There were three poems — all of them upon the Most Holy Trinity, and so sublime and devout that they seem to enkindle the reader. In this house at Cuerva we have some which begin:

"Far away in the beginning,

Dwelt the Word in God Most High."'

The frequent references to keeping his verses in his head and the popular exaggeration of the hardships (great though these were) which the Saint had to endure in Toledo have led some writers to affirm that he did not in fact write these poems in prison but committed them to memory and transferred them to paper at some later date. The evidence of M. Magdalena, however, would appear to be decisive. We know, too, that the second of St. John of the Cross's gaolers, Fray Juan de Santa Mar'a, was a kindly man who did all he could to lighten his captive's sufferings; and his superiors would probably not have forbidden him writing materials provided he wrote no letters.

It seems, then, that the Saint wrote in Toledo the first seventeen (or perhaps thirty) stanzas of the 'Spiritual Canticle,' the nine parts of the poem 'Far away in the beginning . . .,' the paraphrase of the psalm Super flumina Babylonis and the poem 'How well I know the fount . . .' This was really a considerable output of work, for, except perhaps when his gaoler allowed him to go into another room, he had no light but that of a small oil-lamp or occasionally the infiltration of daylight that penetrated a small interior window.

Apart from the statement of M. Magdalena already quoted, little more is known of what the Saint wrote in El Calvario than of what he wrote in Toledo. From an amplification made by herself of the sentences to which we have referred it appears that almost the whole of what she had copied was taken from her; as the short extracts transcribed by her are very similar to passages from the Saint's writings we may perhaps conclude that much of the other material was also incorporated in them. In that case he may well have completed a fair proportion of the Ascent of Mount Carmel before leaving Beas.

It was in El Calvario, too, and for the nuns of Beas, that the Saint drew the plan called the 'Mount of Perfection' (referred to by M. Magdalena[and in the Ascent of Mount Carmel and reproduced as the frontispiece to this volume) of which copies were afterwards multiplied and distributed among Discalced houses. Its author wished it to figure at the head of all his treatises, for it is a graphical representation of the entire mystic way, from the starting-point of the beginner to the very summit of perfection. His first sketch, which still survives, is a rudimentary and imperfect one; before long, however, as M. Magdalena tells us, he evolved another that was fuller and more comprehensive.

Just as we owe to PP. Gracien and Salazar many precious relics of St. Teresa, so we owe others of St. John of the Cross to M. Magdalena. Among the most valuable of these is her own copy of the 'Mount,' which, after her death, went to the 'Desert' of Our Lady of the Snows established by the Discalced province of Upper Andalusia in the diocese of Granada. It was found there by P. Andres de la Encarnacion, of whom we shall presently speak, and who immediately made a copy of it, legally certified as an exact one and now in the National Library of Spain (MS. 6,296).

The superiority of the second plan over the first is very evident. The first consists simply of three parallel lines corresponding to three different paths — one on either side of the Mount, marked 'Road of the spirit of imperfection' and one in the centre marked 'Path of Mount Carmel. Spirit of perfection.' In the spaces between the paths are written the celebrated maxims which appear in Book I, Chapter xiii, of the Ascent of Mount Carmel, in a somewhat different form, together with certain others. At the top of the drawing are the words 'Mount Carmel,' which are not found in the second plan, and below them is the legend: 'There is no road here, for there is no law for the righteous man,' together with other texts from Scripture.

The second plan represents a number of graded heights, the loftiest of which is planted with trees. Three paths, as in the first sketch, lead from the base of the mount, but they are traced more artistically and have a more detailed ascetic and mystical application. Those on either side, which denote the roads of imperfection, are broad and somewhat tortuous and come to an end before the higher stages of the mount are reached. The centre road, that of perfection, is at first very narrow but gradually broadens and leads right up to the summit of the mountain, which only the perfect attain and where they enjoy the iuge convivium — the heavenly feast. The different zones of religious perfection, from which spring various virtues, are portrayed with much greater detail than in the first plan. As we have reproduced the second plan in this volume, it need not be described more fully.

We know that St. John of the Cross used the 'Mount' very, frequently for all kinds of religious instruction. 'By means of this drawing,' testified one of his disciples, 'he used to teach us that, in order to attain to perfection, we must not desire the good things of earth, nor those of Heaven; but that we must desire naught save to seek and strive after the glory and honour of God our Lord in all things . . . and this "Mount of Perfection" the said holy father himself expounded to this Witness when he was his superior in the said priory of Granada.'

It seems not improbable that the Saint continued writing chapters of the Ascent and the Spiritual Canticle while he was Rector at Baeza, whether in the College itself, or in El Castellar, where he was accustomed often to go into retreat. It was certainly here that he wrote the remaining stanzas of the Canticle (as M. Magdalena explicitly tells us in words already quoted), except the last five, which he composed rather later, at Granada. One likes to think that these loveliest of his verses were penned by the banks of the Guadalimar, in the woods of the Granja de Santa Ann, where he was in the habit of passing long hours in communion with God. At all events the stanzas seem more in harmony with such an atmosphere than with that of the College.

With regard to the last five stanzas, we have definite evidence from a Beas nun, M. Francisca de la Madre de Dios, who testifies in the Beatification process (April 2, 1618) as follows:

And so, when the said holy friar John of the Cross was in this convent one Lent (for his great love for it brought him here from the said city of Granada, where he was prior, to confess the nuns and preach to them) he was preaching to them one day in the parlour, and this witness observed that on two separate occasions he was rapt and lifted up from the ground; and when he came to himself he dissembled and said: 'You saw how sleep overcame me!' And one day he asked this witness in what her prayer consisted, and she replied: 'In considering the beauty of God and in rejoicing that He has such beauty.' And the Saint was so pleased with this that for some days he said the most sublime things concerning the beauty of God, at which all marvelled. And thus, under the influence of this love, he composed five stanzas, beginning 'Beloved, let us sing, And in thy beauty see ourselves portray'd.' And in all this he showed that there was in his breast a great love of God.

From a letter which this nun wrote from Beas in 1629 to P. Jeronimo de San José, we gather that the stanzas were actually written at Granada and brought to Beas, where

. . . with every word that we spoke to him we seemed to be opening a door to the fruition of the great treasures and riches which God had stored up in his soul.

If there is a discrepancy here, however, it is of small importance; there is no doubt as to the approximate date of the composition of these stanzas and of their close connection with Beas.

The most fruitful literary years for St. John of the Cross were those which he spent at Granada. Here he completed the Ascent and wrote all his remaining treatises. Both M. Magdalena and the Saint's closest disciple, P. Juan Evangelista, bear witness to this. The latter writes from Granada to P. Jeronimo de San José, the historian of the Reform:

With regard to having seen our venerable father write the books, I saw him write them all; for, as I have said, I was ever at his side. The Ascent of Mount Carmel and the Dark Night he wrote here at Granada, little by little, continuing them only with many breaks. The Living Flame of Love he also wrote in this house, when he was Vicar-Provincial, at the request of Doa Ana de Pealosa, and he wrote it in fifteen days when he was very busy here with an abundance of occupations. The first thing that he wrote was Whither hast vanished? and that too he wrote here; the stanzas he had written in the prison at Toledo.

In another letter (February 18, 1630), he wrote to the same correspondent:

With regard to our holy father's having written his books in this home, I will say what is undoubtedly true — namely, that he wrote here the commentary on the stanzas Whither hast vanished? and the Living Flame of Love, for he began and ended them in my time. The Ascent of Mount Carmel I found had been begun when I came here to take the habit, which was a year and a half after the foundation of this house; he may have brought it from yonder already begun. But the Dark Night he certainly wrote here, for I saw him writing a part of it, and this is certain, because I saw it.

These and other testimonies might with advantage be fuller and more concrete, but at least they place beyond doubt the facts that we have already set down. Summarizing our total findings, we may assert that part of the 'Spiritual Canticle,' with perhaps the 'Dark Night,' and the other poems enumerated, were written in the Toledo prison; that at the request of some nuns he wrote at El Calvario (1578-79) a few chapters of the Ascent and commentaries on some of the stanzas of the 'Canticle'; that he composed further stanzas at Baeza (1579-81), perhaps with their respective commentaries; and that, finally, he completed the Canticle and the Ascent at Granada and wrote the whole of the Dark Night and of the Living Flame — the latter in a fortnight. All these last works he wrote before the end of 1585, the first year in which he was Vicar-Provincial.

Other writings, most of them brief, are attributed to St. John of the Cross; they will be discussed in the third volume of this edition, in which we shall publish the minor works which we accept as genuine. The authorship of his four major prose works — the Ascent, Dark Night, Spiritual Canticle and Living Flame — no one has ever attempted to question, even though the lack of extant autographs and the large number of copies have made it difficult to establish correct texts. To this question we shall return later.

The characteristics of the writings of St. John of the Cross are so striking that it would be difficult to confuse them with those of any other writer. His literary personality stands out clearly from that of his Spanish contemporaries who wrote on similar subjects. Both his style and his methods of exposition bear the marks of a strong individuality.

If some of these derive from his native genius and temperament, others are undoubtedly reflections of his education and experience. The Aristotelian-Thomistic philosophy, then at the height of its splendour, which he learned so thoroughly in the classrooms of Salamanca University, characterizes the whole of his writings, giving them a granite-like solidity even when their theme is such as to defy human speculation. Though the precise extent of his debt to this Salamancan training in philosophy has not yet been definitely assessed, the fact of its influence is evident to every reader. It gives massiveness, harmony and unity to both the ascetic and the mystical work of St. John of the Cross — that is to say, to all his scientific writing.

Deeply, however, as St. John of the Cross drew from the Schoolmen, he was also profoundly indebted to many other writers. He was distinctly eclectic in his reading and quotes freely (though less than some of his Spanish contemporaries) from the Fathers and from the mediaeval mystics, especially from St. Thomas, St. Bonaventura, Hugh of St. Victor and the pseudo-Areopagite. All that he quotes, however, he makes his own, with the result that his chapters are never a mass of citations loosely strung together, as are those of many other Spanish mystics of his time.

When we study his treatises — principally that great composite work known as the Ascent of Mount Carmel and the Dark Night — we have the impression of a master-mind that has scaled the heights of mystical science and from their summit looks down upon and dominates the plain below and the paths leading upward. We may well wonder what a vast contribution to the subject he would have made had he been able to expound all the eight stanzas of his poem since he covered so much ground in expounding no more than two. Observe with what assurance and what mastery of subject and method he defines his themes and divides his arguments, even when treating the most abstruse and controversial questions. The most obscure phenomena he appears to illumine, as it were, with one lightning flash of understanding, as though the explanation of them were perfectly natural and easy. His solutions of difficult problems are not timid, questioning and loaded with exceptions, but clear, definite and virile like the man who proposes them. No scientific field, perhaps, has so many zones which are apt to become vague and obscure as has that of mystical theology; and there are those among the Saint's predecessors who seem to have made their permanent abode in them. They give the impression of attempting to cloak vagueness in verbosity, in order to avoid being forced into giving solutions of problems which they find insoluble. Not so St. John of the Cross. A scientific dictator, if such a person were conceivable, could hardly express himself with greater clarity. His phrases have a decisive, almost a chiselled quality; where he errs on the side of redundance, it is not with the intention of cloaking uncertainty, but in order that he may drive home with double force the truths which he desires to impress.

No less admirable are, on the one hand, his synthetic skill and the logic of his arguments, and, on the other, his subtle and discriminating analyses, which weigh the finest shades of thought and dissect each subject with all the accuracy of science. To his analytical genius we owe those finely balanced statements, orthodox yet bold and fearless, which have caused clumsier intellects to misunderstand him. It is not remarkable that this should have occurred. The ease with which the unskilled can misinterpret genius is shown in the history of many a heresy.

How much of all this St. John of the Cross owed to his studies of scholastic philosophy in the University of Salamanca, it is difficult to say. If we examine the history of that University and read of its severe discipline we shall be in no danger of under-estimating the effect which it must have produced upon so agile and alert an intellect. Further, we note the constant parallelisms and the comparatively infrequent (though occasionally important) divergences between the doctrines of St. John of the Cross and St. Thomas, to say nothing of the close agreement between the views of St. John of the Cross and those of the Schoolmen on such subjects as the passions and appetites, the nature of the soul, the relations between soul and body. Yet we must not forget the student tag: Quod natura non dat, Salamtica non praestat. Nothing but natural genius could impart the vigour and the clarity which enhance all St. John of the Cross's arguments and nothing but his own deep and varied experience could have made him what he may well be termed — the greatest psychologist in the history of mysticism.

Eminent, too, was St. John of the Cross in sacred theology. The close natural connection that exists between dogmatic and mystical theology and their continual interdependence in practice make it impossible for a Christian teacher to excel in the latter alone. Indeed, more than one of the heresies that have had their beginnings in mysticism would never have developed had those who fell into them been well grounded in dogmatic theology. The one is, as it were, the lantern that lights the path of the other, as St. Teresa realized when she began to feel the continual necessity of consulting theological teachers. If St. John of the Cross is able to climb the greatest heights of mysticism and remain upon them without stumbling or dizziness it is because his feet are invariably well shod with the truths of dogmatic theology. The great mysteries — those of the Trinity, the Creation, the Incarnation and the Redemption — and such dogmas as those concerning grace, the gifts of the Spirit, the theological virtues, etc., were to him guide-posts for those who attempted to scale, and to lead others to scale, the symbolic mount of sanctity.

It will be remembered that the Saint spent but one year upon his theological course at the University of Salamanca, for which reason many have been surprised at the evident solidity of his attainments. But, apart from the fact that a mind so keen and retentive as that of Fray Juan de San Mat'as could absorb in a year what others would have failed to imbibe in the more usual two or three, we must of necessity assume a far longer time spent in private study. For in one year he could not have studied all the treatises of which he clearly demonstrates his knowledge — to say nothing of many others which he must have known. His own works, apart from any external evidence, prove him to have been a theologian of distinction.

In both fields, the dogmatic and the mystical he was greatly aided by his knowledge of Holy Scripture, which he studied continually, in the last years of his life, to the exclusion, as it would seem, of all else. Much of it he knew by heart; the simple devotional talks that he was accustomed to give were invariably studded with texts, and he made use of passages from the Bible both to justify and to illustrate his teaching. In the mystical interpretation of Holy Scripture, as every student of mysticism knows, he has had few equals even among his fellow Doctors of the Church Universal.

Testimonies to his mastery of the Scriptures can be found in abundance. P. Alonso de la Madre de Dios, el Asturicense, for example, who was personally acquainted with him, stated in 1603 that 'he had a great gift and facility for the exposition of the Sacred Scripture, principally of the Song of Songs, Ecclesiasticus, Ecclesiastes, the Proverbs and the Psalms of David.' His spiritual daughter, that same Magdalena del Esp'ritus Santo to whom we have several times referred, affirms that St. John of the Cross would frequently read the Gospels to the nuns of Beas and expound the letter and the spirit to them.[1 Fray Juan Evangelista says in a well-known passage:

He was very fond of reading in the Scriptures, and I never once saw him read any other books than the Bible,[almost all of which he knew by heart, St. Augustine Contra Haereses and the Flos Sanctorum. When occasionally he preached (which was seldom) or gave informal addresses [pleticas], as he more commonly did, he never read from any book save the Bible. His conversation, whether at recreation or at other times, was continually of God, and he spoke so delightfully that, when he discoursed upon sacred things at recreation, he would make us all laugh and we used greatly to enjoy going out. On occasions when we held chapters, he would usually give devotional addresses after supper, and he never failed to give an address every night.

Fray Pablo de Santa Mar'a, who had also heard the Saint's addresses, wrote thus:

He was a man of the most enkindled spirituality and of great insight into all that concerns mystical theology and matters of prayer; I consider it impossible that he could have spoken so well about all the virtues if he had not been most proficient in the spiritual life, and I really think he knew the whole Bible by heart, so far as one could judge from the various Biblical passages which he would quote at chapters and in the refectory, without any great effort, but as one who goes where the Spirit leads him.

Nor was this admiration for the expository ability of St. John of the Cross confined to his fellow-friars, who might easily enough have been led into hero-worship. We know that he was thought highly of in this respect by the University of Alcala de Henares, where he was consulted as an authority. A Dr. Villegas, Canon of Segovia Cathedral, has left on record his respect for him. And Fray Jer—nimo de San José relates the esteem in which he was held at the University of Baeza, which in his day enjoyed a considerable reputation for Biblical studies:

There were at that time at the University of Baeza many learned and spiritually minded persons, disciples of that great father and apostle Juan de Avila. . . . All these doctors . . . would repair to our venerable father as to an oracle from heaven and would discuss with him both their own spiritual progress and that of souls committed to their charge, with the result that they were both edified and astonished at his skill. They would also bring him difficulties and delicate points connected with Divine letters, and on these, too, he spoke with extraordinary energy and illumination. One of these doctors, who had consulted him and listened to him on various occasions, said that, although he had read deeply in St. Augustine and St. John Chrysostom and other saints, and had found in them greater heights and depths, he had found in none of them that particular kind of spirituality in exposition which this great father applied to Scriptural passages.

The Scriptural knowledge of St. John of the Cross was, as this passage makes clear, in no way merely academic. Both in his literal and his mystical interpretations of the Bible, he has what we may call a 'Biblical sense,' which saves him from such exaggerations as we find in other expositors, both earlier and contemporary. One would not claim, of course, that among the many hundreds of applications of Holy Scripture made by the Carmelite Doctor there are none that can be objected to in this respect; but the same can be said of St. Augustine, St. Ambrose, St. Gregory or St. Bernard, and no one would assert that, either with them or with him, such instances are other than most exceptional.

To the three sources already mentioned in which St. John of the Cross found inspiration we must add a fourth — the works of ascetic and mystical writers. It is not yet possible to assert with any exactness how far the Saint made use of these; for, though partial studies of this question have been attempted, a complete and unbiased treatment of it has still to be undertaken. Here we can do no more than give a few indications of what remains to be done and summarize the present content of our knowledge.

We may suppose that, during his novitiate in Medina, the Saint read a number of devotional books, one of which would almost certainly have been the Imitation of Christ, and others would have included works which were translated into Spanish by order of Cardinal Cisneros. The demands of a University course would not keep him from pursuing such studies at Salamanca; the friar who chose a cell from the window of which he could see the Blessed Sacrament, so that he might spend hours in its company, would hardly be likely to neglect his devotional reading. But we have not a syllable of direct external evidence as to the titles of any of the books known to him.

Nor, for that matter, have we much more evidence of this kind for any other part of his life. Both his early Carmelite biographers and the numerous witnesses who gave evidence during the canonization process describe at great length his extraordinary penances, his love for places of retreat beautified by Nature, the long hours that he spent in prayer and the tongue of angels with which he spoke on things spiritual. But of his reading they say nothing except to describe his attachment to the Bible, nor have we any record of the books contained in the libraries of the religious houses that he visited. Yet if, as we gather from the process, he spent little more than three hours nightly in sleep, he must have read deeply of spiritual things by night as well as by day.

Some clues to the nature of his reading may be gained from his own writings. It is true that the clues are slender. He cites few works apart from the Bible and these are generally liturgical books, such as the Breviary. Some of his quotations from St. Augustine, St. Gregory and other of the Fathers are traceable to these sources. Nevertheless, we have not read St. John of the Cross for long before we find ourselves in the full current of mystical tradition. It is not by means of more or less literal quotations that the Saint produces this impression; he has studied his precursors so thoroughly that he absorbs the substance of their doctrine and incorporates it so intimately in his own that it becomes flesh of his flesh. Everything in his writings is fully matured: he has no juvenilia. The mediaeval mystics whom he uses are too often vague and undisciplined; they need someone to select from them and unify them, to give them clarity and order, so that their treatment of mystical theology may have the solidity and substance of scholastic theology. To have done this is one of the achievements of St. John of the Cross.

We are convinced, then, by an internal evidence which is chiefly of a kind in which no chapter and verse can be given, that St. John of the Cross read widely in mediaeval mystical theology and assimilated a great part of what he read. The influence of foreign writers upon Spanish mysticism, though it was once denied, is to-day generally recognized. It was inevitable that it should have been considerable in a country which in the sixteenth century had such a high degree of culture as Spain. Plotinus, in a diluted form, made his way into Spanish mysticism as naturally as did Seneca into Spanish asceticism. Plato and Aristotle entered it through the two greatest minds that Christianity has known — St. Augustine and St. Thomas. The influence of the Platonic theories of love and beauty and of such basic Aristotelian theories as the origin of knowledge is to be found in most of the Spanish mystics, St. John of the Cross among them.

The pseudo-Dionysius was another writer who was considered a great authority by the Spanish mystics. The importance attributed to his works arose partly from the fact that he was supposed to have been one of the first disciples of the Apostles; many chapters from mystical works of those days all over Europe are no more than glosses of the pseudo-Areopagite. He is followed less, however, by St. John of the Cross than by many of the latter's contemporaries.

Other influences upon the Carmelite Saint were St. Gregory, St. Bernard and Hugh and Richard of St. Victor, many of whose maxims were in the mouths of the mystics in the sixteenth century. More important, probably, than any of these was the Fleming, Ruysbroeck, between whom and St. John of the Cross there were certainly many points of contact. The Saint would have read him, not in the original, but in Surius' Latin translation of 1552, copies of which are known to have been current in Spain. Together with Ruysbroeck may be classed Suso, Denis the Carthusian, Herp, Kempis and various other writers.

Many of the ideas and phrases which we find in St. John of the Cross, as in other writers, are, of course, traceable to the common mystical tradition rather than to any definite individual influence. The striking metaphor of the ray of light penetrating the room, for example, which occurs in the first chapter of the pseudo-Areopagite's De Mystica Theologia, has been used continually by mystical writers ever since his time. The figures of the wood consumed by fire, of the ladder, the mirror, the flame of love and the nights of sense and spirit had long since become naturalized in mystical literature. There are many more such examples.

The originality of St. John of the Cross is in no way impaired by his employment of this current mystical language: such an idea might once have been commonly held, but has long ceased to be put forward seriously. His originality, indeed, lies precisely in the use which he made of language that he found near to hand. It is not going too far to liken the place taken by St. John of the Cross in mystical theology to that of St. Thomas in dogmatic; St. Thomas laid hold upon the immense store of material which had accumulated in the domain of dogmatic theology and subjected it to the iron discipline of reason. That St. John of the Cross did the same for mystical theology is his great claim upon our admiration. Through St. Thomas speaks the ecclesiastical tradition of many ages on questions of religious belief; through St. John speaks an equally venerable tradition on questions of Divine love. Both writers combined sainthood with genius. Both opened broad channels to be followed of necessity by Catholic writers through the ages to come till theology shall lose itself in that vast ocean of truth and love which is God. Both created instruments adequate to the greatness of their task: St. Thomas' clear, decisive reasoning processes give us the formula appropriate to each and every need of the understanding; St. John clothes his teaching in mellower and more appealing language, as befits the exponent of the science of love. We may describe the treatises of St. John of the Cross as the true Summa Angelica of mystical theology.

II: Outstanding Qualities and Defects of the Saint's Style

The profound and original thought which St. John of the Cross bestowed upon so abstruse a subject, and upon one on which there was so little classical literature in Spanish when he wrote, led him to clothe his ideas in a language at once energetic, precise and of a high degree of individuality. His style reflects his thought, but it reflects the style of no school and of no other writer whatsoever.

This is natural enough, for thought and feeling were always uppermost in the Saint: style and language take a place entirely subordinate to them. Never did he sacrifice any idea to artistic combinations of words; never blur over any delicate shade of thought to enhance some rhythmic cadence of musical prose. Literary form (to use a figure which he himself might have coined) is only present at all in his works in the sense in which the industrious and deferential servant is present in the ducal apartment, for the purpose of rendering faithful service to his lord and master. This subordination of style to content in the Saint's work is one of its most eminent qualities. He is a great writer, but not a great stylist. The strength and robustness of his intellect everywhere predominate.

This to a large extent explains the negligences which we find in his style, the frequency with which it is marred by repetitions and its occasional degeneration into diffuseness. The long, unwieldy sentences, one of which will sometimes run to the length of a reasonably sized paragraph, are certainly a trial to many a reader. So intent is the Saint upon explaining, underlining and developing his points so that they shall be apprehended as perfectly as may be, that he continually recurs to what he has already said, and repeats words, phrases and even passages of considerable length without scruple. It is only fair to remind the reader that such things were far commoner in the Golden Age than they are to-day; most didactic Spanish prose of that period would be notably improved, from a modern standpoint, if its volume were cut down by about one-third.

Be that as it may, these defects in the prose of St. John of the Cross are amply compensated by the fullness of his phraseology, the wealth and profusion of his imagery, the force and the energy of his argument. He has only to be compared with the didactic writers who were his contemporaries for this to become apparent. Together with Luis de Granada, Luis de Leon, Juan de los angeles and Luis de la Puente,[he created a genuinely native language, purged of Latinisms, precise and eloquent, which Spanish writers have used ever since in writing of mystical theology.

The most sublime of all the Spanish mystics, he soars aloft on the wings of Divine love to heights known to hardly any of them. Though no words can express the loftiest of the experiences which he describes, we are never left with the impression that word, phrase or image has failed him. If it does not exist, he appears to invent it, rather than pause in his description in order to search for an expression of the idea that is in his mind or be satisfied with a prolix paraphrase. True to the character of his thought, his style is always forceful and energetic, even to a fault.

We have said nothing of his poems, for indeed they call for no purely literary commentary. How full of life the greatest of them are, how rich in meaning, how unforgettable and how inimitable, the individual reader may see at a glance or may learn from his own experience. Many of their exquisite figures their author owes, directly or indirectly, to his reading and assimilation of the Bible. Some of them, however, have acquired a new life in the form which he has given them. A line here, a phrase there, has taken root in the mind of some later poet or essayist and has given rise to a new work of art, to many lovers of which the Saint who lies behind it is unknown.

It is perhaps not an exaggeration to say that the verse and prose works combined of St. John of the Cross form at once the most grandiose and the most melodious spiritual canticle to which any one man has ever given utterance. It is impossible, in the space at our disposal, to quote at any length from the Spanish critics who have paid tribute to its comprehensiveness and profundity. We must content ourselves with a short quotation characterizing the Saint's poems, taken from the greatest of these critics, Marcelino Menendez Pelayo, who, besides referring frequently to St. John of the Cross in such of his mature works as the Heterodoxos, Ideas Esteticas and Ciencia Espa–ola, devoted to him a great part of the address which he delivered as a young man at his official reception into the Spanish Academy under the title of 'Mystical Poetry.'

'So sublime,' wrote Menendez Pelayo, 'is this poetry [of St. John of the Cross] that it scarcely seems to belong to this world at all; it is hardly capable of being assessed by literary criteria. More ardent in its passion than any profane poetry, its form is as elegant and exquisite, as plastic and as highly figured as any of the finest works of the Renaissance. The spirit of God has passed through these poems every one, beautifying and sanctifying them on its way.'

III: Diffusion of the Writings of St. John of the Cross — Loss of the Autographs — General Characteristics of the Manuscripts

The outstanding qualities of St. John of the Cross's writings were soon recognized by the earliest of their few and privileged readers. All such persons, of course, belonged to a small circle composed of the Saint's intimate friends and disciples. As time went on, the circle widened repeatedly; now it embraces the entire Church, and countless individual souls who are filled with the spirit of Christianity.

First of all, the works were read and discussed in those loci of evangelical zeal which the Saint had himself enkindled, by his word and example, at Beas, El Calvario, Baeza and Granada. They could not have come more opportunely. St. Teresa's Reform had engendered a spiritual alertness and energy reminiscent of the earliest days of Christianity. Before this could in any way diminish, her first friar presented the followers of them both with spiritual food to nourish and re-create their souls and so to sustain the high degree of zeal for Our Lord which He had bestowed upon them.

In one sense, St. John of the Cross took up his pen in order to supplement the writings of St. Teresa; on several subjects, for example, he abstained from writing at length because she had already treated of them. [2 Much of the work of the two Saints, however, of necessity covers the same ground, and thus the great mystical school of the Spanish Carmelites is reinforced at its very beginnings in a way which must be unique in the history of mysticism. The writings of St. Teresa and St. John of the Cross, though of equal value and identical aim, are in many respects very different in their nature; together they cover almost the entire ground of orthodox mysticism, both speculative and experimental. The Carmelite mystics who came after them were able to build upon a broad and sure foundation.

The writings of St. John of the Cross soon became known outside the narrow circle of his sons and daughters in religion. In a few years they had gone all over Spain and reached Portugal, France and Italy. They were read by persons of every social class, from the Empress Maria of Austria, sister of Philip II, to the most unlettered nuns of St. Teresa's most remote foundations. One of the witnesses at the process for the beatification declared that he knew of no works of which there existed so many copies, with the exception of the Bible.

We may fairly suppose (and the supposition is confirmed by the nature of the extant manuscripts) that the majority of the early copies were made by friars and nuns of the Discalced Reform. Most Discalced houses must have had copies and others were probably in the possession of members of other Orders. We gather, too, from various sources, that even lay persons managed to make or obtain copies of the manuscripts.

How many of these copies, it will be asked, were made directly from the autographs? So vague is the available evidence on this question that it is difficult to attempt any calculation of even approximate reliability. All we can say is that the copies made by, or for, the Discalced friars and nuns themselves are the earliest and most trustworthy, while those intended for the laity were frequently made at third or fourth hand. The Saint himself seems to have written out only one manuscript of each treatise and none of these has come down to us. Some think that he destroyed the manuscripts copied with his own hand, fearing that they might come to be venerated for other reasons than that of the value of their teaching. He was, of course, perfectly capable of such an act of abnegation; once, as we know, in accordance with his own principles, he burned some letters of St. Teresa, which he had carried with him for years, for no other reason than that he realized that he was becoming attached to them.

The only manuscript of his that we possess consists of a few pages of maxims, some letters and one or two documents which he wrote when he was Vicar-Provincial of Andalusia.[So numerous and so thorough have been the searches made for further autographs during the last three centuries that further discoveries of any importance seem most unlikely. We have, therefore, to console ourselves with manuscripts, such as the Sanlœcar de Barrameda Codex of the Spiritual Canticle, which bear the Saint's autograph corrections as warrants of their integrity.

The vagueness of much of the evidence concerning the manuscripts to which we have referred extends to the farthest possible limit — that of using the word 'original' to indicate 'autograph' and 'copy' indifferently. Even in the earliest documents we can never be sure which sense is intended. Furthermore, there was a passion in the seventeenth and eighteenth centuries for describing all kinds of old manuscripts as autographs, and thus we find copies so described in which the hand bears not the slightest resemblance to that of the Saint, as the most superficial collation with a genuine specimen of his hand would have made evident. We shall give instances of this in describing the extant copies of individual treatises. One example of a general kind, however, may be quoted here to show the extent to which the practice spread. In a statement made, with reference to one of the processes, at the convent of Discalced Carmelite nuns of Valladolid, a certain M. Mar'a de la Trinidad deposed 'that a servant of God, a Franciscan tertiary named Ana Mar'a, possesses the originals of the books of our holy father, and has heard that he sent them to the Order.' Great importance was attached to this deposition and every possible measure was taken to find the autographs — needless to say, without result.

With the multiplication of the number of copies of St. John of the Cross's writings, the number of variants naturally multiplied also. The early copies having all been made for devotional purposes, by persons with little or no palaeographical knowledge, many of whom did not even exercise common care, it is not surprising that there is not a single one which can compare in punctiliousness with certain extant eighteenth-century copies of documents connected with St. John of the Cross and St. Teresa. These were made by a painstaking friar called Manuel de Santa Mar'a, whose scrupulousness went so far that he reproduced imperfectly formed letters exactly as they were written, adding the parts that were lacking (e.g., the tilde over the letter –) with ink of another colour.

We may lament that this good father had no predecessor like himself to copy the Saint's treatises, but it is only right to say that the copies we possess are sufficiently faithful and numerous to give us reasonably accurate versions of their originals. The important point about them is that they bear no signs of bad faith, nor even of the desire (understandable enough in those unscientific days) to clarify the sense of their original, or even to improve upon its teaching. Their errors are often gross ones, but the large majority of them are quite easy to detect and put right. The impression to this effect which one obtains from a casual perusal of almost any of these copies is quite definitely confirmed by a comparison of them with copies corrected by the Saint or written by the closest and most trusted of his disciples. It may be added that some of the variants may, for aught we know to the contrary, be the Saint's own work, since it is not improbable that he may have corrected more than one copy of some of his writings, and not been entirely consistent.

There are, broadly speaking, two classes into which the copies (more particularly those of the Ascent and the Dark Night) may be divided. One class aims at a more or less exact transcription; the other definitely sets out to abbreviate. Even if the latter class be credited with a number of copies which hardly merit the name, the former is by far the larger, and, of course, the more important, though it must not be supposed that the latter is unworthy of notice. The abbreviators generally omit whole chapters, or passages, at a time, and, where they are not for the moment doing this, or writing the connecting phrases necessary to repair their mischief, they are often quite faithful to their originals. Since they do not, in general, attribute anything to their author that is not his, no objection can be taken, on moral grounds, to their proceeding, though, in actual fact, the results are not always happy. Their ends were purely practical and devotional and they made no attempt to pass their compendia as full-length transcriptions.

With regard to the Spiritual Canticle and the Living Flame of Love, of each of which there are two redactions bearing indisputable marks of the author's own hand, the classification of the copies will naturally depend upon which redaction each copy the more nearly follows. This question will be discussed in the necessary detail in the introduction to each of these works, and to the individual introductions to the four major treatises we must refer the reader for other details of the manuscripts. In the present pages we have attempted only a general account of these matters. It remains to add that our divisions of each chapter into paragraphs follow the manuscripts throughout except where indicated. The printed editions, as we shall see, suppressed these divisions, but, apart from their value to the modern reader, they are sufficiently nearly identical in the various copies to form one further testimony to their general high standard of reliability.

IV: Integrity of the Saint's Work — Incomplete Condition of the 'Ascent' and the 'Night' — Disputed Questions

The principal lacuna in St. John of the Cross's writings, and, from the literary standpoint, the most interesting, is the lack of any commentary to the last five stanzas of the poem 'Dark Night.' Such a commentary is essential to the completion of the plan which the Saint had already traced for himself in what was to be, and, in spite of its unfinished condition, is in fact, his most rigorously scientific treatise. 'All the doctrine,' he wrote in the Argument of the Ascent, 'whereof I intend to treat in this Ascent of Mount Carmel is included in the following stanzas, and in them is also described the manner of ascending to the summit of the Mount, which is the high estate of perfection which we here call union of the soul with God.' This leaves no doubt but that the Saint intended to treat the mystical life as one whole, and to deal in turn with each stage of the road to perfection, from the beginnings of the Purgative Way to the crown and summit of the life of Union. After showing the need for such a treatise as he proposes to write, he divides the chapters on Purgation into four parts corresponding to the Active and Passive nights of Sense and of Spirit. These, however, correspond only to the first two stanzas of his poem; they are not, as we shall shortly see, complete, but their incompleteness is slight compared with that of the work as a whole.

Did St. John of the Cross, we may ask, ever write a commentary on those last five stanzas, which begin with a description of the state of Illumination:

'Twas that light guided me,
More surely than the noonday's brightest glare —

and end with that of the life of Union:

All things for me that day

Ceas'd, as I slumber'd there,

Amid the lilies drowning all my care?

If we suppose that he did, we are faced with the question of its fate and with the strange fact that none of his contemporaries makes any mention of such a commentary, though they are all prolific in details of far less importance.

Conjectures have been ventured on this question ever since critical methods first began to be applied to St. John of the Cross's writings. A great deal was written about it by P. Andres de la Encarnaci—n, to whom his superiors entrusted the task of collecting and editing the Saint's writings, and whose findings, though they suffer from the defects of an age which from a modern standpoint must be called unscientific, and need therefore to be read with the greatest caution, are often surprisingly just and accurate. P. Andres begins by referring to various places where St. John of the Cross states that he has treated certain subjects and proposes to treat others, about which nothing can be found in his writings. This, he says, may often be due to an oversight on the writer's part or to changes which new experiences might have brought to his mode of thinking. On the other hand, there are sometimes signs that these promises have been fulfilled: the sharp truncation of the argument, for example, at the end of Book III of the Ascent suggests that at least a few pages are missing, in which case the original manuscript must have been mutilated, [for almost all the extant copies break off at the same word. It is unthinkable, as P. Andres says, that the Saint 'should have gone on to write the Night without completing the Ascent, for all these five books are integral parts of one whole, since they all treat of different stages of one spiritual path.'

It may be argued in the same way that St. John of the Cross would not have gone on to write the commentaries on the 'Spiritual Canticle' and the 'Living Flame of Love' without first completing the Dark Night. P. Andres goes so far as to say that the very unwillingness which the Saint displayed towards writing commentaries on the two latter poems indicates that he had already completed the others; otherwise, he could easily have excused himself from the later task on the plea that he had still to finish the earlier.

Again, St. John of the Cross declares very definitely, in the prologue to the Dark Night, that, after describing in the commentary on the first two stanzas the effects of the two passive purgations of the sensual and the spiritual part of man, he will devote the six remaining stanzas to expounding 'various and wondrous effects of the spiritual illumination and union of love with God.' Nothing could be clearer than this. Now, in the commentary on the 'Living Flame,' argues P.

Andres, he treats at considerable length of simple contemplation and adds that he has written fully of it in several chapters of the Ascent and the Night, which he names; but not only do we not find the references in two of the chapters enumerated by him, but he makes no mention of several other chapters in which the references are of considerable fullness. The proper deductions from these facts would seem to be, first, that we do not possess the Ascent and the Night in the form in which the Saint wrote them, and, second, that in the missing chapters he referred to the subject under discussion at much greater length than in the chapters we have.

Further, the practice of St. John of the Cross was not to omit any part of his commentaries when for any reason he was unable or unwilling to write them at length, but rather to abbreviate them. Thus, he runs rapidly through the third stanza of the Night and through the fourth stanza of the Living Flame: we should expect him in the same way to treat the last three stanzas of the Night with similar brevity and rapidity, but not to omit them altogether.

Such are the principal arguments used by P. Andres which have inclined many critics to the belief that St. John of the Cross completed these treatises. Other of his arguments, which to himself were even more convincing, have now lost much weight. The chief of these are the contention that, because a certain Fray Agust'n Antol'nez (b. 1554), in expounding these same poems, makes no mention of the Saint's having failed to expound five stanzas of the Night, he did therefore write an exposition of them; and the supposition that the Living Flame was written before the Spiritual Canticle, and that therefore, when the prologue to the Living Flame says that the author has already described the highest state of perfection attainable in this life, it cannot be referring to the Canticle and must necessarily allude to passages, now lost, from the Dark Night.

Our own judgment upon this much debated question is not easily delivered.

On the one hand, the reasons why St. John of the Cross should have completed his work are perfectly sound ones and his own words in the Ascent and the Dark Night are a clear statement of his intentions. Furthermore, he had ample time to complete it, for he wrote other treatises at a later date and he certainly considered the latter part of the Dark Night to be more important than the former. On the other hand, it is disconcerting to find not even the briefest clear reference to this latter part in any of his subsequent writings, when both the Living Flame and the Spiritual Canticle offered so many occasions for such a reference to an author accustomed to refer his readers to his other treatises. Again, his contemporaries, who were keenly interested in his work, and mention such insignificant things as the Cautions, the Maxims and the 'Mount of Perfection,' say nothing whatever of the missing chapters. None of his biographers speaks of them, nor does P. Alonso de la Madre de Dios, who examined the Saint's writings in detail immediately after his death and was in touch with his closest friends and companions. We are inclined, therefore, to think that the chapters in question were never written.[Is not the following sequence of probable facts the most tenable? We know from P. Juan Evangelista that the Ascent and the Dark Night were written at different times, with many intervals of short or long duration. The Saint may well have entered upon the Spiritual Canticle, which was a concession to the affectionate importunity of M. Ann de Jesœs, with every intention of returning later to finish his earlier treatise.

But, having completed the Canticle, he may equally well have been struck with the similarity between a part of it and the unwritten commentary on the earlier stanzas, and this may have decided him that the Dark Night needed no completion, especially as the Living Flame also described the life of Union. This hypothesis will explain all the facts, and seems completely in harmony with all we know of St. John of the Cross, who was in no sense, as we have already said, a writer by profession. If we accept it, we need not necessarily share the views which we here assume to have been his. Not only would the completion of the Dark Night have given us new ways of approach to so sublime and intricate a theme, but this would have been treated in a way more closely connected with the earlier stages of the mystical life than was possible in either the Living Flame or the Canticle.

We ought perhaps to notice one further supposition of P. Andres, which has been taken up by a number of later critics: that St. John of the Cross completed the commentary which we know as the Dark Night, but that on account of the distinctive nature of the contents of the part now lost he gave it a separate title. The only advantage of this theory seems to be that it makes the hypothesis of the loss of the commentary less improbable. In other respects it is as unsatisfactory as the theory of P. Andres, of which we find a variant in M. Baruzi, that the Saint thought the commentary too bold, and too sublime, to be perpetuated, and therefore destroyed it, or, at least, forbade its being copied. It is surely unlikely that the sublimity of these missing chapters would exceed that of the Canticle or the Living Flame.

This seems the most suitable place to discuss a feature of the works of St. John of the Cross to which allusion is often made — the little interest which he took in their division into books and chapters and his lack of consistency in observing such divisions when he had once made them. A number of examples may be cited. In the first chapter of the Ascent of Mount Carmel, using the words 'part' and 'book' as synonyms, he makes it clear that the Ascent and the Dark Night are to him one single treatise. 'The first night or purgation,' he writes, 'is of the sensual part of the soul, which is treated in the present stanza, and will be treated in the first part of this book. And the second is of the spiritual part; of this speaks the second stanza, which follows; and of this we shall treat likewise, in the second and the third part, with respect to the activity of the soul; and in the fourth part, with respect to its passivity.' The author's intention here is evident. Purgation may be sensual or spiritual, and each of these kinds may be either active or passive. The most logical proceeding would be to divide the whole of the material into four parts or books: two to be devoted to active purgation and two to passive. St. John of the Cross, however, devotes two parts to active spiritual purgation — one to that of the understanding and the other to that of the memory and the will. In the Night, on the other hand, where it would seem essential to devote one book to the passive purgation of sense and another to that of spirit, he includes both in one part, the fourth. In the Ascent, he divides the content of each of his books into various chapters; in the Night, where the argument is developed like that of the Ascent, he makes a division into paragraphs only, and a very irregular division at that, if we may judge by the copies that have reached us. In the Spiritual Canticle and the Living Flame he dispenses with both chapters and paragraphs. The commentary on each stanza here corresponds to a chapter.

Another example is to be found in the arrangement of his expositions. As a rule, he first writes down the stanzas as a whole, then repeats each in turn before expounding it, and repeats each line also in its proper place in the same way. At the beginning of each treatise he makes some general observations — in the form either of an argument and prologue, as in the Ascent; of a prologue and general exposition, as in the Night; of a prologue alone, as in the first redaction of the Canticle and in the Living Flame; or of a prologue and argument, as in the second redaction of the Canticle. In the Ascent and the Night, the first chapter of each book contains the 'exposition of the stanzas,' though some copies describe this, in Book III of the Ascent, as an 'argument.' In the Night, the book dealing with the Night of Sense begins with the usual 'exposition'; that of the Night of the Spirit, however, has nothing to correspond with it.

In the first redaction of the Spiritual Canticle, St. John of the Cross first sets down the poem, then a few lines of 'exposition' giving the argument of the stanza, and finally the commentary upon each line. Sometimes he comments upon two or three lines at once. In the second redaction, he prefaces almost every stanza with an 'annotation,' of which there is none in the first redaction except before the commentary on the thirteenth and fourteenth stanzas. The chief purpose of the 'annotation' is to link the argument of each stanza with that of the stanza preceding it; occasionally the annotation and the exposition are combined.

It is clear from all this that, in spite of his orderly mind, St. John of the Cross was no believer in strict uniformity in matters of arrangement which would seem to demand such uniformity once they had been decided upon. They are, of course, of secondary importance, but the fact that the inconsistencies are the work of St. John of the Cross himself, and not merely of careless copyists, who have enough else to account for, is of real moment in the discussion of critical questions which turn on the Saint's accuracy.

Another characteristic of these commentaries is the inequality of length as between the exposition of certain lines and stanzas. While some of these are dealt with fully, the exposition of others is brought to a close with surprising rapidity, even though it sometimes seems that much more needs to be said: we get the impression that the author was anxious to push his work forward or was pressed for time. He devotes fourteen long chapters of the Ascent to glossing the first two lines of the first stanza and dismisses the three remaining lines in a few sentences. In both the Ascent and the Night, indeed, the stanzas appear to serve only as a pretext for introducing the great wealth of ascetic and mystical teaching which the Saint has gathered together. In the Canticle and the Living Flame, on the other hand, he keeps much closer to his stanzas, though here, too, there is a considerable inequality. One result of the difference in nature between these two pairs of treatises is that the Ascent and the Night are more solidly built and more rigidly doctrinal, whereas in the Canticle and the Flame there is more movement and more poetry.

V: History of the Publication of St. John of the Cross's Writings — the First Edition

It seems strange that mystical works of such surpassing value should not have been published till twenty-seven years after their author's death, for not only were the manuscript copies insufficient to propagate them as widely as those who made them would have desired, but the multiplication of these copies led to an ever greater number of variants in the text. Had it but been possible for the first edition of them to have been published while their author still lived, we might to-day have a perfect text. But the probability is that, if such an idea had occurred to St. John of the Cross, he would have set it aside as presumptuous. In allowing copies to be made he doubtless never envisaged their going beyond the limited circle of his Order.

We have found no documentary trace of any project for an edition of these works during their author's lifetime. The most natural time for a discussion of the matter would have been in September 1586, when the Definitors of the Order, among whom was St. John of the Cross, met in Madrid and decided to publish the works of St. Teresa. Two years earlier, when he was writing the Spiritual Canticle, St. John of the Cross had expressed a desire for the publication of St. Teresa's writings and assumed that this would not be long delayed. As we have seen, he considered his own works as complementary to those of St. Teresa, and one would have thought that the simultaneous publication of the writings of the two Reformers would have seemed to the Definitors an excellent idea.

After his death, it is probable that there was no one at first who was both able and willing to undertake the work of editor; for, as is well known, towards the end of his life the Saint had powerful enemies within his Order who might well have opposed the project, though, to do the Discalced Reform justice, it was brought up as early as ten years after his death. A resolution was passed at the Chapter-General of the Reform held in September 1601, to the effect 'that the works of Fr. Juan de la Cruz be printed and that the Definitors, Fr. Juan de Jesús Mar'a and Fr. Tomas [de Jesús], be instructed to examine and approve them.'[Two years later (July 4, 1603), the same Chapter, also meeting in Madrid, 'gave leave to the Definitor, Fr. Tomas [de Jesús], for the printing of the works of Fr. Juan de la Cruz, first friar of the Discalced Reform.'

It is not known (since the Chapter Book is no longer extant) why the matter lapsed for two years, but Fr. Tomas de Jesús, the Definitor to whom alone it was entrusted on the second occasion, was a most able man, well qualified to edit the works of his predecessor. Why, then, we may wonder, did he not do so? The story of his life in the years following the commission may partly answer this question. His definitorship came to an end in 1604, when he was elected Prior of the 'desert' of San José de las Batuecas. After completing the customary three years in this office, during which time he could have done no work at all upon the edition, he was elected Prior of the Discalced house at Zaragoza. But at this point Paul V sent for him to Rome and from that time onward his life followed other channels.

The next attempt to accomplish the project was successful. The story begins with a meeting between the Definitors of the Order and Fr. José de Jesús Mar'a, the General, at Velez-Melaga, where a new decision to publish the works of St. John of the Cross was taken and put into effect (as a later resolution has it) 'without any delay or condition whatsoever.' The enterprise suffered a setback, only a week after it had been planned, in the death of the learned Jesuit P. Suarez, who was on terms of close friendship with the Discalced and had been appointed one of the censors. But P. Diego de Jesús (Salablanca), Prior of the Discalced house at Toledo, to whom its execution was entrusted, lost no time in accomplishing his task; indeed, one would suppose that he had begun it long before, since early in the next year it was completed and published in Alcala. The volume, entitled Spiritual Works which lead a soul to perfect union with God, has 720 pages and bears the date 1618. The works are preceded by a preface addressed to the reader and a brief summary of the author's 'life and virtues.' An engraving of the 'Mount of Perfection' is included.

There are several peculiarities about this editio princeps. In the first place, although the pagination is continuous, it was the work of two different printers; the reason for this is quite unknown, though various reasons might be suggested. The greatest care was evidently taken so that the work should be well and truly approved: it is recommended, in terms of the highest praise, by the authorities of the University of Alcala, who, at the request of the General of the Discalced Carmelites, had submitted it for examination to four of the professors of that University. No doubt for reasons of safety, the Spiritual Canticle was not included in that edition: it was too much like a commentary on the Song of Songs for such a proceeding to be just then advisable.

We have now to enquire into the merits of the edition of P. Salablanca, which met with such warm approval on its publication, yet very soon afterwards began to be recognized as defective and is little esteemed for its intrinsic qualities to-day.

It must, of course, be realized that critical standards in the early seventeenth century were low and that the first editor of St. John of the Cross had neither the method nor the available material of the twentieth century. Nor were the times favourable for the publication of the works of a great mystic who attempted fearlessly and fully to describe the highest stages of perfection on the road to God. These two facts are responsible for most of the defects of the edition.

For nearly a century, the great peril associated with the mystical life had been that of Illuminism, a gross form of pseudo-mysticism which had claimed many victims among the holiest and most learned, and of which there was such fear that excessive, almost unbelievable, precautions had been taken against it. These precautions, together with the frequency and audacity with which Illuminists invoked the authority and protection of well-known contemporary ascetic and mystical writers, give reality to P. Salablanca's fear lest the leaders of the sect might shelter themselves behind the doctrines of St. John of the Cross and so call forth the censure of the Inquisition upon passages which seemed to him to bear close relation to their erroneous teaching. It was for this definite reason, and not because of an arbitrary meticulousness, that P. Salablanca omitted or adapted such passages as those noted in Book I, Chapter viii of the Ascent of Mount Carmel and in a number of chapters in Book II. A study of these, all of which are indicated in the footnotes to our text, is of great interest.

Less important are a large number of minor corrections made with the intention of giving greater precision to some theological concept; the omission of lines and even paragraphs which the editor considered redundant, as in fact they frequently are; and corrections made with the aim of lending greater clearness to the argument or improving the style. A few changes were made out of prudery: such are the use of sensitivo for sensual, the suppression of phrases dealing with carnal vice and the omission of several paragraphs from that chapter of the Dark Night — which speaks of the third deadly sin of beginners. There was little enough reason for these changes: St. John of the Cross is particularly inoffensive in his diction and may, from that point of view, be read by a child.

The sum total of P. Salablanca's mutilations is very considerable. There are more in the Ascent and the Living Flame than in the Dark Night; but hardly a page of the editio princeps is free from them and on most pages they abound. It need not be said that they are regrettable. They belong to an age when the garments of dead saints were cut up into small fragments and distributed among the devout and when their cells were decked out with indifferent taste and converted into oratories. It would not have been considered sufficient had the editor printed the text of St. John of the Cross as he found it and glossed it to his liking in footnotes; another editor would have put opposite interpretations upon it, thus cancelling out the work of his predecessor. Even the radical mutilations of P. Salablanca did not suffice, as will now be seen, to protect the works of the Saint from the Inquisition.

VI: Denunciation of the 'Works' to the Inquisition — Defence of Them Made by Fr. Basilo Ponce De Leîn — Editions of the Seventeenth and Eighteenth Centuries

Neither the commendations of University professors nor the scissors of a meticulous editor could save the treatises of St. John of the Cross from that particular form of attack which, more than all others, was feared in the seventeenth century. We shall say nothing here of the history, nature and procedure of the Spanish Inquisition, which has had its outspoken antagonists and its unreasoning defenders but has not yet been studied with impartiality. It must suffice to set down the facts as they here affect our subject.

Forty propositions, then, were extracted from the edition of 1618 and presented to the Holy Office for condemnation with the object of causing the withdrawal of the edition from circulation. The attempt would probably have succeeded but for the warm, vigorous and learned defence put up by the Augustinian Fray Basilio Ponce de Leon, a theological professor in the University of Salamanca and a nephew of the Luis de Leon who wrote the Names of Christ and took so great an interest in the works of St. Teresa.

It was in the very convent of San Felipe in Madrid where thirty-five years earlier Fray Luis had written his immortal eulogy of St. Teresa that Fray Basilio, on July 11, 1622, signed a most interesting 'Reply' to the objections which had been raised to the Alcala edition of St. John of the Cross. Although we propose, in our third volume, to reproduce Fray Basilio's defence, it is necessary to our narrative to say something of it here, for it is the most important of all extant documents which reveal the vicissitudes in the history of the Saint's teaching.

Before entering upon an examination of the censured propositions, the learned Augustinian makes some general observations, which must have carried great weight as coming from so high a theological authority. He recalls the commendations of the edition by the professors of the University of Alcala 'where the faculty of theology is so famous,' and by many others, including several ministers of the Holy Office and two Dominicans who 'without dispute are among the most learned of their Order.' Secondly, he refers to the eminently saintly character of the first friar of the Discalced Reform: 'it is not to be presumed that God would set a man whose teaching is so evil . . . as is alleged, to be the comer-stone of so great a building.' Thirdly, he notes how close a follower was St. John of the Cross of St. Teresa, a person who was singularly free from any taint of unorthodoxy. And finally he recalls a number of similar attacks on works of this kind, notably that on Laredo's Ascent of Mount Sion, which have proved to be devoid of foundation, and points out that isolated 'propositions' need to be set in their context before they can be fairly judged.

Fray Basilio next refutes the charges brought against the works of St. John of the Cross, nearly all of which relate to his teaching on the passivity of the faculties in certain degrees of contemplation. Each proposition he copies and afterwards defends, both by argument and by quotations from the Fathers, from the medieval mystics and from his own contemporaries. It is noteworthy that among these authorities he invariably includes St. Teresa, who had been beatified in 1614, and enjoyed an undisputed reputation. This inclusion, as well as being an enhancement of his defence, affords a striking demonstration of the unity of thought existing between the two great Carmelites.

Having expounded the orthodox Catholic teaching in regard to these matters, and shown that the teaching of St. John of the Cross is in agreement with it, Fray Basilio goes on to make clear the true attitude of the Illuminists and thus to reinforce his contentions by showing how far removed from this is the Saint's doctrine.

Fray Basilio's magnificent defence of St. John of the Cross appears to have had the unusual effect of quashing the attack entirely: the excellence of his arguments, backed by his great authority, was evidently unanswerable. So far as we know, the Inquisition took no proceedings against the Alcala edition whatsoever. Had this at any time been prohibited, we may be sure that Llorente would have revealed the fact, and, though he refers to the persecution of St. John of the Cross during his lifetime, he is quite silent about any posthumous condemnation of his writings.

The editio princeps was reprinted in 1619, with a different pagination and a few corrections, in Barcelona.[Before these two editions were out of print, the General of the Discalced Carmelites had entrusted an able historian of the Reform, Fray Jeronimo de San José, with the preparation of a new one. This was published at Madrid, in 1630. It has a short introduction describing its scope and general nature, a number of new and influential commendations and an admirable fifty-page 'sketch' of St. John of the Cross by the editor which has been reproduced in most subsequent editions and has probably done more than any other single work to make known the facts of the Saint's biography. The great feature of this edition, however, is the inclusion of the Spiritual Canticle, placed (by an error, as a printer's note explains) at the end of the volume, instead of before the Living Flame, which is, of course, its proper position.

The inclusion of the Canticle is one of the two merits that the editor claims for his new edition. The other is that he 'prints both the Canticle and the other works according to their original manuscripts, written in the hand of the same venerable author.' This claim is, of course, greatly exaggerated, as what has been said above with regard to the manuscripts will indicate. Not only does Fray Jeronimo appear to have had no genuine original manuscript at all, but of the omissions of the editio princeps it is doubtful if he makes good many more than one in a hundred. In fact, with very occasional exceptions, he merely reproduces the princeps — omissions, interpolations, well-meant improvements and all.

In Fray Jeronimo's defence it must be said that the reasons which moved his predecessor to mutilate his edition were still potent, and the times had not changed. It is more surprising that for nearly three centuries the edition of 1630 should have been followed by later editors. The numerous versions of the works which saw the light in the later seventeenth and the eighteenth century added a few poems, letters and maxims to the corpus of work which he presented and which assumed great importance as the Saint became better known and more deeply venerated. But they did no more. It suffices, therefore, to enumerate the chief of them.

The Barcelona publisher of the 1619 edition produced a new edition in 1635, which is a mere reproduction of that of 1630. A Madrid edition of 1649, which adds nine letters, a hundred maxims and a small collection of poems, was reproduced in 1672 (Madrid), 1679 (Madrid), 1693 (Barcelona) and 1694 (Madrid), the last reproduction being in two volumes. An edition was also published in Barcelona in 1700.

If we disregard a 'compendium' of the Saint's writings published in Seville in 1701, the first eighteenth-century edition was published in Seville in 1703 — the most interesting of those that had seen the light since 1630. It is well printed on good paper in a folio volume and its editor, Fr. Andres de Jesús Mar'a, claims it, on several grounds, as an advance on preceding editions. First, he says, 'innumerable errors of great importance' have been corrected in it; then, the Spiritual Canticle has been amended according to its original manuscript 'in the hand of the same holy doctor, our father, kept and venerated in our convent of Discalced Carmelite nuns at Jaen'; next, he adds two new poems and increases the number of maxims from 100 to 365; and lastly, the letters are increased from nine to seventeen, all of which are found in P. Jeronimo de San José's history. The first of these claims is as great an exaggeration as was P. Jeronimo's; to the second we shall refer in our introduction to the Spiritual Canticle. The third and fourth, however, are justified, and for these, as for a few minor improvements, the editor deserves every commendation.

The remaining years of the eighteenth century produced few editions; apart from a reprint (1724) of the compendium of 1701, the only one known to us is that published at Pamplona in 1774, after which nearly eighty years were to pass before any earlier edition was so much as reprinted. Before we resume this bibliographical narrative, however, we must go back over some earlier history.

VII: New Denunciations and Defences — Fray Nicolas De Jesús Maria — the Carmelite School and the Inquisition

We remarked, apropos of the edition of 1630, that the reasons which led Fray Diego de Jesús to mutilate his texts were still in existence when Fray Jeronimo de San Jose prepared his edition some twelve years later. If any independent proof of this statement is needed, it may be found in the numerous apologias that were published during the seventeenth century, not only in Spain, but in Italy, France, Germany and other countries of Europe. If doctrines are not attacked, there is no occasion to write vigorous defences of them.

Following the example of Fray Basilio Ponce de Leon, a professor of theology in the College of the Reform at Salamanca, Fray Nicholas de Jesús Mar'a, wrote a learned Latin defence of St. John of the Cross in 1631, often referred to briefly as the Elucidatio. [It is divided into two parts, the first defending the Saint against charges of a general kind that were brought against his writings, and the second upholding censured propositions taken from them. On the general ground, P. Nicholas reminds his readers that many writers who now enjoy the highest possible reputation were in their time denounced and unjustly persecuted. St. Jerome was attacked for his translation of the Bible from Hebrew into Latin; St. Augustine, for his teaching about grace and free-will. The works of St. Gregory the Great were burned at Rome; those of St. Thomas Aquinas at Paris. Most mediaeval and modern mystics have been the victims of persecution — Ruysbroeck, Tauler and even St. Teresa. Such happenings, he maintains, have done nothing to lessen the eventual prestige of these authors, but rather have added to it.

Nor, he continues, can the works of any author fairly be censured, because misguided teachers make use of them to propagate their false teaching. No book has been more misused by heretics than Holy Scripture and few books of value would escape if we were to condemn all that had been so treated. Equally worthless is the objection that mystical literature is full of difficulties which may cause the ignorant and pusillanimous to stumble.

Apart from the fact that St. John of the Cross is clearer and more lucid than most of his contemporaries, and that therefore the works of many of them would have to follow his own into oblivion, the same argument might again be applied to the Scriptures. Who can estimate the good imparted by the sacred books to those who read them in a spirit of uprightness and simplicity? Yet what books are more pregnant with mystery and with truths that are difficult and, humanly speaking, even inaccessible?

But (continues P. Nicolas), even if we allow that parts of the work of St. John of the Cross, for all the clarity of his exposition, are obscure to the general reader, it must be remembered that much more is of the greatest attraction and profit to all. On the one hand, the writings of the Saint represent the purest sublimation of Divine love in the pilgrim soul, and are therefore food for the most advanced upon the mystic way. On the other, every reader, however slight his spiritual progress, can understand the Saint's ascetic teaching: his chapters on the purgation of the senses, mortification, detachment from all that belongs to the earth, purity of conscience, the practice of the virtues, and so on. The Saint's greatest enemy is not the obscurity of his teaching but the inflexible logic with which he deduces, from the fundamental principles of evangelical perfection, the consequences which must be observed by those who would scale the Mount. So straight and so hard is the road which he maps out for the climber that the majority of those who see it are at once dismayed.

These are the main lines of P. Nicolas' argument, which he develops at great length. We must refer briefly to the chapter in which he makes a careful synthesis of the teaching of the Illuminists, to show how far it is removed from that of St. John of the Cross. He divides these false contemplatives into four classes. In the first class he places those who suppress all their acts, both interior and exterior, in prayer. In the second, those who give themselves up to a state of pure quiet, with no loving attention to God. In the third, those who allow their bodies to indulge every craving and maintain that, in the state of spiritual intoxication which they have reached, they are unable to commit sin. In the fourth, those who consider themselves to be instruments of God and adopt an attitude of complete passivity, maintaining also that they are unable to sin, because God alone is working in them. The division is more subtle than practical, for the devotees of this sect, with few exceptions, professed the same erroneous beliefs and tended to the same degree of licence in their conduct. But, by isolating these tenets, P. Nicolas is the better able to show the antithesis between them and those of St. John of the Cross.

In the second part of the Elucidatio, he analyses the propositions already treated by Fray Basilio Ponce de Leon, reducing them to twenty and dealing faithfully with them in the same number of chapters. His defence is clear, methodical and convincing and follows similar lines to those adopted by Fray Basilio, to whom its author acknowledges his indebtedness.

Another of St. John of the Cross's apologists is Fray Jose de Jesús Mar'a (Quiroga), who, in a number of his works, both defends and eulogizes him, without going into any detailed examination of the propositions. Fray Jose is an outstanding example of a very large class of writers, for, as Illuminism gave place to Quietism, the teaching of St. John of the Cross became more and more violently impugned and almost all mystical writers of the time referred to him. Perhaps we should single out, from among his defenders outside the Carmelite Order, that Augustinian father, P. Antol'nez, to whose commentary on three of the Saint's works we have already made reference.

As the school of mystical writers within the Discalced Carmelite Reform gradually grew — a school which took St. John of the Cross as its leader and is one of the most illustrious in the history of mystical theology — it began to share in the same persecution as had befallen its founder. It is impossible, in a few words, to describe this epoch of purgation, and indeed it can only be properly studied in its proper context — the religious history of the period as a whole. For our purpose, it suffices to say that the works of St. John of the Cross were once more denounced to the Inquisition, though, once more, no notice appears to have been taken of the denunciations, for there exists no record ordering the expurgation or prohibition of the books referred to. The Elucidatio was also denounced, together with several of the works of P. Jose de Jesús Mar'a, at various times in the seventeenth century, and these attacks were of course equivalent to direct attacks on St. John of the Cross. One of the most vehement onslaughts made was levelled against P. José's Subida del Alma a Dios ('Ascent of the Soul to God'), which is in effect an elaborate commentary on St. John of the Cross's teaching. The Spanish Inquisition refusing to censure the book, an appeal against it was made to the Inquisition at Rome. When no satisfaction was obtained in this quarter, P. José's opponents went to the Pope, who referred the matter to the Sacred Congregation of the Index; but this body issued a warm eulogy of the book and the matter thereupon dropped.

In spite of such defeats, the opponents of the Carmelite school continued their work into the eighteenth century. In 1740, a new appeal was made to the Spanish Inquisition to censure P. José's Subida. A document of seventy-three folios denounced no less than one hundred and sixty-five propositions which it claimed to have taken direct from the work referred to, and this time, after a conflict extending over ten years, the book (described as 'falsely attributed' to P. JosŽ) was condemned (July 4, 1750), as 'containing doctrine most perilous in practice, and propositions similar and equivalent to those condemned in Miguel de Molinos.'

We set down the salient facts of this controversy, without commenting upon them, as an instance of the attitude of the eighteenth century towards the mystics in general, and, in particular, towards the school of the Discalced Carmelites. In view of the state and tendencies of thought in these times, the fact of the persecution, and the degree of success that it attained, is not surprising. The important point to bear in mind is that it must be taken into account continually by students of the editions of the Saint's writings and of the history of his teaching throughout the eighteenth and nineteenth centuries.

VIII: Further History of the Editions — P. Andres De La Encarnaciîn — Editions of the Nineteenth and Twentieth Centuries

What has just been said will fully explain the paucity of the editions of St. John of the Cross which we find in the eighteenth century. This century, however, was, scientifically speaking, one of great progress. Critical methods of study developed and became widespread; and there was a great desire to obtain purer and more nearly perfect texts and to discover the original sources of the ideas of great thinkers. These tendencies made themselves felt within the Discalced Carmelite Order, and there also arose a great ambition to republish in their original forms the works both of St. Teresa and of St. John of the Cross. The need was greater in the latter case than in the former; so urgent was it felt to be as to admit of no delay. 'There have been discovered in the works [of St. John of the Cross],' says a document of about 1753, 'many errors, mutilations and other defects the existence of which cannot be denied.'[The religious who wrote thus to the Chapter-General of the Reform set out definite and practical schemes for a thorough revision of these works, which were at once accepted. There thus comes into our history that noteworthy friar, P. Andres de la Encarnacion, to whom we owe so much of what we know about the Saint to-day. P. Andres was no great stylist, nor had he the usual Spanish fluency of diction. But he was patient, modest and industrious, and above all he was endowed with a double portion of the critical spirit of the eighteenth century. He was selected for the work of investigation as being by far the fittest person who could be found for it. A decree dated October 6, 1754 ordered him to set to work. As a necessary preliminary to the task of preparing a corrected text of the Saint's writings, he was to spare no effort in searching for every extant manuscript; accordingly he began long journeys through La Mancha and Andalusia, going over all the ground covered by St. John of the Cross in his travels and paying special attention to the places where he had lived for any considerable period. In those days, before the religious persecutions of the nineteenth century had destroyed and scattered books and manuscripts, the archives of the various religious houses were intact. P. Andres and his amanuensis were therefore able to copy and collate valuable manuscripts now lost to us and they at once began to restore the phrases and passages omitted from the editions. Unhappily, their work has disappeared and we can judge of it only at second hand; but it appears to have been in every way meritorious. So far as we can gather from the documents which have come down to us, it failed to pass the rigorous censorship of the Order. In other words, the censors, who were professional theologians, insisted upon making so many corrections that the Superiors, who shared the enlightened critical opinions of P. Andres, thought it better to postpone the publication of the edition indefinitely.

The failure of the project, however, to which P. Andres devoted so much patient labour, did not wholly destroy the fruits of his skill and perseverance. He was ordered to retire to his priory, where he spent the rest of his long life under the burden of a trial the magnitude of which any scholar or studiously minded reader can estimate. He did what he could in his seclusion to collect, arrange and recopy such notes of his work as he could recover from those to whom they had been submitted. His defence of this action to the Chapter-General is at once admirable in the tranquillity of its temper and pathetic in the eagerness and affection which it displays for the task that he has been forbidden to continue:

Inasmuch as I was ordered, some years ago . . . to prepare an exact edition of the works of our holy father, and afterwards was commanded to suspend my labours for just reasons which presented themselves to these our fathers and prevented its accomplishment at the time, I obeyed forthwith with the greatest submissiveness, but, as I found that I had a rich store of information which at some future time might contribute to the publication of a truly illustrious and perfect edition, it seemed to me that I should not be running counter to the spirit of the Order if I gave it some serviceable form, so that I should not be embarrassed by seeing it in a disorderly condition if at some future date it should be proposed to carry into effect the original decisions of the Order.

With humility and submissiveness, therefore, I send to your Reverences these results of my private labours, not because it is in my mind that the work should be recommended, or that, if this is to be done, it should be at any particular time, for that I leave to the disposition of your Reverences and of God, but to the end that I may return to the Order that which belongs to it; for, since I was excused from religious observances for nearly nine years so that I might labour in this its own field, the Order cannot but have a right to the fruits of my labours, nor can I escape the obligation of delivering what I have discovered into its hand. . . .

We cannot examine the full text of the interesting memorandum to the Censors which follows this humble exordium. One of their allegations had been that the credit of the Order would suffer if it became known that passages of the Saint's works had been suppressed by Carmelite editors. P. Andres makes the sage reply: 'There is certainly the risk that this will become known if the edition is made; but there is also a risk that it will become known in any case. We must weigh the risks against each other and decide which proceeding will bring the Order into the greater discredit if one of them materializes.' He fortifies this argument with the declaration that the defects of the existing editions were common knowledge outside the Order as well as within it, and that, as manuscript copies of the Saint's works were also in the possession of many others than Carmelites, there was nothing to prevent a correct edition being made at any time. This must suffice as a proof that P. Andres could be as acute as he was submissive.

Besides collecting this material, and leaving on record his opposition to the short-sighted decision of the Censors, P. Andres prepared 'some Disquisitions on the writings of the Saint, which, if a more skilful hand should correct and improve their style, cannot but be well received.' Closely connected with the Disquisitions are the Preludes in which he glosses the Saint's writings. These studies, like the notes already described, have all been lost— no doubt, together with many other documents from the archives of the Reform in Madrid, they disappeared during the pillaging of the religious houses in the early nineteenth century.

The little of P. Andres' work that remains to us gives a clear picture of the efforts made by the Reform to bring out a worthy edition of St. John of the Cross's writings in the eighteenth century; it is manifestly insufficient, however, to take a modern editor far along the way. Nor, as we have seen, are his judgments by any means to be followed otherwise than with the greatest caution; he greatly exaggerates, too, the effect of the mutilations of earlier editors, no doubt in order to convince his superiors of the necessity for a new edition. The materials for a modern editor are to be found, not in the documents left by P. Andres, but in such Carmelite archives as still exist, and in the National Library of Spain, to which many Carmelite treasures found their way at the beginning of the last century.

The work sent by P. Andres to his superiors was kept in the archives of the Discalced Carmelites, but no new edition was prepared till a hundred and fifty years later. In the nineteenth century such a task was made considerably more difficult by religious persecution; which resulted in the loss of many valuable manuscripts, some of which P. Andres must certainly have examined. For a time, too, the Orders were expelled from Spain, and, on their return, had neither the necessary freedom, nor the time or material means, for such undertakings. In the twenty-seventh volume of the well-known series of classics entitled Biblioteca de Autores Espanoles (1853) the works of St. John of the Cross were reprinted according to the 1703 edition, without its engravings, indices and commendations, and with a 'critical estimate' of the Saint by Pi y Margall, which has some literary value but in other respects fails entirely to do justice to its subject.

Neither the Madrid edition of 1872 nor the Barcelona edition of 1883 adds anything to our knowledge and it was not till the Toledo edition of 1912-14 that a new advance was made. This edition was the work of a young Carmelite friar, P. Gerardo de San Juan de la Cruz, who died soon after its completion. It aims, according to its title, which is certainly justified, at being 'the most correct and complete edition of all that have been published down to the present date.' If it was not as successful as might have been wished, this could perhaps hardly have been expected of a comparatively inexperienced editor confronted with so gigantic a task — a man, too, who worked almost alone and was by temperament and predilection an investigator rather than a critic. Nevertheless, its introductions, footnotes, appended documents, and collection of apocryphal works of the Saint, as well as its text, were all considered worthy of extended study and the edition was rightly received with enthusiasm. Its principal merit will always lie in its having restored to their proper places, for the first time in a printed edition, many passages which had theretofore remained in manuscript.

We have been anxious that this new edition [Burgos, 1929-31] should represent a fresh advance in the task of establishing a definitive text of St. John of the Cross's writings. For this reason we have examined, together with two devoted assistants, every discoverable manuscript, with the result, as it seems to us, that both the form and the content of our author's works are as nearly as possible as he left them.

In no case have we followed any one manuscript exclusively, preferring to assess the value of each by a careful preliminary study and to consider each on its merits, which are described in the introduction to each of the individual works. Since our primary aim has been to present an accurate text, our footnotes will be found to be almost exclusively textual. The only edition which we cite, with the occasional exception of that of 1630, is the princeps, from which alone there is much to be learned. The Latin quotations from the Vulgate are not, of course, given except where they appear in the manuscripts, and, save for the occasional correction of a copyist's error, they are reproduced in exactly the form in which we have found them. Orthography and punctuation have had perforce to be modernized, since the manuscripts differ widely and we have so few autographs that nothing conclusive can be learned of the Saint's own practice.

Introduction

As will be seen from the biographical outline which we have given of the life of St. John of the Cross, this was the first of the Saint's treatises to be written; it was begun at El Calvario, and, after various intervals, due to the author's preoccupation with the business of government and the direction and care of souls, was completed at Granada.

The treatise presents a remarkable outline of Christian perfection from the point at which the soul first seeks to rise from the earth and soar upward towards union with God. It is a work which shows every sign of careful planning and great attention to detail, as an ascetic treatise it is noteworthy for its detailed psychological analysis; as a contribution to mystical theology, for the skill with which it treats the most complicated and delicate questions concerning the Mystic Way.

Both the great Carmelite reformers pay close attention to the early stages of the mystical life, beyond which many never pass, and both give the primacy to prayer as a means of attaining perfection. To St. Teresa prayer is the greatest of all blessings of this life, the channel through which all the favours of God pass to the soul, the beginning of every virtue and the plainly marked highroad which leads to the summit of Mount Carmel. She can hardly conceive of a person in full spiritual health whose life is not one of prayer. Her coadjutor in the Carmelite Reform writes in the same spirit. Prayer, for St. John of the Cross as for St. Teresa, is no mere exercise made up of petition and meditation, but a complete spiritual life which brings in its train all the virtues, increases all the soul's potentialities and may ultimately lead to 'deification' or transformation in God through love. It may be said that the exposition of the life of prayer, from its lowest stages to its highest, is the common aim of these two Saints, which each pursues and accomplishes in a peculiarly individual manner.

St. John of the Cross assumes his reader to be familiar with the rudiments of the spiritual life and therefore omits detailed description of the most elementary of the exercises incumbent upon all Christians. The plan of the Ascent of Mount Carmel (which, properly speaking, embraces its sequel, the Dark Night) follows the lines of the poem with the latter title (p. 10). Into two stanzas of five lines each, St. John of the Cross has condensed all the instruction which he develops in this treatise. In order to reach the Union of Light, the soul must pass through the Dark Night — that is to say, through a series of purifications, during which it is walking, as it were, through a tunnel of impenetrable obscurity and from which it emerges to bask in the sunshine of grace and to enjoy the Divine intimacy.

Through this obscurity the thread which guides the soul is that of 'emptiness' or 'negation.' Only by voiding ourselves of all that is not God can we attain to the possession of God, for two contraries cannot co-exist in one individual, and creature-love is darkness, while God is light, so that from any human heart one of the two cannot fail to drive out the other.

Now the soul, according to the Saint's psychology, is made up of interior and exterior senses and of the faculties. All these must be free from creature impurities in order to be prepared for Divine union. The necessary self-emptying may be accomplished in two ways: by our own efforts, with the habitual aid of grace, and by the action of God exclusively, in which the individual has no part whatsoever. Following this order, the Ascent is divided into two parts, which deal respectively with the 'Active' night and the 'Passive.' Each of these parts consists of several books. Since the soul must be purified in its entirety, the Active Night is logically divided into the Night of Sense and the Night of the Spirit; a similar division is observed in treating of the Passive Night. One book is devoted to the Active Night of Sense; two are needed for the Active Night of the Spirit. Unhappily, however, the treatise was never finished; not only was its author unable to take us out of the night into the day, as he certainly intended to do, but he has not even space to describe the Passive Night in all the fullness of its symbolism.

A brief glance at the outstanding parts of the Ascent of Mount Carmel will give some idea of its nature. The first obstacle which the pilgrim soul encounters is the senses, upon which St. John of the Cross expends his analytical skill in Book I. Like any academic professor (and it will be recalled that he had undergone a complete university course at Salamanca), he outlines and defines his subject, goes over the necessary preliminary ground before expounding it, and treats it, in turn, under each of its natural divisions. He tells us, that is to say, what he understands by the 'dark night'; describes its causes and its stages; explains how necessary it is to union with God; enumerates the perils which beset the soul that enters it; and shows how all desires must be expelled, 'however small they be,' if the soul is to travel through it safely. Finally he gives a complete synthesis of the procedure that must be adopted by the pilgrim in relation to this part of his journey: the force of this is intensified by those striking maxims and distichs which make Chapter xiii of Book I so memorable.

The first thirteen chapters of the Ascent are perhaps the easiest to understand (though they are anything but easy to put into practice) in the entire works of St. John of the Cross. They are all a commentary on the very first line of the poem. The last two chapters of the first book glance at the remaining lines, rather than expound them, and the Saint takes us on at once to Book II, which expounds the second stanza and enters upon the Night of the Spirit.

Here the Saint treats of the proximate means to union with God — namely, faith. He uses the same careful method of exposition, showing clearly how faith is to the soul as a dark night, and how, nevertheless, it is the safest of guides. A parenthetical chapter (v) attempts to give some idea of the nature of union, so that the reader may recognize from afar the goal to which he is proceeding. The author then goes on to describe how the three theological virtues — faith, hope and charity — must 'void and dispose for union' the three faculties of the soul — understanding, memory and will.

He shows how narrow is the way that leads to life and how nothing that belongs to the understanding can guide the soul to union. His illustrations and arguments are far more complicated and subtle than are those of the first book, and give the reader some idea of his knowledge, not only of philosophy and theology, but also of individual souls. Without this last qualification he could never have written those penetrating chapters on the impediments to union — above all, the passages on visions, locutions and revelations — nor must we overlook his description (Chapter xiii) of the three signs that the soul is ready to pass from meditation to contemplation. It may be doubted if in its own field this second book has ever been surpassed. There is no mystic who gives a more powerful impression than St. John of the Cross of an absolute mastery of his subject. No mistiness, vagueness or indecision clouds his writing: he is as clear-cut and definite as can be.

In his third book St. John of the Cross goes on to describe the obstacles to union which come from the memory and the will. Unlike St. Thomas, he considered the memory as a distinct and separate faculty of the soul. Having written, however, at such length of the understanding, he found it possible to treat more briefly of that other faculty, which is so closely related to it. Fourteen chapters (ii-xv) describe the dark night to be traversed by the memory; thirty (xvi-xlv) the passage of the will, impelled by love. The latter part is the more strikingly developed. Four passions — joy, hope, sorrow and fear — invade the will, and may either encompass the soul's perdition, or, if rightly directed, lead it to virtue and union. Once more St. John of the Cross employs his profound familiarity with the human soul to turn it away from peril and guide it into the path of safety. Much that he says, in dealing with passions so familiar to us all, is not only purely ascetic, but is even commonplace to the instructed Christian. Yet these are but parts of a greater whole.

Of particular interest, both intrinsically and as giving a picture of the Saint's own times, are the chapters on ceremonies and aids to devotion — the use of rosaries, medals, pilgrimages, etc. It must be remembered, of course, that he spent most of his active life in the South of Spain, where exaggerations of all kinds, even to-day, are more frequent than in the more sober north. In any case there is less need, in this lukewarm age, to warn Christians against the abuse of these means of grace, and more need, perhaps, to urge them to employ aids that will stimulate and quicken their devotion.

In the seventeenth chapter of this third book, St. John of the Cross enumerates the 'six kinds of good' which can give rise to rejoicing and sets down his intention of treating each of them in turn. He carries out his purpose, but, on entering his last division, subdivides it at considerable length and subsequently breaks off with some brusqueness while dealing with one of these sub-heads, just as he is introducing another subject of particular interest historically — namely, pulpit methods considered from the standpoint of the preacher. In all probability we shall never know what he had to say about the hearers of sermons, or what were his considered judgments on confessors and penitents — though of these judgments he has left us examples elsewhere in this treatise, as well as in others.

We cannot estimate of how much the sudden curtailment of the Ascent of Mount Carmel has robbed us. Orderly as was the mind of St. John of the Cross, he was easily carried away in his expositions, which are apt to be unequal. No one would have suspected, for example, that, after going into such length in treating the first line of his first stanza, he would make such short work of the remaining four. Nor can we disregard the significance of his warning that much of what he had written on the understanding was applicable also to the memory and the will. He may, therefore, have been nearer the end of his theme than is generally supposed. Yet it is equally possible that much more of his subtle analysis was in store for his readers. Any truncation, when the author is a St. John of the Cross, must be considered irreparable.

The Manuscripts

Unfortunately there is no autograph of this treatise extant, though there are a number of early copies, some of which have been made with great care. Others, for various reasons, abbreviate the original considerably. The MSS. belonging to both classes will be enumerated.

Alba de Tormes. The Discalced Carmelite priory of Alba de Tormes has a codex which contains the four principal treatises of St. John of the Cross (Ascent, Dark Night, Spiritual Canticle and Living Flame). This codex belonged from a very early date (perhaps from a date not much later than that of the Saint's death) to the family of the Duke of Alba, which was greatly devoted to the Discalced Carmelite Reform and to St. Teresa, its foundress. It remained in the family until the beginning of the eighteenth century, when it came into the hands of a learned Carmelite, Fray Alonso de la Madre de Dios, who presented it to the Alba monastery on April 15, 1705. The details of this history are given by Fray Alonso himself in a note bearing this date.

For over half a century the MS. was believed to be an autograph, partly, no doubt, on account of its luxurious binding and the respect paid to the noble house whence it came. In February 1761, however, it was examined carefully by P. Manuel de Santa Mar'a, who, by his Superiors' orders, was assisting P. Andres de la Encarnacion in his search for, and study of, manuscripts of the Saint's writings. P. Manuel soon discovered that the opinion commonly held was erroneous — greatly, it would seem, to the disillusionment of his contemporaries. Among the various reasons which he gives in a statement supporting his conclusions is that in two places the author is described as 'santo' — a proof not only that the MS. is not an autograph but also that the copyist had no intention of representing it as such.

Although this copy is carefully made and richly bound — which suggests that it was a gift from the Reform to the house of Alba — it contains many errors, of a kind which indicate that the copyist, well educated though he was, knew little of ascetic or mystical theology. A number of omissions, especially towards the end of the book, give the impression that the copy was finished with haste and not compared with the original on its completion. There is no reason, however, to suppose that the errors and omissions are ever intentional; indeed, they are of such a kind as to suggest that the copyist had not the skill necessary for successful adulteration.

MS. 6,624. This copy, like the next four, is in N.L.M. [National Library of Spain, Madrid], and contains the same works as that of Alba de Tormes. It was made in 1755, under the direction of P. Andres de la Encarnacion, from a manuscript, now lost, which was venerated by the Benedictines of Burgos: this information is found at the end of the volume. P. Andres had evidently a good opinion of the Burgos MS., as he placed this copy in the archives of the Discalced Reform, whence it passed to the National Library early in the nineteenth century.

As far as the Ascent is concerned, this MS. is very similar to that of Alba. With a few notable exceptions, such as the omission of the second half of Book I,

Chapter iv, the errors and omissions are so similar as to suggest a definite relationship, if not a common source.

MS. 13,498. This MS., which gives us the Ascent and the Dark Night, also came from the Archives of the Reform and is now in the National Library. The handwriting might be as early as the end of the sixteenth century. The author did not attempt to make a literal transcription of the Ascent, but summarized where he thought advisable, reducing the number of chapters and abbreviating many of them — this last not so much by the method of paraphrase as by the free omission of phrases and sentences.

MS. 2,201. This, as far as the Ascent is concerned, is an almost literal transcription of the last MS., in a seventeenth-century hand; it was bound in the eighteenth century, when a number of other treatises were added to it, together with some poems by St. John of the Cross and others. The variants as between this MS. and 13,498 are numerous, but of small importance, and seem mainly to have been due to carelessness.

MS. 18,160. This dates from the end of the sixteenth century and contains the four treatises named above, copied in different hands and evidently intended to form one volume. Only the first four chapters of the Ascent are given, together with the title and the first three lines of the fifth chapter. The transcription is poorly done.

MS. 13,507. An unimportant copy, containing only a few odd chapters of the Ascent and others from the remaining works of St. John of the Cross and other writers.

Pamplona. A codex in an excellent state of preservation is venerated by the Discalced Carmelite nuns of Pamplona. It was copied, at the end of the sixteenth century, by a Barcelona Carmelite, M. Magdalena de la Asuncion, and contains a short summary of the four treatises enumerated above, various poems by St. John of the Cross and some miscellaneous writings. The Ascent is abbreviated to the same extent as in 13,498 and 2,201 and by the same methods; many chapters, too, are omitted in their entirety.

Alcaudete. This MS., which contains the Ascent only, was copied by St. John of the Cross's close friend and companion, P. Juan Evangelista, as a comparison with manuscripts (N.L.M., 12,738) written in his well-known and very distinctive hand, puts beyond all doubt. P. Juan, who took the habit of the Reform at Christmas 1582, knew the Saint before this date; was professed by him at Granada in 1583; accompanied him on many of his journeys; saw him write most of his books; and, as his close friend and confessor, was consulted repeatedly by his biographers. It is natural that he should also have acted as the Saint's copyist, and, in the absence of autographs, we should expect no manuscripts to be more trustworthy than copies made by him. Examination of this MS. shows that it is in fact highly reliable. It corrects none of those unwieldy periods in which the Saint's work abounds, and which the editio princeps often thought well to amend, nor, like the early editions and even some manuscripts, does it omit whole paragraphs and substitute others for them. Further, as this copy was being made solely for the use of the Order, no passages are omitted or altered in it because they might be erroneously interpreted as illuministic. It is true that P. Juan Evangelista is not, from the technical standpoint, a perfect copyist, but, frequently as are his slips, they are always easy to recognize.

The Alcaudete MS. was found in the Carmelite priory in that town by P. Andres de la Encarnacion, who first made use of it for his edition. When the priory was abandoned during the religious persecutions of the early nineteenth century, the MS. was lost. Nearly a hundred years passed before it was re-discovered by P. Silverio de Santa Teresa in a second-hand bookshop [and forms a most important contribution to that scholar's edition, which normally follows it]. It bears many signs of frequent use; eleven folios are missing from the body of the MS. (corresponding approximately to Book III, Chapters xxii to xxvi) and several more from its conclusion.

In the footnotes to the Ascent, the following abbreviations are used:

A = MS. of the Discalced Carmelite Friars of Alba.

Alc. = Alcaudete MS.

B = MS. of the Benedictines of Burgos.

C = N.L.M., MS. 13,498.

D = N.L.M., MS. 2,201.

P = MS. of the Discalced Carmelite Nuns of Pamplona.

E.p. = Editio princeps (Alcala, 1618).

Other editions or manuscripts cited are referred to without abbreviation.

Ascent of Mount Carmel

Treats of how the soul may prepare itself in order to attain in a short time to Divine union. Gives very profitable counsels and instruction, both to beginners and to proficients, that they may know how to disencumber themselves of all that is temporal and not to encumber themselves with the spiritual, and to remain in complete detachment and liberty of spirit, as is necessary for Divine union.

Argument

ALL the doctrine whereof I intend to treat in this Ascent of Mount Carmel is included in the following stanzas, and in them is also described the manner of ascending to the summit of the Mount, which is the high estate of perfection which we here call union of the soul with God. And because I must continually base upon them that which I shall say, I have desired to set them down here together, to the end that all the substance of that which is to be written may be seen and comprehended together; although it will be fitting to set down each stanza separately before expounding it, and likewise the lines of each stanza, according as the matter and the exposition require. The poem, then, runs as follows:

Stanzas

Wherein the soul sings of the happy chance which it had in passing through the dark night of faith, in detachment and purgation of itself, to union with the Beloved.

On a dark night, Kindled in love with yearnings — oh, happy chance!
I went forth without being observed, My house being now at rest.
In darkness and secure, By the secret ladder, disguised — oh, happy chance!
In darkness and in concealment, My house being now at rest.
In the happy night, In secret, when none saw me, Nor I beheld aught, Without light or guide, save that which burned in my heart.
This light guided me More surely than the light of noonday,

To the place where he (well I knew who!) was awaiting me — A place where none appeared.

Oh, night that guided me, Oh, night more lovely than the dawn,

Oh, night that joined Beloved with lover, Lover transformed in the Beloved!

Upon my flowery breast, Kept wholly for himself alone,

There he stayed sleeping, and I caressed him, And the fanning of the cedars made a breeze.

The breeze blew from the turret As I parted his locks;

With his gentle hand he wounded my neck And caused all my senses to be suspended.

I remained, lost in oblivion; My face I reclined on the Beloved.

All ceased and I abandoned myself, Leaving my cares forgotten among the lilies.

Prologue

In order to expound and describe this dark night, through which the soul passes in order to attain to the Divine light of the perfect union of the love of God, as far as is possible in this life, it would be necessary to have illumination of knowledge and experience other and far greater than mine; for this darkness and these trials, both spiritual and temporal, through which happy souls are wont to pass in order to be able to attain to this high estate of perfection, are so numerous and so profound that neither does human knowledge suffice for the understanding of them, nor experience for the description of them; for only he that passes this way can understand it, and even he cannot describe it.

Therefore, in order to say a little about this dark night, I shall trust neither to experience nor to knowledge, since both may fail and deceive; but, while not omitting to make such use as I can of these two things, I shall avail myself, in all that, with the Divine favour, I have to say, or at the least, in that which is most important and dark to the understanding, of Divine Scripture; for, if we guide ourselves by this, we shall be unable to stray, since He Who speaks therein is the Holy Spirit. And if aught I stray, whether through my imperfect understanding of that which is said in it or of matters uncollected with it, it is not my intention to depart from the sound sense and doctrine of our Holy Mother the Catholic Church; for in such a case I submit and resign myself wholly, not only to her command, but to whatever better judgment she may pronounce concerning it.

To this end I have been moved, not by any possibility that I see in myself of accomplishing so arduous a task, but by the confidence which I have in the Lord that He will help me to say something to relieve the great necessity which is experienced by many souls, who, when they set out upon the road of virtue, and Our Lord desires to bring them into this dark night that they may pass through it to Divine union, make no progress. At times this is because they have no desire to enter it or to allow themselves to be led into it; at other times, because they understand not themselves and lack competent and alert directors who will guide them to the summit. And so it is sad to see many souls to whom God gives both aptitude and favour with which to make progress (and who, if they would take courage, could attain to this high estate), remaining in an elementary stage of communion with God, for want of will, or knowledge, or because there is none who will lead them in the right path or teach them how to get away from these beginnings. And at length, although Our Lord grants them such favour as to make them to go onward without this hindrance or that, they arrive at their goal very much later, and with greater labour, yet with less merit, because they have not conformed themselves to God, and allowed themselves to be brought freely into the pure and sure road of union. For, although it is true that God is leading them, and that He can lead them without their own help, they will not allow themselves to be led; and thus they make less progress, because they resist Him Who is leading them, and they have less merit, because they apply not their will, and on this account they suffer more. For these are souls who, instead of committing themselves to God and making use of His help, rather hinder God by the indiscretion of their actions or by their resistance; like children who, when their mothers desire to carry them in their arms, start stamping and crying, and insist upon being allowed to walk, with the result that they can make no progress; and, if they advance at all, it is only at the pace of a child.

Wherefore, to the end that all, whether beginners or proficients, may know how to commit themselves to God's guidance, when His Majesty desires to lead them onward, we shall give instruction and counsel, by His help, so that they may be able to understand His will, or, at the least, allow Him to lead them. For some confessors and spiritual fathers, having no light and experience concerning these roads, are wont to hinder and harm such souls rather than to help them on the road; they are like the builders of Babel, who, when told to furnish suitable material, gave and applied other very different material, because they understood not the language, and thus nothing was done. Wherefore, it is a difficult and troublesome thing at such seasons for a soul not to understand itself or to find none who understands it. For it will come to pass that God will lead the soul by a most lofty path of dark contemplation and aridity, wherein it seems to be lost, and, being thus full of darkness and trials, constraints and temptations, will meet one who will speak to it like Job's comforters, and say that it is suffering from melancholy, or low spirits, or a morbid disposition, or that it may have some hidden sin, and that it is for this reason that God has forsaken it. Such comforters are wont to declare immediately that that soul must have been very evil, since such things as these are befalling it.

And there will likewise be those who tell the soul to retrace its steps, since it is finding no pleasure or consolation in the things of God as it did aforetime. And in this way they double the poor soul's trials; for it may well be that the greatest affliction which it is feeling is that of the knowledge of its own miseries, thinking that it sees itself, more clearly than daylight, to be full of evils and sins, for God gives it that light of knowledge in that night of contemplation, as we shall presently show. And, when the soul finds someone whose opinion agrees with its own, and who says that these things must be due to its own fault, its affliction and trouble increase infinitely and are wont to become more grievous than death. And, not content with this, such confessors, thinking that these things proceed from sin, make these souls go over their lives and cause them to make many general confessions, and crucify them afresh; not understanding that this may quite well not be the time for any of such things, and that their penitents should be left in the state of purgation which God gives them, and be comforted and encouraged to desire it until God be pleased to dispose otherwise; for until that time, no matter what the souls themselves may do and their confessors may say, there is no remedy for them.

This, with the Divine favour, we shall consider hereafter, and also how the soul should conduct itself at such a time, and how the confessor must treat it, and what signs there will be whereby it may be known if this is the purgation of the soul; and, in such case, whether it be of sense or of spirit (which is the dark night whereof we speak), and how it may be known if it be melancholy or some other imperfection with respect to sense or to spirit. For there may be some souls who will think, or whose confessors will think, that God is leading them along this road of the dark night of spiritual purgation, whereas they may possibly be suffering only from some of the imperfections aforementioned. And, again, there are many souls who think that they have no aptitude for prayer, when they have very much; and there are others who think that they have much when they have hardly any.

There are other souls who labour and weary themselves to a piteous extent, and yet go backward, seeking profit in that which is not profitable, but is rather a hindrance; and there are still others who, by remaining at rest and in quietness, continue to make great progress. There are others who are hindered and disturbed and make no progress, because of the very consolations and favours that God is granting them in order that they may make progress. And there are many other things on this road that befall those who follow it, both joys and afflictions and hopes and griefs: some proceeding from the spirit of perfection and others from imperfection. Of all these, with the Divine favour, we shall endeavour to say something, so that each soul who reads this may be able to see something of the road that he ought to follow, if he aspire to attain to the summit of this Mount.

And, since this introduction relates to the dark night through which the soul must go to God, let not the reader marvel if it seem to him somewhat dark also. This, I believe, will be so at the beginning when he begins to read; but, as he passes on, he will find himself understanding the first part better, since one part will explain another. And then, if he read it a second time, I believe it will seem clearer to him and the instruction will appear sounder. And if any persons find themselves disagreeing with this instruction, it will be due to my ignorance and poor style; for in itself the matter is good and of the first importance. But I think that, even were it written in a more excellent and perfect manner than it is, only the minority would profit by it, for we shall not here set down things that are very moral and delectable for all spiritual persons who desire to travel toward God by pleasant and delectable ways, but solid and substantial instruction, as well suited to one kind of person as to another, if they desire to pass to the detachment of spirit which is here treated.

Nor is my principal intent to address all, but rather certain persons of our sacred Order of Mount Carmel of the primitive observance, both friars and nuns — since they have desired me to do so — to whom God is granting the favour of setting them on the road to this Mount; who, as they are already detached from the temporal things of this world, will better understand the instruction concerning detachment of spirit.

BOOK THE FIRST

Wherein is described the nature of dark night and how necessary it is to pass through it to Divine union; and in particular this book describes the dark night of sense, and desire, and the evils which these work in the soul.

Chapter 1

Sets down the first stanza. Describes two different nights through which spiritual persons pass, according to the two parts of man, the lower and the higher. Expounds the stanza which follows.

Stanza The First

On a dark night, Kindled in love with yearnings — oh, happy chance! —
I went forth without being observed, My house being now at rest.

IN this first stanzas the soul sings of the happy fortune and chance which it experienced in going forth from all things that are without, and from the desires and imperfections that are in the sensual part of man because of the disordered state of his reason. For the understanding of this it must be known that, for a soul to attain to the state of perfection, it has ordinarily first to pass through two principal kinds of night, which spiritual persons call purgations or purifications of the soul; and here we call them nights, for in both of them the soul journeys, as it were, by night, in darkness.

The first night or purgation is of the sensual part of the soul, which is treated in the present stanza, and will be treated in the first part of this book. And the second is of the spiritual part; of this speaks the second stanza, which follows; and of this we shall treat likewise, in the second and the third part, with respect to the activity of the soul; and in the fourth part, with respect to its passivity.

And this first night pertains to beginners, occurring at the time when God begins to bring them into the state of contemplation; in this night the spirit likewise has a part, as we shall say in due course. And the second night, or purification, pertains to those who are already proficient, occurring at the time when God desires to bring them to the state of union with God. And this latter night is a more obscure and dark and terrible purgation, as we shall say afterwards.

Briefly, then, the soul means by this stanza that it went forth (being led by God) for love of Him alone, enkindled in love of Him, upon a dark night, which is the privation and purgation of all its sensual desires, with respect to all outward things of the world and to those which were delectable to its flesh, and likewise with respect to the desires of its will. This all comes to pass in this purgation of sense; for which cause the soul says that it went forth while its house was still at rest; which house is its sensual part, the desires being at rest and asleep in it, as it is to them. For there is no going forth from the pains and afflictions of the secret places of the desires until these be mortified and put to sleep. And this, the soul says, was a happy chance for it — namely, its going forth without being observed: that is, without any desire of its flesh or any other thing being able to hinder it. And likewise, because it went out by night — which signifies the privation of all these things wrought in it by God, which privation was night for it.

And it was a happy chance that God should lead it into this night, from which there came to it so much good; for of itself the soul would not have succeeded in entering therein, because no man of himself can succeed in voiding himself of all his desires in order to come to God.

This is, in brief, the exposition of the stanza; and we shall now have to go through it, line by line, setting down one line after another, and expounding that which pertains to our purpose. And the same method is followed in the other stanzas, as I said in the Prologue — namely, that each stanza will be set down and expounded, and afterwards each line.

Chapter 11

Explains the nature of this dark night through which the soul says that it has passed on the road to union.

On A Dark Night

We may say that there are three reasons for which this journey made by the soul to union with God is called night. The first has to do with the point from which the soul goes forth, for it has gradually to deprive itself of desire for all the worldly things which it possessed, by denying them to itself; the which denial and deprivation are, as it were, night to all the senses of man. The second reason has to do with the mean, or the road along which the soul must travel to this union — that is, faith, which is likewise as dark as night to the understanding. The third has to do with the point to which it travels — namely, God, Who, equally, is dark night to the soul in this life. These three nights must pass through the soul — or, rather, the soul must pass through them — in order that it may come to Divine union with God.

In the book of the holy Tobias these three kinds of night were shadowed forth by the three nights which, as the angel commanded, were to pass ere the youth Tobias should be united with his bride. In the first he commanded him to burn the heart of the fish in the fire, which signifies the heart that is affectioned to, and set upon, the things of the world; which, in order that one may begin to journey toward God, must be burned and purified from all that is creature, in the fire of the love of God. And in this purgation the devil flees away, for he has power over the soul only when it is attached to things corporeal and temporal.

On the second night the angel told him that he would be admitted into the company of the holy patriarchs, who are the fathers of the faith. For, passing through the first night, which is self-privation of all objects of sense, the soul at once enters into the second night, and abides alone in faith to the exclusion, not of charity, but of other knowledge acquired by the understanding, as we shall say hereafter, which is a thing that pertains not to sense.

On the third night the angel told him that he would obtain a blessing, which is God; Who, by means of the second night, which is faith, continually communicates Himself to the soul in such a secret and intimate manner that He becomes another night to the soul, inasmuch as this said communication is far darker than those others, as we shall say presently. And, when this third night is past, which is the complete accomplishment of the communication of God in the spirit, which is ordinarily wrought in great darkness of the soul, there then follows its union with the Bride, which is the Wisdom of God. Even so the angel said likewise to Tobias that, when the third night was past, he should be united with his bride in the fear of the Lord; for, when this fear of God is perfect, love is perfect, and this comes to pass when the transformation of the soul is wrought through its love.

These three parts of the night are all one night; but, after the manner of night, it has three parts. For the first part, which is that of sense, is comparable to the beginning of night, the point at which things begin to fade from sight. And the second part, which is faith, is comparable to midnight, which is total darkness. And the third part is like the close of night, which is God, the which part is now near to the light of day. And, that we may understand this the better, we shall treat of each of these reasons separately as we proceed.

Chapter III

Speaks of the first cause of this night, which is that of the privation of the desire in all things, and gives the reason for which it is called night.

We here describe as night the privation of every kind of pleasure which belongs to the desire; for, even as night is naught but the privation of light, and, consequently, of all objects that can be seen by means of light, whereby the visual faculty remains unoccupied and in darkness, even so likewise the mortification of desire may be called night to the soul. For, when the soul is deprived of the pleasure of its desire in all things, it remains, as it were, unoccupied and in darkness. For even as the visual faculty, by means of light, is nourished and fed by objects which can be seen, and which, when the light is quenched, are not seen, even so, by means of the desire, the soul is nourished and fed by all things wherein it can take pleasure according to its faculties; and, when this also is quenched, or rather, mortified, the soul ceases to feed upon the pleasure of all things, and thus, with respect to its desire, it remains unoccupied and in darkness.

Let us take an example from each of the faculties. When the soul deprives its desire of the pleasure of all that can delight the sense of hearing, the soul remains unoccupied and in darkness with respect to this faculty. And, when it deprives itself of the pleasure of all that can please the sense of sight, it remains unoccupied and in darkness with respect to this faculty also. And, when it deprives itself of the pleasure of all the sweetness of perfumes which can give it pleasure through the sense of smell, it remains equally unoccupied and in darkness according to this faculty. And, if it also denies itself the pleasure of all food that can satisfy the palate, the soul likewise remains unoccupied and in darkness. And finally, when the soul mortifies itself with respect to all the delights and pleasures that it can receive from the sense of touch, it remains, in the same way, unoccupied and in darkness with respect to this faculty. So that the soul that has denied and thrust away from itself the pleasures which come from all these things, and has mortified its desire with respect to them, may be said to be, as it were, in the darkness of night, which is naught else than an emptiness within itself of all things.

The reason for this is that, as the philosophers say, the soul, as soon as God infuses it into the body, is like a smooth, blank board upon which nothing is painted; and, save for that which it experiences through the senses, nothing is communicated to it, in the course of nature, from any other source. And thus, for as long as it is in the body, it is like one who is in a dark prison and who knows nothing, save what he is able to see through the windows of the said prison; and, if he saw nothing through them, he would see nothing in any other way. And thus the soul, save for that which is communicated to it through the senses, which are the windows of its prison, could acquire nothing, in the course of nature, in any other way.

Wherefore, if the soul rejects and denies that which it can receive through the senses, we can quite well say that it remains, as it were, in darkness and empty; since, as appears from what has been said, no light can enter it, in the course of nature, by any other means of illumination than those aforementioned. For, although it is true that the soul cannot help hearing and seeing and smelling and tasting and touching, this is of no greater import, nor, if the soul denies and rejects the object, is it hindered more than if it saw it not, heard it not, etc. Just so a man who desires to shut his eyes will remain in darkness, like the blind man who has not the faculty of sight. And to this purpose David says these words: Pauper sum ego, et in laboribus a indenture mea. Which signifies: I am poor and in labours from my youth. He calls himself poor, although it is clear that he was rich, because his will was not set upon riches, and thus it was as though he were really poor. But if he had not been really poor and had not been so in his will, he would not have been truly poor, for his soul, as far as its desire was concerned, would have been rich and replete. For that reason we call this detachment night to the soul, for we are not treating here of the lack of things, since this implies no detachment on the part of the soul if it has a desire for them; but we are treating of the detachment from them of the taste and desire, for it is this that leaves the soul free and void of them, although it may have them; for it is not the things of this world that either occupy the soul or cause it harm, since they enter it not, but rather the will and desire for them, for it is these that dwell within it.

This first kind of night, as we shall say hereafter, belongs to the soul according to its sensual part, which is one of the two parts, whereof we spoke above, through which the soul must pass in order to attain to union.

Let us now say how meet it is for the soul to go forth from its house into this dark night of sense, in order to travel to union with God.

Chapter IV

Wherein is declared how necessary it is for the soul truly to pass through this dark night of sense, which is mortification of desire, in order that it may journey to union with God.

The reason for which it is necessary for the soul, in order to attain to Divine union with God, to pass through this dark night of mortification of the desires and denial of pleasures in all things, is because all the affections which it has for creatures are pure darkness in the eyes of God, and, when the soul is clothed in these affections, it has no capacity for being enlightened and possessed by the pure and simple light of God, if it first cast them not from it; for light cannot agree with darkness; since, as Saint John says: Tenebroe eam non comprehenderunt. That is: The darkness could not receive the light.

The reason is that two contraries (even as philosophy teaches us) cannot coexist in one person; and that darkness, which is affection set upon the creatures, and light, which is God, are contrary to each other, and have no likeness or accord between one another, even as Saint Paul taught the Corinthians, saying: Quoe conventio luci ad tenebras? That is to say: What communion can there be between light and darkness? Hence it is that the light of Divine union cannot dwell in the soul if these affections first flee not away from it.

In order that we may the better prove what has been said, it must be known that the affection and attachment which the soul has for creatures renders the soul like to these creatures; and, the greater is its affection, the closer is the equality and likeness between them; for love creates a likeness between that which loves and that which is loved. For which reason David, speaking of those who set their affections upon idols, said thus: Similes illis fiant qui faciunt ea: et omnes qui confidunt in eis. Which signifies: Let them that set their heart upon them be like to them. And thus, he that loves a creature becomes as low as that creature, and, in some ways, lower; for love not only makes the lover equal to the object of his love, but even subjects him to it. Hence in the same way it comes to pass that the soul that loves anything else becomes incapable of pure union with God and transformation in Him. For the low estate of the creature is much less capable of union with the high estate of the Creator than is darkness with light. For all things of earth and heaven, compared with God, are nothing, as Jeremias says in these words: Aspexi terram, et ecce vacua erat, et nihil; et coelos, et non erat lux in eis. 'I beheld the earth,' he says, 'and it was void, and it was nothing; and the heavens, and saw that they had no light.' In saying that he beheld the earth void, he means that all its creatures were nothing, and that the earth was nothing likewise. And, in saying that he beheld the heavens and saw no light in them, he says that all the luminaries of heaven, compared with God, are pure darkness. So that in this way all the creatures are nothing; and their affections, we may say, are less than nothing, since they are an impediment to transformation in God and the privation thereof, even as darkness is not only nothing, but less than nothing, since it is privation of light. And even as he that is in darkness comprehends not the light, so the soul that sets its affection upon creatures will be unable to comprehend God; and, until it be purged, it will neither be able to possess Him here below, through pure transformation of love, nor yonder in clear vision. And, for greater clarity, we will now speak in greater detail.

All the being of creation, then, compared with the infinite Being of God, is nothing. And therefore the soul that sets its affection upon the being of creation is likewise nothing in the eyes of God, and less than nothing; for, as we have said, love makes equality and similitude, and even sets the lover below the object of his love. And therefore such a soul will in no wise be able to attain to union with the infinite Being of God; for that which is not can have no communion with that which is. And, coming down in detail to some examples, all the beauty of the creatures, compared with the infinite beauty of God, is the height of deformity even as Solomon says in the Proverbs: Fallax gratia, et vana est pulchritudo. 'Favour is deceitful and beauty is vain.' And thus the soul that is affectioned to the beauty of any creature is the height of deformity in the eyes of God. And therefore this soul that is deformed will be unable to become transformed in beauty, which is God, since deformity cannot attain to beauty; and all the grace and beauty of the creatures, compared with the grace of God, is the height of misery and of uncomeliness. Wherefore the soul that is ravished by the graces and beauties of the creatures has only supreme misery and unattractiveness in the eyes of God; and thus it cannot be capable of the infinite grace and loveliness of God; for that which has no grace is far removed from that which is infinitely gracious; and all the goodness of the creatures of the world, in comparison with the infinite goodness of God, may be described as wickedness. 'For there is naught good, save only God.' And therefore the soul that sets its heart upon the good things of the world is supremely evil in the eyes of God. And, even as wickedness comprehends not goodness, even so such a soul cannot be united with God, Who is supreme goodness.

All the wisdom of the world and all human ability, compared with the infinite wisdom of God, are pure and supreme ignorance, even as Saint Paul writes ad Corinthios, saying: Sapientia hujus mundi stultitia est apud Deum. 'The wisdom of this world is foolishness with God.' Wherefore any soul that makes account of all its knowledge and ability in order to come to union with the wisdom of God is supremely ignorant in the eyes of God and will remain far removed from that wisdom; for ignorance knows not what wisdom is, even as Saint Paul says that this wisdom seems foolishness to God; since, in the eyes of God, those who consider themselves to be persons with a certain amount of knowledge are very ignorant, so that the Apostle, writing to the Romans, says of them: Dicentes enim se esse sapientes, stulti facti sunt. That is: Professing themselves to be wise, they became foolish. And those alone acquire wisdom of God who are like ignorant children, and, laying aside their knowledge, walk in His service with love. This manner of wisdom Saint Paul taught likewise ad Corinthios: Si quis videtur inter vos sapiens esse in hoc soeculo, stultus fiat ut sit sapiens. Sapientia enim hujus mundi stultitia est apud Deum. That is: If any man among you seem to be wise, let him become ignorant that he may be wise; for the wisdom of this world is foolishness with God. So that, in order to come to union with the wisdom of God, the soul has to proceed rather by unknowing than by knowing; and all the dominion and liberty of the world, compared with the liberty and dominion of the Spirit of God, is the most abject slavery, affliction and captivity.

Wherefore the soul that is enamoured of prelacy, or of any other such office, and longs for liberty of desire, is considered and treated, in the sight of God, not as a son, but as a base slave and captive, since it has not been willing to accept His holy doctrine, wherein He teaches us that whoso would be greater must be less, and whoso would be less must be greater. And therefore such a soul will be unable to attain to that true liberty of spirit which is attained in His Divine union. For slavery can have no part with liberty; and liberty cannot dwell in a heart that is subject to desires, for this is the heart of a slave; but it dwells in the free man, because he has the heart of a son. It was for this cause that Sara bade her husband Abraham cast out the bondwoman and her son, saying that the son of the bondwoman should not be heir with the son of the free woman.

And all the delights and pleasures of the will in all the things of the world, in comparison with all those delights which are God, are supreme affliction, torment and bitterness. And thus he that sets his heart upon them is considered, in the sight of God, as worthy of supreme affliction, torment and bitterness; and thus he will be unable to attain to the delights of the embrace of union with God, since he is worthy of affliction and bitterness. All the wealth and glory of all creation, in comparison with the wealth which is God, is supreme poverty and wretchedness. Thus the soul that loves and possesses creature wealth is supremely poor and wretched in the sight of God, and for that reason will be unable to attain to that wealth and glory which is the state of transformation in God; for that which is miserable and poor is supremely far removed from that which is supremely rich and glorious.

And therefore Divine Wisdom, grieving for such as these, who make themselves vile, low, miserable and poor, because they love the things in this world which seem to them so rich and beautiful, addresses an exclamation to them in the Proverbs, saying: O viri, ad vos clamito, et vox mea ad filios hominum. Intelligite, parvuli, astutiam, et insipientes, animadvertite. Audite quia de rebus magnis locutura sum. And farther on he continues: Mecum sunt divitoe, et gloria, opes superboe et justicia. Melior est fructus meus auro, et lapide pretioso, et genimina mea argento electo. In viis justitioe ambulo, in medio semitarum judicii, ut ditem diligentes me, et thesauros eorum repleam. Which signifies: O ye men, to you I call, and my voice is to the sons of men. Attend, little ones, to subtlety and sagacity; ye that are foolish, take notice. Hear, for I have to speak of great things. With me are riches and glory, high riches and justice. Better is the fruit that ye will find in me than gold and precious stones; and my generation — namely, that which ye will engender of me in your souls — is better than choice silver. I walk in the ways of justice, in the midst of the paths of judgment, that I may enrich those that love me and fill their treasures perfectly. — Herein Divine Wisdom speaks to all those that set their hearts and affections upon anything of the world, according as we have already said. And she calls them 'little ones,' because they make themselves like to that which they love, which is little. And therefore she tells them to be subtle and to take note that she is treating of great things and not of things that are little like themselves. That the great riches and the glory that they love are with her and in her, and not where they think. And that high riches and justice dwell in her; for, although they think the things of this world to be all this, she tells them to take note that her things are better, saying that the fruit that they will find in them will be better for them than gold and precious stones; and that which she engenders in souls is better than the choice silver which they love; by which is understood any kind of affection that can be possessed in this life.

Chapter V

Wherein the aforementioned subject is treated and continued, and it is shown by passages and figures from Holy Scripture how necessary it is for the soul to journey to God through this dark night of the mortification of desire in all things.

From what has been said it may be seen in some measure how great a distance there is between all that the creatures are in themselves and that which God is in Himself, and how souls that set their affections upon any of these creatures are at as great a distance as they from God; for, as we have said, love produces equality and likeness. This distance was clearly realized by Saint Augustine, who said in the Sololoquies, speaking with God: 'Miserable man that I am, when will my littleness and imperfection be able to have fellowship with Thy uprightness? Thou indeed art good, and I am evil; Thou art merciful, and I am impious; Thou art holy, I am miserable; Thou art just, I am unjust; Thou art light, I am blind; Thou, life, I, death; Thou, medicine, I, sick; Thou, supreme truth, I, utter vanity.' All this is said by this Saint.

Wherefore, it is supreme ignorance for the soul to think that it will be able to pass to this high estate of union with God if first it void not the desire of all things, natural and supernatural, which may hinder it, according as we shall explain hereafter; for there is the greatest possible distance between these things and that which comes to pass in this estate, which is naught else than transformation in God. For this reason Our Lord, when showing us this path, said through Saint Luke: Qui non renuntiat omnibus quoe possidet, non potest meus esse discipulus. This signifies: He that renounces not all things that he possesses with his will cannot be My disciple. And this is evident; for the doctrine that the Son of God came to teach was contempt for all things, whereby a man might receive as a reward the Spirit of God in himself. For, as long as the soul rejects not all things, it has no capacity to receive the Spirit of God in pure transformation.

Of this we have a figure in Exodus, wherein we read that God gave not the children of Israel the food from Heaven, which was manna, until the flour which they had brought from Egypt failed them. By this is signified that first of all it is meet to renounce all things, for this angels' food is not fitting for the palate that would find delight in the food of men. And not only does the soul become incapable of receiving the Divine Spirit when it stays and pastures on other strange pleasures, but those souls greatly offend the Divine Majesty who desire spiritual food and are not content with God alone, but desire rather to intermingle desire and affection for other things. This can likewise be seen in the same book of Holy Scripture, wherein it is said that, not content with that simplest of food, they desired and craved fleshly food. And that Our Lord was greatly wroth that they should desire to intermingle a food that was so base and so coarse with one that was so noble and so simple; which, though it was so, had within itself the sweetness and substance of all foods. Wherefore, while they yet had the morsels in their mouths, as David says likewise: Ira Dei descendit super eos. The wrath of God came down upon them, sending fire from Heaven and consuming many thousands of them; for God held it an unworthy thing that they should have a desire for other food when He had given them food from Heaven.

Oh, did spiritual persons but know how much good and what great abundance of spirit they lose through not seeking to raise up their desires above childish things, and how in this simple spiritual food they would find the sweetness of all things, if they desired not to taste those things! But such food gives them no pleasure, for the reason why the children of Israel received not the sweetness of all foods that was contained in the manna was that they would not reserve their desire for it alone. So that they failed to find in the manna all the sweetness and strength that they could wish, not because it was not contained in the manna, but because they desired some other thing. Thus he that will love some other thing together with God of a certainty makes little account of God, for he weighs in the balance against God that which, as we have said, is at the greatest possible distance from God.

It is well known by experience that, when the will of a man is affectioned to one thing, he prizes it more than any other; although some other thing may be much better, he takes less pleasure in it. And if he wishes to enjoy both, he is bound to wrong the more important, because he makes an equality between them. Wherefore, since there is naught that equals God, the soul that loves some other thing together with Him, or clings to it, does Him a grievous wrong. And if this is so, what would it be doing if it loved anything more than God?

It is this, too, that was denoted by the command of God to Moses that he should ascend the Mount to speak with Him: He commanded him not only to ascend it alone, leaving the children of Israel below, but not even to allow the beasts to feed over against the Mount. By this He signified that the soul that is to ascend this mount of perfection, to commune with God, must not only renounce all things and leave them below, but must not even allow the desires, which are the beasts, to pasture over against this mount — that is, upon other things which are not purely God, in Whom — that is, in the state of perfection — every desire ceases. So he that journeys on the road and makes the ascent to God must needs be habitually careful to quell and mortify the desires; and the greater the speed wherewith a soul does this, the sooner will it reach the end of its journey. Until these be quelled, it cannot reach the end, however much it practise the virtues, since it is unable to attain to perfection in them; for this perfection consists in voiding and stripping and purifying the soul of every desire. Of this we have another very striking figure in Genesis, where we read that, when the patriarch Jacob desired to ascend Mount Bethel, in order to build an altar there to God whereon he should offer Him sacrifice, he first commanded all his people to do three things: one was that they should cast away from them all strange gods; the second, that they should purify themselves; the third, that they should change their garments.

By these three things it is signified that any soul that will ascend this mount in order to make of itself an altar whereon it may offer to God the sacrifice of pure love and praise and pure reverence, must, before ascending to the summit of the mount, have done these three things aforementioned perfectly. First, it must cast away all strange gods — namely, all strange affections and attachments; secondly, it must purify itself of the remnants which the desires aforementioned have left in the soul, by means of the dark night of sense whereof we are speaking, habitually denying them and repenting itself of them; and thirdly, in order to reach the summit of this high mount, it must have changed its garments, which, through its observance of the first two things, God will change for it, from old to new, by giving it a new understanding of God in God, the old human understanding being cast aside; and a new love of God in God, the will being now stripped of all its old desires and human pleasures, and the soul being brought into a new state of knowledge and profound delight, all other old images and forms of knowledge having been cast away, and all that belongs to the old man, which is the aptitude of the natural self, quelled, and the soul clothed with a new supernatural aptitude with respect to all its faculties. So that its operation, which before was human, has become Divine, which is that that is attained in the state of union, wherein the soul becomes naught else than an altar whereon God is adored in praise and love, and God alone is upon it. For this cause God commanded that the altar whereon the Ark of the Covenant was to be laid should be hollow within; so that the soul may understand how completely empty of all things God desires it to be, that it may be an altar worthy of the presence of His Majesty. On this altar it was likewise forbidden that there should be any strange fire, or that its own fire should ever fail; and so essential was this that, because Nadab and Abiu, who were the sons of the High Priest Aaron, offered strange fire upon His Altar, Our Lord was wroth and slew them there before the altar. By this we are to understand that the love of God must never fail in the soul, so that the soul may be a worthy altar, and so that no other love must be mingled with it.

God permits not that any other thing should dwell together with Him. Wherefore we read in the First Book the Kings that, when the Philistines put the Ark of the Covenant into the temple where their idol was, the idol was cast down upon the ground at the dawn of each day, and broken to pieces. And He permits and wills that there should be only one desire where He is, which is to keep the law of God perfectly, and to bear upon oneself the Cross of Christ. And thus naught else is said in the Divine Scripture to have been commanded by God to be put in the Ark, where the manna was, save the book of the Law, and the rod Moses, which signifies the Cross. For the soul that aspires naught else than the keeping of the law of the Lord perfectly and the bearing of the Cross of Christ will be a true Ark, containing within itself the true manna, which is God, when that soul attains to a perfect possession within itself of this law and this rod, without any other thing soever.

Chapter VI

Wherein are treated two serious evils caused in the soul by the desires, the one evil being privative and the other positive.

In order that what we have said may be the more clearly and fully understood, it will be well to set down here and state how these desires are the cause of two serious evils in the soul: the one is that they deprive it of the Spirit of God, and the other is that the soul wherein they dwell is wearied, tormented, darkened, defiled and weakened, according to that which is said in Jeremias, Chapter II: *Duo mala fecit Populus meus: dereliquerunt fontem aquoe vivoe, et foderunt sibi cisternas, dissipatas, quoe continere non valent aquas.* Which signifies: They have forsaken Me, Who am the fountain of living water, and they have hewed them out broken cisterns, that can hold no water. Those two evils — namely, the privative and the positive — may be caused by any disordered act of the desire. And, speaking first of all, of the privative, it is clear from the very fact that the soul becomes affectioned to a thing which comes under the head of creature, that the more the desire for that thing fills the soul, the less capacity has the soul for God; inasmuch as two contraries, according to the philosophers, cannot coexist in one person; and further, since, as we said in the fourth chapter, affection for God and affection for creatures are contraries, there cannot be contained within one will affection for creatures and affection for God. For what has the creature to do with the Creator? What has sensual to do with spiritual? Visible with invisible? Temporal with eternal? Food that is heavenly, spiritual and pure with food that is of sense alone and is purely sensual? Christ like poverty of spirit with attachment to aught soever?

Wherefore, as in natural generation no form can be introduced unless the preceding, contrary form is first expelled from the subject, which form, while present, is an impediment to the other by reason of the contrariety which the two have between each other; even so, for as long as the soul is subjected to the sensual spirit, the spirit which is pure and spiritual cannot enter it. Wherefore our Saviour said through Saint Matthew: Non est bonum sumere panem filiorum, et mittere canibus. That is: It is not meet to take the children's bread and to cast it to the dogs. And elsewhere, too, he says through the same Evangelist: Nolite sanctum dare canibus. Which signifies: Give not that which is holy to the dogs. In these passages Our Lord compares those who renounce their creature-desires, and prepare themselves to receive the Spirit of God in purity, to the children of God; and those who would have their desire feed upon the creatures, to dogs. For it is given to children to eat with their father at table and from his dish, which is to feed upon His Spirit, and to dogs are given the crumbs which fall from the table.

From this we are to learn that all created things are crumbs that have fallen from the table of God. Wherefore he that feeds ever upon the creatures is rightly called a dog, and therefore the bread is taken from the children, because they desire not to rise above feeding upon the crumbs, which are created things, to the Uncreated Spirit of their Father. Therefore, like dogs, they are ever hungering, and justly so, because the crumbs serve to whet their appetite rather than to satisfy their hunger. And thus David says of them: Famem patientur ut canes, et circuibunt civitatem. Si vero non fuerint saturati, et murmurabunt. Which signifies: They shall suffer hunger like dogs and shall go round about the city, and, if they find not enough to fill them, they shall murmur. For this is the nature of one that has desires, that he is ever discontented and dissatisfied, like one that suffers hunger; for what has the hunger which all the creatures suffer to do with the fullness which is caused by the Spirit of God? Wherefore this fullness that is uncreated cannot enter the soul, if there be not first cast out that other created hunger which belongs to the desire of the soul; for, as we have said two contraries cannot dwell in one person, the which contraries in this case are hunger and fullness.

From what has been said it will be seen how much greater is the work of God in the cleansing and the purging of a soul from these contrarieties than in the creating of that soul from nothing. For thee contrarieties, these contrary desires and affections, are more completely opposed to God and offer Him greater resistance than does nothingness; for nothingness resists not at all. And let this suffice with respect to the first of the important evils which are inflicted upon the soul by the desires — namely, resistance to the Spirit of God — since much has been said of this above.

Let us now speak of the second effect which they cause in the soul. This is of many kinds, because the desires weary the soul and torment and darken it, and defile it and weaken it. Of these five things we shall speak separately, in their turn.

With regard to the first, it is clear that the desires weary and fatigue the soul; for they are like restless and discontented children, who are ever demanding this or that from their mother, and are never contented. And even as one that digs because he covets a treasure is wearied and fatigued, even so is the soul weary and fatigued in order to attain that which its desires demand of it; and although in the end it may attain it, it is still weary, because it is never satisfied; for, after all, the cisterns which it is digging are broken, and cannot hold water to satisfy thirst. And thus, as Isaias says: Lassus adhuc sitit, et anima ejus vacua est. Which signifies: His desire is empty. And the soul that has desires is wearied and fatigued; for it is like a man that is sick of a fever, who finds himself no better until the fever leaves him, and whose thirst increases with every moment. For, as is said in the Book of Job: Cum satiatus fuerit, arctabitur, oestuabit, et omnis dolor irruet super eum. Which signifies: When he has satisfied his desire, he will be the more oppressed and straitened; the heat of desire hath increased in his soul and thus every sorrow will fall upon him. The soul is wearied and fatigued by its desires, because it is wounded and moved and disturbed by them as is water by the winds; in just the same way they disturb it, allowing it not to rest in any place or in any thing soever. And of such a soul says Isaias: Cor impii quasi mare fervens. 'The heart of the wicked man is like the sea when it rages.' And he is a wicked man that conquers not his desires. The soul that would fain satisfy its desires grows wearied and fatigued; for it is like one that, being an hungered, opens his mouth that he may sate himself with wind, whereupon, instead of being satisfied, his craving becomes greater, for the wind is no food for him. To this purpose said Jeremias: In desiderio animoe sum attraxit ventum amoris sui. As though he were to say: In the desire of his will he snuffed up the wind of his affection. And he then tries to describe the aridity wherein such a soul remains, and warns it, saying: Prohibe pedem tuum a nuditate, et guttur tuum a siti. Which signifies: Keep thy foot (that is, thy thought) from being bare and thy throat from thirst (that is to say, thy will from the indulgence of the desire which causes greater dryness); and, even as the lover is wearied and fatigued upon the day of his hopes, when his attempt has proved to be vain, so the soul is wearied and fatigued by all its desires and by indulgence in them, since they all cause it greater emptiness and hunger; for, as is often said, desire is like the fire, which increases as wood is thrown upon it, and which, when it has consumed the wood, must needs die.

And in this regard it is still worse with desire; for the fire goes down when the wood is consumed, but desire, though it increases when fuel is added to it, decreases not correspondingly when the fuel is consumed; on the contrary, instead of going down, as does the fire when its fuel is consumed, it grows weak through weariness, for its hunger is increased and its food diminished. And of this Isaias speaks, saying: Declinabit ad dexteram, et esuriet: et comedet ad sinistram, et non saturabitur. This signifies: He shall turn to the right hand, and shall be hungry; and he shall eat on the left hand, and shall not be filled. For they that mortify not their desires, when they 'turn,' justly see the fullness of the sweetness of spirit of those who are at the right hand of God, which fullness is not granted to themselves; and justly, too, when they eat on the left hand, by which is meant the satisfaction of their desire with some creature comfort, they are not filled, for, leaving aside that which alone can satisfy, they feed on that which causes them greater hunger. It is clear, then, that the desires weary and fatigue the soul.

Chapter VII

Wherein is shown how the desires torment the soul. This is proved likewise by comparison and quotations.

The second kind of positive evil which the desires cause the soul is in their tormenting and afflicting of it, after the manner of one who is in torment through being bound with cords from which he has no relief until he be freed. And of these David says: Funes peccatorum circumplexi sunt me. The cords of my sins, which are my desires, have constrained me round about. And, even as one that lies naked upon thorns and briars is tormented and afflicted, even so is the soul tormented and afflicted when it rests upon its desires. For they take hold upon it and distress it and cause it pain, even as do thorns. Of these David says likewise: Circumdederunt me sicut apes: et exarserunt sicut ignis in spinis. Which signifies: They compassed me about like bees, wounding me with their stings, and they were enkindled against me, like fire among thorns; for in the desires, which are the thorns, increases the fire of anguish and torment. And even as the husbandman, coveting the harvest for which he hopes, afflicts and torments the ox in the plough, even so does concupiscence afflict a soul that is subject to its desire to attain that for which it longs. This can be clearly seen in that desire which Dalila had to know whence Samson derived his strength that was so great, for the Scripture says that it fatigued and tormented her so much that it caused her to swoon, almost to the point of death, and she said: Defecit anima ejus, et ad mortem usque lassata est.

The more intense is the desire, the greater is the torment which it causes the soul. So that the torment increases with the desire; and the greater are the desires which possess the soul, the greater are its torments; for in such a soul is fulfilled, even in this life, that which is said in the Apocalypse concerning Babylon, in these words: Quantum glorificavit se, et in deliciis fuit, tantum date illi tormentum, et luctum. That is: As much as she has wished to exalt and fulfil her desires, so much give ye to her torment and anguish. And even as one that falls into the hands of his enemies is tormented and afflicted, even so is the soul tormented and afflicted that is led away by its desires. Of this there is a figure in the Book of the Judges, wherein it may be read that that strong man, Samson, who at one time was strong and free and a judge of Israel, fell into the power of his enemies, and they took his strength from him, and put out his eyes, and bound him in a mill, to grind corn, wherein they tormented and afflicted him greatly; and thus it happens to the soul in which these its enemies, the desires, live and rule; for the first thing that they do is to weaken the soul and blind it, as we shall say below; and then they afflict and torment it, binding it to the mill of concupiscence; and the bonds with which it is bound are its own desires.

Wherefore God, having compassion on these that with such great labour, and at such cost to themselves, go about endeavouring to satisfy the hunger and thirst of their desire in the creatures, says to them through Isaias: Omnes sitientes, venite ad aquas; et qui non habetis argentum, properate, emite, el comedite: venite, emite absque argento vinum et lac. Quare appenditis argentum non in panibus, et laborem vestrum non in saturitate? As though He were to say: All ye that have thirst of desire, come to the waters, and all ye that have no silver of your own will and desires, make haste; buy from Me and eat; come and buy from Me wine and milk (that is, spiritual sweetness and peace) without the silver of your own will, and without giving Me any labour in exchange for it, as ye give for your desires. Wherefore do ye give the silver of your will for that which is not bread — namely, that of the Divine Spirit — and set the labour of your desires upon that which cannot satisfy you? Come, hearkening to Me, and ye shall eat the good that ye desire and your soul shall delight itself in fatness.

This attaining to fatness is a going forth from all pleasures of the creatures; for the creatures torment, but the Spirit of God refreshes. And thus He calls us through Saint Matthew, saying: Venite ad me omnes, qui laboratis et onerati estis, et ego reficiam vos, et invenietis requiem animabus vestris. As though He were to say: All ye that go about tormented, afflicted and burdened with the burden of your cares and desires, go forth from them, come to Me, and I will refresh you and ye shall find for your souls the rest which your desires take from you, wherefore they are a heavy burden, for David says of them: Sicut onus grave gravatoe sunt super me.

Chapter VIII

Wherein is shown how the desires darken and blind the soul.

The third evil that the desires cause in the soul is that they blind and darken it. Even as vapours darken the air and allow not the bright sun to shine; or as a mirror that is clouded over cannot receive within itself a clear image; or as water defiled by mud reflects not the visage of one that looks therein; even so the soul that is clouded by the desires is darkened in the understanding and allows neither the sun of natural reason nor that of the supernatural Wisdom of God to shine upon it and illumine it clearly. And thus David, speaking to this purpose, says: Comprehenderunt me iniquitates meoe, et non potui, ut viderem. Which signifies: Mine iniquities have taken hold upon me, and I could have no power to see.

And, at this same time, when the soul is darkened in the understanding, it is benumbed also in the will, and the memory becomes dull and disordered in its due operation. For, as these faculties in their operations depend upon the understanding, it is clear that, when the understanding is impeded, they will become disordered and troubled. And thus David says: Anima mea turbata est valde. That is: My soul is sorely troubled. Which is as much as to say, 'disordered in its faculties.' For, as we say, the understanding has no more capacity for receiving enlightenment from the wisdom of God than has the air, when it is dark, for receiving enlightenment from the sun; neither has the will any power to embrace God within itself in pure love, even as the mirror that is clouded with vapour has no power to reflect clearly within itself any visage, and even less power has the memory which is clouded by the darkness of desire to take clearly upon itself the form of the image of God, just as the muddled water cannot show forth clearly the visage of one that looks at himself therein.

Desire blinds and darkens the soul; for desire, as such, is blind, since of itself it has no understanding in itself, the reason being to it always, as it were, a child leading a blind man. And hence it comes to pass that, whensoever the soul is guided by its desire, it becomes blind; for this is as if one that sees were guided by one that sees not, which is, as it were, for both to be blind. And that which follows from this is that which Our Lord says through Saint Matthew: Si coecus coeco ducatum proestet, ambo in foveam cadunt. 'If the blind lead the blind, both fall into the pit.' Of little use are its eyes to a moth, since desire for the beauty of the light dazzles it and leads it into the flame. And even so we may say that one who feeds upon desire is like a fish that is dazzled, upon which the light acts rather as darkness, preventing it from seeing the snares which the fishermen are preparing for it. This is very well expressed by David himself, where he says of such persons: Supercecidit ignis, et non viderunt solem. Which signifies: There came upon them the fire, which burns with its heat and dazzles with its light. And it is this that desire does to the soul, enkindling its concupiscence and dazzling its understanding so that it cannot see its light. For the cause of its being thus dazzled is that when another light of a different kind is set before the eye, the visual faculty is attracted by that which is interposed so that it sees not the other; and, as the desire is set so near to the soul as to be within the soul itself, the soul meets this first light and is attracted by it; and thus it is unable to see the light of clear understanding, neither will see it until the dazzling power of desire is taken away from it.

For this reason one must greatly lament the ignorance of certain men, who burden themselves with extraordinary penances and with many other voluntary practices, and think that this practice or that will suffice to bring them to the union of Divine Wisdom; but such will not be the case if they endeavour not diligently to mortify their desires. If they were careful to bestow half of that labour on this, they would profit more in a month than they profit by all the other practices in many years. For, just as it is necessary to till the earth if it is to bear fruit, and unless it be tilled it bears naught but weeds, just so is mortification of the desires necessary if the soul is to profit. Without this mortification, I make bold to say, the soul no more achieves progress on the road to perfection and to the knowledge of God of itself, however many efforts it may make, than the seed grows when it is cast upon untilled ground. Wherefore the darkness and rudeness of the soul will not be taken from it until the desires be quenched. For these desires are like cataracts, or like motes in the eye, which obstruct the sight until they be taken away.

And thus David, realizing how blind are these souls, and how completely impeded from beholding the light of truth, and how wroth is God with them, speaks to them, saying: Priusquam intelligerent spinoe vestroe rhamnum: sicut viventes, sic in ira absorber eos. And this is as though He had said: Before your thorns (that is, your desires) harden and grow, changing from tender thorns into a thick hedge and shutting out the sight of God even as oft-times the living find their thread of life broken in the midst of its course, even so will God swallow them up in His wrath. For the desires that are living in the soul, so that it cannot understand Him, will be swallowed up by God by means of chastisement and correction, either in this life or in the next, and this will come to pass through purgation. And He says that He will swallow them up in wrath, because that which is suffered in the mortification of the desires is punishment for the ruin which they have wrought in the soul.

Oh, if men but knew how great is the blessing of Divine light whereof they are deprived by this blindness which proceeds from their affections and desires, and into what great hurts and evils these make them to fall day after day, for so long as they mortify them not! For a man must not rely upon a clear understanding, or upon gifts that he has received from God, and think that he may indulge his affection or desire, and will not be blinded and darkened, and fall gradually into a worse estate. For who would have said that a man so perfect in wisdom and the gifts of God as was Solomon would have been reduced to such blindness and torpor of the will as to make altars to so many idols and to worship them himself, when he was old? Yet no more was needed to bring him to this than the affection which he had for women and his neglect to deny the desires and delights of his heart. For he himself says concerning himself, in Ecclesiastes, that he denied not his heart that which it demanded of him. And this man was capable of being so completely led away by his desires that, although it is true that at the beginning he was cautious, nevertheless, because he denied them not, they gradually blinded and darkened his understanding, so that in the end they succeeded in quenching that great light of wisdom which God had given him, and therefore in his old age he forsook God.

And if unmortified desires could do so much in this man who knew so well the distance that lies between good and evil, what will they not be capable of accomplishing by working upon our ignorance? For we, as God said to the prophet Jonas concerning the Ninivites, cannot discern between our right hand and our left. At every step we hold evil to be good, and good, evil, and this arises from our own nature. What, then, will come to pass if to our natural darkness is added the hindrance of desire? Naught but that which Isaias describes thus: Palpavimus, sicut coeci parietem, et quasi absque oculis attreetavimus: impegimus meridie, quasi in tenebris. The prophet is speaking with those who love to follow these their desires. It is as if he had said: We have groped for the wall as though we were blind, and we have been groping as though we had no eyes, and our blindness has attained to such a point that we have stumbled at midday as though it were in the darkness. For he that is blinded by desire has this property, that, when he is set in the midst of truth and of that which is good for him, he can no more see them than if he were in darkness.

Chapter IX

Wherein is described how the desires defile the soul. This is proved by comparisons and quotations from Holy Scripture.

The fourth evil which the desires cause in the soul is that they stain and defile it, as is taught in Ecclesiasticus, in these words: Qui tetigerit picem, inquinabitur ab ea. This signifies: He that toucheth pitch shall be defiled with it. And a man touches pitch when he allows the desire of his will to be satisfied by any creature. Here it is to be noted that the Wise Man compares the creatures to pitch; for there is more difference between excellence of soul and the best of the creatures than there is between pure diamond, or fine gold, and pitch. And just as gold or diamond, if it were heated and placed upon pitch, would become foul and be stained by it, inasmuch as the heat would have cajoled and allured the pitch, even so the soul that is hot with desire for any creature draws forth foulness from it through the heat of its desire and is stained by it. And there is more difference between the soul and other corporeal creatures than between a liquid that is highly clarified and mud that is most foul. Wherefore, even as such a liquid would be defiled if it were mingled with mud, so is the soul defiled that clings to creatures, since by doing this it becomes like to the said creatures. And in the same way that traces of soot would defile a face that is very lovely and perfect, even in this way do disordered desires befoul and defile the soul that has them, the which soul is in itself a most lovely and perfect image of God.

Wherefore Jeremias, lamenting the ravages of foulness which these disordered affections cause in the soul, speaks first of its beauty, and then of its foulness, saying: Candidiores sunt Nazaroei ejus nive, nitidiores lacte, rubicundiores ebore antiquo, sapphiro pulchriores. Denigrata est super carbones facies eorum, et non sunt cogniti in plateis. Which signifies: Its hair — that is to say, that of the soul — is more excellent in whiteness than the snow, clearer than milk, and ruddier than old ivory, and lovelier than the sapphire stone. Their face has now become blacker than coal and they are not known in the streets. By the hair we here understand the affections and thoughts of the soul, which, ordered as God orders them — that is, in God Himself — are whiter than snow, and clearer than milk, and ruddier than ivory, and lovelier than the sapphire. By these four things is understood every kind of beauty and excellence of corporeal creatures, higher than which, says the writer, are the soul and its operations, which are the Nazarites or the hair aforementioned; the which Nazarites, being unruly, with their lives ordered in a way that God ordered not — that is, being set upon the creatures — have their face (says Jeremias) made and turned blacker than coal.

All this harm, and more, is done to the beauty of the soul by its unruly desires for the things of this world; so much so that, if we set out to speak of the foul and vile appearance that the desires can give the soul, we should find nothing, however full of cobwebs and worms it might be, not even the corruption of a dead body, nor aught else that is impure and vile, nor aught that can exist and be imagined in this life, to which we could compare it. For, although it is true that the unruly soul, in its natural being, is as perfect as when God created it, yet, in its reasonable being, it is vile, abominable, foul, black and full of all the evils that are here being described, and many more. For, as we shall afterwards say, a single unruly desire, although there be in it no matter of mortal sin, suffices to bring a soul into such bondage, foulness and vileness that it can in no wise come to accord with God in union until the desire be purified. What, then, will be the vileness of the soul that is completely unrestrained with respect to its own passions and given up to its desires, and how far removed will it be from God and from His purity?

It is impossible to explain in words, or to cause to be understood by the understanding, what variety of impurity is caused in the soul by a variety of desires. For, if it could be expressed and understood, it would be a wondrous thing, and one also which would fill us with pity, to see how each desire, in accordance with its quality and degree, be it greater or smaller, leaves in the soul its mark and deposit of impurity and vileness, and how one single disorder of the reason can be the source of innumerable different impurities, some greater, some less, each one after its kind. For, even as the soul of the righteous man has in one single perfection, which is uprightness of soul, innumerable gifts of the greatest richness, and many virtues of the greatest loveliness, each one different and full of grace after its kind according to the multitude and the diversity of the affections of love which it has had in God, even so the unruly soul, according to the variety of the desires which it has for the creatures, has in itself a miserable variety of impurities and meannesses, wherewith it is endowed by the said desires.

The variety of these desires is well illustrated in the Book of Ezechiel, where it is written that God showed this Prophet, in the interior of the Temple, painted around its walls, all likenesses of creeping things which crawl on the ground, and all the abomination of unclean beasts. And then God said to Ezechiel: 'Son of man, hast thou not indeed seen the abominations that these do, each one in the secrecy of his chamber?' And God commanded the Prophet to go in farther and he would see greater abominations; and he says that he there saw women seated, weeping for Adonis, the god of love. And God commanded him to go in farther still, and he would see yet greater abominations, and he says that he saw there five-and-twenty old men whose backs were turned toward the Temple.

The diversity of creeping things and unclean beasts that were painted in the first chamber of the Temple are the thoughts and conceptions which the understanding fashions from the lowly things of earth, and from all the creatures, which are painted, just as they are, in the temple of the soul, when the soul embarrasses its understanding with them, which is the soul's first habitation. The women that were farther within, in the second habitation, weeping for the god Adonis, are the desires that are in the second faculty of the soul, which is the will; the which are, as it were, weeping, inasmuch as they covet that to which the will is affectioned, which are the creeping things painted in the understandings. And the men that were in the third habitation are the images and representations of the creatures, which the third part of the soul — namely memory — keeps and reflects upon within itself. Of these it is said that their backs are turned toward the Temple because when the soul, according to these three faculties, completely and perfectly embraces anything that is of the earth, it can be said to have its back turned toward the Temple of God, which is the right reason of the soul, which admits within itself nothing that is of creatures.

And let this now suffice for the understanding of this foul disorder of the soul with respect to its desires. For if we had to treat in detail of the lesser foulness which these imperfections and their variety make and cause in the soul, and that which is caused by venial sins, which is still greater than that of the imperfections, and their great variety, and likewise that which is caused by the desires for mortal sin, which is complete foulness of the soul, and its great variety, according to the variety and multitude of all these three things, we should never end, nor would the understanding of angels suffice to understand it. That which I say, and that which is to the point for my purpose, is that any desire, although it be for but the smallest imperfection, stains and defiles the soul.

Chapter X

Wherein is described how the desires weaken the soul in virtue and make it lukewarm.

The fifth way in which the desires harm the soul is by making it lukewarm and weak, so that it has no strength to follow after virtue and to persevere therein. For as the strength of the desire, when it is set upon various aims, is less than if it were set wholly on one thing alone, and as, the more are the aims whereon it is set, the less of it there is for each of them, for this cause philosophers say that virtue in union is stronger than if it be dispersed. Wherefore it is clear that, if the desire of the will be dispersed among other things than virtue, it must be weaker as regards virtue. And thus the soul whose will is set upon various trifles is like water, which, having a place below wherein to empty itself, never rises; and such a soul has no profit. For this cause the patriarch Jacob compared his son Ruben to water poured out, because in a certain sin he had given rein to his desires. And he said: 'Thou art poured out like water; grow thou not.' As though he had said: Since thou art poured out like water as to the desires, thou shalt not grow in virtue. And thus, as hot water, when uncovered, readily loses heat, and as aromatic spices, when they are unwrapped, gradually lose the fragrance and strength of their perfume, even so the soul that is not recollected in one single desire for God loses heat and vigour in its virtue. This was well understood by David, when he said, speaking with God: I will keep my strength for Thee. That is, concentrating the strength of my desires upon Thee alone.

And the desires weaken the virtue of the soul, because they are to it like the shoots that grow about a tree, and take away its virtue so that it cannot bring forth so much fruit. And of such souls as these says the Lord: Voe proegnantibus, et nutrientibus in illis diebus. That is: Woe to them that in those days are with child and to them that give suck. This being with child and giving suck is understood with respect to the desires; which, if they be not pruned, will ever be taking more virtue from the soul, and will grow to the harm of the soul, like the shoots upon the tree. Wherefore Our Lord counsels us, saying: Have your loins girt about — the loins signifying here the desires. And indeed, they are also like leeches, which are ever sucking the blood from the veins, for thus the Preacher terms them when he says: The leeches are the daughters — that is, the desires — saying ever: Daca, daca.

From this it is clear that the desires bring no good to the soul but rather take from it that which it has; and, if it mortify them not, they will not cease till they have wrought in it that which the children of the viper are said to work in their mother; who, as they are growing within her womb, consume her and kill her, and they themselves remain alive at her cost. Just so the desires that are not mortified grow to such a point that they kill the soul with respect to God because it has not first killed them. And they alone live in it. Wherefore the Preacher says: Aufer a me Domine ventris concupiscentias.

And, even though they reach not this point, it is very piteous to consider how the desires that live in this poor soul treat it, how unhappy it is with regard to itself, how dry with respect to its neighbours, and how weary and slothful with respect to the things of God. For there is no evil humour that makes it as wearisome and difficult for a sick man to walk, or gives him a distaste for eating comparable to the weariness and distaste for following virtue which is given to a soul by desire for creatures. And thus the reason why many souls have no diligence and eagerness to gain virtue is, as a rule, that they have desires and affections which are not pure and are not fixed upon God.

Chapter XI

Wherein it is proved necessary that the soul that would attain to Divine union should be free from desires, however slight they be.

I expect that for a long time the reader has been wishing to ask whether it be necessary, in order to attain to this high estate of perfection, to undergo first of all total mortification in all the desires, great and small, or if it will suffice to mortify some of them and to leave others, those at least which seem of little moment. For it appears to be a severe and most difficult thing for the soul to be able to attain to such purity and detachment that it has no will and affection for anything.

To this I reply: first, that it is true that all the desires are not equally hurtful, nor do they all equally embarrass the soul. I am speaking of those that are voluntary, for the natural desires hinder the soul little, if at all, from attaining to union, when they are not consented to nor pass beyond the first movements (I mean, all those wherein the rational will has had no part, whether at first or afterward); and to take away these — that is, to mortify them wholly in this life — is impossible. And these hinder not the soul in such a way as to prevent its attainment to Divine union, even though they be not, as I say, wholly mortified; for the natural man may well have them, and yet the soul may be quite free from them according to the rational spirit. For it will sometimes come to pass that the soul will be in the full union of the prayer of quiet in the will at the very time when these desires are dwelling in the sensual part of the soul, and yet the higher part, which is in prayer, will have nothing to do with them. But all the other voluntary desires, whether they be of mortal sin, which are the gravest, or of venial sin, which are less grave, or whether they be only of imperfections, which are the least grave of all, must be driven away every one, and the soul must be free from them all, howsoever slight they be, if it is to come to this complete union; and the reason is that the state of this Divine union consists in the soul's total transformation, according to the will, in the will of God, so that, there may be naught in the soul that is contrary to the will of God, but that, in all and through all, its movement may be that of the will of God alone.

It is for this reason that we say of this state that it is the making of two wills into one — namely, into the will of God, which will of God is likewise the will of the soul. For if this soul desired any imperfection that God wills not, there would not be made one will of God, since the soul would have a will for that which God has not. It is clear, then, that for the soul to come to unite itself perfectly with God through love and will, it must first be free from all desire of the will, howsoever slight. That is, that it must not intentionally and knowingly consent with the will to imperfections, and it must have power and liberty to be able not so to consent intentionally. I say knowingly, because, unintentionally and unknowingly, or without having the power to do otherwise, it may well fall into imperfections and venial sins, and into the natural desires whereof we have spoken; for of such sins as these which are not voluntary and surreptitious it is written that the just man shall fall seven times in the day and shall rise up again. But of the voluntary desires, which, though they be for very small things, are, as I have said, intentional venial sins, any one that is not conquered suffices to impede union. I mean, if this habit be not mortified; for sometimes certain acts of different desires have not as much power when the habits are mortified. Still, the soul will attain to the stage of not having even these, for they likewise proceed from a habit of imperfection. But some habits of voluntary imperfections, which are never completely conquered, prevent not only the attainment of Divine union, but also progress in perfection.

These habitual imperfections are, for example, a common custom of much speaking, or some slight attachment which we never quite wish to conquer — such as that to a person, a garment, a book, a cell, a particular kind of food, tittle-tattle, fancies for tasting, knowing or hearing certain things, and suchlike. Any one of these imperfections, if the soul has become attached and habituated to it, is of as great harm to its growth and progress in virtue as though it were to fall daily into many other imperfections and usual venial sins which proceed not from a habitual indulgence in any habitual and harmful attachment, and will not hinder it so much as when it has attachment to anything. For as long as it has this there is no possibility that it will make progress in perfection, even though the imperfection be extremely slight. For it comes to the same thing whether a bird be held by a slender cord or by a stout one; since, even if it be slender, the bird will be well held as though it were stout, for so long as it breaks it not and flies not away. It is true that the slender one is the easier to break; still, easy though it be, the bird will not fly away if it be not broken. And thus the soul that has attachment to anything, however much virtue it possess, will not attain to the liberty of Divine union. For the desire and the attachment of the soul have that power which the sucking-fish is said to have when it clings to a ship; for, though but a very small fish, if it succeed in clinging to the ship, it makes it incapable of reaching the port, or of sailing on at all. It is sad to see certain souls in this plight; like rich vessels, they are laden with wealth and good works and spiritual exercises, and with the virtues and the favours that God grants them; and yet, because they have not the resolution to break with some whim or attachment or affection (which all come to the same thing), they never make progress or reach the port of perfection, though they would need to do no more than make one good flight and thus to snap that cord of desire right off, or to rid themselves of that sucking-fish of desire which clings to them.

It is greatly to be lamented that, when God has granted them strength to break other and stouter cords — namely, affections for sins and vanities — they should fail to attain to such blessing because they have not shaken off some childish thing which God had bidden them conquer for love of Him, and which is nothing more than a thread or a hair. And, what is worse, not only do they make no progress, but because of this attachment they fall back, lose that which they have gained, and retrace that part of the road along which they have travelled at the cost of so much time and labour; for it is well known that, on this road, not to go forward is to turn back, and not to be gaining is to be losing. This Our Lord desired to teach us when He said: 'He that is not with Me is against Me; and he that gathereth not with Me scattereth.' He that takes not the trouble to repair the vessel, however slight be the crack in it, is likely to spill all the liquid that is within it. The Preacher taught us this clearly when he said: He that contemneth small things shall fall by little and little. For, as he himself says, a great fire cometh from a single spark. And thus one imperfection is sufficient to lead to another; and these lead to yet more; wherefore you will hardly ever see a soul that is negligent in conquering one desire, and that has not many more arising from the same weakness and imperfection that this desire causes. In this way they are continually filling; we have seen many persons to whom God has been granting the favour of leading them a long way, into a state of great detachment and liberty, yet who, merely through beginning to indulge some slight attachment, under the pretext of doing good, or in the guise of conversation and friendship, often lose their spirituality and desire for God and holy solitude, fall from the joy and wholehearted devotion which they had in their spiritual exercises, and cease not until they have lost everything; and this because they broke not with that beginning of sensual desire and pleasure and kept not themselves in solitude for God.

Upon this road we must ever journey in order to attain our goal; which means that we must ever be mortifying our desires and not indulging them; and if they are not all completely mortified we shall not completely attain. For even as a log of wood may fail to be transformed in the fire because a single degree of heat is wanting to it, even so the soul will not be transformed in God if it have but one imperfection, although it be something less than voluntary desire; for, as we shall say hereafter concerning the night of faith, the soul has only one will, and that will, if it be embarrassed by aught and set upon by aught, is not free, solitary, and pure, as is necessary for Divine transformation.

Of this that has been said we have a figure in the Book of the Judges, where it is related that the angel came to the children of Israel and said to them that, because they had not destroyed that forward people, but had made a league with some of them, they would therefore be left among them as enemies, that they might be to them an occasion of stumbling and perdition. And just so does God deal with certain souls: though He has taken them out of the world, and slain the giants, their sins, and destroyed the multitude of their enemies, which are the occasions of sin that they encountered in the world, solely that they may enter this Promised Land of Divine union with greater liberty, yet they harbour friendship and make alliance with the insignificant peoples — that is, with imperfections — and mortify them not completely; therefore Our Lord is angry, and allows them to fall into their desires and go from bad to worse.

In the Book of Josue, again, we have a figure of what has just been said — where we read that God commanded Josue, at the time that he had to enter into possession of the Promised Land, to destroy all things that were in the city of Jericho, in such wise as to leave therein nothing alive, man or woman, young or old, and to slay all the beasts, and to take naught, neither to covet aught, of all the spoils. This He said that we may understand how, if a man is to enter this Divine union, all that lives in his soul must die, both little and much, small and great, and that the soul must be without desire for all this, and detached from it, even as though it existed not for the soul, neither the soul for it. This Saint Paul teaches us clearly in his epistle ad Corinthios, saying: 'This I say to you, brethren, that the time is short; it remains, and it behoves you, that they that have wives should be as if they had none; and they that weep for the things of this world, as though they wept not; and they that rejoice, as if they rejoiced not; and they that buy, as though they possessed not; and they that use this world, as if they used it not.' This the Apostle says to us in order to teach us how complete must be the detachment of our soul from all things if it is to journey to God.

Chapter XII

Which treats of the answer to another question, explaining what the desires are that suffice to cause the evils aforementioned in the soul.

We might write at greater length upon this matter of the night of sense, saying all that there is to say concerning the harm which is caused by the desires, not only in the ways aforementioned, but in many others. But for our purpose that which has been said suffices; for we believe we have made it clear in what way the mortification of these desires is called night, and how it behoves us to enter this night in order to journey to God. The only thing that remains, before we treat of the manner of entrance therein, in order to bring this part to a close, is a question concerning what has been said which might occur to the reader.

It may first be asked if any desire can be sufficient to work and produce in the soul the two evils aforementioned — namely, the privative, which consists in depriving the soul of the grace of God, and the positive, which consists in producing within it the five serious evils whereof we have spoken. Secondly, it may be asked if any desire, however slight it be and of whatever kind, suffices to produce all these together, or if some desires produce some and others produce others. If, for example, some produce torment; others, weariness; others, darkness, etc.

Answering this question, I say, first of all, that with respect to the privative evil — which consists in the soul's being deprived of God — this is wrought wholly, and can only be wrought, by the voluntary desires, which are of the matter of mortal sin; for they deprive the soul of grace in this life, and of glory, which is the possession of God, in the next. In the second place, I say that both those desires which are of the matter of mortal sin, and the voluntary desires, which are of the matter of venial sin, and those that are of the matter of imperfection, are each sufficient to produce in the soul all these positive evils together; the which evils, although in a certain way they are privative, we here call positive, since they correspond to a turning towards the creature, even as the privative evils correspond to a turning away from God. But there is this difference, that the desires which are of mortal sin produce total blindness, torment, impurity, weakness, etc. Those others, however, which are of the matter of venial sin or imperfection, produce not these evils in a complete and supreme degree, since they deprive not the soul of grace, upon the loss of which depends the possession of them, since the death of the soul is their life; but they produce them in the soul remissly, proportionately to the remission of grace which these desires produce in the soul. So that desire which most weakens grace will produce the most abundant torment, blindness and defilement.

It should be noted, however, that, although each desire produces all these evils, which we here term positive, there are some which, principally and directly, produce some of them, and others which produce others, and the remainder are produced consequently upon these. For, although it is true that one sensual desire produces all these evils, yet its principal and proper effect is the defilement of soul and body. And, although one avaricious desire produces them all, its principal and direct result is to produce misery. And, although similarly one vainglorious desire produces them all, its principal and direct result is to produce darkness and blindness. And, although one gluttonous desire produces them all, its principal result is to produce lukewarmness in virtue. And even so is it with the rest.

And the reason why any act of voluntary desire produces in the soul all these effects together lies in the direct contrariety which exists between them and all the acts of virtue which produce the contrary effects in the soul. For, even as an act of virtue produces and begets in the soul sweetness, peace, consolation, light, cleanness and fortitude altogether, even so an unruly desire causes torment, fatigue, weariness, blindness and weakness. All the virtues grow through the practice of any one of them, and all the vices grow through the practice of any one of them likewise, and the remnants of each grow in the soul. And although all these evils are not evident at the moment when the desire is indulged, since the resulting pleasure gives no occasion for them, yet the evil remnants which they leave are clearly perceived, whether before or afterwards. This is very well illustrated by that book which the angel commanded Saint John to eat, in the Apocalypse, the which book was sweetness to his mouth, and in his belly bitterness. For the desire, when it is carried into effect, is sweet and appears to be good, but its bitter taste is felt afterwards; the truth of this can be clearly proved by anyone who allows himself to be led away by it. Yet I am not ignorant that there are some men so blind and insensible as not to feel this, for, as they do not walk in God, they are unable to perceive that which hinders them from approaching Him.

I am not writing here of the other natural desires which are not voluntary, and of thoughts that go not beyond the first movements, and other temptations to which the soul is not consenting; for these produce in the soul none of the evils aforementioned. For, although a person who suffers from them may think that the passion and disturbance which they then produce in him are defiling and blinding him, this is not the case; rather they are bringing him the opposite advantages. For, in so far as he resists them, he gains fortitude, purity, light and consolation, and many blessings, even as Our Lord said to Saint Paul: That virtue was made perfect in weakness. But the voluntary desires work all the evils aforementioned, and more. Wherefore the principal care of spiritual masters is to mortify their disciples immediately with respect to any desire soever, by causing them to remain without the objects of their desires, in order to free them from such great misery.

Chapter XIII

Wherein is described the manner and way which the soul must follow in order to enter this night of sense.

It now remains for me to give certain counsels whereby the soul may know how to enter this night of sense and may be able so to do. To this end it must be known that the soul habitually enters this night of sense in two ways: the one is active; the other passive. The active way consists in that which the soul can do, and does, of itself, in order to enter therein, whereof we shall now treat in the counsels which follow. The passive way is that wherein the soul does nothing, and God works in it, and it remains, as it were, patient. Of this we shall treat in the fourth book, where we shall be treating of beginners. And because there, with the Divine favour, we shall give many counsels to beginners, according to the many imperfections which they are apt to have while on this road, I shall not spend time in giving many here. And this, too, because it belongs not to this place to give them, as at present we are treating only of the reasons for which this journey is called a night, and of what kind it is, and how many parts it has. But, as it seems that it would be incomplete, and less profitable than it should be, if we gave no help or counsel here for walking in this night of desires, I have thought well to set down briefly here the way which is to be followed: and I shall do the same at the end of each of the next two parts, or causes, of this night, whereof, with the help of the Lord, I have to treat.

These counsels for the conquering of the desires, which now follow, albeit brief and few, I believe to be as profitable and efficacious as they are concise; so that one who sincerely desires to practice them will need no others, but will find them all included in these.

First, let him have an habitual desire to imitate Christ in everything that he does, conforming himself to His life; upon which life he must meditate so that he may know how to imitate it, and to behave in all things as Christ would behave.

Secondly, in order that he may be able to do this well, every pleasure that presents itself to the senses, if it be not purely for the honour and glory of God, must be renounced and completely rejected for the love of Jesus Christ, Who in this life had no other pleasure, neither desired any, than to do the will of His Father, which He called His meat and food. I take this example. If there present itself to a man the pleasure of listening to things that tend not to the service and honour of God, let him not desire that pleasure, nor desire to listen to them; and if there present itself the pleasure of looking at things that help him not Godward, let him not desire the pleasure or look at these things; and if in conversation or in aught else soever such pleasure present itself, let him act likewise. And similarly with respect to all the senses, in so far as he can fairly avoid the pleasure in question; if he cannot, it suffices that, although these things may be present to his senses, he desires not to have this pleasure. And in this wise he will be able to mortify and void his senses of such pleasure, as though they were in darkness. If he takes care to do this, he will soon reap great profit.

For the mortifying and calming of the four natural passions, which are joy, hope, fear and grief, from the concord and pacification whereof come these and other blessings, the counsels here following are of the greatest help, and of great merit, and the source of great virtues.

Strive always to prefer, not that which is easiest, but that which is most difficult;

Not that which is most delectable, but that which is most unpleasing;

Not that which gives most pleasure, but rather that which gives least;

Not that which is restful, but that which is wearisome;

Not that which is consolation, but rather that which is disconsolateness;

Not that which is greatest, but that which is least;

Not that which is loftiest and most precious, but that which is lowest and most despised;

Not that which is a desire for anything, but that which is a desire for nothing;

Strive to go about seeking not the best of temporal things, but the worst.

Strive thus to desire to enter into complete detachment and emptiness and poverty, with respect to everything that is in the world, for Christ's sake.

And it is meet that the soul embrace these acts with all its heart and strive to subdue its will thereto. For, if it perform them with its heart, it will very quickly come to find in them great delight and consolation, and to act with order and discretion.

These things that have been said, if they be faithfully put into practice, are quite sufficient for entrance into the night of sense; but, for greater completeness, we shall describe another kind of exercise which teaches us to mortify the concupiscence of the flesh and the concupiscence of the eyes, and the pride of life, which, says Saint John, are the things that reign in the world, from which all the other desires proceed.

First, let the soul strive to work in its own despite, and desire all to do so. Secondly, let it strive to speak in its own despite and desire all to do so. Third, let it strive to think humbly of itself, in its own despite, and desire all to do so.

To conclude these counsels and rules, it will be fitting to set down here those lines which are written in the Ascent of the Mount, which is the figure that is at the beginning of this book; the which lines are instructions for ascending to it, and thus reaching the summit of union. For, although it is true that that which is there spoken of is spiritual and interior, there is reference likewise to the spirit of imperfection according to sensual and exterior things, as may be seen by the two roads which are on either side of the path of perfection. It is in this way and according to this sense that we shall understand them here; that is to say, according to that which is sensual. Afterwards, in the second part of this night, they will be understood according to that which is spiritual.

The lines are these:

In order to arrive at having pleasure in everything,
Desire to have pleasure in nothing.

In order to arrive at possessing everything,
Desire to possess nothing.

In order to arrive at being everything,
Desire to be nothing.

In order to arrive at knowing everything,
Desire to know nothing.

In order to arrive at that wherein thou hast no pleasure,
Thou must go by a way wherein thou hast no pleasure.

In order to arrive at that which thou knowest not,
Thou must go by a way that thou knowest not.

In order to arrive at that which thou possessest not,
Thou must go by a way that thou possessest not.

In order to arrive at that which thou art not,
Thou must go through that which thou art not.

When thy mind dwells upon anything,
Thou art ceasing to cast thyself upon the All.

For, in order to pass from the all to the All,
Thou hast to deny thyself wholly in all.

And, when thou comest to possess it wholly,
Thou must possess it without desiring anything.

For, if thou wilt have anything in having all,

Thou hast not thy treasure purely in God.

In this detachment the spiritual soul finds its quiet and repose; for, since it covets nothing, nothing wearies it when it is lifted up, and nothing oppresses it when it is cast down, because it is in the centre of its humility; but when it covets anything, at that very moment it becomes wearied.

Chapter XIV

Wherein is expounded the second line of the stanza.
Kindled in love with yearnings.

Now that we have expounded the first line of this stanza, which treats of the night of sense, explaining what this night of sense is, and why it is called night; and now that we have likewise described the order and manner which are to be followed for a soul to enter therein actively, the next thing to be treated in due sequence is its properties and effects, which are wonderful, and are described in the next lines of the stanza aforementioned, upon which I will briefly touch for the sake of expounding the said lines, as I promised in the Prologue; and I will then pass on at once to the second book, treating of the other part of this night, which is the spiritual.

The soul, then, says that, 'kindled in love with yearnings,' it passed through this dark night of sense and came out thence to the union of the Beloved. For, in order to conquer all the desires and to deny itself the pleasures which it has in everything, and for which its love and affection are wont to enkindle the will that it may enjoy them, it would need to experience another and a greater enkindling by an other and a better love, which is that of its Spouse; to the end that, having its pleasure set upon Him and deriving from Him its strength, it should have courage and constancy to deny itself all other things with ease. And, in order to conquer the strength of the desires of sense, it would need, not only to have love for its Spouse, but also to be enkindled by love and to have yearnings. For it comes to pass, and so it is, that with such yearnings of desire the sensual nature is moved and attracted toward sensual things, so that, if the spiritual part be not enkindled with other and greater yearnings for that which is spiritual, it will be unable to throw off the yoke of nature or to enter this night of sense, neither will it have courage to remain in darkness as to all things, depriving itself of desire for them all.

And the nature and all the varieties of these yearnings of love which souls experience in the early stages of this road to union; and the diligent means and contrivances which they employ in order to leave their house, which is self-will, during the night of the mortification of their senses; and how easy, and even sweet and delectable, these yearnings for the Spouse make all the trials and perils of this night to appear to them, this is not the place to describe, neither is such description possible; for it is better to know and meditate upon these things than to write of them. And so we shall pass on to expound the remaining lines in the next chapter.

Chapter XV

Wherein are expounded the remaining lines of the aforementioned stanza.
. . . oh, happy chance! —
I went forth without being observed, My house being now at rest.

These lines take as a metaphor the miserable estate of captivity, a man's deliverance from which, when none of the gaolers' hinder his release, he considers a 'happy chance.' For the soul, on account of original sin, is truly as it were a captive in this mortal body, subject to the passions and desires of nature, from bondage and subjection to which it considers its having gone forth without being observed as a 'happy chance' — having gone forth, that is, without being impeded or engulfed by any of them.

For to this end the soul profited by going forth upon a 'dark night' — that is, in the privation of all pleasures and mortification of all desires, after the manner whereof we have spoken. And by its 'house being now at rest' is meant the sensual part, which is the house of all the desires, and is now at rest because they have all been overcome and lulled to sleep. For until the desires are lulled to sleep through the mortification of the sensual nature, and until at last the sensual nature itself is at rest from them, so that they make not war upon the spirit, the soul goes not forth to true liberty and to the fruition of union with its Beloved.

BOOK THE SECOND

Wherein is treated the proximate means of ascending to union with God, which is faith; and wherein therefore is described the second part of this night, which, as we said, belongs to the spirit, and is contained in the second stanza, which is as follows.

Chapter I

Stanza the Second

In darkness and secure, By the secret ladder, disguised — oh, happy chance! — In darkness and in concealment, My house being now at rest.

In this second stanza the soul sings of the happy chance which it experienced in stripping the spirit of all spiritual imperfections and desires for the possession of spiritual things. This was a much greater happiness to, by reason of the greater difficulty that there is in putting to rest this house of the spiritual part, and of being able to enter this interior darkness, which is spiritual detachment from all things, whether sensual or spiritual, and leaning on pure faith alone and an ascent thereby to God. The soul here calls this a 'ladder,' and 'secret,' because all the rungs and parts of it are secret and hidden from all sense and understanding. And thus the soul has remained in darkness as to all light of sense and understanding, going forth beyond all limits of nature and reason in order to ascend by this Divine ladder of faith, which attains and penetrates even to the heights of God. The soul says that it was travelling 'disguised,' because the garments and vesture which it wears and its natural condition are changed into the Divine, as it ascends by faith. And it was because of this disguise that it was not recognized or impeded, either by time or by reason or by the devil; for none of these things can harm one that journeys in faith. And not only so, but the soul travels in such wise concealed and hidden and is so far from all the deceits of the devil that in truth it journeys (as it also says here) 'in darkness and in concealment' — that is to say, hidden from the devil, to whom the light of faith is more than darkness.

And thus the soul that journeys through this night, we may say, journeys in concealment and in hiding from the devil, as will be more clearly seen hereafter. Wherefore the soul says that it went forth 'in darkness and secure'; for one that has such happiness as to be able to journey through the darkness of faith, taking faith for his guide, like to one that is blind, and leaving behind all natural imaginings and spiritual reasonings, journeys very securely, as we have said. And so the soul says furthermore that it went forth through this spiritual night, its 'house being now at rest' — that is to say, its spiritual and rational parts. When, therefore, the soul attains to union which is of God, its natural faculties are at rest, as are likewise its impulses and yearnings of the senses, in its spiritual part. For this cause the soul says not here that it went forth with yearnings, as in the first night of sense. For, in order to journey in the night of sense, and to strip itself of that which is of sense, it needed yearnings of sense-love so that it might go forth perfectly; but, in order to put to rest the house of its spirit, it needs no more than denial of all faculties and pleasures and desires of the spirit in pure faith. This attained, the soul is united with the Beloved in a union of simplicity and purity and love and similitude.

And it must be remembered that the first stanza, speaking of the sensual part, says that the soul went forth upon 'a dark night,' and here, speaking of the spiritual part, it says that it went forth 'in darkness.' For the darkness of the spiritual part is by far the greater, even as darkness is a greater obscurity than that of night. For, however dark a night may be, something can always be seen, but in true darkness nothing can be seen; and thus in the night of sense there still remains some light, for the understanding and reason remain, and are not blinded. But this spiritual night, which is faith, deprives the soul of everything, both as to understanding and as to sense. And for this cause the soul in this night says that it was journeying 'in darkness and secure,' which it said not in the other. For, the less the soul works with its own ability, the more securely it journeys, because it journeys more in faith. And this will be expounded at length in the course of this second book, wherein it will be necessary for the devout reader to proceed attentively, because there will be said herein things of great importance to the person that is truly spiritual. And, although they are somewhat obscure, some of them will pave the way to others, so that I believe they will all be quite clearly understood.

Chapter 11

Which begins to treat of the second part or cause of this night, which is faith. Proves by two arguments how it is darker than the first and than the third.

We now go on to treat of the second part of this night, which is faith; this is the wondrous means which, as we said, leads to the goal, which is God, Who, as we said, is also to the soul, naturally, the third cause or part of this night. For faith, which is the means, is compared with midnight. And thus we may say that it is darker for the soul either than the first part or, in a way, than the third; for the first part, which is that of sense, is compared to the beginning of night, or the time when sensible objects can no longer be seen, and thus it is not so far removed from light as is midnight. The third part, which is the period preceding the dawn, is quite close to the light of day, and it, too, therefore, is not so dark as midnight; for it is now close to the enlightenment and illumination of the light of day, which is compared with God. For, although it is true, if we speak after a natural manner, that God is as dark a night to the soul as is faith, still, when these three parts of the night are over, which are naturally night to the soul, God begins to illumine the soul by supernatural means with the ray of His Divine light; which is the beginning of the perfect union that follows, when the third night is past, and it can thus be said to be less dark.

It is likewise darker than the first night, for this belongs to the lower part of man, which is the sensual part, and, consequently, the more exterior; and this second part, which is of faith, belongs to the higher part of man, which is the rational part, and, in consequence, more interior and more obscure, since it deprives it of the light of reason, or, to speak more clearly, blinds it; and thus it is aptly compared to midnight, which is the depth of night and the darkest part thereof.

We have now to prove how this second part, which is faith, is night to the spirit, even as the first part is night to sense. And we shall then also describe the things that are contrary to it, and how the soul must prepare itself actively to enter it. For, concerning the passive part, which is that which God works in it, when He brings it into that night, we shall speak in its place, which I intend shall be the third book.

Chapter III

How faith is dark night to the soul. This is proved with arguments and quotations and figures from Scripture.

Faith, say the theologians, is a habit of the soul, certain and obscure. And the reason for its being an obscure habit is that it makes us believe truths revealed by God Himself, which transcend all natural light, and exceed all human understanding, beyond all proportion. Hence it follows that, for the soul, this excessive light of faith which is given to it is thick darkness, for it overwhelms greater things and does away with small things, even as the light of the sun overwhelms all other lights whatsoever, so that when it shines and disables our visual faculty they appear not to be lights at all. So that it blinds it and deprives it of the sight that has been given to it, inasmuch as its light is great beyond all proportion and transcends the faculty of vision. Even so the light of faith, by its excessive greatness, oppresses and disables that of the understanding; for the latter, of its own power, extends only to natural knowledge, although it has a faculty for the supernatural, whenever Our Lord is pleased to give it supernatural activity.

Wherefore a man can know nothing by himself, save after a natural manner, which is only that which he attains by means of the senses. For this cause he must have the phantasms and the forms of objects present in themselves and in their likenesses; otherwise it cannot be, for, as philosophers say: Ab objecto et potentia paritur notitia. That is: From the object that is present and from the faculty, knowledge is born in the soul. Wherefore, if one should speak to a man of things which he has never been able to understand, and whose likeness he has never seen, he would have no more illumination from them whatever than if naught had been said of them to him. I take an example. If one should say to a man that on a certain island there is an animal which he has never seen, and give him no idea of the likeness of that animal, that he may compare it with others that he has seen, he will have no more knowledge of it, or idea of its form, than he had before, however much is being said to him about it. And this will be better understood by another and a more apt example. If one should describe to a man that was born blind, and has never seen any colour, what is meant by a white colour or by a yellow, he would understand it but indifferently, however fully one might describe it to him; for, as he has never seen such colours or anything like them by which he may judge them, only their names would remain with him; for these he would be able to comprehend through the ear, but not their forms or figures, since he has never seen them.

Even so is faith with respect to the soul; it tells us of things which we have never seen or understood, nor have we seen or understood aught that resembles them, since there is naught that resembles them at all. And thus we have no light of natural knowledge concerning them, since that which we are told of them bears no relation to any sense of ours; we know it by the ear alone, believing that which we are taught, bringing our natural light into subjection and treating it as if it were not. For, as Saint Paul says, Fides ex auditu. As though he were to say: Faith is not knowledge which enters by any of the senses, but is only the consent given by the soul to that which enters through the ear.

And faith far transcends even that which is indicated by the examples given above. For not only does it give no information and knowledge, but, as we have said, it deprives us of all other information and knowledge, and blinds us to them, so that they cannot judge it well. For other knowledge can be acquired by the light of the understanding; but the knowledge that is of faith is acquired without the illumination of the understanding, which is rejected for faith; and in its own light, if that light be not darkened, it is lost. Wherefore Isaias said: Si non credideritis, non intelligetis. That is: If ye believe not, ye shall not understand. It is clear, then, that faith is dark night for the soul, and it is in this way that it gives it light; and the more the soul is darkened, the greater is the light that comes to it. For it is by blinding that it gives light, according to this saying of Isaias. For if ye believe not, ye shall not (he says) have light. And thus faith was foreshadowed by that cloud which divided the children of Israel and the Egyptians when the former were about to enter the Red Sea, whereof Scripture says: Erat nubes tenebrosa, et illuminans noctem. This is to say that that cloud was full of darkness and gave light to the night.

A wondrous thing it is that, though it was dark, it should give light to the night. This was said to show that faith, which is a black and dark cloud to the soul (and likewise is night, since in the presence of faith the soul is deprived of its natural light and is blinded), can with its darkness give light and illumination to the darkness of the soul, for it was fitting that the disciples should thus be like the master. For man, who is in darkness, could not fittingly be enlightened save by other darkness, even as David teaches us, saying: Dies diei eructat verbum et nox nocti indicat scientiam. Which signifies: Day unto day uttereth and aboundeth in speech, and night unto night showeth knowledge. Which, to speak more clearly, signifies: The day, which is God in bliss, where it is day to the blessed angels and souls who are now day, communicates and reveals to them the Word, which is His Son, that they may know Him and enjoy Him. And the night, which is faith in the Church Militant, where it is still night, shows knowledge is night to the Church, and consequently to every soul, which knowledge is night to it, since it is without clear beatific wisdom; and, in the presence of faith, it is blind as to its natural light.

So that which is to be inferred from this that faith, because it is dark night, gives light to the soul, which is in darkness, that there may come to be fulfilled that which David likewise says to this purpose, in these works: Et nox illuminatio mea in deliciis meis. Which signifies: the night will be illumination in my delights. Which is as much as to say: In the delights of my pure contemplation and union with God, the night of faith shall be my guide. Wherein he gives it clearly to be understood that the soul must be in darkness in order to have light for this road.

Chapter IV

Treats in general of how the soul likewise must be in darkness, in so far as this rests with itself, to the end that it may be effectively guided by faith to the highest contemplation.

It is now, I think, becoming clear how faith is dark night to the soul, and how the soul likewise must be dark, or in darkness as to its own light so that it may allow itself to be guided by faith to this high goal of union. But, in order that the soul may be able to do this, it will now be well to continue describing, in somewhat greater detail, this darkness which it must have, in order that it may enter into this abyss of faith. And thus in this chapter I shall speak of it in a general way; and hereafter, with the Divine favour, I shall continue to describe more minutely the way in which the soul is to conduct itself that it may neither stray therein nor impede this guide.

I say, then, that the soul, in order to be effectively guided to this state by faith, must not only be in darkness with respect to that part that concerns the creatures and temporal things, which is the sensual and the lower part (whereof we have already treated), but that likewise it must be blinded and darkened according to the part which has respect to God and to spiritual things, which is the rational and higher part, whereof we are now treating. For, in order that one may attain supernatural transformation, it is clear that he must be plunged into darkness and carried far away from all contained in his nature that is sensual and rational. For the word supernatural means that which soars above the natural self; the natural self, therefore, remains beneath it. For, although this transformation and union is something that cannot be comprehended by human ability and sense, the soul must completely and voluntarily void itself of all that can enter into it, whether from above or from below — I mean according to the affection and will — so far as this rests with itself. For who shall prevent God from doing that which He will in the soul that is resigned, annihilated and detached? But the soul must be voided of all such things as can enter its capacity, so that, however many supernatural experiences it may have, it will ever remain as it were detached from them and in darkness. It must be like to a blind man, leaning upon dark faith, taking it for guide and light, and leaning upon none of the things that he understands, experiences, feels and imagines. For all these are darkness, which will cause him to stray; and faith is above all that he understands and experiences and feels and imagines. And, if he be not blinded as to this, and remain not in total darkness, he attains not to that which is greater — namely, that which is taught by faith.

A blind man, if he be not quite blind, refuses to be led by a guide; and, since he sees a little, he thinks it better to go in whatever happens to be the direction which he can distinguish, because he sees none better; and thus he can lead astray a guide who sees more than he, for after all it is for him to say where he shall go rather than for the guide. In the same way a soul may lean upon any knowledge of its own, or any feeling or experience of God, yet, however great this may be, it is very little and far different from what God is; and, in going along this road, a soul is easily led astray, or brought to a standstill, because it will not remain in faith like one that is blind, and faith is its true guide.

It is this that was meant by Saint Paul when he said: Accedentem ad Deum oportet credere quod est. Which signifies: He that would journey towards union with God must needs believe in His Being. As though he had said: He that would attain to being joined in a union with God must not walk by understanding, neither lean upon experience or feeling or imagination, but he must believe in His being, which is not perceptible to the understanding, neither to the desire nor to the imagination nor to any other sense, neither can it be known in this life at all. Yea, in this life, the highest thing that can be felt and experienced concerning God is infinitely remote from God and from the pure possession of Him. Isaias and Saint Paul say: Nec oculus vidit, nec auris audivit, nec in cor hominis ascendit, qua praeparavit Deus iis, qui diligunt illum. Which signifies: That which God hath prepared for them that love Him neither eye hath seen, nor ear heard, neither hath it entered into the heart or thought of man. So, however much the soul aspires to be perfectly united through grace in this life with that to which it will be united through glory in the next (which, as Saint Paul here says, eye hath not seen, nor ear heard, neither hath it entered into the heart of man in the flesh), it is clear that, in order perfectly to attain to union in this life through grace and through love, a soul must be in darkness with respect to all that can enter through the eye, and to all that can be received through the ear, and can be imagined with the fancy, and understood with the heart, which here signifies the soul. And thus a soul is greatly impeded from reaching this high estate of union with God when it clings to any understanding or feeling or imagination or appearance or will or manner of its own, or to any other act or to anything of its own, and cannot detach and strip itself of all these. For, as we say, the goal which it seeks lies beyond all this, yea, beyond even the highest thing that can be known or experienced; and thus a soul must pass beyond everything to unknowing.

Wherefore, upon this road, to enter upon the road is to leave the road; or, to express it better, it is to pass on to the goal and to leave one's own way, and to enter upon that which has no way, which is God. For the soul that attains to this state has no longer any ways or methods, still less is it attached to ways and methods, or is capable of being attached to them. I mean ways of understanding, or of perception, or of feeling. Nevertheless it has within itself all ways, after the way of one that possesses nothing, yet possesses all things. For, if it have courage to pass beyond its natural limitations, both interiorly and exteriorly, it enters within the limits of the supernatural, which has no way, yet in substance has all ways. Hence for the soul to arrive at these limits is for it to leave these limits, in each case going forth out of itself a great way, from this lowly state to that which is high above all others.

Wherefore, passing beyond all that can be known and understood, both spiritually and naturally, the soul will desire with all desire to come to that which in this life cannot be known, neither can enter into its heart. And, leaving behind all that it experiences and feels, both temporally and spiritually, and all that it is able to experience and feel in this life, it will desire with all desire to come to that which surpasses all feeling and experience. And, in order to be free and void to that end, it must in no wise lay hold upon that which it receives, either spiritually or sensually, within itself (as we shall explain presently, when we treat this in detail), considering it all to be of much less account. For the more emphasis the soul lays upon what it understands, experiences and imagines, and the more it esteems this, whether it be spiritual or no, the more it loses of the supreme good, and the more it is hindered from attaining thereto. And the less it thinks of what it may have, however much this be, in comparison with the highest good, the more it dwells upon that good and esteems it, and, consequently, the more nearly it approaches it. And in this wise the soul approaches a great way towards union, in darkness, by means of faith, which is likewise dark, and in this wise faith wondrously illumines it. It is certain that, if the soul should desire to see, it would be in darkness much more quickly, with respect to God, than would one who opens his eyes to look upon the great brightness of the sun.

Wherefore, by blinding itself in its faculties upon this road, the soul will see the light, even as the Saviour says in the Gospel, in this wise: In judicium veni in hunc mundum: ut qui non vident, videant, et qui vident, caeci fiant. That is: I am come into this world for judgment; that they which see not may see, and that they which see may become blind. This, as it will be supposed, is to be understood of this spiritual road, where the soul that is in darkness, and is blinded as regards all its natural and proper lights, will see supernaturally; and the soul that would depend upon any light of its own will become the blinder and will halt upon the road to union.

And, that we may proceed with less confusion, I think it will be necessary to describe, in the following chapter, the nature of this that we call union of the soul with God; for, when this is understood, that which we shall say hereafter will become much clearer. And so I think the treatment of this union comes well at this point, as in its proper place. For, although the thread of that which we are expounding is interrupted thereby, this is not done without a reason, since it serves to illustrate in this place the very thing that is being described. The chapter which follows, then, will be a parenthetical one, placed, as it were, between the two terms of an enthymeme, since we shall afterwards have to treat in detail of the three faculties of the soul, with respect to the three logical virtues, in relation to this second night.

Chapter V

Wherein is described what is meant by union of the soul with God. A comparison is given.

From what has been said above it becomes clear to some extent what we mean by union of the soul with God; what we now say about it, therefore, will be the better understood. It is not my intention here to treat of the divisions of this union, nor of its parts, for I should never end if I were to begin now to explain what is the nature of union of the understanding, and what is that of union according to the will, and likewise according to the memory; and likewise what is transitory and what permanent in the union of the said faculties; and then what is meant by total union, transitory and permanent, with regard to the said faculties all together. All this we shall treat gradually in our discourse — speaking first of one and then of another. But here this is not to the point in order to describe what we have to say concerning them; it will be explained much more fittingly in its place, when we shall again be treating the same matter, and shall have a striking illustration to add to the present explanation, so that everything will then be considered and explained and we shall judge of it better.

Here I treat only of this permanent and total union according to the substance of the soul and its faculties with respect to the obscure habit of union: for with respect to the act, we shall explain later, with the Divine favour, how there can be no permanent union in the faculties, in this life, but a transitory union only.

In order, then, to understand what is meant by this union whereof we are treating, it must be known that God dwells and is present substantially in every soul, even in that of the greatest sinner in the world. And this kind of union is ever wrought between God and all the creatures, for in it He is preserving their being: if union of this kind were to fail them, they would at once become annihilated and would cease to be. And so, when we speak of union of the soul with God, we speak not of this substantial union which is continually being wrought, but of the union and transformation of the soul with God, which is not being wrought continually, but only when there is produced that likeness that comes from love; we shall therefore term this the union of likeness, even as that other union is called substantial or essential. The former is natural, the latter supernatural. And the latter comes to pass when the two wills — namely that of the soul and that of God — are conformed together in one, and there is naught in the one that repugnant to the other. And thus, when the soul rids itself totally of that which is repugnant to the Divine will and conforms not with it, it is transformed in God through love.

This is to be understood of that which is repugnant, not only in action, but likewise in habit, so that not only must the voluntary acts of imperfection cease, but the habits of any such imperfections must be annihilated. And since no creature whatsoever, and none of its actions or abilities, can conform or can attain to that which is God, therefore must the soul be stripped of all things created, and of its own actions and abilities — namely, of its understanding, perception and feeling — so that, when all that is unlike God and unconformed to Him is cast out, the soul may receive the likeness of God; and nothing will then remain in it that is not the will of God and it will thus be transformed in God. Wherefore, although it is true that, as we have said, God is ever in the soul, giving it, and through His presence conserving within it, its natural being, yet He does not always communicate supernatural being to it. For this is communicated only by love and grace, which not all souls possess; and all those that possess it have it not in the same degree; for some have attained more degrees of love and others fewer. Wherefore God communicates Himself most to that soul that has progressed farthest in love; namely, that has its will in closest conformity with the will of God. And the soul that has attained complete conformity and likeness of will is totally united and transformed in God supernaturally. Wherefore, as has already been explained, the more completely a soul is wrapped up in the creatures and in its own abilities, by habit and affection, the less preparation it has for such union; for it gives not God a complete opportunity to transform it supernaturally. The soul, then, needs only to strip itself of these natural dissimilarities and contrarieties, so that God, Who is communicating Himself naturally to it, according to the course of nature, may communicate Himself to it supernaturally, by means of grace.

And it is this that Saint John desired to explain when he said: Qui non ex sanguinibus, neque ex voluntate carnis, neque ex voluntate viri, sed ex Deo nati sunt. As though he had said: He gave power to be sons of God — that is, to be transformed in God — only to those who are born, not of blood — that is, not of natural constitution and temperament — neither of the will of the flesh — that is, of the free will of natural capacity and ability — still less of the will of man — wherein is included every way and manner of judging and comprehending with the understanding. He gave power to none of these to become sons of God, but only to those that are born of God — that is, to those who, being born again through grace, and dying first of all to everything that is of the old man, are raised above themselves to the supernatural, and receive from God this rebirth and adoption, which transcends all that can be imagined. For, as Saint John himself says elsewhere: Nisi quis renatus fuerit ex aqua, et Spiritu Sancto, non potest videre regnum Dei. This signifies: He that is not born again in the Holy Spirit will not be able to see this kingdom of God, which is the state of perfection; and to be born again in the Holy Spirit in this life is to have a soul most like to God in purity, having in itself no admixture of imperfection, so that pure transformation can be wrought in it through participation of union, albeit not essentially.

In order that both these things may be the better understood, let us make a comparison. A ray of sunlight is striking a window. If the window is in any way stained or misty, the sun's ray will be unable to illumine it and transform it into its own light, totally, as it would if it were clean of all these things, and pure; but it will illumine it to a lesser degree, in proportion as it is less free from those mists and stains; and will do so to a greater degree, in proportion as it is cleaner from them, and this will not be because of the sun's ray, but because of itself; so much so that, if it be wholly pure and clean, the ray of sunlight will transform it and illumine it in such wise that it will itself seem to be a ray and will give the same light as the ray. Although in reality the window has a nature distinct from that of the ray itself, however much it may resemble it, yet we may say that that window is a ray of the sun or is light by participation. And the soul is like this window, whereupon is ever beating (or, to express it better, wherein is ever dwelling) this Divine light of the Being of God according to nature, which we have described.

In thus allowing God to work in it, the soul (having rid itself of every mist and stain of the creatures, which consists in having its will perfectly united with that of God, for to love is to labour to detach and strip itself for God's sake of all that is not God) is at once illumined and transformed in God, and God communicates to it His supernatural Being, in such wise that it appears to be God Himself, and has all that God Himself has. And this union comes to pass when God grants the soul this supernatural favour, that all the things of God and the soul are one in participant transformation; and the soul seems to be God rather than a soul, and is indeed God by participation; although it is true that its natural being, though thus transformed, is as distinct from the Being of God as it was before, even as the window has likewise a nature distinct from that of the ray, though the ray gives it brightness.

This makes it clearer that the preparation of the soul for this union, as we said, is not that it should understand or perceive or feel or imagine anything, concerning either God or aught else, but that it should have purity and love —

that is, perfect resignation and detachment from everything for God's sake alone; and, as there can be no perfect transformation if there be not perfect purity, and as the enlightenment, illumination and union of the soul with God will be according to the proportion of its purity, in greater or in less degree; yet the soul will not be perfect, as I say, if it be not wholly and perfectly bright and clean.

This will likewise be understood by the following comparison. A picture is truly perfect, with many and most sublime beauties and delicate and subtle illuminations, and some of its beauties are so fine and subtle that they cannot be completely realized, because of their delicacy and excellence. Fewer beauties and less delicacy will be seen in this picture by one whose vision is less clear and refined; and he whose vision is somewhat more refined will be able to see in it more beauties and perfections; and, if another person has a vision still more refined, he will see still more perfection; and, finally, he who has the clearest and purest faculties will see the most beauties and perfections of all; for there is so much to see in the picture that, however far one may attain, there will ever remain higher degrees of attainment.

After the same manner we may describe the condition of the soul with relation to God in this enlightenment or transformation. For, although it is true that a soul, according to its greater or lesser capacity, may have attained to union, yet not all do so in an equal degree, for this depends upon what the Lord is pleased to grant to each one. It is in this way that souls see God in Heaven; some more, some less; but all see Him, and all are content, for their capacity is satisfied.

Wherefore, although in this life here below we find certain souls enjoying equal peace and tranquillity in the state of perfection, and each one of them satisfied, yet some of them may be many degrees higher than others. All, however, will be equally satisfied, because the capacity of each one is satisfied. But the soul that attains not to such a measure of purity as is in conformity with its capacity never attains true peace and satisfaction, since it has not attained to the possession of that detachment and emptiness in its faculties which is required for simple union.

Chapter VI

Wherein is described how it is the three theological virtues that perfect the three faculties of the soul, and how the said virtues produce emptiness and darkness within them.

Having now to endeavour to show how the three faculties of the soul — understanding, memory and will — are brought into this spiritual night, which is the means to Divine union, it is necessary first of all to explain in this chapter how the three theological virtues — faith, hope and charity — which have respect to the three faculties aforesaid as their proper supernatural objects, and by means whereof the soul is united with God according to its faculties, produce the same emptiness and darkness, each one in its own faculty. Faith, in the understanding; hope, in the memory; and charity, in the will. And afterwards we shall go on to describe how the understanding is perfected in the darkness of faith; and the memory in the emptiness of hope; and likewise how the will must be buried by withdrawing and detaching every affection so that the soul may journey to God. This done, it will be clearly seen how necessary it is for the soul, if it is to walk securely on this spiritual road, to travel through this dark night, leaning upon these three virtues, which empty it of all things and make it dark with respect to them. For, as we have said, the soul is not united with God in this life through understanding, nor through enjoyment, nor through the imagination, nor through any sense whatsoever; but only through faith, according to the understanding; and through hope, according to the memory; and through love, according to the will.

These three virtues, as we have said, all cause emptiness in the faculties: faith, in the understanding, causes an emptiness and darkness with respect to understanding; hope, in the memory, causes emptiness of all possessions; and charity causes emptiness in the will and detachment from all affection and from rejoicing in all that is not God. For, as we see, faith tells us what cannot be understood with the understanding. Wherefore Saint Paul spoke of it ad Hebraeos after this manner: Fides est sperandarum substantia rerum, argumentum non apparentium. This we interpret as meaning that faith is the substance of things hoped for; and, although the understanding may be firmly and certainly consenting to them, they are not things that are revealed to the understanding, since, if they were revealed to it, there would be no faith. So faith, although it brings certainty to the understanding, brings it not clearness, but obscurity.

Then, as to hope, there is no doubt but that it renders the memory empty and dark with respect both to things below and to things above. For hope always relates to that which is not possessed; for, if it were possessed, there would be no more hope. Wherefore Saint Paul says ad Romanos: Spes, quae videtur, non est spes: nam quod videt quis, quid sperat? That is to say: Hope that is seen is not hope; for what a man seeth — that is, what a man possesseth — how doth he hope for it? This virtue, then, also produces emptiness, for it has to do with that which is not possessed and not with that which is possessed.

Similarity, charity causes emptiness in the will with respect to all things, since it obliges us to love God above them all; which cannot be unless we withdraw our affection from them in order to set it wholly upon God. Wherefore Christ says, through Saint Luke: Qui non renuntiat omnibus quae possidet, non potest meus esse discipulus. Which signifies: He that renounces not all that he possesses with the will cannot be My disciple. And thus all these three virtues set the soul in obscurity and emptiness with respect to all things.

And here we must consider that parable which our Redeemer related in the eleventh chapter of Saint Luke, wherein He said that a friend had to go out at midnight in order to ask his friend for three loaves; the which loaves signify these three virtues. And he said that he asked for them at midnight in order to signify that the soul that is in darkness as to all things must acquire these three virtues according to its faculties and must perfect itself in them in this night. In the sixth chapter of Isaias we read that the two seraphim whom this Prophet saw on either side of God had each six wings; with two they covered their feet, which signified the blinding and quenching of the affections of the will with respect to all things for the sake of God; and with two they covered their face, which signified the darkness of the understanding in the presence of God; and with the other two they flew. This is to signify the flight of hope to the things that are not possessed, when it is raised above all that it can possess, whether below or above, apart from God.

To these three virtues, then, we have to lead the three faculties of the soul, informing each faculty by each one of them, and stripping it and setting it in darkness concerning all things save only these three virtues. And this is the spiritual night which just now we called active; for the soul does that which in it lies in order to enter therein. And even as, in the night of sense, we described a method of voiding the faculties of sense of their sensible objects, with regard to the desire, so that the soul might go forth from the beginning of its course to the mean, which is faith; even so, in this spiritual night, with the favour of God, we shall describe a method whereby the spiritual faculties are voided and purified of all that is not God, and are set in darkness concerning these three virtues, which, as we have said, are the means and preparation for the union of the soul with God.

In this method is found all security against the crafts of the devil and against the efficacy of self-love and its ramifications, which is wont most subtly to deceive and hinder spiritual persons on their road, when they know not how to become detached and to govern themselves according to these three virtues; and thus they are never able to reach the substance and purity of spiritual good, nor do they journey by so straight and short a road as they might.

And it must be noted that I am now speaking particularly to those who have begun to enter the state of contemplation, because as far as this concerns beginners it must be described somewhat more amply, as we shall note in the second book, God willing, when we treat of the properties of these beginners.

Chapter VII

Wherein is described how strait is the way that leads to eternal life and how completely detached and disencumbered must be those that will walk in it. We begin to speak of the detachment of the understanding.

We have now to describe the detachment and purity of the three faculties of the soul and for this are necessary a far greater knowledge and spirituality than mine, in order to make clear to spiritual persons how strait is this road which, said Our Saviour, leads to life; so that, persuaded of this, they may not marvel at the emptiness and detachment to which, in this night, we have to abandon the faculties of the soul.

To this end must be carefully noted the words which Our Saviour used, in the seventh chapter of Saint Matthew, concerning this road, as follows: Quam angusta porta, et arcta via est, quae ducit ad vitam, et pauci sunt, qui inveniunt eam. This signifies: How strait is the gate and how narrow the way that leadeth unto life, and few there are that find it! In this passage we must carefully note the emphasis and insistence which are contained in that word Quam. For it is as if He had said: In truth the way is very strait, more so than you think. And likewise it is to be noted that He says first that the gate is strait, to make it clear that, in order for the soul to enter by this gate, which is Christ, and which comes at the beginning of the road, the will must first be straitened and detached in all things sensual and temporal, and God must be loved above them all; which belongs to the night of sense, as we have said.

He then says that the way is narrow — that is to say, the way of perfection — in order to make it clear that, to travel upon the way of perfection, the soul has not only to enter by the strait gate, emptying itself of things of sense, but has also to straiten itself, freeing and disencumbering itself completely in that which pertains to the spirit. And thus we can apply what He says of the strait gate to the sensual part of man; and what He says of the narrow road we can understand of the spiritual or the rational part; and, when He says 'Few there are that find it,' the reason of this must be noted, which is that there are few who can enter, and desire to enter, into this complete detachment and emptiness of spirit. For this path ascending the high mountain of perfection leads upward, and is narrow, and therefore requires travellers that have no burden weighing upon them with respect to lower things, neither aught that embarrasses them with respect to higher things: and, as this is a matter wherein we must seek after and attain to God alone, God alone must be the object of our search and attainment.

Hence it is clearly seen that the soul must not only be disencumbered from that which belongs to the creatures, but likewise, as it travels, must be annihilated and detached from all that belongs to its spirit. Wherefore Our Lord, instructing us and leading us into this road, gave, in the eighth chapter of St. Mark, that wonderful teaching of which I think it may almost be said that, the more necessary it is for spiritual persons, the less it is practised by them. As this teaching is so important and so much to our purpose, I shall reproduce it here in full, and expound it according to its genuine, spiritual sense. He says, then, thus: Si quis vult me sequi, deneget semetipsum: et tollat crucem suam, et sequatur me. Qui enim voluerit animam suam salvam facere, perdet eam: qui autem perdiderit animam suam propter me. . . salvam lacier eam. This signifies: If any man will follow My road, let him deny himself and take up his cross and follow Me. For he that will save his soul shall lose it; but he that loses it for My sake, shall gain it.

Oh, that one could show us how to understand, practise and experience what this counsel is which our Saviour here gives us concerning self-denial, so that spiritual persons might see in how different a way they should conduct themselves upon this road from that which many of them think proper! For they believe that any kind of retirement and reformation of life suffices; and others are content with practising the virtues and continuing in prayer and pursuing mortification; but they attain not to detachment and poverty or selflessness or spiritual purity (which are all one), which the Lord here commends to us; for they prefer feeding and clothing their natural selves with spiritual feelings and consolations, to stripping themselves of all things, and denying themselves all things, for God's sake. For they think that it suffices to deny themselves worldly things without annihilating and purifying themselves of spiritual attachment. Wherefore it comes to pass that, when there presents itself to them any of this solid and perfect spirituality, consisting in the annihilation of all sweetness in God, in aridity, distaste and trial, which is the true spiritual cross, and the detachment of the spiritual poverty of Christ, they flee from it as from death, and seek only sweetness and delectable communion with God. This is not self-denial and detachment of spirit, but spiritual gluttony. Herein, spiritually, they become enemies of the Cross of Christ; for true spirituality seeks for God's sake that which is distasteful rather than that which is delectable; and inclines itself rather to suffering than to consolation; and desires to go without all blessings for God's sake rather than to possess them; and to endure aridities and afflictions rather than to enjoy sweet communications, knowing that this is to follow Christ and to deny oneself, and that the other is perchance to seek oneself in God, which is clean contrary to love. For to seek oneself in God is to seek the favours and refreshments of God; but to seek God in oneself is not only to desire to be without both of these for God's sake, but to be disposed to choose, for Christ's sake, all that is most distasteful, whether in relation to God or to the world; and this is love of God.

Oh, that one could tell us how far Our Lord desires this self-denial to be carried! It must certainly be like to death and annihilation, temporal, natural and spiritual, in all things that the will esteems, wherein consists all self-denial. And it is this that Our Lord meant when He said: 'He that will save his life, the same shall lose it.' That is to say: He that will possess anything or seek anything for himself, the same shall lose it; and he that loses his soul for My sake, the same shall gain it. That is to say: He who for Christ's sake renounces all that his will can desire and enjoy, and chooses that which is most like to the Cross (which the Lord Himself, through Saint John, describes as hating his soul), the same shall gain it. And this His Majesty taught to those two disciples who went and begged Him for a place on His right hand and on His left; when, giving no countenance to their request for such glory, He offered them the chalice which He had to drink, as a thing more precious and more secure upon this earth than is fruition.

This chalice is death to the natural self, a death attained through the detachment and annihilation of that self, in order that the soul may travel by this narrow path, with respect to all its connections with sense, as we have said, and according to the spirit, as we shall now say; that is, in its understanding and in its enjoyment and in its feeling. And, as a result, not only has the soul made its renunciation as regards both sense and spirit, but it is not hindered, even by that which is spiritual, in taking the narrow way, on which there is room only for self-denial (as the Saviour explains), and the Cross, which is the staff wherewith one may reach one's goal, and whereby the road is greatly lightened and made easy. Wherefore Our Lord said through Saint Matthew: 'My yoke is easy and My burden is light'; which burden is the cross. For if a man resolve to submit himself to carrying this cross — that is to say, if he resolve to desire in truth to meet trials and to bear them in all things for God's sake, he will find in them all great relief and sweetness wherewith he may travel upon this road, detached from all things and desiring nothing. Yet, if he desire to possess anything — whether it come from God or from any other source — with any feeling of attachment, he has not stripped and denied himself in all things; and thus he will be unable to walk along this narrow path or to climb upward by it.

I would, then, that I could convince spiritual persons that this road to God consists not in a multiplicity of meditations nor in ways or methods of such, nor in consolations, although these things may in their own way be necessary to beginners; but that it consists only in the one thing that is needful, which is the ability to deny oneself truly, according to that which is without and to that which is within, giving oneself up to suffering for Christ's sake, and to total annihilation. For the soul that practises this suffering and annihilation will achieve all that those other exercises can achieve, and that can be found in them, and even more. And if a soul be found wanting in this exercise, which is the sum and root of the virtues, all its other methods are so much beating about the bush, and profiting not at all, although its meditations and communications may be as lofty as those of the angels. For progress comes not save through the imitation of Christ, Who is the Way, the Truth and the Life, and no man comes to the Father but by Him, even as He Himself says through Saint John. And elsewhere He says: 'I am the door; by Me if any man enter he shall be saved.' Wherefore, as it seems to me, any spirituality that would fain walk in sweetness and with ease, and flees from the imitation of Christ, is worthless.

And, as I have said that Christ is the Way, and that this Way is death to our natural selves, in things both of sense and of spirit, I will now explain how we are to die, following the example of Christ, for He is our example and light.

In the first place, it is certain that He died as to sense, spiritually, in His life, besides dying naturally, at His death. For, as He said, He had not in His life where to lay His head, and at His death this was even truer.

In the second place, it is certain that, at the moment of His death, He was likewise annihilated in His soul, and was deprived of any relief and consolation, since His Father left Him in the most intense aridity, according to the lower part of His nature. Wherefore He had perforce to cry out, saying: 'My God! My God! 'Why hast Thou forsaken Me?' This was the greatest desolation, with respect to sense, that He had suffered in His life. And thus He wrought herein the greatest work that He had ever wrought, whether in miracles or in mighty works, during the whole of His life, either upon earth or in Heaven, which was the reconciliation and union of mankind, through grace, with God. And this, as I say, was at the moment and the time when this Lord was most completely annihilated in everything. Annihilated, that is to say, with respect to human reputation; since, when men saw Him die, they mocked Him rather than esteemed Him; and also with respect to nature, since His nature was annihilated when He died; and further with respect to the spiritual consolation and protection of the Father, since at that time He forsook Him, that He might pay the whole of man's debt and unite him with God, being thus annihilated and reduced as it were to nothing.

Wherefore David says concerning Him: Ad nihilum redactus sum, et nescivi. This he said that the truly spiritual man may understand the mystery of the gate and of the way of Christ, and so become united with God, and may know that, the more completely he is annihilated for God's sake, according to these two parts, the sensual and the spiritual, the more completely is he united to God and the greater is the work which he accomplishes. And when at last he is reduced to nothing, which will be the greatest extreme of humility, spiritual union will be wrought between the soul and God, which in this life is the greatest and the highest state attainable. This consists not, then, in refreshment and in consolations and spiritual feelings, but in a living death of the Cross, both as to sense and as to spirit — that is, both inwardly and outwardly.

I will not pursue this subject farther, although I have no desire to finish speaking of it, for I see that Christ is known very little by those who consider themselves His friends: we see them seeking in Him their own pleasures and consolations because of their great love for themselves, but not loving His bitter trials and His death because of their great love for Him. I am speaking now of those who consider themselves His friends; for such as live far away, withdrawn from Him, men of great learning and influence, and all others who live yonder, with the world, and are eager about their ambitions and their prelacies, may be said not to know Christ; and their end, however good, will be very bitter. Of such I make no mention in these lines; but mention will be made of them on the Day of Judgment, for to them it was fitting to speak first this word of God, as to those whom God set up as a target for it, by reason of their learning and their high position.

But let us now address the understanding of the spiritual man, and particularly that of the man to whom God has granted the favour of leading him into the state of contemplation (for, as I have said, I am now speaking to these in particular), and let us say how such a man must direct himself toward God in faith, and purify himself from contrary things, constraining himself that he may enter upon this narrow path of obscure contemplation.

Chapter VIII

Which describes in a general way how no creature and no knowledge that can be comprehended by the understanding can serve as a proximate means of Divine union with God.

Before we treat of the proper and fitting means of union with God, which is faith, it behoves us to prove how no thing, created or imagined, can serve the understanding as a proper means of union with God; and how all that the understanding can attain serves it rather as an impediment than as such a means, if it should desire to cling to it. And now, in this chapter, we shall prove this in a general way, and afterwards we shall begin to speak in detail, treating in turn of all kinds of knowledge that the understanding may receive from any sense, whether inward or outward, and of the inconveniences and evils that may result from all these kinds of inward and outward knowledge, when it clings not, as it progresses, to the proper means, which is faith.

It must be understood, then, that, according to a rule of philosophy, all means must be proportioned to the end; that is to say, they must have some connection and resemblance with the end, such as is enough and sufficient for the desired end to be attained through them. I take an example. A man desires to reach a city; he has of necessity to travel by the road, which is the means that brings him to this same city and connects him with it. Another example. Fire is to be combined and united with wood; it is necessary that heat, which is the means, shall first prepare the wood, by conveying to it so many degrees of warmth that it will have great resemblance and proportion to fire. Now if one would prepare the wood by any other than the proper means — namely, with heat — as, for example, with air or water or earth, it would be impossible for the wood to be united with the fire, just as it would be to reach the city without going by the road that leads to it. Wherefore, in order that the understanding may be united with God in this life, so far as is possible, it must of necessity employ that means that unites it with Him and that bears the greatest resemblance to Him.

Here it must be pointed out that, among all the creatures, the highest or the lowest, there is none that comes near to God or bears any resemblance to His Being. For, although it is true that all creatures have, as theologians say, a certain relation to God, and bear a Divine impress (some more and others less, according to the greater or lesser excellence of their nature), yet there is no essential resemblance or connection between them and God — on the contrary, the distance between their being and His Divine Being is infinite. Wherefore it is impossible for the understanding to attain to God by means of the creatures, whether these be celestial or earthly, inasmuch as there is no proportion or resemblance between them. Wherefore, when David speaks of the heavenly creatures, he says: 'There is none among the gods like unto Thee, O Lord'; meaning by the gods the angels and holy souls. And elsewhere: 'O God, Thy way is in the holy place. What God is there so great as our God?' As though he were to say: The way of approach to Thee, O God, is a holy way — that is, the purity of faith. For what God can there be so great? That is to say: What angel will there be so exalted in his being, and what saint so exalted in glory, as to be a proportionate and sufficient road by which a man may come to Thee? And the same David, speaking likewise of earthly and heavenly things both together, says: 'The Lord is high and looketh on lowly things, and the high things He knoweth afar off.' As though he had said: Lofty in His own Being, He sees that the being of things here below is very low in comparison with His lofty Being; and the lofty things, which are the celestial creatures, He sees and knows to be very far from His Being. All the creatures, then, cannot serve as a proportionate means to the understanding whereby it may reach God.

Just so all that the imagination can imagine and the understanding can receive and understand in this life is not, nor can it be, a proximate means of union with God. For, if we speak of natural things, since understanding can understand naught save that which is contained within, and comes under the category of, forms and imaginings of things that are received through the bodily senses, the which things, we have said, cannot serve as means, it can make no use of natural intelligence. And, if we speak of the supernatural (in so far as is possible in this life of our ordinary faculties), the understanding in its bodily prison has no preparation or capacity for receiving the clear knowledge of God; for such knowledge belongs not to this state, and we must either die or remain without receiving it. Wherefore Moses, when he entreated God for this clear knowledge, was told by God that he would be unable to see Him, in these words: 'No man shall see Me and remain alive.' Wherefore Saint John says: 'No man hath seen God at any time, neither aught that is like to Him.' And Saint Paul says, with Isaias: 'Eye hath not seen Him, nor hath ear heard Him, neither hath it entered into the heart of man.' And it is for this reason that, as is said in the Acts of the Apostles, Moses, in the bush, durst not consider for as long as God was present; for he knew that his understanding could make no consideration that was fitting concerning God, corresponding to the sense which he had of God's presence. And of Elias, our father, it is said that he covered his face on the Mount in the presence of God — an action signifying the blinding of his understanding, which he wrought there, daring not to lay so base a hand upon that which was so high, and seeing clearly that whatsoever he might consider or understand with any precision would be very far from God and completely unlike Him.

Wherefore no supernatural apprehension or knowledge in this mortal state can serve as a proximate means to the high union of love with God. For all that can be understood by the understanding, that can be tasted by the will, and that can be invented by the imagination is most unlike to God and bears no proportion to Him, as we have said. All this Isaias admirably explained in that most noteworthy passage, where he says: 'To what thing have ye been able to liken God? Or what image will ye make that is like to Him? Will the workman in iron perchance be able to make a graven image? Or will he that works gold be able to imitate Him with gold, or the silversmith with plates of silver?' By the workman in iron is signified the understanding, the office of which is to form intelligences and strip them of the iron of species and images. By the workman in gold is understood the will, which is able to receive the figure and the form of pleasure, caused by the gold of love. By the silversmith, who is spoken of as being unable to form Him with plates of silver, is understood the memory, with the imagination, whereof it may be said with great propriety that its knowledge and the imaginings that it can invent and make are like plates of silver. And thus it is as though he had said: Neither the understanding with its intelligence will be able to understand aught that is like Him, nor can the will taste pleasure and sweetness that bears any resemblance to that which is God, neither can the memory set in the imagination ideas and images that represent Him. It is clear, then, that none of these kinds of knowledge can lead the understanding direct to God; and that, in order to reach Him, a soul must rather proceed by not understanding than by desiring to understand; and by blinding itself and setting itself in darkness, rather than by opening its eyes, in order the more nearly to approach the ray Divine.

And thus it is that contemplation, whereby the understanding has the loftiest knowledge of God, is called mystical theology, which signifies secret wisdom of God; for it is secret even to the understanding that receives it. For that reason Saint Dionysius calls it a ray of darkness. Of this the prophet Baruch says: 'There is none that knoweth its way, nor any that can think of its paths.' It is clear, then, that the understanding must be blind to all paths that are open to it in order that it may be united with God. Aristotle says that, even as are the eyes of the bat with regard to the sun, which is total darkness to it, even so is our understanding to that which is greater light in God, which is total darkness to us. And he says further that, the loftier and clearer are the things of God in themselves, the more completely unknown and obscure are they to us. This likewise the Apostle affirms, saying: 'The lofty things of God are the least known unto men.'

But we should never end if we continued at this rate to quote authorities and arguments to prove and make clear that among all created things, and things that can be apprehended by the understanding, there is no ladder whereby the understanding can attain to this high Lord. Rather it is necessary to know that, if the understanding should seek to make use of all these things, or of any of them, as a proximate means to such union, they would be not only a hindrance, but even an occasion of numerous errors and delusions in the ascent of this mount.

Chapter IX

How faith is the proximate and proportionate means to the understanding whereby the soul may attain to the Divine union of love. This is proved by passages and figures from Divine Scripture.

From what has been said it is to be inferred that, in order for the understanding to be prepared for this Divine union, it must be pure and void of all that pertains to sense, and detached and freed from all that can clearly be apprehended by the understanding, profoundly hushed and put to silence, and leaning upon faith, which alone is the proximate and proportionate means whereby the soul is united with God; for such is the likeness between itself and God that there is no other difference, save that which exists between seeing God and believing in Him. For, even as God is infinite, so faith sets Him before us as infinite; and, as He is Three and One, it sets Him before us as Three and One; and, as God is darkness to our understanding, even so does faith likewise blind and dazzle our understanding. And thus, by this means alone, God manifests Himself to the soul in Divine light, which passes all understanding. And therefore, the greater is the faith of the soul, the more closely is it united with God. It is this that Saint Paul meant in the passage which we quoted above, where he says: 'He that will be united with God must believe.' That is, he must walk by faith as he journeys to Him, the understanding being blind and in darkness, walking in faith alone; for beneath this darkness the understanding is united with God, and beneath it God is hidden, even as David said in these words: 'He set darkness under His feet. And He rose upon the cherubim, and flew upon the wings of the wind. And He made darkness, and the dark water, His hiding-place.'

By his saying that He set darkness beneath His feet, and that He took the darkness for a hiding-place, and that His tabernacle round about Him was in the dark water, is denoted the obscurity of the faith wherein He is concealed. And by his saying that He rose upon the cherubim and flew upon the wings of the winds, is understood His soaring above all understanding. For the cherubim denote those who understand or contemplate. And the wings of the winds signify the subtle and lofty ideas and conceptions of spirits, above all of which is His Being, and to which none, by his own power, can attain.

This we learn from an illustration in the Scriptures. When Solomon had completed the building of the Temple, God came down in darkness and filled the Temple so that the children of Israel could not see; whereupon Solomon spake and said: 'The Lord hath promised that He will dwell in darkness'. Likewise He appeared in darkness to Moses on the Mount, where God was concealed. And whensoever God communicated Himself intimately, He appeared in darkness, as may be seen in Job, where the Scripture says that God spoke with him from the darkness of the air. All these mentions of darkness signify the obscurity of the faith wherein the Divinity is concealed, when It communicates Itself to the soul; which will be ended when, as Saint Paul says, that which is in part shall be ended, which is this darkness of faith, and that which is perfect shall come, which is the Divine light. Of this we have a good illustration in the army of Gedeon, whereof it is said all the soldiers had lamps in their hands, which they saw not, because they had them concealed in the darkness of the pitchers; but, when these pitchers were broken, the light was seen. Just so does faith, which is foreshadowed by those pitchers, contain within itself Divine light; which, when it is ended and broken, at the ending and breaking of this mortal life, will allow the glory and light of the Divinity, which was contained in it, to appear.

It is clear, then, that, if the soul in this life is to attain to union with God, and commune directly with Him, it must unite itself with the darkness whereof Solomon spake, wherein God had promised to dwell, and must draw near to the darkness of the air wherein God was pleased to reveal His secrets to Job, and must take in its hands, in darkness, the jars of Gedeon, that it may have in its hands (that is, in the works of its will) the light, which is the union of love, though it be in the darkness of faith, so that, when the pitchers of this life are broken, which alone have kept from it the light of faith, it may see God face to face in glory.

It now remains to describe in detail all the types of knowledge and the apprehensions which the understanding can receive; the hindrance and the harm which it can receive upon this road of faith; and the way wherein the soul must conduct itself so that, whether they proceed from the senses or from the spirit, they may cause it, not harm, but profit.

Chapter X

Wherein distinction is made between all apprehensions and types of knowledge which can be comprehended by the understanding.

In order to treat in detail of the profit and the harm which may come to the soul, with respect to this means to Divine union which we have described — namely, faith — through the ideas and apprehensions of the understanding, it is necessary here to make a distinction between all the apprehensions, whether natural or supernatural, that the soul may receive, so that then, with regard to each of them in order, we may direct the understanding with greater clearness into the night and obscurity of faith. This will be done with all possible brevity.

It must be known, then, that the understanding can receive knowledge and intelligence by two channels: the one natural and the other supernatural. By the natural channel is meant all that the understanding can understand, whether by means of the bodily senses or by its own power. The supernatural channel is all that is given to the understanding over and above its natural ability and capacity.

Of these kinds of supernatural knowledge, some are corporeal and some are spiritual. The corporeal are two in number: some are received by means of the outward bodily senses; others, by means of the inward bodily senses, wherein is comprehended all that the imagination can comprehend, form and conceive.

The spiritual supernatural knowledge is likewise of two kinds: that which is distinct and special in its nature, and that which is confused, general and dark. Of the distinct and special kind there are four manners of apprehension which are communicated to the spirit without the aid of any bodily sense: these are visions, revelations, locutions and spiritual feelings. The obscure and general type of knowledge is of one kind alone, which is contemplation that is given in faith. To this we have to lead the soul by bringing it thereto through all these other means, beginning with the first and detaching it from them.

Chapter XI

Of the hindrance and harm that may be caused by apprehensions of the understanding which proceed from that which is supernaturally represented to the outward bodily senses; and how the soul is to conduct itself therein.

The first kinds of knowledge whereof we have spoken in the preceding chapter are those that belong to the understanding and come through natural channels. Of these, since we have treated them already in the first book, where we led the soul into the night of sense, we shall here say not a word, for in that place we gave suitable instruction to the soul concerning them. What we have to treat, therefore, in the present chapter, will be solely those kinds of knowledge and those apprehensions which belong to the understanding and come supernaturally, by way of the outward bodily senses — namely, by seeing, hearing, smelling, tasting and touching. With respect to all these there may come, and there are wont to come, to spiritual persons representations and objects of a supernatural kind. With respect to sight, they are apt to picture figures and forms of persons belonging to the life to come — the forms of certain saints, and representations of angels, good and evil, and certain lights and brightnesses of an extraordinary kind. And with the ears they hear certain extraordinary words, sometimes spoken by those figures that they see, sometimes without seeing the person who speaks them. As to the sense of smell, they sometimes perceive the sweetest perfumes with the senses, without knowing whence they proceed. Likewise, as to taste, it comes to pass that they are conscious of the sweetest savours, and, as to touch, they experience great delight — sometimes to such a degree that it is as though all the bones and the marrow rejoice and sing and are bathed in delight; this is like that which we call spiritual unction, which in pure souls proceeds from the spirit and flows into the very members. And this sensible sweetness is a very ordinary thing with spiritual persons, for it comes to them from their sensible affection and devotion, to a greater or a lesser degree, to each one after his own manner.

And it must be known that, although all these things may happen to the bodily senses in the way of God, we must never rely upon them or accept them, but must always fly from them, without trying to ascertain whether they be good or evil; for, the more completely exterior and corporeal they are, the less certainly are they of God. For it is more proper and habitual to God to communicate Himself to the spirit, wherein there is more security and profit for the soul, than to sense, wherein there is ordinarily much danger and deception; for bodily sense judges and makes its estimate of spiritual things by thinking that they are as it feels them to be, whereas they are as different as is the body from the soul and sensuality from reason. For the bodily sense is as ignorant of spiritual things as is a beast of rational things, and even more so.

So he that esteems such things errs greatly and exposes himself to great peril of being deceived; in any case he will have within himself a complete impediment to the attainment of spirituality. For, as we have said, between spiritual things and all these bodily things there exists no kind of proportion whatever. And thus it may always be supposed that such things as these are more likely to be of the devil than of God; for the devil has more influence in that which is exterior and corporeal, and can deceive a soul more easily thereby than by that which is more interior and spiritual.

And the more exterior are these corporeal forms and objects in themselves, the less do they profit the interior and spiritual nature, because of the great distance and the lack of proportion existing between the corporeal and the spiritual. For, although there is communicated by their means a certain degree of spirituality, as is always the case with things that come from God, much less is communicated than would be the case if the same things were more interior and spiritual. And thus they very easily become the means whereby error and presumption and vanity grow in the soul; since, as they are so palpable and material, they stir the senses greatly, and it appears to the judgment of the soul that they are of greater importance because they are more readily felt. Thus the soul goes after them, abandoning faith and thinking that the light which it receives from them is the guide and means to its desired goal, which is union with God. But the more attention it pays to such things, the farther it strays from the true way and means, which are faith.

And, besides all this, when the soul sees that such extraordinary things happen to it, it is often visited, insidiously and secretly by a certain complacency, so that it thinks itself to be of some importance in the eyes of God; which is contrary to humility. The devil, too, knows how to insinuate into the soul a secret satisfaction with itself, which at times becomes very evident; wherefore he frequently represents these objects to the senses, setting before the eyes figures of saints and most beauteous lights; and before the ears words very much dissembled; and representing also sweetest perfumes, delicious tastes and things delectable to the touch; to the end that, by producing desires for such things, he may lead the soul into much evil. These representations and feelings, therefore, must always be rejected; for, even though some of them be of God, He is not offended by their rejection, nor is the effect and fruit which He desires to produce in the soul by means of them any the less surely received because the soul rejects them and desires them not.

The reason for this is that corporeal vision, or feeling in respect to any of the other senses, or any other communication of the most interior kind, if it be of God, produces its effect upon the spirit at the very moment when it appears or is felt, without giving the soul time or opportunity to deliberate whether it will accept or reject it. For, even as God gives these things supernaturally, without effort on the part of the soul, and independently of its capacity, even so likewise, without respect to its effort or capacity, God produces in it the effect that He desires by means of such things; for this is a thing that is wrought and brought to pass in the spirit passively; and thus its acceptance or non-acceptance consists not in the acceptance or the rejection of it by the will. It is as though fire were applied to a person's naked body: it would matter little whether or no he wished to be burned; the fire would of necessity accomplish its work. Just so is it with visions and representations that are good: even though the soul desire it not, they work their effect upon it, chiefly and especially in the soul, rather than in the body. And likewise those that come from the devil (without the consent of the soul) cause it disturbance or aridity or vanity or presumption in the spirit. Yet these are not so effective to work evil as are those of God to work good; for those of the devil can only set in action the first movements of the will, and move it no farther, unless the soul be consenting thereto; and such trouble continues not long unless the soul's lack of courage and prudence be the occasion of its continuance. But the visions that are of God penetrate the soul and move the will to love, and produce their effect, which the soul cannot resist even though it would, any more than the window can resist the sun's rays when they strike

The soul, then, must never presume to desire to receive them, even though, as I say, they be of God; for, if it desire to receive them, there follow six inconveniences.

The first is that faith grows gradually less; for things that are experienced by the senses derogate from faith; since faith, as we have said, transcends every sense. And thus the soul withdraws itself from the means of union with God when it closes not its eyes to all these things of sense.

Secondly, if they be not rejected, they are a hindrance to the spirit, for the soul rests in them and its spirit soars not to the invisible. This was one of the reasons why the Lord said to His disciples that it was needful for Him to go away that the

Holy Spirit might come; so, too, He forbade Mary Magdalene to touch His feet, after His resurrection, that she might be grounded in faith.

Thirdly, the soul becomes attached to these things and advances not to true resignation and detachment of spirit.

Fourthly, it begins to lose the effect of them and the inward spirituality which they cause it, because it sets its eyes upon their sensual aspect, which is the least important. And thus it receives not so fully the spirituality which they cause, which is impressed and preserved more securely when all things of sense are rejected, since these are very different from pure spirit.

Fifthly, the soul begins to lose the favours of God, because it accepts them as though they belonged to it and profits not by them as it should. And to accept them in this way and not to profit by them is to seek after them; but God gives them not that the soul may seek after them; nor should the soul take upon itself to believe that they are of God.

Sixthly, a readiness to accept them opens the door to the devil that he may deceive the soul by other things like to them, which he very well knows how to dissimulate and disguise, so that they may appear to be good; for, as the Apostle says, he can transform himself into an angel of light. Of this we shall treat hereafter, by the Divine favour, in our third book, in the chapter upon spiritual gluttony.

It is always well, then, that the soul should reject these things, and close its eyes to them, whencesoever they come. For, unless it does so, it will prepare the way for those things that come from the devil, and will give him such influence that, not only will his visions come in place of God's, but his visions will begin to increase, and those of God to cease, in such manner that the devil will have all the power and God will have none. So it has happened to many incautious and ignorant souls, who rely on these things to such an extent that many of them have found it hard to return to God in purity of faith; and many have been unable to return, so securely has the devil rooted himself in them; for which reason it is well to resist and reject them all. For, by the rejection of evil visions, the errors of the devil are avoided, and by the rejection of good visions no hindrance is offered to faith and the spirit harvests the fruit of them. And just as, when the soul allows them entrance, God begins to withhold them because the soul is becoming attached to them and is not profiting by them as it should, while the devil insinuates and increases his own visions, where he finds occasion and cause for them; just so, when the soul is resigned, or even averse to them, the devil begins to desist, since he sees that he is working it no harm; and contrariwise God begins to increase and magnify His favours in a soul that is so humble and detached, making it ruler over many things, even as He made the servant who was faithful in small things.

In these favours, if the soul be faithful and humble, the Lord will not cease until He has raised it from one step to another, even to Divine union and transformation. For Our Lord continues to prove the soul and to raise it ever higher, so that He first gives it things that are very unpretentious and exterior and in the order of sense, in conformity with the smallness of its capacity; to the end that, when it behaves as it should, and receives these first morsels with moderation for its strength and sustenance, He may grant it further and better food. If, then, the soul conquer the devil upon the first step, it will pass to the second; and if upon the second likewise, it will pass to the third; and so onward, through all seven mansions, which are the seven steps of love, until the Spouse shall bring it to the cellar of wine of His perfect charity.

Happy the soul that can fight against that beast of the Apocalypse, which has seven heads, set over against these seven steps of love, and which makes war therewith against each one, and strives therewith against the soul in each of these mansions, wherein the soul is being exercised and is mounting step by step in the love of God. And undoubtedly if it strive faithfully against each of these heads, and gain the victory, it will deserve to pass from one step to another, and from one mansion to another, even unto the last, leaving the beast vanquished after destroying its seven heads, wherewith it made so furious a war upon it. So furious is this war that Saint John says in that place that it was given unto the beast to make war against the saints and to be able to overcome them upon each one of these steps of love, arraying against each one many weapons and munitions of war. And it is therefore greatly to be lamented that many who engage in this spiritual battle against the beast do not even destroy its first head by denying themselves the sensual things of the world. And, though some destroy and cut off this head, they destroy not the second head, which is that of the visions of sense whereof we are speaking. But what is most to be lamented is that some, having destroyed not only the first and the second but even the third, which is that of the interior senses, pass out of the state of meditation, and travel still farther onward, and are overcome by this spiritual beast at the moment of their entering into purity of spirit, for he rises up against them once more, and even his first head comes to life again, and the last state of those souls is worse than the first, since, when they fall back, the beast brings with him seven other spirits worse then himself.

The spiritual person, then, has to deny himself all the apprehensions, and the temporal delights, that belong to the outward senses, if he will destroy the first and the second head of this beast, and enter into the first chamber of love, and the second, which is of living faith, desiring neither to lay hold upon, nor to be embarrassed by, that which is given to the senses, since it is this that derogates most from faith.

It is clear, then, that these sensual apprehensions and visions cannot be a means to union, since they bear no proportion to God; and this was one of the reasons why Christ desired that the Magdalene and Saint Thomas should not touch Him. And so the devil rejoices greatly when a soul desires to receive revelations, and when he sees it inclined to them, for he has then a great occasion and opportunity to insinuate errors and, in so far as he is able, to derogate from faith; for, as I have said, he renders the soul that desires them very gross, and at times even leads it into many temptations and unseemly ways.

I have written at some length of these outward apprehensions in order to throw and shed rather more light on the others, whereof we have to treat shortly. There is so much to say on this part of my subject that I could go on and never end. I believe, however, that I am summarizing it sufficiently by merely saying that the soul must take care never to receive these apprehensions, save occasionally on another person's advice, which should very rarely be given, and even then it must have no desire for them. I think that on this part of my subject what I have said is sufficient.

Chapter XII

Which treats of natural imaginary apprehensions. Describes their nature and proves that they cannot be a proportionate means of attainment to union with God. Shows the harm which results from inability to detach oneself from them.

Before we treat of the imaginary visions which are wont to occur supernaturally to the interior sense, which is the imagination and the fancy, it is fitting here, so that we may proceed in order, to treat of the natural apprehensions of this same interior bodily sense, in order that we may proceed from the lesser to the greater, and from the more exterior to the more interior, until we reach the most interior recollection wherein the soul is united with God; this same order we have followed up to this point. For we treated first of all the detachment of the exterior senses from the natural apprehensions of objects, and, in consequence, from the natural power of the desires — this was contained in the first book, wherein we spoke of the night of sense. We then began to detach these same senses from supernatural exterior apprehensions (which, as we have just shown in the last chapter, affect the exterior senses), in order to lead the soul into the night of the spirit.

In this second book, the first thing that has now to be treated is the interior bodily sense — namely, the imagination and the fancy; this we must likewise void of all the imaginary apprehensions and forms that may belong to it by nature, and we must prove how impossible it is that the soul should attain to union with God until its operation cease in them, since they cannot be the proper and proximate means of this union.

It is to be known, then, that the senses whereof we are here particularly speaking are two interior bodily senses which are called imagination and fancy, which subserve each other in due order. For the one sense reasons, as it were, by imagining, and the other forms the imagination, or that which is imagined, by making use of the fancy. For our purpose the discussion of the one is equivalent to that of the other, and, for this reason, when we name them not both, it must be understood that we are speaking of either, as we have here explained. All the things, then, that these senses can receive and fashion are known as imaginations and fancies, which are forms that are represented to these senses by bodily figures and images. This can happen in two ways. The one way is supernatural, wherein representation can be made, and is made, to these senses passively, without any effort of their own; these we call imaginary visions, produced after a supernatural manner, and of these we shall speak hereafter. The other way is natural, wherein, through the ability of the soul, these things can be actively fashioned in it through its operation, beneath forms, figures and images. And thus to these two faculties belongs meditation, which is a discursive action wrought by means of images, forms and figures that are fashioned and imagined by the said senses, as when we imagine Christ crucified, or bound to the column, or at another of the stations; or when we imagine God seated upon a throne with great majesty; or when we consider and imagine glory to be like a most beauteous light, etc.; or when we imagine all kinds of other things, whether Divine or human, that can belong to the imagination. All these imaginings must be cast out from the Soul, which will remain in darkness as far as this sense is concerned, that it may attain to Divine union; for they can bear no proportion to proximate means of union with God, any more than can the bodily imaginings, which serve as objects to the five exterior senses.

The reason of this is that the imagination cannot fashion or imagine anything whatsoever beyond that which it has experienced through its exterior senses — namely, that which it has seen with the eyes, or heard with the ears, etc. At most it can only compose likenesses of those things that it has seen or heard or felt, which are of no more consequence than those which have been received by the senses aforementioned, nor are they even of as much consequence. For, although a man imagines palaces of pearls and mountains of gold, because he has seen gold and pearls, all this is in truth less than the essence of a little gold or of a single pearl, although in the imagination it be greater in quantity and in beauty. And since, as has already been said, no created things can bear any proportion to the Being of God, it follows that nothing that is imagined in their likeness can serve as proximate means to union with Him, but, as we say, quite the contrary.

Wherefore those that imagine God beneath any of these figures, or as a great fire or brightness, or in any other such form, and think that anything like this will be like to Him, are very far from approaching Him. For, although these considerations and forms and manners of meditation are necessary to beginners, in order that they may gradually feed and enkindle their souls with love by means of sense, as we shall say hereafter, and although they thus serve them as remote means to union with God, through which a soul has commonly to pass in order to reach the goal and abode of spiritual repose, yet they must merely pass through them, and not remain ever in them, for in such a manner they would never reach their goal, which does not resemble these remote means, neither has aught to do with them. The stairs of a staircase have naught to do with the top of it and the abode to which it leads, yet are means to the reaching of both; and if the climber left not behind the stairs below him until there were no more to climb, but desired to remain upon any one of them, he would never reach the top of them nor would he mount to the pleasant and peaceful room which is the goal. And just so the soul that is to attain in this life to the union of that supreme repose and blessing, by means of all these stairs of meditations, forms and ideas, must pass though them and have done with them, since they have no resemblance and bear no proportion to the goal to which they lead, which is God. Wherefore Saint Paul says in the Acts of the Apostles: Non debemus aestimare, auro, vel argento, aut lapidi sculpturae artis, et cogitationis hominis, Divinum esse similem. Which signifies: We ought not to think of the Godhead by likening Him to gold or to silver, neither to stone that is formed by art, nor to aught that a man can fashion with his imagination.

Great, therefore, is the error of many spiritual persons who have practised approaching God by means of images and forms and meditations, as befits beginners. God would now lead them on to further spiritual blessings, which are interior and invisible, by taking from them the pleasure and sweetness of discursive meditation; but they cannot, or dare not, or know not how to detach themselves from those palpable methods to which they have grown accustomed. They continually labour to retain them, desiring to proceed, as before, by the way of consideration and meditation upon forms, for they think that it must be so with them always. They labour greatly to this end and find little sweetness or none; rather the aridity and weariness and disquiet of their souls are increased and grow, in proportion as they labour for that earlier sweetness. They cannot find this in that earlier manner, for the soul no longer enjoys that food of sense, as we have said; it needs not this but another food, which is more delicate, more interior and partaking less of the nature of sense; it consists not in labouring with the imagination, but in setting the soul at rest, and allowing it to remain in its quiet and repose, which is more spiritual. For, the farther the soul progresses in spirituality, the more it ceases from the operation of the faculties in particular acts, since it becomes more and more occupied in one act that is general and pure; and thus the faculties that were journeying to a place whither the soul has arrived cease to work, even as the feet stop and cease to move when their journey is over. For if all were motion, one would never arrive, and if all were means, where or when would come the fruition of the end and goal?

It is piteous, then, to see many a one who though his soul would fain tarry in this peace and rest of interior quiet, where it is filled with the peace and refreshment of God, takes from it its tranquillity, and leads it away to the most exterior things, and would make it return and retrace the ground it has already traversed, to no purpose, and abandon the end and goal wherein it is already reposing for the means which led it to that repose, which are meditations. This comes not to pass without great reluctance and repugnance of the soul, which would fain be in that peace that it understands not, as in its proper place; even as one who has arrived, with great labour, and is now resting, suffers pain if he is made to return to his labour. And, as such souls know not the mystery of this new experience, the idea comes to them that they are being idle and doing nothing; and thus they allow not themselves to be quiet, but endeavor to meditate and reason. Hence they are filled with aridity and affliction, because they seek to find sweetness where it is no longer to be found; we may even say of them that the more they strive the less they profit, for, the more they persist after this manner, the worse is the state wherein they find themselves, because their soul is drawn farther away from spiritual peace; and this is to leave the greater for the less, and to retrace the ground already traversed, and to seek to do that which has been done.

To such as these the advice must be given to learn to abide attentively and wait lovingly upon God in that state of quiet, and to pay no heed either to imagination or to its working; for here, as we say, the faculties are at rest, and are working, not actively, but passively, by receiving that which God works in them; and, if they work at times, it is not with violence or with carefully elaborated meditation, but with sweetness of love, moved less by the ability of the soul itself than by God, as will be explained hereafter. But let this now suffice to show how fitting and necessary it is for those who aim at making further progress to be able to detach themselves from all these methods and manners and works of the imagination at the time and season when the profit of the state which they have reached demands and requires it.

And, that it may be understood how this is to be, and at what season, we shall give in the chapter following certain signs which the spiritual person will see in himself and whereby he may know at what time and season he may freely avail himself of the goal mentioned above, and may cease from journeying by means of meditation and the work of the imagination.

Chapter XIII

Wherein are set down the signs which the spiritual person will find in himself whereby he may know at what season it behoves him to leave meditation and reasoning and pass to the state of contemplation.

In order that there may be no confusion in this instruction it will be meet in this chapter to explain at what time and season it behoves the spiritual person to lay aside the task of discursive meditation as carried on through the imaginations and forms and figures above mentioned, in order that he may lay them aside neither sooner nor later than when the Spirit bids him; for, although it is meet for him to lay them aside at the proper time in order that he may journey to God and not be hindered by them, it is no less needful for him not to lay aside the said imaginative meditation before the proper time lest he should turn backward. For, although the apprehensions of these faculties serve not as proximate means of union to the proficient, they serve nevertheless as remote means to beginners in order to dispose and habituate the spirit to spirituality by means of sense, and in order to void the sense, in the meantime, of all the other low forms and images, temporal, worldly and natural. We shall therefore speak here of certain signs and examples which the spiritual person will find in himself, whereby he may know whether or not it will be meet for him to lay them aside at this season.

The first sign is his realization that he can no longer meditate or reason with his imagination, neither can take pleasure therein as he was wont to do aforetime; he rather finds aridity in that which aforetime was wont to captivate his senses and to bring him sweetness. But, for as long as he finds sweetness in meditation, and is able to reason, he should not abandon this, save when his soul is led into the peace and quietness which is described under the third head.

The second sign is a realization that he has no desire to fix his mediation or his sense upon other particular objects, exterior or interior. I do not mean that the imagination neither comes nor goes (for even at times of deep recollection it is apt to move freely), but that the soul has no pleasure in fixing it of set purpose upon other objects.

The third and surest sign is that the soul takes pleasure in being alone, and waits with loving attentiveness upon God, without making any particular meditation, in inward peace and quietness and rest, and without acts and exercises of the faculties — memory, understanding and will — at least, without discursive acts, that is, without passing from one thing to another; the soul is alone, with an attentiveness and a knowledge, general and loving, as we said, but without any particular understanding, and adverting not to that which it is contemplating.

These three signs, at least, the spiritual person must observe in himself, all together, before he can venture safely to abandon the state of meditation and sense, and to enter that of contemplation and spirit.

And it suffices not for a man to have the first alone without the second, for it might be that the reason for his being unable to imagine and meditate upon the things of God, as he did aforetime, was distraction on his part and lack of diligence; for the which cause he must observe in himself the second likewise, which is the absence of inclination or desire to think upon other things; for, when the inability to fix the imagination and sense upon the things of God proceeds from distraction or lukewarmness, the soul then has the desire and inclination to fix it upon other and different things, which lead it thence altogether. Neither does it suffice that he should observe in himself the first and second signs, if he observe not likewise, together with these, the third; for, although he observe his inability to reason and think upon the things of God, and likewise his distaste for thinking upon other and different things, this might proceed from melancholy or from some other kind of humour in the brain or the heart, which habitually produces a certain absorption and suspension of the senses, causing the soul to think not at all, nor to desire or be inclined to think, but rather to remain in that pleasant state of reverie. Against this must be set the third sign, which is loving attentiveness and knowledge, in peace, etc., as we have said.

It is true, however, that, when this condition first begins, the soul is hardly aware of this loving knowledge, and that for two reasons. First, this loving knowledge is apt at the beginning to be very subtle and delicate, and almost imperceptible to the senses. Secondly, when the soul has been accustomed to that other exercise of meditation, which is wholly perceptible, it is unaware, and hardly conscious, of this other new and imperceptible condition, which is purely spiritual; especially when, not understanding it, the soul allows not itself to rest in it, but strives after the former, which is more readily perceptible; so that abundant though the loving interior peace may be, the soul has no opportunity of experiencing and enjoying it. But the more accustomed the soul grows to this, by allowing itself to rest, the more it will grow therein and the more conscious it will become of that loving general knowledge of God, in which it has greater enjoyment than in aught else, since this knowledge causes it peace, rest, pleasure and delight without labour.

And, to the end that what has been said may be the clearer, we shall give, in this chapter following, the causes and reasons why the three signs aforementioned appear to be necessary for the soul that is journeying to pure spirit.

Chapter XIV

Wherein is proved the fitness of these signs, and the reason is given why that which has been said in speaking of them is necessary to progress.

With respect to the first sign whereof we are speaking — that is to say, that the spiritual person who would enter upon the spiritual road (which is that of contemplation) must leave the way of imagination and of meditation through sense when he takes no more pleasure therein and is unable to reason — there are two reasons why this should be done, which may almost be comprised in one. The first is, that in one way the soul has received all the spiritual good which it would be able to derive from the things of God by the path of meditation and reasoning, the sign whereof is that it can no longer meditate or reason as before, and finds no new sweetness or pleasure therein as it found before, because up to that time it had not progressed as far as the spirituality which was in store for it; for, as a rule, whensoever the soul receives some spiritual blessing, it receives it with pleasure, at least in spirit, in that means whereby it receives it and profits by it; otherwise it is astonishing if it profits by it, or finds in the cause of it that help and that sweetness which it finds when it receives it. For this is in agreement with a saying of the philosophers, Quod sapit, nutrit. This is: That which is palatable nourishes and fattens. Wherefore holy Job said: Numquid poterit comedi insulsum, quod non est sale conditum? Can that which is unsavory perchance be eaten when it is not seasoned with salt? It is this cause that the soul is unable to meditate or reason as before: the little pleasure which the spirit finds therein and the little profit which it gains.

The second reason is that the soul at this season has now both the substance and the habit of the spirit of meditation. For it must be known that the end of reasoning and meditation on the things of God is the gaining of some knowledge and love of God, and each time that the soul gains this through meditation, it is an act; and just as many acts, of whatever kind, end by forming a habit in the soul, just so, many of these acts of loving knowledge which the soul has been making one after another from time to time come through repetition to be so continuous in it that they become habitual. This end God is wont also to effect in many souls without the intervention of these acts (or at least without many such acts having preceded it), by setting them at once in contemplation. And thus that which aforetime the soul was gaining gradually through its labour of meditation upon particular facts has now through practice, as we have been saying, become converted and changed into a habit and substance of loving knowledge, of a general kind, and not distinct or particular as before. Wherefore, when it gives itself to prayer, the soul is now like one to whom water has been brought, so that he drinks peacefully, without labour, and is no longer forced to draw the water through the aqueducts of past meditations and forms and figures So that, as soon as the soul comes before God, it makes an act of knowledge, confused, loving, passive and tranquil, wherein it drinks of wisdom and love and delight.

And it is for this cause that the soul feels great weariness and distaste, when, although it is in this condition of tranquillity, men try to make it meditate and labour in particular acts of knowledge. For it is like a child, which, while receiving the milk that has been collected and brought together for it in the breast, is taken from the breast and then forced to try to gain and collect food by its own diligent squeezing and handling. Or it is like one who has removed the rind from a fruit, and is tasting the substance of the fruit, when he is forced to cease doing this and to try to begin removing the said rind, which has been removed already. He finds no rind to remove, and yet he is unable to enjoy the substance of the fruit which he already had in his hand; herein he is like to one who leaves a prize which he holds for another which he holds not.

And many act thus when they begin to enter this state; they think that the whole business consists in a continual reasoning and learning to understand particular things by means of images and forms, which are to the spirit as rind. When they find not these in that substantial and loving quiet wherein their soul desires to remain, and wherein it understands nothing clearly, they think that they are going astray and wasting time, and they begin once more to seek the rind of their imaginings and reasonings, but find it not, because it has already been removed. And thus they neither enjoy the substance nor make progress in meditation, and they become troubled by the thought that they are turning backward and are losing themselves. They are indeed losing themselves, though not in the way they think, for they are becoming lost to their own senses and to their first manner of perception; and this means gain in that spirituality which is being given them. The less they understand, however, the farther they penetrate into the night of the spirit, whereof we are treating in this book, through the which night they must pass in order to be united with God, in a union that transcends all knowledge.

With respect to the second sign, there is little to say, for it is clear that at this season the soul cannot possibly take pleasure in other and different objects of the imagination, which are of the world, since, as we have said, and for the reasons already mentioned, it has no pleasure in those which are in closest conformity with it — namely, those of God. Only as has been noted above, the imaginative faculty in this state of recollection is in the habit of coming and going and varying of its own accord; but neither according to the pleasure nor at the will of the soul, which is troubled thereby, because its peace and joy are disturbed.

Nor do I think it necessary to say anything here concerning the fitness and necessity of the third sign whereby the soul may know if it is to leave the meditation aforementioned, which is a knowledge of God or a general and loving attentiveness to Him. For something has been said of this in treating of the first sign, and we shall treat of it again hereafter, when we speak in its proper place of this confused and general knowledge, which will come after our description of all the particular apprehensions of the understanding. But we will speak of one reason alone by which it may clearly be seen how, when the contemplative has to turn aside from the way of meditation and reasoning, he needs this general and loving attentiveness or knowledge of God. The reason is that, if the soul at that time had not this knowledge of God or this realization of His presence, the result would be that it would do nothing and have nothing; for, having turned aside from meditation (by means whereof the soul has been reasoning with its faculties of sense), and being still without contemplation, which is the general knowledge whereof we are speaking, wherein the soul makes use of its spiritual faculties — namely, memory, understanding and will — these being united in this knowledge which is then wrought and received in them, the soul would of necessity be without any exercise in the things of God, since the soul can neither work, nor can it receive that which has been worked in it, save only by way of these two kinds of faculty, that of sense and that of spirit. For, as we have said, by means of the faculties of sense it can reason and search out and gain knowledge of things and by means of the spiritual faculties it can have fruition of the knowledge which it has already received in these faculties aforementioned, though the faculties themselves take no part herein.

And thus the difference between the operation of these two kinds of faculty in the soul is like the difference between working and enjoying the fruit of work which has been done; or like that between the labour of journeying and the rest and quiet which comes from arrival at the goal; or, again, like that between preparing a meal and partaking and tasting of it, when it has been both prepared and masticated, without having any of the labour of cooking it, or it is like the difference between receiving something and profiting by that which has been received. Now if the soul be occupied neither with respect to the operation of the faculties of sense, which is meditation and reasoning, nor with respect to that which has already been received and effected in the spiritual faculties, which is the contemplation and knowledge whereof we have spoken, it will have no occupation, but will be wholly idle, and there would be no way in which it could be said to be employed. This knowledge, then, is needful for the abandonment of the way of meditation and reasoning.

But here it must be made clear that this general knowledge whereof we are speaking is at times so subtle and delicate, particularly when it is most pure and simple and perfect, most spiritual and most interior, that, although the soul be occupied therein, it can neither realize it nor perceive it. This is most frequently the case when we can say that it is in itself most clear, perfect and simple; and this comes to pass when it penetrates a soul that is unusually pure and far withdrawn from other particular kinds of knowledge and intelligence, which the understanding or the senses might fasten upon. Such a soul, since it no longer has those things wherein the understanding and the senses have the habit and custom of occupying themselves, is not conscious of them, inasmuch as it has not its accustomed powers of sense. And it is for this reason that, when this knowledge is purest and simplest and most perfect, the understanding is least conscious of it and thinks of it as most obscure. And similarly, in contrary wise, when it is in itself least pure and simple in the understanding, it seems to the understanding to be clearest and of the greatest importance, since it is clothed in, mingled with or involved in certain intelligible forms which understanding or sense may seize upon.

This will be clearly understood by the following comparison. If we consider a ray of sunlight entering through a window, we see that, the more the said ray is charged with atoms and particles of matter, the more palpable, visible and bright it appears to the eye of sense; yet it is clear that the ray is in itself least pure, clear, simple and perfect at that time, since it is full of so many particles and atoms. And we see likewise that, when it is purest and freest from those particles and atoms, the least palpable and the darkest does it appear to the material eye; and the purer it is, the darker and less apprehensible it appears to it. And if the ray were completely pure and free from all these atoms and particles, even from the minutest specks of dust, it would appear completely dark and invisible to the eye, since everything that could be seen would be absent from it — namely, the objects of sight. For the eye would find no objects whereon to rest, since light is no proper object of vision, but the means whereby that which is visible is seen; so that, if there be no visible objects wherein the sun's ray or any light can be reflected, nothing will be seen. Wherefore, if the ray of light entered by one window and went out by another, without meeting anything that has material form, it would not be seen at all; yet, notwithstanding, that ray of light would be purer and clearer in itself than when it was more clearly seen and perceived through being full of visible objects.

The same thing happens in the realm of spiritual light with respect to the sight of the soul, which is the understanding, and which this general and supernatural knowledge and light whereof we are speaking strikes so purely and simply. So completely is it detached and removed from all intelligible forms, which are objects of the understanding, that it is neither perceived nor observed. Rather, at times (that is, when it is purest), it becomes darkness, because it withdraws the understanding from its accustomed lights, from forms and from fancies, and then the darkness is more clearly felt and realized. But, when this Divine light strikes the soul with less force, it neither perceives darkness nor observes light, nor apprehends aught that it knows, from whatever source; hence at times the soul remains as it were in a great forgetfulness, so that it knows not where it has been or what it has done, nor is it aware of the passage of time. Wherefore it may happen, and does happen, that many hours are spent in this forgetfulness, and, when the soul returns to itself, it believes that less than a moment has passed, or no time at all.

The cause of this forgetfulness is the purity and simplicity of this knowledge which occupies the soul and simplifies, purifies and cleanses it from all apprehensions and forms of the senses and of the memory, through which it acted when it was conscious of time, and thus leaves it in forgetfulness and without consciousness of time. This prayer, therefore, seems to the soul extremely brief, although, as we say, it may last for a long period; for the soul has been united in pure intelligence, which belongs not to time; and this is the brief prayer which is said to pierce the heavens, because it is brief and because it belongs not to time. And it pierces the heavens, because the soul is united in heavenly intelligence; and when the soul awakens, this knowledge leaves in it the effects which it created in it without its being conscious of them, which effects are the lifting up of the spirit to the heavenly intelligence, and its withdrawal and abstraction from all things and forms and figures and memories thereof. It is this that David describes as having happened to him when he returned to himself out of this same forgetfulness, saying: Vigilavi, et factus sum sicut passer solitarius in tecto. Which signifies: I have watched and I have become like the lonely bird on the house-top. He uses the word 'lonely' to indicate that he was withdrawn and abstracted from all things. And by the house-top he means the elevation of the spirit on high; so that the soul remains as though ignorant of all things, for it knows God only, without knowing how. Wherefore the Bride declares in the Songs that among the effects which that sleep and forgetfulness of hers produced was this unknowing. She says that she came down to the garden, saying: Nescivi. That is: I knew not whence. Although, as we have said, the soul in this state of knowledge believes itself to be doing nothing, and to be entirely unoccupied, because it is working neither with the senses nor with the faculties, it should realize that it is not wasting time. For, although the harmony of the faculties of the soul may cease, its intelligence is as we have said. For this cause the Bride, who was wise, answered this question herself in the Songs, saying: Ego dormio et cor meum vigilat. As though she were to say: Although I sleep with respect to my natural self, ceasing to labour, my heart waketh, being supernaturally lifted up in supernatural knowledge.

But, it must be realized, we are not to suppose that this knowledge necessarily causes this forgetfulness when the soul is in the state that we are here describing: this occurs only when God suspends in the soul the exercise of all its faculties, both natural and spiritual, which happens very seldom, for this knowledge does not always fill the soul entirely. It is sufficient for the purpose, in the case which we are treating, that the understanding should be withdrawn from all particular knowledge, whether temporal or spiritual, and that the will should not desire to think with respect to either, as we have said, for this is a sign that the soul is occupied. And it must be taken as an indication that this is so when this knowledge is applied and communicated to the understanding only, which sometimes happens when the soul is unable to observe it. For, when it is communicated to the will also, which happens almost invariably, the soul does not cease to understand in the very least degree, if it will reflect hereon, that it is employed and occupied in this knowledge, inasmuch as it is conscious of a sweetness of love therein, without particular knowledge or understanding of that which it loves. It is for this reason that this knowledge is described as general and loving; for, just as it is so in the understanding, being communicated to it obscurely, even so is it in the will, sweetness and love being communicated to it confusedly, so that it cannot have a distinct knowledge of the object of its love.

Let this suffice now to explain how meet it is that the soul should be occupied in this knowledge, so that it may turn aside from the way of spiritual meditation, and be sure that, although it seem to be doing nothing, it is well occupied, if it discern within itself these signs. It will also be realized, from the comparison which we have made, that if this light presents itself to the understanding in a more comprehensible and palpable manner, as the sun's ray presents itself to the eye when it is full of particles, the soul must not for that reason consider it purer, brighter and more sublime. It is clear that, as Aristotle and the theologians say, the higher and more sublime is the Divine light, the darker is it to our understanding.

Of this Divine knowledge there is much to say, concerning both itself and the effects which it produces upon contemplatives. All this we reserve for its proper place, for, although we have spoken of it here, there would be no reason for having done so at such length, save our desire not to leave this doctrine rather more confused than it is already, for I confess it is certainly very much so. Not only is it a matter which is seldom treated in this way, either verbally or in writing, being in itself so extraordinary and obscure, but my rude style and lack of knowledge make it more so. Further, since I have misgivings as to my ability to explain it, I believe I often write at too great length and go beyond the limits which are necessary for that part of the doctrine which I am treating. Herein I confess that I sometimes err purposely; for that which is not explicable by one kind of reasoning will perhaps be better understood by another, or by others yet; and I believe, too, that in this way I am shedding more light upon that which is to be said hereafter.

Wherefore it seems well to me also, before completing this part of my treatise, to set down a reply to one question which may arise with respect to the continuance of this knowledge, and this shall be briefly treated in the chapter following.

Chapter XV

Wherein is explained how it is sometimes well for progressives who are beginning to enter upon this general knowledge of contemplation to make use of natural reasoning and the work of the natural faculties.

With regard to that which has been said, there might be raised one question — if progressives (that is, those whom God is beginning to bring into this supernatural knowledge of contemplation whereof we have spoken) must never again, because of this that they are beginning to experience, return to the way of meditation and reasoning and natural forms. To this the answer is that it is not to be understood that such as are beginning to experience this loving knowledge must, as a general rule, never again try to return to meditation; for, when they are first making progress in proficiency, the habit of contemplation is not yet so perfect that they can give themselves to the act thereof whensoever they wish, nor, in the same way, have they reached a point so far beyond meditation that they cannot occasionally meditate and reason in a natural way, as they were wont, using the figures and the steps that they were wont to use, and finding something new in them. Rather, in these early stages, when, by means of the indications already given, they are able to see that the soul is not occupied in that repose and knowledge, they will need to make use of meditation until by means of it they come to acquire in some degree of perfection the habit which we have described. This will happen when, as soon as they seek to meditate, they experience this knowledge and peace, and find themselves unable to meditate and no longer desirous of doing so, as we have said. For until they reach this stage, which is that of the proficient in this exercise, they use sometimes the one and sometimes the other, at different times.

The soul, then, will frequently find itself in this loving or peaceful state of waiting upon God without in any way exercising its faculties — that is, with respect to particular acts — and without working actively at all, but only receiving. In order to reach this state, it will frequently need to make use of meditation, quietly and in moderation; but, when once the soul is brought into this other state, it acts not at all with its faculties, as we have already said. It would be truer to say that understanding and sweetness work in it and are wrought within it, than that the soul itself works at all, save only by waiting upon God and by loving Him without desiring to feel or to see anything. Then God communicates Himself to it passively, even as to one who has his eyes open, so that light is communicated to him passively, without his doing more than keep them open. And this reception of light which is infused supernaturally is passive understanding. We say that the soul works not at all, not because it understands not, but because it understands things without taxing its own industry and receives only that which is given to it, as comes to pass in the illuminations and enlightenments or inspirations of God.

Although in this condition the will freely receives this general and confused knowledge of God, it is needful, in order that it may receive this Divine light more simply and abundantly, only that it should not try to interpose other lights which are more palpable, whether forms or ideas or figures having to do with any kind of meditation; for none of these things is similar to that pure and serene light. So that if at this time the will desires to understand and consider particular things, however spiritual they be, this would obstruct the pure and simple general light of the spirit, by setting those clouds in the way; even as a man might set something before his eyes which impeded his vision and kept from him both the light and the sight of things in front of him.

Hence it clearly follows that, when the soul has completely purified and voided itself of all forms and images that can be apprehended, it will remain in this pure and simple light, being transformed therein into a state of perfection. For, though this light never fails in the soul, it is not infused into it because of the creature forms and veils wherewith the soul is veiled and embarrassed; but, if these impediments and these veils were wholly removed (as will be said hereafter), the soul would then find itself in a condition of pure detachment and poverty of spirit, and, being simple and pure, would be transformed into simple and pure Wisdom, which is the Son of God. For the enamoured soul finds that that which is natural has failed it, and it is then imbued with that which is Divine, both naturally and supernaturally, so that there may be no vacuum in its nature.

When the spiritual person cannot meditate, let him learn to be still in God, fixing his loving attention upon Him, in the calm of his understanding, although he may think himself to be doing nothing. For thus, little by little and very quickly, Divine calm and peace will be infused into his soul, together with a wondrous and sublime knowledge of God, enfolded in Divine love. And let him not meddle with forms, meditations and imaginings, or with any kind of reasoning, lest his soul be disturbed, and brought out of its contentment and peace, which can only result in its experiencing distaste and repugnance. And if, as we have said, such a person has scruples that he is doing nothing, let him note that he is doing no small thing by pacifying the soul and bringing it into calm and peace, unaccompanied by any act or desire, for it is this that Our Lord asks of us, through David, saying: Vacate, et videte quoniam ego sum Deus. As though he had said: Learn to be empty of all things (that is to say, inwardly and outwardly) and you will see that I am God.

Table of Contents

Chapter XVI

Which treats of the imaginary apprehensions that are supernaturally represented in the fancy. Describing how they cannot serve the soul as a proximate means to union with God.

Now that we have treated of the apprehensions which the soul can receive within itself by natural means, and whereon the fancy and the imagination can work by means of reflection, it will be suitable to treat here of the supernatural apprehensions, which are called imaginary visions, which likewise belong to these senses, since they come within the category of images, forms and figures, exactly as do the natural apprehensions.

It must be understood that beneath this term 'imaginary vision' we purpose to include all things which can be represented to the imagination supernaturally by means of any image, form, figure and species. For all the apprehensions and species which, through all the five bodily senses, are represented to the soul, and dwell within it, after a natural manner, may likewise occur in the soul after a supernatural manner, and be represented to it without any assistance of the outward senses. For this sense of fancy, together with memory, is, as it were, an archive and storehouse of the understanding, wherein are received all forms and images that can be understood; and thus the soul has them within itself as it were in a mirror, having received them by means of the five senses, or, as we say, supernaturally; and thus it presents them to the understanding, whereupon the understanding considers them and judges them. And not only so, but the soul can also prepare and imagine others like to those with which it is acquainted.

It must be understood, then, that even as the five outward senses represent the images and species of their objects to these inward senses, even so, supernaturally, as we say, without using the outward senses, both God and the devil can represent the same images and species, and much more beautiful and perfect ones. Wherefore, beneath these images, God often represents many things to the soul, and teaches it much wisdom; this is continually seen in the Scriptures, as when Isaias saw God in His glory beneath the smoke which covered the Temple, and beneath the seraphim who covered their faces and their feet with wings; and as Jeremias saw the rod watching, and Daniel a multitude of visions, etc. And the devil, too, strives to deceive the soul with his visions, which in appearance are good, as may be seen in the Book of the Kings, when he deceived all the prophets of Achab, presenting to their imaginations the horns wherewith he said the King was to destroy the Assyrians, which was a lie. Even such were the visions of Pilate's wife, warning him not to condemn Christ; and there are many other places where it is seen how, in this mirror of the fancy and the imagination, these imaginary visions come more frequently to proficients than do outward and bodily visions. These, as we say, differ not in their nature (that is, as being images and species) from those which enter by the outward senses; but, with respect to the effect which they produce, and in the degree of their perfection, there is a great difference; for imaginary visions are subtler and produce a deeper impression upon the soul, inasmuch as they are supernatural, and are also more interior than the exterior supernatural visions. Nevertheless, it is true that some of these exterior bodily visions may produce a deeper impression; the communication, after all, is as God wills. We are speaking, however, merely as concerns their nature, and in this respect they are more spiritual.

It is to these senses of imagination and fancy that the devil habitually betakes himself with his wiles — now natural, now supernatural; for they are the door and entrance to the soul, and here, as we have said, the understanding comes to take up or set down its goods, as it were in a harbour or in a store-house where it keeps its provisions. And for this reason it is hither that both God and the devil always come with their jewels of supernatural forms and images, to offer them to the understanding; although God does not make use of this means alone to instruct the soul, but dwells within it in substance, and is able to do this by Himself and by other methods.

There is no need for me to stop here in order to give instruction concerning the signs by which it may be known which visions are of God and which not, and which are of one kind and which of another; for this is not my intention, which is only to instruct the understanding herein, that it may not be hindered or impeded as to union with Divine Wisdom by the good visions, neither may be deceived by those which are false.

I say, then, that with regard to all these imaginary visions and apprehensions and to all other forms and species whatsoever, which present themselves beneath some particular kind of knowledge or image or form, whether they be false and come from the devil or are recognized as true and coming from God, the understanding must not be embarrassed by them or feed upon them, neither must the soul desire to receive them or to have them, lest it should no longer be detached, free, pure and simple, without any mode or manner, as is required for union.

The reason of this is that all these forms which we have already mentioned are always represented, in the apprehension of the soul, as we have said, beneath certain modes and manners which have limitations; and that the Wisdom of God, wherewith the understanding is to be united, has no mode or manner, neither is it contained within any particular or distinct kind of intelligence or limit, because it is wholly pure and simple. And as, in order that these two extremes may be united — namely, the soul and Divine Wisdom — it will be necessary for them to attain to agreement, by means of a certain mutual resemblance, hence it follows that the soul must be pure and simple, neither bounded by, nor attached to, any particular kind of intelligence, nor modified by any limitation of form, species and image. As God comes not within any image or form, neither is contained within any particular kind of intelligence, so the soul, in order to reach God, must likewise come within no distinct form or kind of intelligence.

And that there is no form or likeness in God is clearly declared by the Holy Spirit in Deuteronomy, where He says: Vocem verborum ejus audistis, et formam penitus non vidistis. Which signifies: Ye heard the voice of His words, and ye saw in God no form whatsoever. But He says that there was darkness there, and clouds and thick darkness, which are the confused and dark knowledge whereof we have spoken, wherein the soul is united with God. And afterwards He says further: Non vidistis aliquam similitudinem in die, qua locutus est vobis Dominus in Horeb de medio ignis. That is: Ye saw no likeness in God upon the day when He spoke to you on Mount Horeb, out of the midst of the fire.

And that the soul cannot reach the height of God, even as far as is possible in this life, by means of any form and figure, is declared likewise by the same Holy Spirit in the Book of Numbers, where God reproves Aaron and Miriam, the brother and sister of Moses, because they murmured against him, and, desiring to convey to them the loftiness of the state of union and friendship with Him wherein He had placed him, said: Si quis inter vos fuerit Propheta Domini, in visione apparebo ei, vel per somnium loquar ad illum. At non talis servus meus Moyses, qui in omni domo mea fidelissimus est: ore enim ad os loquor ei, et palem, et non per aenigmata, et figuras Dominum videt. Which signifies: If there be any prophet of the Lord among you, I will appear to him in some vision or form, or I will speak with him in his dreams; but there is none like My servant Moses, who is the most faithful in all My house, and I speak with him mouth to mouth, and he sees not God by comparisons, similitudes and figures. Herein He says clearly that, in this lofty state of union whereof we are speaking, God is not communicated to the soul by means of any disguise of imaginary vision or

similitude or form, neither can He be so communicated; but mouth to mouth —
that is, in the naked and pure essence of God, which is the mouth of God in love,
with the naked and pure essence of the soul, which is the mouth of the soul in
love of God.

Wherefore, in order to come to this essential union of love in God, the soul
must have a care not to lean upon imaginary visions, nor upon forms or figures or
particular objects of the understanding; for these cannot serve it as a
proportionate and proximate means to such an end; rather they would disturb it,
and for this reason the soul must renounce them and strive not to have them. For
if in any circumstances they were to be received and prized, it would be for the
sake of profit which true visions bring to the soul and the good effect which they
produce upon it. But, for this to happen, it is not necessary to receive them;
indeed, for the soul's profit, it is well always to reject them. For these imaginary
visions, like the outward bodily visions whereof we have spoken, do the soul good
by communicating to it intelligence or love or sweetness; but for this effect to be
produced by them in the soul it is not necessary that it should desire to receive
them; for, as has also been said above, at this very time when they are present to
the imagination, they produce in the soul and infuse into it intelligence and love,
or sweetness, or whatever effect God wills them to produce. And not only do they
produce this joint effect, but principally, although not simultaneously, they
produce their effect in the soul passively, without its being able to hinder this
effect, even if it so desired, just as it was also powerless to acquire it, although it
had been able previously to prepare itself. For, even as the window is powerless to
impede the ray of sunlight which strikes it, but, when it is prepared by being
cleansed, receives its light passively without any diligence or labour on its own
part, even so the soul, although against its will, cannot fail to receive in itself the
influences and communications of those figures, however much it might desire to
resist them. For the will that is negatively inclined cannot, if coupled with loving
and humble resignation, resist supernatural infusions; only the impurity and
imperfections of the soul can resist them even as the stains upon a window
impede the brightness of the sunlight.

From this it is evident that, when the soul completely detaches itself, in its will
and affection, from the apprehensions of the strains of those forms, images and
figures wherein are clothed the spiritual communications which we have
described, not only is it not deprived of these communications and the blessings
which they cause within it, but it is much better prepared to receive them with
greater abundance, clearness, liberty of spirit and simplicity, when all these
apprehensions are set on one side, for they are, as it were, curtains and veils
covering the spiritual thing that is behind them. And thus, if the soul desire to

feed upon them, they occupy spirit and sense in such a way that the spirit cannot communicate itself simply and freely; for, while they are still occupied with the outer rind, it is clear that the understanding is not free to receive the substance. Wherefore, if the soul at that time desires to receive these forms and to set store by them, it would be embarrassing itself, and contenting itself with the least important part of them — namely, all that it can apprehend and know of them, which is the form and image and particular object of the understanding in question. The most important part of them, which is the spiritual part that is infused into the soul, it can neither apprehend nor understand, nor can it even know what it is, or be able to express it, since it is purely spiritual. All that it can know of them, as we say, according to its manner of understanding, is but the least part of what is in them — namely, the forms perceptible by sense. For this reason I say that what it cannot understand or imagine is communicated to it by these visions, passively, without any effort of its own to understand and without its even knowing how to make such an effort.

Wherefore the eyes of the soul must ever be withdrawn from all these apprehensions which it can see and understand distinctly, which are communicated through sense, and do not make for a foundation of faith, or for reliance on faith, and must be set upon that which it sees not, and which belongs not to sense, but to spirit, which can be expressed by no figure of sense; and it is this which leads the soul to union in faith, which is the true medium, as has been said. And thus these visions will profit the soul substantially, in respect of faith, when it is able to renounce the sensible and intelligible part of them, and to make good use of the purpose for which God gives them to the soul, by casting them aside; for, as we said of corporeal visions, God gives them not so that the soul may desire to have them and to set its affection upon them.

But there arises here this question: If it be true that God gives the soul supernatural visions, but not so that it may desire to have them or be attached to them or set store by them, why does He give them at all, since by their means the soul may fall into many errors and perils, or at the least may find in them such hindrances to further progress as are here described, especially since God can come to the soul, and communicate to it, spiritually and substantially, that which He communicates to it through sense, by means of the sensible forms and visions aforementioned?

We shall answer this question in the following chapter: it involves important teaching, most necessary, as I see it, both to spiritual persons and to those who instruct them. For herein is taught the way and purpose of God with respect to these visions, which many know not, so that they cannot rule themselves or guide themselves to union, neither can they guide others to union, through these visions. For they think that, just because they know them to be true and to come from God, it is well to receive them and to trust them, not realizing that the soul will become attached to them, cling to them and be hindered by them, as it will by things of the world, if it know not how to renounce these as well as those. And thus they think it well to receive one kind of vision and to reject another, causing themselves, and the souls under their care, great labour and peril in discerning between the truth and the falsehood of these visions. But God does not command them to undertake this labour, nor does He desire that sincere and simple souls should be led into this conflict and danger; for they have safe and sound teaching, which is that of the faith, wherein they can go forward.

This, however, cannot be unless they close their eyes to all that is of particular and clear intelligence and sense. For, although Saint Peter was quite certain of that vision of glory which he saw in Christ at the Transfiguration, yet, after having described it in his second canonical Epistle, he desired not that it should be taken for an important and sure testimony, but rather directed his hearers to faith, saying: Et habemus firmiorem propheticum sermonem: cui benefacitis attendentes, quasi lucernoe lucenti in caliginoso loco, donec dies elucescat. Which signifies: And we have a surer testimony than this vision of Tabor — namely, the sayings and words of the prophets who bear testimony to Christ, whereunto ye must indeed cling, as to a candle which gives light in a dark place. If we will think upon this comparison, we shall find therein the teaching which we are now expounding. For, in telling us to look to the faith whereof the prophets spake, as to a candle that shines in a dark place, he is bidding us remain in the darkness, with our eyes closed to all these other lights; and telling us that in this darkness, faith alone, which likewise is dark, will be the light to which we shall cling; for if we desire to cling to these other bright lights — namely, to distinct objects of the understanding — we cease to cling to that dark light, which is faith, and we no longer have that light in the dark place whereof Saint Peter speaks. This place, which here signifies the understanding, which is the candlestick wherein this candle of faith is set, must be dark until the day when the clear vision of God dawns upon it in the life to come, or, in this life, until the day of transformation and union with God to which the soul is journeying.

Chapter XVII

Wherein is described the purpose and manner of God in His communication of spiritual blessings to the soul by means of the senses. Herein is answered the question which has been referred to.

There is much to be said concerning the purpose of God, and concerning the manner wherein He gives these visions in order to raise up the soul from its lowly estate to His Divine union. All spiritual books deal with this and in this treatise of ours the method which we pursue is to explain it; therefore I shall only say in this chapter as much as is necessary to answer our question, which was as follows: Since in these supernatural visions there is so much hindrance and peril to progress, as we have said, why does God, Who is most wise and desires to remove stumbling-blocks and snares from the soul, offer and communicate them to it?

In order to answer this, it is well first of all to set down three fundamental points. The first is from Saint Paul ad Romanos, where he says: Quae autem sunt, a Deo ordinatoe sunt. Which signifies: The works that are done are ordained of God. The second is from the Holy Spirit in the Book of Wisdom, where He says: Disponit omnia suaviter. And this is as though He had said: The wisdom of God, although it extends from one end to another — that is to say, from one extreme to another — orders all things with sweetness. The third is from the theologians, who say that Omnia movet secundum modum eorum. That is, God moves all things according to their nature.

It is clear, then, from these fundamental points, that if God is to move the soul and to raise it up from the extreme depth of its lowliness to the extreme height of His loftiness, in Divine union with Him, He must do it with order and sweetness and according to the nature of the soul itself. Then, since the order whereby the soul acquires knowledge is through forms and images of created things, and the natural way wherein it acquires this knowledge and wisdom is through the senses, it follows that, if God is to raise up the soul to supreme knowledge, and to do so with sweetness, He must begin to work from the lowest and extreme end of the senses of the soul, in order that He may gradually lead it, according to its own nature, to the other extreme of His spiritual wisdom, which belongs not to sense. Wherefore He first leads it onward by instructing it through forms, images and ways of sense, according to its own method of understanding, now naturally, now supernaturally, and by means of reasoning, to this supreme Spirit of God.

It is for this reason that God gives the soul visions and forms, images and other kinds of sensible and intelligible knowledge of a spiritual nature; not that God would not give it spiritual wisdom immediately, and all at once, if the two extremes — which are human and Divine, sense and spirit — could in the ordinary way concur and unite in one single act, without the previous intervention of many other preparatory acts which concur among themselves in order and sweetness, and are a basis and a preparation one for another, like natural agents; so that the first acts serve the second, the second the third, and so onward, in exactly the same way. And thus God brings man to perfection according to the way of man's own nature, working from what is lowest and most exterior up to what is most interior and highest. First, then, He perfects his bodily senses, impelling him to make use of good things which are natural, perfect and exterior, such as hearing sermons and masses, looking on holy things, mortifying the palate at meals and chastening the sense of touch by penance and holy rigour. And, when these senses are in some degree prepared, He is wont to perfect them still further, by bestowing on them certain supernatural favours and gifts, in order to confirm them the more completely in that which is good, offering them certain supernatural communications, such as visions of saints or holy things, in corporeal shape, the sweetest perfumes, locutions, and exceeding great delights of touch, wherewith sense is greatly continued in virtue and is withdrawn from a desire for evil things. And besides this He continues at the same time to perfect the interior bodily senses, whereof we are here treating, such as imagination and fancy, and to habituate them to that which is good, by means of considerations, meditations, and reflections of a sacred kind, in all of which He is instructing the spirit. And, when these are prepared by this natural exercise, God is wont to enlighten and spiritualize them still more by means of certain supernatural visions, which are those that we are here calling imaginary; wherein, as we have said, the spirit, at the same time, profits greatly, for both kinds of vision help to take away its grossness and gradually to reform it. And after this manner God continues to lead the soul step by step till it reaches that which is the most interior of all; not that it is always necessary for Him to observe this order, and to cause the soul to advance exactly in this way, from the first step to the last; sometimes He allows the soul to attain one stage and not another, or leads it from the more interior to the less, or effects two stages of progress together. This happens when God sees it to be meet for the soul, or when He desires to grant it His favours in this way; nevertheless His ordinary method is as has been said.

It is in this way, then, that God instructs the soul and makes it more spiritual, communicating spirituality to it first of all by means of outward and palpable things, adapted to sense, on account of the soul's feebleness and incapacity, so that, by means of the outer husk of those things which in themselves are good, the spirit may make particular acts and receive so many spiritual communications that it may form a habit as to things spiritual, and may acquire actual and substantial spirituality, which is completely removed from every sense. To this, as we have said, the soul cannot attain except very gradually, and in its own way — that is, by means of sense — to which it has ever been attached. And thus, in proportion as the spirit attains more nearly to converse with God, it becomes ever more detached and emptied of the ways of sense, which are those of imaginary meditation and reflection. Wherefore, when the soul attains perfectly to spiritual converse with God, it must of necessity have been voided of all that relates to God and yet might come under the head of sense. Even so, the more closely a thing grows attracted to one extreme, the farther removed and withdrawn it becomes from the other; and, when it comes to rest perfectly in the one, it will also have withdrawn itself perfectly from the other. Wherefore there is a commonly quoted spiritual adage which says: Gustato spiritu, desipit omni caro. Which signifies: After the taste and sweetness of the spirit have been experienced, everything carnal is insipid. That is: No profit or enjoyment is afforded by all the ways of the flesh, wherein is included all communication of sense with the spiritual. And this is clear: for, if it is spirit, it has no more to do with sense; and, if sense can comprehend it, it is no longer pure spirit. For, the more can be known of it by natural apprehension and sense, the less it has of spirit and of the supernatural, as has been explained above.

The spirit that has become perfect, therefore, pays no heed to sense, nor does it receive anything through sense, nor make any great use of it, neither does it need to do so, in its relations with God, as it did aforetime when it had not grown spiritually. It is this that is signified by that passage from Saint Paul's Epistle to the Corinthians which says: Cum essem parvulus, loquebar ut parvulus, sapiebam ut parvulus, cogitabam ut parvulus. Quando autem factus sum vir, evacuavi quae erant parvuli. This signifies: When I was a child, I spake as a child, I knew as a child, I thought as a child; but, when I became a man, I put away childish things. We have already explained how the things of sense, and the knowledge that spirit can derive from them, are the business of a child. Thus, if the soul should desire to cling to them for ever, and not to throw them aside, it would never be aught but a little child; it would speak ever of God as a child, and would know of God as a child, and would think of God as a child; for, clinging to the outer husk of sense, which pertains to the child, it would never attain to the substance of the spirit, which pertains to the perfect man. And thus the soul must not desire to receive the said revelations in order to continue in growth, even though God offer them to it, just as the child must leave the breast in order to accustom its palate to strong meat, which is more substantial.

You will ask, then, if, when the soul is immature, it must take these things, and, when it is grown, must abandon them; even as an infant must take the breast, in order to nourish itself, until it be older and can leave it. I answer that, with respect to meditation and natural reflection by means of which the soul begins to seek God, it is true that it must not leave the breast of sense in order to continue taking in nourishment until the time and season to leave it have arrived, and this comes when God brings the soul into a more spiritual communion, which is contemplation, concerning which we gave instruction in the eleventh chapter of this book. But, when it is a question of imaginary visions, or other supernatural apprehensions, which can enter the senses without the co-operation of man's free will, I say that at no time and season must it receive them, whether the soul be in the state of perfection, or whether in a state less perfect — not even though they come from God. And this for two reasons. The first is that, as we have said, He produces His effect in the soul, without its being able to hinder it, although, as often happens, it can and may hinder visions; and consequently that effect which was to be produced in the soul is communicated to it much more substantially, although not after that manner. For, as we said likewise, the soul cannot hinder the blessings that God desires to communicate to it, since it is not in the soul's power to do so, save when it has some imperfection and attachment; and there is neither imperfection nor attachment in renouncing these things with humility and misgiving. The second reason is that the soul may free itself from the peril and effort inherent in discerning between evil visions and good, and in deciding whether an angel be of light or of darkness. This effort brings the soul no advantage; it merely wastes its time, and hinders it, and becomes to it an occasion of many imperfections and of failure to make progress. The soul concerns not itself, in such a case, with what is important, nor frees itself of trifles in the shape of apprehensions and perceptions of some particular kind. This has already been said in the discussion of corporeal visions; and more will be said on the subject hereafter.

Let it be believed, too, that, if Our Lord were not about to lead the soul in a way befitting its own nature, as we say here, He would never communicate to it the abundance of His Spirit through these aqueducts, which are so narrow — these forms and figures and particular perceptions — by means whereof He gives the soul enlightenment by crumbs. For this cause David says: Mittit crystallum suam sicut buccellas. Which is as much as to say: He sent His wisdom to the souls as in morsels. It is greatly to be lamented that, though the soul has infinite capacity, it should be given its food by morsels conveyed through the senses, by reason of the small degree of its spirituality and its incapacitation by sense. Saint Paul was also grieved by this lack of preparation and this incapability of men for receiving the Spirit, when he wrote to the Corinthians, saying: 'I, brethren, when I came to you, could not speak to you as to spiritual persons, but as to carnal; for ye could not receive it, neither can ye now.' Tamquam parvulis in Christo lac potum vobis dedi, non escam. That is: I have given you milk to drink, as to infants in Christ, and not solid food to eat.

It now remains, then, to be pointed out that the soul must not allow its eyes to rest upon that outer husk — namely, figures and objects set before it supernaturally. These may be presented to the exterior senses, as are locutions and words audible to the ear; or, to the eyes, visions of saints, and of beauteous radiance; or perfumes to the sense of smell; or tastes and sweetnesses to the palate; or other delights to the touch, which are wont to proceed from the spirit, a thing that very commonly happens to spiritual persons. Or the soul may have to avert its eyes from visions of interior sense, such as imaginary visions, all of which it must renounce entirely. It must set its eyes only upon the spiritual good which they produce, striving to preserve it in its works and to practise that which is for the due service of God, paying no heed to those representations nor desiring any pleasure of sense. And in this way the soul takes from these things only that which God intends and wills — namely, the spirit of devotion — for there is no other important purpose for which He gives them; and it casts aside that which He would not give if these gifts could be received in the spirit without it, as we have said — namely, the exercise and apprehension of the senses.

Chapter XVIII

Which treats of the harm that certain spiritual masters may do to souls when they direct them not by a good method with respect to the visions aforementioned. Describes also how these visions may cause deception even though they be of God.

In this matter of visions we cannot be as brief as we should desire, since there is so much to say about them. Although in substance we have said what is relevant in order to explain to the spiritual person how he is to behave with regard to the visions aforementioned, and to the master who directs him, the way in which he is to deal with his disciple, yet it will not be superfluous to go into somewhat greater detail about this doctrine, and to give more enlightenment as to the harm which can ensue, either to spiritual souls or to the masters who direct them, if they are over-credulous about them, although they be of God.

The reason which has now moved me to write at length about this is the lack of discretion, as I understand it, which I have observed in certain spiritual masters. Trusting to these supernatural apprehensions, and believing that they are good and come from God, both masters and disciples have fallen into great error and found themselves in dire straits, wherein is fulfilled the saying of Our Saviour: Si coecus coeco ducatum praestet, ambo in foveam cadunt. Which signifies: If a blind man lead another blind man, both fall into the pit. And He says not 'shall fall,' but 'fall.' For they may fall without falling into error, since the very venturing of the one to guide the other is going astray, and thus they fall in this respect alone, at the very least. And, first of all, there are some whose way and method with souls that experience these visions cause them to stray, or embarrass them with respect to their visions, or guide them not along the road in some way (for which reason they remain without the true spirit of faith) and edify them not in faith, but lead them to speak highly of those things. By doing this they make them realize that they themselves set some value upon them, or make great account of them, and, consequently, their disciples do the same. Thus their souls have been set upon these apprehensions, instead of being edified in faith, so that they may be empty and detached, and freed from those things and can soar to the heights of dark faith. All this arises from the terms and language which the soul observes its master to employ with respect to these apprehensions; somehow it very easily develops a satisfaction and an esteem for them, which is not in its own control, and which averts its eyes from the abyss of faith.

And the reason why this is so easy must be that the soul is so greatly occupied with these things of sense that, as it is inclined to them by nature, and is likewise disposed to enjoy the apprehension of distinct and sensible things, it has only to observe in its confessor, or in some other person, a certain esteem and appreciation for them, and not merely will it at once conceive the same itself, but also, without its realizing the fact, its desire will become lured away by them, so that it will feed upon them and will be ever more inclined toward them and will set a certain value upon them. And hence arise many imperfections, at the very least; for the soul is no longer as humble as before, but thinks that all this is of some importance and productive of good, and that it is itself esteemed by God, and that He is pleased and somewhat satisfied with it, which is contrary to humility. And thereupon the devil secretly sets about increasing this, without the soul's realizing it, and begins to suggest ideas to it about others, as to whether they have these things or have them not, or are this or are that; which is contrary to holy simplicity and spiritual solitude.

There is much more to be said about these evils, and of how such souls, unless they withdraw themselves, grow not in faith, and also of how there are other evils of the same kind which, although they be not so palpable and recognizable as these, are subtler and more hateful in the Divine eyes, and which result from not living in complete detachment. Let us, however, leave this subject now, until we come to treat of the vice of spiritual gluttony and of the other six vices, whereof, with the help of God, many things will be said, concerning these subtle and delicate stains which adhere to the spirit when its director cannot guide it in detachment.

Let us now say something of this manner wherein certain confessors deal with souls, and instruct them ill. And of a truth I could wish that I knew how to describe it, for I realize that it is a difficult thing to explain how the spirit of the disciple grows in conformity with that of his spiritual father, in a hidden and secret way; and this matter is so tedious that it wearies me, for it seems impossible to speak of the one thing without describing the other also, as they are spiritual things, and the one corresponds with the other.

But it is sufficient to say here that I believe, if the spiritual father has an inclination toward revelations of such a kind that they mean something to him, or satisfy or delight his soul, it is impossible but that he will impress that delight and that aim upon the spirit of his disciple, even without realizing it, unless the disciple be more advanced than he; and, even in this latter case, he may well do him grievous harm if he continue with him. For, from that inclination of the spiritual father toward such visions, and the pleasure which he takes in them, there arises a certain kind of esteem for them, of which, unless he watch it carefully, he cannot fail to communicate some indication or impression to other persons; and if any other such person is like-minded and has a similar inclination, it is impossible, as I understand, but that there will be communicated from the one to the other a readiness to apprehend these things and a great esteem for them.

But we need not now go into detail about this. Let us speak of the confessor who, whether or no he be inclined toward these things, has not the prudence that he ought to have in disencumbering the soul of his disciple and detaching his desire from them, but begins to speak to him about these visions and devotes the greater part of his spiritual conversation to them, as we have said, giving him signs by which he may distinguish good visions from evil. Now, although it is well to know this, there is no reason for him to involve the soul in such labour, anxiety and peril. By paying no heed to visions, and refusing to receive them, all this is prevented, and the soul acts as it should. Nor is this all, for such confessors, when they see that their penitents are receiving visions from God, beg them to entreat God to reveal them to themselves also, or to say such and such things to them, with respect to themselves or to others, and the foolish souls do so, thinking that it is lawful to desire knowledge by this means. For they suppose that, because God is pleased to reveal or say something by supernatural means, in His own way or for His own purpose, it is lawful for them to desire Him to reveal it to them, and even to entreat Him to do so.

And, if it come to pass that God answers their petition and reveals it, they become more confident, thinking that, because God answers them, it is His will and pleasure to do so; whereas, in reality, it is neither God's will nor His pleasure. And they frequently act or believe according to that which He has revealed to them, or according to the way wherein He has answered them; for, as they are attached to that manner of communion with God, the revelation makes a great impression upon them and their will acquiesces in it. They take a natural pleasure in their own way of thinking and therefore naturally acquiesce in it; and frequently they go astray. Then they see that something happens in a way they had not expected; and they marvel, and then begin to doubt if the thing were of God, since it happens not, and they see it not, according to their expectations. At the beginning they thought two things: first, that the vision was of God, since at the beginning it agreed so well with their disposition, and their natural inclination to that kind of thing may well have been the cause of this agreement, as we have said; and secondly that, being of God, it would turn out as they thought or expected.

And herein lies a great delusion, for revelations or locutions which are of God do not always turn out as men expect or as they imagine inwardly. And thus they must never be believed or trusted blindly, even though they are known to be revelations or answers or sayings of God. For, although they may in themselves be certain and true, they are not always so in their causes, and according to our manner of understanding, as we shall prove in the chapter following. And afterwards we shall further say and prove that, although God sometimes gives a supernatural answer to that which is asked of Him, it is not His pleasure to do so, and sometimes, although He answers, He is angered.

Chapter XIX

Wherein is expounded and proved how, although visions and locutions which come from God are true, we may be deceived about them. This is proved by quotations from Divine Scripture.

For two reasons we have said that, although visions and locutions which come from God are true, and in themselves are always certain, they are not always so with respect to ourselves. One reason is the defective way in which we understand them; and the other, the variety of their causes. In the first place, it is clear that they are not always as they seem, nor do they turn out as they appear to our manner of thinking. The reason for this is that, since God is vast and boundless, He is wont, in His prophecies, locutions and revelations, to employ ways, concepts and methods of seeing things which differ greatly from such purpose and method as can normally be understood by ourselves; and these are the truer and the more certain the less they seem so to us. This we constantly see in the Scriptures. To many of the ancients many prophecies and locutions of God came not to pass as they expected, because they understood them after their own manner, in the wrong way, and quite literally. This will be clearly seen in these passages.

In Genesis, God said to Abraham, when He had brought him to the land of the Chanaanites: Tibi dabo terram hanc. Which signifies, I will give thee this land. And when He had said it to him many times, and Abraham was by now very Domine, unde scire possum, quod possessurus sim eam? That old, and He had never given it to him, though He had said this to him, Abraham answered God once again and said: Lord, whereby or by what sign am I to know that I am to possess it? Then God revealed to him that he was not to possess it in person, but that his sons would do so after four hundred years; and Abraham then understood the promise, which in itself was most true; for, in giving it to his sons for love of him, God was giving it to himself. And thus Abraham was deceived by the way in which he himself had understood the prophecy. If he had then acted according to his own understanding of it, those that saw him die without its having been given to him might have erred greatly; for they were not to see the time of its fulfilment. And, as they had heard him say that God would give it to him, they would have been confounded and would have believed it to have been false.

Likewise to his grandson Jacob, when Joseph his son brought him to Egypt because of the famine in Chanaan, and when he was on the road, God appeared and said: Jacob, Jacob, noli timere, descende in Aegiptum, quia in gentem magnam faciam te ibi. Ego descendam tecum illuc. . . . Et inde adducam te revertentem. Which signifies: Jacob, fear not; go down into Egypt, and I will go down there with thee; and, when thou goest forth thence again, I will bring thee out and guide thee. This promise, as it would seem according to our own manner of understanding, was not fulfilled, for, as we know, the good old man Jacob died in Egypt and never left it alive. The word of God was to be fulfilled in his children, whom He brought out thence after many years, being Himself their guide upon the way. It is clear that anyone who had known of this promise made by God to Jacob would have considered it certain that Jacob, even as he had gone to Egypt alive, in his own person, by the command and favour of God, would of a certainty leave it, alive and in his own person, in the same form and manner as he went there, since God had promised him a favourable return; and such a one would have been deceived, and would have marvelled greatly, when he saw him die in Egypt, and the promise, in the sense in which he understood it, remain unfulfilled. And thus, while the words of God are in themselves most true, it is possible to be greatly mistaken with regard to them.

In the Judges, again, we read that, when all the tribes of Israel had come together to make war against the tribe of Benjamin, in order to punish a certain evil to which that tribe had been consenting, they were so certain of victory because God had appointed them a captain for the war, that, when twenty-two thousand of their men were conquered and slain, they marvelled very greatly; and, going into the presence of God, they wept all that day, knowing not the cause of the fall, since they had understood that the victory was to be theirs. And, when they enquired of God if they should give battle again or no, He answered that they should go and fight against them. This time they considered victory to be theirs already, and went out with great boldness, and were conquered again the second time, with the loss of eighteen thousand of their men. Thereat they were greatly confused, and knew not what to do, seeing that God had commanded them to fight and yet each time they were vanquished, though they were superior to their enemies in number and strength, for the men of Benjamin were no more than twenty-five thousand and seven hundred and they were four hundred thousand. And in this way they were mistaken in their manner of understanding the words of God. His words were not deceptive, for He had not told them that they would conquer, but that they should fight; for by these defeats God wished to chastise a certain neglect and presumption of theirs, and thus to humble them. But, when in the end He answered that they would conquer, it was so, although they conquered only after the greatest stratagem and toil.

In this way, and in many other ways, souls are oftentimes deceived with respect to locutions and revelations that come from God, because they interpret them according to their apparent sense and literally; whereas, as has already been explained, the principal intention of God in giving these things is to express and convey the spirit that is contained in them, which is difficult to understand. And the spirit is much more pregnant in meaning than the letter, and is very extraordinary, and goes far beyond its limits. And thus, he that clings to the letter, or to a locution or to the form or figure of a vision, which can be apprehended, will not fail to go far astray, and will forthwith fall into great confusion and error, because he has guided himself by sense according to these visions, and not allowed the spirit to work in detachment from sense. Littera enim occidit, spiritus autem vivificat, as Saint Paul says. That is: The letter killeth and the spirit giveth life. Wherefore in this matter of sense the letter must be set aside, and the soul must remain in darkness, in faith, which is the spirit, and this cannot be comprehended by sense.

For which cause, many of the children of Israel, because they took the sayings and prophecies of the prophets according to the strict letter, and these were not fulfilled as they expected, came to make little account of them and believed them not; so much so, that there grew up a common saying among them — almost a proverb, indeed — which turned prophets into ridicule. Of this Isaias complains, speaking and exclaiming in the manner following: Quem docebit Dominus scientiam? et quem intelligere faciet auditum? ablactatos a lacte, avulsos ab uberibus. Quia manda remanda, manda remanda, expecta reexpecta, expecta reexpecta, modicum ibi, modicum ibi. In loquela enim labii, et lingua altera loquetur ad populum istum. This signifies: To whom shall God teach knowledge? And whom shall He make to understand His word and prophecy? Only them that are already weaned from the milk and drawn away from the breasts. For all say (that is, concerning the prophecies): Promise and promise again; wait and wait again; wait and wait again; a little there, a little there; for in the words of His lips and in another tongue will He speak to this people. Here Isaias shows quite clearly that these people were turning prophecies into ridicule, and that it was in mockery that they repeated this proverb: 'Wait and then wait again.' They meant that the prophecies were never fulfilled for them, for they were wedded to the letter, which is the milk of infants, and to their own sense, which is the breasts, both of which contradict the greatness of spiritual knowledge. Wherefore he says: To whom shall He teach the wisdom of His prophecies? And whom shall He make to understand His doctrine, save them that are already weaned from the milk of the letter and from the breasts of their own senses? For this reason these people understand it not, save according to this milk of the husk and letter, and these breasts of their own sense, since they say: Promise and promise again; wait and wait again, etc. For it is in the doctrine of the mouth of God, and not in their own doctrine, and it is in another tongue than their own, that God shall speak to them.

And thus, in interpreting prophecy, we have not to consider our own sense and language, knowing that the language of God is very different from ours, and that it is spiritual language, very far removed from our understanding and exceedingly difficult. So much so is it that even Jeremias, though a prophet of God, when he sees that the significance of the words of God is so different from the sense commonly attributed to them by men, is himself deceived by them and defends the people, saying: Heu, heu, heu, Domine Deus, ergone decipisti populum istum et Jerusalem, dicens: Pax erit vobis; et ecce pervenit gladius usque ad animam? Which signifies: Ah, ah, ah, Lord God, hast Thou perchance deceived this people and Jerusalem, saying, 'Peace will come upon you,' and seest Thou here that the sword reacheth unto their soul? For the peace that God promised them was that which was to be made between God and man by means of the Messiah Whom He was to send them, whereas they understood it of temporal peace; and therefore, when they suffered wars and trials, they thought that God was deceiving them, because there befell them the contrary of that which they expected. And thus they said, as Jeremias says likewise: Exspectavimus pacem, et non erat bonum. That is: We have looked for peace and there is no boon of peace. And thus it was impossible for them not to be deceived, since they took the prophecy merely in its literal sense. For who would fail to fall into confusion and to go astray if he confined himself to a literal interpretation of that prophecy which David spake concerning Christ, in the seventy-first Psalm, and of all that he says therein, where he says: Et dominabitur a mari usque ad mare; et a flumine usque ad terminos orbis terrarum. That is: He shall have dominion from one sea even to the other sea, and from the river even unto the ends of the earth. And likewise in that which he says in the same place: Liberabit pauperem a potente, et pauperem, cui non erat adjutor. Which signifies: He shall deliver the poor man from the power of the mighty, and the poor man that had no helper. But later it became known that Christ was born in a low state and lived in poverty and died in misery; not only had He no dominion over the earth, in a temporal sense, while He lived, but He was subject to lowly people, until He died under the power of Pontius Pilate. And not only did He not deliver poor men — namely, His disciples — from the hands of the mighty, in a temporal sense, but He allowed them to be slain and persecuted for His name's sake.

The fact is that these prophecies concerning Christ had to be understood spiritually, in which sense they were entirely true. For Christ was not only Lord of earth alone, but likewise of Heaven, since He was God; and the poor who were to follow Him He was not only to redeem and free from the power of the devil, that mighty one against whom they had no helper, but also to make heirs of the Kingdom of Heaven. And thus God was speaking, in the most important sense, of Christ, and of the reward of His followers, which was an eternal kingdom and eternal liberty; and they understood this, after their own manner, in a secondary sense, of which God takes small account, namely that of temporal dominion and temporal liberty, which in God's eyes is neither kingdom nor liberty at all. Wherefore, being blinded by the insufficiency of the letter, and not understanding its spirit and truth, they took the life of their God and Lord, even as Saint Paul said in these words: Qui enim habitabant Jerusalem, et principes ejus, hunc ignorantes et voces prophetarum, quae per omne Sabbatum leguntur, judicantes impleverunt. Which signifies: They that dwelt in Jerusalem, and her rulers, not knowing Who He was, nor understanding the sayings of the prophets, which are read every Sabbath day, have fulfilled them by judging Him.

And to such a point did they carry this inability to understand the sayings of God as it behoved them, that even His own disciples, who had gone about with Him, were deceived, as were those two who, after His death, were going to the village of Emmaus, sad and disconsolate, saying: Nos autem sperabamus quod ipse esset redempturus Israel. We hoped that it was He that should have redeemed Israel. They, too, understood that this dominion and redemption were to be temporal; but Christ our Redeemer, appearing to them, reproved them as foolish and heavy and gross of heart as to their belief in the things that the prophets had spoken. And, even when He was going to Heaven, some of them were still in that state of grossness of heart, and asked Him, saying: Domine, si in tempore hoc restitues Regnum Israel. That is: Lord, tell us if Thou wilt restore at this time the kingdom of Israel. The Holy Spirit causes many things to be said which bear another sense than that which men understand; as can be seen in that which he caused to be said by Caiphas concerning Christ: that is was meet that one man should die lest all the people should perish. This he said not of his own accord; and he said it and understood it in one sense, and the Holy Spirit in another.

From this it is clear that, although sayings and revelations may be of God, we cannot always be sure of their meaning; for we can very easily be greatly deceived by them because of our manner of understanding them. For they are all an abyss and a depth of the spirit, and to try to limit them to what we can understand concerning them, and to what our sense can apprehend, is nothing but to attempt to grasp the air, and to grasp some particle in it that the hand touches: the air disappears and nothing remains.

The spiritual teacher must therefore strive that the spirituality of his disciple be not cramped by attempts to interpret all supernatural apprehensions, which are no more than spiritual particles, lest he come to retain naught but these, and have no spirituality at all. But let the teacher wean his disciple from all visions and locutions, and impress upon him the necessity of dwelling in the liberty and darkness of faith, wherein are received spiritual liberty and abundance, and consequently the wisdom and understanding necessary to interpret sayings of God. For it is impossible for a man, if he be not spiritual, to judge of the things of God or understand them in a reasonable way, and he is not spiritual when he judges them according to sense; and thus, although they come to him beneath the disguise of sense, he understands them not. This Saint Paul well expresses in these words: Animalis autem homo non percipit ea quoe sunt spiritus Dei: stultitia enim est illi, et non potest intelligere: quia de spiritualibus examinatur. Spiritualis autem judicat omnia. Which signifies: The animal man perceives not the things which are of the Spirit of God, for unto him they are foolishness and he cannot understand them because they are spiritual; but he that is spiritual judges all things. By the animal man is here meant one that uses sense alone; by the spiritual man, one that is not bound or guided by sense. Wherefore it is temerity to presume to have intercourse with God by way of a supernatural apprehension effected by sense, or to allow anyone else to do so.

And that this may be the better understood let us here set down a few examples. Let us suppose that a holy man is greatly afflicted because his enemies persecute him, and that God answers him, saying: I will deliver thee from all thine enemies. This prophecy may be very true, yet, notwithstanding, his enemies may succeed in prevailing, and he may die at their hands. And so if a man should understand this after a temporal manner he would be deceived; for God might be speaking of the true and principal liberty and victory, which is salvation, whereby the soul is delivered, free and made victorious over all its enemies, and much more truly so and in a higher sense than if it were delivered from them here below. And thus, this prophecy was much more true and comprehensive than the man could understand if he interpreted it only with respect to this life; for, when God speaks, His words are always to be taken in the sense which is most important and profitable, whereas man, according to his own way and purpose, may understand the less important sense, and thus may be deceived. This we see in that prophecy which David makes concerning Christ in the second Psalm saying: Reges eos in virga ferrea, et tamquam vas figuli confringes eos. That is: Thou shalt rule all the people with a rod of iron and thou shalt dash them in pieces like a vessel of clay. Herein God speaks of the principal and perfect dominion, which is eternal dominion; and it was in this sense that it was fulfilled, and not in the less important sense, which was temporal, and which was not fulfilled in Christ during any part of His temporal life.

Let us take another example. A soul has great desires to be a martyr. It may happen that God answers him, saying: Thou shalt be a martyr. This will give him inwardly great comfort and confidence that he is to be martyred; yet it may come to pass that he dies not the death of a martyr, and notwithstanding this the promise may be true. Why, then, is it not fulfilled literally? Because it will be fulfilled, and is capable of being fulfilled, according to the most important and essential sense of that saying — namely, in that God will have given that soul the love and the reward which belong essentially to a martyr; and thus in truth He gives to the soul that which it formally desired and that which He promised it. For the formal desire of the soul was, not that particular manner of death, but to do God a martyr's service, and to show its love for Him as a martyr does. For that manner of death is of no worth in itself without this love, the which love and the showing forth thereof and the reward belonging to the martyr may be given to it more perfectly by other means. So that, though it may not die like a martyr, the soul is well satisfied that it has been given that which it sired. For, when they are born of living love, such desires, and others like them, although they be not fulfilled in the way wherein they are described and understood, are fulfilled in another and a better way, and in a way which honours God more greatly than that which they might have asked. Wherefore David says: Desiderium pauperum exaudivit Dominus. That is: The Lord has granted the poor their desire. And in the Proverbs Divine Wisdom says: Desiderium suum justis dabitur. 'The just shall be given their desire.' Hence, then, since we see that many holy men have desired many particular things for God's sake, and that in this life their desires have not been granted them, it is a matter of faith that, as their desires were just and true, they have been fulfilled for them perfectly in the next life. Since this is truth, it would also be truth for God to promise it to them in this life, saying to them: Your desire shall be fulfilled; and for it not to be fulfilled in the way which they expected.

In this and other ways, the words and visions of God may be true and sure and yet we may be deceived by them, through being unable to interpret them in a high and important sense, which is the sense and purpose wherein God intends them. And thus the best and surest course is to train souls in prudence so that they flee from these supernatural things, by accustoming them, as we have said, to purity of spirit in dark faith, which is the means of union.

Chapter XX

Wherein is proved by passages from Scripture how the sayings and words of God, though always true, do not always rest upon stable causes.

We have now to prove the second reason why visions and words which come from God, although in themselves they are always true, are not always stable in their relation to ourselves. This is because of their causes, whereon they are founded; for God often makes statements founded upon creatures and their effects, which are changeable and liable to fail, for which reason the statements which are founded upon them are liable also to be changeable and to fail; for, when one thing depends on another, if one fails, the other fails likewise. It is as though God should say: In a year's time I shall send upon this kingdom such or such a plague; and the cause and foundation for this warning is a certain offence which has been committed against God in that kingdom. If the offence should cease or change, the punishment might cease; yet the threat was true because it was founded upon the fault committed at the time, and, if this had continued, it would have been carried out.

This, we see, happened in the city of Ninive, where God said: Adhuc quadraginta dies, et Ninive subvertetur. Which signifies: Yet forty days and Ninive shall be destroyed. This was not fulfilled, because the cause of the threat ceased — namely, the sins of the city, for which it did penace — but, if this had not been so, the prophecy would have been carried into effect. We read likewise in the Third Book of the Kings that, when King Achab had committed a very great sin, God sent to phophesy a great punishment — our father Elias being the messenger — which should come upon his person, upon his house and upon his kingdom. And, because Achab rent his garments with grief and clothed himself in haircloth and fasted, and slept in sackcloth and went about in a humble and contrite manner, God sent again, by the same prophet, to declare to him these words: Quia igitur humiliatus est mei causa, non inducam malum in diebus ejus, sed in diebus filii sui. Which signifies: Inasmuch as Achab has humbled himself for love of Me, I will not send the evil whereof I spake in his days, but in the days of his son. Here we see that, because Achab changed his spirit and his former affection, God likewise changed His sentence.

From this we may deduce, as regards the matter under discussion, that, although God may have revealed or affirmed something to a soul, whether good or evil, and whether relating to that soul itself or to others, this may, to a greater or a lesser extent, be changed or altered or entirely withdrawn, according to the change or variation in the affection of this soul, or the cause whereon God based His judgment, and thus it would not be fulfilled in the way expected, and oftentimes none would have known why, save only God. For God is wont to declare and teach and promise many things, not that they may be understood or possessed at the time, but that they may be understood at a later time, when it is fitting that a soul may have light concerning them, or when their effect is attained. This, as we see, He did with His disciples, to whom He spake many parables, and pronounced many judgments, the wisdom whereof they understood not until the time when they had to preach it, which was when the Holy Spirit came upon them, of Whom Christ had said to them that He would explain to them all the things that He had spoken to them in His life. And, when Saint John speaks of that entry of Christ into Jerusalem, he says: Haec non cognoverunt discipuli ejus primum: sed quando glorificatus est Jesus, tunc recordati sunt quia haec erant scripta de eo. And thus there may pass through the soul many detailed messages from God which neither the soul nor its director will understand until the proper time.

Likewise, in the First Book of the Kings, we read that, when God was wroth against Heli, a priest of Israel, for his sins in not chastising his sons, he sent to him by Samuel to say, among other words, these which follow: Loquens locutus sum, ut domus tua, et domus patris tui, ministraret in conspectu meo, usque in sempiternum. Verumtamen absit hoc a me. And this is as though He had said: In very truth I said aforetime that thy house and the house of thy father should serve Me continually in the priesthood in my presence for ever, but this purpose is far from Me; I will not do this thing. For this office of the priesthood was founded for giving honour and glory to God, and to this end God has promised to give it to the father of Heli for ever if he failed not. But, when Heli failed in zeal for the honour of God (for, as God Himself complained when He sent him the message, he honoured his sons more than God, overlooking their sins so as not to offend them), the promise also failed which would have held good for ever if the good service and zeal of Heli had lasted for ever. And thus there is no reason to think that, because sayings and revelations come from God, they must invariably come to pass in their apparent sense, especially when they are bound up with human causes which may vary, change, or alter.

And when they are dependent upon these causes God Himself knows, though He does not always declare it, but pronounces the saying, or makes the revelation, and sometimes says nothing of the condition, as when He definitely told the Ninivites that they would be destroyed after forty days. At other times, he lays down the condition, as He did to Roboam, saying to him: 'If thou wilt keep My commandments, as my servant David, I will be with thee even as I was with him, and will set thee up a house as I did to My servant David'. But, whether He declares it or no, the soul must not rely upon its own understanding; for it is impossible to understand the hidden truths of God which are in His sayings, and the multitude of their meanings. He is above the heavens, and speaks according to the way of eternity; we blind souls are upon the earth and understand only the ways of flesh and time. It was for that reason, I believe, that the Wise Man said: 'God is in Heaven, and thou are upon earth; wherefore be not thou lengthy or hasty in speaking.'

You will perhaps ask me: Why, if we are not to understand these things, or to play any part in them, does God communicate them to us? I have already said that everything will be understood in its own time by the command of Him Who spake it, and he whom God wills shall understand it, and it will be seen that it was fitting; for God does naught save with due cause and in truth. Let it be realized, therefore, that there is no complete understanding of the meaning of the sayings and things of God, and that this meaning cannot be decided by what it seems to be, without great error, and, in the end, grievous confusion. This was very well known to the prophets, into whose hands was given the word of God, and who found it a sore trial to prophesy concerning the people; for, as we have said, many of the people saw that things came not to pass literally, as they were told them, for which cause they laughed at the prophets and mocked them greatly; so much that Jeremias went as far as to say: 'They mock me all the day long, they scorn and despise me every one, for I have long been crying against evil and promising them destruction; and the word of the Lord has been made a reproach and a derision to me continually. And I said, I must not remember Him, neither speak any more in His name.' Herein, although the holy prophet was speaking with resignation and in the form of a weak man who cannot endure the ways and workings of God, he clearly indicates the difference between the way wherein the Divine sayings are fulfilled and the ordinary meaning which they appear to have; for the Divine prophets were treated as mockers, and suffered so much from their prophecy that Jeremias himself said elsewhere: Formido et laqueus facta est nobis vaticinatio et contritio. Which signifies: Prophecy has become to us fear and snares and contradiction of spirit.

And the reason why Jonas fled when God sent him to preach the destruction of Ninive was this, namely, that he knew the different meanings of the sayings of God with respect to the understanding of men and with respect to the causes of the sayings. And thus, lest they should mock him when they saw that his prophecy was not fulfilled, he went away and lied in order not to prophesy; and thus he remained waiting all the forty days outside the city, to see if his prophecy was fulfilled; and, when it was not fulfilled, he was greatly afflicted, so much so that he said to God: Obsecro, Domine, numquid non hoc est verbum meum, cum adhuc essem in terra mea? propter hoc praeoccupavi, ut fugerem in Tharsis. That is: I pray Thee, O Lord, is not this what I said when I was yet in my own country? Therefore was I vexed, and fled away to Tharsis. And the saint was wroth and besought God to take away his life.

Why, then, must we marvel that God should speak and reveal certain things to souls which come not to pass in the sense wherein they understand them? For, if God should affirm or represent such or such a thing to the soul, whether good or evil, with respect to itself or to another, and if that thing be founded upon a certain affection or service or offence of that soul, or of another, at that time, with respect to God, so that, if the soul persevere therein, it will be fulfilled; yet even then its fulfillment is not certain, since it is not certain that the soul will persevere. Wherefore we must rely, not upon understanding, but upon faith.

Chapter XXI

Wherein is explained how at times, although God answers the prayers that are addressed to Him, He is not pleased that we should use such methods. It is also shown how, although He condescend to us and answer us, He is oftentimes wroth.

Certain spiritual men, as we have said, assure themselves that it is a good thing to display curiosity, as they sometimes do, in striving to know certain things by supernatural methods, thinking that, because God occasionally answers their importunity, this is a good method and pleasing to Him. Yet the truth is that, although He may answer them, the method is not good, neither is it pleasing to God, but rather it is displeasing to Him; and not only so, but oftentimes He is greatly offended and wroth. The reason for this is that it is lawful for no creature to pass beyond the limits that God has ordained for its governance after the order of nature. He has laid down rational and natural limits for man's governance; wherefore to desire to pass beyond them is not lawful, and to desire to seek out and attain to anything by supernatural means is to go beyond these natural limits. It is therefore an unlawful thing, and it is therefore not pleasing to God, for He is offended by all that is unlawful. King Achaz was well aware of this, since, although Isaias told him from God to ask for a sign, he would not do so, saying: *Non petam, et non tentabo Dominum.* That is: I will not ask such a thing, neither will I tempt God. For it is tempting God to seek to commune with Him by extraordinary ways, such as those that are supernatural.

But why, you will say, if it be a fact that God is displeased, does He sometimes answer? I reply that it is sometimes the devil who answers. And, if it is God Who answers, I reply that He does so because of the weakness of the soul that desires to travel along that road, lest it should be disconsolate and go backward, or lest it should think that God is wroth with it and should be overmuch afflicted; or for other reasons known to God, founded upon the weakness of that soul, whereby God sees that it is well that He should answer it and deigns to do so in that way. In a like manner, too, does He treat many weak and tender souls, granting them favours and sweetness in sensible converse with Himself, as has been said above;

this is not because He desires or is pleased that they should commune with Him after that manner or by these methods; it is that He gives to each one, as we have said, after the manner best suited to him. For God is like a spring, whence everyone draws water according to the vessel which he carries. Sometimes a soul is allowed to draw it by these extraordinary channels; but it follows not from this that it is lawful to draw water by them, but only that God Himself can permit this, when, how and to whom He wills, and for what reason He wills, without the party concerned having any right in the matter. And thus, as we say, He sometimes deigns to satisfy the desire and the prayer of certain souls, whom, since they are good and sincere, He wills not to fail to succour, lest He should make them sad, but it is not because He is pleased with their methods that He wills it. This will be the better understood by the following comparison.

The father of a family has on his table many and different kinds of food, some of which are better than others. A child is asking him for a certain dish, not the best, but the first that meets its eye, and it asks for this dish because it would rather eat of it than any other; and as the father sees that, even if he gives it the better kind of food, it will not take it, but will have that which it asks for, since that alone pleases it, he gives it that, regretfully, lest it should take no food at all and be miserable. In just this way, we observe, did God treat the children of Israel when they asked Him for a king: He gave them one, but unwillingly, because it was not good for them. And thus He said to Samuel: Audi vocem populi in omnibus quae loquuntur tibi: non enim te objecerunt, sed me. Which signifies: Hearken unto the voice of this people and grant them the king whom they ask of thee, for they have not rejected thee but Me, that I should not reign over them. In this same way God condescends to certain souls, and grants them that which is not best for them, because they will not or cannot walk by any other road. And thus certain souls attain to tenderness and sweetness of spirit or sense; and God grants them this because they are unable to partake of the stronger and more solid food of the trials of the Cross of His Son, which He would prefer them to take, rather than aught else.

I consider, however, that the desire to know things by supernatural means is much worse than the desire for other spiritual favours pertaining to the senses; for I cannot see how the soul that desires them can fail to commit, at the least, venial sin, however good may be its aims, and however far advanced it may be on the road to perfection; and if anyone should bid the soul desire them, and consent to it, he sins likewise. For there is no necessity for any of these things, since the soul has its natural reason and the doctrine and law of the Gospel, which are quite sufficient for its guidance, and there is no difficulty or necessity that cannot be solved and remedied by these means, which are very pleasing to God and of great profit to souls; and such great use must we make of our reason and of Gospel doctrine that, if certain things be told us supernaturally, whether at our desire or no, we must receive only that which is in clear conformity with reason and Gospel law. And then we must receive it, not because it is revelation, but because it is reason, and not allow ourselves to be influenced by the fact that it has been revealed. Indeed, it is well in such a case to look at that reason and examine it very much more closely than if there had been no revelation concerning it; inasmuch as the devil utters many things that are true, and that will come to pass, and that are in conformity with reason, in order that he may deceive.

Wherefore, in all our needs, trials and difficulties, there remains to us no better and surer means than prayer and hope that God will provide for us, by such means as He wills. This is the advice given to us in the Scriptures, where we read that, when King Josaphat was greatly afflicted and surrounded by enemies, the saintly King gave himself to prayer, saying to God: Cum ignoremus quid facere debeamus, hoc solum habemus residue, ut oculos nostros dirigamus ad re. Which is as though he had said: When means fail and reason is unable to succour us in our necessities, it remains for us only to lift up our eyes to Thee, that Thou mayest succour us as is most pleasing to Thee.

And further, although this has also been made clear, it will be well to prove, from certain passages of Scripture, that, though God may answer such requests, He is none the less sometimes wroth. In the First Book of the Kings it is said that, when King Saul begged that the prophet Samuel, who was now dead, might speak to him, the said prophet appeared to him, and that God was wroth with all this, since Samuel at once reproved Saul for having done such a thing, saying: Quare inquietasti me, ut suscitarer? That is: Why hast thou disquieted me, in causing me to arise? We also know that, in spite of having answered the children of Israel and given them the meat that they besought of Him, God was nevertheless greatly incensed against them; for He sent fire from Heaven upon them as a punishment, as we read in the Pentateuch, and as David relates in these words: Adhuc escape eorum erant in ore ipsorum, et ira Dei descendit super cos. Which signifies: Even as they had the morsels in their months, the wrath of God came down upon them. And likewise we read in Numbers that God was greatly wroth with Balaam the prophet, because he went to the Madianites when Balac their king sent for him, although God had bidden him go, because he desired to go and had begged it of God; and while he was yet in the way there appeared to him an angel with a sword, who desired to slay him, and said to him: Perversa est via tua, mihique contraria. 'Thy way is perverse and contrary to Me.' For which cause he desired to slay him.

After this manner and many others God deigns to satisfy the desires of souls though He be wroth with them. Concerning this we have many testimonies in Scripture, and, in addition, many illustrations, though in a matter that is so clear these are unnecessary. I will merely say that to desire to commune with God by such means is a most perilous thing, more so than I can express, and that one who is affectioned to such methods will not fail to err greatly and will often find himself in confusion. Anyone who in the past has prized them will understand me from his own experience. For over and above the difficulty that there is in being sure that one is not going astray in respect of locutions and visions which are of God, there are ordinarily many of these locutions and visions which are of the devil; for in his converse with the soul the devil habitually wears the same guise as God assumes in His dealings with it, setting before it things that are very like to those which God communicates to it, insinuating himself, like the wolf in sheep's clothing, among the flock, with a success so nearly complete that he can hardly be recognized. For, since he says many things that are true, and in conformity with reason, and things that come to pass as he describes them, it is very easy for the soul to be deceived, and to think that, since these things come to pass as he says, and the future is correctly foretold, this can be the work of none save God; for such souls know not that it is a very easy thing for one that has clear natural light to be acquainted, as to their causes, with things, or with many of them, which have been or shall be. And since the devil has a very clear light of this kind, he can very easily deduce effect from cause, although it may not always turn out as he says, because all causes depend upon the will of God. Let us take an example.

The devil knows that the constitution of the earth and the atmosphere, and the laws ruling the sun, are disposed in such manner and in such degree that, when a certain moment has arrived, it will necessarily follow, according to the laws of nature laid down for these elements, that they will infect people with pestilence, and he knows in what places this will be more severe and in what places less so. Here you have a knowledge of pestilence in respect of its causes. What a wonderful thing it seems when the devil reveals this to a soul, saying: 'In a year or in six months from now there will be pestilence,' and it happens as he says! And yet this is a prophecy of the devil. In the same way he may have a knowledge of earthquakes, and, seeing that the bowels of the earth are filling with air, will say: 'At such a time there will be an earthquake.' Yet this is only natural knowledge, for the possession of which it suffices for the spirit to be free from the passions of the soul, even as Boetius says in these words: Si vis claro lumine cernere verum, gaudia pelle, timorem, spemque fugato, nec dolor adsit. That is:

If thou desire to know truths with the clearness of nature, cast from thee rejoicing and fear and hope and sorrow.

And likewise supernatural events and happenings may be known, in their causes, in matters concerning Divine Providence, which deals most justly and surely as is required by their good or evil causes as regards the sons of men. For one may know by natural means that such or such a person, or such or such a city, or some other place, is in such or such necessity, or has reached such or such a point, so that God, according to His providence and justice, must deal with such a person or thing in the way required by its cause, and in the way that is fitting for it, whether by means of punishment or of reward, as the cause merits. And then one can say: 'At such a time God will give you this, or will do this, or that will come to pass, of a surety.' It was this that holy Judith said to Holofernes, when, in order to persuade him that the children of Israel would without fail be destroyed, she first related to him many of their sins and the evil deeds that they did. And then she said: Et, quoniam haec faciunt, certum est quod in perditionem dabuntur. Which signifies: Since they do these things, it is certain that they will be destroyed. This is to know the punishment in the cause, and it is as though she had said: It is certain that such sins must be the cause of such punishments, at the hand of God Who is most just. And as the Divine Wisdom says: Per quae quis peccat, per haec et torquetur. With respect to that and for that wherein a man sins, therein is he punished.

The devil may have knowledge of this, not only naturally, but also by the experience which he has of having seen God do similar things, and he can foretell it and do so correctly. Again, holy Tobias was aware of the punishment of the city of Ninive because of its cause, and he thus admonished his son, saying: 'Behold, son, in the hour when I and thy mother die, go thou forth from this land, for it will not remain.' Video enim quia iniquitas ejus finem dabit ei. I see clearly that its own iniquity will be the cause of its punishment, which will be that it shall be ended and destroyed altogether. This might have been known by the devil as well as by Tobias, not only because of the iniquity of the city, but by experience, since they had seen that for the sins of the world God destroyed it in the Flood, and that the Sodomites, too, perished for their sins by fire; but Tobias knew it also through the Divine Spirit.

And the devil may know that one Peter cannot, in the course of nature, live more than so many years, and he may foretell this; and so with regard to many other things and in many ways that it is impossible to recount fully — nor can one even begin to recount many of them, since they are most intricate and subtle — he insinuates falsehoods; from which a soul cannot free itself save by fleeing from all revelations and visions and locutions that are supernatural. Wherefore God is justly angered with those that receive them, for He sees that it is temerity on their part to expose themselves to such great peril and presumption and curiosity, and things that spring from pride, and are the root and foundation of vainglory, and of disdain for the things of God, and the beginning of many evils to which many have come. Such persons have succeeded in angering God so greatly that He has of set purpose allowed them to go astray and be deceived and to blind their own spirits and to leave the ordered paths of life and give rein to their vanities and fancies, according to the word of Isaias, where he says: Dominus miscuit in medio ejus spiritum vertiginis. Which is as much to say: The Lord hath mingled in the midst thereof the spirit of dissension and confusion. Which in our ordinary vernacular signifies the spirit of misunderstanding. What Isaias is here very plainly saying is to our purpose, for he is speaking of those who were endeavouring by supernatural means to know things that were to come to pass. And therefore he says that God mingled in their midst the spirit of misunderstanding; not that God willed them, in fact, to have the spirit of error, or gave it to them, but that they desired to meddle with that to which by nature they could not attain. Angered by this, God allowed them to act foolishly, giving them no light as to that wherewith He desired not that they should concern themselves. And thus the Prophet says that God mingled that spirit in them, privatively. And in this sense God is the cause of such an evil — that is to say, He is the privative cause, which consists in His withdrawal of His light and favour, to such a point that they must needs fall into error.

And in this way God gives leave to the devil to blind and deceive many, when their sins and audacities merit it; and this the devil can do and does successfully, and they give him credence and believe him to be a good spirit; to such a point that, although they may be quite persuaded that he is not so, they cannot undeceive themselves, since, by the permission of God, there has already been insinuated into them the spirit of misunderstanding, even as we read was the case with the prophets of King Achab, whom God permitted to be deceived by a lying spirit, giving the devil leave to deceive them, and saying: Decipies, et praevalebis; egredere, et fac ita. Which signifies: Thou shalt prevail with thy falsehood, and shalt deceive them; go forth and do so. And so well was he able to work upon the prophets and the King, in order to deceive them, that they would not believe the prophet Micheas, who prophesied the truth to them, saying the exact contrary of that which the others had prophesied, and this came to pass because God permitted them to be blinded, since their affections were attached to that which they desired to happen to them, and God answered them according to their desires and wishes; and this was a most certain preparation and means for their being blinded and deceived, which God allowed of set purpose.

Thus, too, did Ezechiel prophesy in the name of God. Speaking against those who began to desire to have knowledge direct from God, from motives of curiosity, according to the vanity of their spirit, he says: When such a man comes to the prophet to enquire of Me through him, I, the Lord, will answer him by Myself, and I will set my face in anger against that man; and, as to the prophet, when he has gone astray in that which was asked of him, Ego Dominus decepi prophetam illum. That is: I, the Lord, have deceived that prophet. This is to be taken to mean, by not succouring him with His favour so that he might not be deceived; and this is His meaning when He says: I the Lord will answer him by Myself in anger — that is, God will withdraw His grace and favour from that man. Hence necessarily follows deception by reason of his abandonment by God. And then comes the devil and makes answer according to the pleasure and desire of that man, who, being pleased thereat, since the answers and communications are according to his will, allows himself to be deceived greatly.

It may appear that we have to some extent strayed from the purpose that we set down in the title of this chapter, which was to prove that, although God answers, He sometimes complains. But, if it be carefully considered, all that has been said goes to prove or intention; for it all shows that God desires not that we should wish for such visions, since He makes it possible for us to be deceived by them in so many ways.

Chapter XXII

Wherein is solved a difficulty — namely, why it is not lawful, under the law of grace, to ask anything of God by supernatural means, as it was under the old law. This solution is proved by a passage from Saint Paul.

Difficulties keep coming to our mind, and thus we cannot progress with the speed that we should desire. For as they occur to us, we are obliged of necessity to clear them up, so that the truth of this teaching may ever be plain and carry its full force. But there is always this advantage in these difficulties, that, although they somewhat impede our progress, they serve nevertheless to make our intention the clearer and more explicit, as will be the case with the present one.

In the previous chapter, we said that it is not the will of God that souls should desire to receive anything distinctly, by supernatural means, through visions, locutions, etc. Further, we saw in the same chapter, and deduced from the testimonies which were there brought forward from Scripture, that such communion with God was employed in the Old Law and was lawful; and that not only was it lawful, but God commanded it. And when they used not this opportunity, God reproved them, as is to be seen in Isaias, where God reproves the children of Israel because they desired to go down to Egypt without first enquiring of Him, saying: Et os meum non interrogastis. That is: Ye asked not first at My own mouth what was fitting. And likewise we read in Josue that, when the children of Israel themselves are deceived by the Gabaonites, the Holy Spirit reproves them for this fault, saying: Susceperunt ergo de cibariis eorum, et os Domini non interrogaverunt. Which signifies: They took of their victuals and they enquired not at the mouth of God. Furthermore, we see in the Divine Scripture that Moses always enquired of God, as did King David and all the kings of Israel with regard to their wars and necessities, and the priests and prophets of old, and God answered and spake with them and was not wroth, and it was well done; and if they did it not it would be ill done; and this is the truth. Why, then, in the new law — the law of grace — may it not now be as it was aforetime?

To this it must be replied that the principal reason why in the law of Scripture the enquiries that were made of God were lawful, and why it was fitting that prophets and priests should seek visions and revelations of God, was because at that time faith had no firm foundation, neither was the law of the Gospel established; and thus it was needful that men should enquire of God and that He should speak, whether by words or by visions and revelations or whether by figures and similitudes or by many other ways of expressing His meaning. For all that He answered and spake and revealed belonged to the mysteries of our faith and things touching it or leading to it. And, since the things of faith are not of man, but come from the mouth of God Himself, God Himself reproved them because they enquired not at His mouth in their affairs, so that He might answer, and might direct their affairs and happenings toward the faith, of which at that time they had no knowledge, because it was not yet founded. But now that the faith is founded in Christ, and in this era of grace, the law of the Gospel has been made manifest, there is no reason to enquire of Him in that manner, nor for Him to speak or to answer as He did then. For, in giving us, as He did, His Son, which is His Word — and He has no other — He spake to us all together, once and for all, in this single Word, and He has no occasion to speak further.

And this is the sense of that passage with which Saint Paul begins, when he tries to persuade the Hebrews that they should abandon those first manners and ways of converse with God which are in the law of Moses, and should set their eyes on Christ alone, saying: Multifariam multisque modis olim Deus loquens patribus in Prophetis: novissime autem diebus istis locutus est nobis in Filio. And this is as though he had said: That which God spake of old in the prophets to our fathers, in sundry ways and divers manners, He has now, at last, in these days, spoken to us once and for all in the Son. Herein the Apostle declares that God has become, as it were, dumb, and has no more to say, since that which He spake aforetime, in part to the prophets, He has now spoken altogether in Him, giving us the All, which is His Son.

Wherefore he that would now enquire of God, or seek any vision or revelation, would not only be acting foolishly, but would be committing an offence against God, by setting his eyes altogether upon Christ, and seeking no new thing or aught beside. And God might answer him after this manner, saying: If I have spoken all things to thee in My Word, Which is My Son, and I have no other word, what answer can I now make to thee, or what can I reveal to thee which is greater than this? Set thine eyes on Him alone, for in Him I have spoken and revealed to thee all things, and in Him thou shalt find yet more than that which thou askest and desirest. For thou askest locutions and revelations, which are the part; but if thou set thine eyes upon Him, thou shalt find the whole; for He is My complete locution and answer, and He is all My vision and all My revelation; so that I have spoken to thee, answered thee, declared to thee and revealed to thee, in giving Him to thee as thy brother, companion and master, as ransom and prize. For since that day when I descended upon Him with My Spirit on Mount Tabor, saying: Hic est filius meus dilectus, in quo mihi bene complacui, ipsum audite (which is to say: This is My beloved Son, in Whom I am well pleased; hear ye Him), I have left off all these manners of teaching and answering, and I have entrusted this to Him. Hear Him; for I have no more faith to reveal, neither have I any more things to declare. For, if I spake aforetime, it was to promise Christ; and, if they enquired of Me, their enquiries were directed to petitions for Christ and expectancy concerning Him, in Whom they should find every good thing (as is now set forth in all the teaching of the Evangelists and the Apostles); but now, any who would enquire of Me after that manner, and desire Me to speak to him or reveal aught to him, would in a sense be asking Me for Christ again, and asking Me for more faith, and be lacking in faith, which has already been given in Christ; and therefore he would be committing a great offence against My beloved Son, for not only would he be lacking in faith, but he would be obliging Him again first of all to become incarnate and pass through life and death. Thou shalt find naught to ask Me, or to desire of Me, whether revelations or visions; consider this well, for thou shalt find that all has been done for thee and all has been given to thee — yea, and much more also — in Him.

If thou desirest Me to answer thee with any word of consolation, consider My Son, Who is subject to Me, and bound by love of Me, and afflicted, and thou shalt see how fully He answers thee. If thou desirest Me to expound to thee secret things, or happenings, set thine eyes on Him alone, and thou shalt find the most secret mysteries, and the wisdom and wondrous things of God, which are hidden in Him, even as My Apostle says: In quo sunt omnes thesauri sapientiae et scientiae Dei absconditi. That is: In this Son of God are hidden all the treasures of wisdom and knowledge of God. These treasures of wisdom shall be very much more sublime and delectable and profitable for thee than the things that thou desiredst to know. Herein the same Apostle gloried, saying: That he had not declared to them that he knew anything, save Jesus Christ and Him crucified. And if thou shouldst still desire other Divine or bodily revelations and visions, look also at Him made man, and thou shalt find therein more than thou thinkest, for the Apostle says likewise: In ipso habitat omnis plenitudo Divinitatis corporaliter. Which signifies: In Christ dwelleth all the fullness of the Godhead bodily.

It is not fitting, then, to enquire of God by supernatural means, nor is it necessary that He should answer; since all the faith has been given us in Christ, and there is therefore no more of it to be revealed, nor will there ever be. And he that now desires to receive anything in a supernatural manner, as we have said, is, as it were, finding fault with God for not having given us a complete sufficiency in His Son. For, although such a person may be assuming the faith, and believing it, nevertheless he is showing a curiosity which belongs to faithlessness. We must not expect, then, to receive instruction, or aught else, in a supernatural manner. For, at the moment when Christ gave up the ghost upon the Cross, saying, Consummatum est, which signifies, 'It is finished,' an end was made, not only of all these forms, but also of all those other ceremonies and rites of the Old Law. And so we must now be guided in all things by the law of Christ made man, and by that of His Church, and of His ministers, in a human and a visible manner, and by these means we must remedy our spiritual weaknesses and ignorances, since in these means we shall find abundant medicine for them all. If we leave this path, we are guilty not only of curiosity, but of great audacity: nothing is to be believed in a supernatural way, save only that which is the teaching of Christ made man, as I say, and of His ministers, who are men. So much so that Saint Paul says these words: Quod si Angelus de coelo evengelizaverit, praterquam quod evangelizavimus vobis, anathema sit. That is to say: If any angel from Heaven preach any other gospel unto you than that which we men preach unto you, let him be accursed and excommunicate.

Wherefore, since it is true that we must ever be guided by that which Christ taught us, and that all things else are as nothing, and are not to be believed unless they are in conformity with it, he who still desires to commune with God after the manner of the Old Law acts vainly. Furthermore, it was not lawful at that time for everyone to enquire of God, neither did God answer all men, but only the priests and prophets, from whose mouths it was that the people had to learn law and doctrine; and thus, if a man desire to know anything of God, he enquired of Him through the prophet or the priest and not of God Himself. And, if David enquired of God at certain times upon his own account, he did this because he was a prophet, and yet, even so, he did it not without the priestly vestment as it is clear was the case in the First Book of the Kings, where he said to Abimelech the priest: Applica ad me Ephod — which ephod was one of the priestly vestments, having which he then spake with God. But at other times he spake with God through the prophet Nathan and other prophets. And by the mouths of these prophets and of the priests men were to believe that that which was said to them came from God; they were not to believe it because of their own opinions.

And thus, men were not authorized or empowered at that time to give entire credence to what was said by God, unless it were approved by the mouths of priests and prophets. For God is so desirous that the government and direction of every man should be undertaken by another man like himself, and that every man should be ruled and governed by natural reason, that He earnestly desires us not to give entire credence to the things that He communicates to us supernaturally, nor to consider them as being securely and completely confirmed until they pass through this human aqueduct of the mouth of man. And thus, whenever He says or reveals something to a soul, He gives this same soul to whom He says it a kind of inclination to tell it to the person to whom it is fitting that it should be told. Until this has been done, it is not wont to give entire satisfaction, because the man has not taken it from another man like himself. We see in the Book of the Judges that the same thing happened to the captain Gedeon, to whom God had said many times that he should conquer the Madianites, yet he was fearful and full of doubts (for God had allowed him to retain that weakness) until he heard from the mouth of men what God had said to him. And it came to pass that, when God saw he was weak, He said to him: 'Rise up and go down to the camp.' Et cum audieris quid loquantur, tunc confortabuntur manus tuae, et securior ad hostium castra descendes. That is: When thou shalt hear what men are saying there, then shalt thou receive strength in that which I have said to thee, and thou shalt go down with greater security to the hosts of the enemy. And so it came to pass that, having heard a dream related by one of the Madianites to another, wherein the Madianite had dreamed that Gedeon should conquer them, he was greatly strengthened, and began to prepare for the battle with great joy. From this it can be seen that God desired not that he should feel secure, since He gave him not the assurance by supernatural means alone, but caused him first to be strengthened by natural means.

And even more surprising is the thing that happened in this connection to Moses, when God had commanded him, and given him many instructions, which He continued with the signs of the wand changed into a serpent and of the leprous hand, enjoining him to go and set free the children of Israel. So weak was he and so uncertain about this going forward that, although God was angered, he had not the courage to summon up the complete faith necessary for going, until God encouraged him through his brother Aaron, saying: Aaron frater tuus Levites, scio quod eloquent sit: ecce ipse egredietur in occursum tuum, vidensque te, laetabitur corde. Loquere ad eum, en pone verba mea in ore ejus: et ego ero in ore tuo, et in ore illius, etc. Which is as though He had said: I know that thy brother Aaron is an eloquent man: behold, he will come forth to meet thee, and, when he seeth thee, he will be glad at heart; speak to him and tell him all My words, and I will be in thy mouth and in his mouth, so that each of you shall believe that which is in the mouth of the other.

Having heard these words, Moses at once took courage, in the hope of finding consolation in the counsel which his brother was to give him; for this is a characteristic of the humble soul, which dares not converse alone with God, neither can be completely satisfied without human counsel and guidance. And that this should be given to it is the will of God, for He draws near to those who come together to converse of truth, in order to expound and confirm it in them, upon a foundation of natural reason, even as He said that He would do when Moses and Aaron should come together — namely, that He would be in the mouth of the one and in the mouth of the other. Wherefore He said likewise in the Gospel that *Ubi fuerint duo vel tres congregati in nomine meo, ibi sum ego in medio eorum.* That is: Where two or three have come together, in order to consider that which is for the greater honour and glory of My name, there am I in the midst of them. That is to say, I will make clear and confirm in their hearts the truths of God. And it is to be observed that He said not: Where there is one alone, there will I be; but: Where there are at least two. In this way He showed that God desires not that any man by himself alone should believe his experiences to be of God, or should act in conformity with them, or rely upon them, but rather should believe the Church and her ministers, for God will not make clear and confirm the truth in the heart of one who is alone, and thus such a one will be weak and cold.

Hence comes that whereon the Preacher insists, where he says: *Vae soli, quia cum ceciderit, non habet sublevantem se. Si dormierint duo, fovebuntur mutuo; unus quomodo calefiet? et si quispiam praevaluerit contra unum, duo resistent ei.* Which signifies: Woe to the man that is alone, for when he falleth he hath none to raise him up. If two sleep together, the one shall give warmth to the other (that is to say: with the warmth of God Who is between them); but one alone, how shall he be warm? That is to say: How shall he be other than cold as to the things of God? And if any man can fight and prevail against one enemy (that is, the devil, who can fight and prevail against those that are alone and desire to be alone as regards the things of God), two men together will resist him — that is, the disciple and the master who come together to know and dost the truth. And until this happens such a man is habitually weak and feeble in the truth, however often he may have heard it from God; so much so that, despite the many occasions on which Saint Paul preached the Gospel, which he said that he had heard, not of men, but of God, he could not be satisfied until he had gone to consult with Saint Peter and the Apostles, saying: *Ne forte in vacuum currerem, aut cucurrissem.* Which signifies: Perchance he should run, or had run, in vain, having no assurance of himself, until man had given him assurance. This seems a noteworthy thing, O Paul, that He Who revealed to thee this Gospel could not likewise reveal to thee the assurance of the fault which thou mightest have committed in preaching the truth concerning Him.

Herein it is clearly shown that a man must not rely upon the things that God reveals, save in the way that we are describing; for, even in cases where a person is in possession of certainty, as Saint Paul was certain of his Gospel (since he had already begun to preach it), yet, although the revelation be of God, man may still err with respect to it, or in things relating to it. For, although God reveals one thing, He reveals not always the other; and oftentimes He reveals something without revealing the way in which it is to be done. For ordinarily He neither performs nor reveals anything that can be accomplished by human counsel and effort, although He may commune with the soul for a long time, very lovingly. Of this Saint Paul was very well aware, since, as we say, although he knew that the Gospel was revealed to him by God, he went to take counsel with Saint Peter. And we see this clearly in the Book of Exodus, where God had communed most familiarly with Moses, yet had never given him that salutary counsel which was given him by his father-in-law Jethro — that is to say, that he should choose other judges to assist him, so that the people should not be waiting from morning till night. This counsel God approved, though it was not He Who had given it to him, for it was a thing that fell within the limits of human judgment and reason. With respect to Divine visions and revelations and locutions, God is not wont to reveal them, for He is ever desirous that men should make such use of their own reason as is possible, and all such things have to be governed by reason, save those that are of faith, which transcend all judgment and reason, although these are not contrary to faith.

Wherefore let none think that, because it may be true that God and the saints commune with him familiarly about many things, they will of necessity explain to him the faults that he commits with regard to anything, if it be possible for him to recognize these faults by other means. He can have no assurance about this; for, as we read came to pass in the Acts of the Apostles, Saint Peter, though a prince of the Church, who was taught directly by God, went astray nevertheless with respect to a certain ceremony that was in use among the Gentiles, and God was silent. So far did he stray that Saint Paul reproved him, as he affirms, saying: Cum vidissem, quod non recte ad veritatem Evangelii ambularent, dixi coram omnibus: Si tu judaeus cum sis, gentiliter vivis, quomodo Gentes cogis judaizare? Which signifies: When I saw (says Saint Paul) that the disciples walked not uprightly according to the truth of the Gospel, I said to Peter before them all: If thou, being a Jew, as thou art, livest after the manner of the Gentiles, how feignest thou to force the Gentiles to live as do the Jews? And God reproved not Saint Peter

Himself for this fault, for that stimulation was a thing that had to do with reason, and it was possible for him to know it by rational means.

Wherefore on the day of judgment God will punish for their many faults and sins many souls with whom He may quite habitually have held converse here below, and to whom He may have given much light and virtue; for, as to those things that they have known that they ought to do, they have been neglectful, and have relied upon that converse that they have had with God and upon the virtue that He has given them. And thus, as Christ says in the Gospel, they will marvel at that time, saying: Domine, Domine, nonne in nomine tuo prophetavimus, et in nomine tuo daemonia ejecimus, et in nomine tuo virtutes multas fecimus? That is: Lord, Lord, were the prophecies that Thou spakest to us perchance not prophesied in Thy name? And in Thy name cast we not out devils? And in Thy name performed we not many miracles and mighty works? And the Lord says that He will answer them in these words: Et tunc confitebor illis, quia numquam novi vos: discedite a me omnes qui operamini iniquitatem. That is to say: Depart from Me, ye workers of iniquity, for I never knew you. Of the number of these was the prophet Balaam and others like to him, who, though God spake with them and gave them thanks, were sinners. But the Lord will likewise give their proportion of reproof to His friends and chosen ones, with whom He communed familiarly here below, as to the faults and sins of neglect that they may have committed; whereof there was no need that God should Himself warn them, since He had already warned them through the natural reason and law that He had given to them.

In concluding this part of my subject, therefore, I say, and I infer from what has already been said, that anything, of whatsoever kind, received by the soul through supernatural means, must clearly and plainly, fully and simply, be at once communicated to the spiritual director. For although there may seem no reason to speak of it, or to spend time upon doing so, since the soul is acting safely, as we have said, if it rejects it and neither pays heed to it nor desires it — especially if it be a question of visions or revelations or other supernatural communications, which are either quite clear or very nearly so — nevertheless, it is very necessary to give an account of all these, although it may seem to the soul that there is no reason for so doing. And this for three causes. First, because, as we have said, God communicates many things, the effect, power, light and certainty whereof He confirms not wholly in the soul, until, as we have said, the soul consults him whom God has given to it as a spiritual judge, which is he that has the power to bind or to loose, and to approve or to blame, as we have shown by means of the passages quoted above; and we can show it clearly by experience, for we see humble souls to whom these things come to pass, and who, after discussing them with the proper persons, experience a new satisfaction, power, light and certainty; so much so that to some it seems that they have no effect upon them, nor do they even belong to them, until they have communicated them to the director, whereupon they are given to them anew.

The second cause is that the soul habitually needs instruction upon the things that come to pass within it, so that it may be led by that means to spiritual poverty and detachment, which is the dark night. For if it begins to relinquish this instruction — even when it desires not the things referred to — it will gradually, without realizing it, become callous as it treads the spiritual road, and draw near again to the road of sense; and it is partly with respect to this that these distinct things happen.

The third cause is that, for the sake of the humility and submission and mortification of the soul, it is well to relate everything to the director, even though he make no account of it all and consider it of no importance. There are some souls who greatly dislike speaking of such things, because they think them to be unimportant, and know not how the person to whom they should relate them will receive them; but this is lack of humility, and for that very reason it is needful for them to submit themselves and relate these things. And there are others who are very timid in relating them, because they see no reason why they should have these experiences, which seem to belong to saints, as well as other things which they are sorry to have to describe; for which cause they think there is no reason to speak of them because they make no account of them; but for this very reason it is well for them to mortify themselves and relate them, until in time they come to speak of them humbly, unaffectedly, submissively and readily, and after this they will always find it easy to do so.

But, with respect to what has been said, it must be pointed out that, although we have insisted so much that such things should be set aside, and that confessors should not encourage their penitents to discuss them, it is not well that spiritual fathers should show displeasure in regard to them, or should seek to avoid speaking of them or despise them, or make their penitents reserved and afraid to mention them, for it would be the means of causing them many inconveniences if the door were closed upon their relating them. For, since they are a means and manner whereby God guides such souls, there is no reason for thinking ill of them or for being alarmed or scandalized by them; but rather there is a reason for proceeding very quietly and kindly, for encouraging these souls and giving them an opportunity to speak of these things; if necessary, they must be exhorted to speak; and, in view of the difficulty that some souls experience in describing such matters, this is sometimes quite essential. Let confessors direct their penitents into faith, advising them frankly to turn away their eyes from all such things, teaching them how to void the desire and the spirit of them, so that they may make progress, and giving them to understand how much more precious in God's sight is one work or act of the will performed in charity than are all the visions and communications that they may receive from Heaven, since these imply neither merit nor demerit. Let them point out, too, that many souls who have known nothing of such things have made incomparably greater progress than others who have received many of them.

Chapter XXIII

Which begins to treat of the apprehensions of the understanding that come in a purely spiritual way, and describes their nature.

Although the instruction that we have given with respect to the apprehensions of the understanding which come by means of sense is somewhat brief, in comparison with what might be said about them, I have not desired to write of them at greater length; I believe, indeed, that I have already been too lengthy for the fulfillment of my present intention, which is to disencumber the understanding of them and direct the soul into the night of faith. Wherefore we shall now begin to treat of those other four apprehensions of the understanding, which, as we said in the tenth chapter, are purely spiritual — namely, visions, revelations, locutions and spiritual feelings. These we call purely spiritual, for they do not (as do those that are corporeal and imaginary) communicate themselves to the understanding by way of the corporeal senses; but, without the intervention of any inward or outward corporeal sense, they present themselves to the understanding, clearly and distinctly, by supernatural means, passively — that is to say, without the performance of any act or operation on the part of the soul itself, at the least actively.

It must be known, then, that, speaking broadly and in general terms, all these four apprehensions may be called visions of the soul; for we term the understanding of the soul also its sight. And since all these apprehensions are intelligible to the understanding, they are described, in a spiritual sense, as 'visible.' And thus the kinds of intelligence that are formed in the understanding may be called intellectual visions. Now, since all the objects of the other senses, which are all that can be seen, and all that can be heard, and all that can be smelt and tasted and touched, are objects of the understanding in so far as they fall within the limits of truth or falsehood, it follows that, just as to the eyes of the body all that is visible in a bodily way causes bodily vision, even so, to the spiritual eyes of the soul — namely, the understanding — all that is intelligible causes spiritual vision; for, as we have said, for the soul to understand is for it to see. And thus, speaking generally, we may call these four apprehensions visions. This cannot be said, however, of the other senses, for no one of them is capable, as such, of receiving the object of another one.

But, since these apprehensions present themselves to the soul in the same way as they do to the various senses, it follows that, speaking properly and specifically, we shall describe that which the understanding receives by means of sight (because it can see things spiritually, even as the eyes can see bodily) as a vision; and that which it receives by apprehending and understanding new things (as it were through the hearing, when it hears things that are not heard) we describe as revelation; and that which it receives by means of hearing we call locution; and that which it receives through the other senses, such as the perception of sweet spiritual fragrance, and spiritual taste and of spiritual delight which the soul may joy supernaturally, we call spiritual feelings. From all these the soul derives spiritual vision or intelligence, without any kind of apprehension concerning form, image or figure of natural fancy or imagination; these things are communicated to the soul directly by supernatural means and a supernatural process.

Of these, likewise (even as we said of the other imaginary corporeal apprehensions), it is well that we should here disencumber the understanding, leading and directing it by means of them into the spiritual night of faith, to the Divine and substantial union of God; lest, by letting such things encumber and stultify it, it should be hindered upon the road to solitude and detachment from all things, which is necessary to that end. For, although these apprehensions are nobler and more profitable and much more certain than those which are corporeal and imaginary, inasmuch as they are interior and purely spiritual, and are those which the devil is least able to counterfeit, since they are communicated to the soul more purely and subtly without any effort of its own or of the imagination, at least actively, yet not only may the understanding be encumbered by them upon this road, but it is possible for it, through its own imprudence, to be sorely deceived.

And although, in one sense, we might conclude with these four kinds of apprehension, by treating them all together and giving advice which applies to them all, as we have given concerning all the others — namely, that they should neither be desired nor aspired to — yet, since we shall presently throw more light upon the way in which this is to be done, and certain things will be said in connection with them, it will be well to treat of each one of them in particular, and thus we shall now speak of the first apprehensions, which are intellectual or spiritual visions.

Chapter XXIV

Which treats of two kinds of spiritual vision that come supernaturally.

Speaking now strictly of those visions which are spiritual, and are received without the intervention of any bodily sense, I say that there are two kinds of vision than can be received by the understanding: the one kind is of corporeal substances; the other, of incorporeal or separated substances. The corporeal visions have respect to all material things that are in Heaven and on earth, which the soul is able to see, even while it is still in the body, by the aid of a certain supernatural illumination, derived from God, wherein it is able to see all things that are not present, both in Heaven and on earth, even as Saint John saw, as we read in the twenty-first chapter of the Apocalypse, where he describes and relates the excellence of the celestial Jerusalem, which he saw in Heaven. Even so, again, we read of Saint Benedict that in a spiritual vision he saw the whole world. This vision, says Saint Thomas in the first of his Quodlibets, was in the light that is derived from above, as we have said.

The other visions, which are of incorporeal substances, cannot be seen by the aid of this derived illumination, whereof we are here speaking, but only by another and a higher illumination which is called the illumination of glory. And thus these visions of incorporeal substances, such as angels and soul, are not of this life, neither can they be seen in the mortal body; for, if God were pleased to communicate them to the soul, in essence as they are, the soul would at once go forth from the flesh and would be loosed from this mortal life. For this reason God said to Moses, when he entreated Him to show him His Essence: Non videbit me homo, et vivet. That is: Man shall not see Me and be able to remain alive. Wherefore, when the children of Israel thought that they were to see God, or had seen Him, or some angel, they feared death, as we read in the Book of Exodus, where, fearing these things, they said: Non loquatur nobis Dominus, ne forte moriamur. As if they had said: Let not God communicate Himself to us openly, lest we die. And likewise in the Book of Judges, Manue, father of Samson, thought that he and his wife had seen in essence the angel who spake with them (and who had appeared to them in the form of a most beautiful man) and he said to his wife: Morte moriemur, quida vidimus Dominum. Which signifies: We shall die, because we have seen the Lord.

And thus these visions occur not in this life, save occasionally and fleetingly, when, making an exception to the conditions which govern our natural life, God so allows it. At such times He totally withdraws the spirit from this life, and the natural functions of the body are supplied by His favour. This is why, at the time when it is thought that Saint Paul saw these (namely, the incorporeal substances in the third heaven), that Saint says: Sive in corpore, nescio, sive extra corpus, nescio, Deus scit. That is, he was raptured, and of that which he saw he says that he knows not if it was in the body or out of the body, but that God knows. Herein it is clearly seen that the limits of natural means of communication were passed, and that this was the work of God. Likewise, it is believed that God showed His Essence to Moses, for we read that God said to him that He would set him in the cleft of the rock, and would protect him, by covering him with His right hand, and protecting him so that he should not die when His glory passed; the which glory passed indeed, and was shown to him fleetingly, and the natural life of Moses was protected by the right hand of God. But these visions that were so substantial — like that of Saint Paul and Moses, and that of our father Elias, when he covered his face at the gentle whisper of God — although they are fleeting, occur only very rarely — indeed, hardly ever and to very few; for God performs such a thing in those that are very strong in the spirit of the Church and the law of God, as were the three men named above.

But, although these visions of spiritual substances cannot be unveiled and be clearly seen in this life by the understanding, they can nevertheless be felt in the substance of the soul, with the sweetest touches and unions, all of which belongs to spiritual feelings, whereof, with the Divine favour, we shall treat presently; for our pen is being directed and guided to these — that is to say, to the Divine bond and union of the soul with Divine Substance. We shall speak of this when we treat of the dark and confused mystical understanding which remains to be described, wherein we shall show how, by means of this dark and loving knowledge, God is united with the soul in a lofty and Divine degree; for, after some manner, this dark and loving knowledge, which is faith, serves as a means to Divine union in this life, even as, in the next life, the light of glory serves as an intermediary to the clear vision of God.

Let us, then, now treat of the visions of corporeal substances, received spiritually in the soul, which come after the manner of bodily visions. For, just as the eyes see bodily visions by means of natural light, even so does the soul, through the understanding, by means of supernaturally derived light, as we have said, see those same natural things inwardly, together with others, as God wills; the difference between the two kinds of vision is only in the mode and manner of them. For spiritual and intellectual visions are much clearer and subtler than those which pertain to the body. For, when God is pleased to grant this favour to the soul, He communicates to it that supernatural light whereof we speak, wherein the soul sees the things that God wills it to see, easily and most clearly, whether they be of Heaven or of earth, and the absence or presence of them is no hindrance to the vision. And it is at times as though a door were opened before it into a great brightness, through which the soul sees a light, after the manner of a lightning flash, which, on a dark night, reveals things suddenly, and causes them to be clearly and distinctly seen, and then leaves them in darkness, although the forms and figures of them remain in the fancy. This comes to pass much more perfectly in the soul, because those things that the spirit has seen in that light remain impressed upon it in such a way that whensoever it observes them it sees them in itself as it saw them before; even as in a mirror the forms that are in it are seen whensoever a man looks in it, and in such a way that those forms of the things that he has seen are never wholly removed from his soul, although in course of time they become somewhat remote.

The effect which these visions produce in the soul is that of quiet, illumination, joy like that of glory, sweetness, purity and love, humility and inclination or elevation of the spirit in God; sometimes more so, at other times less; with sometimes more of one thing, at other times more of another, according to the spirit wherein they are received and according as God wills.

The devil likewise can produce these visions, by means of a certain natural light, whereby he brings things clearly before the mind, through spiritual suggestion, whether they be present or absent. There is that passage in Saint Matthew, which says of the devil and Christ: Ostendit omnia regna mundi, et gloriam eorum. That is so say: He showed Him all the kingdoms of the world and the glory of them. Concerning this certain doctors say that he did it by spiritual suggestion, for it was not possible to make Him see so much with the bodily eyes as all the kingdoms of the world and the glory of them. But there is much difference between these visions that are caused by the devil and those that are of God. For the effects produced in the soul by the devil's visions are not like those produced by good visions; the former produce aridity of spirit as to communion with God and an inclination to esteem oneself highly, and to receive and set store by the visions aforesaid, and in no wise do they produce the gentleness of humility and love of God. Neither do the forms of such visions remain impressed upon the soul with the sweetness and brightness of the others; nor do they last, but are quickly effaced from the soul, save when the soul greatly esteems them, in which case this high esteem itself causes it to recall them naturally, but with great aridity of spirit, and without producing that effect of love and humility which is produced by good visions when the soul recalls them.

These visions, inasmuch as they are of creatures, wherewith God has no essential conformity or proportion, cannot serve the understanding as a proximate means to union with God. And thus the soul must conduct itself in a purely negative way concerning them, as in the other things that we have described, in order that it may progress by the proximate means — namely, by faith. Wherefore the soul must make no store of treasure of the forms of such visions as remain impressed upon it, neither must it lean upon them; for to do this would be to be encumbered with those forms, images and persons which remain inwardly within it, and thus the soul would not progress toward God by denying itself all things. For, even if these forms should be permanently set before the soul, they will not greatly hinder this progress, if the soul has no desire to set store by them. For, although it is true that the remembrance of them impels the soul to a certain love of God and contemplation, yet it is impelled and exalted much more by pure faith and detachment in darkness from them all, without its knowing how or whence it comes to it. And thus it will come to pass that the soul will go forward, enkindled with yearnings of purest love for God, without knowing whence they come to it, or on what they are founded. The fact is that, while faith has become ever more deeply rooted and infused in the soul by means of that emptiness and darkness and detachment from all things, or spiritual poverty, all of which may be spoken of as one and the same thing, at the same time the charity of God has become rooted and infused in the soul ever more deeply also. Wherefore, the more the soul desires obscurity and annihilation with respect to all the outward or inward things that it is capable of receiving, the more is it infused by faith, and, consequently, by love and hope, since all these three theological virtues go together.

But at certain times the soul neither understands this love nor feels it; for this love resides, not in sense, with its tender feelings, but in the soul, with fortitude and with a courage and daring that are greater than they were before, though sometimes it overflows into sense and produces gentle and tender feelings. Wherefore, in order to attain to that love, joy and delight which such visions produce and cause in the soul, it is well that soul should have fortitude and mortification and love, so that it may desire to remain in emptiness and darkness as to all things, and to build its love and joy upon that which it neither sees nor feels, neither can see nor feel in this life, which is God, Who is incomprehensible and transcends all things. It is well, then, for us to journey to Him by denying ourselves everything. For otherwise, even if the soul be so wise, humble and strong that the devil cannot deceive it by visions or cause it to fall into some sin of presumption, as he is wont to do, he will not allow it to make progress; for he set obstacles in the way of spiritual detachment and poverty of spirit and emptiness in faith, which is the essential condition for union of the soul with God.

And, as the same teaching that we gave in the nineteenth and twentieth chapters, concerning supernatural apprehensions and visions of sense, holds good for these visions, we shall not spend more time here in describing them.

Chapter XXV

Which treats of revelations, describing their nature and making a distinction between them.

According to the order which we are here following, we have next to treat of the second kind of spiritual apprehension, which we have described above as revelations, and which properly belongs to the spirit of prophecy. With respect to this, it must first be known that revelation is naught else than the discovery of some hidden truth or the manifestation of some secret or mystery. Thus God may cause the soul to understand something by making clear to the understanding the truth concerning it, or He may reveal to the soul certain things which He is doing or proposes to do.

Accordingly, we may say that there are two kinds of revelation. The first is the disclosure to the understanding of truths which are properly called intellectual knowledge or intelligence; the second is the manifestation of secrets, which are called revelations with more propriety than the others. For the first kind cannot strictly be called revelations, since they consist in this, that God causes the soul to understand naked truths, not only with respect to temporal things, but likewise with respect to spiritual things, revealing them to the soul clearly and openly. These I have desired to treat under the heading of revelations: first, because they have close kinship and similarity with them: secondly, in order not to multiply distinctions.

According to this method, then, we shall now be well able to divide revelations into two kinds of apprehension. The one kind we shall call intellectual knowledge, and the other, the manifestation of secrets and hidden mysteries of God. With these we shall conclude in two chapters as briefly as we may, and in this chapter following we shall treat of the first.

Chapter XXVI

Which treats of the intuition of naked truths in the understanding, explaining how they are of two kinds and how the soul is to conduct itself with respect to them.

In order to speak properly of this intuition of naked truths which is conveyed to the understanding, the writer would need God to take his hand and to guide his pen; for know, dear reader, that what they are to the soul cannot be expressed in words. But, since I speak not of them here of set purpose, but only that through them I may instruct the soul and lead it to Divine union, I shall suffer myself to speak of them here in a brief and modified form, as is sufficient for the fulfillment of that intention.

This kind of vision (or, to speak more properly, of knowledge of naked truths) is very different from that of which we have just spoken in the twenty-fourth chapter. For it is not like seeing bodily things with the understanding; it consists rather in comprehending and seeing with the understanding the truths of God, whether of things that are, that have been or that will be, which is in close conformity with the spirit of prophecy, as perchance we shall explain hereafter.

Here it is to be observed that this kind of knowledge is distinguishable according to two divisions: the one kind comes to the soul with respect to the Creator; the other with respect to creatures, as we have said. And, although both kinds are very delectable to the soul, yet the delight caused in it by the kind that relates to God is comparable to nothing whatsoever, and there are no words or terms wherein it can be described. This kind of knowledge is of God Himself, and the delight is in God Himself, whereof David says: 'There is naught soever like to Him.' For this kind of knowledge comes to the soul in direct relation to God, when the soul, after a most lofty manner, has a perception of some attribute of God — of His omnipotence, of His might, of His goodness and sweetness, etc.; and, whensoever it has such a perception, that which is perceived cleaves to the soul. Inasmuch as this is pure contemplation, the soul clearly sees that there is no way wherein it can say aught concerning it, save to speak in certain general terms, of the abundance of delight and blessing which it has felt, and this is expressed by souls that experience it; but not to the end that what the soul has experienced and perceived may be wholly apprehended.

And thus David, speaking for himself when something of this kind had happened to him, used only common and general terms, saying: Judicia Domini vera, justificata in semetipsa. Desiderabilia super aurum et lapidem pretiosum multum; et dulciora super mel et favum. Which signifies: The judgments of God — that is, the virtues and attributes which we perceive in God — are in themselves true, justified, more to be desired than gold and very much more than precious stones, and sweeter than the honeycomb and honey. And concerning Moses we read that, when God gave him a most lofty manifestation of knowledge from Himself on an occasion when He passed before him, he said only that which can be expressed in the common terms above mentioned. And it was so that, when the Lord passed before him in that manifestation of knowledge, Moses quickly prostrated himself upon the ground, saying: Dominator Domine Deus, misericors et clemens, patiens, et multae miserationis, ac verax. Qui custodis misericordiam in millia. Which signifies: Ruler, Lord, God, merciful and clement, patient, and of great compassion, and true, that keepest mercy promised unto thousands. Here it is seen that Moses could not express that which he had learned from God in one single manifestation of knowledge, and therefore he expressed and gave utterance to it in all these words. And although at times, when such knowledge is given to a soul, words are used, the soul is well aware that it has expressed no part of what it has felt; for it knows that there is no fit name by which it can name it. And thus Saint Paul, when he was granted that lofty knowledge of God, made no attempt to describe it, saying only that it was not lawful for man to speak of it.

These Divine manifestations of knowledge which have respect to God never relate to particular matters, inasmuch as they concern the Chief Beginning, and therefore can have no particular reference, unless it be a question of some truth concerning a thing less than God, which is involved in the perception of the whole; but these Divine manifestations themselves — no, in no way whatsoever. And these lofty manifestations of knowledge can come only to the soul that attains to union with God, for they are themselves that union; and to receive them is equivalent to a certain contact with the Divinity which the soul experiences, and thus it is God Himself Who is perceived and tasted therein. And, although He cannot be experienced manifestly and clearly, as in glory, this touch of knowledge and delight is nevertheless so sublime and profound that it penetrates the substance of the soul, and the devil cannot meddle with it or produce any manifestation like to it, for there is no such thing, neither is there aught that compares with it, neither can he infuse pleasure or delight that is like to it; for such kinds of knowledge savour of the Divine Essence and of eternal life, and the devil cannot counterfeit a thing so lofty.

Nevertheless he might make some pretence of imitating it, by representing to the soul certain great matters and things which enchant the senses and can readily be perceived by them, and endeavoring to persuade the soul that these are God; but he cannot do this in such wise that they enter into the substance of the soul and of a sudden renew it and enkindle it with love, as do the manifestations of God. For there are certain kinds of knowledge, and certain of these touches effected by God in the substance of the soul, which enrich it after such wise that not only does one of them suffice to take from the soul once and for all the whole of the imperfections that it had itself been unable to throw off during its whole life, but it leaves the soul full of virtues and blessings from God.

And these touches are so delectable to the soul, and the delight they produce is so intimate, that if it received only one of them it would consider itself well rewarded for all the trials that it had suffered in this life, even had they been innumerable; and it is so greatly encouraged and given such energy to suffer many things for God's sake that it suffers especially in seeing that it is not suffering more.

The soul cannot attain to these lofty degrees of knowledge by means of any comparison or imagination of its own, because they are loftier than all these; and so God works them in the soul without making use of its own capacities. Wherefore, at certain times, when the soul is least thinking of it and least desiring it, God is wont to give it these Divine touches, by causing it certain remembrances of Himself. And these are sometimes suddenly caused in the soul by its mere recollection of certain things — sometimes of very small things. And they are so readily perceived that at times they cause not only the soul, but also the body, to tremble. But at other times they come to pass in the spirit when it is very tranquil, without any kind of trembling, but with a sudden sense of delight and spiritual refreshment.

At other times, again, they come when the soul repeats or hears some word, perhaps from Scripture or possibly from some other source; but they are not always equally efficacious and sensible, for oftentimes they are extremely faint; yet, however faint they may be, one of these recollections and touches of God is more profitable to the soul than many other kinds of knowledge or many meditations upon the creatures and the works of God. And, since these manifestations of knowledge come to the soul suddenly, and independently of its own free will, it must neither desire to have them, nor desire not to have them; but must merely be humble and resigned concerning them, and God will perform His work how and when He wills.

And I say not that the soul should behave in the same negative manner with regard to these apprehensions as with regard to the rest, for, as we have said, they are a part of the union towards which we are leading the soul, to which end we are teaching it to detach and strip itself of all other apprehensions. And the means by which God will do this must be humility and suffering for love of God with resignation as regards all reward; for these favours are not granted to the soul which still cherishes attachments, inasmuch as they are granted through a very special love of God toward the soul which loves Him likewise with great detachment. It is to this that the Son of God referred, in Saint John, when He said: Qui autem diligit rag, diligetur a Patre meo, et ego diligam eum, et manifestabo ei me ipsum. Which signifies: He that loves Me shall be loved by My Father, and I will love him and will manifest Myself to him. Herein are included the kinds of knowledge and touches to which we are referring, which God manifests to the soul that truly loves Him.

The second kind of knowledge or vision of interior truths is very different from this that we have described, since it is of things lower than God. And herein is included the perception of the truth of things in themselves, and that of the events and happenings which come to pass among men. And this knowledge is of such a kind that, when the soul learns these truths, they sink into it, independently of any suggestion from without, to such an extent that, although it may be given a different interpretation of them, it cannot make inward assent to this, even though it endeavor to do so by putting forth a great effort; for within the spirit it is learning otherwise through the spirit that is teaching it that thing, which is equivalent to seeing it clearly. This pertains to the spirit of prophecy and to the grace which Saint Paul calls the gift of the discernment of spirits. Yet, although the soul holds something which it understands to be quite certain and true, as we have said, and although it may be unable to cease giving it that passive interior consent, it must not therefore cease to believe and to give the consent of reason to that which its spiritual director tells it and commands it, even though this may be quite contrary to its own feelings, so that it may be directed in faith to Divine union, to which a soul must journey by believing rather than by understanding.

Concerning both these things we have clear testimonies in Scripture. For, with respect to the spiritual knowledge of things that may be acquired, the Wise Man says these words: Ipse dedit mihi horum, quae sunt, scientiam veram, ut sciam dispositionem orbis terrarum, et virtutes elementorum, initium et consummationem temporum, viccissitudinum permutationes, et consummationes temporum, et morum mutationes, divisiones temporum, et anni cursus, et stellarum dispositiones, naturas animalium et iras bestiarum, vim ventorum, et cogitationes hominum, differentias virgultorum, et virtutes radicum, et quaecumque sunt abscondita, et improvisa didici: omnium enim artifex docuit me sapientia. Which signifies: God hath given me true knowledge of things that are: to know the disposition of the round world and the virtues of the elements; the beginning, and ending, and midst of the times, the alterations in the changes and the consummations of the seasons, and the changes of customs, the divisions of the seasons, the courses of the year and the dispositions of the stars; the natures of animals, and the furies of the beasts, the strength and virtue of the winds, and the thoughts of men; the diversities in plants and trees and the virtues of roots and all things that are hidden, and those that are not foreseen: all these I learned, for Wisdom, which is the worker of all things, taught me. And although this knowledge which the Wise Man here says that God gave him concerning all things was infused and general, the passage quoted furnishes sufficient evidence for all particular kinds of knowledge which God infuses into souls, by supernatural means, when He wills. And this not that He may give them a general habit of knowledge as He gave to Solomon in the matters aforementioned; but that He may reveal to them at times certain truths with respect to any of all these things that the Wise Man here enumerates. Although it is true that into many souls Our Lord infuses habits which relate to many things, yet these are never of so general a kind as they were in the case of Solomon. The differences between them are like to those between the gifts distributed by God which are enumerated by Saint Paul; among these he sets wisdom, knowledge, faith, prophecy, discernment or knowledge of spirits, understanding of tongues, interpretation of spoken words, etc. All these kinds of knowledge are infused habits, which God gives freely to whom He will, whether naturally or supernaturally; naturally, as to Balaam, to other idolatrous prophets and to many sybils, to whom He gave the spirit of prophecy; and supernaturally, as to the holy prophets and apostles and other saints.

But over and above these habits or graces freely bestowed, what we say is that persons who are perfect or are making progress in perfection are wont very commonly to receive enlightenment and knowledge of things present or absent; these they know through their spirit, which is already enlightened and purged. We can interpret that passage from the Proverbs in this sense, namely: Quomodo in aquis resplendent vultus prospicientium sic corda hominum manifesta sunt proudentibus. Even as there appear in the waters the faces of those that look therein, so the hearts of men are manifest to the prudent. This is understood of those that have the wisdom of saints, which the sacred Scripture calls prudence. And in this way these spirits sometimes learn of other things also, although not whensoever they will; for this belongs only to those that have the habit, and even to these it belongs not always and with respect to all things, for it depends upon God's will to help them.

But it must be known that those whose spirits are purged can learn by natural means with great readiness, and some more readily than others, that which is in the inward spirit or heart, and the inclinations and talents of men, and this by outward indications, albeit very slight ones, as words, movements and other signs. For, even as the devil can do this, since he is spirit, even so likewise can the spiritual man, according to the words of the Apostle, who says: Spiritualis autem judicat omnia. 'He that is spiritual judgeth all things.' And again he says: Spiritus enim omnia scrutatur, etiam profunda Dei. 'The spirit searcheth all things, yea, the deep things of God.' Wherefore, although spiritual persons cannot by nature know thoughts, or things that are in the minds of others, they may well interpret them through supernatural enlightenment or by signs. And, although they may often be deceived in their interpretation of signs, they are more generally correct. Yet we must trust neither to the one means nor to the other, for the devil meddles herein greatly, and with much subtlety, as we shall afterwards say, and thus we must ever renounce such kinds of knowledge.

And that spiritual persons may have knowledge of the deeds and happenings of men, even though they be elsewhere, we have witness and example in the Fourth Book of the Kings, where Giezi, the servant of our father Eliseus, desired to hide from him the money which he had received from Naaman the Syrian, and Eliseus said: Nonne cor meum in praesenti erat, quando reversus est homo de curru suo in occursum tui? 'Was not my heart perchance present, when Naaman turned back from his chariot and went to meet thee? This happens spiritually; the spirit sees it as though it were happening in its presence. And the same thing is proved in the same book, where we read likewise of the same Eliseus, that, knowing all that the King of Syria did with his princes in his privy chamber, he told it to the King of Israel, and thus the counsels of the King of Syria were of no effect; so much so that, when the King of Syria saw that all was known, he said to his people: Why do ye not tell me which of you is betraying me to the King of Israel? And then one of his servants said: Nequaquam, Domine mi Rex, sed Eliseus Propheta, qui est in Israel, indicat Regi Israel omnia verba, quaecumque locutus fueris in conclavi tuo. 'It is not so, my lord, O King, but Eliseus, the prophet that is in Israel, telleth the king of Israel all the words that thou speakest in thy privy chamber.'

Both kinds of this knowledge of things, as well as other kinds of knowledge, come to pass in the soul passively, so that for its own part it does naught. For it will come to pass that, when a person is inattentive to a matter and it is far from his mind, there will come to him a vivid understanding of what he is hearing or reading, and that much more clearly than could be conveyed by the sound of the words; and at times, though he understand not the words, as when they are in Latin and he knows not that tongue, the knowledge of their meaning comes to him, despite his not understanding them.

With regard to the deceptions which the devil can bring about, and does bring about, concerning this kind of knowledge and understanding, there is much that might be said, for the deceptions which he effects in this way are very great and very difficult to unmask. Inasmuch as, through suggestion, he can represent to the soul many kinds of intellectual knowledge and implant them so firmly that it appears impossible that they should not be true, he will certainly cause the soul to believe innumerable falsehoods if it be not humble and cautious. For suggestion has sometimes great power over the soul, above all when it is to some extent aided by the weakness of sense, causing the knowledge which it conveys to sink into the soul with such great power, persuasiveness and determination that the soul needs to give itself earnestly to prayer and to exert great strength if it is to cast it off. For at times the devil is accustomed to represent to the soul the sins of others, and evil consciences and evil souls, falsely but very vividly, and all this he does to harm the soul, trusting that it may spread abroad his revelations, and that thus more sins may be committed, for which reason he fills the soul with zeal by making it believe that these revelations are granted it so that it may commend the persons concerned to God. Now, though it is true that God sometimes sets before holy souls the necessities of their neighbours, so that they may commend them to God or relieve them, even as we read that He revealed to Jeremias the weakness of the prophet Baruch, that he might give him counsel concerning it, yet it is more often the devil who does this, and speaks falsely about it, in order to cause infamy, sin and discouragement, whereof we have very great experience. And at other times he implants other kinds of knowledge with great assurance, and persuades the soul to believe them.

Such knowledge as this, whether it be of God or no, can be of very little assistance to the progress of the soul on its journey to God if the soul desire it and be attached to it; on the contrary, if it were not scrupulous in rejecting it, not only would it be hindered on its road, but it would even be greatly harmed and led far astray. For all the perils and inconveniences which, as we have said, may be involved in the supernatural apprehensions whereof we have treated up to this point, may occur here, and more also. I will not, therefore, treat more fully of this matter here, since sufficient instruction about it has already been given in past chapters; I will only say that the soul must always be very scrupulous in rejecting these things, and seek to journey to God by the way of unknowing; and must ever relate its experiences to its spiritual confessor, and be ever attentive to his counsel.

Let the confessor guide the soul past this, laying no stress upon it, for it is of no kind of importance for the road to union; for when these things are granted to the soul passively they always leave in it such effect as God wills shall remain, without necessity for the soul to exert any diligence in the matter. And thus it seems to me that there is no reason to describe here either the effect which is produced by true knowledge, or that which comes from false knowledge, for this would be wearisome and never-ending. For the effects of this knowledge cannot all be described in a brief instruction, the knowledge being great and greatly varied, and its effects being so likewise, since good knowledge produces good effects, and evil knowledge, evil effects, etc. In saying that all should be rejected, we have said sufficient for the soul not to go astray.

Chapter XXVII

Which treats of the second kind of revelation, namely, the disclosure of hidden secrets. Describes the way in which these may assist the soul toward union with God, and the way in which they may be a hindrance; and how the devil may deceive the soul greatly in this matter.

We were saying that the second kind of revelation was the manifestation of hidden mysteries and secrets. This may come to pass in two ways. The first with respect to that which God is in Himself, wherein is included the revelation of the mystery of the Most Holy Trinity and Unity of God. The second is with respect to that which God is in His works, and herein are included the other articles of our Catholic faith, and the propositions deducible from them which may be laid down explicitly as truths. In these are included and comprised a great number of the revelations of the prophets, of promises and threatenings of God, and of other things which have happened and shall happen concerning this matter of faith. Under this second head we may also include many other particular things which God habitually reveals, both concerning the universe in general as also in particular concerning kingdoms, provinces and states and families and particular persons. Of these we have examples in abundance in the Divine writings, both of the one kind and of the other, especially in all the Prophets, wherein are found revelations of all these kinds. As this is a clear and plain matter, I will not here spend time in quoting these examples, but will only say that these revelations do not come to pass by word alone, but that God gives them in many ways and manners, sometimes by word alone, sometimes by signs and figures alone, and by images and similitudes alone, sometimes in more than one way at once, as is likewise to be seen in the Prophets, particularly throughout the Apocalypse, where we find not only all the kinds of revelation which we have described, but likewise the ways and manners to which we are here referring.

As to these revelations which are included under our second head, God grants them still in our time to whom He will. He is wont, for example, to reveal to some persons how many days they still have to live, or what trials they are to suffer, or what is to befall such and such a person, or such and such a kingdom, etc. And even as regards the mysteries of our faith, He will reveal and expound to the spirit the truths concerning them, although, since this has already been revealed once, it is not properly to be termed revelation, but is more correctly a manifestation or explanation of what has been revealed already.

In this kind of revelation the devil may meddle freely. For, as revelations of this nature come ordinarily through words, figures and similitudes, etc., the devil may very readily counterfeit others like them, much more so than when the revelations are in spirit alone. Wherefore, if with regard to the first and the second kind of revelation which we are here describing, as touching our faith, there be revealed to us anything new, or different, we must in no wise give our consent to it, even though we had evidence that it was spoken by an angel from Heaven. For even so says Saint Paul, in these words: Licet nos, gut Angelus de coelo evangelizet vobis praeterquam quod evangelizavimus vobis, anathema sit. Which signifies: Even though an angel from Heaven declare or preach unto you aught else than that which we have preached unto you, let him be anathema.

Since, then, there are no more articles to be revealed concerning the substance of our faith than those which have already been revealed to the Church, not only must anything new which may be revealed to the soul concerning this be rejected, but it behoves the soul to be cautious and pay no heed to any novelties implied therein, and for the sake of the purity of the soul it behoves it to rely on faith alone. Even though the truths already revealed to it be revealed again, it will believe them, not because they are now revealed anew, but because they have already been sufficiently revealed to the Church: indeed, it must close its understanding to them, holding simply to the doctrine of the Church and to its faith, which, as Saint Paul says, enters through hearing. And let not its credence and intellectual assent be given to these matters of the faith which have been revealed anew, however fitting and true they may seem to it, if it desire not to be deceived. For, in order to deceive the soul and to instil falsehoods into it, the devil first feeds it with truths and things that are probable in order to give it assurance and afterwards to deceive it. He resembles one that sews leather with a bristle, first piercing the leather with the sharp bristle, after which enters the soft thread; the thread could not enter unless the bristle guided it.

And let this be considered carefully; for, even were it true that there was no peril in such deception, yet it greatly behoves the soul not to desire to understand clearly things that have respect to the faith, so that it may preserve the merit of faith, in its purity and entirety, and likewise that it may come, in this night of the understanding, to the Divine light of Divine union. And it is equally necessary to consider any new revelation with ones eyes closed, and holding fast the prophecies of old, for the Apostle Saint Peter, though he had seen the glory of the Son of God after some manner on Mount Tabor, wrote, in his canonical epistle, these words: Et habemus firmiorem propheticum sermonem; cui bene factitis attendentes, etc. Which is as though he had said: Although the vision that we have seen of Christ on the Mount is true, the word of the prophecy that is revealed to us is firmer and surer, and, if ye rest your soul upon it, ye do well.

And if it is true that, for the reasons already described, it behoves the soul to close its eyes to the aforementioned revelations which come to it, and which concern the propositions of the faith, how much more necessary will it be neither to receive nor to give credit to other revelations relating to different things, wherein the devil habitually meddles so freely that I believe it impossible for a man not to be deceived in many of them unless he strive to reject them, such an appearance of truth and security does the devil give them? For he brings together so many appearances and probabilities, in order that they may be believed, and plants them so firmly in the sense and the imagination, that it seems to the person affected that what he says will certainly happen; and in such a way does he cause the soul to grasp and hold them, that, if it have not humility, it will hardly be persuaded to reject them and made to believe the contrary. Wherefore, the soul that is pure, cautious, simple and humble must resist revelations and other visions with as much effort and care as though they were very perilous temptations. For there is no need to desire them; on the contrary, there is need not too desire them, if we are to reach the union of love. It is this that Solomon meant when he said: 'What need has a man to desire and seek things that are above his natural capacity?' As though we were to say: He has no necessity, in order to be perfect, to desire supernatural things by supernatural means, which are above his capacity.

And as the objections that can be made to this have already been answered, in the nineteenth and twentieth chapter of this book, I refer the reader to these, saying only that the soul must keep itself from all revelations in order to journey, in purity and without error, in the night of faith, to union.

Chapter XXVIII

Which treats of interior locutions that may come to the spirit supernaturally. Says of what kinds they are.

The discreet reader has ever need to bear in mind the intent and end which I have in this book, which is the direction of the soul, through all its apprehensions, natural and supernatural, without deception or hindrance, in purity of faith, to Divine union with God. If he does this, he will understand that, although with respect to apprehensions of the soul and the doctrine that I am expounding I give not such copious instruction neither do I particularize so much or make so many divisions as the understanding perchance requires, I am not being over-brief in this matter. For with respect to all this I believe that sufficient cautions, explanations and instructions are given for the soul to be enabled to behave prudently in every contingency, outward or inward, so as to make progress. And this is the reason why I have so briefly dismissed the subject of prophetic apprehensions and the other subjects allied to it; for there is so much more to be said of each of them, according to the differences and the ways and manners that are wont to be observed in each, that I believe one could never know it all perfectly. I am content that, as I believe, the substance and the doctrine thereof have been given, and the soul has been warned of the caution which it behoves it to exercise in this respect, and also concerning all other things of the same kind that may come to pass within it.

I will now follow the same course with regard to the third kind of apprehension, which, we said, was that of supernatural locutions, which are apt to come to the spirits of spiritual persons without the intervention of any bodily sense. These, although they are of many kinds, may, I believe, all be reduced to three, namely: successive, formal and substantial. I describe as successive certain words and arguments which the spirit is wont to form and fashion when it is inwardly recollected. Formal words are certain clear and distinct words which the spirit receives, not from itself, but from a third person, sometimes when it is recollected and sometimes when it is not. Substantial words are others which also come to the spirit formally, sometimes when it is recollected and sometimes when it is not; these cause in the substance of the soul that substance and virtue which they signify. All these we shall here proceed to treat in their order.

Chapter XXIX

Which treats of the first kind of words that the recollected spirit sometimes forms within itself. Describes the cause of these and the profit and the harm which there may be in them.

These successive words always come when the spirit is recollected and absorbed very attentively in some meditation; and, in its reflections upon that same matter whereon it is thinking, it proceeds from one stage to another, forming words and arguments which are very much to the point, with great facility and distinctiveness, and by means of its reasoning discovers things which it knew not with respect to the subject of its reflections, so that it seems not to be doing this itself, but rather it seems that another person is supplying the reasoning within its mind or answering its questions or teaching it. And in truth it has good cause for thinking this, for the soul itself is reasoning with itself and answering itself as though it were two persons convening together; and in some ways this is really so; for, although it is the spirit itself that works as an instrument, the Holy Spirit oftentimes aids it to produce and form those true reasonings, words and conceptions. And thus it utters them to itself as though to a third person. For, as at that time the understanding is recollected and united with the truth of that whereon it is thinking, and the Divine Spirit is likewise united with it in that truth, as it is always united in all truth, it follows that, when the understanding communicates in this way with the Divine Spirit by means of this truth, it begins to form within itself, successively, those other truths which are connected with that whereon it is thinking, the door being opened to it and illumination being given to it continually by the Holy Spirit Who teaches it. For this is one of the ways wherein the Holy Spirit teaches.

And when the understanding is illumined and taught in this way by this master, and comprehends these truths, it begins of its own accord to form the words which relate to the truths that are communicated to it from elsewhere. So that we may say that the voice is the voice of Jacob and the hands are the hand of Esau. And one that is in this condition will be unable to believe that this is so, but will think that the sayings and the words come from a third person. For such a one knows not the facility with which the understanding can form words inwardly, as though they came from a third person, and having reference to conceptions and truths which have in fact been communicated to it by a third person.

And although it is true that, in this communication and enlightenment of the understanding, no deception is produced in the soul itself, nevertheless, deception may, and does, frequently occur in the formal words and reasonings which the understanding bases upon it. For, inasmuch as this illumination which it receives is at times very subtle and spiritual, so that the understanding cannot attain to a clear apprehension of it, and it is the understanding that, as we say, forms the reasonings of its own accord, it follows that those which it forms are frequently false, and on other occasions are only apparently true, or are imperfect. For since at the outset the soul began to seize the truth, and then brought into play the skilfulness or the clumsiness of its own weak understanding, its perception of the truth may easily be modified by the instability of its own faculties of comprehension, and act all the time exactly as though a third person were speaking.

I knew a person who had these successive locutions: among them were some very true and substantial ones concerning the most holy Sacrament of the Eucharist, but others were sheer heresy. And I am appalled at what happens in these days — namely, when some soul with the very smallest experience of meditation, if it be conscious of certain locutions of this kind in some state of recollection, at once christens them all as coming from God, and assumes that this is the case, saying: 'God said to me . . .'; 'God answered me . . .'; whereas it is not so at all, but, as we have said, it is for the most part they who are saying these things to themselves.

And, over and above this, the desire which people have for locutions, and the pleasure which comes to their spirits from them, lead them to make answer to themselves and then to think that it is God Who is answering them and speaking to them. They therefore commit great blunders unless they impose a strict restraint upon themselves, and unless their director obliges them to abstain from these kinds of reflection. For they are apt to gain from them mere nonsensical talk and impurity of soul rather than humility and mortification of spirit, if they think, 'This was indeed a great thing' and 'God was speaking'; whereas it will have been little more than nothing, or nothing at all, or less than nothing. For, if humility and charity be not engendered by such experiences, and mortification and holy simplicity and silence, etc., what can be the value of them? I say, then, that these things may hinder the soul greatly in its progress to Divine union because, if it pay heed to them, it is led far astray from the abyss of faith, where the understanding must remain in darkness, and must journey in darkness, by love and in faith, and not by much reasoning.

And if you ask me why the understanding must be deprived of these truths, since through them it is illumined by the Spirit of God, and thus they cannot be evil, I reply that the Holy Spirit illumines the understanding which is recollected, and illumines it according to the manner of its recollection, and that the understanding cannot find any other and greater recollection than in faith; and thus the Holy Spirit will illumine it in naught more than in faith. For the purer and the more refined in faith is the soul, the more it has of the infused charity of God; and the more charity it has, the more is it illumined and the more gifts of the Holy Spirit are communicated to it, for charity is the cause and the means whereby they are communicated to it. And although it is true that, in this illumination of truths, the Holy Spirit communicates a certain light to the soul, this is nevertheless as different in quality from that which is in faith, wherein is no clear understanding, as is the most precious gold from the basest metal; and, with regard to its quantity, the one is as much greater than the other as the sea is greater than a drop of water. For in the one manner there is communicated to the soul wisdom concerning one or two or three truths, etc., but in the other there is communicated to it all the wisdom of God in general, which is the Son of God, Who communicates Himself to the soul in faith.

And if you tell me that this is all good, and that the one impedes not the other, I reply that it impedes it greatly if the soul sets store by it; for to do this is to occupy itself with things which are clear and of little importance, yet which are sufficient to hinder the communication of the abyss of faith, wherein God supernaturally and secretly instructs the soul, and exalts it in virtues and gifts in a way that it knows not. And the profit which these successive communications will bring us cannot come by our deliberately applying the understanding to them, for if we do this they will rather lead us astray, even as Wisdom says to the soul in the Songs: 'Turn away thine eyes from me, for they make me to fly away.' That is so say: They make me to fly far away from thee and to set myself higher. We must therefore not apply the understanding to that which is being supernaturally communicated to it, but simply and sincerely apply the will to God with love, for it is through love that these good things are communicated and through love they will be communicated in greater abundance than before. For if the ability of the natural understanding or of other faculties be brought actively to bear upon these things which are communicated supernaturally and passively, its imperfect nature will not reach them, and thus they will perforce be modified according to the capacity of the understanding, and consequently will perforce be changed; and thus the understanding will necessarily go astray and begin to form reasonings within itself, and there will no longer be anything supernatural or any semblance thereof, but all will be merely natural and most erroneous and unworthy.

But there are certain types of understanding so quick and subtle that, when they become recollected during some meditation, they invent conceptions, and begin naturally, and with great facility, to form these conceptions into the most lifelike words and arguments, which they think, without any doubt, come from God. Yet all the time they come only from the understanding, which, with its natural illumination, being to some extent freed from the operation of the senses, is able to effect all this, and more, without any supernatural aid. This happens very commonly, and many persons are greatly deceived by it, thinking that they have attained to a high degree of prayer and are receiving communications from God, wherefore they either write this down or cause it to be written. And it turns out to be nothing, and to have the substance of no virtue, and it serves only to encourage them in vanity.

Let these persons learn to be intent upon naught, save only upon grounding the will in humble love, working diligently, suffering and thus imitating the Son of God in His life and mortifications, for it is by this road that a man will come to all spiritual good, rather than by much inward reasoning.

In this type of locution — namely, in successive interior words — the devil frequently intervenes, especially in the case of such as have some inclination or affection for them. At times when such persons begin to be recollected, the devil is accustomed to offer them ample material for distractions, forming conceptions or words by suggestion in their understanding, and then corrupting and deceiving it most subtly with things that have every appearance of being true. And this is one of the manners wherein he communicates with those who have made some implicit or expressed compact with him; as with certain heretics, especially with certain heresiarchs, whose understanding he fills with most subtle, false and erroneous conceptions and arguments.

From what has been said, it is evident that these successive locutions may proceed in the understanding from three causes, namely: from the Divine Spirit, Who moves and illumines the understanding; from the natural illumination of the same understanding; and from the devil, who may speak to the soul by suggestion. To describe now the signs and indications by which a man may know when they proceed from one cause and when from another would be somewhat difficult, as also to give examples and indications. It is quite possible, however, to give some general signs, which are these. When in its words and conceptions the soul finds itself loving God, and at the same time is conscious not only of love but also of humility and reverence, it is a sign that the Holy Spirit is working within it, for, whensoever He grants favours, He grants them with this accompaniment. When the locutions proceed solely from the vivacity and brilliance of the understanding, it is the understanding that accomplishes everything, without the operation of the virtues (although the will, in the knowledge and illumination of those truths, may love naturally); and, when the meditation is over, the will remains dry, albeit inclined neither to vanity nor to evil, unless the devil should tempt it afresh about this matter. This, however, is not the case when the locutions have been prompted by a good spirit; for then, as a rule, the will is afterwards affectioned to God and inclined to well-doing. At certain times, nevertheless, it will happen that, although the communication has been the work of a good spirit, the will remains in aridity, since God ordains it so for certain causes which are of assistance to the soul. At other times the soul will not be very conscious of the operations or motions of those virtues, yet that which it has experienced will be good. Wherefore I say that the difference between these locutions is sometimes difficult to recognize, by reason of the varied effects which they produce; but these which have now been described are the most common, although sometimes they occur in greater abundance and sometimes in less. But those that come from the devil are sometimes difficult to understand and recognize, for, although it is true that as a rule they leave the will in aridity with respect to love of God, and the mind inclined to vanity, self-esteem or complacency, nevertheless they sometimes inspire the soul with a false humility and a fervent affection of the will rooted in self-love, so that at times a person must be extremely spiritually-minded to recognize it. And this the devil does in order the better to protect himself; for he knows very well how sometimes to produce tears by the feelings which he inspires in a soul, in order that he may continue to implant in it the affections that he desires. But he always strives to move its will so that it may esteem those interior communications, attach great importance to them, and, as a result, give itself up to them and be occupied in that which is not virtue, but is rather the occasion of losing virtue as the soul may have.

Let us remember, then, this necessary caution, both as to the one type of locution and as to the other, so that we may not be deceived or hindered by them. Let us treasure none of them, but think only of learning to direct our will determinedly to God, fulfilling His law and His holy counsels perfectly, which is the wisdom of the Saints, and contenting ourselves with knowing the mysteries and truths

with the simplicity and truth wherewith the Church sets them before us. For this is sufficient to enkindle the will greatly, so that we need not pry into other deep and curious things wherein it is a wonder if there is no peril. For with respect to this Saint Paul says: It is not fitting to know more than it behoves us to know. And let this suffice with respect to this matter of successive words.

Chapter XXX

Which treats of the interior words that come to the spirit formally by supernatural means. Warns the reader of the harm which they may do and of the caution that is necessary in order that the soul may not be deceived by them.

The interior words belonging to the second type are formal words, which at certain times come to the spirit by supernatural means, without the intervention of any of the senses, sometimes when the spirit is recollected and at other times when it is not. I call them formal because they are communicated to the spirit formally by a third person, the spirit itself playing no part in this. And they are therefore very different from those which we have just described; because not only is there this difference, that they come without any such intervention of the spirit itself as takes place in the other case; but also, as I say, they sometimes come when the spirit is not recollected and even when it is far from thinking of the subject of what is being said to it. This is not so in the first type of locution — namely, that of successive words — which always has some relation to the subject which the soul is considering.

These words are sometimes very clearly formed and sometimes less so; for they are frequently like conceptions in which something is said to the spirit, whether in the form of a reply to it or in that of another manner of address. Sometimes there is only one word; sometimes there are two or more; sometimes the words succeed one another like those already described, for they are apt to be continuous, either instructing the soul or discussing something with it; and all this comes to pass without any part being played therein by the spirit, for it is just as though one person were speaking with another. In this way, we read, it came to pass with Daniel, who says that the angel spoke within him. This was a formal and successive discourse within his spirit, which instructed him, even as the angel declared at the time, saying that he had come to instruct him.

When these words are no more than formal, the effect which they produce upon the soul is not great. For ordinarily they serve only to instruct or illumine with respect to one thing; and, in order to produce this effect, it is not necessary that they should produce any other effect more efficacious than the purpose to which they are leading. And when they are of God they invariably work this in the soul; for they make it ready and quick to do that which it is commanded or instructed to do; yet at times they take not from it the repugnance or the difficulty which it feels, but are rather wont to increase these, according as God ordains for the better instruction, increased humility and greater good of the soul. And this repugnance most commonly occurs when the soul is commanded to do things of a high order, or things of a kind that may exalt it; when things are commanded it that conduce to its greater lowliness and humility, it responds with more readiness and ease. And thus we read in Exodus that, when God commanded Moses to go to Pharao and driver the people, he showed such great repugnance that He had to command him three times to do it and to perform signs for him; and all this was of no avail until God gave him Aaron for a companion to take part of the honour.

When, on the other hand, the words and communications are of the devil, it comes to pass that the soul responds with more ease and readiness to things that are of greater weight, and for lowlier things it conceives repugnance. The fact is that God so greatly abhors seeing souls attracted by high position that, even when He commands and obliges them to accept such positions, He desires them not to be ready and anxious to command. It is this readiness which God commonly inspires in the soul, through these formal words, that constitutes one great difference between them and those other successive words: the latter move not the spirit so much, neither do they inspire it with such readiness, since they are less formal, and since the understanding has more to do with them. Nevertheless successive words may sometimes produce a greater effect by reason of the close communication that there is at times between the Divine Spirit and the human. It is in the manner of their coming that there is a great difference between the two kinds of locution. With respect to formal words the soul can have no doubt as to whether or no it is pronouncing them itself, for it sees quite ready that it is not, especially when it has not been thinking of the subject of that which has been said to it; and even when it has been so thinking it feels very clearly and distinctly that the words come from elsewhere.

The soul must no more attach importance to all these formal words than to the other, or successive, words; for, apart from the fact that to do so would occupy the spirit with that which is not a legitimate and proximate means to union with God — namely, faith — it might also very easily cause it to be deceived by the devil. For sometimes it is hardly possible to know what words are spoken by a good spirit, and what by an evil spirit. By their effects they can hardly be distinguished at all, since neither kind produces effects of much importance: sometimes, indeed, with imperfect souls, words which come from the devil have more efficacy than have these others, which come from a good spirit, with souls that are spiritual. The soul, then, must take no account of what these words may express, nor attach any importance to them, whether the spirit from which they come be good or evil. But the words must be repeated to an experienced confessor, or to a discreet and learned person, that he may give instruction and see what it is well to do, and impart his advice; and the soul must behave, with regard to them, in a resigned and negative way. And, if such an expert person cannot be found, it is better to attach no importance to these words and to repeat them to nobody; for it is easy to find persons who will ruin the soul rather than edify it. Souls must not be given into the charge of any kind of director, since in so grave a matter it is of the greatest importance whether one goes astray or acts rightly.

And let it be carefully noted that a soul should never act according to its own opinion or accept anything of what these locutions express, without much reflection and without taking advice of another. For strange and subtle deceptions may arise in this matter; so much so that I myself believe that the soul that does not set itself against accepting such things cannot fail to be deceived by many of them.

And since we have treated of these deceptions and perils, and of the caution to be observed with regard to them, in Chapters seventeen, eighteen, nineteen and twenty of this book, I refer the reader to these and say no more on this matter here; I only repeat that my chief instruction is that the soul should attach no importance to these things in any way.

Chapter XXXI

Which treats of the substantial words that come interiorly to the spirit. Describes the difference between them and formal words, and the profit which they bring and the resignation and respect which the soul must observe with regard to them.

The third kind of interior words, we said, is called substantial. These substantial words, although they are likewise formal, since they are impressed upon the soul in a definitely formal way, differ, nevertheless, in that substantial words produce vivid and substantial effects upon the soul, whereas words which are merely formal do not. So that, although it is true that every substantial word is formal, every formal word is not therefore substantial, but only, as we said above, such a word as impresses substantially on the soul that which it signifies. It is as if Our Lord were to say formally to the soul: 'Be thou good'; it would then be substantially good. Or as if He were to say to it: 'Love thou Me'; it would then have and feel within itself the substance of love for God. Or as if it feared greatly and He said to it: 'Fear thou not'; it would at once feel within itself great fortitude and tranquility. For the saying of God, and His word, as the Wise Man says, is full of power; and thus that which He says to the soul He produces substantially within it. For it is this that David meant when he said: 'See, He will give to His voice a voice of virtue.' And even so with Abraham, when He said to him: 'Walk in My presence and be perfect': he was then perfect and walked ever in the fear of God. And this is the power of His word in the Gospel, wherewith He healed the sick, raised the dead, etc., by no more than a word. And after this manner He gives certain souls locutions which are substantial; and they are of such moment and price that they are life and virtue and incomparable good to the soul; for one of these words works greater good within the soul than all that the soul itself has done throughout its life.

With respect to these words, the soul should do nothing. It should neither desire them nor refrain from desiring them; it should neither reject them nor fear them. It should do nothing in the way of executing what these words express, for these substantial words are never pronounced by God in order that the soul may translate them into action, but that He may so translate them within the soul; herein they differ from formal and successive words. And I say that the soul must neither desire nor refrain from desiring, since its desire is not necessary for God to translate these words into effect, nor is it sufficient for the soul to refrain from desiring in order for the said effect not to be produced. Let the soul rather be resigned and humble with respect to them. It must not reject them, since the effect of these words remains substantially within it and is full of the good which comes from God. As the soul receives this good passively, its action is at no time of any importance. Nor should it fear any deception; for neither the understanding nor the devil can intervene herein, nor can they succeed in passively producing this substantial effect in the soul, in such a way that the effect and habit of the locution may be impressed upon it, unless the soul should have given itself to the devil by a voluntary compact, and he should have dwelt in it as its master, and impressed upon it these effects, not of good, but of evil. Inasmuch as that soul would be already voluntarily united to him in perversity, the devil might easily impress upon it the effects of his sayings and words with evil intent. For we see by experience that in many things and even upon good souls he works great violence, by means of suggestion, making his suggestions very efficacious; and if they were evil he might work in them the consummation of these suggestions. But he cannot leave upon a soul effects similar to those of locutions which are good; for there is no comparison between the locutions of the devil and those of God. The former are all as though they were not, in comparison with the latter, neither do they produce any effect at all compared with the effect of these. For this cause God says through Jeremias: 'What has the chaff to do with the wheat? Are not My words perchance as fire, and as a hammer that breaketh the rock in pieces?' And thus these substantial words are greatly conducive to the union of the soul with God; and the more interior they are, the more substantial are they, and the greater is the profit that they bring. Happy is the soul to whom God addresses these words. Speak, Lord, for Thy servant heareth.

Chapter XXXII

Which treats of the apprehensions received by the understanding from interior feelings which come supernaturally to the soul. Describes their cause, and the manner wherein the soul must conduct itself so that they may not obstruct its road to union with God.

It is now time to treat of the fourth and last kind of intellectual apprehension which we said might come to the understanding through the spiritual feelings which are frequently produced supernaturally in the souls of spiritual persons and which we count amongst the distinct apprehensions of the understanding.

These distinct spiritual feelings may be of two kinds. The first kind is in the affection of the will. The second, in the substance of the soul. Each of these may be of many kinds. Those of the will, when they are of God, are most sublime; but those that are of the substance of the soul are very high and of great good and profit. As to these, neither the soul nor he that treats with it can know or understand the cause whence they proceed, or what are the acts whereby God may grant it these favours; for they depend not upon any works performed by the soul, nor upon its meditations, although both these things are a good preparation for them: God grants these favours to whom He wills and for what reason He wills. For it may come to pass that a person will have performed many good works, yet that He will not give him these touches of His favour; and another will have done far fewer good works, yet He will give him them to a most sublime degree and in great abundance. And thus it is not needful that the soul should be actually employed and occupied in spiritual things (although it is much better that it should be so employed if it is to have these favours) for God to give it these touches in which the soul experiences the said feelings; for in the majority of cases the soul is completely heedless of them. Of these touches, some are distinct and pass quickly away; others are less distinct and last longer.

These feelings, inasmuch as they are feelings only, belong not to the understanding but to the will; and thus I refrain, of set purpose, from treating of them here, nor shall I do so until we treat of the night and purgation of the will in its affections: this will be in the third book, which follows this. But since frequently, and even in the majority of cases, apprehensions and knowledge and intelligence overflow from them into the understanding, it would be well to make mention of them here, for that reason only. It must be known, then, that from these feelings, both from those of the will and from those which are in the substance of the soul, whether they are caused suddenly by the touches of God, or are durable and successive, an apprehension of knowledge or intelligence frequently overflows, as I say, into the understanding; and this is normally a most sublime perception of God, most delectable to the understanding, to which no name can be given, any more than to the feeling whence it overflows. And these manifestations of knowledge are sometimes of one kind and sometimes of another; sometimes they are clearer and more sublime, according to the nature of the touches which come from God and which produce the feelings whence they proceed, and according also to their individual characteristics.

It is unnecessary here to spend a great store of words in cautioning and directing the understanding, through these manifestations of knowledge, in faith, to union with God. For albeit the feelings which we have described are produced passively in the soul, without any effective assistance to that end on its own part, even so likewise is the knowledge of them received passively in the understanding, in a way called by the philosophers 'passible,' wherein the understanding plays no part. Wherefore, in order not to go astray on their account nor to impede the profit which comes from them, the understanding must do nothing in connection with these feelings, but must conduct itself passively, and not interfere by applying to them its natural capacity. For, as we have said is the case with successive locutions, the understanding, with its activity, would very easily disturb and ruin the effect of these delicate manifestations of knowledge, which are a delectable supernatural intelligence that human nature cannot attain or apprehend by its own efforts, but only by remaining in a state of receptivity. And thus the soul must not strive to attain them or desire to receive them, lest the understanding should form other manifestations of its own, or the devil should make his entry with still more that are different from them and false. This he may very well do by means of the feelings aforementioned, or of those which he can himself infuse into the soul that devotes itself to these kinds of knowledge. Let the soul be resigned, humble and passive herein, for, since it receives this knowledge passively from God, He will communicate it whensoever He is pleased, if He sees the soul to be humble and detached. And in this way the soul will do nothing to counteract the help which these kinds of knowledge give it in its progress toward Divine union, which help is great; for these touches are all touches of union, which is wrought passively in the soul.

What has been said concerning this suffices, for no matter what may happen to the soul with respect to the understanding, cautions and instructions have been given it in the sections already mentioned. And although a case may appear to be different and to be in no way included herein, there is none that cannot be referred to one of these, and thus may be deduced the instruction necessary for it.

BOOK THE THIRD

Which treats of the purgation of the active night of the memory and will. Gives instruction how the soul is to behave with respect to the apprehensions of these two faculties, that it may come to union with God, according to the two faculties aforementioned, in perfect hope and charity.

Chapter 1

The first faculty of the soul, which is the understanding, has now been instructed, through all its apprehensions, in the first theological virtue, which is faith, to the end that, according to this faculty, the soul may be united with God by means of the purity of faith. It now remains to do likewise with respect to the other two faculties of the soul, which are memory and will, and to purify them likewise with respect to their apprehensions, to the end that, according to these two faculties also, the soul may come to union with God in perfect hope and charity. This will briefly be effected in this third book. We have now concluded our treatment of the understanding, which is the receptacle of all other objects according to its mode of operation; and in treating of this we have gone a great part of the whole way. It is therefore unnecessary for us to write at equal length with respect to these faculties; for it is not possible that, if the spiritual man instructs his understanding in faith according to the doctrine which has been given him, he should not, in so doing, instruct the other two faculties in the other two virtues likewise; for the operations of each faculty depend upon the others.

But since, in order to follow our manner of procedure, and in order, too, that we may be the better understood, we must necessarily speak of the proper and determinate matter, we shall here be obliged to set down the apprehensions proper to each faculty, and first, those of the memory, making here such distinction between them as suffices for our purpose. This we shall be able to deduce from the distinction between their objects, which are three: natural, imaginary and spiritual; according to which there are likewise three kinds of knowledge which come from the memory, namely: natural and supernatural, imaginary and spiritual.

All these, by the Divine favour, we shall treat here in due course, beginning with natural knowledge, which pertains to the most exterior objects. And we shall then treat of the affections of the will, wherewith we shall conclude this third book of the active spiritual night.

Chapter II

Which treats of the natural apprehensions of the memory and describes how the soul must be voided of them in order to be able to attain to union with God according to this faculty.

It is necessary that, in each of these books, the reader should bear in mind the purpose of which we are speaking. For otherwise there may arise within him many such questions with respect to what he is reading as might by this time be occurring to him with respect to what we have said of the understanding, and shall say now of the memory, and afterwards shall say of the will. For, seeing how we annihilate the faculties with respect to their operations, it may perhaps seem to him that we are destroying the road of spiritual practice rather than constructing it.

This would be true if we were seeking here only to instruct beginners, who are best prepared through these apprehensible and discursive apprehensions. But, since we are here giving instruction to those who would progress farther in contemplation, even to union with God, to which end all of these means and exercises of sense concerning the faculties must recede into the background, and be put to silence, to the end that God may of His own accord work Divine union in the soul, it is necessary to proceed by this method of disencumbering and emptying the soul, and causing it to reject the natural jurisdiction and operations of the faculties, so that they may become capable of infusion and illumination from supernatural sources; for their capacity cannot attain to so lofty an experience, but will rather hinder it, if it be not disregarded.

And thus, if it be true, as it is, that the soul must proceed in its growing knowledge of God by learning that which He is not rather than that which He is, in order to come to Him, it must proceed by renouncing and rejecting, to the very uttermost, everything in its apprehensions that it is possible to renounce, whether this be natural or supernatural. We shall proceed with this end in view with regard to the memory, drawing it out from its natural state and limitations, and causing it to rise above itself — that is, above all distinct knowledge and apprehensible possession — to the supreme hope of God, Who is incomprehensible.

Beginning, then, with natural knowledge, I say that natural knowledge in the memory consists of all the kinds of knowledge that the memory can form concerning the objects of the five bodily senses — namely: hearing, sight, smell, taste and touch — and all kinds of knowledge of this type which it is possible to form and fashion. Of all these forms and kinds of knowledge the soul must strip and void itself, and it must strive to lose the imaginary apprehension of them, so that there may be left in it no kind of impression of knowledge, nor trace of aught soever, but rather the soul must remain barren and bare, as if these forms had never passed through it, and in total oblivion and suspension. And this cannot happen unless the memory be annihilated as to all its forms, if it is to be united with God. For it cannot happen save by total separation from all forms which are not God; for God comes beneath no definite form or kind of knowledge whatsoever, as we have said in treating of the night of the understanding. And since, as Christ says, no man can serve two masters, the memory cannot be united both with God and with forms and distinct kinds of knowledge and, as God has no form or image that can be comprehended by the memory, it follows that, when the memory is united with God (as is seen, too, every day by experience), it remains without form and without figure, its imagination being lost and itself being absorbed in a supreme good, and in a great oblivion, remembering nothing. For that Divine union voids its fancy and sweeps it clean of all forms and kinds of knowledge and raises it to the supernatural.

Now there sometimes comes to pass here a notable thing; for occasionally, when God brings about these touches of union in the memory, the brain (where memory has its seat) is so perceptibly upset that it seems as if it becomes quite inert, and its judgment and sense are lost. This is sometimes more perceptible and sometimes less so, according to the strength of this touch, and then, by reason of this union, the memory is voided and purged, as I say, of all kinds of knowledge. It remains in oblivion — at times in complete oblivion — so that it has to put forth a great effort and to labour greatly in order to remember anything.

And sometimes this oblivion of the memory and suspension of the imagination reach such a point, because of the union of the memory with God, that a long time passes without the soul's perceiving it, or knowing what has taken place during that period. And, as the imaginative faculty is then in suspension, it feels naught that is done to it, not even things that cause pain; for without imagination there is no feeling, not even coming through thought, since this exists not. And, to the end that God may bring about these touches of union, the soul must needs withdraw its memory from all apprehensible kinds of knowledge. And it is to be noted that these suspensions come not to pass in those that are already perfect, since they have attained to perfect union, and these suspensions belong to the beginnings of union.

Someone will remark that all this seems very well, but that it leads to the destruction of the natural use and course of the faculties, and reduces man to the state of a beast — a state of oblivion and even worse — since he becomes incapable of reasoning or of remembering his natural functions and necessities. It will be argued that God destroys not nature, but rather perfects it; and that from this teaching there necessarily follows its destruction, when that which pertains to morality and reason is not practised and is forgotten, neither is that which is natural practised; for (it will be said) none of these things can be remembered, as the soul is deprived of forms and kinds of knowledge which are the means of remembrance.

To this I reply that, the more nearly the memory attains to union with God, the more do distinct kinds of knowledge become perfected within it, until it loses them entirely — namely, when it attains to the state of union in perfection. And thus, at the beginning, when this is first taking place, the soul cannot but fall into great oblivion with respect to all things, since forms and kinds of knowledge are being erased from it; and therefore it is very negligent concerning its outward behaviour and usage — forgetting to eat or drink, and being uncertain if it has done this or no, if it has seen this or no, if it has said this or no — because of the absorption of the memory in God. But when once it attains to the habit of union, which is a supreme blessing, it no longer has these periods of oblivion, after this manner, in that which pertains to natural and moral reason; actions which are seemly and necessary, indeed, it performs with a much greater degree of pection, although it performs them no longer by means of forms and manners of knowledge pertaining to the memory. For, when it has the habit of union, which is a supernatural state, memory and the other faculties fail it completely in their natural functions, and pass beyond their natural limitations, even to God, Who is supernatural. And thus, when the memory is transformed in God, it cannot receive impressions of forms or kinds of knowledge. Wherefore the functions of the memory and of the other faculties in this state are all Divine; for, when at last God possesses the faculties and has become the entire master of them, through their transformation into Himself, it is He Himself Who moves and commands them divinely, according to His Divine Spirit and will; and the result of this is that the operations of the soul are not distinct, but all that it does is of God, and its operations are Divine, so that, even as Saint Paul says, he that is joined unto God becomes one spirit with Him.

Hence it comes to pass that the operations of the soul in union are of the Divine Spirit and are Divine. And hence it comes that the actions of such souls are only those that are seemly and reasonable, and not those that are ill-beseeming. For the Spirit of God teaches them that which they ought to know, and causes them to be ignorant of that which it behoves them not to know, and to remember that which they have to remember, with or without forms, and to forget that which they should forget; and it makes them love that which they have to love, and not to love that which is not in God. And thus, all the first motions of the faculties of such souls are Divine and it is not to be wondered at that the motions and operations of these faculties should be Divine, since they are transformed in the Divine Being.

Of these operations I will give a few examples. Let this be one. A person asks another who is in this state to commend him to God. This person will not remember to do so by means of any form or kind of knowledge that remains in his memory concerning that other person; if it be right that he should recommend him to God (which will be if God desires to receive a prayer for that person), He will move his will and give him a desire to pray for him; and if God desires not such prayer, that other person will not be able nor will desire to pray,' though he make great efforts to do so; and at times God will cause him to pray for others of whom he has no knowledge nor has ever heard. And this is because, as I have said, God alone moves the faculties of these souls to do those works which are meet, according to the will and ordinance of God, and they cannot be moved to do others; and thus the works and prayers of these souls are always effectual. Such were those of the most glorious Virgin Our Lady, who, being raised to this high estate from the beginning, had never the form of any creature imprinted in her soul, neither was moved by such, but was invariably guided by the Holy Spirit.

Another example. At a certain time a person in this state has to attend to some necessary business. He will remember it by no kind of form, but, without his knowing how, it will come to his soul, at the time and in the manner that it ought to come, and that without fail.

And not only in these things does the Holy Spirit give such persons light, but also in many others, relating both to the present and to the future, and even, in many cases, as regards those absent from them; and although at times this comes to pass through intellectual forms, it frequently happens without the intervention of any forms that can be apprehended, so that these persons know not how they know. But this comes to them from the Divine Wisdom; for, since these souls exercise themselves in knowing and apprehending nothing with the faculties, they come in general, as we have said in the Mount, to know everything, according to that which the Wise Man says: 'The worker of all things, who is Wisdom, taught me all things.'

You will say, perhaps, that the soul will be unable to void and deprive its memory of all forms and fancies to such an extent as to be able to attain to so lofty a state; for there are two things so difficult that their accomplishment surpasses human ability and strength, namely, to throw off with one's natural powers that which is natural, which is hard enough, and to attain and be united to the supernatural, which is much more difficult — indeed, to speak the truth, is impossible with natural ability alone. The truth, I repeat, is that God must place the soul in this supernatural state; but the soul, as far as in it lies, must be continually preparing itself; and this it can do by natural means, especially with the help that God is continually giving it. And thus, as the soul, for its own part, enters into this renunciation and self-emptying of forms, so God begins to give it the possession of union; and this God works passively in the soul, as we shall say, Deo dante, when we treat of the passive night of the soul. And thus, when it shall please God, and according to the manner of the soul's preparation, He will grant it the habit of perfect and Divine union.

And the Divine effects which God produces in the soul when He has granted it this habit, both as to the understanding and as to the memory and will, we shall not describe in this account of the soul's active purgation and night, for this alone will not bring the soul to Divine union. We shall speak of these effects, however, in treating of the passive night, by means of which is brought about the union of the soul with God. And so I shall speak here only of the necessary means whereby the memory may place itself actively in this night and purgation, as far as lies in its power. And these means are that the spiritual man must habitually exercise caution, after this manner. All the things that he hears, sees, smells, tastes, or touches, he must be careful not to store up or collect in his memory, but he must allow himself to forget them immediately, and this he must accomplish, if need be, with the same efficacy as that with which others contrive to remember them, so that there remains in his memory no knowledge or image of them whatsoever. It must be with him as if they existed not in the world, and his memory must be left free and disencumbered of them, and be tied to no consideration, whether from above or from below; as if he had no faculty of memory; he must freely allow everything to fall into oblivion as though all things were a hindrance to him; and in fact everything that is natural, if one attempt to make use of it in supernatural matters, is a hindrance rather than a help.

And if those questions and objections which arose above with respect to the understanding should also arise here (the objections, that is to say, that the soul is doing nothing, is wasting its time and is depriving itself of spiritual blessings which it might well receive through the memory), the answer to this has already been given, and will be given again farther on, in our treatment of the passive night; wherefore there is no need for us to dwell upon it here. It is needful only to observe that, although at certain times the benefit of this suspension of forms and of all knowledge may not be realized, the spiritual man must not for that reason grow weary, for in His own time God will not fail to succour him. To attain so great a blessing it behoves the soul to endure much and to suffer with patience and hope.

And, although it is true that hardly any soul will be found that is moved by God in all things and at all times, and has such continual union with God that, without the mediation of any form, its faculties are ever moved divinely, there are nevertheless souls who in their operations are very habitually moved by God, and these are not they that are moved of themselves, for, as Saint Paul says, the sons of God who are transformed and united in God, are moved by the Spirit of God, that is, are moved to perform Divine work in their faculties. And it is no marvel that their operations should be Divine, since the union of the soul is Divine.

Chapter III

Wherein are described three kinds of evil which come to the soul when it enters not into darkness with respect to knowledge and reflections in the memory. Herein is described the first.

To three kinds of evil and inconvenience the spiritual man is subject when he persists in desiring to make use of all natural knowledge and reflections of the memory in order to journey toward God, or for any other purpose: two of these are positive and one is privative. The first comes from things of the world; the second, from the devil; the third, which is privative, is the impediment and hindrance to Divine union caused and effected in the soul.

The first evil, which comes from the world, consists in the subjection of the soul, through knowledge and reflection, to many kinds of harm, such as falsehoods, imperfections, desires, opinions, loss of time, and many other things which breed many kinds of impurity in the soul. And it is clear that the soul must of necessity fall into many perils of falsehood, when it admits knowledge and reasoning; for oftentimes that which is true must appear false, and that which is certain, doubtful; and contrariwise; for there is scarcely a single truth of which we can have complete knowledge. From all these things the soul is free if the memory enters into darkness with respect to every kind of reflection and knowledge.

Imperfections meet the soul at every step if it sets its memory upon that which it has heard, seen, touched, smelt and tasted; for there must then perforce cling to it some affection, whether this be of pain, of fear, of hatred, of vain hope, vain enjoyment, vainglory, etc.; for all these are, at the least, imperfections, and at times are downright venial sins; and they leave much impurity most subtly in the soul, even though the reflections and the knowledge have relation to God. And it is also clear that they engender desires within the soul, for these arise naturally from the knowledge and reflections aforementioned, and if one wishes only to have this knowledge and these reflections, even that is a desire. And it is clearly seen that many occasions of judging others will come likewise; for, in using its memory, the soul cannot fail to come upon that which is good and bad in others, and, in such a case, that which is evil oftentimes seems good, and that which is good, evil. I believe there is none who can completely free himself from all these kinds of evil, save by blinding his memory and leading it into darkness with regard to all these things.

And if you tell me that a man is well able to conquer all these things when they come to him, I reply that, if he sets store by knowledge, this is simply and utterly impossible; for countless imperfections and follies insinuate themselves into such knowledge, some of which are so subtle and minute that, without the soul's realization thereof, they cling to it of their own accord, even as pitch clings to the man that touches it; so that it is better to conquer once for all by denying the memory completely. You will say likewise that by so doing the soul deprives itself of many good thoughts and meditations upon God, which are of great profit to it and whereby God grants it favours. I reply that to this end purity of soul is of the greatest profit, which means that there clings to the soul no creature affection, or temporal affection, or effective advertence; which I believe cannot but cling to the soul because of the imperfection which the faculties have in their own operations. Wherefore it is best to learn to silence the faculties and to cause them to be still, so that God may speak. For, as we have said, in order to attain to this state the natural operations must be completely disregarded, and this happens, as the Prophet says, when the soul comes into solitude, according to these its faculties, and God speaks to its heart.

And if you again reply, saying that the soul will have no blessing unless it meditates upon God and allows its memory to reflect upon Him, and that many distractions and negligences will continually enter it, I say that it is impossible, if the memory be recollected with regard both to things of the next life and to things here below, that evils or distractions should enter it, nor any other follies or vices (the which things always enter when the memory wanders), since there is no exit or entrance for them. This would come to pass if, when we had shut the door upon considerations and reflections concerning things above, we opened it to things below; but in this state we shut the door to all things whence distraction may come, causing the memory to be still and dumb, and the ear of the spirit to be attentive, in silence, to God alone, saying with the Prophet: 'Speak, Lord, for Thy servant heareth.' It was thus that the Spouse in the Songs said that his Bride should be, in these words: 'My sister is a garden enclosed and a fountain sealed up' — that is to say, enclosed and sealed up against all things that may enter.

Let the soul, then, remain 'enclosed,' without anxieties and troubles, and He that entered in bodily form to His disciples when the doors were shut, and gave them peace, though they neither knew nor thought that this was possible nor knew how it was possible, will enter spiritually into the soul, without its knowing how He does so, when the doors of its faculties — memory, understanding and will — are enclosed against all apprehensions. And He will fill them with peace, coming down upon the soul, as the prophet says, like a river of peace, and taking it from all the misgivings and suspicions, disturbances and darknesses which caused it to fear that it was lost or was on the way to being so. Let it not grow careless about prayer, and let it wait in detachment and emptiness, for its blessings will not tarry.

Chapter IV

Which treats of the second kind of evil that may come to the soul from the devil by way of the natural apprehensions of the memory.

The second positive evil that may come to the soul by means of the knowledge of the memory proceeds from the devil, who by this means obtains great influence over it. For he can continually bring it new forms, kinds of knowledge and reflections, by means whereof he can taint the soul with pride, avarice, wrath, envy, etc., and cause it unjust hatred, or vain love, and deceive it in many ways. And besides this, he is wont to leave impressions, and to implant them in the fancy, in such wise that those that are false appear true, and those that are true, false, And finally all the worst deceptions which are caused by the devil, and the evils that he brings to the soul, enter by way of knowledge and reflections of the memory, Thus if the memory enter into darkness with respect to them all, and be annihilated in its oblivion to them, it shuts the door altogether upon this evil which proceeds from the devil, and frees itself from all these things, which is a great blessing. For the devil has no power over the soul unless it be through the operations of its faculties, principally by means of knowledge, whereupon depend almost all the other operations of the other faculties. Wherefore, if the memory be annihilated with respect to them, the devil can do naught; for he finds no foothold, and without a foothold he is powerless.

I would that spiritual persons might clearly see how many kinds of harm are wrought by evil spirits in their souls by means of the memory, when they devote themselves frequently to making use of it, and how many kinds of sadness and affliction and vain and evil joys they have, both with respect to their thoughts about God, and also with respect to the things of the world; and how many impurities are left rooted in their spirits; and likewise how greatly they are distracted from the highest recollection, which consists in the fixing of the whole soul, according to its faculties, upon the one incomprehensible Good, and in withdrawing it from all things that can be apprehended, since these are not incomprehensible Good. This is a great good (although less good results from this emptiness than from the soul's fixing itself upon God), simply because it is the cause whereby the soul frees itself from any griefs and afflictions and sorrows, over and above the imperfections and sins from which it is freed.

Chapter V

Of the third evil which comes to the soul by way of the distinct natural knowledge or the memory.

The third evil which comes to the soul through the natural apprehensions of the memory is privative; for these apprehensions can hinder moral good and deprive us of spiritual good. And, in order that we may first of all explain how these apprehensions hinder moral good in the soul, it must be known that moral good consists in the restraining of the passions and the curbing of disorderly desires, from which restraint there come to the soul tranquillity, peace and rest, and moral virtues, all of which things are moral good. This restraining and curbing of the passions cannot be truly accomplished by the soul that forgets not and withdraws not itself from things pertaining to itself, whence arise the affections; and no disturbances ever arise in the soul save through the apprehensions of the memory. For, when all things are forgotten, there is naught that can disturb peace or that moves the desires; since, as they say, that which the eye sees not the heart desires not.

This we are constantly learning by experience; for we observe that, whenever the soul begins to think of any matter, it is moved and disturbed, either much or little, with respect to that thing, according to the nature of its apprehension. If it be a troublesome and grievous matter, the soul finds sadness in it; if pleasant, desire and joy, and so forth. Wherefore the result of the changing of that apprehension is necessarily disturbance; and thus the soul is now joyful, now sad; now it hates, now loves; and it cannot continue in one and the same attitude (which is an effect of moral tranquillity save when it strives to forget all things. It is clear, then, that knowledge greatly hinders the good of the moral virtues in the soul.

Again, what has been said clearly proves that an encumbered memory also hinders spiritual good; for the soul that is disturbed, and has no foundation of moral good, is to that extent incapable of spiritual good, which impresses itself only upon souls that are restrained and at peace. And besides this, if the soul pays attention and heed to the apprehensions of the memory — seeing that it can attend to but one thing at a time — and busies itself with things that can be apprehended, such as the knowledge of the memory, it is not possible for it to be free to attend to the incomprehensible, which is God. For, in order to approach God, the soul must proceed by not comprehending rather than by comprehending; it must exchange the mutable and comprehensible for the immutable and incomprehensible.

Chapter VI

Of the benefits which come to the soul from forgetfulness and emptiness of all thoughts and knowledge which it may have in a natural way with respect to the memory.

From the evils which, as we have said, come to the soul through the apprehensions of the memory, we can likewise infer the benefits which are contrary to them and come to the soul as a result of its forgetting them and emptying itself of them. For, as natural philosophy puts it, the same doctrine which serves for one thing serves likewise for the contrary. In the first place, the soul enjoys tranquillity and peace of mind, since it is freed from the disturbance and the changeableness which arise from thoughts and ideas of the memory, and consequently, which is more important, it enjoys purity of conscience and soul. And herein the soul has ample preparation for the acquiring of Divine and human wisdom, and of the virtues.

In the second place, it is freed from many suggestions, temptations and motions of the devil, which he infuses into the soul by means of thoughts and ideas, causing it to fall into many impurities and sins, as David says in these words: 'They have thought and spoken wickedness.' And thus, when these thoughts have been completely removed, the devil has naught wherewith to assault the soul by natural means.

In the third place, the soul has within itself, through this recollection of itself and this forgetfulness as to all things, a preparedness to be moved by the Holy Spirit and taught by Him, for, as the Wise Man says, He removes Himself from thoughts that are without understanding. Even if a man received no other benefit from this forgetfulness and emptiness of the memory than being freed thereby from troubles and disturbances, it would be a great gain and good for him. For the troubles and storms which adverse things and happenings arouse in the soul are of no use or help for bringing peace and calm; indeed, as a rule, they make things worse and also harm the soul itself. Wherefore David said: 'Of a truth every man is disquieted in vain.' For it is clear that to disquiet oneself is always vain since it brings profit to none. And thus, even if everything came to an end and were destroyed, and if all things went wrong and turned to adversity, it would be vain to disturb oneself; for such disturbance hurts a man rather than relieves him. Whereas to bear everything with equable and peaceful tranquillity not only brings the soul the profit of many blessings, but likewise causes it, even in the midst of its adversities, to form a truer judgment about them and to find a fitting remedy.

For this reason Solomon, being well acquainted both with the evil and with the benefit of which we are speaking, said: 'I knew that there was naught better for man than to rejoice and to do good in his life.' By this he meant that, in everything that happens to us, howsoever adverse it be, we should rejoice rather than be disturbed, so that we may not lose a blessing which is greater than any kind of prosperity — namely, tranquillity and peace of mind in all things, which, whether they bring adversity or prosperity, we must bear in the same manner. This a man would never lose if he were not only to forget all kinds of knowledge and put aside all thoughts, but would even withdraw himself from hearing, sight and commerce with others, in so far as was possible for him. Our nature is so frail and unstable that, however well it be disciplined, it will hardly fail to stumble upon the remembrance of things which will disturb and change a mind that was in peace and tranquillity when it remembered them not. For this cause said Jeremias: 'With memory I will remember, and my soul will fail me for pain.'

Chapter VII

Which treats or the second kind or apprehension of the memory — namely, imaginary apprehensions — and of supernatural knowledge.

Although in writing of natural apprehensions of the first kind we also gave instruction concerning the imaginary, which are likewise natural, it was well to make this division because of the love which the memory always has for other forms and kinds of knowledge, which are of supernatural things, such as visions, revelations, locutions and feelings which come in a supernatural way. When these things have passed through the soul, there is wont to remain impressed upon it some image, form, figure or idea, whether in the soul or in the memory or fancy, at times very vividly and effectively. Concerning these images it is also needful to give advice, lest the memory be encumbered with them and they be a hindrance to its union with God in perfect and pure hope.

I say that the soul, in order to attain that blessing, must never reflect upon the clear and distinct objects which may have passed through its mind by supernatural means, in such a way as to preserve within itself the forms and figures and knowledge of those things. For we must ever bear in mind this principle: the greater heed the soul gives to any clear and distinct apprehensions, whether natural or supernatural, the less capacity and preparation it has for entering into the abyss of faith, wherein are absorbed all things else. For, as has been said, no supernatural forms or kinds of knowledge which can be apprehended by the memory are God, and, in order to reach God, the soul must void itself of all that is not God. The memory must also strip itself of all these forms and kinds of knowledge, that it may unite itself with God in hope. For all possession is contrary to hope, which, as Saint Paul says, belongs to that which is not possessed. Wherefore, the more the memory dispossesses itself, the greater is its hope; and the more it has of hope, the more it has of union with God; for, with respect to God, the more the soul hopes, the more it attains. And it hopes most when it is most completely dispossessed; and, when it shall be perfectly dispossessed, it will remain with the perfect possession of God, in Divine union. But there are many who will not deprive themselves of the sweetness and delight which memory finds in those forms and notions, wherefore they attain not to supreme possession and perfect sweetness. For he that renounces not all that he possesses cannot be the disciple of Christ.

Chapter VIII

Of the evils which may be caused in the soul by the knowledge of supernatural things, if it reflect upon them. Says how many these evils are.

The spiritual man incurs the risk of five kinds of evil if he pays heed to, and reflects upon, these forms and ideas which are impressed upon him by the things which pass through his mind in a supernatural way.

The first is that he is frequently deceived, and mistakes one thing for another. The second is that he is like to fall, and is exposed to the danger of falling, into some form of presumption or vanity. The third is that the devil has many occasions of deceiving him by means of the apprehensions aforementioned. The fourth is that he is hindered as to union in hope with God. The fifth is that, for the most part, he has a low judgment of God.

As to the first evil, it is clear that, if the spiritual man pays heed to these forms and notions, and reflects upon them, he must frequently be deceived in his judgment of them; for, as no man can have a complete understanding of the things that pass through his imagination naturally, nor a perfect and certain judgment about them, he will be much less able still to have this with respect to supernatural things, which are above our capacity to understand, and occur but rarely. Wherefore he will often think that what comes but from his fancy pertains to God; and often, too, that what is of God is of the devil, and what is of the devil is of God. And very often there will remain with him deap-seated impressions of forms and ideas concerning the good and evil of others, or of himself, together with other figures which have been presented to him: these he will consider to be most certain and true, when in fact they will not be so, but very great falsehoods. And others will be true, and he will judge them to be false, although this error I consider safer, as it is apt to arise from humility.

And, even if he be not deceived as to their truth, he may well be deceived as to their quantity or quality, thinking that little things are great, and great things, little. And with respect to their quality, he may consider what is in his imagination to be this or that, when it is something quite different; he may put, as Isaias says, darkness for light, and light for darkness, or bitter for sweet, and sweet for bitter. And finally, even though he be correct as to one thing, it will be a marvel if he goes not astray with respect to the next; for, although he may not desire to apply his judgment to the judging of them, yet, if he apply it in paying heed to them, this will be sufficient to make some evil to cling to him as a result of it, at least passively; if not evil of this kind, then of one of the four other kinds of which we shall shortly speak.

It behoves the spiritual man, therefore, lest he fall into this evil of being deceived in his judgment, not to desire to apply his judgment in order to know the nature of his own condition or feelings, or the nature of such and such a vision, idea or feeling; neither should he desire to know it or to pay heed to it. This he should only desire in order to speak of it to his spiritual father, and to be taught by him how to void his memory of these apprehensions. For, whatever may be their intrinsic nature, they cannot help him to love God as much as the smallest act of living faith and hope performed in the emptiness and renunciation of all things.

Chapter IX

Of the second kind of evil, which is the peril of falling into self-esteem and vain presumption.

The supernatural apprehensions of the memory already described are also a frequent occasion to spiritual persons of falling into some kind of presumption or vanity, if they give heed to them and set store by them. For, even as he who knows nothing of them is quite free from falling into this vice, since he sees in himself no occasion of presumption, even so, in contrary wise, he that has experience of them has close at hand an occasion for thinking himself to be something, since he possesses these supernatural communications. For, although it is true that he may attribute them to God, hold himself to be unworthy of them, and give God the thanks, yet nevertheless there is wont to remain in his spirit a certain secret satisfaction, and a self-esteem and a sense of their value, from which, without his knowledge, there will come to him great spiritual pride.

This may be observed very clearly by such as will consider the dislike and aversion caused them by any who do not praise their spirituality, or esteem the experiences which they enjoy, and the mortification which they suffer when they think or are told that others have just those same experiences, or even superior ones. All this arises from secret self-esteem and pride, and they can never quite realize that they are steeped in pride up to their very eyes. For they think that a certain degree of recognition of their own wretchedness suffices, and, although they have this, they are full of secret self-esteem and self-satisfaction, taking more delight in their own spirituality and spiritual gifts than in those of others. They are like the Pharisee who gave thanks to God that he was not as other men, and that he practised such and such virtues, whereat he was satisfied with himself and presumed thereon. Such men, although they may not use the Pharisee's actual words, habitually resemble him in spirit. And some of them even become so proud that they are worse than the devil. For, observing in themselves, as they imagine, certain apprehensions and feelings concerning God which are devout and sweet, they become self-satisfied to such an extent that they believe themselves to be very near God; and those that are not like themselves they consider very low and despise them after the manner of the Pharisee.

In order to flee from this pestilent evil, abhorrent in the eyes of God, they must consider two things. First, that virtue consists not in apprehensions and feelings concerning God, howsoever sublime they be, nor in anything of this kind that a man can feel within himself; but, on the contrary, in that which has nothing to do with feeling — namely, a great humility and contempt of oneself and of all that pertains to oneself, firmly rooted in the soul and keenly felt by it; and likewise in being glad that others feel in this very way concerning oneself and in not wishing to be of any account in the esteem of others.

Secondly, it must be noted that all visions, revelations and feelings coming from Heaven, and any thoughts that may proceed from these, are of less worth than the least act of humility. And humility is one of the effects of charity, which esteems not its own things nor strives to attain them; nor thinks evil, save of itself; nor thinks any good thing of itself, but only of others. It is well, therefore, that these supernatural apprehensions should not attract men's eyes, but that they should strive to forget them in order that they may be free.

Chapter X

Of the third evil that may come to the soul from the devil, through the imaginary apprehensions of the memory.

From all that has been said above it may be clearly understood and inferred how great is the evil that may come to the soul from the devil by way of these supernatural apprehensions. For not only can he represent to the memory and the fancy many false forms and ideas, which seem true and good, impressing them on spirit and sense with great effectiveness and certifying them to be true by means of suggestion (so that it appears to the soul that it cannot be otherwise, but that everything is even as he represents it; for, as he transfigures himself into an angel of light, he appears as light to the soul); but he may also tempt the soul in many ways with respect to true knowledge, which is of God, moving its desires and affections, whether spiritual or sensual, in unruly fashion with respect to these; for, if the soul takes pleasure in such apprehensions, it is very easy for the devil to cause its desires and affections to grow within it, and to make it fall into spiritual gluttony and other evils.

And, in order the better to do this, he is wont to suggest and give pleasure, sweetness and delight to the senses with respect to these same things of God, so that the soul is corrupted and bewildered by that sweetness, and is thus blinded with that pleasure and sets its eyes on pleasure rather than on love (or, at least, very much more than upon love), and gives more heed to the apprehensions than to the detachment and emptiness which are found in faith and hope and love of God. And from this he may go on gradually to deceive the soul and cause it to believe his falsehoods with great facility. For to the soul that is blind falsehood no longer appears to be falsehood, nor does evil appear to be evil, etc.; for darkness appears to be light, and light, darkness; and hence that soul comes to commit a thousand foolish errors, whether with respect to natural things, or to moral things, or to spiritual things; so that that which was wine to it becomes vinegar. All this happens to the soul because it began not, first of all, by denying itself the pleasure of those supernatural things. At first this is a small matter, and not very harmful, and the soul has therefore no misgivings, and allows it to continue, and it grows, like the grain of mustard seed, into a tall tree. For a small error at the beginning, as they say, becomes a great error in the end.

Wherefore, in order to flee from this great evil, which comes from the devil, the soul must not desire to have any pleasure in such things, because such pleasure will most surely lead it to become blind and to fall. For of their own nature, and without the help of the devil, pleasure and delight and sweetness blinds the soul. And this was the meaning of David when he said: 'Perhaps darkness shall blind me in my delights and I shall have the night for my light.'

Chapter XI

Of the fourth evil that comes to the soul from the distinct supernatural apprehensions of the memory, which is the hindrance that it interposes to union.

Concerning this fourth evil there is not much to be said, since it has already been treated again and again in this third book, wherein we have proved how, in order that the soul may come to union with God in hope, it must renounce every possession of the memory; for, in order that its hope in God may be perfect, it must have naught in the memory that is not God. And, as we have likewise said, no form or figure or image or other kind of knowledge that may come to the memory can be God, neither can be like Him, whether it be of heaven or of earth, natural or supernatural, even as David teaches, when he says: 'Lord, among the gods there is none like unto Thee.'

Wherefore, if the memory desires to pay heed to any of these things, it hinders the soul from reaching God; first, because it encumbers it, and next because, the more the soul has of possession, the less it has of hope. Wherefore it is needful for the soul to be stripped of the distinct forms and the knowledge of supernatural things, and to become oblivious to them, so that the memory may cause no hindrance to its union with God in perfect hope.

Chapter XII

Of the fifth evil that may come to the soul in supernatural imaginary forms and apprehensions, which is a low and unseemly judgment or God.

No less serious is the fifth evil that comes to the soul from its desire to retain in the memory and imagination the said forms and images of things that are supernaturally communicated to it, above all if it desires to use them as a means to Divine union. For it is a very easy thing to judge of the Being and greatness of God less worthily and nobly than befits His incomprehensible nature; for, although our reason and judgment may form no express conception that God is like any one of these things, yet the very esteeming of these apprehensions, if in fact the soul esteems them, makes and causes it not to esteem God, or not to feel concerning Him, as highly as faith teaches, since faith tells us that He is incomparable, incomprehensible, and so forth. For, quite apart from the fact that the soul takes from God all that it gives to the creature, it is natural that its esteem of these apprehensible things should lead it to make a certain inward comparison between such things and God, which would prevent it from judging and esteeming God as highly as it ought. For the creatures, whether terrestrial or celestial, and all distinct images and kinds of knowledge, both natural and supernatural, that can be encompassed by the faculties of the soul, however lofty they be in this life, have no comparison or proportion with the Being of God, since God falls within no genus and no species, whereas the creatures do, or so the theologians tell us. And the soul in this life is not capable of receiving in a clear and distinct manner aught save that which falls within genus and species. For this cause Saint John says that no man hath seen God at any time. And Isaias says it has not entered into the heart of man what God is like. And God said to Moses that he could not see Him while he was in this mortal state. Wherefore he that encumbers his memory and the other faculties of the soul with that which they can comprehend cannot esteem God, neither feel concerning Him, as he ought.

Let us make a comparison on a lower level. It is clear that the more a man fixes his eyes upon the servants of a king, and the more notice he takes of them, the less notice does he take of the king himself, and the less does he esteem him; for, although this comparison may not be formally and distinctly present in the understanding, it is inherent in the act, since, the more attention the man gives to the servants, the more he takes from their lord; and he cannot have a very high opinion of the king if the servants appear to him to be of any importance while they are in the presence of the king, their lord. Even so does the soul treat its God when it pays heed to the creatures aforementioned. This comparison, however, is on a very low level, for, as we have said, God is of another being than His creatures in that He is infinitely far from them all. For this reason they must all be banished from sight, and the soul must withdraw its gaze from them in all their forms, that it may yet gaze on God through faith and hope.

Wherefore those who not only pay heed to the imaginary apprehensions aforementioned, but suppose God to be like some of them, and think that by means of them they will be able to attain to union with God, have already gone far astray and will ever continue to lose the light of faith in the understanding, through which this faculty is united with God; neither will they grow in the loftiness of hope, by means whereof the memory is united with God in hope, which must be brought about through disunion from all that is of the imagination.

Chapter XIII

Of the benefits which the soul receives through banishing from itself the apprehensions of the imagination. This chapter answers a certain objection and explains a difference which exists between apprehensions that are imaginary, natural and supernatural.

The benefits that come from voiding the imagination of imaginary forms can be clearly observed in the five evils aforementioned which they inflict upon the soul, if it desires to retain them, even as we also said of the natural forms. But, apart from these, there are other benefits for the spirit — namely, those of great rest and quiet. For, setting aside that natural rest which the soul obtains when it is free from images and forms, it likewise becomes free from anxiety as to whether they are good or evil, and as to how it must behave with respect to the one and to the other. Nor has it to waste the labour and time of its spiritual masters by requiring them to decide if these things are good or evil, and if they are of this kind or of another; for the soul has no need to desire to know all this if it pays no heed to them. The time and energies which it would have wasted in dealing with these images and forms can be better employed in another and a more profitable exercise, which is that of the will with respect to God, and in having a care to seek detachment and poverty of spirit and sense, which consists in desiring earnestly to be without any consoling support that can be apprehended, whether interior or exterior. This we practise well when we desire and strive to strip ourselves of these forms, since from this there will proceed no less a benefit than that of approach to God (Who has no image, neither form nor figure), and this will be the greater according as the soul withdraws itself the more completely from all forms, images and figures of the imagination.

But perchance you will say: 'Why do many spiritual persons counsel the soul to strive to profit by the communications and feelings which come from God, and to desire to receive them from Him, that it may have something to give Him; since, if He gives us nothing, we shall give Him nothing likewise? And wherefore does Saint Paul say: 'Quench not the spirit?' And the Spouse to the Bride: "Set Me as a seal upon thy heart and as a seal upon thine arm?" This certainly denotes some kind of apprehension. And, according to the instruction given above, not only must all this not be striven after, but, even though God sends it, it must be rejected and cast aside. But surely it is clear that, since God gives it, He gives it to a good purpose, and it will have a good effect. We must not throw away pearls. And it is even a kind of pride to be unwilling to receive the things of God, as if we could do without them and were self-sufficient.'

In order to meet this objection it is necessary to recall what we said in the fifteenth and sixteenth chapters of the second book, where to a great extent the difficulty is solved. For we said there that the good that overflows in the soul from supernatural apprehensions, when they come from a good source, is produced passively in the soul at that very instant when they are represented to the senses, without the working of any operation of the faculties. Wherefore it is unnecessary for the will to perform the act of receiving them; for, as we have also said, if at that time the soul should try to labour with its faculties, the effect of its own base and natural operation would be to hinder the supernatural graces which God is even then working in it rather than that, through these apprehensions, God should cause it to derive any benefit from its active labour. Nay, rather, as the spirituality coming from those imaginary apprehensions is given passively to the soul, even so must the soul conduct itself passively with respect to them, setting no store by its inward or outward actions. To do this is to preserve the feelings that have their source in God, for in this way they are not lost through the soul's base manner of working. And this is not quenching the spirit; for the spirit would be quenched by the soul if it desired to behave in any other manner than that whereby God is leading it. And this it would be doing if, when God had given it spiritual graces passively, as He does in these apprehensions, it should then desire to exert itself actively with respect to them, by labouring with its understanding or by seeking to find something in them. And this is clear because, if the soul desires to labour at that time with its own exertions, its work cannot be more than natural, for of itself it is capable of no more; for supernaturally it neither moves itself nor can move itself — it is God that moves it and brings it to this state. And thus, if the soul at that time desires to labour with its own exertions (as far as lies in its power), its active working will hinder the passive work that God is communicating to it, which is spirit. It will be setting itself to its own work, which is of another and an inferior kind than that which God communicates to it; for the work of God is passive and supernatural, and that of the soul is active and natural; and in this way the soul would therefore be quenching the spirit.

That this activity of the soul is an inferior one is also clear from the fact that the faculties of the soul cannot, of their own power, reflect and act, save upon some form, figure and image, and this is the rind and accident of the substance and spirit which lie beneath this rind and accident. This substance and spirit unite not with the faculties of the soul in true understanding and love, save when at last the operation of the faculties ceases. For the aim and end of this operation is only that the substance which can be understood and loved and which lies beneath these forms may come to be received in the soul. The difference, therefore, between active and passive operation, and the superiority of the latter, corresponds to the difference between that which is being done and that which is done already, or between that which a man tries to attain and effect and that which is already effected. Hence it may likewise be inferred that, if the soul should desire to employ its faculties actively on these supernatural apprehensions, wherein God, as we have said, bestows the spirit of them passively, it would be doing nothing less than abandoning what it had already done, in order to do it again, neither would it enjoy what it had done, nor could it produce any other result by these actions of its own, save that of impeding what had been done already. For, as we say, the faculties cannot of their own power attain to the spirituality which God bestows upon the soul without any operation of their own. And thus the soul would be directly quenching the spirituality which God infuses through these imaginary apprehensions aforementioned if it were to set any store by them; wherefore it must set them aside, and take up a passive and negative attitude with regard to them. For at that time God is moving the soul to things which are above its own power and knowledge. For this cause the Prophet said: 'I will stand upon my watch and set my step upon my tower, and I will watch to see that which will be said to me.' This is as though he were to say: I will stand on guard over my faculties and I will take no step forward as to my actions, and thus I shall be able to contemplate that which will be said to me — that is, I shall understand and enjoy that which will be communicated to me supernaturally.

And the passage which has been quoted concerning the Spouse is to be understood as referring to the love that He entreats of the Bride, the office of which love between two lovers is to make one like to the other in the most vital part of them. Wherefore He tells her to set Him as a seal upon her heart, where all the arrows strike that leave the quiver of love, which arrows are the actions and motives of love. So they will all strike Him Who is there as a mark for them; and thus all will be for Him, so that the soul will become like Him through the actions and motions of love, until it be transformed in Him. Likewise he bids her set Him as a seal upon her arm, because the arm performs the exercise of love, for by the arm the Beloved is sustained and comforted.

Therefore all that the soul has to endeavour to do with respect to all the apprehensions which come to it from above, whether imaginary or of any other kind — it matters not if they be visions, locutions, feelings or revelations — is to make no account of the letter or the rind (that is, of what is signified or represented or given to be understood), but to pay heed only to the possession of the love of God which they cause interiorly within the soul. And in this case the soul will make account, not of feelings of sweetness or delight, nor of figures, but of the feelings of love which they cause it. And with this sole end in view it may at times recall that image and apprehension caused it by love, in order to set the spirit on its course of love. For, though the effect of that apprehension be not so great afterwards, when it is recalled, as it was on the first occasion when it was communicated, yet, when it is recalled, love is renewed, and the mind is lifted up to God, especially when the recollection is of certain figures, images or feelings which are supernatural, and are wont to be sealed and imprinted upon the soul in such a way that they continue for a long time — some of them, indeed, never leave the soul. And those that are thus sealed upon the soul produce in it Divine effects of love, sweetness, light and so forth, on almost every occasion when the soul returns to them, sometimes more so and sometimes less; for it was to this end that they were impressed upon it. And thus this is a great favour for the soul on which God bestows it, for it is as though it had within itself a mine of blessings.

The figures which produce effects such as these are deeply implanted in the soul, and are not like other images and forms that are retained in the fancy. And thus the soul has no need to have recourse to this faculty when it desires to recall them, for it sees that it has them within itself, and that they are as an image seen in the mirror. When it comes to pass that any soul has such figures formally within itself, it will then do well to recall them to the effect of love to which I have referred, for they will be no hindrance to the union of love in faith, since the soul will not desire to be absorbed in the figure, but only to profit by the love; it will immediately set aside the figure, which thus will rather be a help to it.

Only with great difficulty can it be known when these images are imprinted upon the soul, and when upon the fancy. For those which touch the fancy are as apt to occur very frequently as are the others; for certain persons are accustomed habitually to have imaginary visions in their imagination and fancy, which are presented to them in one form with great frequency; sometimes because the apprehensive power of the organ concerned is very great, and, however little they reflect upon it, that habitual figure is at once presented to, and outlined upon, their fancy; sometimes because it is the work of the devil; sometimes, again, because it is the work of God; but the visions are not formally imprinted upon the soul. They may be known, however, by their effects. For those that are natural, or that come from the devil, produce no good effect upon the soul, however frequently they be recalled, nor work its spiritual renewal, but the contemplation of them simply produces aridity. Those that are good, however, produce some good effect when they are recalled, like that which was produced in the soul upon the first occasion. But the formal images which are imprinted upon the soul almost invariably produce some effect in it, whensoever they are remembered.

He that has experienced these will readily distinguish the one kind from the other, for the great difference between them is very clear to anyone that has experience of them. I will merely say that those which are formally and durably imprinted upon the soul are of very rare occurrence. But, whether they be of this kind or of that, it is good for the soul to desire to understand nothing, save God alone, through faith, in hope. And if anyone makes the objection that to reject these things, if they are good, appears to be pride, I reply that it is not so, but that it is prudent humility to profit by them in the best way, as has been said, and to be guided by that which is safest.

Chapter XIV

Which treats of spiritual knowledge in so far as it may concern the memory.

We classed spiritual forms of knowledge as the third division of the apprehensions of the memory, not because they belong to the bodily sense of the fancy, as do the others, for they have no bodily form and image, but because they are likewise apprehensible by spiritual memory and reminiscence. Now, after the soul has had experience of one of these apprehensions, it can recall it whensoever it will; and this is not by the effigy and image that the apprehension has left in the bodily sense, for, since this is of bodily form, as we say, it has no capacity for spiritual forms; but because it recalls it, intellectually and spiritually, by means of that form which it has left impressed upon the soul, which is likewise a formal or spiritual form or notion or image, whereby it is recalled, or by means of the effect that it has wrought. It is for this reason that I place these apprehensions among those of the memory, although they belong not to the apprehensions of the fancy.

What these kinds of knowledge are, and how the soul is to conduct itself with respect to them in order to attain to union with God, are sufficiently described in the twenty-fourth chapter of the second book, where we treated this knowledge as apprehensions of the understanding. Let this be referred to, for we there described how it was of two kinds: either uncreated or of the creatures. I speak now only of things relating to my present purpose — namely, how the memory must behave with respect to them in order to attain to union. And I say, as I have just said of formal knowledge in the preceding chapter (for this, being of created things, is of the same kind), that these apprehensions my be recalled when they produce good effects, not that they may be dwelt upon, but that they may quicken the soul's love and knowledge of God. But, unless the recollection of them produces good effects, let the memory never give them even passing attention. With regard to uncreated knowledge, I say that the soul should try to recall it as often as possible, for it will produce most beneficial effects. As we said above, it produces touches and impressions of union with God, which is the aim towards which we are directing the soul. And by no form, image or figure which can be impressed upon the soul does the memory recall these (for these touches and impressions of union with the Creator have no form), but only by the effects which they have produced upon it of light, love, joy and spiritual renewal, and so forth, some of which are wrought anew in the soul whensoever they are remembered.

Chapter XV

Which sets down the general method whereby the spiritual person must govern himself with respect to this sense.

In order to conclude this discussion on the memory, it will be well at this point to give the spiritual reader an account of the method which he must observe, and which is of universal application, in order that he may be united with God according to this sense. For, although what has been said makes the subject quite clear, it will nevertheless be more easily apprehended if we summarize it here. To this end it must be remembered that, since our aim is the union of the soul with God in hope, according to the memory, and since that which is hoped for is that which is not possessed, and since, the less we possess of other things, the greater scope and the greater capacity have we for hoping, and consequently the greater hope, therefore, the more things we possess, the less scope and capacity is there for hoping, and consequently the less hope have we. Hence, the more the soul dispossesses the memory of forms and things which may be recalled by it, which are not God, the more will it set its memory upon God, and the emptier will its memory become, so that it may hope for Him Who shall fill it. What must be done, then, that the soul may live in the perfect and pure hope of God is that, whensoever these distinct images, forms and ideas come to it, it must not rest in them, but must turn immediately to God, voiding the memory of them entirely, with loving affection. It must neither think of these things nor consider them beyond the degree which is necessary for the understanding and performing of its obligations, if they have any concern with these. And this it must do without setting any affection or inclination upon them, so that they may produce no effects in the soul. And thus a man must not fail to think and recall that which he ought to know and do, for, provided he preserves no affection or attachments, this will do him no harm. For this matter the lines of the Mount, which are in the thirteenth chapter of the first book, will be of profit.

But here it must be borne in mind that this doctrine ours does not agree, nor do we desire that it should agree, with the doctrine of those pestilent men, who, inspired by Satanic pride and envy, have desired to remove from the eyes of the faithful the holy and necessary use, and the worthy adoration, of images of God and of the saints. This teaching of ours is very different from that; for we say not here, as they do, that images should not exist, and should not be adored; we simply explain the difference between images and God. We exhort men to pass beyond that which is superficial that they may not be hindered from attaining to the living truth beneath it, and to make no more account of the former than suffices for attainment to the spiritual. For means are good and necessary to an end; and images are means which serve to remind us of God and of the saints. But when we consider and attend to the means more than is necessary for treating them as such, they disturb and hinder us as much, in their own way, as any different thing; the more so, when we treat of supernatural visions and images, to which I am specially referring, and with respect to which arise many deceptions and perils. For, with respect to the remembrance and adoration and esteem of images, which the Catholic Church sets before us, there can be no deception or peril, because naught is esteemed therein other than that which is represented; nor does the remembrance of them fail to profit the soul, since they are not preserved in the memory save with love for that which they represent; and, provided the soul pays no more heed to them than is necessary for this purpose, they will ever assist it to union with God, allowing the soul to soar upwards (when God grants it that favour) from the superficial image to the living God, forgetting every creature and everything that belongs to creatures.

Chapter XVI

Which begins to treat of the dark night of the will. Makes a division between the affections of the will.

We should have accomplished nothing by the purgation of the understanding in order to ground it in the virtue of faith, and by the purgation of the memory in order to ground it in hope, if we purged not the will also according to the third virtue, which is charity, whereby the works that are done in faith live and have great merit, and without it are of no worth. For, as Saint James says: 'Without works of charity, faith is dead.' And, now that we have to treat of the active detachment and night of this faculty, in order to form it and make it perfect in this virtue of the charity of God, I find no more fitting authority than that which is written in the sixth chapter of Deuteronomy, where Moses says: 'Thou shalt love the Lord thy God with thy whole heart and with thy whole soul and with thy whole strength.' Herein is contained all that the spiritual man ought to do, and all that I have here to teach him, so that he may truly attain to God, through union of the will, by means of charity. For herein man is commanded to employ all the faculties and desires and operations and affections of his soul in God, so that all the ability and strength of his soul may serve for no more than this, according to that which David says, in these words: Fortitudinem meam ad te custodiam.

The strength of the soul consists in its faculties, passions and desires, all of which are governed by the will. Now when these faculties, passions and desires are directed by the will toward God, and turned away from all that is not God, then the strength of the soul is kept for God, and thus the soul is able to love God with all its strength. And, to the end that the soul may do this, we shall here treat of the purgation from the will of all its unruly affections, whence arise unruly operations, affections and desires, and whence also arises its failure to keep all its strength for God. These affections and passions are four, namely: Joy, hope, grief and fear. These passions, when they are controlled by reason according to the way of God, so that the soul rejoices only in that which is purely the honour and glory of God, and hopes for naught else, neither grieves save for things that concern this, neither fears aught save God alone, it is clear that the strength and ability of the soul are being directed toward God and kept for Him. For, the more the soul rejoices in any other thing than God, the less completely will it centre its rejoicing in God; and the more it hopes in aught else, the less will it hope in God; and so with the other passions.

And in order to give fuller instructions concerning this, we shall treat, in turn and in detail, as is our custom, of each of these four passions and of the desires of the will. For the whole business of attaining to union with God consists in purging the will from its affections and desires; so that thus it may no longer be a base, human will, but may become a Divine will, being made one with the will of God.

These four passions have the greater dominion in the soul, and assail it the more vehemently, when the will is less strongly attached to God and more dependent on the creatures. For then it rejoices very readily at things that merit not rejoicing, hopes in that which brings no profit, grieves over that in which perchance it ought to rejoice, and fears where there is no reason for fearing.

From these affections, when they are unbridled, arise in the soul all the vices and imperfections which it possesses, and likewise, when they are ordered and composed, all its virtues. And it must be known that, if one of them should become ordered and controlled by reason, the rest will become so likewise; for these four passions of the soul are so closely and intimately united to one another that the actual direction of one is the virtual direction of the others; and if one be actually recollected the other three will virtually and proportionately be recollected likewise. For, if the will rejoice in anything it will as a result hope for the same thing to the extent of its rejoicing, and herein are virtually included grief and fear with regard to the same thing; and, in proportion as desire for these is taken away, fear and grief concerning them are likewise gradually lost, and hope for them is removed. For the will, with these four passions, is denoted by that figure which was seen by Ezechiel, of four beasts with one body, which had four faces; and the wings of the one were joined to those of the other, and each one went straight before his face, and when they went forward they turned not back. And thus in the same manner the wings of each one of these affections are joined to those of each of the others, so that, in whichever direction one of them turns — that is, in its operation — the others of necessity go with it virtually also; and, when one of them descends, as is there said, they must all descend, and, when one is lifted up, they will all be lifted up. Where thy hope is, thither will go thy joy and fear and grief; and, if thy hope returns, the others will return, and so of the rest.

Wherefore thou must take note that, wheresoever one of these passions is, thither will go likewise the whole soul and the will and the other faculties, and they will all live as captives to this passion, and the other three passions will be living in it also, to afflict the soul with their captivity, and not to allow it to fly upward to the liberty and rest of sweet contemplation and union. For this cause Boetius told thee that, if thou shouldst desire to understand truth with clear light, thou must cast from thee joys, hope, fear and grief. For, as long as these passions reign, they allow not the soul to remain in the tranquillity and peace which are necessary for the wisdom which, by natural or supernatural means, it is capable of receiving.

Chapter XVII

Which begins to treat of the first affections of the will. Describes the nature of joy and makes a distinction between the things in which the will can rejoice.

The first of the passions of the soul and affections of the will is joy, which, in so far as concerns that which we propose to say about it, is naught else than a satisfaction of the will together with esteem for something which it considers desirable; for the will never rejoices save when an object affords it appreciation and satisfaction. This has reference to active joy, which arises when the soul clearly and distinctly understands the reason for its rejoicing, and when it is in its own power to rejoice or not. There is another and a passive joy, a condition in which the will may find itself rejoicing without understanding clearly and distinctly the reason for its rejoicing, and which also occurs at times when it does understand this; but it is not in the soul's power to rejoice or not. Of this condition we shall speak hereafter. For the present we shall speak of joy when it is active and voluntary and arises from things that are distinct and clear.

Joy may arise from six kinds of good things or blessings, namely: temporal, natural, sensual, moral, supernatural and spiritual. Of these we shall speak in their order, controlling the will with regard to them so that it may not be encumbered by them and fail to place the strength of its joy in God. To this end it is well to presuppose one fundamental truth, which will be as a staff whereon we should ever lean as we progress; and it will be well to have understood it, because it is the light whereby we should be guided and whereby we may understand this doctrine, and direct our rejoicing in all these blessings to God. This truth is that the will must never rejoice save only in that which is to the honour and glory of God; and that the greatest honour we can show to Him is that of serving Him according to evangelical perfection; and anything that has naught to do with this is of no value and profit to man.

Chapter XVIII

Which treats of joy with respect to temporal blessings. Describes how joy in them must be directed to God.

The first kind of blessing of which we have spoken is temporal. And by temporal blessings we here understand riches, rank, office and other things that men desire; and children, relatives, marriages, etc.: all of which are things wherein the will may rejoice. But it is clear how vain a thing it is for men to rejoice in riches, titles, rank, office and other such things which they are wont to desire; for, if a man were the better servant of God for being rich, he ought to rejoice in riches; but in fact they are rather a cause for his giving offence to God, even as the Wise Man teaches, saying: 'Son, if thou be rich, thou shalt not be free from sin.' Although it is true that temporal blessings do not necessarily of themselves cause sin, yet, through the frailty of its affections, the heart of man habitually clings to them and fails God (which is a sin, for to fail God is sin); it is for this cause that the Wise Man says: 'Thou shalt not be free from sin.' For this reason the Lord described riches, in the Gospel, as thorns, in order to show that he who touches them with the will shall be wounded by some sin. And that exclamation which He makes in the Gospel, saying: 'How hardly shall they that have riches enter the Kingdom of the heavens' — that is to say, they that have joy in riches — clearly shows that man must not rejoice in riches, since he exposes himself thereby to such great peril. And David, in order to withdraw us from this peril, said likewise: 'If riches abound, set not your heart on them.' And I will not here quote further testimony on so clear a matter.

For in that case I should never cease quoting Scripture, nor should I cease describing the evils which Solomon imputes to riches in Ecclesiastes. Solomon was a man who had possessed great riches, and, knowing well what they were, said: 'All things that are under the sun are vanity of vanities, vexation of spirit and vain solicitude of the mind.' And he that loves riches, he said, shall reap no fruit from them. And he adds that riches are kept to the hurt of their owner, as we see in the Gospel, where it was said from Heaven to the man that rejoiced because he had kept many fruits for many years: 'Fool, this night shall thy soul be required of thee to give account thereof, and whose shall be that which thou has provided?' And finally, David teaches us the same, saying: 'Let us have no envy when our neighbour becomes rich, for it will profit him nothing in the life to come;' meaning thereby that we might rather have pity on him.

It follows, then, that a man must neither rejoice in riches when he has them, nor when his brother has them, unless they help them to serve God. For if ever it is allowable to rejoice in them, it will be when they are spent and employed in the service of God, for otherwise no profit will be derived from them. And the same is to be understood of other blessings (titles, offices, etc.), in all of which it is vain to rejoice if a man feel not that God is the better served because of them and the way to eternal life is made more secure. And as it cannot be clearly known if this is so (if God is better served, etc.), it would be a vain thing to rejoice in these things deliberately, since such a joy cannot be reasonable. For, as the Lord says: 'If a man gain all the world, he may yet lose his soul.' There is naught, then, wherein to rejoice save in the fact that God is better served.

Neither is there cause for rejoicing in children because they are many, or rich, or endowed with natural graces and talents and the good things of fortune, but only if they serve God. For Absalom, the son of David, found neither his beauty nor his riches nor his lineage of any service to him because he served not God. Hence it was a vain thing to have rejoiced in such a son. For this reason it is also a vain thing for men to desire to have children, as do some who trouble and disturb everyone with their desire for them, since they know not if such children will be good and serve God. Nor do they know if their satisfaction in them will be turned into pain; nor if the comfort and consolation which they should have from them will change to disquiet and trial; and the honour which they should bring them, into dishonour; nor if they will cause them to give greater offence to God, as happens to many. Of these Christ says that they go round about the sea and the land to enrich them and to make them doubly the children of perdition which they are themselves.

Wherefore, though all things smile upon a man and all that he does turns out prosperously, he ought to have misgivings rather than to rejoice; for these things increase the occasion and peril of his forgetting God. For this cause Solomon says, in Ecclesiastes, that he was cautious: 'Laughter I counted error and to rejoicing I said, "Why art thou vainly deceived?"' Which is as though he had said: When things smiled upon me I counted it error and deception to rejoice in them; for without doubt it is a great error and folly on the part of a man if he rejoice when things are bright and pleasant for him, knowing not of a certainty that there will come to him thence some eternal good. The heart of the fool, says the Wise Man, is where there is mirth, but that of the wise man is where there is sorrow. For mirth blinds the heart and allows it not to consider things and ponder them; but sadness makes a man open his eyes and look at the profit and the harm of them. And hence it is that, as he himself says, anger is better than laughter. Wherefore it is better to go to the house of mourning than to the house of feasting; for in the former is figured the end of all men, as the Wise Man says likewise.

It would therefore be vanity for a woman or her husband to rejoice in their marriage when they know not clearly that they are serving God better thereby. They ought rather to feel confounded, since matrimony is a cause, as Saint Paul says, whereby each one sets his heart upon the other and keeps it not wholly with God. Wherefore he says: 'If thou shouldst find thyself free from a wife, desire not to seek a wife; while he that has one already should walk with such freedom of heart as though he had her not.' This, together with what we have said concerning temporal blessings, he teaches us himself, in these words: 'This is certain; as I say to you, brethren, the time is short; it remaineth that they also who have wives be as if they had none; and they that weep, as them that weep not; and they that rejoice, as them that rejoice not; and they that buy, as them that possess not; and they that use this world, as them that use it not.' All this he says to show us that we must not set our rejoicings upon any other thing than that which tends to the service of God, since the rest is vanity and a thing which profits not; for joy that is not according to God can bring the soul no profit.

Chapter XIX

Of the evils that may befall the soul when it sets its rejoicing upon temporal blessings.

If we had to describe the evils which encompass the soul when it sets the affections of its will upon temporal blessings, neither ink nor paper would suffice us and our time would be too short. For from very small beginnings a man may attain to great evils and destroy great blessings; even as from a spark of fire, if it be not quenched, may be enkindled great fires which set the world ablaze. All these evils have their root and origin in one important evil of a privative kind that is contained in this joy — namely, withdrawal from God. For even as, in the soul that is united with Him by the affection of its will, there are born all blessings, even so, when it withdraws itself from Him because of this creature affection, there beset it all evils and disasters proportionately to the joy and affection wherewith it is united with the creature; for this is inherent in withdrawal from God. Wherefore a soul may expect the evils which assail it to be greater or less according to the greater or lesser degree of its withdrawal from God. These evils may be extensive or intensive; for the most part they are both together.

This privative evil, whence, we say, arise other privative and positive evils, has four degrees, each one worse than the other. And, when the soul compasses the fourth degree, it will have compassed all the evils and depravities that arise in this connection. These four degrees are well indicated by Moses in Deuteronomy in these words, where he says: 'The beloved grew fat and kicked. He grew fat and became swollen and gross. He forsook God his Maker and departed from God his Salvation.'

This growing fat of the soul, which was loved before it grew fat, indicates absorption in this joy of creatures. And hence arises the first degree of this evil, namely the going backward; which is a certain blunting of the mind with regard to God, an obscuring of the blessings of God like the obscuring of the air by mist, so that it cannot be clearly illumined by the light of the sun. For, precisely when the spiritual person sets his rejoicing upon anything, and gives rein to his desire for foolish things, he becomes blind as to God, and the simple intelligence of his judgment becomes clouded, even as the Divine Spirit teaches in the Book of Wisdom, saying: 'the use and association of vanity and scorn obscureth good things, and inconstancy of desire overturneth and perverteth the sense and judgment that are without malice.' Here the Holy Spirit shows that, although there be no malice conceived in the understanding of the soul, concupiscence and rejoicing in creatures suffice of themselves to create in the soul the first degree of this evil, which is the blunting of the mind and the darkening of the judgment, by which the truth is understood and each thing honestly judged as it is.

Holiness and good judgment suffice not to save a man from falling into this evil, if he gives way to concupiscence or rejoicing in temporal things. For this reason God warned us by uttering these words through Moses: 'Thou shalt take no gifts, which blind even the prudent.' And this was addressed particularly to those who were to be judges; for these have need to keep their judgment clear and alert, which they will be unable to do if they covet and rejoice in gifts. And for this cause likewise God commanded Moses to appoint judges from those who abhorred avarice, so that their judgment should not be blunted with the lust of the passions. And thus he says not only that they should not desire it, but that they should abhor it. For, if a man is to be perfectly defended from the affection of love, he must preserve an abhorrence of it, defending himself by means of the one thing against its contrary. The reason why the prophet Samuel, for example, was always so upright and enlightened a judge is that (as he said in the Book of the Kings) he had never received a gift from any man.

The second degree of this privative evil arises from the first, which is indicated in the words following the passage already quoted, namely: 'He grew fat and became swollen and gross.' And thus this second degree is dilation of the will through the acquisition of greater liberty in temporal things; which consists in no longer attaching so much importance to them, nor troubling oneself about them, nor esteeming so highly the joy and pleasure that come from created blessings. And this will have arisen in the soul from its having in the first place given rein to rejoicing; for, through giving way to it, the soul has become swollen with it, as is said in that passage, and that fatness of rejoicing and desire has mused it to dilate and extend its will more freely toward the creatures. And this brings with it great evils. For this second degree causes the soul to withdraw itself from the things of God, and from holy practices, and to take no pleasure in them, because it takes pleasure in other things and devotes itself continually to many imperfections and follies and to joys and vain pleasures.

And when this second degree is consummated, it withdraws a man wholly from the practices which he followed continually and makes his whole mind and covetousness to be given to secular things. And those who are affected by this second degree not only have their judgment and understanding darkened so that they cannot recognize truth and justice, like those who are in the first degree, but they are also very weak and lukewarm and careless in acquiring knowledge of, and in practising, truth and justice, even as Isaias says of them in these words: 'They all love gifts and allow themselves to be carried away by rewards, and they judge not the orphan, neither doth the cause of the widow come unto them that they may give heed to it.' This comes not to pass in them without sin, especially when to do these things is incumbent upon them because of their office. For those who are affected by this degree are not free from malice as are those of the first degree. And thus they withdraw themselves more and more from justice and virtues, since their will reaches out more and more in affection for creatures. Wherefore, the characteristics of those who are in this second degree are great lukewarmness in spiritual things and failure to do their duty by them; they practise them from formality or from compulsion or from the habit which they have formed of practising them, rather than because they love them.

The third degree of this privative evil is a complete falling away from God, neglect to fulfil His law in order not to lose worldly things and blessings, and relapse into mortal sin through covetousness. And this third degree is described in the words following the passage quoted above, which says: 'He forsook God his Maker.' In this degree are included all who have the faculties of the soul absorbed in things of the world and in riches and commerce, in such a way that they care nothing for fulfilling the obligations of the law of God. And they are very forgetful and dull with respect to that which touches their salvation, and have a correspondingly greater ardour and shrewdness with respect to things of the world. So much so that in the Gospel Christ calls them children of this world, and says of them that they are more prudent and acute in their affairs than are the children of light in their own. And thus they are as nothing in God's business, whereas in the world's business they are everything. And these are the truly avaricious, who have extended and dispersed their desire and joy on things created, and this with such affection that they cannot be satisfied; on the contrary, their desire and their thirst grow all the more because they are farther withdrawn from the only source that could satisfy them, which is God. For it is of these that God Himself speaks through Jeremias, saying: 'They have forsaken Me, Who am the fountain of living water, and they have digged to themselves broken cisterns that can hold no water.' And this is the reason why the covetous man finds naught among the creatures wherewith he can quench his thirst, but only that which increases it. These persons are they that fall into countless kinds of sin through love of temporal blessings and the evils which afflict them are innumerable. And of these David says: Transierunt in affectum cordis.

The fourth degree of this privative evil is indicated in the last words of our passage, which says: 'And he departed from God his Salvation.' To this degree come those of the third degree whereof we have just spoken. For, through his not giving heed to setting his heart upon the law of God because of temporal blessings, the soul of the covetous man departs far from God according to his memory, understanding and will, forgetting Him as though He were not his God, which comes to pass because he has made for himself a god of money and of temporal blessings, as Saint Paul says when he describes avarice as slavery to idols. For this fourth degree leads a man as far as to forget God, and to set his heart, which he should have set formally upon God, formally upon money, as though he had no god beside.

To this fourth degree belong those who hesitate not to subject Divine and supernatural things to temporal things, as to their God, when they ought to do the contrary, and subject temporal things to God, if they considered Him as their God, as would be in accordance with reason. To these belonged the iniquitous Balaam, who sold the grace that God had given to him. And also Simon Magus, who thought to value the grace of God in terms of money, and desired to buy it. In doing this he showed a greater esteem for money; and he thought there were those who similarly esteemed it, and would give grace for money. There are many nowadays who in many other ways belong to this fourth degree; their reason is darkened to spiritual things by covetousness; they serve money and not God, and are influenced by money and not by God, putting first the cost of a thing and not its Divine worth and reward, and in many ways making money their principal god and end, and setting it before the final end, which is God.

To this last degree belong also those miserable souls who are so greatly in love with their own goods that they take them for their god, so much so that they scruple not to sacrifice their lives for them, when they see that this god of theirs is suffering some temporal harm. They abandon themselves to despair and take their own lives for their miserable ends, showing by their own acts how wretched is the reward which such a god as theirs bestows. For when they can no longer hope for aught from him he gives them despair and death; and those whom he pursues not to this last evil of death he condemns to a dying life in the griefs of anxiety and in many other miseries, allowing no mirth to enter their heart, and naught that is of earth to bring them satisfaction. They continually pay the tribute of their heart to money by their yearning for it and hoarding of it for the final calamity of their just perdition, as the Wise Man warns them, saying: 'Riches are kept to the hurt of their owner.'

And to this fourth degree belong those of whom Saint Paul says: Tradidit illos in reprobum sensum. For joy, when it strives after possessions as its final goal, drags man down to these evils. But those on whom it inflicts lesser evils are also to be sorely pitied, since, as we have said, their souls are driven far backward upon the way of God. Wherefore, as David says: Be not thou afraid when a man shall be made rich: that is, envy him not, thinking that he outstrips thee, for, when he dieth, he shall carry nothing away, neither shall his glory nor his joy descend with him.

Chapter XX

Of the benefits that come to the soul from its withdrawal of joy from temporal things.

The spiritual man, then, must look carefully to it that his heart and his rejoicing begin not to lay hold upon temporal things; he must fear lest from being little it should grow to be great, and should increase from one degree to another. For little things, in time, become great; and from a small beginning there comes in the end a great matter, even as a spark suffices to set a mountain on fire and to burn up the whole world. And let him never be self-confident because his attachment is small, and fail to uproot it instantly because he thinks that he will do so later. For if, when it is so small and in its beginnings, he has not the courage to make an end of it, how does he suppose, and presume, that he will be able to do so when it is great and more deeply rooted. The more so since Our Lord said in the Gospel: 'He that is unfaithful in little will be unfaithful also in much.' For he that avoids the small sin will not fall into the great sin; but great evil is inherent in the small sin, since it has already penetrated within the fence and wall of the heart; and as the proverb says: Once begun, half done. Wherefore David warns us, saying: 'Though riches abound, let us not apply our heart to them.'

Although a man might not do this for the sake of God and of the obligations of Christian perfection, he should nevertheless do it because of the temporal advantages that result from it, to say nothing of the spiritual advantages, and he should free his heart completely from all rejoicing in the things mentioned above. And thus, not only will he free himself from the pestilent evils which we have described in the last chapter, but, in addition to this, he will withdraw his joy from temporal blessings and acquire the virtue of liberality, which is one of the principal attributes of God, and can in no wise coexist with covetousness. Apart from this, he will acquire liberty of soul, clarity of reason, rest, tranquillity and peaceful confidence in God and a true reverence and worship of God which comes from the will. He will find greater joy and recreation in the creatures through his detachment from them, for he cannot rejoice in them if he look upon them with attachment to them as to his own. Attachment is an anxiety that, like a bond, ties the spirit down to the earth and allows it no enlargement of heart. He will also acquire, in his detachment from things, a clear conception of them, so that he can well understand the truths relating to them, both naturally and supernaturally. He will therefore enjoy them very differently from one who is attached to them, and he will have a great advantage and superiority over such a one. For, while he enjoys them according to their truth, the other enjoys them according to their falseness; the one appreciates the best side of them and the other the worst; the one rejoices in their substance; the other, whose sense is bound to them, in their accident. For sense cannot grasp or attain to more than the accident, but the spirit, purged of the clouds and species of accident, penetrates the truth and worth of things, for this is its object. Wherefore joy, like a cloud, darkens the judgment, since there can be no voluntary joy in creatures without voluntary attachment, even as there can be no joy which is passion when there is no habitual attachment in the heart; and the renunciation and purgation of such joy leave the judgment clear, even as the mists leave the air clear when they are scattered.

This man, then, rejoices in all things — since his joy is dependent upon none of them — as if he had them all; and this other, through looking upon them with a particular sense of ownership, loses in a general sense all the pleasure of them all. This former man, having none of them in his heart, possesses them all, as Saint Paul says, in great freedom. This latter man, inasmuch as he has something of them through the attachment of his will, neither has nor possesses anything; it is rather they that have possessed his heart, and he is, as it were, a sorrowing captive. Wherefore, if he desire to have a certain degree of joy in creatures, he must of necessity have an equal degree of disquietude and grief in his heart, since it is seized and possessed by them. But he that is detached is untroubled by anxieties, either in prayer or apart from it; and thus, without losing time, he readily gains great spiritual treasure. But the other man loses everything, running to and fro upon the chain by which his heart is attached and bound; and with all his diligence he can still hardly free himself for a short time from this bond of thought and rejoicing by which his heart is bound. The spiritual man, then, must restrain the first motion of his heart towards creatures, remembering the premiss which we have here laid down, that there is naught wherein a man must rejoice, save in his service of God, and in his striving for His glory and honour in all things, directing all things solely to this end and turning aside from vanity in them, looking in them neither for his own joy nor for his consolation.

There is another very great and important benefit in this detachment of the rejoicing from creatures — namely, that it leaves the heart free for God. This is the dispositive foundation of all the favours which God will grant to the soul, and without this disposition He grants them not. And they are such that, even from the temporal standpoint, for one joy which the soul renounces for love of Him and for the perfection of the Gospel, He will give him a hundred in this life, as His Majesty promises in the same Gospel. But, even were there not so high a rate of interest, the spiritual man should quench these creature joys in his soul because of the displeasure which they give to God. For we see in the Gospel that, simply because that rich man rejoiced at having laid up for many years, God was so greatly angered that He told him that his soul would be brought to account on that same night. Therefore, we must believe that, whensoever we rejoice vainly, God is beholding us and preparing some punishment and bitter draught according to our deserts, so that the pain which results from the joy may sometimes be a hundred times greater than the joy. For, although it is true, as Saint John says on this matter, in the Apocalypse, concerning Babylon, that as much as she had rejoiced and lived in delights, so much torment and sorrow should be given her, yet this is not to say that the pain will not be greater than the joy, which indeed it will be, since for brief pleasures are given eternal torments. The words mean that there shall be nothing without its particular punishment, for He Who will punish the idle word will not pardon vain rejoicing.

Chapter XXI

Which describes how it is vanity to set the rejoicing of the will upon the good things of nature, and how the soul must direct itself, by means of them, to God.

By natural blessings we here understand beauty, grace, comeliness, bodily constitution and all other bodily endowments; and likewise, in the soul, good understanding, discretion and other things that pertain to reason. Many a man sets his rejoicing upon all these gifts, to the end that he himself, or those that belong to him, may possess them, and for no other reason, and gives no thanks to God Who bestows them on him so that He may be better known and loved by him because of them. But to rejoice for this cause alone is vanity and deception, as Solomon says in these words: 'Deceitful is grace and vain is beauty; the woman who fears God, she shall be praised.' Here he teaches us that a man ought rather to be fearful because of these natural gifts, since he may easily be distracted by them from the love of God, and, if he be attracted by them, he may fall into vanity and be deceived. For this reason bodily grace is said to be deceptive because it deceives a man in the ways and attracts him to that which beseems him not, through vain joy and complacency, either in himself or in others that have such grace. And it is said that beauty is vain because it causes a man to fall in many ways when he esteems it and rejoices in it, for he should rejoice only if he serves God or others through it. But he ought rather to fear and harbour misgivings lest perchance his natural graces and gifts should be a cause of his offending God, either by his vain presumption or by the extreme affection with which he regards them. Wherefore he that has such gifts should be cautious and live carefully, lest, by his vain ostentation, he give cause to any man to withdraw his heart in the smallest degree from God. For these graces and gifts of nature are so full of provocation and occasion of evil, both to him that possesses them and to him that looks upon them, that there is hardly any who entirely escapes from binding and entangling his heart in them. We have heard that many spiritual persons, who had certain of these gifts, had such fear of this that they prayed God to disfigure them, lest they should be a cause and occasion of any vain joy or affection to themselves or to others, and God granted their prayer.

The spiritual man, then, must purge his will, and make it to be blind to this vain rejoicing, bearing in mind that beauty and all other natural gifts are but earth, and that they come from the earth and will return thither; and that grace and beauty are the smoke and vapour belonging to this same earth; and that they must be held and esteemed as such by any man who desires not to fall into vanity, but will direct his heart to God in these matters, with rejoicing and gladness, because God is in Himself all these beauties and graces in the most eminent degree, and is infinitely high above all created things. And, as David says, they are all like a garment and shall grow old and pass away, and He alone remains immutable for ever. Wherefore, if in all these matters a man direct not his rejoicing to God, it will ever be false and deceptive. For of such a man is that saying of Solomon to be understood, where he addresses joy in the creatures, saying: 'To joy I said: "Why art thou vainly deceived?"' That is, when the heart allows itself to be attracted by the creatures.

Chapter XXII

Of the evils which come to the soul when it sets the rejoicing of its will upon the good things of nature.

Although many of these evils and benefits that I am describing in treating of these kinds of joy are common to all, yet, because they follow directly from joy and detachment from joy (although comprised under any one of these six divisions which I am treating), therefore I speak under each heading of some evils and benefits which are also found under another, since these, as I say, are connected with that joy which belongs to them all. But my principal intent is to speak of the particular evils and benefits which come to the soul, with respect to each thing, through its rejoicing or not rejoicing in it. These I call particular evils, because they are primarily and immediately caused by one particular kind of rejoicing, and are not, save in a secondary and mediate sense, caused by another. The evil of spiritual lukewarmness, for example, is caused directly by any and every kind of joy, and this evil is therefore common to all these six kinds; but fornication is a particular evil, which is the direct result only of joy in the good things of nature of which we are speaking.

The spiritual and bodily evils, then, which directly and effectively come to the soul when it sets its rejoicing on the good things of nature are reduced to six principal evils. The first is vainglory, presumption, pride and disesteem of our neighbour; for a man cannot cast eyes of esteem on one thing without taking them from the rest. From this follows, at the least, a real disesteem for everything else; for naturally, by setting our esteem on one thing, we withdraw our heart from all things else and set it upon the thing esteemed; and from this real contempt it is very easy to fall into an intentional and voluntary contempt for all these other things, in particular or in general, not only in the heart, but also in speech, when we say that such a thing or such a person is not like such another. The second evil is the moving of the senses to complacency and sensual delight and lust. The third evil comes from falling into adulation and vain praise, wherein is deception and vanity, as Isaias says in these words: 'My people, he that praises thee deceives thee.' And the reason is that, although we sometimes speak the truth when we praise grace and beauty, yet it will be a marvel if there is not some evil enwrapped therein or if the person praised is not plunged into vain complacency and rejoicing, or his imperfect intentions and affections are not directed thereto. The fourth evil is of a general kind: it is a serious blunting of the reason and the spiritual sense, such as is effected by rejoicing in temporal good things. In one way, indeed, it is much worse. For as the good things of nature are more closely connected with man than are temporal good things, the joy which they give leaves an impression and effect and trace upon the senses more readily and more effectively, and deadens them more completely. And thus reason and judgment are not free, but are clouded with that affection of joy which is very closely connected with them; and from this arises the fifth evil, which is distraction of the mind by created things. And hence arise and follow lukewarmness and weakness of spirit, which is the sixth evil, and is likewise of a general kind; this is apt to reach such a pitch that a man may find the things of God very tedious and troublesome, and at last even come to abhor them. In this rejoicing purity of spirit is invariably lost — at least, in its essence. For, if any spirituality is discerned, it will be of such a gross and sensual kind as to be hardly spiritual or interior or recollected at all, since it will consist rather in pleasure of sense than in strength of spirit. Since, then, the spirituality of the soul is of so low and weak a character at that time as not to quench the habit of this rejoicing (for this habit alone suffices to destroy pure spirituality, even when the soul is not consenting to the acts of rejoicing), the soul must be living, so to say, in the weakness of sense rather than in the strength of the spirit. Otherwise, it will be seen in the perfection and fortitude which the soul will have when the occasion demands it. Although I do not deny that many virtues may exist together with serious imperfections, no pure or delectable inward spirituality can exist while these joys are not quenched; for the flesh reigns within, warring against the spirit, and, although the spirit may be unconscious of the evil, yet at the least it causes it secret distraction.

Returning now to speak of that second evil, which contains within itself innumerable other evils, it is impossible to describe with the pen or to express in words the lengths to which it can go, but this is not unknown or secret, nor is the extent of the misery that arises from the setting of our rejoicing on natural beauty and graces. For every day we hear of its causing numerous deaths, the loss by many of their honour, the commission of many insults, the dissipation of much wealth, numerous cases of emulation and strife, of adultery, rape and fornication, and of the fall of many holy men, comparable in number to that third part of the stars of Heaven which was swept down by the tail of the serpent on earth. The fine gold has lost its brilliance and lustre and is become mire; and the notable and noble men of Sion, who were clothed in finest gold, are counted as earthen pitchers that are broken and have become potsherds. How far does the poison of this evil not penetrate?

And who drinks not, either little or much, from this golden chalice of the Babylonian woman of the Apocalypse? She seats herself on that great beast, that had seven heads and ten crowns, signifying that there is scarce any man, whether high or low, saint or sinner, who comes not to drink of her wine, to some extent enslaving his heart thereby, for, as is said of her in that place, all the kings of the earth have become drunken with the wine of her prostitution. And she seizes upon all estates of men, even upon the highest and noblest estate — the service of the sanctuary and the Divine priesthood — setting her abominable cup, as Daniel says, in the holy place, and leaving scarcely a single strong man without making him to drink, either little or much, from the wine of this chalice, which is vain rejoicing. For this reason it is said that all the kings of the earth have become drunken with this wine, for very few will be found, however holy they may have been, that have not been to some extent stupefied and bewildered by this draught of the joy and pleasure of natural graces and beauty.

This phrase 'have become drunken' should be noted. For, however little a man may drink of the wine of this rejoicing, it at once takes hold upon the heart, and stupefies it and works the evil of darkening the reason, as does wine to those who have been corrupted by it. So that, if some antidote be not at once taken against this poison, whereby it may be quickly expelled, the life of the soul is endangered. Its spiritual weakness will increase, bringing it to such a pass that it will be like Samson, when his eyes were put out and the hair of his first strength was cut off, and like Samson it will see itself grinding in the mills, a captive among its enemies; and afterwards, peradventure, it will die the second death among its enemies, even as did he, since the drinking of this rejoicing will produce in them spiritually all those evils that were produced in him physically, and does in fact produce them in many persons to this day. Let his enemies come and say to him afterwards, to his great confusion: Art thou he that broke the knotted cords, that tore asunder the lions, slew the thousand Philistines, broke down the gates and freed himself from all his enemies?

Let us conclude, then, by giving the instruction necessary to counteract this poison. And let it be this: As soon as thy heart feels moved by this vain joy in the good things of nature, let it remember how vain a thing it is to rejoice in aught save the service of God, how perilous and how pernicious. Let it consider how great an evil it was for the angels to rejoice and take pleasure in their natural endowments and beauty, since it was this that plunged them into the depths of shame. Let them think, too, how many evils come to men daily through this same vanity, and let them therefore resolve in good time to employ the remedy which the poet commends to those who begin to grow affectioned to such things. 'Make haste now,' he says, 'and use the remedy at the beginning; for when evil things have had time to grow in the heart, remedy and medicine come late.' Look not upon the wine, as the Wise Man says, when its colour is red and when it shines in the glass; it enters pleasantly and bites like a viper and sheds abroad poison like a basilisk.

Chapter XXIII

Of the benefits which the soul receives from not setting its rejoicing upon the good things of nature.

Many are the benefits which come to the soul through the withdrawal of its heart from this rejoicing; for, besides preparing itself for the love of God and the other virtues, it makes a direct way for its own humility, and for a general charity toward its neighbours. For, as it is not led by the apparent good things of nature, which are deceitful, into affection for anyone, the soul remains free and able to love them all rationally and spiritually, as God wills them to be loved. Here it must be understood that none deserves to be loved, save for the virtue that is in him. And, when we love in this way, it is very pleasing to the will of God, and also brings great freedom; and if there be attachment in it, there is greater attachment to God. For, in that case, the more this love grows, the more grows our love toward God; and, the more grows our love toward God, the greater becomes our love for our neighbour. For, when love is grounded in God, the reason for all love is one and the same and the cause of all love is one and the same also.

Another excellent benefit comes to the soul from its renunciation of this kind of rejoicing, which is that it fulfils and keeps the counsel of Our Saviour which He gives us through Saint Matthew. 'Let him that will follow Me', He says, 'deny himself.' This the soul could in no wise do if it were to set its rejoicing upon the good things of nature; for he that makes any account of himself neither denies himself nor follows Christ.

There is another great benefit in the renunciation of this kind of rejoicing, which is that it produces great tranquillity in the soul, empties it of distractions and brings recollection to the senses, especially to the eyes. For the soul that desires not to rejoice in these things desires neither to look at them nor to attach the other senses to them, lest it should be attracted or entangled by them. Nor will it spend time or thought upon them, being like the prudent serpent, which stops its ears that it may not hear the charmers lest they make some impression upon it. For, by guarding its doors, which are the senses, the soul guards itself safely and increases its tranquillity and purity.

There is another benefit of no less importance to those that have become proficient in the mortification of this kind of rejoicing, which is that evil things and the knowledge of them neither make an impression upon them nor stain them as they do those to whom they still give any delight. Wherefore the renunciation and mortification of this rejoicing result in spiritual cleanness of soul and body; that is, of spirit and sense; and the soul comes to have an angelical conformity with God, and becomes, both in spirit and in body, a worthy temple of the Holy Spirit. This cannot come to pass if the heart rejoices in natural graces and good things. For this reason it is not necessary to have given consent to any evil thing, or to have remembrance of such; for that rejoicing suffices to stain the soul and the senses with impurity by means of the knowledge of evil; for, as the Wise Man says, the Holy Spirit will remove Himself from thoughts that are without understanding — that is, without the higher reason that has respect to God.

Another benefit of a general kind follows, which is that, besides freeing ourselves from the evils and dangers aforementioned, we are delivered also from countless vanities, and from many other evils, both spiritual and temporal; and especially from falling into the small esteem in which are held all those that are seen to glory or rejoice in the said natural gifts, whether in their own or in those of others. And thus these souls are held and esteemed as wise and prudent, as indeed are all those who take no account of these things, but only of that which pleases God.

From these said benefits follows the last, which is a generosity of the soul, as necessary to the service of God as is liberty of spirit, whereby temptations are easily vanquished and trials faithfully endured, and whereby, too, the virtues grow and become prosperous.

Chapter XXIV

Which treats of the third kind of good thing whereon the will may set the affection of rejoicing, which kind pertains to sense. Indicates what these good things are and of how many kinds, and how the will has to be directed to God and purged of this rejoicing.

We have next to treat of rejoicing with respect to the good things of sense, which is the third kind of good thing wherein we said that the will may rejoice. And it is to be noted that by the good things of sense we here understand everything in this life that can be apprehended by the senses of sight, hearing, smell, taste or touch, and by the interior fashioning of imaginary reflections, all of which things belong to the bodily senses, interior and exterior.

And, in order to darken the will and purge it of rejoicing with respect to these sensible objects, and direct it to God by means of them, it is necessary to assume one truth, which is that, as we have frequently said, the sense of the lower part of man which is that whereof we are treating, is not, neither can be, capable of knowing or understanding God as God is. So that the eye cannot see Him, or aught that is like Him; neither can the ear hear His voice, or any sound that resembles it; neither can the sense of smell perceive a perfume so sweet as He; neither can the taste detect a savour so sublime and delectable; neither can the touch feel a movement so delicate and full of delight, nor aught like to it; neither can His form or any figure that represents Him enter into the thought or imagination. Even as says Isaias: 'Eye hath not seen Him, nor hath ear heard Him, neither hath it entered into the heart of man.'

And here it must be noted that the senses may receive pleasure and delight, either from the spirit, by means of some communication that it receives from God interiorly, or from outward things communicated to them. And, as has been said, neither by way of the spirit nor by that of sense can the sensual part of the soul know God. For, since it has no capacity for attaining to such a point, it receives in the senses both that which is of the spirit and that which is of sense, and receives them in no other way. Wherefore it would be at the least but vanity to set the rejoicing of the will upon pleasure caused by any of these apprehensions, and it would be hindering the power of the will from occupying itself with God and from setting its rejoicing upon Him alone. This the soul cannot perfectly accomplish, save by purging itself and remaining in darkness as to rejoicing of this kind, as also with respect to other things.

I said advisedly that if the rejoicing of the will were to rest in any of these things it would be vanity. But, when it does not rest upon them, but, as soon as the will finds pleasure in that which it hears, sees and does, soars upward to rejoice in God — so that its pleasure acts as a motive and strengthens it to that end — this is very good. In such a case not only need the said motions not be shunned when they cause this devotion and prayer, but the soul may profit by them, and indeed should so profit, to the end that it may accomplish this holy exercise. For there are souls who are greatly moved by objects of sense to seek God. But much circumspection must be observed herein and the resulting effects must be considered; for oftentimes many spiritual persons indulge in the recreations of sense aforementioned under the pretext of offering prayer and devotion to God; and they do this in a way which must be described as recreation rather than prayer, and which gives more pleasure to themselves than to God. And, although the intention that they have is toward God, the effect which they produce is that of recreation of sense, wherein they find weakness and imperfection, rather than revival of the will and surrender thereof to God.

I wish, therefore, to propose a test whereby it may be seen when these delights of the senses aforementioned are profitable and when they are not. And it is that, whensoever a person hears music and other things, and sees pleasant things, and is conscious of sweet perfumes, or tastes things that are delicious, or feels soft touches, if his thought and the affection of his will are at once centred upon God and if that thought of God gives him more pleasure than the movement of sense which causes it, and save for that he finds no pleasure in the said movement, this is a sign that he is receiving benefit therefrom, and that this thing of sense is a help to his spirit. In this way such things may be used, for then such things of sense subserve the end for which God created and gave them, which is that He should be the better loved and known because of them. And it must be known, furthermore, that one upon whom these things of sense cause the pure spiritual effect which I describe has no desire for them, and makes hardly any account of them, though they cause him great pleasure when they are offered to him, because of the pleasure which, as I have said, they cause him in God. He is not, however, solicitous for them, and when they are offered to him, as I say, his will passes from them at once and he abandons it to God and sets it upon Him.

The reason why he cares little for these motives, although they help him on his journey to God, is that the spirit which is ready to go by every means and in every way to God is so completely nourished and prepared and satisfied by the spirit of God that it lacks nothing and desires nothing; or, if it desires anything to that end, the desire at once passes and is forgotten, and the soul makes no account of it. But one that feels not this liberty of spirit in these things and pleasures of sense, but whose will rests in these pleasures and feeds upon them, is greatly harmed by them and should withdraw himself from the use of them. For, although his reason may desire to employ them to journey to God, yet, inasmuch as his desire finds pleasure in them which is according to sense, and their effect is ever dependent upon the pleasure which they give, he is certain to find hindrance in them rather than help, and harm rather than profit. And, when he sees that the desire for such recreation reigns in him, he must mortify it; for, the stronger it becomes, the more imperfection he will have and the greater will be his weakness.

So whatever pleasure coming from sense presents itself to the spiritual person, and whether it come to him by chance or by design, he must make use of it only for God, lifting up to Him the rejoicing of his soul so that his rejoicing may be useful and profitable and perfect; realizing that all rejoicing which implies not renunciation and annihilation of every other kind of rejoicing, although it be with respect to something apparently very lofty, is vain and profits not, but is a hindrance towards the union of the will in God.

Chapter XXV

Which treats of the evils that afflict the soul when it desires to set the rejoicing of its will upon the good things of sense.

In the first place, if the soul does not darken and quench the joy which may arise within it from the things of sense, and direct its rejoicing to God, all the general kinds of evil which we have described as arising from every other kind of rejoicing follow from this joy in the things of sense: such evils are darkness in the reason, lukewarmness, spiritual weariness, etc. But, to come to details, many are the evils, spiritual, bodily and sensual, into which the soul may fall through this rejoicing.

First of all, from joy in visible things, when the soul denies not itself therein in order to reach God, there may come to it, directly, vanity of spirit and distraction of the mind, unruly covetousness, immodesty, outward and inward unseemliness, impurity of thought, and envy.

From joy in hearing useless things there may directly arise distraction of the imagination, gossiping, envy, rash judgements and vacillating thoughts; and from these arise many other and pernicious evils.

From joy in sweet perfumes, there arise loathing of the poor, which is contrary to the teaching of Christ, dislike of serving others, unruliness of heart in humble things, and spiritual insensibility, at least to a degree proportionate with its desire for this joy.

From joy in the savour of meat and drink, there arise directly such gluttony and drunkenness, wrath, discord and want of charity with one's neighbours and with the poor, as had that Epulon, who fared sumptuously every day, with Lazarus. Hence arise bodily disorders, infirmities and evil motions, because the incentives to luxury become greater. Directly, too, there arises great spiritual torpor, and the desire for spiritual things is corrupted, so that the soul can derive no enjoyment or satisfaction from them nor can even speak of them. From this joy is likewise born distraction of the other senses and of the heart, and discontent with respect to many things.

From joy in the touch of soft things arise many more evils and more pernicious ones, which more quickly cause sense to overflow into spirit, and quench all spiritual strength and vigour. Hence arises the abominable vice of effeminacy, or the incentives thereto, according to the proportion of joy of this kind which is experienced. Hence luxury increases, the mind becomes effeminate and timid, and the senses grow soft and delicate and are predisposed to sin and evil. Vain gladness and joy are infused into the heart; the tongue takes to itself licence and the eyes roam unrestrainedly; and the remaining senses are blunted and deadened, according to the measure of this desire. The judgment is put to confusion, being nourished by spiritual folly and insipidity; moral cowardice and inconstancy increase; and, by the darkness of the soul and the weakness of the heart, fear is begotten even where no fear is. At times, again, this joy begets a spirit of confusion, and insensibility with respect to conscience and spirit; wherefore the reason is greatly enfeebled, and is affected in such a way that it can neither take nor give good counsel, and remains incapable of moral and spiritual blessings and becomes as useless as a broken vessel.

All these evils are caused by this kind of rejoicing — in some more intensely, according to the intensity of their rejoicing, and also according to the complacency or weakness or variableness of the person who yields to it. For there are natures that will receive more detriment from a slight occasion of sin than will others from a great one.

Finally, from joy of this kind in touch, a person may fall into as many evils and perils as those which we have described as concerning the good things of nature; and, since these have already been described, I do not detail them here; neither do I describe many other evils wrought thus, such as a falling-off in spiritual exercises and bodily penance and lukewarmness and lack of devotion in the use of the sacraments of penance and of the Eucharist.

Chapter XXVI

Of the benefits that come to the soul from self-denial in rejoicing as to things of sense, which benefits are spiritual and temporal.

Marvellous are the benefits that the soul derives from self-denial in this rejoicing: some of these are spiritual and some temporal.

The first is that the soul, by restraining its rejoicing as to things of sense, is restored from the distraction into which it has fallen through excessive use of the senses, and is recollected in God. The spirituality and the virtues that it has acquired are preserved; nay, they are increased and increase continually.

The second spiritual benefit which comes from self-denial in rejoicing as to things of sense is exceeding great. We may say with truth that that which was sensual becomes spiritual, and that which was animal becomes rational; and even that the soul is journeying from a human life to a portion which is angelical; and that, instead of being temporal and human, it becomes celestial and divine. For, even as a man who seeks the pleasure of things of sense and sets his rejoicing upon them neither merits nor deserves any other name than those which we have given him — that is, sensual, animal, temporal, etc. — even so, when he exalts his rejoicing above these things of sense, he merits all those other names — to wit, spiritual, celestial, etc.

And it is clear that this is true; for, although the use of the senses and the power of sensuality are contrary, as the Apostle says, to the power and the exercises of spirituality, it follows that, when the one kind of power is diminished and brought to an end, the other contrary kinds, the growth of which was hindered by the first kinds, are increased. And thus, when the spirit is perfected (which is the higher part of the soul and the part that has relations with God and receives His communications), it merits all these attributes aforementioned, since it is perfected in the heavenly and spiritual gifts and blessings of God. Both these things are proved by Saint Paul, who calls the sensual man (namely, the man that directs the exercise of his will solely to sense) the animal man, who perceives not the things of God. But this other man, who lifts up his will to God, he calls the spiritual man, saying that this man penetrates and judges all things, even the deep things of God. Therefore the soul gains herein the marvellous benefit of a disposition well able to receive the blessings and spiritual gifts of God.

The third benefit is that the pleasures and the rejoicing of the will in temporal matters are very greatly increased; for, as the Saviour says, they shall receive an hundredfold in this life. So that, if thou deniest thyself one joy, the Lord will give thee an hundredfold in this life, both spiritually and temporally; and likewise, for one joy that thou hast in these things of sense, thou shalt have an hundredfold of affliction and misery. For, through the eye that is purged from the joys of sight, there comes to the soul a spiritual joy, directed to God in all things that are seen, whether Divine or profane. Through the ear that is purged from the joy of hearing, there comes to the soul joy most spiritual an hundredfold, directed to God in all that it hears, whether Divine or profane. Even so is it with the other senses when they are purged. For, even as in the state of innocence all that our first parents saw and said and ate in Paradise furnished them with greater sweetness of contemplation, so that the sensual part of their nature might be duly subjected to, and ordered by, reason; even so the man whose senses are purged from all things of sense and made subject to the spirit receives, in their very first motion, the delight of delectable knowledge and contemplation of God.

Wherefore, to him that is pure, all things, whether high or low, are an occasion of greater good and further purity; even as the man that is impure is apt to derive evil from things both high and low, because of his impurity. But he that conquers not the joy of desire will not enjoy the serenity of habitual rejoicing in God through His creatures and works. In the man that lives no more according to sense, all the operations of the senses and faculties are directed to Divine contemplation. For, as it is true in good philosophy that each thing operates according to its being, and to the life that it lives, so it is clear, beyond contradiction, that, if the soul lives a spiritual life, the animal life being mortified, it must be journeying straight to God, since all its spiritual actions and motions pertain to the life of the spirit. Hence it follows that such a man, being pure in heart, finds in all things a knowledge of God which is joyful and pleasant, chaste, pure, spiritual, glad and loving.

From what has been said I deduce the following doctrine — namely that, until a man has succeeded in so habituating his senses to the purgation of the joys of sense that from their first motion he is gaining the benefit aforementioned of directing all his powers to God, he must needs deny himself joy and pleasure with respect to these powers, so that he may withdraw his soul from the life of sense. He must fear that since he is not yet spiritual, he may perchance derive from the practice of these things a pleasure and an energy which is of sense rather than of spirit; that the energy which is of sense may predominate in all his actions; and that this may lead to an increase of sensuality and may sustain and nurture it. For, as Our Saviour says, that which is born of the flesh is flesh, and that which is born of the spirit is spirit. Let this be closely considered, for it is the truth. And let not him that has not yet mortified his pleasure in things of sense dare to make great use of the power and operation of sense with respect to them, thinking that they will help him to become more spiritual; for the powers of the soul will increase the more without the intervention of these things of sense — that is, if it quench the joy and desire for them rather than indulge its pleasure in them.

There is no need to speak of the blessings of glory that, in the life to come, result from the renunciation of these joys. For, apart from the fact that the bodily gifts of the life of glory, such as agility and clarity, will be much more excellent than in those souls who have not denied themselves, there will be an increase in the essential glory of the soul corresponding to its love of God, for Whose sake it has renounced the things of sense aforementioned. For every momentary, fleeting joy that has been renounced, as Saint Paul says, there shall be laid up an exceeding weight of glory eternally. And I will not here recount the other benefits, whether moral, temporal or spiritual, which result from this night of rejoicing; for they all are those that have already been described, and to a more eminent degree; since these joys that are renounced are more closely linked to the natural man, and therefore he that renounces them acquires thereby a more intimate purity.

Chapter XXVII

Which begins to treat of the fourth kind of good — namely, the moral. Describes wherein this consists, and in what manner joy of the will therein is lawful.

The fourth kind of good wherein the will may rejoice is moral. By this we here understand the virtues, and the habits of the virtues, in so far as these are moral, and the practice of any virtue, and the practice of works of mercy, the keeping of the law of God, and of that of the commonweal, and the putting into practice of all good intentions and inclinations.

These kinds of moral good, when they are possessed and practised, deserve perhaps more than any of the other kinds aforementioned that the will should rejoice in them. For a man may rejoice in his own affairs for one of two reasons, or for both reasons together — namely, for that which they are in themselves, or for the good which they imply and bring with them as a means and instrument. We shall find that the possession of the three kinds of good already mentioned merits no rejoicing of the will. For of themselves, as has been said, they do no good to man, nor in themselves have they any good, since they are so fleeting and frail; rather, as we have likewise said, they cause and bring him trouble and grief and affliction of spirit. Now, although they might merit that man should rejoice in them for the second reason — which is that he may profit by them for journeying to God — this is so uncertain that, as we commonly see, they more often harm man than bring him profit. But good things of a moral kind merit a certain degree of rejoicing in him that possesses them, and this for the first reason — namely, for their intrinsic nature and worth. For they bring with them peace and tranquillity, and a right and ordered use of the reason and actions that are consistent therewith, so that a man cannot, humanly speaking, have anything better in this life.

Thus, since these virtues deserve to be loved and esteemed, humanly speaking, for their own sakes, a man may well rejoice in the possession of them, and may practise them for that which they are in themselves, and for the blessing which they bring to man in human and temporal form. In this way and for this reason philosophers and wise men and princes of old esteemed and praised them, and endeavoured to possess and practise them; and, although they were heathen, and regarded them only in a temporal manner, merely considering the blessings which they knew would result from them — temporal, corporeal and natural — they not only obtained by means of them the temporal renown and benefits which they sought, but, apart from this, God, Who loves all that is good (even in barbarians and heathen) and, as the Wise Man says, hinders the doing of naught that is good, gave them longer life, greater honour, dominion and peace (as He did for example to the Romans), because they made just laws; for He subjected nearly the whole world to them, and gave rewards of a temporal kind for their good customs to those who because of their unbelief were incapable of eternal reward. For God loves moral good so much that, merely because Solomon asked wisdom of Him that he might teach his people, govern them justly and bring them up in good customs, God Himself was greatly pleased with him, and told him that, because he had asked for wisdom to that end, this should be given him, and there should also be given him that which he had not asked, namely, riches and honour, so that no king, either in the past or in the future, should be like him.

But, although the Christian should rejoice in this first way in the moral good that he possesses and in the good works of a temporal kind which he does, since they lead to the temporal blessings which we have described, he must not allow his joy to stop at this first stage (as we have said the heathen did, because their spiritual sight extended not beyond the things of this mortal life); but, since he has the light of faith, wherein he hopes for eternal life, without which nothing that belongs to this life and the next will be of any value to him, he must rejoice principally and solely in the possession and employment of this moral good after the second manner — namely, in that by doing these works for the love of God he will gain eternal life. And thus he should set his eyes and his rejoicing solely on serving and honouring God with his good customs and virtues. For without this intention the virtues are of no worth in the sight of God, as is seen in the ten virgins of the Gospel, who had all kept their virginity and done good works; and yet, because the joy of five of them was not of the second kind (that is, because they had not directed their joy to God), but was rather after the first and vain kind, for they rejoiced in the possession of their good works, they were cast out from Heaven with no acknowledgement or reward from the Bridegroom. And likewise many persons of old had many virtues and practised good works, and many Christians have them nowadays and accomplish great acts, which will profit them nothing for eternal life, because they have not sought in them the glory and honour which belong to God alone. The Christian, then, must rejoice, not in the performing of good works and the following of good customs, but in doing them for the love of God alone, without respect too aught else soever. For, inasmuch as good works that are done to serve God alone will have the greater reward in glory, the greater will be the confusion in the presence of God of those who have done them for other reasons.

The Christian, then, if he will direct his rejoicing to God with regard to moral good, must realize that the value of his good works, fasts, alms, penances, etc., is based, not upon the number or the quality of them, but upon the love of God which inspires him to do them; and that they are the more excellent when they are performed with a purer and sincerer love of God, and when there is less in them of self-interest, joy, pleasure, consolation and praise, whether with reference to this world or to the next. Wherefore the heart must not be set upon pleasure, consolation and delight, and the other interests which good works and practices commonly bring with them, but it must concentrate its rejoicing upon God. It must desire to serve Him in its good works, and purge itself from this other rejoicing, remaining in darkness with respect to it and desiring that God alone shall have joy in its good works and shall take secret pleasure therein, without any other intention and delight than those relating to the honour and glory of God. And thus, with respect to this moral good, the soul will concentrate all the strength of its will upon God.

Chapter XXVIII

Of seven evils into which a man may fall if he set the rejoicing of his will upon moral good.

The principal evils into which a man may fall through vain rejoicing in his good works and habits I find to be seven; and they are very hurtful because they are spiritual.

The first evil is vanity, pride, vainglory and presumption; for a man cannot rejoice in his works without esteeming them. And hence arise boasting and like things, as is said of the Pharisee in the Gospel, who prayed and congratulated himself before God, boasting that he fasted and did other good works.

The second evil is usually linked with this: it is our judging others, by comparison with ourselves, as wicked and imperfect, when it seems to us that their acts and good works are inferior to our own; we esteem them the less highly in our hearts, and at times also in our speech. This evil was likewise that of the Pharisee, for in his prayer he said: 'I thank Thee that I am not as other men are: robbers, unjust and adulterers.' So that by one single act he fell into these two evils, esteeming himself and despising others, as do many nowadays, saying: I am not like such a man, nor do I do this and that, as does such or such a man. And many of these are even worse than the Pharisee. He, it is true, not only despised others, but also pointed to an individual, saying: 'Nor am I like this publican.' But they, not satisfied with either of these things, go so far as to be angry and envious when they see that others are praised, or do more, or are of greater use, than themselves.

The third evil is that, as they look for pleasure in their good works, they usually perform them only when they see that some pleasure and praise will result from them. And thus, as Christ says, they do everything ut videantur ab hominibus, and work not for the love of God alone.

The fourth evil follows from this. It is that they will have no reward from God, since they have desired in this life to have joy or consolation or honour or some other kind of interest as a result of their good works: of such the Saviour says that herein they have received their reward. And thus they have had naught but the labour of their work and are confounded, and receive no reward. There is so much misery among the sons of men which has to do with this evil that I myself believe that the greater number of good works which they perform in public are either vicious or will be of no value to them, or are imperfect in the sight of God, because they are not detached from these human intentions and interests. For what other judgment can be formed of some of the actions which certain men perform, and of the memorials which they set up, when they will not perform these actions at all unless they are surrounded by human respect and honour, which are the vanity of life, or unless they can perpetuate in these memorials their name, lineage or authority, even setting up their emblems and escutcheons in the very churches, as if they wished to set themselves, in the stead of images, in places where all bend the knee? In these good works which some men perform, may it not be said that they are worshipping themselves more than God? This is certainly true if they perform them for the reason described and otherwise would not perform them at all. But leaving aside these, which are the worst cases, how many are there who fall into these evils in their good works in many ways? Some wish to be praised, others to be thanked, others enumerate their good works and desire that this person and that shall know of them, and indeed the whole world; and sometimes they wish an intermediary to present their alms, or to perform other of their charitable deeds, so that more may be known of them; and some desire all these things. This is the sounding of the trumpet, which, says the Saviour in the Gospel, vain men do, for which reason they shall have no reward for their works from God.

In order to flee from this evil, such persons must hide their good works so that God alone may see them, and must not desire anyone to take notice of them. And they must hide them, not only from others, but even from themselves. That is to say, they must find no satisfaction in them, nor esteem them as if they were of some worth, nor derive pleasure from them at all. It is this that is spiritually indicated in those words of Our Lord: 'Let not thy left hand know what they right hand doeth. Which is as much to say: Esteem not with thy carnal and temporal eye the work that thou doest spiritually. And in this way the strength of the will is concentrated upon God, and a good deed bears fruit in His sight; so that not only will it not be lost, but it will be of great merit. And in this sense must be understood that passage from Job: 'If I have kissed my hand with my mouth, which is a great sin and iniquity, and my heart hath rejoiced in secret.' Here by the hand is understood good works, and by the mouth is understood the will which finds satisfaction in them. And since this is, as we say, finding satisfaction in oneself, he says: If my heart hath rejoiced in secret, which is a great iniquity against God and a denial of Him. And this is as though he were to say that he had no satisfaction, neither did his heart rejoice in secret.

The fifth of these evils is that such persons make no progress on the road of perfection. For, since they are attached to the pleasure and consolation which they find in their good works, it follows that, when they find no such pleasure and consolation in their good works and exercises, which ordinarily happens when God desires to lead them on, by giving them the dry bread of the perfect and taking from them the milk of babes, in order to prove their strength and to purge their delicate appetites so that they may be able to enjoy the food of grown men, they commonly faint and cease to persevere, because their good works give them no pleasure. In this way may be spiritually understood these words of the Wise Man: 'Dying flies spoil the sweetness of ointment.' For, when any mortification comes to these persons, they die to their good works and cease to practise them; and thus they lose their perseverance, wherein are found sweetness of spirit and interior consolation.

The sixth of these evils is that such persons commonly deceive themselves, thinking that the things and good works which give them pleasure must be better than those that give them none. They praise and esteem the one kind and depreciate the other; yet as a rule those works whereby a man is most greatly mortified (especially when he is not proficient in perfection) are more acceptable and precious in the sight of God, by reason of the self-denial which a man must observe in performing them, than are those wherein he finds consolation and which may very easily be an occasion of self-seeking. And in this connection Micheas says of them: Malum manuum suarum dicunt bonum. That is: That which is bad in their works they call good. This comes to them because of the pleasure which they take in their good works, instead of thinking only of giving pleasure to God. The extent to which this evil predominates, whether in spiritual men or in ordinary persons, would take too long to describe, for hardly anyone can be found who is moved to do such works simply for God's sake, without the attraction of some advantage of consolation or pleasure, or some other consideration.

The seventh evil is that, in so far as a man stifles not vain rejoicing in moral works, he is to that extent incapable of receiving reasonable counsel and instruction with regard to good works that he should perform. For he is lettered by the habit of weakness that he has acquired through performing good works with attachment to vain rejoicing; so that he cannot consider the counsel of others as best, or, even if he considers it to be so, he cannot follow it, through not having the necessary strength of mind. Such persons as this are greatly weakened in charity toward God and their neighbour; for the self-love with respect to their good works in which they indulge causes their charity to grow cold.

Chapter XXIX

Of the benefits which come to the soul through the withdrawal of its rejoicing from moral good.

Very great are the benefits which come to the soul when it desires not to set the vain rejoicing of its will on this kind of good. For, in the first place, it is freed from falling into many temptations and deceits of the devil, which are involved in rejoicing in these good works, as we may understand by that which is said in Job, namely: 'He sleepeth under the shadow, in the covert of the reed and in moist places.' This he applies to the devil, who deceives the soul in the moisture of rejoicing and in the vanity of the reed — that is, in vain works. And it is no wonder if the soul is secretly deceived by the devil in this rejoicing; for, apart altogether from his suggestions, vain rejoicing is itself deception. This is especially true when there is any boasting of heart concerning these good works, as Jeremias well says in these words: Arrogantia tua decepit te. For what greater deception is there than boasting? And from this the soul that purges itself from this rejoicing is freed.

The second benefit is that the soul performs its good works with greater deliberation and perfection than it can if there be in them the passion of joy and pleasure. For, because of this passion of joy, the passions of wrath and concupiscence are so strong that they will not submit to reason, but ordinarily cause a man to be inconsistent in his actions and purposes, so that he abandons some and takes up others, and begins a thing only to abandon it without completing any part of it. For, since he acts under the influence of pleasure, and since pleasure is variable, being much stronger in some natures than in others, it follows that, when this pleasure ceases, both the action and its purpose cease, important though they may be. To such persons the joy which they have in their work is the soul and the strength thereof; and, when the joy is quenched, the work ceases and perishes, and they persevere therein no longer. It is of such persons that Christ says: 'They receive the word with joy, and then the devil taketh it away from them, lest they should persevere.' And this is because they have no strength and no roots save in the joy aforementioned. To take and to withdraw their will, therefore, from this rejoicing is the cause of their perseverance and success. This benefit, then, is a great one, even as the contrary evil is great likewise. The wise man sets his eyes upon the substance and benefit of his work, not upon the pleasure and delight which it gives him; and so he is not beating the air, but derives from his work a stable joy, without any meed of bitterness.

The third benefit is divine. It is that, when vain joy in these good works is quenched, the soul becomes poor in spirit, which is one of the blessings spoken of by the Son of God when He says: 'Blessed are the poor in spirit, for theirs is the Kingdom of Heaven.'

The fourth benefit is that he that denies himself this joy will be meek, humble and prudent in his actions. For he will not act impetuously and rapidly, through being impelled by the wrath and concupiscence which belong to joy; neither presumptuously, through being affected by the esteem of his own work which he cherishes because of the joy that he has in it; neither incautiously, through being blinded by joy.

The fifth benefit is that he becomes pleasing to God and man, and is freed from spiritual sloth, gluttony and avarice, and from spiritual envy and from a thousand other vices.

Chapter XXX

Which begins to treat of the fifth kind of good wherein the will may rejoice, which is the supernatural. Describes the nature of these supernatural good things, and how they are distinguished from the spiritual, and how joy in them is to be directed to God.

It now behoves us to treat of the fifth kind of good thing wherein the soul may rejoice, which is the supernatural. By this term we here understand all the gifts and graces given by God which transcend natural virtue and capacity and are called gratis datae. Such as these are the gifts of wisdom and knowledge which God gave to Solomon, and the graces whereof Saint Paul speaks — namely, faith, gifts of healing, the working of miracles, prophecy, knowledge and discernment of spirits, interpretation of words and likewise the gift of tongues.

These good things, it is true, are also spiritual, like those of the same kind of which we have to speak presently; yet, since the two are so different, I have thought well to make a distinction between them. The practice of these has an intimate relation with the profit of man, and it is with a view to this profit and to this end that God gives them. As Saint Paul says: 'The spirit is given to none save for the profit of the rest;' this is to be understood of these graces. But the use and practice of spiritual graces has to do with the soul and God alone, and with God and the soul, in the communion of understanding and will, etc., as we shall say hereafter. And thus there is a difference in their object, since spiritual graces have to do only with the Creator and the soul; whereas supernatural graces have to do with the creature, and furthermore differ in substance, and therefore in their operation, and thus of necessity the instruction which we give concerning them differs also.

Speaking now of supernatural graces and gifts as we here understand them, I say that, in order to purge ourselves of vain joy in them, it is well here to notice two benefits which are comprised in this kind of gift — namely, temporal and spiritual. The temporal benefits are the healing of infirmities, the receiving of their sight by the blind, the raising of the dead, the casting out of devils, prophesying concerning the future so that men may take heed to themselves, and other things of the kind. The spiritual and eternal benefit is that God is known and served through these good works by him that performs them, or by those in whom and in whose presence they are performed.

With respect to the first kind of benefit — namely, the temporal — supernatural works and miracles merit little or no rejoicing on the part of the soul; for, without the second kind of benefit, they are of little or no importance to man, since they are not in themselves a means for uniting the soul with God, as charity is. And these supernatural works and graces may be performed by those who are not in a state of grace and charity, whether they truly give thanks and attribute their gifts to God, as did the wicked prophet Balaam, and Solomon, or whether they perform them falsely, through the agency of the devil, as did Simon Magus, or by means of other secrets of nature. These works and marvels, if any of them were to be of any profit to him that worked them, would be true works given by God. And Saint Paul teaches us what these are worth without the second kind of benefit, saying: 'Though I speak with the tongues of men and of angels, and have not charity, I am become as a sounding bell or metal. And though I have prophecy and know all mysteries and all knowledge; and though I have all faith, even as much as may remove mountains, and have not charity, I am nothing, etc.' Wherefore Christ will refuse the requests of many who have esteemed their good works in this way, when they beg Him for glory because of them, saying: Lord, have we not prophesied in Thy name and worked many miracles? Then Christ will say to them: 'Depart from Me, workers of iniquity.'

A man, then, should rejoice, not when he has such graces and makes use of them, but when he reaps from them the second spiritual fruit, namely that of serving God in them with true charity, for herein is the fruit of eternal life. For this cause Our Saviour reproved the disciples who were rejoicing because they cast out devils, saying: 'Desire not to rejoice in this, that devils are subject to you, but rather because your names are written in the book of life.' This, according to good theology, is as much as to say: Rejoice if your names are written in the book of life. By this it is understood that a man should not rejoice save when he is walking in the way of life, which he may do by performing good works in charity; for where is the profit and what is the worth in the sight of God of aught that is not love of God? And this love is not perfect if it be not strong and discreet in purging the will of joy in all things, and if it be not set upon doing the will of God alone. And in this manner the will is united with God through these good things which are supernatural.

Chapter XXXI

Of the evils which come to the soul when it sets the rejoicing of the will upon this kind of good.

Thee principal evils, it seems to me, may come to the soul when it sets its rejoicing upon supernatural good. These are: that it may deceive and be deceived; that it may fall away from the faith; and that it may indulge in vainglory or some other such vanity.

As to the first of these, it is a very easy thing to deceive others, and to deceive oneself, by rejoicing in this kind of operation. And the reason is that, in order to know which of these operations are false and which are true, and how and at what time they should be practised, much counsel and much light from God are needful, both of which are greatly impeded by joy in these operations and esteem for them. And this for two reasons: first, because joy blunts and obscures the judgment; second, because, when a man has joy in these things, not only does he the more quickly become eager for them, but he is also the more impelled to practise them out of the proper season. And even supposing the virtues and operations which are practised to be genuine, these two defects suffice for us to be frequently deceived in them, either through not understanding them as they should be understood, or through not profiting by them and not using them at the times and in the ways that are most meet. For, although it is true that, when God gives these gifts and graces, He gives light by which to see them, and the impulse whereby a man may know at what times and in what ways to use them; yet these souls, through the attachment and imperfection which they may have with regard to them, may greatly err, by not using them with the perfection that God desires of them therein, and in the way and at the time that He wills. We read that Balaam desired to do this, when, against the will of God, he determined to go and curse the people of Israel, for which reason God was wroth and purposed to slay him. And Saint James and Saint John desired to call down fire from Heaven upon the Samaritans because they gave not lodging to Our Saviour, and for this He reproved them.

Here it is evident that these persons were led to determine to perform these works, when it was not meet for them to do so, by a certain imperfect passion, which was inherent in their joy in them and esteem for them. For, when no such imperfection exists, the soul is moved and determined to perform these virtues only in the manner wherein God so moves it, and at His time, and until then it is not right that they should be performed. It was for this reason that God complained of certain prophets, through Jeremias, saying: 'I sent not the prophets, and they ran; I spake not to them, and they prophesied.' And later He says: 'They deceived My people by their lying and their miracles, when I had not commanded them, neither had I sent them.' And in that place He says of them likewise: 'They see the visions of their heart, and speak of them' ; which would not happen if they had not this abominable attachment to these works.

From these passages it is to be understood that the evil of this rejoicing not only leads men to make wicked and perverse use of these graces given by God, as did Balaam and those of whom the prophet here says that they worked miracles whereby they deceived the people, but it even leads them to use these graces without having been given them by God, like those who prophesied their own fancies and published the visions which they invented or which the devil represented to them. For, when the devil sees them affectioned to these things, he opens a wide field to them, gives them abundant material and interferes with them in many ways; whereupon they spread their sails and become shamelessly audacious in the freedom wherewith they work these marvels.

Nor does the evil stop here. To such a point does their joy in these works and their eagerness for them extend that, if before they had a secret compact with the devil (and many of them do in fact perform these works by such secret compacts), it now makes them bold enough to work with him by an explicit and manifest compact, submitting themselves to him, by agreement, as his disciples and allies. Hence we have wizards, enchanters, magicians, soothsayers and sorcerers. And so far does the joy of these persons in their works carry them that, not only do they seek to purchase gifts and graces with money, as did Simon Magus, in order to serve the devil, but they even strive to obtain sacred things, and (which cannot be said without trembling) Divine things, for even the very Body of our Lord Jesus Christ has been seen to be usurped for the use of their wicked deeds and abominations. May God here extend and show to them His great mercy!

Everyone will clearly understand how pernicious are such persons to themselves and how prejudicial to Christianity. It may be noted here that all those magicians and soothsayers who lived among the children of Israel, whom Saul destroyed out of the land, because they desired to imitate the true prophets of God, had fallen into such abominations and deceits.

He, then, that has supernatural gifts and graces ought to refrain from desiring to practise them, and from rejoicing in so doing, nor ought he to care to exercise them; for God, Who gives Himself to such persons, by supernatural means, for the profit of His Church and of its members, will move them likewise supernaturally in such a manner and at such time as He desires. As He commanded His faithful ones to take no thought as to what they were to say, or as to how they were to say it, since this is the supernatural business of faith, it will likewise be His will (as these operations are no less a supernatural matter) that a man should wait and allow God to work by moving his heart, since it is in the virtue of this working that there will be wrought all virtue. The disciples (so we read in the Acts of the Apostles), although these graces and gifts had been infused within them, prayed to God, beseeching Him to be pleased to stretch forth His hand in making signs and performing works of healing through them, that they might introduce the faith of our Lord Jesus Christ into men's hearts.

From this first evil may proceed the second, which is a falling away from the faith; this can come to pass after two manners. The first has respect to others; for, when a man sets out, unseasonably and needlessly, to perform a marvel or a mighty work, apart from the fact that this is tempting God, which is a great sin, it may be that he will not succeed, and will engender in the hearts of men discredit and contempt for the faith. For, although at times such persons may succeed because for other reasons and purposes God so wills it, as in the case of Saul's witch (if it be true that it was indeed Samuel who appeared on that occasion), they will not always so succeed; and, when they do so, they go astray none the less and are blameworthy for having used these graces when it was not fitting. The second manner in which we may fall away is in ourselves and has respect to the merit of faith; for, if a man make much account of these miracles, he ceases to lean upon the substantial practice of faith, which is an obscure habit; and thus, where signs and witnesses abound, there is less merit in believing. In this way Saint Gregory says that faith has no merit when human reason provides experience. And thus these marvels are never worked by God save when they are really necessary for belief. Therefore, to the end that His disciples should not be without merit, though they had experience of His resurrection, He did many things before He showed Himself to them, so that they should believe Him without seeing Him. To Mary Magdalene, first of all, He showed the empty tomb, and afterwards bade the angels speak to her (for, as Saint Paul says, faith comes by hearing); so that, having heard, she should believe before she saw. And, although she saw Him, it was as an ordinary man, that, by the warmth of His presence, He might completely instruct her in the belief which she lacked. And He first sent to tell His disciples, with the women, and afterwards they went to see the tomb. And, as to those who went to Emmaus, He first of all enkindled their hearts in faith so that they might see Him, dissembling with them as He walked. And finally He reproved them all because they had not believed those who had announced to them His resurrection. And He reproved Saint Thomas because he desired to have the witness of His wounds, by telling him that they who saw Him not and yet believed Him were blessed.

And thus it is not the will of God that miracles should be wrought: when He works them, He does so, as it were, because He cannot do otherwise. And for this cause He reproved the Pharisees because they believed not save through signs, saying: 'Unless ye see marvels and signs, ye believe not.' Those, then, who love to rejoice in these supernatural works lose much in the matter of faith.

The third evil is that, because of their joy in these works, men commonly fall into vainglory or some other vanity. For even their joy in these wonders, when it is not, as we have said, purely in God and for God, is vanity; which is evident in the reproof given by Our Lord to the disciples because they had rejoiced that devils were subject to them; for which joy, if it had not been vain, He would not have reproved them.

Chapter XXXII

Of two benefits which are derived from the renunciation of rejoicing in the matter of the supernatural graces.

Besides the benefits which the soul gains by being delivered from the three evils aforementioned through its renunciation of this joy, it acquires two excellent benefits. The first is that it magnifies and exalts God: the second is that it exalts itself. For God is exalted in the soul after two manners: first, by the withdrawal of the heart and the joy of the will from all that is not God, in order that they may be set upon Him alone. This David signified in the verse which we quoted when we began to speak of the night of this faculty; namely: 'Man shall attain to a lofty heart, and God shall be exalted.' For, when the heart is raised above all things, the soul is exalted above them all.

And, because in this way the soul centres itself in God alone, God is exalted and magnified, when He reveals to the soul His excellence and greatness; for, in this elevation of joy, God bears witness of Who He Himself is. This cannot be done save if the will be voided of joy and consolation with respect to all things, even as David said also, in these words: 'Be still and see that I am God.' And again he says: 'In a desert land, dry and pathless, have I appeared before Thee, to see Thy power and Thy glory.' And, since it is true that God is exalted by the fixing of the soul's rejoicing upon detachment from all things, He is much more highly exalted when the soul withdraws itself from the most wondrous of these things in order to fix its rejoicing on Him alone. For these, being supernatural, are of a nobler kind; and thus for the soul to cast them aside, in order to set its rejoicing upon God alone, is for it to attribute greater glory and excellence to God than to them. For, the more and the greater things a man despises for the sake of another, the more does he esteem and exalt that other.

Furthermore, God is exalted after the second manner when the will is withdrawn from this kind of operation; for, the more God is believed and served without testimonies and signs, the more He is exalted by the soul, for it believes more concerning God than signs and miracles can demonstrate.

The second benefit wherein the soul is exalted consists in this, that, withdrawing the will from all desire for apparent signs and testimonies, it is exalted in purest faith, which God increases and infuses within it much more intensely. And, together with this, He increases in it the other two theological virtues, which are charity and hope, wherein the soul enjoys the highest Divine knowledge by means of the obscure and detached habit of faith; and it enjoys great delight of love by means of charity, whereby the will rejoices in naught else than in the living God; and likewise it enjoys satisfaction in the memory by means of hope. All this is a wondrous benefit, which leads essentially and directly to the perfect union of the soul with God.

Chapter XXXIII

Which begins to treat of the sixth kind of good wherein the soul may rejoice. Describes its nature and makes the first division under this head.

Since the intention of this work of ours is to lead the spirit through these good things of the spirit even to the Divine union of the soul with God, it will not behove both myself and the reader to give our consideration to this matter with particular care. For, in speaking of this sixth kind of good, we have to treat of the good things of the spirit, which are those that are of the greatest service to this end. For it is quite certain, and quite an ordinary occurrence, that some persons, because of their lack of knowledge, make use of spiritual things with respect only to sense, and leave the spirit empty. There will scarcely be anyone whose spirit is not to a considerable degree corrupted by sweetness of sense; since, if the water be drunk up before it reaches the spirit, the latter becomes dry and barren.

Coming to this matter, then, I say that by good things of the spirit I understand all those that influence and aid the soul in Divine things and in its intercourse with God, and the communications of God to the soul.

Beginning by making a division between these supreme kinds of good, I say that good things of the spirit are of two kinds: the one kind is delectable and the other painful. And each of these kinds is likewise of two manners; for the delectable kind consists of clear things that are distinctly understood, and also of things that are not understood clearly or distinctly. The painful kind, likewise, may be of clear and distinct things, or of things dark and confused.

Between all these we may likewise make distinctions with respect to the faculties of the soul. For some kinds of spiritual good, being of knowledge, pertain to the understanding; others, being of affection, pertain to the will; and others, inasmuch as they are imaginary, pertain to the memory.

We shall leave for later consideration those good things that are painful, since they pertain to the passive night, in treating of which we shall have to speak of them; and likewise the delectable blessings which we described as being of things confused and not distinct, of which we shall treat hereafter, since they pertain to that general, confused and loving knowledge wherein is effected the union of the soul with God, and which we passed over in the second book, deferring it so that we might treat of it later when we should make a division between the apprehensions of the understanding. We shall speak here and now of those delectable blessings which are of things clear and distinct.

Chapter XXXIV

Of those good things of the spirit which can be distinctly apprehended by the understanding and the memory. Describes how the will is to behave in the matter of rejoicing in them.

We might spend much time here upon the multitude of the apprehensions of the memory and the understanding, teaching how the will is to conduct itself with regard to the joy that it may have in them, had we not treated of this at length in the second and the third book. But, since we there spoke of the manner wherein it behoves these two faculties to act with respect to them, in order that they may take the road to Divine union, and since it behoves the will to conduct itself likewise as regards rejoicing in them, it is unnecessary to go over this here; for it suffices to say that wheresoever we there said that those faculties should void themselves of this or that apprehension, it is to be understood also that the will should likewise be voided of joy in them. And in the way wherein it is said that memory and understanding are to conduct themselves with regard to all these apprehensions, the will must conduct itself likewise; for, since the understanding and the other faculties cannot admit or reject anything unless the will intervene therein, it is clear that the same teaching that serves for the one will serve also for the other.

It may there be seen, then, what is requisite in this case, for the soul will fall into all the evils and perils to which we there referred if it cannot direct the rejoicing of the will to God in all those apprehensions.

Chapter XXXV

Of the delectable spiritual good things which can be distinctly apprehended by the will.
Describes the kinds of these.

We can reduce all the kinds of good which can distinctly cause joy to the will to four: namely, motive, provocative, directive and perfective. Of these we shall speak in turn, each in its order; and first, of the motive kind — namely, images and portraits of saints, oratories and ceremonies.

As touching images and portraits, there may be much vanity and vain rejoicing in these. For, though they are most important for Divine worship and most necessary to move the will to devotion, as is shown by the approval given to them and the use made of them by our Mother Church (for which reason it is always well that we should employ them, in order to awaken our lukewarmness), there are many persons who rejoice rather in the painting and decoration of them than in what they represent.

The use of images has been ordained by the Church for two principal ends — namely, that we may reverence the saints in them, and that the will may be moved and devotion to the saints awakened by them. When they serve this purpose they are beneficial and the use of them is necessary; and therefore we must choose those that are most true and lifelike, and that most move the will to devotion, and our eyes must ever be fixed upon this motive rather than upon the value and cunning of their workmanship and decoration. For, as I say, there are some who pay more attention to the cunning with which an image is made, and to its value, than to what it represents; and that interior devotion which they ought to direct spiritually to the saint whom they see not, forgetting the image at once, since it serves only as a motive, they squander upon the cunning and the decoration of its outward workmanship. In this way sense is pleased and delighted, and the love and rejoicing of the will remain there. This is a complete hindrance to true spirituality, which demands annihilation of the affections as to all particular things.

This will become quite clear from the detestable custom which certain persons observe with regard to images in these our days. Holding not in abhorence the vain trappings of the world, they adorn images with the garments which from time to time vain persons invent in order to satisfy their own pleasures and vanities. So they clothe images with garments reprehensible even in themselves, a kind of vanity which was, and is still, abhorrent to the saints whom the images represent. Herein, with their help, the devil succeeds in canonizing his vanities, by clothing the saints with them, not without causing them great displeasure. And in this way the honest and grave devotion of the soul, which rejects and spurns all vanity and every trace of it, becomes with them little more than a dressing of dolls; some persons use images merely as idols upon which they have set their rejoicing. And thus you will see certain persons who are never tired of adding one image to another, and wish them to be of this or that kind and workmanship, and to be placed in this or that manner, so as to be pleasing to sense; and they make little account of the devotion of the heart. They are as much attached to them as was Michas to his idols, or as was Laban; for the one ran out of his house crying aloud because they were being taken from him; and the other, having made a long journey and been very wroth because of them, disturbed all the household stuff of Jacob, in searching for them.

The person who is truly devout sets his devotion principally upon that which is invisible; he needs few images and uses few, and chooses those that harmonize with the Divine rather than with the human, clothing them, and with them himself, in the garments of the world to come, and following its fashions rather than those of this world. For not only does an image belonging to this world in no way influence his desire; it does not even lead him to think of this world, in spite of his having before his eyes something worldly, akin to the world's interests. Nor is his heart attached to the images that he uses; if they are taken from him, he grieves very little, for he seeks within himself the living image, which is Christ crucified, for Whose sake he even desires that all should be taken from him and he should have nothing. Even when the motives and means which lead him closest to God are taken from him, he remains in tranquility. For the soul is nearer perfection when it is tranquil and joyous, though it be deprived of these motives, than if it has possession of them together with desire and attachment. For, although it is good to be pleased to have such images as assist the soul to greater devotion (for which reason it is those which move it most that must always be chosen), yet it is something far removed from perfection to be so greatly attached to them as to possess them with attachment, so that, if they are taken away from the soul, it becomes sad.

Let the soul be sure that, the more closely it is attached to an image or a motive, the less will its devotion and prayer mount to God. For, although it is true that, since some are more appropriate than others, and excite devotion more than others, it is well, for this reason alone, to be more affectioned to some than to others, as I have just now said, yet there must be none of the attachment and affection which I have described. Otherwise, that which has to sustain the spirit in its flight to God, in total forgetfulness, will be wholly occupied by sense, and the soul will be completely immersed in a delight afforded it by what are but instruments. These instruments I have to use, but solely in order to assist me in devotion; and, on account of my imperfection, they may well serve me as a hindrance, no less so than may affection and attachment to anything else.

7. But, though perhaps in this matter of images you may think that there is something to be said on the other side, if you have not clearly understood how much detachment and poverty of spirit is required by perfection, at least you cannot excuse the imperfection which is commonly indulged with regard to rosaries; for you will hardly find anyone who has not some weakness with regard to these, desiring them to be of this workmanship rather than of that, or of this colour or metal rather than of that, or decorated in some one style or in some other. Yet no one style is better than another for the hearing of a prayer by God, for this depends upon the simple and true heart, which looks at no more than pleasing God, and, apart from the question of indulgences, cares no more for one rosary than for another.

Our vain concupiscence is of such a nature and quality that it tries to establish itself in everything; and it is like the worm which destroys healthy wood, and works upon things both good and evil. For what else is your desire to have a rosary of cunning workmanship, and your wish that it shall be of one kind rather than of another, but the fixing of your rejoicing upon the instrument? It is like desiring to choose one image rather than another, and considering, not if it will better awaken Divine love within you, but only if it is more precious and more cunningly made. If you employed your desire and rejoicing solely in the love of God, you would care nothing for any of these considerations. It is most vexatious to see certain spiritual persons so greatly attached to the manner and workmanship of these instruments and motives, and to the curiosity and vain pleasure which they find in them: you will never see them satisfied; they will be continually leaving one thing for another, and forgetting and forsaking spiritual devotion for these visible things, to which they have affection and attachment, sometimes of just the same kind as that which a man has to temporal things; and from this they receive no small harm.

Chapter XXXVI

Which continues to treat of images, and describes the ignorance which certain persons have with respect to them.

There is much that might be said of the stupidity which many persons display with regard to images; their foolishness reaches such a point that some of them place more confidence in one kind of image than in another, believing that God will hear them more readily because of these than because of those, even when both represent the same thing, as when there are two of Christ or two of Our Lady. And this happens because they have more affection for the one kind of workmanship than for the other; which implies the crudest ideas concerning intercourse with God and the worship and honour that are owed to Him, which has solely to do with the faith and the purity of heart of him that prays. For if God sometimes grants more favours by means of one image rather than by another of the same kind, it is not because there is more virtue to this effect in one than in another (however much difference there may be in their workmanship), but because some persons better awaken their own devotion by one than by another. If they had the same devotion for the one as for the other (or even without the use of either), they would receive the same favours from God.

Hence the reason for which God works miracles and grants favours by means of one kind of image rather than by another is not that these should be esteemed more than those, but to the end that, by means of the wonder that they cause, there may be awakened sleeping devotion and the affection of the faithful for prayer. And hence it comes that, as the contemplation of the image at that time enkindles devotion and makes us to continue in prayer (both these being means whereby God hears and grants that which is asked of Him), therefore, at that time and by means of that same image, God continues to work favours and miracles because of the prayer and affection which are then shown; for it is certain that God does it not because of the image, which in itself is no more than a painted thing, but because of the devotion and faith which the person has toward the saint whom it represents. And so, if you had the same devotion and faith in Our

Lady before one image representing her as before another, since the person represented is the same (and even, as we have said, if you had no such image at all), you would receive the same favours. For it is clear from experience that, when God grants certain favours and works miracles, He does so as a rule by means of certain images which are not well carved or cunningly formed or painted, so that the faithful may attribute nothing to the figure or the painting.

Furthermore, Our Lord is frequently wont to grant these favours by means of those images that are most remote and solitary. One reason for this is that the effort necessary to journey to them causes the affections to be increased and makes the act of prayer more earnest. Another reason is that we may withdraw ourselves from noise and from people when we pray, even as did the Lord. Wherefore he that makes a pilgrimage does well if he makes it at a time when no others are doing so, even though the time be unusual. I should never advise him to make a pilgrimage when a great multitude is doing so; for, as a rule, on these occasions, people return in a state of greater distraction than when they went. And many set out on these pilgrimages and make them for recreation rather than for devotion. Where there is devotion and faith, then, any image will suffice; but, if there is none, none will suffice. Our Saviour was a very living image in the world; and yet those that had no faith, even though they went about with Him and saw His wondrous works, derived no benefit from them. And this was the reason why, as the Evangelist says, He did few mighty works in His own country.

I desire also to speak here of certain supernatural effects which are sometimes produced by certain images upon particular persons. To certain images God gives a particular spiritual influence upon such persons, so that the figure of the image and the devotion caused by it remain fixed in the mind, and the person has them ever present before him; and so, when he suddenly thinks of the image, the spiritual influence which works upon him is of the same kind as when he saw it — sometimes it is less, but sometimes it is even greater — yet, from another image, although it be of more perfect workmanship, he will not obtain the same spiritual effect.

Many persons, too, have devotion to one kind of workmanship rather than to another, and to some they will have no more than a natural inclination and affection, just as we prefer seeing one person's face to another's. And they will naturally become more attracted to a particular image, and will keep it more vividly in their imagination, even though it be not as beautiful as others, just because their nature is attracted to that kind of form and figure which it represents. And some persons will think that the affection which they have for such or such an image is devotion, whereas it will perhaps be no more than natural inclination and affection. Again, it may happen that, when they look at an image, they will see it move, or make signs and gestures and indications, or speak. This, and the variety of supernatural effects caused by images of which we have here been speaking, are, it is true, quite frequently good and true effects, produced by God either to increase devotion or so that the soul may have some support on which to lean, because it is somewhat weak, and so that it may not be distracted. Yet frequently, again, they are produced by the devil in order to cause deception and harm. We shall therefore give instruction concerning this in the chapter following.

Chapter XXXVII

Of how the rejoicing of the will must be directed, by way of the images, to God, so that the soul may not go astray because of them or be hindered by them.

Just as images are of great benefit for remembering God and the saints, and for moving the will to devotion when they are used in the ordinary way, as is fitting, so they will lead to great error if, when supernatural happenings come to pass in connection with them, the soul should not be able to conduct itself as is fitting for its journey to God. For one of the means by which the devil lays hold on incautious souls, with great ease, and obstructs the way of spiritual truth for them, is the use of extraordinary and supernatural happenings, of which he gives examples by means of images, both the material and corporeal images used by the Church, and also those which he is wont to fix in the fancy in relation to such or such a saint, or an image of him, transforming himself into an angel of light that he may deceive. For in those very means which we possess for our relief and help the astute devil contrives to hide himself in order to catch us when we are least prepared. Wherefore it is concerning good things that the soul that is good must ever have the greatest misgivings, for evil things bear their own testimony with them.

Hence, in order to avoid all the evils which may happen to the soul in this connection, which are its being hindered from soaring upward to God, or its using images in an unworthy and ignorant manner, or its being deceived by them through natural or supernatural means, all of which are things that we have touched upon above; and in order likewise to purify the rejoicing of the will in them and by means of them to lead the soul to God, for which reason the Church recommends their use, I desire here to set down only one warning, which will suffice for everything; and this warning is that, since images serve us as a motive for invisible things, we must strive to set the motive and the affection and the rejoicing of our will only upon that which in fact they represent. Let the faithful soul, then, be careful that, when he sees the image, he desire not that his senses should be absorbed by it, whether the image be corporeal or imaginary, whether beautifully made, whether richly adorned, whether the devotion that it causes be of sense or of spirit, whether it produce supernatural manifestations or no. The soul must on no account set store by these accidents, nor even regard them, but must raise up its mind from the image to that which it represents, centering the sweetness and rejoicing of its will, together with the prayer and devotion of its spirit, upon God or upon the saint who is being invoked; for that which belongs to the living reality and to the spirit should not be usurped by sense and by the painted object. If the soul do this, it will not be deceived, for it will set no store by anything that the image may say to it, nor will it occupy its sense or its spirit in such a way that they cannot travel freely to God, nor will it place more confidence in one image than in another. And an image which would cause the soul devotion by supernatural means will now do so more abundantly, since the soul will now go with its affections directly to God. For, whensoever God grants these and other favours, He does so by inclining the affection of the joy of the will to that which is invisible, and this He wishes us also to do, by annihilating the power and sweetness of the faculties with respect to these visible things of sense.

Chapter XXXVIII

Continues to describe motive good. Speaks of oratories and places dedicated to prayer.

I think it has now been explained how the spiritual person may find as great imperfection in the accidents of images, by setting his pleasure and rejoicing upon them, as in other corporeal and temporal things, and perchance imperfection more perilous still. And I say perchance more perilous, because, when a person says that the objects of his rejoicing are holy, he feels more secure, and fears not to cling to them and become attached to them in a natural way. And thus such a person is sometimes greatly deceived, thinking himself to be full of devotion because he perceives that he takes pleasure in these holy things, when, perchance, this is due only to his natural desire and temperament, which lead him to this just as they lead him to other things.

Hence it arises (we are now beginning to treat of oratories) that there are some persons who never tire of adding to their oratories images of one kind and then of another, and take pleasure in the order and array in which they set them out, so that these oratories may be well adorned and pleasing to behold. Yet they love God no more when their oratories are ornate than when they are simple — nay, rather do they love Him less, since, as we have said, the pleasure which they set upon their painted adornments is stolen from the living reality. It is true that all the adornment and embellishment and respect that can be lavished upon images amounts to very little, and that therefore those who have images and treat them with a lack of decency and reverence are worthy of severe reproof, as are those who have images so ill-carved that they take away devotion rather than produce it, for which reason some image-makers who are very defective and unskilled in this art should be forbidden to practise it. But what has that to do with the attachment and affection and desire which you have for these outward adornments and decorations, when your senses are absorbed by them in such a way that your heart is hindered from journeying to God, and from loving Him and forgetting all things for love of Him? If you fail in the latter aim for the sake of the former, not only will God not esteem you for it, but He will even chasten you for not having sought His pleasure in all things rather than your own. This you may clearly gather from the description of that feast which they made for His Majesty when He entered Jerusalem. They received Him with songs and with branches, and the Lord wept; for their hearts were very far removed from Him and they paid Him reverence only with outward adornments and signs. We may say of them that they were making a festival for themselves rather than for God; and this is done nowadays by many, who, when there is some solemn festival in a place, are apt to rejoice because of the pleasure which they themselves will find in it — whether in seeing or in being seen, or whether in eating or in some other selfish thing — rather than to rejoice at being acceptable to God. By these inclinations and intentions they are giving no pleasure to God. Especially is this so when those who celebrate festivals invent ridiculous and undevout things to intersperse in them, so that they may incite people to laughter, which causes them greater distraction. And other persons invent things which merely please people rather than move them to devotion.

And what shall I say of persons who celebrate festivals for reasons connected with their own interests? They alone, and God Who sees them, know if their regard and desire are set upon such interests rather than upon the service of God. Let them realize, when they act in any of these ways, that they are making festivals in their own honour rather than in that of God. For that which they do for their own pleasure, or for the pleasure of men, God will not account as done for Himself. Yea, many who take part in God's festivals will be enjoying themselves even while God is wroth with them, as He was with the children of Israel when they made a festival, and sang and danced before their idol, thinking that they were keeping a festival in honour of God; of whom He slew many thousands. Or again, as He was with the priests Nabad and Abiu, the sons of Aaron, whom He slew with the censers in their hands, because they offered strange fire. Or as with the man that entered the wedding feast ill-adorned and ill-garbed, whom the king commanded to be thrown into outer darkness, bound hand and foot. By this it may be known how ill God suffers these irreverences in assemblies that are held for His service. For how many festivals, O my God, are made Thee by the sons of men to the devil's advantage rather than to Thine! The devil takes a delight in them, because such gatherings bring him business, as they might to a trader. And how often wilt Thou say concerning them: 'This people honoureth Me with their lips alone, but their heart is far from Me, for they serve Me from a wrong cause!' For the sole reason for which God must be served is that He is Who He is, and not for any other mediate ends. And thus to serve Him for other reasons than solely that He is Who He is, is to serve Him without regard for Him as the Ultimate Reason.

Returning now to oratories, I say that some persons deck them out for their own pleasure rather than for the pleasure of God; and some persons set so little account by the devotion which they arouse that they think no more of them than of their own secular antechambers; some, indeed, think even less of them, for they take more pleasure in the profane than in the Divine.

But let us cease speaking of this and speak only of those who are more particular — that is to say, of those who consider themselves devout persons. Many of these centre their desire and pleasure upon their oratory and its adornments, to such an extent that they squander on them all the time that they should be employing in prayer to God and interior recollection. They cannot see that, by not arranging their oratory with a view to the interior recollection and peace of the soul, they are as much distracted by it as by anything else, and will find the pleasure which they take in it a continual occasion of unrest, and more so still if anyone endeavors to deprive them of it.

Chapter XXXIX

Of the way in which oratories and churches should be used, in order to direct the spirit to God.

With regard to the direction of the spirit to God through this kind of good, it is well to point out that it is certainly lawful, and even expedient, for beginners to find some sensible sweetness and pleasure in images, oratories and other visible objects of devotion, since they have not yet weaned or detached their desire from things of the world, so that they can leave the one pleasure for the other. They are like a child holding something in one of its hands; to make it loosen its hold upon it we give it something else to hold in the other hand lest it should cry because both its hands are empty. But the spiritual person that would make progress must strip himself of all those pleasures and desires wherein the will can rejoice, for pure spirituality is bound very little to any of those objects, but only to interior recollection and mental converse with God. So, although he makes use of images and oratories, he does so only fleetingly; his spirit at once comes to rest in God and he forgets all things of sense.

Wherefore, although it is best to pray where there is most decency, yet notwithstanding one should choose the place where sense and spirit are least hindered from journeying to God. Here we should consider that answer made by Our Saviour to the Samaritan woman, when she asked Him which was the more fitting place wherein to pray, the temple or the mountain, and He answered her that true prayer was not connected with the mountain or with the temple, but that those who adored the Father and were pleasing to Him were those that adored Him in spirit and in truth. Wherefore, although churches and pleasant places are set apart and furnished for prayer (for a church must not be used for aught else), yet, for a matter as intimate as converse held with God, one should choose that place which gives sense the least occupation and the least encouragement. And thus it must not be a place that is pleasant and delectable to sense (like the places that some habitually contrive to find), for otherwise, instead of the recollection of the spirit in God, naught will be achieved save recreation and pleasure and delight of sense. Wherefore it is good to choose a place that is solitary, and even wild, so that the spirit may resolutely and directly soar upward to God, and not be hindered or detained by visible things; for, although these sometimes help to raise up the spirit, it is better to forget them at once and to rest in God. For this reason Our Saviour was wont to choose solitary places for prayer, and such as occupied the senses but little, in order to give us an example. He chose places that lifted up the soul to God, such as mountains, which are lifted up above the earth, and are ordinarily bare, thus offering no occasion for recreation of the senses.

The truly spiritual man, then, is never tied to a place of prayer because of its suitability in this way or in that, nor does he even consider such a thing, for, if he did so, he would still be tied to sense. But, to the end that he may attain interior recollection, and forget everything, he chooses the places most free from sensible objects and attractions, withdrawing his attention from all these, that he may be able to rejoice in his God and be far removed from all things created. But it is a remarkable thing to see some spiritual persons, who waste all their time in setting up oratories and furnishing places which please their temperaments or inclinations, yet make little account of interior recollection, which is the most important thing, but of which they have very little. If they had more of it, they would be incapable of taking pleasure in those methods and manners of devotion, which would simply weary them.

Chapter XL

Which continues to direct the spirit to interior recollection with reference to what has been said.

The reason, then, why some spiritual persons never enter perfectly into the true joys of the spirit is that they never succeed in raising their desire for rejoicing above these things that are outward and visible. Let such take note that, although the visible oratory and temple is a decent place set apart for prayer, and an image is a motive to prayer, the sweetness and delight of the soul must not be set upon the motive or the visible temple, lest the soul should forget to pray in the living temple, which is the interior recollection of the soul. The Apostle, to remind us of this, said: 'See that your bodies are living temples of the Holy Spirit, Who dwelleth in you.' And this thought is suggested by the words of Christ which we have quoted, namely that they who truly adore God must needs adore Him in spirit and in truth. For God takes little heed of your oratories and your places set apart for prayer if your desire and pleasure are bound to them, and thus you have little interior detachment, which is spiritual poverty and renunciation of all things that you may possess.

In order, then, to purge the will from vain desire and rejoicing in this matter, and to lead it to God in your prayer, you must see only to this, that your conscience is pure, and your will perfect with God, and your spirit truly set upon Him. Then, as I have said, you should choose the place that is the farthest withdraw and the most solitary that you can find, and devote all the rejoicing of the will to calling upon God and glorifying Him; and you should take no account of those whims about outward things, but rather strive to renounce them. For, if the soul be attached to the delight of sensible devotion, it will never succeed in passing onward to the power of spiritual delight, which is found in spiritual detachment coming through interior recollection.

Chapter XLI

Of certain evils into which those persons fall who give themselves to pleasure in sensible objects and who frequent places of devotion in the way that has been described.

Many evils, both interior and exterior, come to the spiritual person when he desires to follow after sweetness of sense in these matters aforementioned. For, as regards the spirit, he will never attain to interior spiritual recollection, which consists in neglecting all such things, and in causing the soul to forget all this sensible sweetness, and to enter into true recollection, and to acquire the virtues by dint of effort. As regards exterior things, he will become unable to dispose himself for prayer in all places, but will be confined to places that are to his taste; and thus he will often fail in prayer, because, as the saying goes, he can understand no other book than his own village.

Furthermore, this desire leads such persons into great inconstancy. Some of them never continue in one place or even always in one state: now they will be seen in one place, now in another; now they will go to one hermitage, now to another; now they will set up this oratory, now that. Some of them, again, wear out their lives in changing from one state or manner of living to another. For, as they possess only the sensible fervour and joy to be found in spiritual things, and have never had the strength to attain spiritual recollection by the renunciation of their own will, and submitting to suffering inconveniences, whenever they see a place which they think well suited for devotion, or any kind of life or state well adapted to their temperament and inclination, they at once go after it and leave the condition or state in which they were before. And, as they have come under the influence of that sensible pleasure, it follows that they soon seek something new, for sensible pleasure is not constant, but very quickly fails.

Chapter XLII

Of three different kinds of place for devotion and of how the will should conduct itself with regard to them.

I can think of three kinds of place by means of which God is wont to move the will to devotion. The first consists in certain dispositions of the ground and situation, which, by means of a pleasing effect of variety, whether obtained by the arrangement of the ground or of trees, or by means of quiet solitude, naturally awaken devotion. These places it is beneficial to use, if they at once lead the will to God and cause it to forget the places themselves, even as, in order to reach one's journey's end, it is advisable not to pause and consider the means and motive of the journey more than is necessary. For those who strive to refresh their desires and to gain sensible sweetness will rather find spiritual aridity and distraction; for spiritual sweetness and satisfaction are not found save in interior recollection.

When they are in such a place, therefore, they should forget it and strive to be inwardly with God, as though they were not in that place at all. For, if they be attached to the pleasure and delight of the place, as we have said, they are seeking refreshment of sense and instability of spirit rather than spiritual repose. The anchorites and other holy hermits, who in the most vast and pleasing wildernesses selected the smallest places that sufficed for them, built there the smallest cells and caves, in which to imprison themselves. Saint Benedict was in such a place for three years, and another — namely, Saint Simon — bound himself with a cord that he might have no more liberty nor go any farther than to places within its reach; and even so did many who are too numerous ever to be counted. Those saints understood very clearly that, if they quenched not the desire and eagerness for spiritual sweetness and pleasure, they could not attain to spirituality.

The second kind is of a more special nature, for it relates to certain places (not necessarily deserts, but any places whatsoever) where God is accustomed to grant to a few special persons certain very delectable spiritual favours; ordinarily, such a place attracts the heart of the person who has received a favour there, and sometimes gives him great desires and yearnings to return to it; although, when he goes there, what happened to him before is not repeated, since this is not within his control. For God grants these favours when and how and where He pleases, without being tied to any place or time, nor to the free-will of the person to whom He grants them. Yet it is good to go and pray in such places at times if the desire is free from attachment; and this for three reasons. First, because although, as we said, God is not bound to any place, it would seem that He has willed to be praised by a soul in the place where He has granted it a favour. Secondly, because in that place the soul is more mindful to give thanks to God for that which it has received there. Thirdly, because, by remembering that favour, the soul's devotion is the more keenly awakened.

It is for these reasons that a man should go to such places, and not because he thinks that God is bound to grant him favours there, in such a way as to be unable to grant them wheresoever He wills, for the soul is a fitter and more comely place for God than any physical place. Thus we read in Holy Scripture that Abraham built an altar in the very place where God appeared to him, and invoked His holy name there, and that afterwards, coming from Egypt, he returned by the same road where God had appeared to him, and called upon God there once more at the same altar which he had built. Jacob, too, marked the place where God had appeared to him, leaning upon a ladder, by raising there a stone which he anointed with oil. And Agar gave a name to the place where the angel had appeared to her, and prized it highly, saying: 'Of a truth I have here seen the back of Him that seeth me.'

The third kind consists of certain special places which God chooses that He may be called upon and served there, such as Mount Sinai, where He gave the law to Moses. And the place that He showed Abraham, that he might sacrifice his son there. And likewise Mount Horeb, where He appeared to our father Elias.

The reason for which God chooses these places rather than others, that He may be praised there, is known to Himself alone. What it behoves us to know is that all is for our advantage, and that He will hear our prayers there, and also in any place where we pray to Him with perfect faith; although there is much greater opportunity for us to be heard in places dedicated to His service, since the Church has appointed and dedicated those places to that end.

Chapter XLIII

Which treats of other motives for prayer that many persons use — namely, a great variety of ceremonies.

The useless joys and the imperfect attachment which many persons have to the things which we have described are perhaps to some extent excusable, since these persons act more or less innocently with regard to them. But the great reliance which some persons place in many kinds of ceremonies introduced by uninstructed persons who lack the simplicity of faith is intolerable. Let us here disregard those which bear various extraordinary names or use terms that signify nothing, and also other things that are not sacred which persons who are foolish and gross and mistrustful in spirit are wont to interpolate in their prayers. For these are clearly evil, and involve sin, and many of them imply a secret compact with the devil; by such means these persons provoke God to wrath and not to mercy, wherefore I treat them not here.

I wish to speak solely of those ceremonies into which enters nothing of a suspicious nature, and of which many people make use nowadays with indiscreet devotion, attributing such efficacy and faith to these ways and manners wherein they desire to perform their devotions and prayers, that they believe that, if they fail to the very slightest extent in them, or go beyond their limits, God will not be served by them nor will He hear them. They place more reliance upon these methods and kinds of ceremony than upon the reality of their prayer, and herein they greatly offend and displease God. I refer, for example, to a Mass at which there must be so many candles, neither more nor fewer; which has to be said by the priest in such or such a way; and must be at such or such an hour, and neither sooner nor later; and must be after a certain day, neither sooner nor later; and the prayers and stations must be made at such and such times, with such or such ceremonies, and neither sooner nor later nor in any other manner; and the person who makes them must have such or such qualities or qualifications. And there are those who think that, if any of these details which they have laid down be wanting, nothing is accomplished.

And, what is worse, and indeed intolerable, is that certain persons desire to feel some effect in themselves, or to have their petitions fulfilled, or to know that the purpose of these ceremonious prayers of theirs will be accomplished. This is nothing less than to tempt God and to anger Him greatly, so much so that He sometimes gives leave to the devil to deceive them, making them feel and understand things that are far removed from the benefit of their soul, which they deserve because of the attachment that they show in their prayers, not desiring God's will, rather than their own desires, to be done therein; and thus, because they place not their whole confidence in God, nothing goes well with them.

Chapter XLIV

Of the manner wherein the rejoicing and strength of the will must be directed to God through these devotions.

Let these persons, then, know that, the more reliance they place on these things and ceremonies, the less confidence they have in God, and that they will not obtain of God that which they desire. There are certain persons who pray for their own ends rather than for the honour of God. Although they suppose that a thing will be done if it be for the service of God, and not otherwise, yet, because of their attachment to it and the vain rejoicing which they have in it, they multiply a large number of petitions for a thing, when it would be better for them to substitute others of greater importance to them, such as for the true cleansing of their consciences, and for a real application to things concerning their own salvation, leaving to a much later season all those other petitions of theirs which are not of this kind. And in this way they would attain that which is of the greatest importance to them, and at the same time all the other things that are good for them (although they might not have prayed for them), much better and much earlier than if they had expended all their energy on those things. For this the Lord promised, through the Evangelist, saying: 'Seek ye first and principally the Kingdom of God and His righteousness, and all these other things shall be added unto you.'

This is the seeking and the asking that is most pleasing to God, and, in order to obtain the fulfilment of the petitions which we have in our hearts, there is no better way than to direct the energy of our prayer to the thing that most pleases God. For then not only will He give that which we ask of Him, which is salvation, but also that which He sees to be fitting and good for us, although we pray not for it. This David makes clear in a psalm where he says: 'The Lord is nigh unto those that call upon Him in truth, that beg Him for the things that are in the highest degree true, such as salvation; for of these he then says: 'He will fulfill the will of them that fear Him, and will hear their cries, and will save them. For God is the guardian of those that truly love Him.' And thus, this nearness to God of which

David here speaks is naught else than His being ready to satisfy them and grant them even that which it has not passed through their minds to ask. Even so we read that, because Solomon did well in asking God for a thing that was pleasing to Him — namely, wisdom to lead and rule his people righteously — God answered him, saying: 'Because more than aught else thou didst desire wisdom, and askedst not victory over thine enemies, with their deaths, nor riches, nor long life, I will not only give thee the wisdom that thou askest to rule My people righteously, but I will likewise give thee that which thou hast not asked — namely, riches and substance and glory — so that neither before thee nor after thee shall there be any king like unto thee.' And this He did, giving him peace also from his enemies, so that all around him should pay tribute to him and trouble him not: We read of a similar incident in Genesis, where God promised Abraham to increase the generation of his lawful son, like the stars of Heaven, even as he had asked of Him, and said to him: 'Likewise I will increase the son of the bondwoman, for he is thy son.'

In this way, then, the strength of the will and its rejoicing must be directed to God in our petitions, and we must not be anxious to cling to ceremonial inventions which are not used or approved by the Catholic Church. We must leave the method and manner of saying Mass to the priest, whom the Church sets there in her place, giving him her orders as to how he is to do it. And let not such persons use new methods, as if they knew more than the Holy Spirit and His Church. If, when they pray in their simplicity, God hears them not, let them not think that He will hear them any the more however many may be their inventions. For God is such that, if they behave towards Him as they should, and conformably to His nature, they will do with Him whatsoever they will; but, if they act from selfish ends, they cannot speak with Him.

With regard to further ceremonies connected with prayer and other devotions, let not the will be set upon other ceremonies and forms of prayer than those which Christ taught us. For it is clear that, when His disciples besought Him that He would teach them to pray, He would tell them all that is necessary in order that the Eternal Father may hear us, since He knew the Father's nature so well. Yet all that He taught them was the Pater Noster, with its seven petitions, wherein are included all our needs, both spiritual and temporal; and He taught them not many other kinds of prayer, either in words or in ceremonies. On the contrary, He told them that when they prayed they ought not to desire to speak much, since our heavenly Father knows well what is meet for us. He charged them only, but with great insistence, that they should persevere in prayer (that is, in the prayer of the Pater Noster), saying elsewhere: 'It behoves us always to pray and never to fail.' But He taught not a variety of petitions, but rather that our petitions should be repeated frequently and with fervour and care. For, as I say, in them is contained all that is the will of God and all that is meet for us. Wherefore, when His Majesty drew near three times to the Eternal Father, He prayed all these three times, using those very words of the Pater Noster, as the Evangelists tell us, saying: 'Father, if it cannot be but that I must drink this cup, Thy will be done.' And the ceremonies which He taught us to use in our prayers are only two. Either we are to pray in the secret place of our chamber, where without noise and without paying heed to any we can pray with the most perfect and pure heart, as He said in these words: 'When thou shalt pray, enter into thy chamber and shut the door and pray.' Or else He taught us to go to a solitary and desert place, as He Himself did, and at the best and quietest time of night. And thus there is no reason to fix any limit of time, or any appointed days, or to set apart one time more than another for our devotions, neither is there any reason to use other forms, in our words and prayers, nor phrases with double meanings, but only those which the Church uses and in the manner wherein she uses them; for all are reduced to those which we have described — namely, the Pater Noster.

I do not for this reason condemn — nay, I rather approve — the fixing of days on which certain persons sometimes arrange to make their devotions, such as novenas, or other such things. I condemn only their conduct as concerns the fixity of their methods and the ceremonies with which they practise them. Even so did Judith rebuke and reprove the people of Bethulia because they had limited God as to the time wherein they awaited His mercy, saying: 'Do ye set God a time for his mercies?' To do this, she says, is not to move God to clemency, but to awaken His wrath.

Chapter XLV

Which treats of the second kind of distinct good, wherein the will may rejoice vainly.

The second kind of distinct and delectable good wherein the will may rejoice vainly is that which provokes or persuades us to serve God and which we have called provocative. This class comprises preachers, and we might speak of it in two ways, namely, as affecting the preachers themselves and as affecting their hearers. For, as regards both, we must not fail to observe that both must direct the rejoicing of their will to God, with respect to this exercise.

In the first place, it must be pointed out to the preacher, if he is to cause his people profit and not to embarrass himself with vain joy and presumption, that preaching is a spiritual exercise rather than a vocal one. For, although it is practised by means of outward words, its power and efficacy reside not in these but in the inward spirit. Wherefore, however lofty be the doctrine that is preached, and however choice the rhetoric and sublime the style wherein it is clothed, it brings as a rule no more benefit than is present in the spirit of the preacher. For, although it is true that the word of God is of itself efficacious, according to those words of David, 'He will give to His voice a voice of virtue,' yet fire, which has also a virtue — that of burning — will not burn when the material is not prepared.

To the end that the preacher's instruction may exercise its full force, there must be two kinds of preparation: that of the preacher and that of the hearer; for as a rule the benefit derived from a sermon depends upon the preparation of the teacher. For this reason it is said that, as is the master, so is wont to be the disciple. For, when in the Acts of the Apostles those seven sons of that chief priest of the Jews were wont to cast out devils in the same form as Saint Paul, the devil rose up against them, saying: 'Jesus I confess and Paul I know, but you, who are ye?' And then, attacking them, he stripped and wounded them. This was only because they had not the fitting preparation, and not because Christ willed not that they should do this in His name. For the Apostles once found a man, who was not a disciple, casting out a devil in the name of Christ, and they forbade him, and the Lord reproved them for it, saying: 'Forbid him not, for no man that has done any mighty works in My name shall be able to speak evil of Me after a brief space of time.' But He is angry with those who, though teaching the law of God, keep it not, and, which preaching spirituality, possess it not. For this reason God says, through Saint Paul: 'Thou teachest others and teachest not thyself. Thou who preachest that men should not steal, stealest.' And through David the Holy Spirit says: 'To the sinner, God said: "Why dost thou declare My justice and take My law in thy mouth, when thou hast hated discipline and cast My words behind thee?"' Here it is made plain that He will give them no spirituality whereby they may bear fruit.

It is a common matter of observation that, so far as we can judge here below, the better is the life of the preacher, the greater is the fruit that he bears, however undistinguished his style may be, however small his rhetoric and however ordinary his instruction. For it is the warmth that comes from the living spirit that clings; whereas the other kind of preacher will produce very little profit, however sublime be his style and his instruction. For, although it is true that a good style and gestures and sublime instruction and well-chosen language influence men and produce much effect when accompanied by true spirituality, yet without this, although a sermon gives pleasure and delight to the sense and the understanding, very little or nothing of its sweetness remains in the will. As a rule, in this case, the will remains as weak and remiss with regard to good works as it was before. Although marvelous things may have been marvellously said by the preacher, they serve only to delight the ear, like a concert of music or a peal of bells; the spirit, as I say, goes no farther from its habits than before, since the voice has no virtue to raise one that is dead from his grave.

Little does it matter that one kind of music should sound better than another if the better kind move me not more than the other to do good works. For, although marvellous things may have been said, they are at once forgotten if they have not fired the will. For, not only do they of themselves bear little fruit, but the fastening of the sense upon the pleasure that it finds in that sort of instruction hinders the instruction from passing to the spirit, so that only the method and the accidents of what has been said are appreciated, and the preacher is praised for this characteristic or for that, and followed from such motives as these rather than because of the purpose of amendment of life which he has inspired. This doctrine is well explained to the Corinthians by Saint Paul, where he says: 'I, brethren, when I came to you, came not preaching Christ with loftiness of instruction and of wisdom, and my words and my preaching consisted not in the rhetoric of human wisdom, but in the showing forth of the spirit and of the truth.'

Although the intention of the Apostle here, like my own intention, is not to condemn good style and rhetoric and phraseology, for, on the contrary, these are of great importance to the preacher, as in everything else, since good phraseology and style raise up and restore things that are fallen and ruined, even as bad phraseology ruins and destroys good things . . .

Dark Night of the Soul

"He soars on the wings of Divine love . . ."

"It is perhaps not an exaggeration to say that the verse and prose works combined of St. John of the Cross form at once the most grandiose and the most melodious spiritual canticle to which any one man has ever given utterance.

The most sublime of all the Spanish mystics, he soars aloft on the wings of Divine love to heights known to hardly any of them. . . . True to the character of his thought, his style is always forceful and energetic, even to a fault.

When we study his treatises— principally that great composite work known as the Ascent of Mount Carmel and the Dark Night— we have the impression of a mastermind that has scaled the heights of mystical science; and from their summit looks down upon and dominates the plain below and the paths leading upward. . . . Nowhere else, again, is he quite so appealingly human; for, though he is human even in his loftiest and sublimest passages, his intermingling of philosophy with mystical theology; makes him seem particularly so. These treatises are a wonderful illustration of the theological truth that graced far from destroying nature, ennobles and dignifies it, and of the agreement always found between the natural and the supernatural— between the principles of sound reason and the sublimest manifestations of Divine grace."

E. Allison Peers

Table of Contents

Principal Abbreviations

A.V.—Authorized Version of the Bible (1611).

D.V.—Douai Version of the Bible (1609).

C.W.S.T.J.—The Complete Works of Saint Teresa of Jesus, translated and edited by E. Allison Peers from the critical edition of P. Silverio de Santa Teresa, C.D. London, Sheed and Ward, 1946. 3 vols.

H.—E. Allison Peers: Handbook to the Life and Times of St. Teresa and St. John of the Cross. London, Burns Oates and Washbourne, 1953.

LL.—The Letters of Saint Teresa of Jesus, translated and edited by E. Allison Peers from the critical edition of P. Silverio de Santa Teresa, C.D. London, Burns Oates and Washbourne, 1951. 2 vols.

N.L.M.—National Library of Spain (Biblioteca Nacional), Madrid.

Obras (P. Silv.)—Obras de San Juan de la Cruz, Doctor de la Iglesia, editadas y anotadas por el P. Silverio de Santa Teresa, C.D. Burgos, 1929-31. 5 vols.

S.S.M.—E. Allison Peers: Studies of the Spanish Mystics. Vol. I, London, Sheldon Press, 1927; 2nd ed., London, S.P.C.K., 1951. Vol. II, London, Sheldon Press, 1930.

Sobrino.—Jose Antonio de Sobrino, S.J.: Estudios sobre San Juan de la Cruz y nuevos textos de su obra. Madrid, 1950.

Introduction

Somewhat reluctantly, out of respect for a venerable tradition, we publish the Dark Night as a separate treatise, though in reality it is a continuation of the Ascent of Mount Carmel and fulfils the undertakings given in it:

The first night or purgation is of the sensual part of the soul, which is treated in the present stanza, and will be treated in the first part of this book. And the second is of the spiritual part; of this speaks the second stanza, which follows; and of this we shall treat likewise, in the second and the third part, with respect to the activity of the soul; and in the fourth part, with respect to its passivity.

This 'fourth part' is the Dark Night. Of it the Saint writes in a passage which follows that just quoted:

And the second night, or purification, pertains to those who are already proficient, occurring at the time when God desires to bring them to the state of union with God. And this latter night is a more obscure and dark and terrible purgation, as we shall say afterwards.

In his three earlier books he has written of the Active Night, of Sense and of Spirit; he now proposes to deal with the Passive Night, in the same order. He has already taught us how we are to deny and purify ourselves with the ordinary help of grace, in order to prepare our senses and faculties for union with God through love. He now proceeds to explain, with an arresting freshness, how these same senses and faculties are purged and purified by God with a view to the same end—that of union. The combined description of the two nights completes the presentation of active and passive purgation, to which the Saint limits himself in these treatises, although the subject of the stanzas which he is glossing is a much wider one, comprising the whole of the mystical life and ending only with the Divine embraces of the soul transformed in God through love.

The stanzas expounded by the Saint are taken from the same poem in the two treatises. The commentary upon the second, however, is very different from that upon the first, for it assumes a much more advanced state of development. The Active Night has left the senses and faculties well prepared, though not completely prepared, for the reception of Divine influences and illuminations in greater abundance than before. The Saint here postulates a principle of dogmatic theology—that by himself, and with the ordinary aid of grace, man cannot attain to that degree of purgation which is essential to his transformation in God. He needs Divine aid more abundantly. 'However greatly the soul itself labours,' writes the Saint, 'it cannot actively purify itself so as to be in the least degree prepared for the Divine union of perfection of love, if God takes not its hand and purges it not in that dark fire.'

The Passive Nights, in which it is God Who accomplishes the purgation, are based upon this incapacity. Souls 'begin to enter' this dark night when God draws them forth from the state of beginners—which is the state of those that meditate on the spiritual road—and begins to set them in the state of progressives—which is that of those who are already contemplatives—to the end that, after passing through it, they may arrive at the state of the perfect, which is that of the Divine union of the soul with God.

Before explaining the nature and effects of this Passive Night, the Saint touches, in passing, upon certain imperfections found in those who are about to enter it and which it removes by the process of purgation. Such travellers are still untried proficients, who have not yet acquired mature habits of spirituality and who therefore still conduct themselves as children. The imperfections are examined one by one, following the order of the seven deadly sins, in chapters (ii-viii) which once more reveal the author's skill as a director of souls. They are easy chapters to understand, and of great practical utility, comparable to those in the first book of the Ascent which deal with the active purgation of the desires of sense.

In Chapter viii, St. John of the Cross begins to describe the Passive Night of the senses, the principal aim of which is the purgation or stripping of the soul of its imperfections and the preparation of it for fruitive union. The Passive Night of Sense, we are told, is 'common' and 'comes to many,' whereas that of Spirit 'is the portion of very few.' The one is 'bitter and terrible' but 'the second bears no comparison with it,' for it is 'horrible and awful to the spirit.'6 A good deal of literature on the former Night existed in the time of St. John of the Cross and he therefore promises to be brief in his treatment of it. Of the latter, on the other hand, he will 'treat more fully . . . since very little has been said of this, either in speech or in writing, and very little is known of it, even by experience.'

Having described this Passive Night of Sense in Chapter viii, he explains with great insight and discernment how it may be recognized whether any given aridity is a result of this Night or whether it comes from sins or imperfections, or from frailty or lukewarmness of spirit, or even from indisposition or 'humours' of the body. The Saint is particularly effective here, and we may once more compare this chapter with a similar one in the Ascent (II, xiii)—that in which he fixes the point where the soul may abandon discursive meditation and enter the contemplation which belongs to loving and simple faith.

Both these chapters have contributed to the reputation of St. John of the Cross as a consummate spiritual master. And this not only for the objective value of his observations, but because, even in spite of himself, he betrays the sublimity of his own mystical experiences. Once more, too, we may admire the crystalline transparency of his teaching and the precision of the phrases in which he clothes it. To judge by his language alone, one might suppose at times that he is speaking of mathematical, rather than of spiritual operations.

In Chapter x, the Saint describes the discipline which the soul in this Dark Night must impose upon itself; this, as might be logically deduced from the Ascent, consists in 'allowing the soul to remain in peace and quietness,' content 'with a peaceful and loving attentiveness toward God.' Before long it will experience enkindlings of love (Chapter xi), which will serve to purify its sins and imperfections and draw it gradually nearer to God; we have here, as it were, so many stages of the ascent of the Mount on whose summit the soul attains to transforming union. Chapters xii and xiii detail with great exactness the benefits that the soul receives from this aridity, while Chapter xiv briefly expounds the last line of the first stanza and brings to an end what the Saint desires to say with respect to the first Passive Night.

At only slightly greater length St. John of the Cross describes the Passive Night of the Spirit, which is at once more afflictive and more painful than those which have preceded it. This, nevertheless, is the Dark Night par excellence, of which the Saint speaks in these words: 'The night which we have called that of sense may and should be called a kind of correction and restraint of the desire rather than purgation. The reason is that all the imperfections and disorders of the sensual part have their strength and root in the spirit, where all habits, both good and bad, are brought into subjection, and thus, until these are purged, the rebellions and depravities of sense cannot be purged thoroughly.'

Spiritual persons, we are told, do not enter the second night immediately after leaving the first; on the contrary, they generally pass a long time, even years, before doing so, for they still have many imperfections, both habitual and actual (Chapter ii). After a brief introduction (Chapter iii), the Saint describes with some fullness the nature of this spiritual purgation or dark contemplation referred to in the first stanza of his poem and the varieties of pain and affliction caused by it, whether in the soul or in its faculties (Chapters iv-viii). These chapters are brilliant beyond all description; in them we seem to reach the culminating point of their author's mystical experience; any excerpt from them would do them an injustice. It must suffice to say that St. John of the Cross seldom again touches those same heights of sublimity.

Chapter ix describes how, although these purgations seem to blind the spirit, they do so only to enlighten it again with a brighter and intenser light, which it is preparing itself to receive with greater abundance. The following chapter makes the comparison between spiritual purgation and the log of wood which gradually becomes transformed through being immersed in fire and at last takes on the fire's own properties. The force with which the familiar similitude is driven home impresses indelibly upon the mind the fundamental concept of this most sublime of all purgations. Marvellous, indeed, are its effects, from the first enkindlings and burnings of Divine love, which are greater beyond comparison than those produced by the Night of Sense, the one being as different from the other as is the body from the soul. 'For this (latter) is an enkindling of spiritual love in the soul, which, in the midst of these dark confines, feels itself to be keenly and sharply wounded in strong Divine love, and to have a certain realization and foretaste of God.' No less wonderful are the effects of the powerful Divine illumination which from time to time enfolds the soul in the splendours of glory. When the effects of the light that wounds and yet illumines are combined with those of the enkindlement that melts the soul with its heat, the delights experienced are so great as to be ineffable.

The second line of the first stanza of the poem is expounded in three admirable chapters (xi-xiii), while one short chapter (xiv) suffices for the three lines remaining. We then embark upon the second stanza, which describes the soul's security in the Dark Night—due, among other reasons, to its being freed 'not only from itself, but likewise from its other enemies, which are the world and the devil.'

This contemplation is not only dark, but also secret (Chapter xvii), and in Chapter xviii is compared to the 'staircase' of the poem. This comparison suggests to the Saint an exposition (Chapters xviii, xix) of the ten steps or degrees of love which comprise St. Bernard's mystical ladder. Chapter xxi describes the soul's 'disguise,' from which the book passes on (Chapters xxii, xxiii) to extol the 'happy chance' which led it to journey 'in darkness and concealment' from its enemies, both without and within.

Chapter xxiv glosses the last line of the second stanza—'my house being now at rest.' Both the higher and the lower 'portions of the soul' are now tranquillized and prepared for the desired union with the Spouse, a union which is the subject that the Saint proposed to treat in his commentary on the five remaining stanzas. As far as we know, this commentary was never written. We have only the briefest outline of what was to have been covered in the third, in which, following the same effective metaphor of night, the Saint describes the excellent properties of the spiritual night of infused contemplation, through which the soul journeys with no other guide or support, either outward or inward, than the Divine love 'which burned in my heart.'

It is difficult to express adequately the sense of loss that one feels at the premature truncation of this eloquent treatise. We have already given our opinion upon the commentaries thought to have been written on the final stanzas of the 'Dark Night.' Did we possess them, they would explain the birth of the light—'dawn's first breathings in the heav'ns above'—which breaks through the black darkness of the Active and the Passive Nights; they would tell us, too, of the soul's further progress towards the Sun's full brightness. It is true, of course, that some part of this great gap is filled by St. John of the Cross himself in his other treatises, but it is small compensation for the incomplete state in which he left this edifice of such gigantic proportions that he should have given us other and smaller buildings of a somewhat similar kind. Admirable as are the Spiritual Canticle and the Living Flame of Love, they are not so completely knit into one whole as is this great double treatise. They lose both in flexibility and in substance through the closeness with which they follow the stanzas of which they are the exposition. In the Ascent and the Dark Night, on the other hand, we catch only the echoes of the poem, which are all but lost in the resonance of the philosopher's voice and the eloquent tones of the preacher. Nor have the other treatises the learning and the authority of these. Nowhere else does the genius of St. John of the Cross for infusing philosophy into his mystical dissertations find such an outlet as here. Nowhere else, again, is he quite so appealingly human; for, though he is human even in his loftiest and sublimest passages, this intermingling of philosophy with mystical theology makes him seem particularly so. These treatises are a wonderful illustration of the theological truth that grace, far from destroying nature, ennobles and dignifies it, and of the agreement always found between the natural and the supernatural—between the principles of sound reason and the sublimest manifestations of Divine grace.

Manuscripts of the Dark Night

The autograph of the Dark Night, like that of the Ascent of Mount Carmel, is unknown to us: the second seems to have disappeared in the same period as the first. There are extant, however, as many as twelve early copies of the Dark Night, some of which, though none of them is as palaeographically accurate as the best copy of the Ascent, are very reliable; there is no trace in them of conscious adulteration of the original or of any kind of modification to fit the sense of any passage into a preconceived theory. We definitely prefer one of these copies to the others but we nowhere follow it so literally as to incorporate in our text its evident discrepancies from its original.

MS. 3,446. An early MS. in the clear masculine hand of an Andalusian: MS. 3,446 in the National Library, Madrid. Like many others, this MS. was transferred to the library from the Convento de San Hermenegildo at the time of the religious persecutions in the early nineteenth century; it had been presented to the Archives of the Reform by the Fathers of Los Remedios, Seville—a Carmelite house founded by P. Grecián in 1574. It has no title and a fragment from the Living Flame of Love is bound up with it.

This MS. has only two omissions of any length; these form part respectively of Book II, Chapters xix and xxiii, dealing with the Passive Night of the Spirit. It has many copyist's errors. At the same time, its antiquity and origin, and the good faith of which it shows continual signs, give it, in our view, primacy over the other copies now to come under consideration. It must be made clear, nevertheless, that there is no extant copy of the Dark Night as trustworthy and as skilfully made as the Alcaudete MS. of the Ascent.

MS. of the Carmelite Nuns of Toledo. Written in three hands, all early. Save for a few slips of the copyist, it agrees with the foregoing; a few of its errors have been corrected. It bears no title, but has a long sub-title which is in effect a partial summary of the argument.

MS. of the Carmelite Nuns of Valladolid. This famous convent, which was one of St. Teresa's foundations, is very rich in Teresan autographs, and has also a number of important documents relating to St. John of the Cross, together with some copies of his works. That here described is written in a large, clear hand and probably dates from the end of the sixteenth century. It has a title similar to that of the last-named copy. With few exceptions it follows the other most important MSS.

MS. Alba de Tormes. What has been said of this in the introduction to the Ascent (Image Books edition, pp. 6-7) applies also to the Dark Night. It is complete, save for small omissions on the part of the amanuensis, the 'Argument' at the beginning of the poem, the verses themselves and a few lines from Book II, Chapter vii.

MS. 6,624. This copy is almost identical with the foregoing. It omits the 'Argument' and the poem itself but not the lines from Book II, Chapter vii.

MS. 8,795. This contains the Dark Night, Spiritual Canticle, Living Flame of Love, a number of poems by St. John of the Cross and the Spiritual Colloquies between Christ and the soul His Bride. It is written in various hands, all very early and some feminine. A note by P. Andrés de la Encarnación, on the reverse of the first folio, records that the copy was presented to the Archives of the Reform by the Discalced Carmelite nuns of Baeza. This convent was founded in 1589, two years before the Saint's death, and the copy may well date from about this period. On the second folio comes the poem 'I entered in—I knew not where.' On the reverse of the third folio begins a kind of preface to the Dark Night, opening with the words: 'Begin the stanzas by means of which a soul may occupy itself and become fervent in the love of God. It deals with the Dark Night and is divided into two books. The first treats of the purgation of sense, and the second of the spiritual purgation of man. It was written by P. Fr. Juan de la Cruz, Discalced Carmelite.' On the next folio, a so-called 'Preface: To the Reader' begins: 'As a beginning and an explanation of these two purgations of the Dark Night which are to be expounded hereafter, this chapter will show how narrow is the path that leads to eternal life and how completely detached and disencumbered must be those that are to enter thereby.' This fundamental idea is developed for the space of two folios. There follows a sonnet on the Dark Night, and immediately afterwards comes the text of the treatise.

The copy contains many errors, but its only omission is that of the last chapter. There is no trace in it of any attempt to modify its original; indeed, the very nature and number of the copyist's errors are a testimony to his good faith.

MS. 12,658. A note by P. Andrés states that he acquired it in Madrid but has no more detailed recollection of its provenance. 'The Dark Night,' it adds, 'begins on folio 43; our holy father is described simply as "the second friar of the new Reformation," which is clear evidence of its antiquity.'

The Codex contains a number of opuscules, transcribed no doubt with a devotional aim by the copyist. Its epoch is probably the end of the sixteenth century; it is certainly earlier than the editions. There is no serious omission except that of six lines of the 'Argument.' The authors of the other works copied include St. Augustine, B. Juan de Ávila, P. Baltasar Álvarez and P. Tomás de Jesús.

The copies which remain to be described are all mutilated or abbreviated and can be disposed of briefly:

MS. 13,498. This copy omits less of the Dark Night than of the Ascent but few pages are without their omissions. In one place a meticulous pair of scissors has removed the lower half of a folio on which the Saint deals with spiritual luxury.

MS. of the Carmelite Friars of Toledo. Dates from early in the seventeenth century and has numerous omissions, especially in the chapters on the Passive Night of the Spirit. The date is given (in the same hand as that which copies the title) as 1618. This MS. also contains an opuscule by Suso and another entitled 'Brief compendium of the most eminent Christian perfection of P. Fr. Juan de la Cruz.'

MS. 18,160. The copyist has treated the Dark Night little better than the Ascent; except from the first ten and the last three chapters, he omits freely.

MS. 12,411. Entitled by its copyist 'Spiritual Compendium,' this MS. contains several short works of devotion, including one by Ruysbroeck. Of St. John of the Cross's works it copies the Spiritual Canticle as well as the Dark Night; the latter is headed: 'Song of one soul alone.' It also contains a number of poems, some of them by the Saint, and many passages from St. Teresa. It is in several hands, all of the seventeenth century. The copy of the Dark Night is most unsatisfactory; there are omissions and abbreviations everywhere.

M.S. of the Carmelite Nuns of Pamplona. This MS. also omits and abbreviates continually, especially in the chapters on the Passive Night of Sense, which are reduced to a mere skeleton.

Editio princeps. This is much more faithful to its original in the Dark Night than in the Ascent. Both the passages suppressed and the interpolations are relatively few and unimportant. Modifications of phraseology are more frequent and alterations are also made with the aim of correcting hyperbaton. In the first book about thirty lines are suppressed; in the second, about ninety. All changes which are of any importance have been shown in the notes.

The present edition. We have given preference, as a general rule, to MS. 3,446, subjecting it, however, to a rigorous comparison with the other copies. Mention has already been made in the introduction to the Ascent (Image Books edition, pp. lxiii-lxvi) of certain apparent anomalies and a certain lack of uniformity in the Saint's method of dividing his commentaries. This is nowhere more noticeable than in the Dark Night. Instead of dividing his treatise into books, each with its proper title, the Saint abandons this method and uses titles only occasionally. As this makes comprehension of his argument the more difficult, we have adopted the divisions which were introduced by P. Salablanca and have been copied by successive editors.

M. Baruzi (Bulletin Hispanique, 1922, Vol. xxiv, pp. 18-40) complains that this division weighs down the spiritual rhythm of the treatise and interrupts its movement. We do not agree. In any case, we greatly prefer the gain of clarity, even if the rhythm occasionally halts, to the other alternative—the constant halting of the understanding. We have, of course, indicated every place where the title is taken from the editio princeps and was not the work of the author.

The following abbreviations are adopted in the footnotes:

A = MS. of the Discalced Carmelite Friars of Alba.

B = MS. 6,624 (National Library, Madrid).

Bz. = MS. 8,795 (N.L.M.).

C = MS. 13,498 (N.L.M.).

G = MS. 18,160 (N.L.M.).

H = MS. 3,446 (N.L.M.).

M = MS. of the Discalced Carmelite Nuns of Toledo.

Mtr. = MS. 12,658.

P = MS. of the Discalced Carmelite Friars of Toledo.

V = MS. of the Discalced Carmelite Nuns of Valladolid.

E.p. = Editio princeps (1618).

MS. 12,411 and the MS. of the Discalced Carmelite nuns of Pamplona are cited without abbreviations.

Exposition of the stanzas describing the method followed by the soul in its journey upon the spiritual road to the attainment of the perfect union of love with God, to the extent that is possible in this life. Likewise are described the properties belonging to the soul that has attained to the said perfection, according as they are contained in the same stanzas.

Prologue

In this book are first set down all the stanzas which are to be expounded; afterwards, each of the stanzas is expounded separately, being set down before its exposition; and then each line is expounded separately and in turn, the line itself also being set down before the exposition. In the first two stanzas are expounded the effects of the two spiritual purgations: of the sensual part of man and of the spiritual part. In the other six are expounded various and wondrous effects of the spiritual illumination and union of love with God.

Stanzas of the Soul

On a dark night,
Kindled in love with yearnings
—oh, happy chance!
I went forth without being observed,
My house being now at rest.

In darkness and secure,
By the secret ladder, disguised
—oh, happy chance!
In darkness and in concealment,
My house being now at rest.

In the happy night,
In secret, when none saw me,
Nor I beheld aught,
Without light or guide,
Save that which burned in my heart.

This light guided me
More surely than the light of noonday
To the place where he (well I knew who!) was awaiting me
— A place where none appeared.

Oh, night that guided me,
Oh, night more lovely than the dawn,
Oh, night that joined Beloved with lover,
Lover transformed in the Beloved!

Upon my flowery breast,
Kept wholly for himself alone,
There he stayed sleeping, and I caressed him,
And the fanning of the cedars made a breeze.

The breeze blew from the turret
As I parted his locks;
With his gentle hand he wounded my neck
And caused all my senses to be suspended.

I remained, lost in oblivion;
My face I reclined on the Beloved.
All ceased and I abandoned myself,
Leaving my cares forgotten among the lilies.

Begins the exposition of the stanzas which treat of the way and manner which the soul follows upon the road of the union of love with God.

Before we enter upon the exposition of these stanzas, it is well to understand here that the soul that utters them is now in the state of perfection, which is the union of love with God, having already passed through severe trials and straits, by means of spiritual exercise in the narrow way of eternal life whereof Our Saviour speaks in the Gospel, along which way the soul ordinarily passes in order to reach this high and happy union with God. Since this road (as the Lord Himself says likewise) is so strait, and since there are so few that enter by it, the soul considers it a great happiness and good chance to have passed along it to the said perfection of love, as it sings in this first stanza, calling this strait road with full propriety 'dark night,' as will be explained hereafter in the lines of the said stanza. The soul, then, rejoicing at having passed along this narrow road whence so many blessings have come to it, speaks after this manner.

BOOK THE FIRST

Which treats of the Night of Sense.

Stanza the First

On a dark night, Kindled in love with yearnings—oh, happy chance!— I went forth without being observed, My house being now at rest.

Exposition

In this first stanza the soul relates the way and manner which it followed in going forth, as to its affection, from itself and from all things, and in dying to them all and to itself, by means of true mortification, in order to attain to living the sweet and delectable life of love with God; and it says that this going forth from itself and from all things was a 'dark night,' by which, as will be explained hereafter, is here understood purgative contemplation, which causes passively in the soul the negation of itself and of all things referred to above.

And this going forth it says here that it was able to accomplish in the strength and ardour which love for its Spouse gave to it for that purpose in the dark contemplation aforementioned. Herein it extols the great happiness which it found in journeying to God through this night with such signal success that none of the three enemies, which are world, devil and flesh (who are they that ever impede this road), could hinder it; inasmuch as the aforementioned night of purgative contemplation lulled to sleep and mortified, in the house of its sensuality, all the passions and desires with respect to their mischievous desires and motions. The line, then, says: On a dark night

Chapter 1

Sets down the first line and begins to treat of the imperfections of beginners.

Into this dark night souls begin to enter when God draws them forth from the state of beginners—which is the state of those that meditate on the spiritual road—and begins to set them in the state of progressives—which is that of those who are already contemplatives—to the end that, after passing through it, they may arrive at the state of the perfect, which is that of the Divine union of the soul with God. Wherefore, to the end that we may the better understand and explain what night is this through which the soul passes, and for what cause God sets it therein, it will be well here to touch first of all upon certain characteristics of beginners (which, although we treat them with all possible brevity, will not fail to be of service likewise to the beginners themselves), in order that, realizing the weakness of the state wherein they are, they may take courage, and may desire that God will bring them into this night, wherein the soul is strengthened and confirmed in the virtues, and made ready for the inestimable delights of the love of God. And, although we may tarry here for a time, it will not be for longer than is necessary, so that we may go on to speak at once of this dark night.

It must be known, then, that the soul, after it has been definitely converted to the service of God, is, as a rule, spiritually nurtured and caressed by God, even as is the tender child by its loving mother, who warms it with the heat of her bosom and nurtures it with sweet milk and soft and pleasant food, and carries it and caresses it in her arms; but, as the child grows bigger, the mother gradually ceases caressing it, and, hiding her tender love, puts bitter aloes upon her sweet breast, sets down the child from her arms and makes it walk upon its feet, so that it may lose the habits of a child and betake itself to more important and substantial occupations. The loving mother is like the grace of God, for, as soon as the soul is regenerated by its new warmth and fervour for the service of God, He treats it in the same way; He makes it to find spiritual milk, sweet and delectable, in all the things of God, without any labour of its own, and also great pleasure in spiritual exercises, for here God is giving to it the breast of His tender love, even as to a tender child.

Therefore, such a soul finds its delight in spending long periods—perchance whole nights—in prayer; penances are its pleasures; fasts its joys; and its consolations are to make use of the sacraments and to occupy itself in Divine things. In the which things spiritual persons (though taking part in them with great efficacy and persistence and using and treating them with great care) often find themselves, spiritually speaking, very weak and imperfect. For since they are moved to these things and to these spiritual exercises by the consolation and pleasure that they find in them, and since, too, they have not been prepared for them by the practice of earnest striving in the virtues, they have many faults and imperfections with respect to these spiritual actions of theirs; for, after all, any man's actions correspond to the habit of perfection attained by him. And, as these persons have not had the opportunity of acquiring the said habits of strength, they have necessarily to work like feebler children, feebly. In order that this may be seen more clearly, and likewise how much these beginners in the virtues lacks with respect to the works in which they so readily engage with the pleasure aforementioned, we shall describe it by reference to the seven capital sins, each in its turn, indicating some of the many imperfections which they have under each heading; wherein it will be clearly seen how like to children are these persons in all they do. And it will also be seen how many blessings the dark night of which we shall afterwards treat brings with it, since it cleanses the soul and purifies it from all these imperfections.

Chapter II

Of certain spiritual imperfections which beginners have with respect to the habit of pride.

As these beginners feel themselves to be very fervent and diligent in spiritual things and devout exercises, from this prosperity (although it is true that holy things of their own nature cause humility) there often comes to them, through their imperfections, a certain kind of secret pride, whence they come to have some degree of satisfaction with their works and with themselves. And hence there comes to them likewise a certain desire, which is somewhat vain, and at times very vain, to speak of spiritual things in the presence of others, and sometimes even to teach such things rather than to learn them. They condemn others in their heart when they see that they have not the kind of devotion which they themselves desire; and sometimes they even say this in words, herein resembling the Pharisee, who boasted of himself, praising God for his own good works and despising the publican.

In these persons the devil often increases the fervour that they have and the desire to perform these and other works more frequently, so that their pride and presumption may grow greater. For the devil knows quite well that all these works and virtues which they perform are not only valueless to them, but even become vices in them. And such a degree of evil are some of these persons wont to reach that they would have none appear good save themselves; and thus, in deed and word, whenever the opportunity occurs, they condemn them and slander them, beholding the mote in their brother's eye and not considering the beam which is in their own; they strain at another's gnat and themselves swallow a camel.

Sometimes, too, when their spiritual masters, such as confessors and superiors, do not approve of their spirit and behavior (for they are anxious that all they do shall be esteemed and praised), they consider that they do not understand them, or that, because they do not approve of this and comply with that, their confessors are themselves not spiritual. And so they immediately desire and contrive to find some one else who will fit in with their tastes; for as a rule they desire to speak of spiritual matters with those who they think will praise and esteem what they do, and they flee, as they would from death, from those who disabuse them in order to lead them into a safe road—sometimes they even harbour ill-will against them. Presuming thus, they are wont to resolve much and accomplish very little. Sometimes they are anxious that others shall realize how spiritual and devout they are, to which end they occasionally give outward evidence thereof in movements, sighs and other ceremonies; and at times they are apt to fall into certain ecstasies, in public rather than in secret, wherein the devil aids them, and they are pleased that this should be noticed, and are often eager that it should be noticed more.

Many such persons desire to be the favorites of their confessors and to become intimate with them, as a result of which there beset them continual occasions of envy and disquiet. They are too much embarrassed to confess their sins nakedly, lest their confessors should think less of them, so they palliate them and make them appear less evil, and thus it is to excuse themselves rather than to accuse themselves that they go to confession. And sometimes they seek another confessor to tell the wrongs that they have done, so that their own confessor shall think they have done nothing wrong at all, but only good; and thus they always take pleasure in telling him what is good, and sometimes in such terms as make it appear to be greater than it is rather than less, desiring that he may think them to be good, when it would be greater humility in them, as we shall say, to depreciate it, and to desire that neither he nor anyone else should consider them of account.

Some of these beginners, too, make little of their faults, and at other times become over-sad when they see themselves fall into them, thinking themselves to have been saints already; and thus they become angry and impatient with themselves, which is another imperfection. Often they beseech God, with great yearnings, that He will take from them their imperfections and faults, but they do this that they may find themselves at peace, and may not be troubled by them, rather than for God's sake; not realizing that, if He should take their imperfections from them, they would probably become prouder and more presumptuous still. They dislike praising others and love to be praised themselves; sometimes they seek out such praise. Herein they are like the foolish virgins, who, when their lamps could not be lit, sought oil from others.

From these imperfections some souls go on to develop many very grave ones, which do them great harm. But some have fewer and some more, and some, only the first motions thereof or little beyond these; and there are hardly any such beginners who, at the time of these signs of fervour, fall not into some of these errors. But those who at this time are going on to perfection proceed very differently and with quite another temper of spirit; for they progress by means of humility and are greatly edified, not only thinking naught of their own affairs, but having very little satisfaction with themselves; they consider all others as far better, and usually have a holy envy of them, and an eagerness to serve God as they do. For the greater is their fervour, and the more numerous are the works that they perform, and the greater is the pleasure that they take in them, as they progress in humility, the more do they realize how much God deserves of them, and how little is all that they do for His sake; and thus, the more they do, the less are they satisfied. So much would they gladly do from charity and love for Him, that all they do seems to them naught; and so greatly are they importuned, occupied and absorbed by this loving anxiety that they never notice what others do or do not; or if they do notice it, they always believe, as I say, that all others are far better than they themselves. Wherefore, holding themselves as of little worth, they are anxious that others too should thus hold them, and should despise and depreciate that which they do. And further, if men should praise and esteem them, they can in no wise believe what they say; it seems to them strange that anyone should say these good things of them.

Together with great tranquillity and humbleness, these souls have a deep desire to be taught by anyone who can bring them profit; they are the complete opposite of those of whom we have spoken above, who would fain be always teaching, and who, when others seem to be teaching them, take the words from their mouths as if they knew them already. These souls, on the other hand, being far from desiring to be the masters of any, are very ready to travel and set out on another road than that which they are actually following, if they be so commanded, because they never think that they are right in anything whatsoever. They rejoice when others are praised; they grieve only because they serve not God like them. They have no desire to speak of the things that they do, because they think so little of them that they are ashamed to speak of them even to their spiritual masters, since they seem to them to be things that merit not being spoken of. They are more anxious to speak of their faults and sins, or that these should be recognized rather than their virtues; and thus they incline to talk of their souls with those who account their actions and their spirituality of little value. This is a characteristic of the spirit which is simple, pure, genuine and very pleasing to God. For as the wise Spirit of God dwells in these humble souls, He moves them and inclines them to keep His treasures secretly within and likewise to cast out from themselves all evil. God gives this grace to the humble, together with the other virtues, even as He denies it to the proud.

These souls will give their heart's blood to anyone that serves God, and will help others to serve Him as much as in them lies. The imperfections into which they see themselves fall they bear with humility, meekness of spirit and a loving fear of God, hoping in Him. But souls who in the beginning journey with this kind of perfection are, as I understand, and as has been said, a minority, and very few are those who we can be glad do not fall into the opposite errors. For this reason, as we shall afterwards say, God leads into the dark night those whom He desires to purify from all these imperfections so that He may bring them farther onward.

Chapter III

Of some imperfections which some of these souls are apt to have, with respect to the second capital sin, which is avarice, in the spiritual sense.

Many of these beginners have also at times great spiritual avarice. They will be found to be discontented with the spirituality which God gives them; and they are very disconsolate and querulous because they find not in spiritual things the consolation that they would desire. Many can never have enough of listening to counsels and learning spiritual precepts, and of possessing and reading many books which treat of this matter, and they spend their time on all these things rather than on works of mortification and the perfecting of the inward poverty of spirit which should be theirs. Furthermore, they burden themselves with images and rosaries which are very curious; now they put down one, now take up another; now they change about, now change back again; now they want this kind of thing, now that, preferring one kind of cross to another, because it is more curious. And others you will see adorned with agnusdeis and relics and tokens, like children with trinkets. Here I condemn the attachment of the heart, and the affection which they have for the nature, multitude and curiosity of these things, inasmuch as it is quite contrary to poverty of spirit which considers only the substance of devotion, makes use only of what suffices for that end and grows weary of this other kind of multiplicity and curiosity. For true devotion must issue from the heart, and consist in the truth and substances alone of what is represented by spiritual things; all the rest is affection and attachment proceeding from imperfection; and in order that one may pass to any kind of perfection it is necessary for such desires to be killed.

I knew a person who for more than ten years made use of a cross roughly formed from a branch that had been blessed, fastened with a pin twisted round it; he had never ceased using it, and he always carried it about with him until I took it from him; and this was a person of no small sense and understanding. And I saw another who said his prayers using beads that were made of bones from the spine of a fish; his devotion was certainly no less precious on that account in the sight of God, for it is clear that these things carried no devotion in their workmanship or value. Those, then, who start from these beginnings and make good progress attach themselves to no visible instruments, nor do they burden themselves with such, nor desire to know more than is necessary in order that they may act well; for they set their eyes only on being right with God and on pleasing Him, and therein consists their covetousness. And thus with great generosity they give away all that they have, and delight to know that they have it not, for God's sake and for charity to their neighbour, no matter whether these be spiritual things or temporal. For, as I say, they set their eyes only upon the reality of interior perfection, which is to give pleasure to God and in naught to give pleasure to themselves.

But neither from these imperfections nor from those others can the soul be perfectly purified until God brings it into the passive purgation of that dark night whereof we shall speak presently. It befits the soul, however, to contrive to labour, in so far as it can, on its own account, to the end that it may purge and perfect itself, and thus may merit being taken by God into that Divine care wherein it becomes healed of all things that it was unable of itself to cure. Because, however greatly the soul itself labours, it cannot actively purify itself so as to be in the least degree prepared for the Divine union of perfection of love, if God takes not its hand and purges it not in that dark fire, in the way and manner that we have to describe.

Chapter IV

Of other imperfections which these beginners are apt to have with respect to the third sin, which is luxury.

Many of these beginners have many other imperfections than those which I am describing with respect to each of the deadly sins, but these I set aside, in order to avoid prolixity, touching upon a few of the most important, which are, as it were, the origin and cause of the rest. And thus, with respect to this sin of luxury (leaving apart the falling of spiritual persons into this sin, since my intent is to treat of the imperfections which have to be purged by the dark night), they have many imperfections which might be described as spiritual luxury, not because they are so, but because the imperfections proceed from spiritual things. For it often comes to pass that, in their very spiritual exercises, when they are powerless to prevent it, there arise and assert themselves in the sensual part of the soul impure acts and motions, and sometimes this happens even when the spirit is deep in prayer, or engaged in the Sacrament of Penance or in the Eucharist. These things are not, as I say, in their power; they proceed from one of three causes.

The first cause from which they often proceed is the pleasure which human nature takes in spiritual things. For when the spirit and the sense are pleased, every part of a man is moved by that pleasure to delight according to its proportion and nature. For then the spirit, which is the higher part, is moved to pleasure and delight in God; and the sensual nature, which is the lower part, is moved to pleasure and delight of the senses, because it cannot possess and lay hold upon aught else, and it therefore lays hold upon that which comes nearest to itself, which is the impure and sensual. Thus it comes to pass that the soul is in deep prayer with God according to the spirit, and, on the other hand, according to sense it is passively conscious, not without great displeasure, of rebellions and motions and acts of the senses, which often happens in Communion, for when the soul receives joy and comfort in this act of love, because this Lord bestows it (since it is to that end that He gives Himself), the sensual nature takes that which is its own likewise, as we have said, after its manner. Now as, after all, these two parts are combined in one individual, they ordinarily both participate in that which one of them receives, each after its manner; for, as the philosopher says, everything that is received is in the recipient after the manner of the same recipient. And thus, in these beginnings, and even when the soul has made some progress, its sensual part, being imperfect, oftentimes receives the Spirit of God with the same imperfection. Now when this sensual part is renewed by the purgation of the dark night which we shall describe, it no longer has these weaknesses; for it is no longer this part that receives aught, but rather it is itself received into the Spirit. And thus it then has everything after the manner of the Spirit.

The second cause whence these rebellions sometimes proceed is the devil, who, in order to disquiet and disturb the soul, at times when it is at prayer or is striving to pray, contrives to stir up these motions of impurity in its nature; and if the soul gives heed to any of these, they cause it great harm. For through fear of these not only do persons become lax in prayer—which is the aim of the devil when he begins to strive with them—but some give up prayer altogether, because they think that these things attack them more during that exercise than apart from it, which is true, since the devil attacks them then more than at other times, so that they may give up spiritual exercises. And not only so, but he succeeds in portraying to them very vividly things that are most foul and impure, and at times are very closely related to certain spiritual things and persons that are of profit to their souls, in order to terrify them and make them fearful; so that those who are affected by this dare not even look at anything or meditate upon anything, because they immediately encounter this temptation. And upon those who are inclined to melancholy this acts with such effect that they become greatly to be pitied since they are suffering so sadly; for this trial reaches such a point in certain persons, when they have this evil humour, that they believe it to be clear that the devil is ever present with them and that they have no power to prevent this, although some of these persons can prevent his attack by dint of great effort and labour. When these impurities attack such souls through the medium of melancholy, they are not as a rule freed from them until they have been cured of that kind of humour, unless the dark night has entered the soul, and rids them of all impurities, one after another.

The third source whence these impure motions are apt to proceed in order to make war upon the soul is often the fear which such persons have conceived for these impure representations and motions. Something that they see or say or think brings them to their mind, and this makes them afraid, so that they suffer from them through no fault of their own.

There are also certain souls of so tender and frail a nature that, when there comes to them some spiritual consolation or some grace in prayer, the spirit of luxury is with them immediately, inebriating and delighting their sensual nature in such manner that it is as if they were plunged into the enjoyment and pleasure of this sin; and the enjoyment remains, together with the consolation, passively, and sometimes they are able to see that certain impure and unruly acts have taken place. The reason for this is that, since these natures are, as I say, frail and tender, their humours are stirred up and their blood is excited at the least disturbance. And hence come these motions; and the same thing happens to such souls when they are enkindled with anger or suffer any disturbance or grief.

Sometimes, again, there arises within these spiritual persons, whether they be speaking or performing spiritual actions, a certain vigour and bravado, through their having regard to persons who are present, and before these persons they display a certain kind of vain gratification. This also arises from luxury of spirit, after the manner wherein we here understand it, which is accompanied as a rule by complacency in the will.

Some of these persons make friendships of a spiritual kind with others, which oftentimes arise from luxury and not from spirituality; this may be known to be the case when the remembrance of that friendship causes not the remembrance and love of God to grow, but occasions remorse of conscience. For, when the friendship is purely spiritual, the love of God grows with it; and the more the soul remembers it, the more it remembers the love of God, and the greater the desire it has for God; so that, as the one grows, the other grows also. For the spirit of God has this property, that it increases good by adding to it more good, inasmuch as there is likeness and conformity between them. But, when this love arises from the vice of sensuality aforementioned, it produces the contrary effects; for the more the one grows, the more the other decreases, and the remembrance of it likewise. If that sensual love grows, it will at once be observed that the soul's love of God is becoming colder, and that it is forgetting Him as it remembers that love; there comes to it, too, a certain remorse of conscience. And, on the other hand, if the love of God grows in the soul, that other love becomes cold and is forgotten; for, as the two are contrary to one another, not only does the one not aid the other, but the one which predominates quenches and confounds the other, and becomes strengthened in itself, as the philosophers say. Wherefore Our Saviour said in the Gospel: 'That which is born of the flesh is flesh, and that which is born of the Spirit is spirit.' That is to say, the love which is born of sensuality ends in sensuality, and that which is of the spirit ends in the spirit of God and causes it to grow. This is the difference that exists between these two kinds of love, whereby we may know them.

When the soul enters the dark night, it brings these kinds of love under control. It strengthens and purifies the one, namely that which is according to God; and the other it removes and brings to an end; and in the beginning it causes both to be lost sight of, as we shall say hereafter.

Chapter V

Of the imperfections into which beginners fall with respect to the sin of wrath.

By reason of the concupiscence which many beginners have for spiritual consolations, their experience of these consolations is very commonly accompanied by many imperfections proceeding from the sin of wrath; for, when their delight and pleasure in spiritual things come to an end, they naturally become embittered, and bear that lack of sweetness which they have to suffer with a bad grace, which affects all that they do; and they very easily become irritated over the smallest matter—sometimes, indeed, none can tolerate them. This frequently happens after they have been very pleasantly recollected in prayer according to sense; when their pleasure and delight therein come to an end, their nature is naturally vexed and disappointed, just as is the child when they take it from the breast of which it was enjoying the sweetness. There is no sin in this natural vexation, when it is not permitted to indulge itself, but only imperfection, which must be purged by the aridity and severity of the dark night.

There are other of these spiritual persons, again, who fall into another kind of spiritual wrath: this happens when they become irritated at the sins of others, and keep watch on those others with a sort of uneasy zeal. At times the impulse comes to them to reprove them angrily, and occasionally they go so far as to indulge it and set themselves up as masters of virtue. All this is contrary to spiritual meekness.

There are others who are vexed with themselves when they observe their own imperfectness, and display an impatience that is not humility; so impatient are they about this that they would fain be saints in a day. Many of these persons purpose to accomplish a great deal and make grand resolutions; yet, as they are not humble and have no misgivings about themselves, the more resolutions they make, the greater is their fall and the greater their annoyance, since they have not the patience to wait for that which God will give them when it pleases Him; this likewise is contrary to the spiritual meekness aforementioned, which cannot be wholly remedied save by the purgation of the dark night. Some souls, on the other hand, are so patient as regards the progress which they desire that God would gladly see them less so.

Chapter VI

Of imperfections with respect to spiritual gluttony.

With respect to the fourth sin, which is spiritual gluttony, there is much to be said, for there is scarce one of these beginners who, however satisfactory his progress, falls not into some of the many imperfections which come to these beginners with respect to this sin, on account of the sweetness which they find at first in spiritual exercises. For many of these, lured by the sweetness and pleasure which they find in such exercises, strive more after spiritual sweetness than after spiritual purity and discretion, which is that which God regards and accepts throughout the spiritual journey. Therefore, besides the imperfections into which the seeking for sweetness of this kind makes them fall, the gluttony which they now have makes them continually go to extremes, so that they pass beyond the limits of moderation within which the virtues are acquired and wherein they have their being. For some of these persons, attracted by the pleasure which they find therein, kill themselves with penances, and others weaken themselves with fasts, by performing more than their frailty can bear, without the order or advice of any, but rather endeavouring to avoid those whom they should obey in these matters; some, indeed, dare to do these things even though the contrary has been commanded them.

These persons are most imperfect and unreasonable; for they set bodily penance before subjection and obedience, which is penance according to reason and discretion, and therefore a sacrifice more acceptable and pleasing to God than any other. But such one-sided penance is no more than the penance of beasts, to which they are attracted, exactly like beasts, by the desire and pleasure which they find therein. Inasmuch as all extremes are vicious, and as in behaving thus such persons are working their own will, they grow in vice rather than in virtue; for, to say the least, they are acquiring spiritual gluttony and pride in this way, through not walking in obedience. And many of these the devil assails, stirring up this gluttony in them through the pleasures and desires which he increases within them, to such an extent that, since they can no longer help themselves, they either change or vary or add to that which is commanded them, as any obedience in this respect is so bitter to them. To such an evil pass have some persons come that, simply because it is through obedience that they engage in these exercises, they lose the desire and devotion to perform them, their only desire and pleasure being to do what they themselves are inclined to do, so that it would probably be more profitable for them not to engage in these exercises at all.

You will find that many of these persons are very insistent with their spiritual masters to be granted that which they desire, extracting it from them almost by force; if they be refused it they become as peevish as children and go about in great displeasure, thinking that they are not serving God when they are not allowed to do that which they would. For they go about clinging to their own will and pleasure, which they treat as though it came from God; and immediately their directors take it from them, and try to subject them to the will of God, they become peevish, grow faint-hearted and fall away. These persons think that their own satisfaction and pleasure are the satisfaction and service of God.

There are others, again, who, because of this gluttony, know so little of their own unworthiness and misery and have thrust so far from them the loving fear and reverence which they owe to the greatness of God, that they hesitate not to insist continually that their confessors shall allow them to communicate often. And, what is worse, they frequently dare to communicate without the leave and consent of the minister and steward of Christ, merely acting on their own opinion, and contriving to conceal the truth from him. And for this reason, because they desire to communicate continually, they make their confessions carelessly, being more eager to eat than to eat cleanly and perfectly, although it would be healthier and holier for them had they the contrary inclination and begged their confessors not to command them to approach the altar so frequently: between these two extremes, however, the better way is that of humble resignation. But the boldness referred to is a thing that does great harm, and men may fear to be punished for such temerity.

These persons, in communicating, strive with every nerve to obtain some kind of sensible sweetness and pleasure, instead of humbly doing reverence and giving praise within themselves to God. And in such wise do they devote themselves to this that, when they have received no pleasure or sweetness in the senses, they think that they have accomplished nothing at all. This is to judge God very unworthily; they have not realized that the least of the benefits which come from this Most Holy Sacrament is that which concerns the senses; and that the invisible part of the grace that it bestows is much greater; for, in order that they may look at it with the eyes of faith, God oftentimes withholds from them these other consolations and sweetnesses of sense. And thus they desire to feel and taste God as though He were comprehensible by them and accessible to them, not only in this, but likewise in other spiritual practices. All this is very great imperfection and completely opposed to the nature of God, since it is Impurity in faith.

These persons have the same defect as regards the practice of prayer, for they think that all the business of prayer consists in experiencing sensible pleasure and devotion and they strive to obtain this by great effort, wearying and fatiguing their faculties and their heads; and when they have not found this pleasure they become greatly discouraged, thinking that they have accomplished nothing. Through these efforts they lose true devotion and spirituality, which consist in perseverance, together with patience and humility and mistrust of themselves, that they may please God alone. For this reason, when they have once failed to find pleasure in this or some other exercise, they have great disinclination and repugnance to return to it, and at times they abandon it. They are, in fact, as we have said, like children, who are not influenced by reason, and who act, not from rational motives, but from inclination. Such persons expend all their effort in seeking spiritual pleasure and consolation; they never tire therefore, of reading books; and they begin, now one meditation, now another, in their pursuit of this pleasure which they desire to experience in the things of God. But God, very justly, wisely and lovingly, denies it to them, for otherwise this spiritual gluttony and inordinate appetite would breed innumerable evils. It is, therefore, very fitting that they should enter into the dark night, whereof we shall speak, that they may be purged from this childishness.

These persons who are thus inclined to such pleasures have another very great imperfection, which is that they are very weak and remiss in journeying upon the hard road of the Cross; for the soul that is given to sweetness naturally has its face set against all self-denial, which is devoid of sweetness.

These persons have many other imperfections which arise hence, of which in time the Lord heals them by means of temptations, aridities and other trials, all of which are part of the dark night. All these I will not treat further here, lest I become too lengthy; I will only say that spiritual temperance and sobriety lead to another and a very different temper, which is that of mortification, fear and submission in all things. It thus becomes clear that the perfection and worth of things consist not in the multitude and the pleasantness of one's actions, but in being able to deny oneself in them; this such persons must endeavour to compass, in so far as they may, until God is pleased to purify them indeed, by bringing them into the dark night, to arrive at which I am hastening on with my account of these imperfections.

Chapter VII

Of imperfections with respect to spiritual envy and sloth.

With respect likewise to the other two vices, which are spiritual envy and sloth, these beginners fail not to have many imperfections. For, with respect to envy, many of them are wont to experience movements of displeasure at the spiritual good of others, which cause them a certain sensible grief at being outstripped upon this road, so that they would prefer not to hear others praised; for they become displeased at others' virtues and sometimes they cannot refrain from contradicting what is said in praise of them, depreciating it as far as they can; and their annoyance thereat grows because the same is not said of them, for they would fain be preferred in everything. All this is clean contrary to charity, which, as Saint Paul says, rejoices in goodness. And, if charity has any envy, it is a holy envy, comprising grief at not having the virtues of others, yet also joy because others have them, and delight when others outstrip us in the service of God, wherein we ourselves are so remiss.

With respect also to spiritual sloth, beginners are apt to be irked by the things that are most spiritual, from which they flee because these things are incompatible with sensible pleasure. For, as they are so much accustomed to sweetness in spiritual things, they are wearied by things in which they find no sweetness. If once they failed to find in prayer the satisfaction which their taste required (and after all it is well that God should take it from them to prove them), they would prefer not to return to it: sometimes they leave it; at other times they continue it unwillingly. And thus because of this sloth they abandon the way of perfection (which is the way of the negation of their will and pleasure for God's sake) for the pleasure and sweetness of their own will, which they aim at satisfying in this way rather than the will of God.

And many of these would have God will that which they themselves will, and are fretful at having to will that which He wills, and find it repugnant to accommodate their will to that of God. Hence it happens to them that oftentimes they think that that wherein they find not their own will and pleasure is not the will of God; and that, on the other hand, when they themselves find satisfaction, God is satisfied. Thus they measure God by themselves and not themselves by God, acting quite contrarily to that which He Himself taught in the Gospel, saying: That he who should lose his will for His sake, the same should gain it; and he who should desire to gain it, the same should lose it.

These persons likewise find it irksome when they are commanded to do that wherein they take no pleasure. Because they aim at spiritual sweetness and consolation, they are too weak to have the fortitude and bear the trials of perfection. They resemble those who are softly nurtured and who run fretfully away from everything that is hard, and take offense at the Cross, wherein consist the delights of the spirit. The more spiritual a thing is, the more irksome they find it, for, as they seek to go about spiritual matters with complete freedom and according to the inclination of their will, it causes them great sorrow and repugnance to enter upon the narrow way, which, says Christ, is the way of life.

Let it suffice here to have described these imperfections, among the many to be found in the lives of those that are in this first state of beginners, so that it may be seen how greatly they need God to set them in the state of proficients. This He does by bringing them into the dark night whereof we now speak; wherein He weans them from the breasts of these sweetnesses and pleasures, gives them pure aridities and inward darkness, takes from them all these irrelevances and puerilities, and by very different means causes them to win the virtues. For, however assiduously the beginner practises the mortification in himself of all these actions and passions of his, he can never completely succeed—very far from it—until God shall work it in him passively by means of the purgation of the said night. Of this I would fain speak in some way that may be profitable; may God, then, be pleased to give me His Divine light, because this is very needful in a night that is so dark and a matter that is so difficult to describe and to expound.

The line, then, is: In a dark night.

Chapter VIII

Wherein is expounded the first line of the first stanza, and a beginning is made of the explanation of this dark night.

This night, which, as we say, is contemplation, produces in spiritual persons two kinds of darkness or purgation, corresponding to the two parts of man's nature—namely, the sensual and the spiritual. And thus the one night or purgation will be sensual, wherein the soul is purged according to sense, which is subdued to the spirit; and the other is a night or purgation which is spiritual, wherein the soul is purged and stripped according to the spirit, and subdued and made ready for the union of love with God. The night of sense is common and comes to many: these are the beginners; and of this night we shall speak first. The night of the spirit is the portion of very few, and these are they that are already practised and proficient, of whom we shall treat hereafter.

The first purgation or night is bitter and terrible to sense, as we shall now show. The second bears no comparison with it, for it is horrible and awful to the spirit, as we shall show presently. Since the night of sense is first in order and comes first, we shall first of all say something about it briefly, since more is written of it, as of a thing that is more common; and we shall pass on to treat more fully of the spiritual night, since very little has been said of this, either in speech or in writing, and very little is known of it, even by experience.

Since, then, the conduct of these beginners upon the way of God is ignoble, and has much to do with their love of self and their own inclinations, as has been explained above, God desires to lead them farther. He seeks to bring them out of that ignoble kind of love to a higher degree of love for Him, to free them from the ignoble exercises of sense and meditation (wherewith, as we have said, they go seeking God so unworthily and in so many ways that are unbefitting), and to lead them to a kind of spiritual exercise wherein they can commune with Him more abundantly and are freed more completely from imperfections. For they have now had practice for some time in the way of virtue and have persevered in meditation and prayer, whereby, through the sweetness and pleasure that they have found therein, they have lost their love of the things of the world and have gained some degree of spiritual strength in God; this has enabled them to some extent to refrain from creature desires, so that for God's sake they are now able to suffer a light burden and a little aridity without turning back to a time which they found more pleasant. When they are going about these spiritual exercises with the greatest delight and pleasure, and when they believe that the sun of Divine favour is shining most brightly upon them, God turns all this light of theirs into darkness, and shuts against them the door and the source of the sweet spiritual water which they were tasting in God whensoever and for as long as they desired. (For, as they were weak and tender, there was no door closed to them, as Saint John says in the Apocalypse, iii,). And thus He leaves them so completely in the dark that they know not whither to go with their sensible imagination and meditation; for they cannot advance a step in meditation, as they were wont to do afore time, their inward senses being submerged in this night, and left with such dryness that not only do they experience no pleasure and consolation in the spiritual things and good exercises wherein they were wont to find their delights and pleasures, but instead, on the contrary, they find insipidity and bitterness in the said things. For, as I have said, God now sees that they have grown a little, and are becoming strong enough to lay aside their swaddling clothes and be taken from the gentle breast; so He sets them down from His arms and teaches them to walk on their own feet; which they feel to be very strange, for everything seems to be going wrong with them.

To recollected persons this commonly happens sooner after their beginnings than to others, inasmuch as they are freer from occasions of backsliding, and their desires turn more quickly from the things of the world, which is necessary if they are to begin to enter this blessed night of sense. Ordinarily no great time passes after their beginnings before they begin to enter this night of sense; and the great majority of them do in fact enter it, for they will generally be seen to fall into these aridities.

With regard to this way of purgation of the senses, since it is so common, we might here adduce a great number of quotations from Divine Scripture, where many passages relating to it are continually found, particularly in the Psalms and the Prophets. However, I do not wish to spend time upon these, for he who knows not how to look for them there will find the common experience of this purgation to be sufficient.

Chapter IX

Of the signs by which it will be known that the spiritual person is walking along the way of this night and purgation of sense.

But since these aridities might frequently proceed, not from the night and purgation of the sensual desires aforementioned, but from sins and imperfections, or from weakness and lukewarmness, or from some bad humour or indisposition of the body, I shall here set down certain signs by which it may be known if such aridity proceeds from the aforementioned purgation, or if it arises from any of the aforementioned sins. For the making of this distinction I find that there are three principal signs.

The first is whether, when a soul finds no pleasure or consolation in the things of God, it also fails to find it in any thing created; for, as God sets the soul in this dark night to the end that He may quench and purge its sensual desire, He allows it not to find attraction or sweetness in anything whatsoever. In such a case it may be considered very probable that this aridity and insipidity proceed not from recently committed sins or imperfections. For, if this were so, the soul would feel in its nature some inclination or desire to taste other things than those of God; since, whenever the desire is allowed indulgence in any imperfection, it immediately feels inclined thereto, whether little or much, in proportion to the pleasure and the love that it has put into it. Since, however, this lack of enjoyment in things above or below might proceed from some indisposition or melancholy humour, which oftentimes makes it impossible for the soul to take pleasure in anything, it becomes necessary to apply the second sign and condition.

The second sign whereby a man may believe himself to be experiencing the said purgation is that the memory is ordinarily centred upon God, with painful care and solicitude, thinking that it is not serving God, but is backsliding, because it finds itself without sweetness in the things of God. And in such a case it is evident that this lack of sweetness and this aridity come not from weakness and lukewarmness; for it is the nature of lukewarmness not to care greatly or to have any inward solicitude for the things of God. There is thus a great difference between aridity and lukewarmness, for lukewarmness consists in great weakness and remissness in the will and in the spirit, without solicitude as to serving God; whereas purgative aridity is ordinarily accompanied by solicitude, with care and grief as I say, because the soul is not serving God. And, although this may sometimes be increased by melancholy or some other humour (as it frequently is), it fails not for that reason to produce a purgative effect upon the desire, since the desire is deprived of all pleasure and has its care centred upon God alone. For, when mere humour is the cause, it spends itself in displeasure and ruin of the physical nature, and there are none of those desires to sense God which belong to purgative aridity. When the cause is aridity, it is true that the sensual part of the soul has fallen low, and is weak and feeble in its actions, by reason of the little pleasure which it finds in them; but the spirit, on the other hand, is ready and strong.

For the cause of this aridity is that God transfers to the spirit the good things and the strength of the senses, which, since the soul's natural strength and senses are incapable of using them, remain barren, dry and empty. For the sensual part of a man has no capacity for that which is pure spirit, and thus, when it is the spirit that receives the pleasure, the flesh is left without savour and is too weak to perform any action. But the spirit, which all the time is being fed, goes forward in strength, and with more alertness and solicitude than before, in its anxiety not to fail God; and if it is not immediately conscious of spiritual sweetness and delight, but only of aridity and lack of sweetness, the reason for this is the strangeness of the exchange; for its palate has been accustomed to those other sensual pleasures upon which its eyes are still fixed, and, since the spiritual palate is not made ready or purged for such subtle pleasure, until it finds itself becoming prepared for it by means of this arid and dark night, it cannot experience spiritual pleasure and good, but only aridity and lack of sweetness, since it misses the pleasure which aforetime it enjoyed so readily.

These souls whom God is beginning to lead through these solitary places of the wilderness are like to the children of Israel, to whom in the wilderness God began to give food from Heaven, containing within itself all sweetness, and, as is there said, it turned to the savour which each one of them desired. But withal the children of Israel felt the lack of the pleasures and delights of the flesh and the onions which they had eaten aforetime in Egypt, the more so because their palate was accustomed to these and took delight in them, rather than in the delicate sweetness of the angelic manna; and they wept and sighed for the fleshpots even in the midst of the food of Heaven. To such depths does the vileness of our desires descend that it makes us to long for our own wretched food and to be nauseated by the indescribable blessings of Heaven.

But, as I say, when these aridities proceed from the way of the purgation of sensual desire, although at first the spirit feels no sweetness, for the reasons that we have just given, it feels that it is deriving strength and energy to act from the substance which this inward food gives it, the which food is the beginning of a contemplation that is dark and arid to the senses; which contemplation is secret and hidden from the very person that experiences it; and ordinarily, together with the aridity and emptiness which it causes in the senses, it gives the soul an inclination and desire to be alone and in quietness, without being able to think of any particular thing or having the desire to do so. If those souls to whom this comes to pass knew how to be quiet at this time, and troubled not about performing any kind of action, whether inward or outward, neither had any anxiety about doing anything, then they would delicately experience this inward refreshment in that ease and freedom from care. So delicate is this refreshment that ordinarily, if a man have desire or care to experience it, he experiences it not; for, as I say, it does its work when the soul is most at ease and freest from care; it is like the air which, if one would close one's hand upon it, escapes.

In this sense we may understand that which the Spouse said to the Bride in the Songs, namely: 'Withdraw thine eyes from me, for they make me to soar aloft.' For in such a way does God bring the soul into this state, and by so different a path does He lead it that, if it desires to work with its faculties, it hinders the work which God is doing in it rather than aids it; whereas aforetime it was quite the contrary. The reason is that, in this state of contemplation, which the soul enters when it forsakes meditation for the state of the proficient, it is God Who is now working in the soul; He binds its interior faculties, and allows it not to cling to the understanding, nor to have delight in the will, nor to reason with the memory. For anything that the soul can do of its own accord at this time serves only, as we have said, to hinder inward peace and the work which God is accomplishing in the spirit by means of that aridity of sense. And this peace, being spiritual and delicate, performs a work which is quiet and delicate, solitary, productive of peace and satisfaction and far removed from all those earlier pleasures, which were very palpable and sensual. This is the peace which, says David, God speaks in the soul to the end that He may make it spiritual. And this leads us to the third point.

The third sign whereby this purgation of sense may be recognized is that the soul can no longer meditate or reflect in the imaginative sphere of sense as it was wont, however much it may of itself endeavour to do so. For God now begins to communicate Himself to it, no longer through sense, as He did aforetime, by means of reflections which joined and sundered its knowledge, but by pure spirit, into which consecutive reflections enter not; but He communicates Himself to it by an act of simple contemplation, to which neither the exterior nor the interior senses of the lower part of the soul can attain. From this time forward, therefore, imagination and fancy can find no support in any meditation, and can gain no foothold by means thereof.

With regard to this third sign, it is to be understood that this embarrassment and dissatisfaction of the faculties proceed not from indisposition, for, when this is the case, and the indisposition, which never lasts for long, comes to an end, the soul is able once again, by taking some trouble about the matter, to do what it did before, and the faculties find their wonted support. But in the purgation of the desire this is not so: when once the soul begins to enter therein, its inability to reflect with the faculties grows ever greater. For, although it is true that at first, and with some persons, the process is not as continuous as this, so that occasionally they fail to abandon their pleasures and reflections of sense (for perchance by reason of their weakness it was not fitting to wean them from these immediately), yet this inability grows within them more and more and brings the workings of sense to an end, if indeed they are to make progress, for those who walk not in the way of contemplation act very differently. For this night of aridities is not usually continuous in their senses. At times they have these aridities; at others they have them not. At times they cannot meditate; at others they can. For God sets them in this night only to prove them and to humble them, and to reform their desires, so that they go not nurturing in themselves a sinful gluttony in spiritual things. He sets them not there in order to lead them in the way of the spirit, which is this contemplation; for not all those who walk of set purpose in the way of the spirit are brought by God to contemplation, nor even the half of them—why, He best knows. And this is why He never completely weans the senses of such persons from the breasts of meditations and reflections, but only for short periods and at certain seasons, as we have said.

Chapter X

Of the way in which these souls are to conduct themselves in this dark night.

During the time, then, of the aridities of this night of sense (wherein God effects the change of which we have spoken above, drawing forth the soul from the life of sense into that of the spirit—that is, from meditation to contemplation—wherein it no longer has any power to work or to reason with its faculties concerning the things of God, as has been said), spiritual persons suffer great trials, by reason not so much of the aridities which they suffer, as of the fear which they have of being lost on the road, thinking that all spiritual blessing is over for them and that God has abandoned them since they find no help or pleasure in good things. Then they grow weary, and endeavour (as they have been accustomed to do) to concentrate their faculties with some degree of pleasure upon some object of meditation, thinking that, when they are not doing this and yet are conscious of making an effort, they are doing nothing. This effort they make not without great inward repugnance and unwillingness on the part of their soul, which was taking pleasure in being in that quietness and ease, instead of working with its faculties. So they have abandoned the one pursuit, yet draw no profit from the other; for, by seeking what is prompted by their own spirit, they lose the spirit of tranquillity and peace which they had before. And thus they are like to one who abandons what he has done in order to do it over again, or to one who leaves a city only to re-enter it, or to one who is hunting and lets his prey go in order to hunt it once more. This is useless here, for the soul will gain nothing further by conducting itself in this way, as has been said.

These souls turn back at such a time if there is none who understands them; they abandon the road or lose courage; or, at the least, they are hindered from going farther by the great trouble which they take in advancing along the road of meditation and reasoning. Thus they fatigue and overwork their nature, imagining that they are failing through negligence or sin. But this trouble that they are taking is quite useless, for God is now leading them by another road, which is that of contemplation, and is very different from the first; for the one is of meditation and reasoning, and the other belongs neither to imagination nor yet to reasoning.

It is well for those who find themselves in this condition to take comfort, to persevere in patience and to be in no wise afflicted. Let them trust in God, Who abandons not those that seek Him with a simple and right heart, and will not fail to give them what is needful for the road, until He bring them into the clear and pure light of love. This last He will give them by means of that other dark night, that of the spirit, if they merit His bringing them thereto.

The way in which they are to conduct themselves in this night of sense is to devote themselves not at all to reasoning and meditation, since this is not the time for it, but to allow the soul to remain in peace and quietness, although it may seem clear to them that they are doing nothing and are wasting their time, and although it may appear to them that it is because of their weakness that they have no desire in that state to think of anything. The truth is that they will be doing quite sufficient if they have patience and persevere in prayer without making any effort. What they must do is merely to leave the soul free and disencumbered and at rest from all knowledge and thought, troubling not themselves, in that state, about what they shall think or meditate upon, but contenting themselves with merely a peaceful and loving attentiveness toward God, and in being without anxiety, without the ability and without desired to have experience of Him or to perceive Him. For all these yearnings disquiet and distract the soul from the peaceful quiet and sweet ease of contemplation which is here granted to it.

And although further scruples may come to them—that they are wasting their time, and that it would be well for them to do something else, because they can neither do nor think anything in prayer—let them suffer these scruples and remain in peace, as there is no question save of their being at ease and having freedom of spirit. For if such a soul should desire to make any effort of its own with its interior faculties, this means that it will hinder and lose the blessings which, by means of that peace and ease of the soul, God is instilling into it and impressing upon it. It is just as if some painter were painting or dyeing a face; if the sitter were to move because he desired to do something, he would prevent the painter from accomplishing anything and would disturb him in what he was doing. And thus, when the soul desires to remain in inward ease and peace, any operation and affection or attentions wherein it may then seek to indulge will distract it and disquiet it and make it conscious of aridity and emptiness of sense. For the more a soul endeavours to find support in affection and knowledge, the more will it feel the lack of these, which cannot now be supplied to it upon that road.

Wherefore it behoves such a soul to pay no heed if the operations of its faculties become lost to it; it is rather to desire that this should happen quickly. For, by not hindering the operation of infused contemplation that God is bestowing upon it, it can receive this with more peaceful abundance, and cause its spirit to be enkindled and to burn with the love which this dark and secret contemplation brings with it and sets firmly in the soul. For contemplation is naught else than a secret, peaceful and loving infusion from God, which, if it be permitted, enkindles the soul with the spirit of love, according as the soul declares in the next lines, namely:
Kindled in love with yearnings.

Chapter XI

Wherein are expounded the three lines of the stanza.

This enkindling of love is not as a rule felt at the first, because it has not begun to take hold upon the soul, by reason of the impurity of human nature, or because the soul has not understood its own state, as we have said, and has therefore given it no peaceful abiding-place within itself. Yet sometimes, nevertheless, there soon begins to make itself felt a certain yearning toward God; and the more this increases, the more is the soul affectioned and enkindled in love toward God, without knowing or understanding how and whence this love and affection come to it, but from time to time seeing this flame and this enkindling grow so greatly within it that it desires God with yearning of love; even as David, when he was in this dark night, said of himself in these words, namely: 'Because my heart was enkindled (that is to say, in love of contemplation), my reins also were changed': that is, my desires for sensual affections were changed, namely from the way of sense to the way of the spirit, which is the aridity and cessation from all these things whereof we are speaking. And I, he says, was dissolved in nothing and annihilated, and I knew not; for, as we have said, without knowing the way whereby it goes, the soul finds itself annihilated with respect to all things above and below which were accustomed to please it; and it finds itself enamoured, without knowing how. And because at times the enkindling of love in the spirit grows greater, the yearnings for God become so great in the soul that the very bones seem to be dried up by this thirst, and the natural powers to be fading away, and their warmth and strength to be perishing through the intensity of the thirst of love, for the soul feels that this thirst of love is a living thirst. This thirst David had and felt, when he said: 'My soul thirsted for the living God.' Which is as much as to say: A living thirst was that of my soul. Of this thirst, since it is living, we may say that it kills. But it is to be noted that the vehemence of this thirst is not continuous, but occasional although as a rule the soul is accustomed to feel it to a certain degree.

But it must be noted that, as I began to say just now, this love is not as a rule felt at first, but only the dryness and emptiness are felt whereof we are speaking. Then in place of this love which afterwards becomes gradually enkindled, what the soul experiences in the midst of these aridities and emptinesses of the faculties is an habitual care and solicitude with respect to God, together with grief and fear that it is not serving Him. But it is a sacrifice which is not a little pleasing to God that the soul should go about afflicted and solicitous for His love. This solicitude and care leads the soul into that secret contemplation, until, the senses (that is, the sensual part) having in course of time been in some degree purged of the natural affections and powers by means of the aridities which it causes within them, this Divine love begins to be enkindled in the spirit. Meanwhile, however, like one who has begun a cure, the soul knows only suffering in this dark and arid purgation of the desire; by this means it becomes healed of many imperfections, and exercises itself in many virtues in order to make itself meet for the said love, as we shall now say with respect to the line following:

Oh, happy chance!

When God leads the soul into this night of sense in order to purge the sense of its lower part and to subdue it, unite it and bring it into conformity with the spirit, by setting it in darkness and causing it to cease from meditation (as He afterwards does in order to purify the spirit to unite it with God, as we shall afterwards say), He brings it into the night of the spirit, and (although it appears not so to it) the soul gains so many benefits that it holds it to be a happy chance to have escaped from the bonds and restrictions of the senses of or its lower self, by means of this night aforesaid; and utters the present line, namely: Oh, happy chance! With respect to this, it behoves us here to note the benefits which the soul finds in this night, and because of which it considers it a happy chance to have passed through it; all of which benefits the soul includes in the next line, namely:

I went forth without being observed.

This going forth is understood of the subjection to its sensual part which the soul suffered when it sought God through operations so weak, so limited and so defective as are those of this lower part; for at every step it stumbled into numerous imperfections and ignorances, as we have noted above in writing of the seven capital sins. From all these it is freed when this night quenches within it all pleasures, whether from above or from below, and makes all meditation darkness to it, and grants it other innumerable blessings in the acquirement of the virtues, as we shall now show. For it will be a matter of great pleasure and great consolation, to one that journeys on this road, to see how that which seems to the soul so severe and adverse, and so contrary to spiritual pleasure, works in it so many blessings. These, as we say, are gained when the soul goes forth, as regards its affection and operation, by means of this night, from all created things, and when it journeys to eternal things, which is great happiness and good fortune: first, because of the great blessing which is in the quenching of the desire and affection with respect to all things; secondly, because they are very few that endure and persevere in entering by this strait gate and by the narrow way which leads to life, as says Our Saviour. The strait gate is this night of sense, and the soul detaches itself from sense and strips itself thereof that it may enter by this gate, and establishes itself in faith, which is a stranger to all sense, so that afterwards it may journey by the narrow way, which is the other night—that of the spirit—and this the soul afterwards enters in order in journey to God in pure faith, which is the means whereby the soul is united to God. By this road, since it is so narrow, dark and terrible (though there is no comparison between this night of sense and that other, in its darkness and trials, as we shall say later), they are far fewer that journey, but its benefits are far greater without comparison than those of this present night. Of these benefits we shall now begin to say something, with such brevity as is possible, in order that we may pass to the other night.

Chapter XII

Of the benefits which this night causes in the soul.

This night and purgation of the desire, a happy one for the soul, works in it so many blessings and benefits (although to the soul, as we have said, it rather seems that blessings are being taken away from it) that, even as Abraham made a great feast when he weaned his son Isaac, even so is there joy in Heaven because God is now taking this soul from its swaddling clothes, setting it down from His arms, making it to walk upon its feet, and likewise taking from it the milk of the breast and the soft and sweet food proper to children, and making it to eat bread with crust, and to begin to enjoy the food of robust persons. This food, in these aridities and this darkness of sense, is now given to the spirit, which is dry and emptied of all the sweetness of sense. And this food is the infused contemplation whereof we have spoken.

This is the first and principal benefit caused by this arid and dark night of contemplation: the knowledge of oneself and of one's misery. For, besides the fact that all the favours which God grants to the soul are habitually granted to them enwrapped in this knowledge, these aridities and this emptiness of the faculties, compared with the abundance which the soul experienced aforetime and the difficulty which it finds in good works, make it recognize its own lowliness and misery, which in the time of its prosperity it was unable to see. Of this there is a good illustration in the Book of Exodus, where God, wishing to humble the children of Israel and desiring that they should know themselves, commanded them to take away and strip off the festal garments and adornments wherewith they were accustomed to adorn themselves in the Wilderness, saying: 'Now from henceforth strip yourselves of festal ornaments and put on everyday working dress, that ye may know what treatment ye deserve.' This is as though He had said: Inasmuch as the attire that ye wear, being proper to festival and rejoicing, causes you to feel less humble concerning yourselves than ye should, put off from you this attire, in order that henceforth, seeing yourselves clothed with vileness, ye may know that ye merit no more, and may know who ye are. Wherefore the soul knows the truth that it knew not at first, concerning its own misery; for, at the time when it was clad as for a festival and found in God much pleasure, consolation and support, it was somewhat more satisfied and contented, since it thought itself to some extent to be serving God. It is true that such souls may not have this idea explicitly in their minds; but some suggestion of it at least is implanted in them by the satisfaction which they find in their pleasant experiences. But, now that the soul has put on its other and working attire—that of aridity and abandonment—and now that its first lights have turned into darkness, it possesses these lights more truly in this virtue of self-knowledge, which is so excellent and so necessary, considering itself now as nothing and experiencing no satisfaction in itself; for it sees that it does nothing of itself neither can do anything. And the smallness of this self-satisfaction, together with the soul's affliction at not serving God, is considered and esteemed by God as greater than all the consolations which the soul formerly experienced and the works which it wrought, however great they were, inasmuch as they were the occasion of many imperfections and ignorances. And from this attire of aridity proceed, as from their fount and source of self-knowledge, not only the things which we have described already, but also the benefits which we shall now describe and many more which will have to be omitted.

In the first place, the soul learns to commune with God with more respect and more courtesy, such as a soul must ever observe in converse with the Most High. These it knew not in its prosperous times of comfort and consolation, for that comforting favour which it experienced made its craving for God somewhat bolder than was fitting, and discourteous and ill-considered. Even so did it happen to Moses, when he perceived that God was speaking to him; blinded by that pleasure and desire, without further consideration, he would have made bold to go to Him if God had not commanded him to stay and put off his shoes. By this incident we are shown the respect and discretion in detachment of desire wherewith a man is to commune with God. When Moses had obeyed in this matter, he became so discreet and so attentive that the Scripture says that not only did he not make bold to draw near to God, but that he dared not even look at Him. For, having taken off the shoes of his desires and pleasures, he became very conscious of his wretchedness in the sight of God, as befitted one about to hear the word of God. Even so likewise the preparation which God granted to Job in order that he might speak with Him consisted not in those delights and glories which Job himself reports that he was wont to have in his God, but in leaving him naked upon a dung-hill, abandoned and even persecuted by his friends, filled with anguish and bitterness, and the earth covered with worms. And then the Most High God, He that lifts up the poor man from the dunghill, was pleased to come down and speak with him there face to face, revealing to him the depths and heights of His wisdom, in a way that He had never done in the time of his prosperity.

And here we must note another excellent benefit which there is in this night and aridity of the desire of sense, since we have had occasion to speak of it. It is that, in this dark night of the desire (to the end that the words of the Prophet may be fulfilled, namely: 'Thy light shall shine in the darkness'), God will enlighten the soul, giving it knowledge, not only of its lowliness and wretchedness, as we have said, but likewise of the greatness and excellence of God. For, as well as quenching the desires and pleasures and attachments of sense, He cleanses and frees the understanding that it may understand the truth; for pleasure of sense and desire, even though it be for spiritual things, darkens and obstructs the spirit, and furthermore that straitness and aridity of sense enlightens and quickens the understanding, as says Isaias. Vexation makes us to understand how the soul that is empty and disencumbered, as is necessary for His Divine influence, is instructed supernaturally by God in His

Divine wisdom, through this dark and arid night of contemplation, as we have said; and this instruction God gave not in those first sweetnesses and joys.

This is very well explained by the same prophet Isaias, where he says: 'Whom shall God teach His knowledge, and whom shall He make to understand the hearing?' To those, He says, that are weaned from the milk and drawn away from the breasts. Here it is shown that the first milk of spiritual sweetness is no preparation for this Divine influence, neither is there preparation in attachment to the breast of delectable meditations, belonging to the faculties of sense, which gave the soul pleasure; such preparation consists rather in the lack of the one and withdrawal from the other. Inasmuch as, in order to listen to God, the soul needs to stand upright and to be detached, with regard to affection and sense, even as the Prophet says concerning himself, in these words: I will stand upon my watch (this is that detachment of desire) and I will make firm my step (that is, I will not meditate with sense), in order to contemplate (that is, in order to understand that which may come to me from God). So we have now arrived at this, that from this arid night there first of all comes self-knowledge, whence, as from a foundation, rises this other knowledge of God. For which cause Saint Augustine said to God: 'Let me know myself, Lord, and I shall know Thee.' For, as the philosophers say, one extreme can be well known by another.

And in order to prove more completely how efficacious is this night of sense, with its aridity and its desolation, in bringing the soul that light which, as we say, it receives there from God, we shall quote that passage of David, wherein he clearly describes the great power which is in this night for bringing the soul this lofty knowledge of God. He says, then, thus: 'In the desert land, waterless, dry and pathless, I appeared before Thee, that I might see Thy virtue and Thy glory.' It is a wondrous thing that David should say here that the means and the preparation for his knowledge of the glory of God were not the spiritual delights and the many pleasures which he had experienced, but the aridities and detachments of his sensual nature, which is here to be understood by the dry and desert land. No less wondrous is it that he should describe as the road to his perception and vision of the virtue of God, not the Divine meditations and conceptions of which he had often made use, but his being unable to form any conception of God or to walk by meditation produced by imaginary consideration, which is here to be understood by the pathless land. So that the means to a knowledge of God and of oneself is this dark night with its aridities and voids, although it leads not to a knowledge of Him of the same plenitude and abundance that comes from the other night of the spirit, since this is only, as it were, the beginning of that other.

Likewise, from the aridities and voids of this night of the desire, the soul draws spiritual humility, which is the contrary virtue to the first capital sin, which, as we said, is spiritual pride. Through this humility, which is acquired by the said knowledge of self, the soul is purged from all those imperfections whereinto it fell with respect to that sin of pride, in the time of its prosperity. For it sees itself so dry and miserable that the idea never even occurs to it that it is making better progress than others, or outstripping them, as it believed itself to be doing before. On the contrary, it recognizes that others are making better progress than itself.

And hence arises the love of its neighbours, for it esteems them, and judges them not as it was wont to do aforetime, when it saw that itself had great fervour and others not so. It is aware only of its own wretchedness, which it keeps before its eyes to such an extent that it never forgets it, nor takes occasion to set its eyes on anyone else. This was described wonderfully by David, when he was in this night, in these words: 'I was dumb and was humbled and kept silence from good things and my sorrow was renewed.' This he says because it seemed to him that the good that was in his soul had so completely departed that not only did he neither speak nor find any language concerning it, but with respect to the good of others he was likewise dumb because of his grief at the knowledge of his misery.

In this condition, again, souls become submissive and obedient upon the spiritual road, for, when they see their own misery, not only do they hear what is taught them, but they even desire that anyone soever may set them on the way and tell them what they ought to do. The affective presumption which they sometimes had in their prosperity is taken from them; and finally, there are swept away from them on this road all the other imperfections which we noted above with respect to this first sin, which is spiritual pride.

Chapter XIII

Of other benefits which this night of sense causes in the soul.

With respect to the soul's imperfections of spiritual avarice, because of which it coveted this and that spiritual thing and found no satisfaction in this and that exercise by reason of its covetousness for the desire and pleasure which it found therein, this arid and dark night has now greatly reformed it. For, as it finds not the pleasure and sweetness which it was wont to find, but rather finds affliction and lack of sweetness, it has such moderate recourse to them that it might possibly now lose, through defective use, what aforetime it lost through excess; although as a rule God gives to those whom He leads into this night humility and readiness, albeit with lack of sweetness, so that what is commanded them they may do for God's sake alone; and thus they no longer seek profit in many things because they find no pleasure in them.

With respect to spiritual luxury, it is likewise clearly seen that, through this aridity and lack of sensible sweetness which the soul finds in spiritual things, it is freed from those impurities which we there noted; for we said that, as a rule, they proceeded from the pleasure which overflowed from spirit into sense.

But with regard to the imperfections from which the soul frees itself in this dark night with respect to the fourth sin, which is spiritual gluttony, they may be found above, though they have not all been described there, because they are innumerable; and thus I will not detail them here, for I would fain make an end of this night in order to pass to the next, concerning which we shall have to pronounce grave words and instructions. Let it suffice for the understanding of the innumerable benefits which, over and above those mentioned, the soul gains in this night with respect to this sin of spiritual gluttony, to say that it frees itself from all those imperfections which have there been described, and from many other and greater evils, and vile abominations which are not written above, into which fell many of whom we have had experience, because they had not reformed their desire as concerning this inordinate love of spiritual sweetness. For in this arid and dark night wherein He sets the soul, God has restrained its concupiscence and curbed its desire so that the soul cannot feed upon any pleasure or sweetness of sense, whether from above or from below; and this He continues to do after such manner that the soul is subjected, reformed and repressed with respect to concupiscence and desire. It loses the strength of its passions and concupiscence and it becomes sterile, because it no longer consults its likings. Just as, when none is accustomed to take milk from the breast, the courses of the milk are dried up, so the desires of the soul are dried up. And besides these things there follow admirable benefits from this spiritual sobriety, for, when desire and concupiscence are quenched, the soul lives in spiritual tranquillity and peace; for, where desire and concupiscence reign not, there is no disturbance, but peace and consolation of God.

From this there arises another and a second benefit, which is that the soul habitually has remembrance of God, with fear and dread of backsliding upon the spiritual road, as has been said. This is a great benefit, and not one of the least that results from this aridity and purgation of the desire, for the soul is purified and cleansed of the imperfections that were clinging to it because of the desires and affections, which of their own accord deaden and darken the soul.

There is another very great benefit for the soul in this night, which is that it practices several virtues together, as, for example, patience and longsuffering, which are often called upon in these times of emptiness and aridity, when the soul endures and perseveres in its spiritual exercises without consolation and without pleasure. It practises the charity of God, since it is not now moved by the pleasure of attraction and sweetness which it finds in its work, but only by God. It likewise practises here the virtue of fortitude, because, in these difficulties and insipidities which it finds in its work, it brings strength out of weakness and thus becomes strong. All the virtues, in short—the theological and also the cardinal and moral—both in body and in spirit, are practised by the soul in these times of aridity.

And that in this night the soul obtains these four benefits which we have here described (namely, delight of peace, habitual remembrance and thought of God, cleanness and purity of soul and the practice of the virtues which we have just described), David tells us, having experienced it himself when he was in this night, in these words: 'My soul refused consolations, I had remembrance of God, I found consolation and was exercised and my spirit failed.' And he then says: 'And I meditated by night with my heart and was exercised, and I swept and purified my spirit'—that is to say, from all the affections.

With respect to the imperfections of the other three spiritual sins which we have described above, which are wrath, envy and sloth, the soul is purged hereof likewise in this aridity of the desire and acquires the virtues opposed to them; for, softened and humbled by these aridities and hardships and other temptations and trials wherein God exercises it during this night, it becomes meek with respect to God, and to itself, and likewise with respect to its neighbour. So that it is no longer disturbed and angry with itself because of its own faults, nor with its neighbour because of his, neither is it displeased with God, nor does it utter unseemly complaints because He does not quickly make it holy.

Then, as to envy, the soul has charity toward others in this respect also; for, if it has any envy, this is no longer a vice as it was before, when it was grieved because others were preferred to it and given greater advantage. Its grief now comes from seeing how great is its own misery, and its envy (if it has any) is a virtuous envy, since it desires to imitate others, which is great virtue.

Neither are the sloth and the irksomeness which it now experiences concerning spiritual things vicious as they were before. For in the past these sins proceeded from the spiritual pleasures which the soul sometimes experienced and sought after when it found them not. But this new weariness proceeds not from this insuffficiency of pleasure, because God has taken from the soul pleasure in all things in this purgation of the desire.

Besides these benefits which have been mentioned, the soul attains innumerable others by means of this arid contemplation. For often, in the midst of these times of aridity and hardship, God communicates to the soul, when it is least expecting it, the purest spiritual sweetness and love, together with a spiritual knowledge which is sometimes very delicate, each manifestation of which is of greater benefit and worth than those which the soul enjoyed aforetime; although in its beginnings the soul thinks that this is not so, for the spiritual influence now granted to it is very delicate and cannot be perceived by sense.

Finally, inasmuch as the soul is now purged from the affections and desires of sense, it obtains liberty of spirit, whereby in ever greater degree it gains the twelve fruits of the Holy Spirit. Here, too, it is wondrously delivered from the hands of its three enemies—devil, world and flesh; for, its pleasure and delight of sense being quenched with respect to all things, neither the devil nor the world nor sensuality has any arms or any strength wherewith to make war upon the spirit.

These times of aridity, then, cause the soul to journey in all purity in the love of God, since it is no longer influenced in its actions by the pleasure and sweetness of the actions themselves, as perchance it was when it experienced sweetness, but only by a desire to please God. It becomes neither presumptuous nor self-satisfied, as perchance it was wont to become in the time of its prosperity, but fearful and timid with regard to itself, finding in itself no satisfaction whatsoever; and herein consists that holy fear which preserves and increases the virtues. This aridity, too, quenches natural energy and concupiscence, as has also been said. Save for the pleasure, indeed, which at certain times God Himself infuses into it, it is a wonder if it finds pleasure and consolation of sense, through its own diligence, in any spiritual exercise or action, as has already been said.

There grows within souls that experience this arid night concern for God and yearnings to serve Him, for in proportion as the breasts of sensuality, wherewith it sustained and nourished the desires that it pursued, are drying up, there remains nothing in that aridity and detachment save the yearning to serve God, which is a thing very pleasing to God. For, as David says, an afflicted spirit is a sacrifice to God.

When the soul, then, knows that, in this arid purgation through which it has passed, it has derived and attained so many and such precious benefits as those which have here been described, it tarries not in crying, as in the stanza of which we are expounding the lines, 'Oh, happy chance!—I went forth without being observed.' That is, 'I went forth' from the bonds and subjection of the desires of sense and the affections, 'without being observed'—that is to say, without the three enemies aforementioned being able to keep me from it. These enemies, as we have said, bind the soul as with bonds, in its desires and pleasures, and prevent it from going forth from itself to the liberty of the love of God; and without these desires and pleasures they cannot give battle to the soul, as has been said.

When, therefore, the four passions of the soul—which are joy, grief, hope and fear—are calmed through continual mortification; when the natural desires have been lulled to sleep, in the sensual nature of the soul, by means of habitual times of aridity; and when the harmony of the senses and the interior faculties causes a suspension of labour and a cessation from the work of meditation, as we have said (which is the dwelling and the household of the lower part of the soul), these enemies cannot obstruct this spiritual liberty, and the house remains at rest and quiet, as says the following line:

My house being now at rest.

Chapter XIV

Expounds this last line of the first stanza.

When this house of sensuality was now at rest—that is, was mortified—its passions being quenched and its desires put to rest and lulled to sleep by means of this blessed night of the purgation of sense, the soul went forth, to set out upon the road and way of the spirit, which is that of progressives and proficients, and which, by another name, is called the way of illumination or of infused contemplation, wherein God Himself feeds and refreshes the soul, without meditation, or the soul's active help. Such, as we have said, is the night and purgation of sense in the soul. In those who have afterwards to enter the other and more formidable night of the spirit, in order to pass to the Divine union of love of God (for not all pass habitually thereto, but only the smallest number), it is wont to be accompanied by formidable trials and temptations of sense, which last for a long time, albeit longer in some than in others. For to some the angel of Satan presents himself—namely, the spirit of fornication—that he may buffet their senses with abominable and violent temptations, and trouble their spirits with vile considerations and representations which are most visible to the imagination, which things at times are a greater affliction to them than death.

At other times in this night there is added to these things the spirit of blasphemy, which roams abroad, setting in the path of all the conceptions and thoughts of the soul intolerable blasphemies. These it sometimes suggests to the imagination with such violence that the soul almost utters them, which is a grave torment to it.

At other times another abominable spirit, which Isaias calls Spiritus vertiginis, is allowed to molest them, not in order that they may fall, but that it may try them. This spirit darkens their senses in such a way that it fills them with numerous scruples and perplexities, so confusing that, as they judge, they can never, by any means, be satisfied concerning them, neither can they find any help for their judgment in counsel or thought. This is one of the severest goads and horrors of this night, very closely akin to that which passes in the night of the spirit.

As a rule these storms and trials are sent by God in this night and purgation of sense to those whom afterwards He purposes to lead into the other night (though not all reach it), to the end that, when they have been chastened and buffeted, they may in this way continually exercise and prepare themselves, and continually accustom their senses and faculties to the union of wisdom which is to be bestowed upon them in that other night. For, if the soul be not tempted, exercised and proved with trials and temptations, it cannot quicken its sense of Wisdom. For this reason it is said in Ecclesiasticus: 'He that has not been tempted, what does he know? And he that has not been proved, what are the things that he recognizes?' To this truth Jeremias bears good witness, saying: 'Thou didst chastise me, Lord, and I was instructed.' And the most proper form of this chastisement, for one who will enter into Wisdom, is that of the interior trials which we are here describing, inasmuch as it is these which most effectively purge sense of all favours and consolations to which it was affected, with natural weakness, and by which the soul is truly humiliated in preparation for the exaltation which it is to experience.

For how long a time the soul will be held in this fasting and penance of sense, cannot be said with any certainty; for all do not experience it after one manner, neither do all encounter the same temptations. For this is meted out by the will of God, in conformity with the greater or the smaller degree of imperfection which each soul has to purge away. In conformity, likewise, with the degree of love of union to which God is pleased to raise it, He will humble it with greater or less intensity or in greater or less time. Those who have the disposition and greater strength to suffer, He purges with greater intensity and more quickly. But those who are very weak are kept for a long time in this night, and these He purges very gently and with slight temptations. Habitually, too, He gives them refreshments of sense so that they may not fall away, and only after a long time do they attain to purity of perfection in this life, some of them never attaining to it at all. Such are neither properly in the night nor properly out of it; for, although they make no progress, yet, in order that they may continue in humility and self-knowledge, God exercises them for certain periods and at certain times in those temptations and aridities; and at other times and seasons He assists them with consolations, lest they should grow faint and return to seek the consolations of the world. Other souls, which are weaker, God Himself accompanies, now appearing to them, now moving farther away, that He may exercise them in His love; for without such turnings away they would not learn to reach God.

But the souls which are to pass on to that happy and high estate, the union of love, are wont as a rule to remain for a long time in these aridities and temptations, however quickly God may lead them, as has been seen by experience. It is time, then, to begin to treat of the second night.

BOOK THE SECOND

Of the Dark Night of the Spirit.

Chapter I

Which begins to treat of the dark nights of the spirit and says at what time it begins.

The soul which God is about to lead onward is not led by His Majesty into this night of the spirit as soon as it goes forth from the aridities and trials of the first purgation and night of sense; rather it is wont to pass a long time, even years, after leaving the state of beginners, in exercising itself in that of proficients. In this latter state it is like to one that has come forth from a rigorous imprisonment; it goes about the things of God with much greater freedom and satisfaction of the soul, and with more abundant and inward delight than it did at the beginning before it entered the said night. For its imagination and faculties are no longer bound, as they were before, by meditation and anxiety of spirit, since it now very readily finds in its spirit the most serene and loving contemplation and spiritual sweetness without the labour of meditation; although, as the purgation of the soul is not complete (for the principal part thereof, which is that of the spirit, is wanting, without which, owing to the communication that exists between the one part and the other, since the subject is one only, the purgation of sense, however violent it may have been, is not yet complete and perfect), it is never without certain occasional necessities, aridities, darknesses and perils which are sometimes much more intense than those of the past, for they are as tokens and heralds of the coming night of the spirit, and are not of as long duration as will be the night which is to come. For, having passed through a period, or periods, or days of this night and tempest, the soul soon returns to its wonted serenity; and after this manner God purges certain souls which are not to rise to so high a degree of love as are others, bringing them at times, and for short periods, into this night of contemplation and purgation of the spirit, causing night to come upon them and then dawn, and this frequently, so that the words of David may be fulfilled, that He sends His crystal—that is, His contemplation—like morsels, although these morsels of dark contemplation are never as intense as is that terrible night of contemplation which we are to describe, into which, of set purpose, God brings the soul that He may lead it to Divine union.

This sweetness, then, and this interior pleasure which we are describing, and which these progressives find and experience in their spirits so easily and so abundantly, is communicated to them in much greater abundance than aforetime, overflowing into their senses more than was usual previously to this purgation of sense; for, inasmuch as the sense is now purer, it can more easily feel the pleasures of the spirit after its manner. As, however, this sensual part of the soul is weak and incapable of experiencing the strong things of the spirit, it follows that these proficients, by reason of this spiritual communication which is made to their sensual part endure therein many frailties and sufferings and weaknesses of the stomach, and in consequence are fatigued in spirit. For, as the Wise Man says: 'The corruptible body presseth down the soul.' Hence comes it that the communications that are granted to these souls cannot be very strong or very intense or very spiritual, as is required for Divine union with God, by reason of the weakness and corruption of the sensual nature which has a part in them. Hence arise the raptures and trances and dislocations of the bones which always happen when the communications are not purely spiritual—that is, are not given to the spirit alone, as are those of the perfect who are purified by the second night of the spirit, and in whom these raptures and torments of the body no longer exist, since they are enjoying liberty of spirit, and their senses are now neither clouded nor transported.

And in order that the necessity for such souls to enter this night of the spirit may be understood, we will here note certain imperfections and perils which belong to these proficients.

Chapter 11

Describes other imperfections which belong to these proficients.

These proficients have two kinds of imperfection: the one kind is habitual; the other actual. The habitual imperfections are the imperfect habits and affections which have remained all the time in the spirit, and are like roots, to which the purgation of sense has been unable to penetrate. The difference between the purgation of these and that of this other kind is the difference between the root and the branch, or between the removing of a stain which is fresh and one which is old and of long standing. For, as we said, the purgation of sense is only the entrance and beginning of contemplation leading to the purgation of the spirit, which, as we have likewise said, serves rather to accommodate sense to spirit than to unite spirit with God. But there still remain in the spirit the stains of the old man, although the spirit thinks not that this is so, neither can it perceive them; if these stains be not removed with the soap and strong lye of the purgation of this night, the spirit will be unable to come to the purity of Divine union.

These souls have likewise the hebetudo mentis and the natural roughness which every man contracts through sin, and the distraction and outward clinging of the spirit, which must be enlightened, refined and recollected by the afflictions and perils of that night. These habitual imperfections belong to all those who have not passed beyond this state of the proficient; they cannot coexist, as we say, with the perfect state of union through love.

To actual imperfections all are not liable in the same way. Some, whose spiritual good is so superficial and so readily affected by sense, fall into greater difficulties and dangers, which we described at the beginning of this treatise. For, as they find so many and such abundant spiritual communications and apprehensions, both in sense and in spirit wherein they oftentimes see imaginary and spiritual visions (for all these things, together with other delectable feelings, come to many souls in this state, wherein the devil and their own fancy very commonly practise deceptions on them), and, as the devil is apt to take such pleasure in impressing upon the soul and suggesting to it the said apprehensions and feelings, he fascinates and deludes it with great ease unless it takes the precaution of resigning itself to God, and of protecting itself strongly, by means of faith, from all these visions and feelings. For in this state the devil causes many to believe in vain visions and false prophecies; and strives to make them presume that God and the saints are speaking with them; and they often trust their own fancy. And the devil is also accustomed, in this state, to fill them with presumption and pride, so that they become attracted by vanity and arrogance, and allow themselves to be seen engaging in outward acts which appear holy, such as raptures and other manifestations. Thus they become bold with God, and lose holy fear, which is the key and the custodian of all the virtues; and in some of these souls so many are the falsehoods and deceits which tend to multiply, and so inveterate do they grow, that it is very doubtful if such souls will return to the pure road of virtue and true spirituality. Into these miseries they fall because they are beginning to give themselves over to spiritual feelings and apprehensions with too great security, when they were beginning to make some progress upon the way.

There is much more that I might say of these imperfections and of how they are the more incurable because such souls consider them to be more spiritual than the others, but I will leave this subject. I shall only add, in order to prove how necessary, for him that would go farther, is the night of the spirit, which is purgation, that none of these proficients, however strenuously he may have laboured, is free, at best, from many of those natural affections and imperfect habits, purification from which, we said, is necessary if a soul is to pass to Divine union.

And over and above this (as we have said already), inasmuch as the lower part of the soul still has a share in these spiritual communications, they cannot be as intense, as pure and as strong as is needful for the aforesaid union; wherefore, in order to come to this union, the soul must needs enter into the second night of the spirit, wherein it must strip sense and spirit perfectly from all these apprehensions and from all sweetness, and be made to walk in dark and pure faith, which is the proper and adequate means whereby the soul is united with God, according as Osee says, in these words: 'I will betroth thee—that is, I will unite thee—with Me through faith.'

Chapter III

Annotation for that which follows.

These souls, then, have now become proficients, because of the time which they have spent in feeding the senses with sweet communications, so that their sensual part, being thus attracted and delighted by spiritual pleasure, which came to it from the spirit, may be united with the spirit and made one with it; each part after its own manner eating of one and the same spiritual food and from one and the same dish, as one person and with one sole intent, so that thus they may in a certain way be united and brought into agreement, and, thus united, may be prepared for the endurance of the stern and severe purgation of the spirit which awaits them. In this purgation these two parts of the soul, the spiritual and the sensual, must be completely purged, since the one is never truly purged without the other, the purgation of sense becoming effective when that of the spirit has fairly begun. Wherefore the night which we have called that of sense may and should be called a kind of correction and restraint of the desire rather than purgation. The reason is that all the imperfections and disorders of the sensual part have their strength and root in the spirit, where all habits, both good and bad, are brought into subjection, and thus, until these are purged, the rebellions and depravities of sense cannot be purged thoroughly.

Wherefore, in this night following, both parts of the soul are purged together, and it is for this end that it is well to have passed through the corrections of the first night, and the period of tranquillity which proceeds from it, in order that, sense being united with spirit, both may be purged after a certain manner and may then suffer with greater fortitude. For very great fortitude is needful for so violent and severe a purgation, since, if the weakness of the lower part has not first been corrected and fortitude has not been gained from God through the sweet and delectable communion which the soul has afterwards enjoyed with Him, its nature will not have the strength or the disposition to bear it.

Therefore, since these proficients are still at a very low stage of progress, and follow their own nature closely in the intercourse and dealings which they have with God, because the gold of their spirit is not yet purified and refined, they still think of God as little children, and speak of God as little children, and feel and experience God as little children, even as Saint Paul says, because they have not reached perfection, which is the union of the soul with God. In the state of union, however, they will work great things in the spirit, even as grown men, and their works and faculties will then be Divine rather than human, as will afterwards be said. To this end God is pleased to strip them of this old man and clothe them with the new man, who is created according to God, as the Apostle says, in the newness of sense. He strips their faculties, affections and feelings, both spiritual and sensual, both outward and inward, leaving the understanding dark, the will dry, the memory empty and the affections in the deepest affliction, bitterness and constraint, taking from the soul the pleasure and experience of spiritual blessings which it had aforetime, in order to make of this privation one of the principles which are requisite in the spirit so that there may be introduced into it and united with it the spiritual form of the spirit, which is the union of love. All this the Lord works in the soul by means of a pure and dark contemplation, as the soul explains in the first stanza. This, although we originally interpreted it with reference to the first night of sense, is principally understood by the soul of this second night of the spirit, since this is the principal part of the purification of the soul. And thus we shall set it down and expound it here again in this sense.

Chapter IV

Sets down the first stanza and the exposition thereof.

On a dark night, Kindled in love with yearnings—oh, happy chance!—I went forth without being observed, My house being now at rest.

Exposition

Interpreting this stanza now with reference to purgation, contemplation or detachment or poverty of spirit, which here are almost one and the same thing, we can expound it after this manner and make the soul speak thus: In poverty, and without protection or support in all the apprehensions of my soul—that is, in the darkness of my understanding and the constraint of my will, in affliction and anguish with respect to memory, remaining in the dark in pure faith, which is dark night for the said natural faculties, the will alone being touched by grief and afflictions and yearnings for the love of God—I went forth from myself—that is, from my low manner of understanding, from my weak mode of loving and from my poor and limited manner of experiencing God, without being hindered therein by sensuality or the devil.

This was a great happiness and a good chance for me; for, when the faculties had been perfectly annihilated and calmed, together with the passions, desires and affections of my soul, wherewith I had experienced and tasted God after a lowly manner, I went forth from my own human dealings and operations to the operations and dealings of God. That is to say, my understanding went forth from itself, turning from the human and natural to the Divine; for, when it is united with God by means of this purgation, its understanding no longer comes through its natural light and vigour, but through the Divine Wisdom wherewith it has become united. And my will went forth from itself, becoming Divine; for, being united with Divine love, it no longer loves with its natural strength after a lowly manner, but with strength and purity from the Holy Spirit; and thus the will, which is now near to God, acts not after a human manner, and similarly the memory has become transformed into eternal apprehensions of glory. And finally, by means of this night and purgation of the old man, all the energies and affections of the soul are wholly renewed into a Divine temper and Divine delight.

There follows the line: On a dark night.

Chapter V

Sets down the first line and begins to explain how this dark contemplation is not only night for the soul but is also grief and torment.

This dark night is an inflowing of God into the soul, which purges it from its ignorances and imperfections, habitual natural and spiritual, and which is called by contemplatives infused contemplation, or mystical theology. Herein God secretly teaches the soul and instructs it in perfection of love without its doing anything, or understanding of what manner is this infused contemplation. Inasmuch as it is the loving wisdom of God, God produces striking effects in the soul for, by purging and illumining it, He prepares it for the union of love with God. Wherefore the same loving wisdom that purges the blessed spirits and enlightens them is that which here purges the soul and illumines it.

But the question arises: Why is the Divine light (which as we say, illumines and purges the soul from its ignorances) here called by the soul a dark night? To this the answer is that for two reasons this Divine wisdom is not only night and darkness for the soul, but is likewise affliction and torment. The first is because of the height of Divine Wisdom, which transcends the talent of the soul, and in this way is darkness to it; the second, because of its vileness and impurity, in which respect it is painful and afflictive to it, and is also dark.

In order to prove the first point, we must here assume a certain doctrine of the philosopher, which says that, the clearer and more manifest are Divine things in themselves the darker and more hidden are they to the soul naturally; just as, the clearer is the light, the more it blinds and darkens the pupil of the owl, and, the more directly we look at the sun, the greater is the darkness which it causes in our visual faculty, overcoming and overwhelming it through its own weakness. In the same way, when this Divine light of contemplation assails the soul which is not yet wholly enlightened, it causes spiritual darkness in it; for not only does it overcome it, but likewise it overwhelms it and darkens the act of its natural intelligence. For this reason Saint Dionysius and other mystical theologians call this infused contemplation a ray of darkness—that is to say, for the soul that is not enlightened and purged—for the natural strength of the intellect is transcended and overwhelmed by its great supernatural light. Wherefore David likewise said: That near to God and round about Him are darkness and cloud; not that this is so in fact, but that it is so to our weak understanding, which is blinded and darkened by so vast a light, to which it cannot attain. For this cause the same David then explained himself, saying: 'Through the great splendour of His presence passed clouds'—that is, between God and our understanding. And it is for this cause that, when God sends it out from Himself to the soul that is not yet transformed, this illumining ray of His secret wisdom causes thick darkness in the understanding.

And it is clear that this dark contemplation is in these its beginnings painful likewise to the soul; for, as this Divine infused contemplation has many excellences that are extremely good, and the soul that receives them, not being purged, has many miseries that are likewise extremely bad, hence it follows that, as two contraries cannot coexist in one subject—the soul—it must of necessity have pain and suffering, since it is the subject wherein these two contraries war against each other, working the one against the other, by reason of the purgation of the imperfections of the soul which comes to pass through this contemplation. This we shall prove inductively in the manner following.

In the first place, because the light and wisdom of this contemplation is most bright and pure, and the soul which it assails is dark and impure, it follows that the soul suffers great pain when it receives it in itself, just as, when the eyes are dimmed by humours, and become impure and weak, the assault made upon them by a bright light causes them pain. And when the soul suffers the direct assault of this Divine light, its pain, which results from its impurity, is immense; because, when this pure light assails the soul, in order to expel its impurity, the soul feels itself to be so impure and miserable that it believes God to be against it, and thinks that it has set itself up against God. This causes it sore grief and pain, because it now believes that God has cast it away: this was one of the greatest trials which Job felt when God sent him this experience, and he said: 'Why hast Thou set me contrary to Thee, so that I am grievous and burdensome to myself?' For, by means of this pure light, the soul now sees its impurity clearly (although darkly), and knows clearly that it is unworthy of God or of any creature. And what gives it most pain is that it thinks that it will never be worthy and that its good things are all over for it. This is caused by the profound immersion of its spirit in the knowledge and realization of its evils and miseries; for this Divine and dark light now reveals them all to the eye, that it may see clearly how in its own strength it can never have aught else. In this sense we may understand that passage from David, which says: 'For iniquity Thou hast corrected man and hast made his soul to be undone and consumed: he wastes away as the spider.'

The second way in which the soul suffers pain is by reason of its weakness, natural, moral and spiritual; for, when this Divine contemplation assails the soul with a certain force, in order to strengthen it and subdue it, it suffers such pain in its weakness that it nearly swoons away. This is especially so at certain times when it is assailed with somewhat greater force; for sense and spirit, as if beneath some immense and dark load, are in such great pain and agony that the soul would find advantage and relief in death. This had been experienced by the prophet Job, when he said: 'I desire not that He should have intercourse with me in great strength, lest He oppress me with the weight of His greatness.'

Beneath the power of this oppression and weight the soul feels itself so far from being favoured that it thinks, and correctly so, that even that wherein it was wont to find some help has vanished with everything else, and that there is none who has pity upon it. To this effect Job says likewise: 'Have pity upon me, have pity upon me, at least ye my friends, because the hand of the Lord has touched me.' A thing of great wonder and pity is it that the soul's weakness and impurity should now be so great that, though the hand of God is of itself so light and gentle, the soul should now feel it to be so heavy and so contrary, though it neither weighs it down nor rests upon it, but only touches it, and that mercifully, since He does this in order to grant the soul favours and not to chastise it.

Chapter VI

Of other kinds of pain that the soul suffers in this night.

The third kind of suffering and pain that the soul endures in this state results from the fact that two other extremes meet here in one, namely, the Divine and the human. The Divine is this purgative contemplation, and the human is the subject—that is, the soul. The Divine assails the soul in order to renew it and thus to make it Divine; and, stripping it of the habitual affections and attachments of the old man, to which it is very closely united, knit together and conformed, destroys and consumes its spiritual substance, and absorbs it in deep and profound darkness. As a result of this, the soul feels itself to be perishing and melting away, in the presence and sight of its miseries, in a cruel spiritual death, even as if it had been swallowed by a beast and felt itself being devoured in the darkness of its belly, suffering such anguish as was endured by Jonas in the belly of that beast of the sea. For in this sepulchre of dark death it must needs abide until the spiritual resurrection which it hopes for.

A description of this suffering and pain, although in truth it transcends all description, is given by David, when he says: 'The lamentations of death compassed me about; the pains of hell surrounded me; I cried in my tribulation.' But what the sorrowful soul feels most in this condition is its clear perception, as it thinks, that God has abandoned it, and, in His abhorrence of it, has flung it into darkness; it is a grave and piteous grief for it to believe that God has forsaken it. It is this that David also felt so much in a like case, saying: 'After the manner wherein the wounded are dead in the sepulchres,' being now cast off by Thy hand, so that Thou rememberest them no more, even so have they set me in the deepest and lowest lake, in the dark places and in the shadow of death, and Thy fury is confirmed upon me and all Thy waves Thou hast brought in upon me.' For indeed, when this purgative contemplation is most severe, the soul feels very keenly the shadow of death and the lamentations of death and the pains of hell, which consist in its feeling itself to be without God, and chastised and cast out, and unworthy of Him; and it feels that He is wroth with it. All this is felt by the soul in this condition—yea, and more, for it believes that it is so with it for ever.

It feels, too, that all creatures have forsaken it, and that it is contemned by them, particularly by its friends. Wherefore David presently continues, saying: 'Thou hast put far from me my friends and acquaintances; they have counted me an abomination.' To all this will Jonas testify, as one who likewise experienced it in the belly of the beast, both bodily and spiritually. 'Thou hast cast me forth (he says) into the deep, into the heart of the sea, and the flood hath compassed me; all its billows and waves have passed over me. And I said, "I am cast away out of the sight of Thine eyes, but I shall once again see Thy holy temple" (which he says, because God purifies the soul in this state that it may see His temple); the waters compassed me, even to the soul, the deep hath closed me round about, the ocean hath covered my head, I went down to the lowest parts of the mountains; the bars of the earth have shut me up for ever.' By these bars are here understood, in this sense, imperfections of the soul, which have impeded it from enjoying this delectable contemplation.

The fourth kind of pain is caused in the soul by another excellence of this dark contemplation, which is its majesty and greatness, from which arises in the soul a consciousness of the other extreme which is in itself—namely, that of the deepest poverty and wretchedness: this is one of the chiefest pains that it suffers in this purgation. For it feels within itself a profound emptiness and impoverishment of three kinds of good, which are ordained for the pleasure of the soul which are the temporal, the natural and the spiritual; and finds itself set in the midst of the evils contrary to these, namely, miseries of imperfection, aridity and emptiness of the apprehensions of the faculties and abandonment of the spirit in darkness. Inasmuch as God here purges the soul according to the substance of its sense and spirit, and according to the interior and exterior faculties, the soul must needs be in all its parts reduced to a state of emptiness, poverty and abandonment and must be left dry and empty and in darkness. For the sensual part is purified in aridity, the faculties are purified in the emptiness of their perceptions and the spirit is purified in thick darkness.

All this God brings to pass by means of this dark contemplation; wherein the soul not only suffers this emptiness and the suspension of these natural supports and perceptions, which is a most afflictive suffering (as if a man were suspended or held in the air so that he could not breathe), but likewise He is purging the soul, annihilating it, emptying it or consuming in it (even as fire consumes the mouldiness and the rust of metal) all the affections and imperfect habits which it has contracted in its whole life. Since these are deeply rooted in the substance of the soul, it is wont to suffer great undoings and inward torment, besides the said poverty and emptiness, natural and spiritual, so that there may here be fulfilled that passage from Ezechiel which says: 'Heap together the bones and I will burn them in the fire; the flesh shall be consumed and the whole composition shall be burned and the bones shall be destroyed.' Herein is understood the pain which is suffered in the emptiness and poverty of the substance of the soul both in sense and in spirit. And concerning this he then says: 'Set it also empty upon the coals, that its metal may become hot and molten, and its uncleanness may be destroyed within it, and its rust may be consumed.' Herein is described the grave suffering which the soul here endures in the purgation of the fire of this contemplation, for the Prophet says here that, in order for the rust of the affections which are within the soul to be purified and destroyed, it is needful that, in a certain manner, the soul itself should be annihilated and destroyed, since these passions and imperfections have become natural to it.

Wherefore, because the soul is purified in this furnace like gold in a crucible, as says the Wise Man, it is conscious of this complete undoing of itself in its very substance, together with the direst poverty, wherein it is, as it were, nearing its end, as may be seen by that which David says of himself in this respect, in these words: 'Save me, Lord (he cries to God), for the waters have come in even unto my soul; I am made fast in the mire of the deep and there is no place where I can stand; I am come into the depth of the sea and a tempest hath overwhelmed me; I have laboured crying, my throat has become hoarse, mine eyes have failed whilst I hope in my God.' Here God greatly humbles the soul in order that He may afterwards greatly exalt it; and if He ordained not that, when these feelings arise within the soul, they should speedily be stilled, it would die in a very short space; but there are only occasional periods when it is conscious of their greatest intensity. At times, however, they are so keen that the soul seems to be seeing hell and perdition opened. Of such are they that in truth go down alive into hell, being purged here on earth in the same manner as there, since this purgation is that which would have to be accomplished there. And thus the soul that passes through this either enters not that place at all, or tarries there but for a very short time; for one hour of purgation here is more profitable than are many there.

Chapter VII

Continues the same matter and considers other afflictions end constraints of the will.

The afflictions and constraints of the will are now very great likewise, and of such a kind that they sometimes transpierce the soul with a sudden remembrance of the evils in the midst of which it finds itself, and with the uncertainty of finding a remedy for them. And to this is added the remembrance of times of prosperity now past; for as a rule souls that enter this night have had many consolations from God, and have rendered Him many services, and it causes them the greater grief to see that they are far removed from that happiness and unable to enter into it. This was also described by Job, who had had experience of it, in these words: 'I, who was wont to be wealthy and rich, am suddenly undone and broken to pieces; He hath taken me by my neck; He hath broken me and set me up for His mark to wound me; He hath compassed me round about with His lances; He hath wounded all my loins; He hath not spared; He hath poured out my bowels on the earth; He hath broken me with wound upon wound; He hath assailed me as a strong giant; I have sewed sackcloth upon my skin and have covered my flesh with ashes; my face is become swollen with weeping and mine eyes are blinded.'

So many and so grievous are the afflictions of this night, and so many passages of Scripture are there which could be cited to this purpose, that time and strength would fail us to write of them, for all that can be said thereof is certainly less than the truth. From the passages already quoted some idea may be gained of them. And, that we may bring the exposition of this line to a close and explain more fully what is worked in the soul by this night, I shall tell what Jeremias felt about it, which, since there is so much of it, he describes and bewails in many words after this manner: 'I am the man that see my poverty in the rod of His indignation; He hath threatened me and brought me into darkness and not into light. So far hath He turned against me and hath converted His hand upon me all the day! My skin and my flesh hath He made old; He hath broken my bones; He hath made a fence around me and compassed me with gall and trial; He hath set me in dark places, as those that are dead for ever. He hath made a fence around me and against me, that I may not go out; He hath made my captivity heavy. Yea, and when I have cried and have entreated, He hath shut out my prayer. He hath enclosed my paths and ways out with square stones; He hath thwarted my steps. He hath set ambushes for me; He hath become to me a lion in a secret place. He hath turned aside my steps and broken me in pieces, He hath made me desolate; He hath bent His bow and set me as a mark for His arrow. He hath shot into my reins the daughters of His quiver. I have become a derision to all the people, and laughter and scorn for them all the day. He hath filled me with bitterness and hath made me drunken with wormwood. He hath broken my teeth by number; He hath fed me with ashes. My soul is cast out from peace; I have forgotten good things. And I said: "Mine end is frustrated and cut short, together with my desire and my hope from the Lord. Remember my poverty and my excess, the wormwood and the gall. I shall be mindful with remembrance and my soul shall be undone within me in pains.'"

All these complaints Jeremias makes about these pains and trials, and by means of them he most vividly depicts the sufferings of the soul in this spiritual night and purgation. Wherefore the soul that God sets in this tempestuous and horrible night is deserving of great compassion. For, although it experiences much happiness by reason of the great blessings that must arise on this account within it, when, as Job says, God raises up profound blessings in the soul out of darkness, and brings up to light the shadow of death, so that, as David says, His light comes to be as was His darkness; yet notwithstanding, by reason of the dreadful pain which the soul is suffering, and of the great uncertainty which it has concerning the remedy for it, since it believes, as this prophet says here, that its evil will never end, and it thinks, as David says likewise, that God set it in dark places like those that are dead, and for this reason brought its spirit within it into anguish and troubled its heart, it suffers great pain and grief, since there is added to all this (because of the solitude and abandonment caused in it by this dark night) the fact that it finds no consolation or support in any instruction nor in a spiritual master. For, although in many ways its director may show it good reason for being comforted because of the blessings which are contained in these afflictions, it cannot believe him. For it is so greatly absorbed and immersed in the realization of those evils wherein it sees its own miseries so clearly, that it thinks that, as its director observes not that which it sees and feels, he is speaking in this manner because he understands it not; and so, instead of comfort, it rather receives fresh affliction, since it believes that its director's advice contains no remedy for its troubles. And, in truth, this is so; for, until the Lord shall have completely purged it after the manner that He wills, no means or remedy is of any service or profit for the relief of its affliction; the more so because the soul is as powerless in this case as one who has been imprisoned in a dark dungeon, and is bound hand and foot, and can neither move nor see, nor feel any favour whether from above or from below, until the spirit is humbled, softened and purified, and grows so keen and delicate and pure that it can become one with the Spirit of God, according to the degree of union of love which His mercy is pleased to grant it; in proportion to this the purgation is of greater or less severity and of greater or less duration.

But, if it is to be really effectual, it will last for some years, however severe it be; since the purgative process allows intervals of relief wherein, by the dispensation of God, this dark contemplation ceases to assail the soul in the form and manner of purgation, and assails it after an illuminative and a loving manner, wherein the soul, like one that has gone forth from this dungeon and imprisonment, and is brought into the recreation of spaciousness and liberty, feels and experiences great sweetness of peace and loving friendship with God, together with a ready abundance of spiritual communication. This is to the soul a sign of the health which is being wrought within it by the said purgation and a foretaste of the abundance for which it hopes. Occasionally this is so great that the soul believes its trials to be at last over. For spiritual things in the soul, when they are most purely spiritual, have this characteristic that, if trials come to it, the soul believes that it will never escape from them, and that all its blessings are now over, as has been seen in the passages quoted; and, if spiritual blessings come, the soul believes in the same way that its troubles are now over, and that blessings will never fail it. This was so with David, when he found himself in the midst of them, as he confesses in these words: 'I said in my abundance: "I shall never be moved."'

This happens because the actual possession by the spirit of one of two contrary things itself makes impossible the actual possession and realization of the other contrary thing; this is not so, however, in the sensual part of the soul, because its apprehension is weak. But, as the spirit is not yet completely purged and cleansed from the affections that it has contracted from its lower part, while changing not in so far as it is spirit, it can be moved to further afflictions in so far as these affections sway it. In this way, as we see, David was afterwards moved, and experienced many ills and afflictions, although in the time of his abundance he had thought and said that he would never be moved. Just so is it with the soul in this condition, when it sees itself moved by that abundance of spiritual blessings, and, being unable to see the root of the imperfection and impurity which still remain within it, thinks that its trials are over.

This thought, however, comes to the soul but seldom, for, until spiritual purification is complete and perfected, the sweet communication is very rarely so abundant as to conceal from the soul the root which remains hidden, in such a way that the soul can cease to feel that there is something that it lacks within itself or that it has still to do. Thus it cannot completely enjoy that relief, but feels as if one of its enemies were within it, and although this enemy is, as it were, hushed and asleep, it fears that he will come to life again and attack it. And this is what indeed happens, for, when the soul is most secure and least alert, it is dragged down and immersed again in another and a worse degree of affliction which is severer and darker and more grievous than that which is past; and this new affliction will continue for a further period of time, perhaps longer than the first. And the soul once more comes to believe that all its blessings are over for ever. Although it had thought during its first trial that there were no more afflictions which it could suffer, and yet, after the trial was over, it enjoyed great blessings, this experience is not sufficient to take away its belief, during this second degree of trial, that all is now over for it and that it will never again be happy as in the past. For, as I say, this belief, of which the soul is so sure, is caused in it by the actual apprehension of the spirit, which annihilates within it all that is contrary to it.

This is the reason why those who lie in purgatory suffer great misgivings as to whether they will ever go forth from it and whether their pains will ever be over. For, although they have the habit of the three theological virtues—faith, hope and charity—the present realization which they have of their afflictions and of their deprivation of God allows them not to enjoy the present blessing and consolation of these virtues. For, although they are able to realize that they have a great love for God, this is no consolation to them, since they cannot think that God loves them or that they are worthy that He should do so; rather, as they see that they are deprived of Him, and left in their own miseries, they think that there is that in themselves which provides a very good reason why they should with perfect justice be abhorred and cast out by God for ever. And thus although the soul in this purgation is conscious that it has a great love for God and would give a thousand lives for Him (which is the truth, for in these trials such souls love their God very earnestly), yet this is no relief to it, but rather brings it greater affliction. For it loves Him so much that it cares about naught beside; when, therefore, it sees itself to be so wretched that it cannot believe that God loves it, nor that there is or will ever be reason why He should do so, but rather that there is reason why it should be abhorred, not only by Him, but by all creatures for ever, it is grieved to see in itself reasons for deserving to be cast out by Him for Whom it has such great love and desire.

Chapter VlII

Of other pains which afflict the soul in this state.

But there is another thing here that afflicts and distresses the soul greatly, which is that, as this dark night has hindered its faculties and affections in this way, it is unable to raise its affection or its mind to God, neither can it pray to Him, thinking, as Jeremias thought concerning himself, that God has set a cloud before it through which its prayer cannot pass. For it is this that is meant by that which is said in the passage referred to, namely: 'He hath shut and enclosed my paths with square stones.' And if it sometimes prays it does so with such lack of strength and of sweetness that it thinks that God neither hears it nor pays heed to it, as this Prophet likewise declares in the same passage, saying: 'When I cry and entreat, He hath shut out my prayer.' In truth this is no time for the soul to speak with God; it should rather put its mouth in the dust, as Jeremias says, so that perchance there may come to it some present hope, and it may endure its purgation with patience. It is God Who is passively working here in the soul; wherefore the soul can do nothing. Hence it can neither pray nor pay attention when it is present at the Divine offices, much less can it attend to other things and affairs which are temporal. Not only so, but it has likewise such distractions and times of such profound forgetfulness of the memory that frequent periods pass by without its knowing what it has been doing or thinking, or what it is that it is doing or is going to do, neither can it pay attention, although it desire to do so, to anything that occupies it.

Inasmuch as not only is the understanding here purged of its light, and the will of its affections, but the memory is also purged of meditation and knowledge, it is well that it be likewise annihilated with respect to all these things, so that that which David says of himself in this purgation may by fulfilled, namely: 'I was annihilated and I knew not.' This unknowing refers to these follies and forgetfulnesses of the memory, which distractions and forgetfulnesses are caused by the interior recollection wherein this contemplation absorbs the soul. For, in order that the soul may be divinely prepared and tempered with its faculties for the Divine union of love, it would be well for it to be first of all absorbed, with all its faculties, in this Divine and dark spiritual light of contemplation, and thus to be withdrawn from all the affections and apprehensions of the creatures, which condition ordinarily continues in proportion to its intensity. And thus, the simpler and the purer is this Divine light in its assault upon the soul, the more does it darken it, void it and annihilate it according to its particular apprehensions and affections, with regard both to things above and to things below; and similarly, the less simple and pure is it in this assault, the less deprivation it causes it and the less dark is it. Now this is a thing that seems incredible, to say that, the brighter and purer is supernatural and Divine light, the more it darkens the soul, and that, the less bright and pure is it, the less dark it is to the soul. Yet this may readily be understood if we consider what has been proved above by the dictum of the philosopher—namely, that the brighter and the more manifest in themselves are supernatural things the darker are they to our understanding.

And, to the end that this may be understood the more clearly, we shall here set down a similitude referring to common and natural light. We observe that a ray of sunlight which enters through the window is the less clearly visible according as it is the purer and freer from specks, and the more of such specks and motes there are in the air, the brighter is the light to the eye. The reason is that it is not the light itself that is seen; the light is but the means whereby the other things that it strikes are seen, and then it is also seen itself, through its reflection in them; were it not for this, neither it nor they would have been seen. Thus if the ray of sunlight entered through the window of one room and passed out through another on the other side, traversing the room, and if it met nothing on the way, or if there were no specks in the air for it to strike, the room would have no more light than before, neither would the ray of light be visible. In fact, if we consider it carefully, there is more darkness where the ray is, since it absorbs and obscures any other light, and yet it is itself invisible, because, as we have said, there are no visible objects which it can strike.

Now this is precisely what this Divine ray of contemplation does in the soul. Assailing it with its Divine light, it transcends the natural power of the soul, and herein it darkens it and deprives it of all natural affections and apprehensions which it apprehended aforetime by means of natural light; and thus it leaves it not only dark, but likewise empty, according to its faculties and desires, both spiritual and natural. And, by thus leaving it empty and in darkness, it purges and illumines it with Divine spiritual light, although the soul thinks not that it has this light, but believes itself to be in darkness, even as we have said of the ray of light, which although it be in the midst of the room, yet, if it be pure and meet nothing on its path, is not visible. With regard, however, to this spiritual light by which the soul is assailed, when it has something to strike—that is, when something spiritual presents itself to be understood, however small a speck it be and whether of perfection or imperfection, or whether it be a judgment of the falsehood or the truth of a thing—it then sees and understands much more clearly than before it was in these dark places. And exactly in the same way it discerns the spiritual light which it has in order that it may readily discern the imperfection which is presented to it; even as, when the ray of which we have spoken, within the room, is dark and not itself visible, if one introduce a hand or any other thing into its path, the hand is then seen and it is realized that that sunlight is present.

Wherefore, since this spiritual light is so simple, pure and general, not appropriated or restricted to any particular thing that can be understood, whether natural or Divine (since with respect to all these apprehensions the faculties of the soul are empty and annihilated), it follows that with great comprehensiveness and readiness the soul discerns and penetrates whatsoever thing presents itself to it, whether it come from above or from below; for which cause the Apostle said: That the spiritual man searches all things, even the deep things of God. For by this general and simple wisdom is understood that which the Holy Spirit says through the Wise Man, namely: That it reaches wheresoever it wills by reason of its purity; that is to say, because it is not restricted to any particular object of the intellect or affection. And this is the characteristic of the spirit that is purged and annihilated with respect to all particular affections and objects of the understanding, that in this state wherein it has pleasure in nothing and understands nothing in particular, but dwells in its emptiness, darkness and obscurity, it is fully prepared to embrace everything to the end that those words of Saint Paul may be fulfilled in it: Nihil habentes, et omnia possidentes. For such poverty of spirit as this would deserve such happiness.

Chapter IX

How, although this night brings darkness to the spirit, it does so in order to illumine it and give it light.

It now remains to be said that, although this happy night brings darkness to the spirit, it does so only to give it light in everything; and that, although it humbles it and makes it miserable, it does so only to exalt it and to raise it up; and, although it impoverishes it and empties it of all natural affection and attachment, it does so only that it may enable it to stretch forward, divinely, and thus to have fruition and experience of all things, both above and below, yet to preserve its unrestricted liberty of spirit in them all. For just as the elements, in order that they may have a part in all natural entities and compounds, must have no particular colour, odour or taste, so as to be able to combine with all tastes odours and colours, just so must the spirit be simple, pure and detached from all kinds of natural affection, whether actual or habitual, to the end that it may be able freely to share in the breadth of spirit of the Divine Wisdom, wherein, through its purity, it has experience of all the sweetness of all things in a certain pre-eminently excellent way. And without this purgation it will be wholly unable to feel or experience the satisfaction of all this abundance of spiritual sweetness. For one single affection remaining in the spirit, or one particular thing to which, actually or habitually, it clings, suffices to hinder it from feeling or experiencing or communicating the delicacy and intimate sweetness of the spirit of love, which contains within itself all sweetness to a most eminent degree.

For, even as the children of Israel, solely because they retained one single affection and remembrance—namely, with respect to the fleshpots and the meals which they had tasted in Egypt—could not relish the delicate bread of angels, in the desert, which was the manna, which, as the Divine Scripture says, held sweetness for every taste and turned to the taste that each one desired; even so the spirit cannot succeed in enjoying the delights of the spirit of liberty, according to the desire of the will, if it be still affectioned to any desire, whether actual or habitual, or to particular objects of understanding, or to any other apprehension. The reason for this is that the affections, feelings and apprehensions of the perfect spirit, being Divine, are of another kind and of a very different order from those that are natural. They are pre-eminent, so that, in order both actually and habitually to possess the one, it is needful to expel and annihilate the other, as with two contrary things, which cannot exist together in one person. Therefore it is most fitting and necessary, if the soul is to pass to these great things, that this dark night of contemplation should first of all annihilate and undo it in its meannesses, bringing it into darkness, aridity, affliction and emptiness; for the light which is to be given to it is a Divine light of the highest kind, which transcends all natural light, and which by nature can find no place in the understanding.

And thus it is fitting that, if the understanding is to be united with that light and become Divine in the state of perfection, it should first of all be purged and annihilated as to its natural light, and, by means of this dark contemplation, be brought actually into darkness. This darkness should continue for as long as is needful in order to expel and annihilate the habit which the soul has long since formed in its manner of understanding, and the Divine light and illumination will then take its place. And thus, inasmuch as that power of understanding which it had aforetime is natural, it follows that the darkness which it here suffers is profound and horrible and most painful, for this darkness, being felt in the deepest substance of the spirit, seems to be substantial darkness. Similarly, since the affection of love which is to be given to it in the Divine union of love is Divine, and therefore very spiritual, subtle and delicate, and very intimate, transcending every affection and feeling of the will, and every desire thereof, it is fitting that, in order that the will may be able to attain to this Divine affection and most lofty delight, and to feel it and experience it through the union of love, since it is not, in the way of nature, perceptible to the will, it be first of all purged and annihilated in all its affections and feelings, and left in a condition of aridity and constraint, proportionate to the habit of natural affections which it had before, with respect both to Divine things and to human. Thus, being exhausted, withered and thoroughly tried in the fire of this dark contemplation, and having driven away every kind of evil spirit (as with the heart of the fish which Tobias set on the coals), it may have a simple and pure disposition, and its palate may be purged and healthy, so that it may feel the rare and sublime touches of Divine love, wherein it will see itself divinely transformed, and all the contrarieties, whether actual or habitual, which it had aforetime, will be expelled, as we are saying.

Moreover, in order to attain the said union to which this dark night is disposing and leading it, the soul must be filled and endowed with a certain glorious magnificence in its communion with God, which includes within itself innumerable blessings springing from delights which exceed all the abundance that the soul can naturally possess. For by nature the soul is so weak and impure that it cannot receive all this. As Isaias says: 'Eye hath not seen, nor ear heard, neither hath it entered into the heart of man, that which God hath prepared, etc.' It is meet, then, that the soul be first of all brought into emptiness and poverty of spirit and purged from all help, consolation and natural apprehension with respect to all things, both above and below. In this way, being empty, it is able indeed to be poor in spirit and freed from the old man, in order to live that new and blessed life which is attained by means of this night, and which is the state of union with God.

And because the soul is to attain to the possession of a sense, and of a Divine knowledge, which is very generous and full of sweetness, with respect to things Divine and human, which fall not within the common experience and natural knowledge of the soul (because it looks on them with eyes as different from those of the past as spirit is different from sense and the Divine from the human), the spirit must be straitened and inured to hardships as regards its common and natural experience, and be brought by means of this purgative contemplation into great anguish and affliction, and the memory must be borne far from all agreeable and peaceful knowledge, and have an intimated sense and feeling that it is making a pilgrimage and being a stranger to all things, so that it seems to it that all things are strange and of a different kind from that which they were wont to be. For this night is gradually drawing the spirit away from its ordinary and common experience of things and bringing it nearer the Divine sense, which is a stranger and an alien to all human ways. It seems now to the soul that it is going forth from its very self, with much affliction. At other times it wonders if it is under a charm or a spell, and it goes about marvelling at the things that it sees and hears, which seem to it very strange and rare, though they are the same that it was accustomed to experience aforetime. The reason of this is that the soul is now becoming alien and remote from common sense and knowledge of things, in order that, being annihilated in this respect, it may be informed with the Divine—which belongs rather to the next life than to this.

The soul suffers all these afflictive purgations of the spirit to the end that it may be begotten anew in spiritual life by means of this Divine inflowing, and in these pangs may bring forth the spirit of salvation, that the saying of Isaias may be fulfilled: 'In Thy sight, O Lord, we have conceived, and we have been as in the pangs of labour, and we have brought forth the spirit of salvation.' Moreover, since by means of this contemplative night the soul is prepared for the attainment of inward peace and tranquillity, which is of such a kind and so delectable that, as the Scripture says, it passes all understanding, it behoves the soul to abandon all its former peace. This was in reality no peace at all, since it was involved in imperfections; but to the soul aforementioned it appeared to be so, because it was following its own inclinations, which were for peace. It seemed, indeed, to be a twofold peace—that is, the soul believed that it had already acquired the peace of sense and that of spirit, for it found itself to be full of the spiritual abundance of this peace of sense and of spirit—as I say, it is still imperfect. First of all, then, it must be purged of that former peace and disquieted concerning it and withdrawn from it. Even so was Jeremias when, in the passage which we quoted from him, he felt and lamented thus, in order to express the calamities of this night that is past, saying: 'My soul is withdrawn and removed from peace.'

This is a painful disturbance, involving many misgivings, imaginings, and strivings which the soul has within itself, wherein, with the apprehension and realization of the miseries in which it sees itself, it fancies that it is lost and that its blessings have gone for ever. Wherefore the spirit experiences pain and sighing so deep that they cause it vehement spiritual groans and cries, to which at times it gives vocal expression; when it has the necessary strength and power it dissolves into tears, although this relief comes but seldom. David describes this very aptly, in a Psalm, as one who has had experience of it, where he says: 'I was exceedingly afflicted and humbled; I roared with the groaning of my heart.' This roaring implies great pain; for at times, with the sudden and acute remembrance of these miseries wherein the soul sees itself, pain and affliction rise up and surround it, and I know not how the affections of the soul could be described save in the similitude of holy Job, when he was in the same trials, and uttered these words: 'Even as the overflowing of the waters, even so is my roaring.' For just as at times the waters make such inundations that they overwhelm and fill everything, so at times this roaring and this affliction of the soul grow to such an extent that they overwhelm it and penetrate it completely, filling it with spiritual pain and anguish in all its deep affections and energies, to an extent surpassing all possibility of exaggeration.

Such is the work wrought in the soul by this night that hides the hopes of the light of day. With regard to this the prophet Job says likewise: 'In the night my mouth is pierced with sorrows and they that feed upon me sleep not.' Now here by the mouth is understood the will, which is transpierced with these pains that tear the soul to pieces, neither ceasing nor sleeping, for the doubts and misgivings which transpierce the soul in this way never cease.

Deep is this warfare and this striving, for the peace which the soul hopes for will be very deep; and the spiritual pain is intimate and delicate, for the love which it will possess will likewise be very intimate and refined. The more intimate and the more perfect the finished work is to be and to remain, the more intimate, perfect and pure must be the labour; the firmer the edifice, the harder the labour. Wherefore, as Job says, the soul is fading within itself, and its vitals are being consumed without any hope. Similarly, because in the state of perfection toward which it journeys by means of this purgative night the soul will attain to the possession and fruition of innumerable blessings, of gifts and virtues, both according to the substance of the soul and likewise according to its faculties, it must needs see and feel itself withdrawn from them all and deprived of them all and be empty and poor without them; and it must needs believe itself to be so far from them that it cannot persuade itself that it will ever reach them, but rather it must be convinced that all its good things are over. The words of Jeremias have a similar meaning in that passage already quoted, where he says: 'I have forgotten good things.'

But let us now see the reason why this light of contemplation, which is so sweet and blessed to the soul that there is naught more desirable (for, as has been said above, it is the same wherewith the soul must be united and wherein it must find all the good things in the state of perfection that it desires), produces, when it assails the soul, these beginnings which are so painful and these effects which are so disagreeable, as we have here said.

This question is easy for us to answer, by explaining, as we have already done in part, that the cause of this is that, in contemplation and the Divine inflowing, there is naught that of itself can cause affliction, but that they rather cause great sweetness and delight, as we shall say hereafter. The cause is rather the weakness and imperfection from which the soul then suffers, and the dispositions which it has in itself and which make it unfit for the reception of them. Wherefore, when the said Divine light assails the soul, it must needs cause it to suffer after the manner aforesaid.

Chapter X

Explains this purgation fully by a comparison.

For the greater clearness of what has been said, and of what has still to be said, it is well to observe at this point that this purgative and loving knowledge or Divine light whereof we here speak acts upon the soul which it is purging and preparing for perfect union with it in the same way as fire acts upon a log of wood in order to transform it into itself; for material fire, acting upon wood, first of all begins to dry it, by driving out its moisture and causing it to shed the water which it contains within itself. Then it begins to make it black, dark and unsightly, and even to give forth a bad odour, and, as it dries it little by little, it brings out and drives away all the dark and unsightly accidents which are contrary to the nature of fire. And, finally, it begins to kindle it externally and give it heat, and at last transforms it into itself and makes it as beautiful as fire. In this respect, the wood has neither passivity nor activity of its own, save for its weight, which is greater, and its substance, which is denser, than that of fire, for it has in itself the properties and activities of fire. Thus it is dry and it dries; it is hot and heats; it is bright and gives brightness; and it is much less heavy than before. All these properties and effects are caused in it by the fire.

In this same way we have to philosophize with respect to this Divine fire of contemplative love, which, before it unites and transforms the soul in itself, first purges it of all its contrary accidents. It drives out its unsightliness, and makes it black and dark, so that it seems worse than before and more unsightly and abominable than it was wont to be. For this Divine purgation is removing all the evil and vicious humours which the soul has never perceived because they have been so deeply rooted and grounded in it; it has never realized, in fact, that it has had so much evil within itself. But now that they are to be driven forth and annihilated, these humours reveal themselves, and become visible to the soul because it is so brightly illumined by this dark light of Divine contemplation (although it is no worse than before, either in itself or in relation to God); and, as it sees in itself that which it saw not before, it is clear to it that not only is it unfit to be seen by God, but deserves His abhorrence, and that He does indeed abhor it. By this comparison we can now understand many things concerning what we are saying and purpose to say.

First, we can understand how the very light and the loving wisdom which are to be united with the soul and to transform it are the same that at the beginning purge and prepare it: even as the very fire which transforms the log of wood into itself, and makes it part of itself, is that which at the first was preparing it for that same purpose.

Secondly, we shall be able to see how these afflictions are not felt by the soul as coming from the said Wisdom, since, as the Wise Man says, all good things together come to the soul with her. They are felt as coming from the weakness and imperfection which belong to the soul; without such purgation, the soul cannot receive its Divine light, sweetness and delight, even as the log of wood, when the fire acts upon it, cannot immediately be transformed until it be made ready; wherefore the soul is greatly afflicted. This statement is fully supported by the Preacher, where he describes all that he suffered in order that he might attain to union with wisdom and to the fruition of it, saying thus: 'My soul hath wrestled with her and my bowels were moved in acquiring her; therefore it shall possess a good possession.'

Thirdly, we can learn here incidentally in what manner souls are afflicted in purgatory. For the fire would have no power over them, even though they came into contact with it, if they had no imperfections for which to suffers. These are the material upon which the fire of purgatory seizes; when that material is consumed there is naught else that can burn. So here, when the imperfections are consumed, the affliction of the soul ceases and its fruition remains.

The fourth thing that we shall learn here is the manner wherein the soul, as it becomes purged and purified by means of this fire of love, becomes ever more enkindled in love, just as the wood grows hotter in proportion as it becomes the better prepared by the fire. This enkindling of love, however, is not always felt by the soul, but only at times when contemplation assails it less vehemently, for then it has occasion to see, and even to enjoy, the work which is being wrought in it, and which is then revealed to it. For it seems that the worker takes his hand from the work, and draws the iron out of the furnace, in order that something of the work which is being done may be seen; and then there is occasion for the soul to observe in itself the good which it saw not while the work was going on. In the same way, when the flame ceases to attack the wood, it is possible to see how much of it has been enkindled.

Fifthly, we shall also learn from this comparison what has been said above—namely, how true it is that after each of these periods of relief the soul suffers once again, more intensely and keenly than before. For, after that revelation just referred to has been made, and after the more outward imperfections of the soul have been purified, the fire of love once again attacks that which has yet to be consumed and purified more inwardly. The suffering of the soul now becomes more intimate, subtle and spiritual, in proportion as the fire refines away the finer, more intimate and more spiritual imperfections, and those which are most deeply rooted in its inmost parts. And it is here just as with the wood, upon which the fire, when it begins to penetrate it more deeply, acts with more force and vehemence in preparing its most inward part to possess it.

Sixthly, we shall likewise learn here the reason why it seems to the soul that all its good is over, and that it is full of evil, since naught comes to it at this time but bitterness; it is like the burning wood, which is touched by no air nor by aught else than by consuming fire. But, when there occur other periods of relief like the first, the rejoicing of the soul will be more interior because the purification has been more interior also.

Seventhly, we shall learn that, although the soul has the most ample joy at these periods (so much so that, as we said, it sometimes thinks that its trials can never return again, although it is certain that they will return quickly), it cannot fail to realize, if it is aware (and at times it is made aware) of a root of imperfection which remains, that its joy is incomplete, because a new assault seems to be threatening it; when this is so, the trial returns quickly. Finally, that which still remains to be purged and enlightened most inwardly cannot well be concealed from the soul in view of its experience of its former purification; even as also in the wood it is the most inward part that remains longest unkindled, and the difference between it and that which has already been purged is clearly perceptible; and, when this purification once more assails it most inwardly, it is no wonder if it seems to the soul once more that all its good is gone, and that it never expects to experience it again, for, now that it has been plunged into these most inward sufferings, all good coming from without is over.

Keeping this comparison, then, before our eyes, together with what has already been said upon the first line of the first stanza concerning this dark night and its terrible properties, it will be well to leave these sad experiences of the soul and to begin to speak of the fruit of its tears and their blessed properties, whereof the soul begins to sing from this second line:

Kindled in love with yearnings,

Chapter XI

Begins to explain the second line of the first stanza. Describes how, as the fruit of these rigorous constraints, the soul finds itself with the vehement passion of Divine love.

In this line the soul describes the fire of love which, as we have said, like the material fire acting upon the wood, begins to take hold upon the soul in this night of painful contemplation. This enkindling now described, although in a certain way it resembles that which we described above as coming to pass in the sensual part of the soul, is in some ways as different from that other as is the soul from the body, or the spiritual part from the sensual. For this present kind is an enkindling of spiritual love in the soul, which, in the midst of these dark confines, feels itself to be keenly and sharply wounded in strong Divine love, and to have a certain realization and foretaste of God, although it understands nothing definitely, for, as we say, the understanding is in darkness.

The spirit feels itself here to be deeply and passionately in love, for this spiritual enkindling produces the passion of love. And, inasmuch as this love is infused, it is passive rather than active, and thus it begets in the soul a strong passion of love. This love has in it something of union with God, and thus to some degree partakes of its properties, which are actions of God rather than of the soul, these being subdued within it passively. What the soul does here is to give its consent; the warmth and strength and temper and passion of love—or enkindling, as the soul here calls it—belong only to the love of God, which enters increasingly into union with it. This love finds in the soul more occasion and preparation to unite itself with it and to wound it, according as all the soul's desires are the more recollected, and are the more withdrawn from and disabled for the enjoyment of aught either in Heaven or in earth.

This takes place to a great extent, as has already been said, in this dark purgation, for God has so weaned all the inclinations and caused them to be so recollected that they cannot find pleasure in anything they may wish. All this is done by God to the end that, when He withdraws them and recollects them in Himself, the soul may have more strength and fitness to receive this strong union of love of God, which He is now beginning to give it through this purgative way, wherein the soul must love with great strength and with all its desires and powers both of spirit and of sense; which could not be if they were dispersed in the enjoyment of aught else. For this reason David said to God, to the end that he might receive the strength of the love of this union with God: 'I will keep my strength for Thee;' that is, I will keep the entire capacity and all the desires and energies of my faculties, nor will I employ their operation or pleasure in aught else than Thyself.

In this way it can be realized in some measure how great and how strong may be this enkindling of love in the spirit, wherein God keeps in recollection all the energies, faculties and desires of the soul, both of spirit and of sense, so that all this harmony may employ its energies and virtues in this love, and may thus attain to a true fulfilment of the first commandment, which sets aside nothing pertaining to man nor excludes from this love anything that is his, but says: 'Thou shalt love thy God with all thy heart and with all thy mind, with all thy soul and with all thy strength.'

When all the desires and energies of the soul, then, have been recollected in this enkindling of love, and when the soul itself has been touched and wounded in them all, and has been inspired with passion, what shall we understand the movements and digressions of all these energies and desires to be, if they find themselves enkindled and wounded with strong love and without the possession and satisfaction thereof, in darkness and doubt? They will doubtless be suffering hunger, like the dogs of which David speaks as running about the city; finding no satisfaction in this love, they keep howling and groaning. For the touch of this love and Divine fire dries up the spirit and enkindles its desires, in order to satisfy its thirst for this Divine love, so much so that it turns upon itself a thousand times and desires God in a thousand ways and manners, with the eagerness and desire of the appetite. This is very well explained by David in a psalm, where he says: 'My soul thirsted for Thee: in how many manners does my soul long for Thee!'—that is, in desires. And another version reads: 'My soul thirsted for Thee, my soul is lost (or perishes) for Thee.'

It is for this reason that the soul says in this line that it was 'kindled in love with yearnings.' For in all the things and thoughts that it revolves within itself, and in all the affairs and matters that present themselves to it, it loves in many ways, and also desires and suffers in the desire in many ways, at all times and in all places, finding rest in naught, and feeling this yearning in its enkindled wound, even as the prophet Job declares, saying: 'As the hart desireth the shadow, and as the hireling desireth the end of his work, so I also had vain months and numbered to myself wearisome and laborious nights. If I lie down to sleep, I shall say: "When shall I arise?" And then I shall await the evening and shall be full of sorrows even until the darkness of night.' Everything becomes cramping to this soul: it cannot live within itself; it cannot live either in Heaven or on earth; and it is filled with griefs until the darkness comes to which Job here refers, speaking spiritually and in the sense of our interpretation. What the soul here endures is afflictions and suffering without the consolation of a certain hope of any light and spiritual good. Wherefore the yearning and the grief of this soul in this enkindling of love are greater because it is multiplied in two ways: first, by the spiritual darkness wherein it finds itself, which afflicts it with its doubts and misgivings; and then by the love of God, which enkindles and stimulates it, and, with its loving wound, causes it a wondrous fear. These two kinds of suffering at such a season are well described by Isaias, where he says: 'My soul desired Thee in the night'—that is, in misery.

This is one kind of suffering which proceeds from this dark night; but, he goes on to say, with my spirit, in my bowels, until the morning, I will watch for Thee. And this is the second way of grieving in desire and yearning which comes from love in the bowels of the spirit, which are the spiritual affections. But in the midst of these dark and loving afflictions the soul feels within itself a certain companionship and strength, which bears it company and so greatly strengthens it that, if this burden of grievous darkness be taken away, it often feels itself to be alone, empty and weak. The cause of this is that, as the strength and efficacy of the soul were derived and communicated passively from the dark fire of love which assailed it, it follows that, when that fire ceases to assail it, the darkness and power and heat of love cease in the soul.

Chapter XII

Shows how this horrible night is purgatory, and how in it the Divine wisdom illumines men on earth with the same illumination that purges and illumines the angels in Heaven.

From what has been said we shall be able to see how this dark night of loving fire, as it purges in the darkness, so also in the darkness enkindles the soul. We shall likewise be able to see that, even as spirits are purged in the next life with dark material fire, so in this life they are purged and cleansed with the dark spiritual fire of love. The difference is that in the next life they are cleansed with fire, while here below they are cleansed and illumined with love only. It was this love that David entreated, when he said: Cor mundum crea in me, Deus, etc. For cleanness of heart is nothing less than the love and grace of God. For the clean of heart are called by our Saviour 'blessed'; which is as if He had called them 'enkindled with love', since blessedness is given by nothing less than love.

And Jeremias well shows how the soul is purged when it is illumined with this fire of loving wisdom (for God never grants mystical wisdom without love, since love itself infuses it), where he says: 'He hath sent fire into my bones, and hath taught me.' And David says that the wisdom of God is silver tried in fire—that is, in purgative fire of love. For this dark contemplation infuses into the soul love and wisdom jointly, to each one according to his capacity and need, enlightening the soul and purging it, in the words of the Wise Man, from its ignorances, as he said was done to himself.

From this we shall also infer that the very wisdom of God which purges these souls and illumines them purges the angels from their ignorances, giving them knowledge, enlightening them as to that which they knew not, and flowing down from God through the first hierarchies even to the last, and thence to men. All the works, therefore, which are done by the angels, and all their inspirations, are said in the Scriptures, with truth and propriety, to be the work of God and of themselves; for ordinarily these inspirations come through the angels, and they receive them likewise one from another without any delay—as quickly as a ray of sunshine is communicated through many windows arranged in order. For although it is true that the sun's ray itself passes through them all, still each one passes it on and infuses it into the next, in a modified form, according to the nature of the glass, and with rather more or rather less power and brightness, according as it is nearer to the sun or farther from it.

Hence it follows that, the nearer to God are the higher spirits and the lower, the more completely are they purged and enlightened with more general purification; and that the lowest of them will receive this illumination very much less powerfully and more remotely. Hence it follows that man, who is the lowest of all those to whom this loving contemplation flows down continually from God, will, when God desires to give it him, receive it perforce after his own manner in a very limited way and with great pain. For, when the light of God illumines an angel, it enlightens him and enkindles him in love, since, being pure spirit, he is prepared for that infusion. But, when it illumines man, who is impure and weak, it illumines him, as has been said above, according to his nature. It plunges him into darkness and causes him affliction and distress, as does the sun to the eye that is weak; it enkindles him with passionate yet afflictive love, until he be spiritualized and refined by this same fire of love; and it purifies him until he can receive with sweetness the union of this loving infusion after the manner of the angels, being now purged, as by the help of the Lord we shall explain later. But meanwhile he receives this contemplation and loving knowledge in the constraint and yearning of love of which we are here speaking.

This enkindling and yearning of love are not always perceived by the soul. For in the beginning, when this spiritual purgation commences, all this Divine fire is used in drying up and making ready the wood (which is the soul) rather than in giving it heat. But, as time goes on, the fire begins to give heat to the soul, and the soul then very commonly feels this enkindling and heat of love. Further, as the understanding is being more and more purged by means of this darkness, it sometimes comes to pass that this mystical and loving theology, as well as enkindling the will, strikes and illumines the other faculty also—that of the understanding—with a certain Divine light and knowledge, so delectably and delicately that it aids the will to conceive a marvellous fervour, and, without any action of its own, there burns in it this Divine fire of love, in living flames, so that it now appears to the soul a living fire by reason of the living understanding which is given to it. It is of this that David speaks in a Psalm, saying: 'My heart grew hot within me, and, as I meditated, a certain fire was enkindled.'

This enkindling of love, which accompanies the union of these two faculties, the understanding and the will, which are here united, is for the soul a thing of great richness and delight; for it is a certain touch of the Divinity and is already the beginning of the perfection of the union of love for which it hopes. Now the soul attains not to this touch of so sublime a sense and love of God, save when it has passed through many trials and a great part of its purgation. But for other touches which are much lower than these, and which are of ordinary occurrence, so much purgation is not needful.

From what we have said it may here be inferred how in these spiritual blessings, which are passively infused by God into the soul, the will may very well love even though the understanding understand not; and similarly the understanding may understand and the will love not. For, since this dark night of contemplation consists of Divine light and love, just as fire contains light and heat, it is not unbefitting that, when this loving light is communicated, it should strike the will at times more effectively by enkindling it with love and leaving the understanding in darkness instead of striking it with light; and, at other times, by enlightening it with light, and giving it understanding, but leaving the will in aridity (as it is also true that the heat of the fire can be received without the light being seen, and also the light of it can be seen without the reception of heat); and this is wrought by the Lord, Who infuses as He wills.

Chapter XIII

Of other delectable effects which are wrought in the soul by this dark night of contemplation.

This type of enkindling will explain to us certain of the delectable effects which this dark night of contemplation works in the soul. For at certain times, as we have just said, the soul becomes enlightened in the midst of all this darkness, and the light shines in the darkness; this mystical intelligence flows down into the understanding and the will remains in dryness—I mean, without actual union of love, with a serenity and simplicity which are so delicate and delectable to the sense of the soul that no name can be given to them. Thus the presence of God is felt, now after one manner, now after another.

Sometimes, too, as has been said, it wounds the will at the same time, and enkindles love sublimely, tenderly and strongly; for we have already said that at certain times these two faculties, the understanding and the will, are united, when, the more they see, the more perfect and delicate is the purgation of the understanding. But, before this state is reached, it is more usual for the touch of the enkindling of love to be felt in the will than for the touch of intelligence to be felt in the understanding.

But one question arises here, which is this: Why, since these two faculties are being purged together, are the enkindling and the love of purgative contemplation at first more commonly felt in the will than the intelligence thereof is felt in the understanding? To this it may be answered that this passive love does not now directly strike the will, for the will is free, and this enkindling of love is a passion of love rather than the free act of the will; for this heat of love strikes the substance of the soul and thus moves the affections passively. And so this is called passion of love rather than a free act of the will, an act of the will being so called only in so far as it is free. But these passions and affections subdue the will, and therefore it is said that, if the soul conceives passion with a certain affection, the will conceives passion; and this is indeed so, for in this manner the will is taken captive and loses its liberty, according as the impetus and power of its passion carry it away. And therefore we can say that this enkindling of love is in the will—that is, it enkindles the desire of the will; and thus, as we say, this is called passion of love rather than the free work of the will. And, because the receptive passion of the understanding can receive intelligence only in a detached and passive way (and this is impossible without its having been purged), therefore until this happens the soul feels the touch of intelligence less frequently than that of the passion of love. For it is not necessary to this end that the will should be so completely purged with respect to the passions, since these very passions help it to feel impassioned love.

This enkindling and thirst of love, which in this case belongs to the spirit, is very different from that other which we described in writing of the night of sense. For, though the sense has also its part here, since it fails not to participate in the labour of the spirit, yet the source and the keenness of the thirst of love is felt in the superior part of the soul—that is, in the spirit. It feels, and understands what it feels and its lack of what it desires, in such a way that all its affliction of sense, although greater without comparison than in the first night of sense, is as naught to it, because it recognizes within itself the lack of a great good which can in no way be measured.

But here we must note that although, at the beginning, when this spiritual night commences, this enkindling of love is not felt, because this fire of love has not begun to take a hold, God gives the soul, in place of it, an estimative love of Himself so great that, as we have said, the greatest sufferings and trials of which it is conscious in this night are the anguished thoughts that it has lost God and the fears that He has abandoned it. And thus we may always say that from the very beginning of this night the soul is touched with yearnings of love, which is now that of estimation, and now again, that of enkindling. And it is evident that the greatest suffering which it feels in these trials is this misgiving; for, if it could be certified at that time that all is not lost and over, but that what is happening to it is for the best—as it is—and that God is not wroth, it would care naught for all these afflictions, but would rejoice to know that God is making use of them for His good pleasure. For the love of estimation which it has for God is so great, even though it may not realize this and may be in darkness, that it would be glad, not only to suffer in this way, but even to die many times over in order to give Him satisfaction. But when once the flame has enkindled the soul, it is wont to conceive, together with the estimation that it already has for God, such power and energy, and such yearning for Him, when He communicates to it the heat of love, that, with great boldness, it disregards everything and ceases to pay respect to anything, such are the power and the inebriation of love and desire. It regards not what it does, for it would do strange and unusual things in whatever way and manner may present themselves, if thereby its soul might find Him Whom it loves.

It was for this reason that Mary Magdalene, though as greatly concerned for her own appearance as she was aforetime, took no heed of the multitude of men who were at the feast, whether they were of little or of great importance; neither did she consider that it was not seemly, and that it looked ill, to go and weep and shed tears among the guests provided that, without delaying an hour or waiting for another time and season, she could reach Him for love of Whom her soul was already wounded and enkindled. And such is the inebriating power and the boldness of love, that, though she knew her Beloved to be enclosed in the sepulchre by the great sealed stone, and surrounded by soldiers who were guarding Him lest His disciples should steal Him away, she allowed none of these things to impede her, but went before daybreak with the ointments to anoint Him.

And finally, this inebriating power and yearning of love caused her to ask one whom she believed to be a gardener and to have stolen Him away from the sepulchre, to tell her, if he had taken Him, where he had laid Him, that she might take Him away; considering not that such a question, according to independent judgment and reason, was foolish; for it was evident that, if the other had stolen Him, he would not say so, still less would he allow Him to be taken away. It is a characteristic of the power and vehemence of love that all things seem possible to it, and it believes all men to be of the same mind as itself. For it thinks that there is naught wherein one may be employed, or which one may seek, save that which it seeks itself and that which it loves; and it believes that there is naught else to be desired, and naught wherein it may be employed, save that one thing, which is pursued by all. For this reason, when the Bride went out to seek her Beloved, through streets and squares, thinking that all others were doing the same, she begged them that, if they found Him, they would speak to Him and say that she was pining for love of Him. Such was the power of the love of this Mary that she thought that, if the gardener would tell her where he had hidden Him, she would go and take Him away, however difficult it might be made for her.

Of this manner, then, are the yearnings of love whereof this soul becomes conscious when it has made some progress in this spiritual purgation. For it rises up by night (that is, in this purgative darkness) according to the affections of the will. And with the yearnings and vehemence of the lioness or the she-bear going to seek her cubs when they have been taken away from her and she finds them not, does this wounded soul go forth to seek its God. For, being in darkness, it feels itself to be without Him and to be dying of love for Him. And this is that impatient love wherein the soul cannot long subsist without gaining its desire or dying. Such was Rachel's desire for children when she said to Jacob: 'Give me children, else shall I die.'

But we have now to see how it is that the soul which feels itself so miserable and so unworthy of God, here in this purgative darkness, has nevertheless strength, and is sufficiently bold and daring, to journey towards union with God. The reason is that, as love continually gives it strength wherewith it may love indeed, and as the property of love is to desire to be united, joined and made equal and like to the object of its love, that it may perfect itself in love's good things, hence it comes to pass that, when this soul is not perfected in love, through not having as yet attained to union, the hunger and thirst that it has for that which it lacks (which is union) and the strength set by love in the will which has caused it to become impassioned, make it bold and daring by reason of the enkindling of its will, although in its understanding, which is still dark and unenlightened, it feels itself to be unworthy and knows itself to be miserable.

I will not here omit to mention the reason why this Divine light, which is always light to the soul, illumines it not as soon as it strikes it, as it does afterwards, but causes it the darkness and the trials of which we have spoken. Something has already been said concerning this, but the question must now be answered directly. The darkness and the other evils of which the soul is conscious when this Divine light strikes it are not darkness or evils caused by this light, but pertain to the soul itself, and the light illumines it so that it may see them. Wherefore it does indeed receive light from this Divine light; but the soul cannot see at first, by its aid, anything beyond what is nearest to it, or rather, beyond what is within it—namely, its darknesses or its miseries, which it now sees through the mercy of God, and saw not aforetime, because this supernatural light illumined it not. And this is the reason why at first it is conscious of nothing beyond darkness and evil; after it has been purged, however, by means of the knowledge and realization of these, it will have eyes to see, by the guidance of this light, the blessings of the Divine light; and, once all these darknesses and imperfections have been driven out from the soul, it seems that the benefits and the great blessings which the soul is gaining in this blessed night of contemplation become clearer.

From what has been said, it is clear that God grants the soul in this state the favour of purging it and healing it with this strong lye of bitter purgation, according to its spiritual and its sensual part, of all the imperfect habits and affections which it had within itself with respect to temporal things and to natural, sensual and spiritual things, its inward faculties being darkened, and voided of all these, its spiritual and sensual affections being constrained and dried up, and its natural energies being attenuated and weakened with respect to all this (a condition which it could never attain of itself, as we shall shortly say). In this way God makes it to die to all that is not naturally God, so that, once it is stripped and denuded of its former skin, He may begin to clothe it anew. And thus its youth is renewed like the eagle's and it is clothed with the new man, which, as the Apostle says, is created according to God. This is naught else but His illumination of the understanding with supernatural light, so that it is no more a human understanding but becomes Divine through union with the Divine. In the same way the will is informed with Divine love, so that it is a will that is now no less than Divine, nor does it love otherwise than divinely, for it is made and united in one with the Divine will and love. So, too, is it with the memory; and likewise the affections and desires are all changed and converted divinely, according to God. And thus this soul will now be a soul of heaven, heavenly, and more Divine than human. All this, as we have been saying, and because of what we have said, God continues to do and to work in the soul by means of this night, illumining and enkindling it divinely with yearnings for God alone and for naught else whatsoever. For which cause the soul then very justly and reasonably adds the third line to the song, which says:

. . . oh, happy chance!—I went forth without being observed.

Chapter XIV

Wherein are set down and explained the last three lines of the first stanza.

This happy chance was the reason for which the soul speaks, in the next lines, as follows:

I went forth without being observed, My house being now at rest.

It takes the metaphor from one who, in order the better to accomplish something, leaves his house by night and in the dark, when those that are in the house are now at rest, so that none may hinder him. For this soul had to go forth to perform a deed so heroic and so rare—namely to become united with its Divine Beloved—and it had to leave its house, because the Beloved is not found save alone and without, in solitude. It was for this reason that the Bride desired to find Him alone, saying: 'Who would give Thee to me, my brother, that I might find Thee alone, without, and that my love might be communicated to Thee.' It is needful for the enamoured soul, in order to attain to its desired end, to do likewise, going forth at night, when all the domestics in its house are sleeping and at rest—that is, when the low operations, passions and desires of the soul (who are the people of the household) are, because it is night, sleeping and at rest. When these are awake, they invariably hinder the soul from seeking its good, since they are opposed to its going forth in freedom. These are they of whom Our Saviour speaks in the Gospel, saying that they are the enemies of man. And thus it would be meet that their operations and motions should be put to sleep in this night, to the end that they may not hinder the soul from attaining the supernatural blessings of the union of love of God, for, while these are alive and active, this cannot be. For all their work and their natural motions hinder, rather than aid, the soul's reception of the spiritual blessings of the union of love, inasmuch as all natural ability is impotent with respect to the supernatural blessings that God, by means of His own infusion, bestows upon the soul passively, secretly and in silence. And thus it is needful that all the faculties should receive this infusion, and that, in order to receive it, they should remain passive, and not interpose their own base acts and vile inclinations.

It was a happy chance for this soul that on this night God should put to sleep all the domestics in its house—that is, all the faculties, passions, affections and desires which live in the soul, both sensually and spiritually. For thus it went forth 'without being observed'—that is, without being hindered by these affections, etc., for they were put to sleep and mortified in this night, in the darkness of which they were left, that they might not notice or feel anything after their own low and natural manner, and might thus be unable to hinder the soul from going forth from itself and from the house of its sensuality. And thus only could the soul attain to the spiritual union of perfect love of God.

Oh, how happy a chance is this for the soul which can free itself from the house of its sensuality! None can understand it, unless, as it seems to me, it be the soul that has experienced it. For such a soul will see clearly how wretched was the servitude in which it lay and to how many miseries it was subject when it was at the mercy of its faculties and desires, and will know how the life of the spirit is true liberty and wealth, bringing with it inestimable blessings. Some of these we shall point out, as we proceed, in the following stanzas, wherein it will be seen more clearly what good reason the soul has to sing of the happy chance of its passage from this dreadful night which has been described above.

Chapter XV

Sets down the second stanza and its exposition.

In darkness and secure, By the secret ladder, disguised—oh, happy chance! In darkness and concealment, My house being now at rest.

In this stanza the soul still continues to sing of certain properties of the darkness of this night, reiterating how great is the happiness which came to it through them. It speaks of them in replying to a certain tacit objection, saying that it is not to be supposed that, because in this night and darkness it has passed through so many tempests of afflictions, doubts, fears and horrors, as has been said, it has for that reason run any risk of being lost. On the contrary, it says, in the darkness of this night it has gained itself. For in the night it has freed itself and escaped subtly from its enemies, who were continually hindering its progress. For in the darkness of the night it changed its garments and disguised itself with three liveries and colours which we shall describe hereafter; and went forth by a very secret ladder, which none in the house knew, the which ladder, as we shall observe likewise in the proper place, is living faith. By this ladder the soul went forth in such complete hiding and concealment, in order the better to execute its purpose, that it could not fail to be in great security; above all since in this purgative night the desires, affections and passions of the soul are put to sleep, mortified and quenched, which are they that, when they were awake and alive, consented not to this.

The first line, then, runs thus:

In darkness and secure.

Chapter XVI

Explains how, though in darkness, the soul walks securely.

The darkness which the soul here describes relates, as we have said, to the desires and faculties, sensual, interior and spiritual, for all these are darkened in this night as to their natural light, so that, being purged in this respect, they may be illumined with respect to the supernatural. For the spiritual and the sensual desires are put to sleep and mortified, so that they can experience nothing, either Divine or human; the affections of the soul are oppressed and constrained, so that they can neither move nor find support in anything; the imagination is bound and can make no useful reflection; the memory is gone; the understanding is in darkness, unable to understand anything; and hence the will likewise is arid and constrained and all the faculties are void and useless; and in addition to all this a thick and heavy cloud is upon the soul, keeping it in affliction, and, as it were, far away from God. It is in this kind of 'darkness' that the soul says here it travelled 'securely.'

The reason for this has been clearly expounded; for ordinarily the soul never strays save through its desires or its tastes or its reflections or its understanding or its affections; for as a rule it has too much or too little of these, or they vary or go astray, and hence the soul becomes inclined to that which behoves it not. Wherefore, when all these operations and motions are hindered, it is clear that the soul is secure against being led astray by them; for it is free, not only from itself, but likewise from its other enemies, which are the world and the devil. For when the affections and operations of the soul are quenched, these enemies cannot make war upon it by any other means or in any other manner.

It follows from this that, the greater is the darkness wherein the soul journeys and the more completely is it voided of its natural operations, the greater is its security. For, as the Prophet says, perdition comes to the soul from itself alone—that is, from its sensual and interior desires and operations; and good, says God, comes from Me alone. Wherefore, when it is thus hindered from following the things that lead it into evil, there will then come to it forthwith the blessings of union with God in its desires and faculties, which in that union He will make Divine and celestial. Hence, at the time of this darkness, if the soul considers the matter, it will see very clearly how little its desire and its faculties are being diverted to things that are useless and harmful; and how secure it is from vainglory and pride and presumption, vain and false rejoicing and many other things. It follows clearly, then, that, by walking in darkness, not only is the soul not lost, but it has even greatly gained, since it is here gaining the virtues.

But there is a question which at once arises here—namely, since the things of God are of themselves profitable to the soul and bring it gain and security, why does God, in this night, darken the desires and faculties with respect to these good things likewise, in such a way that the soul can no more taste of them or busy itself with them than with these other things, and indeed in some ways can do so less? The answer is that it is well for the soul to perform no operation touching spiritual things at that time and to have no pleasure in such things, because its faculties and desires are base, impure and wholly natural; and thus, although these faculties be given the desire and interest in things supernatural and Divine, they could not receive them save after a base and a natural manner, exactly in their own fashion. For, as the philosopher says, whatsoever is received comes to him that receives it after the manner of the recipient. Wherefore, since these natural faculties have neither purity nor strength nor capacity to receive and taste things that are supernatural after the manner of those things, which manner is Divine, but can do so only after their own manner, which is human and base, as we have said, it is meet that its faculties be in darkness concerning these Divine things likewise. Thus, being weaned and purged and annihilated in this respect first of all, they may lose that base and human way of receiving and acting, and thus all these faculties and desires of the soul may come to be prepared and tempered in such a way as to be able to receive, feel and taste that which is Divine and supernatural after a sublime and lofty manner, which is impossible if the old man die not first of all.

Hence it follows that all spiritual things, if they come not from above and be not communicated by the Father of lights to human desire and free will (howsoever much a man may exercise his taste and faculties for God, and howsoever much it may seem to the faculties that they are experiencing these things), will not be experienced after a Divine and spiritual manner, but after a human and natural manner, just as other things are experienced, for spiritual blessings go not from man to God, but come from God to man. With respect to this (if this were the proper place for it) we might here explain how there are many persons whose many tastes and affections and the operations of whose faculties are fixed upon God or upon spiritual things, and who may perhaps think that this is supernatural and spiritual, when it is perhaps no more than the most human and natural desires and actions. They regard these good things with the same disposition as they have for other things, by means of a certain natural facility which they possess for directing their desires and faculties to anything whatever.

If perchance we find occasion elsewhere in this book, we shall treat of this, describing certain signs which indicate when the interior actions and motions of the soul, with respect to communion with God, are only natural, when they are spiritual, and when they are both natural and spiritual. It suffices for us here to know that, in order that the interior motions and acts of the soul may come to be moved by God divinely, they must first be darkened and put to sleep and hushed to rest naturally as touching all their capacity and operation, until they have no more strength.

Therefore, O spiritual soul, when thou seest thy desire obscured, thy affections arid and constrained, and thy faculties bereft of their capacity for any interior exercise, be not afflicted by this, but rather consider it a great happiness, since God is freeing thee from thyself and taking the matter from thy hands. For with those hands, howsoever well they may serve thee, thou wouldst never labour so effectively, so perfectly and so securely (because of their clumsiness and uncleanness) as now, when God takes thy hand and guides thee in the darkness, as though thou wert blind, to an end and by a way which thou knowest not. Nor couldst thou ever hope to travel with the aid of thine own eyes and feet, howsoever good thou be as a walker.

The reason, again, why the soul not only travels securely, when it travels thus in the darkness, but also achieves even greater gain and progress, is that usually, when the soul is receiving fresh advantage and profit, this comes by a way that it least understands—indeed, it quite commonly believes that it is losing ground. For, as it has never experienced that new feeling which drives it forth and dazzles it and makes it depart recklessly from its former way of life, it thinks itself to be losing ground rather than gaining and progressing, since it sees that it is losing with respect to that which it knew and enjoyed, and is going by a way which it knows not and wherein it finds no enjoyment. It is like the traveller, who, in order to go to new and unknown lands, takes new roads, unknown and untried, and journeys unguided by his past experience, but doubtingly and according to what others say. It is clear that such a man could not reach new countries, or add to his past experience, if he went not along new and unknown roads and abandoned those which were known to him. Exactly so, one who is learning fresh details concerning any office or art always proceeds in darkness, and receives no guidance from his original knowledge, for if he left not that behind he would get no farther nor make any progress; and in the same way, when the soul is making most progress, it is travelling in darkness, knowing naught. Wherefore, since God, as we have said, is the Master and Guide of this blind soul, it may well and truly rejoice, once it has learned to understand this, and say: 'In darkness and secure.'

There is another reason why the soul has walked securely in this darkness, and this is because it has been suffering; for the road of suffering is more secure and even more profitable than that of fruition and action: first, because in suffering the strength of God is added to that of man, while in action and fruition the soul is practising its own weaknesses and imperfections; and second, because in suffering the soul continues to practise and acquire the virtues and become purer, wiser and more cautious.

But there is another and a more important reason why the soul now walks in darkness and securely; this emanates from the dark light or wisdom aforementioned. For in such a way does this dark night of contemplation absorb and immerse the soul in itself, and so near does it bring the soul to God, that it protects and delivers it from all that is not God. For this soul is now, as it were, undergoing a cure, in order that it may regain its health—its health being God Himself. His Majesty restricts it to a diet and abstinence from all things, and takes away its appetite for them all. It is like a sick man, who, if he is respected by those in his house, is carefully tended so that he may be cured; the air is not allowed to touch him, nor may he even enjoy the light, nor must he hear footsteps, nor yet the noise of those in the house; and he is given food that is very delicate, and even that only in great moderation—food that is nourishing rather than delectable.

All these particularities (which are for the security and safekeeping of the soul) are caused by this dark contemplation, because it brings the soul nearer to God. For the nearer the soul approaches Him, the blacker is the darkness which it feels and the deeper is the obscurity which comes through its weakness; just as, the nearer a man approaches the sun, the greater are the darkness and the affliction caused him through the great splendour of the sun and through the weakness and impurity of his eyes. In the same way, so immense is the spiritual light of God, and so greatly does it transcend our natural understanding, that the nearer we approach it, the more it blinds and darkens us. And this is the reason why, in Psalm xvii, David says that God made darkness His hiding-place and covering, and His tabernacle around Him dark water in the clouds of the air. This dark water in the clouds of the air is dark contemplation and Divine wisdom in souls, as we are saying. They continue to feel it is a thing which is near Him, as the tabernacle wherein He dwells, when God brings them ever nearer to Himself. And thus, that which in God is supreme light and refulgence is to man blackest darkness, as Saint Paul says, according as David explains in the same Psalm, saying: 'Because of the brightness which is in His presence, passed clouds and cataracts'—that is to say, over the natural understanding, the light whereof, as Isaias says in chapter V: Obtenebrata est in caligine ejus.

Oh, miserable is the fortune of our life, which is lived in such great peril and wherein it is so difficult to find the truth. For that which is most clear and true is to us most dark and doubtful; wherefore, though it is the thing that is most needful for us, we flee from it. And that which gives the greatest light and satisfaction to our eyes we embrace and pursue, though it be the worst thing for us, and make us fall at every step. In what peril and fear does man live, since the very natural light of his eyes by which he has to guide himself is the first light that dazzles him and leads him astray on his road to God! And if he is to know with certainty by what road he travels, he must perforce keep his eyes closed and walk in darkness, that he may be secure from the enemies who inhabit his own house—that is, his senses and faculties.

Well hidden, then, and well protected is the soul in these dark waters, when it is close to God. For, as these waters serve as a tabernacle and dwelling-place for God Himself, they will serve the soul in the same way and for a perfect protection and security, though it remain in darkness, wherein, as we have said, it is hidden and protected from itself, and from all evils that come from creatures; for to such the words of David refer in another Psalm, where he says: 'Thou shalt hide them in the hiding-place of Thy face from the disturbance of men; Thou shalt protect them in Thy tabernacle from the contradiction of tongues.' Herein we understand all kinds of protection; for to be hidden in the face of God from the disturbance of men is to be fortified with this dark contemplation against all the chances which may come upon the soul from men. And to be protected in His tabernacle from the contradiction of tongues is for the soul to be engulfed in these dark waters, which are the tabernacle of David whereof we have spoken. Wherefore, since the soul has all its desires and affections weaned and its faculties set in darkness, it is free from all imperfections which contradict the spirit, whether they come from its own flesh or from other creatures. Wherefore this soul may well say that it journeys 'in darkness and secure.'

There is likewise another reason, which is no less effectual than the last, by which we may understand how the soul journeys securely in darkness; it is derived from the fortitude by which the soul is at once inspired in these obscure and afflictive dark waters of God. For after all, though the waters be dark, they are none the less waters, and therefore they cannot but refresh and fortify the soul in that which is most needful for it, although in darkness and with affliction. For the soul immediately perceives in itself a genuine determination and an effectual desire to do naught which it understands to be an offence to God, and to omit to do naught that seems to be for His service. For that dark love cleaves to the soul, causing it a most watchful care and an inward solicitude concerning that which it must do, or must not do, for His sake, in order to please Him. It will consider and ask itself a thousand times if it has given Him cause to be offended; and all this it will do with much greater care and solicitude than before, as has already been said with respect to the yearnings of love. For here all the desires and energies and faculties of the soul are recollected from all things else, and its effort and strength are employed in pleasing its God alone. After this manner the soul goes forth from itself and from all created things to the sweet and delectable union of love of God, 'In darkness and secure.'

By the secret ladder, disguised.

Chapter XVII

Explains how this dark contemplation is secret.

Three things have to be expounded with reference to three words contained in this present line. Two (namely, 'secret' and 'ladder') belong to the dark night of contemplation of which we are treating; the third (namely, 'disguised') belongs to the soul by reason of the manner wherein it conducts itself in this night. As to the first, it must be known that in this line the soul describes this dark contemplation, by which it goes forth to the union of love, as a secret ladder, because of the two properties which belong to it—namely, its being secret and its being a ladder. We shall treat of each separately.

First, it describes this dark contemplation as 'secret,' since, as we have indicated above, it is mystical theology, which theologians call secret wisdom, and which, as Saint Thomas says is communicated and infused into the soul through love. This happens secretly and in darkness, so as to be hidden from the work of the understanding and of other faculties. Wherefore, inasmuch as the faculties aforementioned attain not to it, but the Holy Spirit infuses and orders it in the soul, as says the Bride in the Songs, without either its knowledge or its understanding, it is called secret. And, in truth, not only does the soul not understand it, but there is none that does so, not even the devil; inasmuch as the Master Who teaches the soul is within it in its substance, to which the devil may not attain, neither may natural sense nor understanding.

And it is not for this reason alone that it may be called secret, but likewise because of the effects which it produces in the soul. For it is secret not only in the darknesses and afflictions of purgation, when this wisdom of love purges the soul, and the soul is unable to speak of it, but equally so afterwards in illumination, when this wisdom is communicated to it most clearly. Even then it is still so secret that the soul cannot speak of it and give it a name whereby it may be called; for, apart from the fact that the soul has no desire to speak of it, it can find no suitable way or manner or similitude by which it may be able to describe such lofty understanding and such delicate spiritual feeling. And thus, even though the soul might have a great desire to express it and might find many ways in which to describe it, it would still be secret and remain undescribed. For, as that inward wisdom is so simple, so general and so spiritual that it has not entered into the understanding enwrapped or cloaked in any form or image subject to sense, it follows that sense and imagination (as it has not entered through them nor has taken their form and colour) cannot account for it or imagine it, so as to say anything concerning it, although the soul be clearly aware that it is experiencing and partaking of that rare and delectable wisdom. It is like one who sees something never seen before, whereof he has not even seen the like; although he might understand its nature and have experience of it, he would be unable to give it a name, or say what it is, however much he tried to do so, and this in spite of its being a thing which he had perceived with the senses. How much less, then, could he describe a thing that has not entered through the senses! For the language of God has this characteristic that, since it is very intimate and spiritual in its relations with the soul, it transcends every sense and at once makes all harmony and capacity of the outward and inward senses to cease and be dumb.

For this we have both authorities and examples in the Divine Scripture. For the incapacity of man to speak of it and describe it in words was shown by Jeremias, when, after God had spoken with him, he knew not what to say, save 'Ah, ah, ah!' This interior incapacity—that is, of the interior sense of the imagination—and also that of the exterior sense corresponding to it was also demonstrated in the case of Moses, when he stood before God in the bush; not only did he say to God that after speaking with Him he knew not neither was able to speak, but also that not even (as is said in the Acts of the Apostles) with the interior imagination did he dare to meditate, for it seemed to him that his imagination was very far away and was too dumb, not only to express any part of that which he understood concerning God, but even to have the capacity to receive aught therefrom. Wherefore, inasmuch as the wisdom of this contemplation is the language of God to the soul, addressed by pure spirit to pure spirit, naught that is less than spirit, such as the senses, can perceive it, and thus to them it is secret, and they know it not, neither can they say it, nor do they desire to do so, because they see it not.

We may deduce from this the reason why certain persons—good and fearful souls—who walk along this road and would like to give an account of their spiritual state to their director, are neither able to do so nor know how. For the reason we have described, they have a great repugnance in speaking of it, especially when their contemplation is of the purer sort, so that the soul itself is hardly conscious of it. Such a person is only able to say that he is satisfied, tranquil and contented and that he is conscious of the presence of God, and that, as it seems to him, all is going well with him; but he cannot describe the state of his soul, nor can he say anything about it save in general terms like these. It is a different matter when the experiences of the soul are of a particular kind, such as visions, feelings, etc., which, being ordinarily received under some species wherein sense participates, can be described under that species, or by some other similitude. But this capacity for being described is not in the nature of pure contemplation, which is indescribable, as we have said, for the which reason it is called secret.

And not only for that reason is it called secret, and is so, but likewise because this mystical knowledge has the property of hiding the soul within itself. For, besides performing its ordinary function, it sometimes absorbs the soul and engulfs it in its secret abyss, in such a way that the soul clearly sees that it has been carried far away from every creature and; has become most remote therefrom; so that it considers itself as having been placed in a most profound and vast retreat, to which no human creature can attain, such as an immense desert, which nowhere has any boundary, a desert the more delectable, pleasant and lovely for its secrecy, vastness and solitude, wherein, the more the soul is raised up above all temporal creatures, the more deeply does it find itself hidden. And so greatly does this abyss of wisdom raise up and exalt the soul at this time, making it to penetrate the veins of the science of love, that it not only shows it how base are all properties of the creatures by comparison with this supreme knowledge and Divine feeling, but likewise it learns how base and defective, and, in some measure, how inapt, are all the terms and words which are used in this life to treat of Divine things, and how impossible it is, in any natural way or manner, however learnedly and sublimely they may be spoken of, to be able to know and perceive them as they are, save by the illumination of this mystical theology. And thus, when by means of this illumination the soul discerns this truth, namely, that it cannot reach it, still less explain it, by common or human language, it rightly calls it secret.

This property of secrecy and superiority over natural capacity, which belongs to this Divine contemplation, belongs to it, not only because it is supernatural, but also inasmuch as it is a road that guides and leads the soul to the perfections of union with God; which, as they are things unknown after a human manner, must be approached, after a human manner, by unknowing and by Divine ignorance. For, speaking mystically, as we are speaking here, Divine things and perfections are known and understood as they are, not when they are being sought after and practised, but when they have been found and practised. To this purpose speaks the prophet Baruch concerning this Divine wisdom: 'There is none that can know her ways nor that can imagine her paths.' Likewise the royal Prophet speaks in this manner concerning this road of the soul, when he says to God: 'Thy lightnings lighted and illumined the round earth; the earth was moved and trembled. Thy way is in the sea and Thy paths are in many waters; and Thy footsteps shall not be known.'

All this, speaking spiritually, is to be understood in the sense wherein we are speaking. For the illumination of the round earth by the lightnings of God is the enlightenment which is produced by this Divine contemplation in the faculties of the soul; the moving and trembling of the earth is the painful purgation which is caused therein; and to say that the way and the road of God whereby the soul journeys to Him is in the sea, and His footprints are in many waters and for this reason shall not be known, is as much as to say that this road whereby the soul journeys to God is as secret and as hidden from the sense of the soul as the way of one that walks on the sea, whose paths and footprints are not known, is hidden from the sense of the body. The steps and footprints which God is imprinting upon the souls that He desires to bring near to Himself, and to make great in union with His Wisdom, have also this property, that they are not known. Wherefore in the Book of Job mention is made of this matter, in these words: 'Hast thou perchance known the paths of the great clouds or the perfect knowledges?' By this are understood the ways and roads whereby God continually exalts souls and perfects them in His Wisdom, which souls are here understood by the clouds. It follows, then, that this contemplation which is guiding the soul to God is secret wisdom.

Chapter XVIII

Explains how this secret wisdom is likewise a ladder.

It now remains to consider the second point—namely, how this secret wisdom is likewise a ladder. With respect to this it must be known that we can call this secret contemplation a ladder for many reasons. In the first place, because, just as men mount by means of ladders and climb up to possessions and treasures and things that are in strong places, even so also, by means of this secret contemplation, without knowing how, the soul ascends and climbs up to a knowledge and possession of the good things and treasures of Heaven. This is well expressed by the royal prophet David, when he says: 'Blessed is he that hath Thy favour and help, for such a man hath placed in his heart ascensions into the vale of tears in the place which he hath appointed; for after this manner the Lord of the law shall give blessing, and they shall go from virtue to virtue as from step to step, and the God of gods shall be seen in Sion.' This God is the treasure of the strong place of Sion, which is happiness.

We may also call it a ladder because, even as the ladder has those same steps in order that men may mount, it has them also that they may descend; even so is it likewise with this secret contemplation, for those same communications which it causes in the soul raise it up to God, yet humble it with respect to itself. For communications which are indeed of God have this property, that they humble the soul and at the same time exalt it. For, upon this road, to go down is to go up, and to go up, to go down, for he that humbles himself is exalted and he that exalts himself is humbled. And besides the fact that the virtue of humility is greatness, for the exercise of the soul therein, God is wont to make it mount by this ladder so that it may descend, and to make it descend so that it may mount, that the words of the Wise Man may thus be fulfilled, namely: 'Before the soul is exalted, it is humbled; and before it is humbled, it is exalted.'

Speaking now in a natural way, the soul that desires to consider it will be able to see how on this road (we leave apart the spiritual aspect, of which the soul is not conscious) it has to suffer many ups and downs, and how the prosperity which it enjoys is followed immediately by certain storms and trials; so much so, that it appears to have been given that period of calm in order that it might be forewarned and strengthened against the poverty which has followed; just as after misery and torment there come abundance and calm. It seems to the soul as if, before celebrating that festival, it has first been made to keep that vigil. This is the ordinary course and proceeding of the state of contemplation until the soul arrives at the state of quietness; it never remains in the same state for long together, but is ascending and descending continually.

The reason for this is that, as the state of perfection, which consists in the perfect love of God and contempt for self, cannot exist unless it have these two parts, which are the knowledge of God and of oneself, the soul has of necessity to be practised first in the one and then in the other, now being given to taste of the one—that is, exaltation—and now being made to experience the other—that is, humiliation—until it has acquired perfect habits; and then this ascending and descending will cease, since the soul will have attained to God and become united with Him, which comes to pass at the summit of this ladder, for the ladder rests and leans upon Him. For this ladder of contemplation, which, as we have said, comes down from God, is prefigured by that ladder which Jacob saw as he slept, whereon angels were ascending and descending, from God to man, and from man to God, Who Himself was leaning upon the end of the ladder. All this, says Divine Scripture, took place by night, when Jacob slept, in order to express how secret is this road and ascent to God, and how different from that of man's knowledge. This is very evident, since ordinarily that which is of the greatest profit in it—namely, to be ever losing oneself and becoming as nothing—is considered the worst thing possible; and that which is of least worth, which is for a soul to find consolation and sweetness (wherein it ordinarily loses rather than gains), is considered best.

But, speaking now somewhat more substantially and properly of this ladder of secret contemplation, we shall observe that the principal characteristic of contemplation, on account of which it is here called a ladder, is that it is the science of love. This, as we have said, is an infused and loving knowledge of God, which enlightens the soul and at the same time enkindles it with love, until it is raised up step by step, even unto God its Creator. For it is love alone that unites and joins the soul with God. To the end that this may be seen more clearly, we shall here indicate the steps of this Divine ladder one by one, pointing out briefly the marks and effects of each, so that the soul may conjecture hereby on which of them it is standing. We shall therefore distinguish them by their effects, as do Saint Bernard and Saint Thomas, for to know them in themselves is not possible after a natural manner, inasmuch as this ladder of love is, as we have said, so secret that God alone is He that measures and weighs it.

Chapter XIX

Begins to explain the ten steps of the mystic ladder of Divine love, according to Saint Bernard and Saint Thomas. The first five are here treated.

We observe, then, that the steps of this ladder of love by which the soul mounts, one by one, to God, are ten. The first step of love causes the soul to languish, and this to its advantage. The Bride is speaking from this step of love when she says: 'I adjure you, daughters of Jerusalem, that, if ye find my Beloved, ye tell Him that I am sick with love.' This sickness, however, is not unto death, but for the glory of God, for in this sickness the soul swoons as to sin and as to all things that are not God, for the sake of God Himself, even as David testifies, saying: 'My soul hath swooned away'—that is, with respect to all things, for Thy salvation. For just as a sick man first of all loses his appetite and taste for all food, and his colour changes, so likewise in this degree of love the soul loses its taste and desire for all things and changes its colour and the other accidentals of its past life, like one in love. The soul falls not into this sickness if excess of heat be not communicated to it from above, even as is expressed in that verse of David which says: Pluviam voluntariam segregabis, Deus, haereditati tuae, et infirmata est, etc. This sickness and swooning to all things, which is the beginning and the first step on the road to God, we clearly described above, when we were speaking of the annihilation wherein the soul finds itself when it begins to climb this ladder of contemplative purgation, when it can find no pleasure, support, consolation or abiding-place in anything soever. Wherefore from this step it begins at once to climb to the second.

The second step causes the soul to seek God without ceasing. Wherefore, when the Bride says that she sought Him by night upon her bed (when she had swooned away according to the first step of love) and found Him not, she said: 'I will arise and will seek Him Whom my soul loveth.' This, as we say, the soul does without ceasing as David counsels it, saying: 'Seek ye ever the face of God, and seek ye Him in all things, tarrying not until ye find Him;' like the Bride, who, having enquired for Him of the watchmen, passed on at once and left them. Mary Magdalene did not even notice the angels at the sepulchre. On this step the soul now walks so anxiously that it seeks the Beloved in all things. In whatsoever it thinks, it thinks at once of the Beloved. Of whatsoever it speaks, in whatsoever matters present themselves, it is speaking and communing at once with the Beloved. When it eats, when it sleeps, when it watches, when it does aught soever, all its care is about the Beloved, as is said above with respect to the yearnings of love. And now, as love begins to recover its health and find new strength in the love of this second step, it begins at once to mount to the third, by means of a certain degree of new purgation in the night, as we shall afterwards describe, which produces in the soul the following effects.

The third step of the ladder of love is that which causes the soul to work and gives it fervour so that it fails not. Concerning this the royal Prophet says: 'Blessed is the man that feareth the Lord, for in His commandments he is eager to labour greatly.' Wherefore if fear, being the son of love, causes within him this eagerness to labour, what will be done by love itself? On this step the soul considers great works undertaken for the Beloved as small; many things as few; and the long time for which it serves Him as short, by reason of the fire of love wherein it is now burning. Even so to Jacob, though after seven years he had been made to serve seven more, they seemed few because of the greatness of his love. Now if the love of a mere creature could accomplish so much in Jacob, what will love of the Creator be able to do when on this third step it takes possession of the soul? Here, for the great love which the soul bears to God, it suffers great pains and afflictions because of the little that it does for God; and if it were lawful for it to be destroyed a thousand times for Him it would be comforted. Wherefore it considers itself useless in all that it does and thinks itself to be living in vain. Another wondrous effect produced here in the soul is that it considers itself as being, most certainly, worse than all other souls: first, because love is continually teaching it how much is due to God; and second, because, as the works which it here does for God are many and it knows them all to be faulty and imperfect, they all bring it confusion and affliction, for it realizes in how lowly a manner it is working for God, Who is so high. On this third step, the soul is very far from vainglory or presumption, and from condemning others. These anxious effects, with many others like them, are produced in the soul by this third step; wherefore it gains courage and strength from them in order to mount to the fourth step, which is that that follows.

The fourth step of this ladder of love is that whereby there is caused in the soul an habitual suffering because of the Beloved, yet without weariness. For, as Saint Augustine says, love makes all things that are great, grievous and burdensome to be almost naught. From this step the Bride was speaking when, desiring to attain to the last step, she said to the Spouse: 'Set me as a seal upon thy heart, as a seal upon thine arm; for love—that is, the act and work of love—is strong as death, and emulation and importunity last as long as hell.' The spirit here has so much strength that it has subjected the flesh and takes as little account of it as does the tree of one of its leaves. In no way does the soul here seek its own consolation or pleasure, either in God, or in aught else, nor does it desire or seek to pray to God for favours, for it sees clearly that it has already received enough of these, and all its anxiety is set upon the manner wherein it will be able to do something that is pleasing to God and to render Him some service such as He merits and in return for what it has received from Him, although it be greatly to its cost. The soul says in its heart and spirit: Ah, my God and Lord! How many are there that go to seek in Thee their own consolation and pleasure, and desire Thee to grant them favours and gifts; but those who long to do Thee pleasure and to give Thee something at their cost, setting their own interests last, are very few. The failure, my God, is not in Thy unwillingness to grant us new favours, but in our neglect to use those that we have received in Thy service alone, in order to constrain Thee to grant them to us continually. Exceeding lofty is this step of love; for, as the soul goes ever after God with love so true, imbued with the spirit of suffering for His sake, His Majesty oftentimes and quite habitually grants it joy, and visits it sweetly and delectably in the spirit; for the boundless love of Christ, the Word, cannot suffer the afflictions of His lover without succouring him. This He affirmed through Jeremias, saying: 'I have remembered thee, pitying thy youth and tenderness, when thou wentest after Me in the wilderness.' Speaking spiritually, this denotes the detachment which the soul now has interiorly from every creature, so that it rests not and nowhere finds quietness. This fourth step enkindles the soul and makes it to burn in such desire for God that it causes it to mount to the fifth, which is that which follows.

The fifth step of this ladder of love makes the soul to desire and long for God impatiently. On this step the vehemence of the lover to comprehend the Beloved and be united with Him is such that every delay, however brief, becomes very long, wearisome and oppressive to it, and it continually believes itself to be finding the Beloved. And when it sees its desire frustrated (which is at almost every moment), it swoons away with its yearning, as says the Psalmist, speaking from this step, in these words: 'My soul longs and faints for the dwellings of the Lord.' On this step the lover must needs see that which he loves, or die; at this step was Rachel, when, for the great longing that she had for children, she said to Jacob, her spouse: 'Give me children, else shall I die.' Here men suffer hunger like dogs and go about and surround the city of God. On this step, which is one of hunger, the soul is nourished upon love; for, even as is its hunger, so is its abundance; so that it rises hence to the sixth step, producing the effects which follow.

Chapter XX

Wherein are treated the other five steps of love.

On the sixth step the soul runs swiftly to God and touches Him again and again; and it runs without fainting by reason of its hope. For here the love that has made it strong makes it to fly swiftly. Of this step the prophet Isaias speaks thus: 'The saints that hope in God shall renew their strength; they shall take wings as the eagle; they shall fly and shall not faint,' as they did at the fifth step. To this step likewise alludes that verse of the Psalm: 'As the hart desires the waters, my soul desires Thee, O God.' For the hart, in its thirst, runs to the waters with great swiftness. The cause of this swiftness in love which the soul has on this step is that its charity is greatly enlarged within it, since the soul is here almost wholly purified, as is said likewise in the Psalm, namely: Sine iniquitate cucurri.And in another Psalm: 'I ran the way of Thy commandments when Thou didst enlarge my heart'; and thus from this sixth step the soul at once mounts to the seventh, which is that which follows.

The seventh step of this ladder makes the soul to become vehement in its boldness. Here love employs not its judgment in order to hope, nor does it take counsel so that it may draw back, neither can any shame restrain it; for the favour which God here grants to the soul causes it to become vehement in its boldness. Hence follows that which the Apostle says, namely: That charity believeth all things, hopeth all things and is capable of all things. Of this step spake Moses, when he entreated God to pardon the people, and if not, to blot out his name from the book of life wherein He had written it. Men like these obtain from God that which they beg of Him with desire. Wherefore David says: 'Delight thou in God and He will give thee the petitions of thy heart.' On this step the Bride grew bold, and said: Osculetur me osculo oris sui. To this step it is not lawful for the soul to aspire boldly, unless it feel the interior favour of the King's sceptre extended to it, lest perchance it fall from the other steps which it has mounted up to this point, and wherein it must ever possess itself in humility. From this daring and power which God grants to the soul on this seventh step, so that it may be bold with God in the vehemence of love, follows the eighth, which is that wherein it takes the Beloved captive and is united with Him, as follows.

The eighth step of love causes the soul to seize Him and hold Him fast without letting Him go, even as the Bride says, after this manner: 'I found Him Whom my heart and soul love; I held Him and I will not let Him go.' On this step of union the soul satisfies her desire, but not continuously. Certain souls climb some way, and then lose their hold; for, if this state were to continue, it would be glory itself in this life; and thus the soul remains therein for very short periods of time. To the prophet Daniel, because he was a man of desires, was sent a command from God to remain on this step, when it was said to him: 'Daniel, stay upon thy step, because thou art a man of desires.' After this step follows the ninth, which is that of souls now perfect, as we shall afterwards say, which is that that follows.

The ninth step of love makes the soul to burn with sweetness. This step is that of the perfect, who now burn sweetly in God. For this sweet and delectable ardour is caused in them by the Holy Spirit by reason of the union which they have with God. For this cause Saint Gregory says, concerning the Apostles, that when the Holy Spirit came upon them visibly they burned inwardly and sweetly through love. Of the good things and riches of God which the soul enjoys on this step, we cannot speak; for if many books were to be written concerning it the greater part would still remain untold. For this cause, and because we shall say something of it hereafter, I say no more here than that after this follows the tenth and last step of this ladder of love, which belongs not to this life.

The tenth and last step of this secret ladder of love causes the soul to become wholly assimilated to God, by reason of the clear and immediate vision of God which it then possesses; when, having ascended in this life to the ninth step, it goes forth from the flesh. These souls, who are few, enter not into purgatory, since they have already been wholly purged by love. Of these Saint Matthew says: Beati mundo corde: quoniam ipsi Deum videbunt. And, as we say, this vision is the cause of the perfect likeness of the soul to God, for, as Saint John says, we know that we shall be like Him. Not because the soul will come to have the capacity of God, for that is impossible; but because all that it is will become like to God, for which cause it will be called, and will be, God by participation.

This is the secret ladder whereof the soul here speaks, although upon these higher steps it is no longer very secret to the soul, since much is revealed to it by love, through the great effects which love produces in it. But, on this last step of clear vision, which is the last step of the ladder whereon God leans, as we have said already, there is naught that is hidden from the soul, by reason of its complete assimilation. Wherefore Our Saviour says: 'In that day ye shall ask Me nothing,' etc. But, until that day, however high a point the soul may reach, there remains something hidden from it—namely, all that it lacks for total assimilation in the Divine Essence. After this manner, by this mystical theology and secret love, the soul continues to rise above all things and above itself, and to mount upward to God. For love is like fire, which ever rises upward with the desire to be absorbed in the centre of its sphere.

Chapter XXI

Which explains the word 'disguised,' and describes the colours of the disguise of the soul in this night.

Now that we have explained the reasons why the soul called this contemplation a 'secret ladder,' it remains for us to explain likewise the word 'disguised,' and the reason why the soul says also that it went forth by this 'secret ladder' in 'disguise.'

For the understanding of this it must be known that to disguise oneself is naught else but to hide and cover oneself beneath another garb and figure than one's own—sometimes in order to show forth, under that garb or figure, the will and purpose which is in the heart to gain the grace and will of one who is greatly loved; sometimes, again, to hide oneself from one's rivals and thus to accomplish one's object better. At such times a man assumes the garments and livery which best represent and indicate the affection of his heart and which best conceal him from his rivals.

The soul, then, touched with the love of Christ the Spouse, and longing to attain to His grace and gain His goodwill, goes forth here disguised with that disguise which most vividly represents the affections of its spirit and which will protect it most securely on its journey from its adversaries and enemies, which are the devil, the world and the flesh. Thus the livery which it wears is of three chief colours—white, green and purple—denoting the three theological virtues, faith, hope and charity. By these the soul will not only gain the grace and goodwill of its Beloved, but it will travel in security and complete protection from its three enemies: for faith is an inward tunic of a whiteness so pure that it completely dazzles the eyes of the understanding. And thus, when the soul journeys in its vestment of faith, the devil can neither see it nor succeed in harming it, since it is well protected by faith—more so than by all the other virtues—against the devil, who is at once the strongest and the most cunning of enemies.

It is clear that Saint Peter could find no better protection than faith to save him from the devil, when he said: Cui resistite fortes in fide. And in order to gain the grace of the Beloved, and union with Him, the soul cannot put on a better vest and tunic, to serve as a foundation and beginning of the other vestments of the virtues, than this white garment of faith, for without it, as the Apostle says, it is impossible to please God, and with it, it is impossible to fail to please Him. For He Himself says through a prophet: Sponsabo te mihi in fide.Which is as much as to say: If thou desirest, O soul, to be united and betrothed to Me, thou must come inwardly clad in faith.

This white garment of faith was worn by the soul on its going forth from this dark night, when, walking in interior constraint and darkness, as we have said before, it received no aid, in the form of light, from its understanding, neither from above, since Heaven seemed to be closed to it and God hidden from it, nor from below, since those that taught it satisfied it not. It suffered with constancy and persevered, passing through those trials without fainting or failing the Beloved, Who in trials and tribulations proves the faith of His Bride, so that afterwards she may truly repeat this saying of David, namely: 'By the words of Thy lips I kept hard ways.'

Next, over this white tunic of faith the soul now puts on the second colour, which is a green vestment. By this, as we said, is signified the virtue of hope, wherewith, as in the first case, the soul is delivered and protected from the second enemy, which is the world. For this green colour of living hope in God gives the soul such ardour and courage and aspiration to the things of eternal life that, by comparison with what it hopes for therein, all things of the world seem to it to be, as in truth they are, dry and faded and dead and nothing worth. The soul now divests and strips itself of all these worldly vestments and garments, setting its heart upon naught that is in the world and hoping for naught, whether of that which is or of that which is to be, but living clad only in the hope of eternal life. Wherefore, when the heart is thus lifted up above the world, not only can the world neither touch the heart nor lay hold on it, but it cannot even come within sight of it.

And thus, in this green livery and disguise, the soul journeys in complete security from this second enemy, which is the world. For Saint Paul speaks of hope as the helmet of salvation—that is, a piece of armour that protects the whole head, and covers it so that there remains uncovered only a visor through which it may look. And hope has this property, that it covers all the senses of the head of the soul, so that there is naught soever pertaining to the world in which they can be immersed, nor is there an opening through which any arrow of the world can wound them. It has a visor, however, which the soul is permitted to use so that its eyes may look upward, but nowhere else; for this is the function which hope habitually performs in the soul, namely, the directing of its eyes upwards to look at God alone, even as David declared that his eyes were directed, when he said: Oculi mei semper ad Dominum.He hoped for no good thing elsewhere, save as he himself says in another Psalm: 'Even as the eyes of the handmaid are set upon the hands of her mistress, even so are our eyes set upon our Lord God, until He have mercy upon us as we hope in Him.'

For this reason, because of this green livery (since the soul is ever looking to God and sets its eyes on naught else, neither is pleased with aught save with Him alone), the Beloved has such great pleasure with the soul that it is true to say that the soul obtains from Him as much as it hopes for from Him. Wherefore the Spouse in the Songs tells the Bride that, by looking upon Him with one eye alone, she has wounded His heart. Without this green livery of hope in God alone it would be impossible for the soul to go forth to encompass this loving achievement, for it would have no success, since that which moves and conquers is the importunity of hope.

With this livery of hope the soul journeys in disguise through this secret and dark night whereof we have spoken; for it is so completely voided of every possession and support that it fixes its eyes and its care upon naught but God, putting its mouth in the dust, if so be there may be hope—to repeat the quotation made above from Jeremias.

Over the white and the green vestments, as the crown and perfection of this disguise and livery, the soul now puts on the third color, which is a splendid garment of purple. By this is denoted the third virtue, which is charity. This not only adds grace to the other two colors, but causes the soul to rise to so lofty a point that it is brought near to God, and becomes very beautiful and pleasing to Him, so that it makes bold to say: 'Albeit I am black, O daughters of Jerusalem, I am comely; wherefore the King hath loved me and hath brought me into His chambers.' This livery of charity, which is that of love, and causes greater love in the Beloved, not only protects the soul and hides it from the third enemy, which is the flesh (for where there is true love of God there enters neither love of self nor that of the things of self), but even gives worth to the other virtues, bestowing on them vigour and strength to protect the soul, and grace and beauty to please the Beloved with them, for without charity no virtue has grace before God. This is the purple which is spoken of in the Songs, upon which God reclines. Clad in this purple livery the soul journeys when (as has been explained above in the first stanza) it goes forth from itself in the dark night, and from all things created, 'kindled in love with yearnings,' by this secret ladder of contemplation, to the perfect union of love of God, its beloved salvation.

This, then, is the disguise which the soul says that it wears in the night of faith, upon this secret ladder, and these are its three colors. They constitute a most fit preparation for the union of the soul with God, according to its three faculties, which are understanding, memory and will. For faith voids and darkens the understanding as to all its natural intelligence, and herein prepares it for union with Divine Wisdom. Hope voids and withdraws the memory from all creature possessions; for, as Saint Paul says, hope is for that which is not possessed; and thus it withdraws the memory from that which it is capable of possessing, and sets it on that for which it hopes. And for this cause hope in God alone prepares the memory purely for union with God. Charity, in the same way, voids and annihilates the affections and desires of the will for whatever is not God, and sets them upon Him alone; and thus this virtue prepares this faculty and unites it with God through love. And thus, since the function of these virtues is the withdrawal of the soul from all that is less than God, their function is consequently that of joining it with God.

And thus, unless it journeys earnestly, clad in the garments of these three virtues, it is impossible for the soul to attain to the perfection of union with God through love. Wherefore, in order that the soul might attain that which it desired, which was this loving and delectable union with its Beloved, this disguise and clothing which it assumed was most necessary and convenient. And likewise to have succeeded in thus clothing itself and persevering until it should obtain the end and aspiration which it had so much desired, which was the union of love, was a great and happy chance, wherefore in this line the soul also says:

Oh, happy chance!

Chapter XXII

Explains the third line of the second stanza.

It is very clear that it was a happy chance for this soul to go forth with such an enterprise as this, for it was its going forth that delivered it from the devil and from the world and from its own sensuality, as we have said. Having attained liberty of spirit, so precious and so greatly desired by all, it went forth from low things to high; from terrestrial, it became celestial; from human, Divine. Thus it came to have its conversation in the heavens, as has the soul in this state of perfection, even as we shall go on to say in what follows, although with rather more brevity.

For the most important part of my task, and the part which chiefly led me to undertake it, was the explanation of this night to many souls who pass through it and yet know nothing about it, as was said in the prologue. Now this explanation and exposition has already been half completed. Although much less has been said of it than might be said, we have shown how many are the blessings which the soul bears with it through the night and how happy is the chance whereby it passes through it, so that, when a soul is terrified by the horror of so many trials, it is also encouraged by the certain hope of so many and such precious blessings of God as it gains therein. And furthermore, for yet another reason, this was a happy chance for the soul; and this reason is given in the following line:

In darkness and in concealment.

Chapter XXIII

Expounds the fourth line and describes the wondrous hiding place wherein the soul is set during this night. Shows how, although the devil has an entrance into other places that are very high, he has none into this.

'In concealment' is as much as to say 'in a hiding-place,' or 'in hiding'; and thus, what the soul here says (namely, that it went forth 'in darkness and in concealment') is a more complete explanation of the great security which it describes itself in the first line of the stanza as possessing, by means of this dark contemplation upon the road of the union of the love of God.

When the soul, then, says 'in darkness and in concealment,' it means that, inasmuch as it journeyed in darkness after the manner aforementioned, it went in hiding and in concealment from the devil and from his wiles and stratagems. The reason why, as it journeys in the darkness of this contemplation, the soul is free, and is hidden from the stratagems of the devil, is that the infused contemplation which it here possesses is infused into it passively and secretly, without the knowledge of the senses and faculties, whether interior or exterior, of the sensual part. And hence it follows that, not only does it journey in hiding, and is free from the impediment which these faculties can set in its way because of its natural weakness, but likewise from the devil; who, except through these faculties of the sensual part, cannot reach or know that which is in the soul, nor that which is taking place within it. Wherefore, the more spiritual, the more interior and the more remote from the senses is the communication, the farther does the devil fall short of understanding it.

And thus it is of great importance for the security of the soul that its inward communication with God should be of such a kind that its very senses of the lower part will remain in darkness and be without knowledge of it, and attain not to it: first, so that it may be possible for the spiritual communication to be more abundant, and that the weakness of its sensual part may not hinder the liberty of its spirit; secondly because, as we say, the soul journeys more securely since the devil cannot penetrate so far. In this way we may understand that passage where Our Saviour, speaking in a spiritual sense, says: 'Let not thy left hand know what thy right hand doth.' Which is as though He had said: Let not thy left hand know that which takes place upon thy right hand, which is the higher and spiritual part of the soul; that is, let it be of such a kind that the lower portion of thy soul, which is the sensual part, may not attain to it; let it be a secret between the spirit and God alone.

It is quite true that oftentimes, when these very intimate and secret spiritual communications are present and take place in the soul, although the devil cannot get to know of what kind and manner they are, yet the great repose and silence which some of them cause in the senses and the faculties of the sensual part make it clear to him that they are taking place and that the soul is receiving a certain blessing from them. And then, as he sees that he cannot succeed in thwarting them in the depth of the soul, he does what he can to disturb and disquiet the sensual part—that part to which he is able to attain—now by means of afflictions, now by terrors and fears, with intent to disquiet and disturb the higher and spiritual part of the soul by this means, with respect to that blessing which it then receives and enjoys. But often, when the communication of such contemplation makes its naked assault upon the soul and exerts its strength upon it, the devil, with all his diligence, is unable to disturb it; rather the soul receives a new and a greater advantage and a securer peace. For, when it feels the disturbing presence of the enemy, then—wondrous thing!—without knowing how it comes to pass, and without any efforts of its own, it enters farther into its own interior depths, feeling that it is indeed being set in a sure refuge, where it perceives itself to be most completely withdrawn and hidden from the enemy. And thus its peace and joy, which the devil is attempting to take from it, are increased; and all the fear that assails it remains without; and it becomes clearly and exultingly conscious of its secure enjoyment of that quiet peace and sweetness of the hidden Spouse, which neither the world nor the devil can give it or take from it. In that state, therefore, it realizes the truth of the words of the Bride about this, in the Songs, namely: 'See how threescore strong men surround the bed of Solomon, etc., because of the fears of the night.' It is conscious of this strength and peace, although it is often equally conscious that its flesh and bones are being tormented from without.

At other times, when the spiritual communication is not made in any great measure to the spirit, but the senses have a part therein, the devil more easily succeeds in disturbing the spirit and raising a tumult within it, by means of the senses, with these terrors. Great are the torment and the affliction which are then caused in the spirit; at times they exceed all that can be expressed. For, when there is a naked contact of spirit with spirit, the horror is intolerable which the evil spirit causes in the good spirit (I mean, in the soul), when its tumult reaches it. This is expressed likewise by the Bride in the Songs, when she says that it has happened thus to her at a time when she wished to descend to interior recollection in order to have fruition of these blessings. She says: 'I went down into the garden of nuts to see the apples of the valleys, and if the vine had flourished. I knew not; my soul troubled me because of the chariots'—that is, because of the chariots and the noise of Aminadab, which is the devil.

At other times it comes to pass that the devil is occasionally able to see certain favours which God is pleased to grant the soul when they are bestowed upon it by the mediation of a good angel; for of those favours which come through a good angel God habitually allows the enemy to have knowledge: partly so that he may do that which he can against them according to the measure of justice, and that thus he may not be able to allege with truth that no opportunity is given him for conquering the soul, as he said concerning Job. This would be the case if God allowed not a certain equality between the two warriors—namely, the good angel and the bad—when they strive for the soul, so that the victory of either may be of the greater worth, and the soul that is victorious and faithful in temptation may be the more abundantly rewarded.

We must observe, therefore, that it is for this reason that, in proportion as God is guiding the soul and communing with it, He gives the devil leave to act with it after this manner. When the soul has genuine visions by the instrumentality of the good angel (for it is by this instrumentality that they habitually come, even though Christ reveal Himself, for He scarcely ever appears in His actual person), God also gives the wicked angel leave to present to the soul false visions of this very type in such a way that the soul which is not cautious may easily be deceived by their outward appearance, as many souls have been. Of this there is a figure in Exodus, where it is said that all the genuine signs that Moses wrought were wrought likewise in appearance by the magicians of Pharao. If he brought forth frogs, they brought them forth likewise; if he turned water into blood, they did the same.

And not only does the evil one imitate God in this type of bodily vision, but he also imitates and interferes in spiritual communications which come through the instrumentality of an angel, when he succeeds in seeing them, as we say (for, as Job said: Omne sublime videt). These, however, as they are without form and figure (for it is the nature of spirit to have no such thing), he cannot imitate and counterfeit like those others which are presented under some species or figure. And thus, in order to attack the soul, in the same way as that wherein it is being visited, his fearful spirit presents a similar vision in order to attack and destroy spiritual things by spiritual. When this comes to pass just as the good angel is about to communicate spiritual contemplation to the soul, it is impossible for the soul to shelter itself in the secrecy and hiding-place of contemplation with sufficient rapidity not to be observed by the devil; and thus he appears to it and produces a certain horror and perturbation of spirit which at times is most distressing to the soul. Sometimes the soul can speedily free itself from him, so that there is no opportunity for the aforementioned horror of the evil spirit to make an impression on it; and it becomes recollected within itself, being favoured, to this end, by the effectual spiritual grace that the good angel then communicates to it.

At other times the devil prevails and encompasses the soul with a perturbation and horror which is a greater affliction to it than any torment in this life could be. For, as this horrible communication passes direct from spirit to spirit, in something like nakedness and clearly distinguished from all that is corporeal, it is grievous beyond what every sense can feel; and this lasts in the spirit for some time, yet not for long, for otherwise the spirit would be driven forth from the flesh by the vehement communication of the other spirit. Afterwards there remains to it the memory thereof, which is sufficient to cause it great affliction.

All that we have here described comes to pass in the soul passively, without its doing or undoing anything of itself with respect to it. But in this connection it must be known that, when the good angel permits the devil to gain this advantage of assailing the soul with this spiritual horror, he does it to purify the soul and to prepare it by means of this spiritual vigil for some great spiritual favour and festival which he desires to grant it, for he never mortifies save to give life, nor humbles save to exalt, which comes to pass shortly afterwards. Then, according as was the dark and horrible purgation which the soul suffered, so is the fruition now granted it of a wondrous and delectable spiritual contemplation, sometimes so lofty that there is no language to describe it. But the spirit has been greatly refined by the preceding horror of the evil spirit, in order that it may be able to receive this blessing; for these spiritual visions belong to the next life rather than to this, and when one of them is seen this is a preparation for the next.

This is to be understood with respect to occasions when God visits the soul by the instrumentality of a good angel, wherein, as has been said, the soul is not so totally in darkness and in concealment that the enemy cannot come within reach of it. But, when God Himself visits it, then the words of this line are indeed fulfilled, and it is in total darkness and in concealment from the enemy that the soul receives these spiritual favours of God. The reason for this is that, as His Majesty dwells substantially in the soul, where neither angel nor devil can attain to an understanding of that which comes to pass, they cannot know the intimate and secret communications which take place there between the soul and God. These communications, since the Lord Himself works them, are wholly Divine and sovereign, for they are all substantial touches of Divine union between the soul and God; in one of which the soul receives a greater blessing than in all the rest, since this is the loftiest degree of prayer in existence.

For these are the touches that the Bride entreated of Him in the Songs, saying: Osculetur me osculo oris sui. Since this is a thing which takes place in such close intimacy with God, whereto the soul desires with such yearnings to attain, it esteems and longs for a touch of this Divinity more than all the other favours that God grants it. Wherefore, after many such favours have been granted to the Bride in the said Songs, of which she has sung therein, she is not satisfied, but entreats Him for these Divine touches, saying: 'Who shall give Thee to me, my brother, that I might find Thee alone without, sucking the breasts of my mother, so that I might kiss Thee with the mouth of my soul, and that thus no man should despise me or make bold to attack me.' By this she denotes the communication which God Himself alone makes to her, as we are saying, far from all the creatures and without their knowledge, for this is meant by 'alone and without, sucking, etc.'—that is, drying up and draining the breasts of the desires and affections of the sensual part of the soul. This takes place when the soul, in intimate peace and delight, has fruition of these blessings, with liberty of spirit, and without the sensual part being able to hinder it, or the devil to thwart it by means thereof. And then the devil would not make bold to attack it, for he would not reach it, neither could he attain to an understanding of these Divine touches in the substance of the soul in the loving substance of God.

To this blessing none attains save through intimate purgation and detachment and spiritual concealment from all that is creature; it comes to pass in the darkness, as we have already explained at length and as we say with respect to this line. The soul is in concealment and in hiding, in the which hiding-place, as we have now said, it continues to be strengthened in union with God through love, wherefore it sings this in the same phrase, saying: 'In darkness and in concealment.'

When it comes to pass that those favours are granted to the soul in concealment (that is, as we have said, in spirit only), the soul is wont, during some of them, and without knowing how this comes to pass, to see itself so far withdrawn and separated according to the higher and spiritual part, from the sensual and lower portion, that it recognizes in itself two parts so distinct from each other that it believes that the one has naught to do with the other, but that the one is very remote and far withdrawn from the other. And in reality, in a certain way, this is so; for the operation is now wholly spiritual, and the soul receives no communication in its sensual part. In this way the soul gradually becomes wholly spiritual; and in this hiding-place of unitive contemplation its spiritual desires and passions are to a great degree removed and purged away. And thus, speaking of its higher part, the soul then says in this last line:

My house being now at rest.

Chapter XXIV

Completes the explanation of the second stanza.

This is as much as to say: The higher portion of my soul being like the lower part also, at rest with respect to its desires and faculties, I went forth to the Divine union of the love of God.

Inasmuch as, by means of that war of the dark night, as has been said, the soul is combated and purged after two manners—namely, according to its sensual and its spiritual part—with its senses, faculties and passions, so likewise after two manners—namely, according to these two parts, the sensual and the spiritual—with all its faculties and desires, the soul attains to an enjoyment of peace and rest. For this reason, as has likewise been said, the soul twice pronounces this line—namely, in this stanza and in the last—because of these two portions of the soul, the spiritual and the sensual, which, in order that they may go forth to the Divine union of love, must needs first be reformed, ordered and tranquillized with respect to the sensual and to the spiritual, according to the nature of the state of innocence which was Adam's. And thus this line which, in the first stanza, was understood of the repose of the lower and sensual portion, is, in this second stanza, understood more particularly of the higher and spiritual part; for which reason it is repeated.

This repose and quiet of this spiritual house the soul comes to attain, habitually and perfectly (in so far as the condition of this life allows), by means of the acts of the substantial touches of Divine union whereof we have just spoken; which, in concealment, and hidden from the perturbation of the devil, and of its own senses and passions, the soul has been receiving from the Divinity, wherein it has been purifying itself, as I say, resting, strengthening and confirming itself in order to be able to receive the said union once and for all, which is the Divine betrothal between the soul and the Son of God. As soon as these two houses of the soul have together become tranquillized and strengthened, with all their domestics—namely, the faculties and desires—and have put these domestics to sleep and made them to be silent with respect to all things, both above and below, this Divine Wisdom immediately unites itself with the soul by making a new bond of loving possession, and there is fulfilled that which is written in the Book of Wisdom, in these words: Dum quietum silentium contineret omnia, et nox in suo cursu medium iter haberet, omnipotens sermo tuus Domine a regalibus sedibus. The same thing is described by the Bride in the Songs, where she says that, after she had passed by those who stripped her of her mantle by night and wounded her, she found Him Whom her soul loved.

The soul cannot come to this union without great purity, and this purity is not gained without great detachment from every created thing and sharp mortification. This is signified by the stripping of the Bride of her mantle and by her being wounded by night as she sought and went after the Spouse; for the new mantle which belonged to the betrothal could not be put on until the old mantle was stripped off. Wherefore, he that refuses to go forth in the night aforementioned to seek the Beloved, and to be stripped of his own will and to be mortified, but seeks Him upon his bed and at his own convenience, as did the Bride, will not succeed in finding Him. For this soul says of itself that it found Him by going forth in the dark and with yearnings of love.

Chapter XXV

Wherein is expounded the third stanza.

In the happy night, In secret, when none saw me, Nor I beheld aught, Without light or guide, save that which burned in my heart.

Exposition

The soul still continues the metaphor and similitude of temporal night in describing this its spiritual night, and continues to sing and extol the good properties which belong to it, and which in passing through this night it found and used, to the end that it might attain its desired goal with speed and security. Of these properties it here sets down three.

The first, it says, is that in this happy night of contemplation God leads the soul by a manner of contemplation so solitary and secret, so remote and far distant from sense, that naught pertaining to it, nor any touch of created things, succeeds in approaching the soul in such a way as to disturb it and detain it on the road of the union of love.

The second property whereof it speaks pertains to the spiritual darkness of this night, wherein all the faculties of the higher part of the soul are in darkness. The soul sees naught, neither looks at aught neither stays in aught that is not God, to the end that it may reach Him, inasmuch as it journeys unimpeded by obstacles of forms and figures, and of natural apprehensions, which are those that are wont to hinder the soul from uniting with the eternal Being of God.

The third is that, although as it journeys it is supported by no particular interior light of understanding, nor by any exterior guide, that it may receive satisfaction therefrom on this lofty road—it is completely deprived of all this by this thick darkness—yet its love alone, which burns at this time, and makes its heart to long for the Beloved, is that which now moves and guides it, and makes it to soar upward to its God along the road of solitude, without its knowing how or in what manner.

There follows the line:

In the happy night.

A Spiritual Canticle of the Soul and the Bridegroom Christ

Table of Contents

Introduction

The present volume of the works of St. John of the Cross contains the explanation of the "Spiritual Canticle of the Soul and the Bridegroom Christ." The two earlier works, the "Ascent of Mount Carmel" and the "Dark Night of the Soul," dealt with the cleansing of the soul, the unremittant war against even the smallest imperfections standing in the way of union with God; imperfections which must be removed, partly by strict self-discipline, partly by the direct intervention of God, Who, searching "the reins and hearts" by means of heavy interior and exterior trials, purges away whatever is displeasing to Him. Although some stanzas refer to this preliminary state, the chief object of the "Spiritual Canticle" is to picture under the Biblical simile of Espousals and Matrimony the blessedness of a soul that has arrived at union with God.

The Canticle was composed during the long imprisonment St. John underwent at Toledo from the beginning of December 1577 till the middle of August of the following year. Being one of the principal supporters of the Reform of St. Teresa, he was also one of the victims of the war waged against her work by the Superiors of the old branch of the Order. St. John's prison was a narrow, stifling cell, with no window, but only a small loophole through which a ray of light entered for a short time of the day, just long enough to enable him to say his office, but affording little facility for reading or writing. However, St. John stood in no need of books. Having for many years meditated on every word of Holy Scripture, the Word of God was deeply written in his heart, supplying abundant food for conversation with God during the whole period of his imprisonment. From time to time he poured forth his soul in poetry; afterwards he communicated his verses to friends.

One of these poetical works, the fruit of his imprisonment, was the "Spiritual Canticle," which, as the reader will notice, is an abridged paraphrase of the Canticle of Canticles, the Song of Solomon, wherein under the image of passionate love are described the mystical sufferings and longings of a soul enamored with God.

From the earliest times the Fathers and Doctors of the Church had recognized the mystical character of the Canticle, and the Church had largely utilized it in her liturgy. But as there is nothing so holy but that it may be abused, the Canticle almost more than any other portion of Holy Scripture, had been misinterpreted by a false Mysticism, such as was rampant in the middle of the sixteenth century. It had come to pass, said the learned and saintly Augustinian, Fray Luis de Leon, that that which was given as a medicine was turned into poison, so that the Ecclesiastical authority, by the Index of 1559, forbade the circulation of the Bible or parts of the Bible in any but the original languages, Hebrew, Greek, and Latin; and no one knew better than Luis de Leon himself how rigorously these rules were enforced, for he had to expiate by nearly five years' imprisonment the audacity of having translated into Castilian the Canticle of Canticles.

Again, one of the confessors of St. Teresa, commonly thought to have been the Dominican, Fray Diego de Yanguas, on learning that the Saint had written a book on the Canticle, ordered her to throw it into the fire, so that we now only possess a few fragments of her work, which, unknown to St. Teresa, had been copied by a nun.

It will now be understood that St. John's poetical paraphrase of the Canticle must have been welcome to many contemplative souls who desired to kindle their devotion with the words of Solomon, but were unable to read them in Latin. Yet the text alone, without explanation, would have helped them little; and as no one was better qualified than the author to throw light on the mysteries hidden under oriental imagery, the Venerable Ann of Jesus, Prioress of the Carmelite convent at Granada, requested St. John to write a commentary on his verses. He at first excused himself, saying that he was no longer in that state of spiritual exuberance in which he had been when composing the Canticle, and that there only remained to him a confused recollection of the wonderful operations of Divine grace during the period of his imprisonment. Ann of Jesus was not satisfied with this answer; she not only knew that St. John had lost nothing of his fervor, though he might no longer experience the same feelings, but she remembered what had happened to St. Teresa under similar circumstances, and believed the same thing might happen to St. John. When St. Teresa was obliged to write on some mystical phenomena, the nature of which she did not fully understand, or whose effect she had forgotten, God granted her unexpectedly a repetition of her former experiences so as to enable her to fully study the matter and report on it. Venerable Ann of Jesus felt sure that if St. John undertook to write an explanation of the Canticle he would soon find himself in the same mental attitude as when he composed it.

St. John at last consented, and wrote the work now before us. The following letter, which has lately come to light, gives some valuable information of its composition. The writer, Magdalen of the Holy Spirit, nun of Veas, where she was professed on August 6, 1577, was intimately acquainted with the Saint.

"When the holy father escaped from prison, he took with him a book of poetry he had written while there, containing the verses commencing `In the beginning was the Word,' and those others: `I know the fountain well which flows and runs, though it is night,' and the canticle, `Where have you hidden yourself?' as far as `O nymphs of Judea' (stanza XVIII.). The remaining verses he composed later on while rector of the college of Baeza (1579 — 81), while some of the explanations were written at Veas at the request of the nuns, and others at Granada. The Saint wrote this book in prison and afterwards left it at Veas, where it was handed to me to make some copies of it. Later on it was taken away from my cell, and I never knew who took it. I was much struck with the vividness and the beauty and subtlety of the words. One day I asked the Saint whether God had given him these words which so admirably explain those mysteries, and He answered: `Child, sometimes God gave them to me, and at other times I sought them myself.'"

The autograph of St. John's work which is preserved at Jaén bears the following title:

"Explanation of Stanzas treating of the exercise of love between the soul and Jesus Christ its Spouse, dealing with and commenting on certain points and effects of prayer; written at the request of Mother Ann of Jesus, prioress of the Discalced Carmelite nuns of St. Joseph's convent, Granada, 1584."

As might be expected, the author dedicated the book to Ann of Jesus, at whose request he had written it. Thus, he began his Prologue with the following words: "Inasmuch as this canticle, Reverend Mother (Religiosa Madre), seems to have been written," etc. A little further on he said: "The stanzas that follow, having been written under the influence of that love which proceeds from the overflowing mystical intelligence, cannot be fully explained. Indeed, I do not purpose any such thing, for my sole purpose is to throw some general light over them, since Your Reverence has asked me to do so, and since this, in my opinion too, is the better course." And again: "I shall, however, pass over the more ordinary (effects of prayer), and treat briefly of the more extraordinary to which they are subject who, by the mercy of God, have advanced beyond the state of beginners. This I do for two reasons: the first is that much is already written concerning beginners; and the second is that I am addressing myself to Your Reverence at your own bidding; for you have received from Our Lord the grace of being led on from the elementary state and led inwards to the bosom of His divine love." He continues thus: "I therefore trust, though I may discuss some points of scholastic theology relating to the interior commerce of the soul with God, that I am not using such language altogether in vain, and that it will be found profitable for pure spirituality. For though Your Reverence is ignorant of scholastic theology, you are by no means ignorant of mystical theology, the science of love, etc."

From these passages it appears quite clearly that the Saint wrote the book for Venerable Ann of Jesus and the nuns of her convent. With the exception of an edition published at Brussels in 1627, these personal allusions have disappeared from both the Spanish text and the translations, nor are they to be found in Mr. Lewis's version. There cannot be the least doubt that they represent St. John's own intention, for they are to be found in his original manuscript. This, containing, in several parts, besides the Explanation of the Spiritual Canticle, various poems by the Saint, was given by him to Ann of Jesus, who in her turn committed it to the care of one of her nuns, Isabelle of the Incarnation, who took it with her to Baeza, where she remained eleven years, and afterwards to Jaén, where she founded a convent of which she became the first prioress. She there caused the precious manuscript to be bound in red velvet with silver clasps and gilt edges. It still was there in 1876, and, for all we know, remains to the present day in the keeping of the said convent. It is a pity that no photographic edition of the writings of St. John (so far as the originals are preserved) has yet been attempted, for there is need for a critical edition of his works.

The following is the division of the work: Stanzas I. to IV. are introductory; V. to XII. refer to the contemplative life in its earlier stages; XIII. to XXI., dealing with what the Saint calls the Espousals, appertain to the Unitive way, where the soul is frequently, but not habitually, admitted to a transient union with God; and XXII. to the end describe what he calls Matrimony, the highest perfection a soul can attain this side of the grave. The reader will find an epitome of the whole system of mystical theology in the explanation of Stanza XXVI.

This work differs in many respects from the "Ascent" and the "Dark Night." Whereas these are strictly systematic, preceding on the line of relentless logic, the "Spiritual Canticle," as a poetical work ought to do, soars high above the divisions and distinctions of the scholastic method. With a boldness akin to that of his Patron Saint, the Evangelist, St. John rises to the highest heights, touching on a subject that should only be handled by a Saint, and which the reader, were he a Saint himself, will do well to treat cautiously: the partaking by the human soul of the Divine Nature, or, as St. John calls it, the Deification of the soul (Stanza XXVI. sqq.), These are regions where the ordinary mind threatens to turn; but St. John, with the knowledge of what he himself had experienced, not once but many times, what he had observed in others, and what, above all, he had read of in Holy Scripture, does not shrink from lifting the veil more completely than probably any Catholic writer on mystical theology has done. To pass in silence the last wonders of God's love for fear of being misunderstood, would have been tantamount to ignoring the very end for which souls are led along the way of perfection; to reveal these mysteries in human language, and say all that can be said with not a word too much, not an uncertain or misleading line in the picture: this could only have been accomplished by one whom the Church has already declared to have been taught by God Himself (divinitus instructus), and whose books She tells us are filled with heavenly wisdom (coelesti sapientia refertos). It is hoped that sooner or later She will proclaim him (what many grave authorities think him to be) a Doctor of the Church, namely, the Doctor of Mystical theology.

As has already been noticed in the Introduction to the "Ascent," the whole of the teaching of St. John is directly derived from Holy Scripture and from the psychological principles of St. Thomas Aquinas. There is no trace to be found of an influence of the Mystics of the Middle Age, with whose writings St. John does not appear to have been acquainted. But throughout this treatise there are many obvious allusions to the writings of St. Teresa, nor will the reader fail to notice the encouraging remark about the publication of her works (stanza xiii, sect. 8). The fact is that the same Venerable Ann of Jesus who was responsible for the composition of St. John's treatise was at the same time making preparations for the edition of St. Teresa's works which a few years later appeared at Salamanca under the editorship of Fray Luis de Leon, already mentioned.

Those of his readers who have been struck with, not to say frightened by, the exactions of St. John in the "Ascent" and the "Dark Night," where he demands complete renunciation of every kind of satisfaction and pleasure, however legitimate in themselves, and an entire mortification of the senses as well as the faculties and powers of the soul, and who have been wondering at his self-abnegation which caused him not only to accept, but even to court contempt, will find here the clue to this almost inhuman attitude. In his response to the question of Our Lord, "What shall I give you for all you have done and suffered for Me?" "Lord, to suffer and be despised for You" — he was not animated by grim misanthropy or stoic indifference, but he had learned that in proportion as the human heart is emptied of Self, after having been emptied of all created things, it is open to the influx of Divine grace. This he fully proves in the "Spiritual Canticle." To be made "partaker of the Divine Nature," as St. Peter says, human nature must undergo a radical transformation. Those who earnestly study the teaching of St. John in his earlier treatises and endeavor to put his recommendations into practice, will see in this and the next volume an unexpected perspective opening before their eyes, and they will begin to understand how it is that the sufferings of this time — whether voluntary or involuntary — are not worthy to be compared with the glory to come that shall be revealed in us.

Mr. Lewis's masterly translation of the works of St. John of the Cross appeared in 1864 under the auspices of Cardinal Wiseman. In the second edition, of 1889, he made numerous changes, without, however, leaving a record of the principles that guided him. Sometimes, indeed, the revised edition is terser than the first, but just as often the old one seems clearer. It is more difficult to understand the reasons that led him to alter very extensively the text of quotations from Holy Scripture. In the first edition he had nearly always strictly adhered to the Douay version, which is the one in official use in the Catholic Church in English-speaking countries. It may not always be as perfect as one would wish it to be, but it must be acknowledged that the wholesale alteration in Mr. Lewis's second edition is, to say the least, puzzling. Even the Stanzas have undergone many changes in the second edition, and it will be noticed that there are some variants in their text as set forth at the beginning of the book, and as repeated at the heading of each chapter.

The present edition, allowing for some slight corrections, is a reprint of that of 1889.

Benedict Zimmerman, Prior, O.C.D.

St. Lukes, Wincanton, Somerset,

Feast of St. Simon Stock,

May 16, 1909.

Prologue

Inasmuch as this canticle seems to have been written with some fervor of love of God, whose wisdom and love are, as is said in the book of Wisdom, so vast that they reach "from end to end," and as the soul, taught and moved by Him, manifests the same abundance and strength in the words it uses, I do not purpose here to set forth all that greatness and fullness the spirit of love, which is fruitful, embodies in it. Yes, rather it would be foolishness to think that the language of love and the mystical intelligence — and that is what these stanzas are — can be at all explained in words of any kind, for the Spirit of our Lord who helps our weakness — as St. Paul says — dwelling in us makes petitions for us with groaning unutterable for that which we cannot well understand or grasp so as to be able to make it known. "The Spirit helps our infirmity . . . the Spirit Himself requests for us with groanings unspeakable." For who can describe that which He shows to loving souls in whom He dwells? Who can set forth in words that which He makes them feel? and, lastly, who can explain that for which they long?

Assuredly no one can do it; not even they themselves who experience it. That is the reason why they use figures of special comparisons and similitudes; they hide somewhat of that which they feel and in the abundance of the Spirit utter secret mysteries rather than express themselves in clear words.

And if these similitudes are not received in the simplicity of a loving mind, and in the sense in which they are uttered, they will seem to be effusions of folly rather than the language of reason; as anyone may see in the divine Canticle of Solomon, and in others of the sacred books, wherein the Holy Spirit, because ordinary and common speech could not convey His meaning, uttered His mysteries in strange terms and similitudes. It follows from this, that after all that the holy doctors have said, and may say, no words of theirs can explain it; nor can words do it; and so, in general, all that is said falls far short of the meaning.

The stanzas that follow having been written under influence of that love which proceeds from the overflowing mystical intelligence, cannot be fully explained. Indeed I do not purpose any such thing, for my sole object is to throw some general light over them, which in my opinion is the better course. It is better to leave the outpourings of love in their own fullness, that everyone may apply them according to the measure of his spirit and power, than to pare them down to one particular sense which is not suited to the taste of everyone. And though I do put forth a particular explanation, still others are not to be bound by it. The mystical wisdom — that is, the love, of which these stanzas speak — does not require to be distinctly understood in order to produce the effect of love and tenderness in the soul, for it is in this respect like faith, by which we love God without a clear comprehension of Him.

I shall therefore be very concise, though now and then unable to avoid some prolixity where the subject requires it, and when the opportunity is offered of discussing and explaining certain points and effects of prayer: many of which being referred to in these stanzas, I must discuss some of them. I shall, however, pass over the more ordinary ones, and treat briefly of the more extraordinary to which they are subject who, by the mercy of God, have advanced beyond the state of beginners. This I do for two reasons: the first is, that much is already written concerning beginners; and the second is, that I am addressing those who have received from our Lord the grace of being led on from the elementary state and are led inwards to the bosom of His divine love.

I therefore trust, though I may discuss some points of scholastic theology relating to the interior commerce of the soul with God, that I am not using such language altogether in vain, and that it will be found profitable for pure spirituality. For though some may be altogether ignorant of scholastic theology by which the divine verities are explained, yet they are not ignorant of mystical theology, the science of love, by which those verities are not only learned, but at the same time are relished also.

And in order that what I am going to say may be the better received, I submit myself to higher judgments, and unreservedly to that of our holy mother the Church, intending to say nothing in reliance on my own personal experience, or on what I have observed in other spiritual persons, nor on what I have heard them say — though I intend to profit by all this — unless I can confirm it with the sanction of the divine writings, at least on those points which are most difficult of comprehension.

The method I propose to follow in the matter is this: first of all, to cite the words of the text and then to give that explanation of them which belongs to the subject before me. I shall now transcribe all the stanzas and place them at the beginning of this treatise. In the next place, I shall take each of them separately, and explain them line by line, each line in its proper place before the explanation.

A Spiritual Canticle of the Soul and the Bridegroom Christ

The Bride
Where have You hidden Yourself,
And abandoned me in my groaning, O my Beloved?
You have fled like the hart,
Having wounded me.
I ran after You, crying; but You were gone.

O shepherds, you who go
Through the sheepcots up the hill,
If you shall see Him
Whom I love the most,
Tell Him I languish, suffer, and die.

In search of my Love
I will go over mountains and strands;
I will gather no flowers,
I will fear no wild beasts;
And pass by the mighty and the frontiers.

O groves and thickets
Planted by the hand of the Beloved;
O verdant meads
Enameled with flowers,
Tell me, has He passed by you?

Answer of the Creatures
A thousand graces diffusing
He passed through the groves in haste,
And merely regarding them
As He passed
Clothed them with His beauty.

The Bride
Oh! who can heal me?
Give me at once Yourself,
Send me no more
A messenger
Who cannot tell me what I wish.

All they who serve are telling me
Of Your unnumbered graces;
And all wound me more and more,
And something leaves me dying,

I know not what, of which they are darkly speaking.

But how you persevere, O life,
Not living where you live;
The arrows bring death
Which you receive
From your conceptions of the Beloved.

Why, after wounding
This heart, have You not healed it?
And why, after stealing it,
Have You thus abandoned it,
And not carried away the stolen prey?

Quench my troubles,
For no one else can soothe them;
And let my eyes behold You,
For You are their light,
And I will keep them for You alone.

Reveal Your presence,
And let the vision and Your beauty kill me,
Behold the malady
Of love is incurable
Except in Your presence and before Your face.

O crystal well!
Oh that on Your silvered surface
You would mirror forth at once
Those eyes desired
Which are outlined in my heart!

Turn them away, O my Beloved!
I am on the wing:

The Bridegroom
Return, My Dove!
The wounded hart
Looms on the hill
In the air of your flight and is refreshed.

My Beloved is the mountains,
The solitary wooded valleys,
The strange islands,

The roaring torrents,
The whisper of the amorous gales;

The tranquil night
At the approaches of the dawn,
The silent music,
The murmuring solitude,
The supper which revives, and enkindles love.

Catch us the foxes,
For our vineyard has flourished;
While of roses
We make a nosegay,
And let no one appear on the hill.

O killing north wind, cease!
Come, south wind, that awakens love!
Blow through my garden,
And let its odors flow,
And the Beloved shall feed among the flowers.

O nymphs of Judea!
While amid the flowers and the rose-trees
The amber sends forth its perfume,
Tarry in the suburbs,
And touch not our thresholds.

Hide yourself, O my Beloved!
Turn Your face to the mountains,
Do not speak,
But regard the companions
Of her who is traveling amidst strange islands.

The Bridegroom
Light-winged birds,
Lions, fawns, bounding does,
Mountains, valleys, strands,
Waters, winds, heat,
And the terrors that keep watch by night;

By the soft lyres
And the siren strains, I adjure you,
Let your fury cease,

And touch not the wall,
That the bride may sleep in greater security.

The bride has entered
The pleasant and desirable garden,
And there reposes to her heart's content;
Her neck reclining
On the sweet arms of the Beloved.

Beneath the apple-tree
There were you betrothed;
There I gave you My hand,
And you were redeemed
Where your mother was corrupted.

The Bride
Our bed is of flowers
By dens of lions encompassed,
Hung with purple,
Made in peace,
And crowned with a thousand shields of gold.

In Your footsteps
The young ones run Your way;
At the touch of the fire
And by the spiced wine,
The divine balsam flows.

In the inner cellar
Of my Beloved have I drunk; and when I went forth
Over all the plain
I knew nothing,
And lost the flock I followed before.

There He gave me His breasts,
There He taught me the science full of sweetness.
And there I gave to Him
Myself without reserve;
There I promised to be His bride.

My soul is occupied,
And all my substance in His service;
Now I guard no flock,

Nor have I any other employment:
My sole occupation is love.

If, then, on the common land
I am no longer seen or found,
You will say that I am lost;
That, being enamored,
I lost myself; and yet was found.

Of emeralds, and of flowers
In the early morning gathered,
We will make the garlands,
Flowering in Your love,
And bound together with one hair of my head.

By that one hair
You have observed fluttering on my neck,
And on my neck regarded,
You were captivated;
And wounded by one of my eyes.

When You regarded me,
Your eyes imprinted in me Your grace:
For this You loved me again,
And thereby my eyes merited
To adore what in You they saw

Despise me not,
For if I was swarthy once
You can regard me now;
Since You have regarded me,
Grace and beauty have You given me.

The Bridegroom
The little white dove
Has returned to the ark with the bough;
And now the turtle-dove
Its desired mate
On the green banks has found.

In solitude she lived,
And in solitude built her nest;
And in solitude, alone

Has the Beloved guided her,
In solitude also wounded with love.

The Bride
Let us rejoice, O my Beloved!
Let us go forth to see ourselves in Your beauty,
To the mountain and the hill,
Where the pure water flows:
Let us enter into the heart of the thicket.

We shall go at once
To the deep caverns of the rock
Which are all secret,
There we shall enter in
And taste of the new wine of the pomegranate.

There you will show me
That which my soul desired;
And there You will give at once,
O You, my life!
That which You gave me the other day.

The breathing of the air,
The song of the sweet nightingale,
The grove and its beauty
In the serene night,
With the flame that consumes, and gives no pains.

None saw it;
Neither did Aminadab appear
The siege was intermitted,
And the cavalry dismounted
At the sight of the waters.

Argument

These stanzas describe the career of a soul from its first entrance on the service of God till it comes to the final state of perfection — the spiritual marriage. They refer accordingly to the three states or ways of the spiritual training — the purgative, illuminative, and unitive ways, some properties and effects of which they explain.

The first stanzas relate to beginners — to the purgative way. The second to the advanced — to the state of spiritual betrothal; that is, the illuminative way. The next to the unitive way — that of the perfect, the spiritual Marriage. The unitive way, that of the perfect, follows the illuminative, which is that of the advanced.

The last stanzas treat of the beatific state, which only the already perfect soul aims at.

Explanation of the Stanzas

The soul, considering the obligations of its state, seeing that "the days of man are short;" that the way of eternal life is straight; that "the just man shall scarcely be saved;" that the things of this world are empty and deceitful; that all die and perish like water poured on the ground; that time is uncertain, the last account strict, perdition most easy, and salvation most difficult; and recognizing also, on the other hand, the great debt that is owing to God, Who has created it solely for Himself, for which the service of its whole life is due, Who has redeemed it for Himself alone, for which it owes Him all else, and the correspondence of its will to His love; and remembering other innumerable blessings for which it acknowledges itself indebted to God even before it was born: and also that a great part of its life has been wasted, and that it will have to render an account of it all from beginning to the end, to the payment of "the last farthing," when God shall "search Jerusalem with lamps;" that it is already late, and perhaps the end of the day: in order to remedy so great an evil, especially when it is conscious that God is grievously offended, and that He has hidden His face from it, because it would forget Him for the creature,-the soul, now touched with sorrow and inward sinking of the heart at the sight of its imminent risks and ruin, renouncing everything and casting them aside without delaying for a day, or even an hour, with fear and groanings uttered from the heart, and wounded with the love of God, begins to invoke the Beloved and says:

Stanza 1: the Bride

Where have You hidden Yourself,
And abandoned me to my sorrow, O my Beloved!
You have fled like the hart,
Having wounded me.
I ran after You, crying; but You were gone.

In this first stanza the soul, enamored of the Word, the Son of God, the Bridegroom, desiring to be united to Him in the clear and substantial vision, sets before Him the anxieties of its love, complaining of His absence. And this the more so because, now pierced and wounded with love, for which it had abandoned all things, even itself, it has still to endure the absence of the Beloved, Who has not released it from its mortal flesh, that it might have the fruition of Him in the glory of eternity. Hence it cries out,

"Where have You hidden Yourself?"

It is as if the soul said, "Show me, O You the Word, my Bridegroom, the place where You are hidden." It asks for the revelation of the divine Essence; for the place where the Son of God is hidden is, according to St. John, "the bosom of the Father," which is the divine Essence, transcending all mortal vision, and hidden from all human understanding, as Isaiah says, speaking to God, "Verily You are a hidden God." From this we learn that the communication and sense of His presence, however great they may be, and the most sublime and profound knowledge of God which the soul may have in this life, are not God essentially, neither have they any affinity with Him, for in very truth He is still hidden from the soul; and it is therefore expedient for it, amid all these grandeurs, always to consider Him as hidden, and to seek Him in His hiding place, saying,

"Where have You hidden Yourself?"

Neither sublime communications nor sensible presence furnish any certain proof of His gracious presence; nor is the absence thereof, and aridity, any proof of His absence from the soul. "If He come to me, I shall not see Him; if He depart, I shall not understand." That is, if the soul have any great communication, or impression, or spiritual knowledge, it must not on that account persuade itself that what it then feels is to enjoy or see God clearly and in His Essence, or that it brings it nearer to Him, or Him to it, however deep such feelings may be. On the other hand, when all these sensible and spiritual communications fail it, and it is itself in dryness, darkness, and desolation, it must not on that account suppose that God is far from it; for in truth the former state is no sign of its being in a state of grace, nor is the latter a sign that it is not; for "man knows not whether he is worthy of love or hatred" in the sight of God.

The chief object of the soul in these words is not to ask only for that affective and sensible devotion, wherein there is no certainty or evidence of the possession of the Bridegroom in this life; but principally for that clear presence and vision of His Essence, of which it longs to be assured and satisfied in the next. This, too, was the object of the bride who, in the divine song desiring to be united to the Divinity of the Bridegroom Word, prayed to the Father, saying, "Show me where You feed, where You lie in the midday." For to ask to be shown the place where He fed was to ask to be shown the Essence of the Divine Word, the Son; because the Father feeds nowhere else but in His only begotten Son, Who is the glory of the Father. In asking to be shown the place where He lies in the midday, was to ask for the same thing, because the Son is the sole delight of the Father, Who lies in no other place, and is comprehended by no other thing, but in and by His beloved Son, in Whom He reposes wholly, communicating to Him His whole Essence, in the "midday," which is eternity, where the Father is ever begetting and the Son ever begotten.

This pasture, then, is the Bridegroom Word, where the Father feeds in infinite glory. He is also the bed of flowers whereupon He reposes with infinite delight of love, profoundly hidden from all mortal vision and every created thing. This is the meaning of the bride-soul when she says,

"Where have You hidden Yourself?"

That the thirsty soul may find the Bridegroom, and be one with Him in the union of love in this life — so far as that is possible — and quench its thirst with that drink which it is possible to drink of at His hands in this life, it will be as well — since that is what the Soul asks of Him — that we should answer for Him, and point out the special spot where He is hidden, that He may be found there in that perfection and sweetness of which this life is capable, and that the soul may not begin to loiter uselessly in the footsteps of its companions.

We must remember that the Word, the Son of God, together with the Father and the Holy Spirit, is hidden in essence and in presence, in the inmost being of the soul. That soul, therefore, that will find Him, must go out from all things in will and affection, and enter into the profoundest self-recollection, and all things must be to it as if they existed not. Hence, St. Augustine says: "I found You not without, O Lord; I sought You without in vain, for You are within," God is therefore hidden within the soul, and the true contemplative will seek Him there in love, saying,

"Where have You hidden Yourself?"

O you soul, then, most beautiful of creatures, who so long to know the place where your Beloved is, that you may seek Him, and be united to Him, you know now that you are yourself that very tabernacle where He dwells, the secret chamber of His retreat where He is hidden. Rejoice, therefore, and exult, because all your good and all your hope is so near you as to be within you; or, to speak more accurately, that you can not be without it, "for lo, the kingdom of God is within you." So says the Bridegroom Himself, and His servant, St. Paul, adds: "You are the temple of the living God." What joy for the soul to learn that God never abandons it, even in mortal sin; how much less in a state of grace!

What more can you desire, what more can you seek without, seeing that within you have your riches, your delight, your satisfaction, your fullness and your kingdom; that is, your Beloved, Whom you desire and seek? Rejoice, then, and be glad in Him with interior recollection, seeing that you have Him so near. Then love Him, then desire Him, then adore Him, and go not to seek Him out of yourself, for that will be but distraction and weariness, and you shall not find Him; because there is no fruition of Him more certain, more ready, or more intimate than that which is within.

One difficulty alone remains: though He is within, yet He is hidden. But it is a great matter to know the place of His secret rest, that He may be sought there with certainty. The knowledge of this is that which you ask for here, O soul, when with loving affection you cry,

"Where have You hidden Yourself?"

You will still urge and say, How is it, then, that I find Him not, nor feel Him, if He is within my soul? It is because He is hidden, and because you hide not yourself also that you may find Him and feel Him; for he that will seek that which is hidden must enter secretly into the secret place where it is hidden, and when he finds it, he is himself hidden like the object of his search. Seeing, then, that the Bridegroom whom you love is "the treasure hidden in the field" of your soul, for which the wise merchant gave all that he had, so you, if you will find Him, must forget all that is yours, withdraw from all created things, and hide yourself in the secret retreat of the spirit, shutting the door upon yourself — that is, denying your will in all things — and praying to your Father in secret. Then you, being hidden with Him, will be conscious of His presence in secret, and will love Him, possess Him in secret, and delight in Him in secret, in a way that no tongue or language can express.

Courage, then, O soul most beautiful, you know now that your Beloved, Whom you desire, dwells hidden within your breast; strive, therefore, to be truly hidden with Him, and then you shall embrace Him, and be conscious of His presence with loving affection. Consider also that He bids you, by the mouth of Isaiah, to come to His secret hiding-place, saying, "Go, . . . enter into your chambers, shut your doors upon you"; that is, all your faculties, so that no created thing shall enter: "be hid a little for a moment," that is, for the moment of this mortal life; for if now during this life which is short, you will "with all watchfulness keep your heart," as the wise man says, God will most assuredly give you, as He has promised by the prophet Isaiah, "hidden treasures and mysteries of secrets." The substance of these secrets is God Himself, for He is the substance of the faith, and the object of it, and the faith is the secret and the mystery. And when that which the faith conceals shall be revealed and made manifest, that is the perfection of God, as St. Paul says, "When that which is perfect is come," then shall be revealed to the soul the substance and mysteries of these secrets.

Though in this mortal life the soul will never reach to the interior secrets as it will in the next, however much it may hide itself, still, if it will hide itself with Moses, "in the hole of the rock" — which is a real imitation of the perfect life of the Bridegroom, the Son of God — protected by the right hand of God, it will merit the vision of the "back parts"; that is, it will reach to such perfection here, as to be united, and transformed by love, in the Son of God, its Bridegroom. So effectually will this be wrought that the soul will feel itself so united to Him, so learned and so instructed in His secrets, that, so far as the knowledge of Him in this life is concerned, it will be no longer necessary for it to say: "Where have You hidden Yourself?"

You know then, O soul, how you are to demean yourself if you will find the Bridegroom in His secret place. But if you will hear it again, hear this one word full of substance and unapproachable truth: Seek Him in faith and love, without seeking to satisfy yourself in anything, or to understand more than is expedient for you to know; for faith and love are the two guides of the blind; they will lead you, by a way you know not, to the secret chamber of God. Faith, the secret of which I am speaking, is the foot that journeys onwards to God, and love is the guide that directs its steps. And while the soul meditates on the mysterious secrets of the faith, it will merit the revelation, on the part of love, of that which the faith involves, namely, the Bridegroom Whom it longs for, in this life by spiritual grace, and the divine union, as we said before, and in the next in essential glory, face to face, hidden now.

But meanwhile, though the soul attains to union, the highest state possible in this life, yet inasmuch as He is still hidden from it in the bosom of the Father, as I have said, the soul longing for the fruition of Him in the life to come, ever cries, "Where have You hidden Yourself?"

You do well, then, O soul, in seeking Him always in His secret place; for you greatly magnify God, and draw near to Him, esteeming Him as far beyond and above all you can reach. Rest, therefore, neither wholly nor in part, on what your faculties can embrace; never seek to satisfy yourself with what you comprehend of God, but rather with what you comprehend not; and never rest on the love of, and delight in, that which you can understand and feel, but rather on that which is beyond your understanding and feeling: this is, as I have said, to seek Him by faith.

God is, as I said before, inaccessible and hidden, and though it may seem that you have found Him, felt Him, and comprehended Him, yet you must ever regard Him as hidden, serve Him as hidden, in secret. Do not be like many unwise, who, with low views of God, think that when they cannot comprehend Him, or be conscious of His presence, that He is then farther away and more hidden, when the contrary is true, namely, that He is nearer to them when they are least aware of it; as the prophet David says, "He put darkness His covert," Thus, when you are near to Him, the very infirmity of your vision makes the darkness palpable; you do well, therefore, at all times, in prosperity as well as in adversity, spiritual or temporal, to look upon God as hidden, and to say to Him, "Where have You hidden Yourself?

And left me to my sorrow, O my Beloved?"

The soul calls Him "my Beloved," the more to move Him to listen to its cry, for God, when loved, most readily listens to the prayer of him who loves Him. Thus He speaks Himself: "If you abide in Me . . . you shall ask whatever thing you will, and it shall be done to you." The soul may then with truth call Him Beloved, when it is wholly His, when the heart has no attachments but Him, and when all the thoughts are continually directed to Him. It was the absence of this that made Delilah say to Samson, "How do you say you love me when your mind is not with me?" The mind comprises the thoughts and the feelings. Some there are who call the Bridegroom their Beloved, but He is not really beloved, because their heart is not wholly with Him. Their prayers are, therefore, not so effectual before God, and they shall not obtain their petitions until, persevering in prayer, they fix their minds more constantly upon God and their hearts more wholly in loving affection upon Him, for nothing can be obtained from God but by love.

The words, "And left me to my sorrow," tell us that the absence of the Beloved is the cause of continual sadness in him who loves; for as such a one loves none else, so, in the absence of the object beloved, nothing can console or relieve him. This is, therefore, a test to discern the true lover of God. Is he satisfied with anything less than God? Do I say satisfied? Yes, if a man possess all things, he cannot be satisfied; the greater his possessions the less will be his satisfaction, for the satisfaction of the heart is not found in possessions, but in detachment from all things and in poverty of spirit. This being so, the perfection of love in which we possess God, by a grace most intimate and special, lives in the soul in this life when it has reached it, with a certain satisfaction, which however is not full, for David, notwithstanding all his perfection, hoped for that in heaven saying, "I shall be satisfied when Your glory shall appear."

Thus, then, the peace and tranquillity and satisfaction of heart to which the soul may attain in this life are not sufficient to relieve it from its groaning, peaceful and painless though it be, while it hopes for that which is still wanting. Groaning belongs to hope, as the Apostle says of himself and others, though perfect, "Ourselves also, who have the first fruits of the Spirit, even we ourselves groan within ourselves, waiting for the adoption of the sons of God." The soul groans when the heart is enamored, for where love wounds there is heard the groaning of the wounded one, complaining feelingly of the absence of the Beloved, especially when, after tasting of the sweet conversation of the Bridegroom, it finds itself suddenly alone, and in aridity, because He has gone away. That is why it cries,

"You have fled like the hart."

Here it is to be observed that in the Canticle of Canticles the bride compares the Bridegroom to the roe and the hart on the mountains — "My Beloved is like a roe and to a fawn of harts" — not only because He is shy, solitary, and avoids companions as the hart, but also for his sudden appearance and disappearance. That is His way in His visits to devout souls in order to comfort and encourage them, and in the withdrawing and absence which He makes them feel after those visits in order to try, humble, and teach them. For that purpose He makes them feel the pain of His absence most keenly, as the following words show:

"Having wounded me."

It is as if it had said, "It was not enough that I should feel the pain and grief which Your absence causes, and from which I am continually suffering, but You must, after wounding me with the arrow of Your love, and increasing my longing and desire to see You, run away from me with the swiftness of the hart, and not permit me to lay hold of You, even for a moment."

For the clearer understanding of this we are to keep in mind that, beside the many kinds of God's visits to the soul, in which He wounds it with love, there are commonly certain secret touches of love, which, like a fiery arrow, pierce and penetrate the soul, and burn it with the fire of love. These are properly called the wounds of love, and it is of these the soul is here speaking. These wounds so inflame the will, that the soul becomes so enveloped with the fire of love as to appear consumed thereby. They make it go forth out of itself, and be renewed, and enter on another life, as the phoenix from the fire.

David, speaking of this, says, "My heart has been inflamed, and my reins have been changed; and I am brought to nothing, and I knew not." The desires and affections, called the reins by the prophet, are all stirred and divinely changed in this burning of the heart, and the soul, through love, melted into nothing, knowing nothing but love. At this time the changing of the reins is a great pain, and longing for the vision of God; it seems to the soul that God treats it with intolerable severity, so much so that the severity with which love treats it seems to the soul unendurable, not because it is wounded — for it considers such wounds to be its salvation — but because it is thus suffering from its love, and because He has not wounded it more deeply so as to cause death, that it may be united to Him in the life of perfect love. The soul, therefore, magnifying its sorrows, or revealing them, says,

"Having wounded me."

The soul says in effect, "You have abandoned me after wounding me, and You have left me dying of love; and then You have hidden Yourself as a hart swiftly running away." This impression is most profound in the soul; for by the wound of love, made in the soul by God, the affections of the will lead most rapidly to the possession of the Beloved, whose touch it felt, and as rapidly also, His absence, and its inability to have the fruition of Him here as it desires. Thereupon succeed the groaning because of His absence; for these visitations of God are not like those which recreate and satisfy the soul, because they are rather for wounding than for healing — more for afflicting than for satisfying it, seeing that they tend rather to quicken the knowledge, and increase the longing, and consequently pain with the longing for the vision of God. They are called the spiritual wounds of love, most sweet to the soul and desirable; and, therefore, when it is thus wounded the soul would willingly die a thousand deaths, because these wounds make it go forth out of itself, and enter into God, which is the meaning of the words that follow:

"I ran after You, crying; but You were gone."

There can be no remedy for the wounds of love but from Him who inflicted them. And so the wounded soul, urged by the vehemence of that burning which the wounds of love occasion, runs after the Beloved, crying to Him for relief. This spiritual running after God has a two-fold meaning. The first is a going forth from all created things, which is effected by hating and despising them; the second, a going forth out of oneself, by forgetting self, which is brought about by the love of God. For when the love of God touches the soul with that vividness of which we are here speaking, it so elevates it, that it goes forth not only out of itself by self-forgetfulness, but it is also drawn away from its own judgment, natural ways and inclinations, crying after God, "O my Bridegroom," as if saying, "By this touch of Yours and wound of love have You drawn me away not only from all created things, but also from myself — for, in truth, soul and body seem now to part — and raised me up to Yourself, crying after You in detachment from all things that I might be attached to You:

"You were gone."

As if saying, "When I sought Your presence, I found You not; and I was detached from all things without being able to cling to You — borne painfully by the gales of love without help in You or in myself." This going forth of the soul in search of the Beloved is the rising of the bride in the Canticle: "I will rise and go about the city; in the streets and the high ways I will seek Him Whom my soul loves. I have sought Him and have not found . . . they wounded me." The rising of the bride — speaking spiritually — is from that which is mean to that which is noble; and is the same with the going forth of the soul out of its own ways and inferior love to the ennobling love of God. The bride says that she was wounded because she found him not; so the soul also says of itself that it is wounded with love and forsaken; that is, the loving soul is ever in pain during the absence of the Beloved, because it has given itself up wholly to Him hoping for the reward of its self-surrender, the Possession of the Beloved. Still the Beloved withholds Himself while the soul has lost all things, and even itself, for Him; it obtains no compensation for its loss, seeing that it is deprived of Him whom it loves.

This pain and sense of the absence of God is wont to be so oppressive in those who are going onwards to the state of perfection, that they would die if God did not interpose when the divine wounds are inflicted upon them. As they have the palate of the will wholesome, and the mind pure and disposed for God, and as they taste in some degree of the sweetness of divine love, which they supremely desire, so they also suffer supremely; for, having but a glimpse of an infinite good which they are not permitted to enjoy, that is to them an ineffable pain and torment.

Stanza II

O shepherds, you who go
Through the sheepcots up the hill,
If you shall see
Him Whom I love,
Tell Him I languish, suffer, and die.

The soul would now employ intercessors and mediators between itself and the Beloved, praying them to make its sufferings and afflictions known. One in love, when he cannot converse personally with the object of his love, will do so in the best way he can. Thus the soul employs its affections, desires, and groanings as messengers well able to manifest the secret of its heart to the Beloved. Accordingly, it calls upon them to do this, saying:

"O shepherds, you who go."

The shepherds are the affections, and desires, and groanings of the soul, for they feed it with spiritual good things. A shepherd is one who feeds: and by means of such God communicates Himself to the soul and feeds it in the divine pastures; for without these groans and desires He communicates but slightly with it.

"You who go."

You who go forth in pure love; for all desires and affections do not reach God, but only those which proceed from sincere love.

"Through the sheepcots up the hill."

The sheepcots are the heavenly hierarchies, the angelic choirs, by whose ministry, from choir to choir, our prayers and sighs ascend to God; that is, to the hill, "for He is the highest eminence, and because in Him, as on a hill, we observe and behold all things, the higher and the lower sheepcots." To Him our prayers ascend, offered by angels, as I have said; so the angel said to Tobit "When you prayed with tears, and buried the dead . . . I offered your prayer to the Lord."

The shepherds also are the angels themselves, who not only carry our petitions to God, but also bring down the graces of God to our souls, feeding them like good shepherds, with the sweet communications and inspirations of God, Who employs them in that ministry. They also protect us and defend us against the wolves, which are the evil spirits. And thus, whether we understand the affections or the angels by the shepherds, the soul calls upon both to be its messengers to the Beloved, and thus addresses them all:

"If you shall see Him,"

That is to say:

If, to my great happiness you shall come into His presence, so that He shall see you and hear your words. God, indeed, knows all things, even the very thoughts of the soul, as He said to Moses, but it is then He beholds our necessities when He relieves them, and hears our prayers when he grants them. God does not see all necessities and hear all petitions until the time appointed shall have come; it is then that He is said to hear and see, as we learn in the book of Exodus. When the children of Israel had been afflicted for four hundred years as serfs in Egypt, God said to Moses, "I have seen the affliction of my people in Egypt, and I have heard their cry, and . . . I am come down to deliver them." And yet He had seen it always. So also St. Gabriel bade Zachariah not to fear, because God had heard his prayer, and would grant him the son, for whom he had been praying for many years; yet God had always heard him. Every soul ought to consider that God, though He does not at once help us and grant our petitions, will still succor us in His own time, for He is, as David says, "a helper in due time in tribulation," if we do not become faint-hearted and cease to pray. This is what the soul means by saying, "If you shall see Him"; that is to say, if the time is come when it shall be His good pleasure to grant my petitions.

"Whom I love the most": that is, whom I love more than all creatures. This is true of the soul when nothing can make it afraid to do and suffer all things in His service. And when the soul can also truly say that which follows, it is a sign that it loves Him above all things:

"Tell Him I languish, suffer, and die."

Here the soul speaks of three things that distress it: namely, languor, suffering, and death; for the soul that truly loves God with a love in some degree perfect, suffers in three ways in His absence, in its three powers ordinarily — the understanding, the will, and the memory. In the understanding it languishes because it does not see God, Who is the salvation of it, as the Psalmist says: "I am your salvation." In the will it suffers, because it possesses not God, Who is its comfort and delight, as David also says: "You shall make them drink of the torrent of Your pleasure." In the memory it dies, because it remembers its privation of all the blessings of the understanding, which are the vision of God, and of the delights of the will, which are the fruition of Him, and that it is very possible also that it may lose Him for ever, because of the dangers and chances of this life. In the memory, therefore, the soul labors under a sensation like that of death, because it sees itself without the certain and perfect fruition of God, Who is the life of the soul, as Moses says: "He is your life."

Jeremiah also, in the Lamentations, speaks of these three things, praying to God, and saying: "Remember my poverty . . . the wormwood and the gall." Poverty relates to the understanding, to which appertain the riches of the knowledge of the Son of God, "in whom all the treasures of wisdom and knowledge are hid." The wormwood, which is a most bitter herb, relates to the will, to which appertains the sweetness of the fruition of God, deprived of which it abides in bitterness. We learn in the Revelation that bitterness appertains spiritually to the will, for the angel said to St. John: "Take the book and eat it up; and it shall make your belly bitter." Here the belly signifies the will. The gall relates not only to the memory, but also to all the powers and faculties of the soul, for it signifies the death thereof, as we learn from Moses speaking of the damned: "Their wine is the gall of dragons, and the venom of asps, which is incurable." This signifies the loss of God, which is the death of the soul.

These three things which distress the soul are grounded on the three theological virtues — faith, charity, and hope, which relate, in the order here assigned them, to the three faculties of the soul — understanding, will, and memory. Observe here that the soul does no more than represent its miseries and pain to the Beloved: for he who loves wisely does not care to ask for that which he wants and desires, being satisfied with hinting at his necessities, so that the beloved one may do what shall to him seem good. Thus the Blessed Virgin at the marriage feast of Cana asked not directly for wine, but only said to her Beloved Son, "They have no wine." The sisters of Lazarus sent to Him, not to ask Him to heal their brother, but only to say that he whom He loved was sick: "Lord, behold, he whom You love is sick."

There are three reasons for this. Our Lord knows what is expedient for us better than we do ourselves. Secondly, the Beloved is more compassionate towards us when He sees our necessities and our resignation. Thirdly, we are more secured against self-love and self-seeking when we represent our necessity, than when we ask for that which we think we need. It is in this way that the soul represents its three necessities; as if it said: "Tell my Beloved, that as I languish, and as He only is my salvation, to save me; that as I am suffering, and as He only is my joy, to give me joy; that as I am dying, and as He only is my life, to give me life."

Stanza III

In search of my Love
I will go over mountains and strands;
I will gather no flowers,

I will fear no wild beasts;
And pass by the mighty and the frontiers.

The soul, observing that its sighs and prayers suffice not to find the Beloved, and that it has not been helped by the messengers it invoked in the first and second stanzas, will not, because its searching is real and its love great, leave undone anything itself can do. The soul that really loves God is not dilatory in its efforts to find the Son of God, its Beloved; and, even when it has done all it could it is still not satisfied, thinking it has done nothing. Accordingly, the soul is now, in this third stanza, actively seeking the Beloved, and saying how He is to be found; namely, in the practice of all virtue and in the spiritual exercises of the active and contemplative life; for this end it rejects all delights and all comforts; and all the power and wiles of its three enemies, the world, the devil, and the flesh, are unable to delay it or hinder it on the road.

"In search of my Love."

Here the soul makes it known that to find God it is not enough to pray with the heart and the tongue, or to have recourse to the help of others; we must also work ourselves, according to our power. God values one effort of our own more than many of others on our behalf; the soul, therefore, remembering the saying of the Beloved, "Seek and you shall find," is resolved on going forth, as I said just now, to seek Him actively, and not rest till it finds Him, as many do who will not that God should cost them anything but words, and even those carelessly uttered, and for His sake will do nothing that will cost them anything. Some, too, will not leave for His sake a place which is to their taste and liking, expecting to receive all the sweetness of God in their mouth and in their heart without moving a step, without mortifying themselves by the abandonment of a single pleasure or useless comfort.

But until they go forth out of themselves to seek Him, however loudly they may cry they will not find Him; for the bride in the Canticle sought Him in this way, but she found Him not until she went out to seek Him: "In my little bed in the nights I have sought Him Whom my soul loves: I have sought Him and have not found Him. I will rise and will go about the city: by the streets and highways I will seek Him Whom my soul loves." She afterwards adds that when she had endured certain trials she "found Him."

He, therefore, who seeks God, consulting his own ease and comfort, seeks Him by night, and therefore finds Him not. But he who seeks Him in the practice of virtue and of good works, casting aside the comforts of his own bed, seeks Him by day; such a one shall find Him, for that which is not seen by night is visible by day. The Bridegroom Himself teaches us this, saying, "Wisdom is clear and never fades away, and is easily seen of them that love her, and is found of them that seek her. She prevents them that covet her, that she first may show herself to them. He that awakes early to seek her shall not labor; for he shall find her sitting at his doors." The soul that will go out of the house of its own will, and abandon the bed of its own satisfaction, will find the divine Wisdom, the Son of God, the Bridegroom waiting at the door without, and so the soul says:

"I will go over mountains and strands."

Mountains, which are lofty, signify virtues, partly on account of their height and partly on account of the toil and labor of ascending them; the soul says it will ascend to them in the practice of the contemplative life. Strands, which are low, signify mortifications, penances, and the spiritual exercises, and the soul will add to the active life that of contemplation; for both are necessary in seeking after God and in acquiring virtue. The soul says, in effect, "In searching after my Beloved I will practice great virtue, and abase myself by lowly mortifications and acts of humility, for the way to seek God is to do good works in Him, and to mortify the evil in ourselves, as it is said in the words that follow:

"I will gather no flowers."

He that will seek after God must have his heart detached, resolute, and free from all evils, and from all goods which are not simply God; that is the meaning of these words. The words that follow describe the liberty and courage which the soul must possess in searching after God. Here it declares that it will gather no flowers by the way — the flowers are all the delights, satisfactions, and pleasures which this life offers, and which, if the soul sought or accepted, would hinder it on the road.

These flowers are of three kinds — temporal, sensual, and spiritual. All of them occupy the heart, and stand in the way of the spiritual detachment required in the way of Christ, if we regard them or rest in them. The soul, therefore, says, that it will not stop to gather any of them, that it may seek after God. It seems to say, I will not set my heart upon riches or the goods of this world; I will not indulge in the satisfactions and ease of the flesh, neither will I consult the taste and comforts of my spirit, in order that nothing may detain me in my search after my Love on the toilsome mountains of virtue. This means that it accepts the counsel of the prophet David to those who travel on this road: "If riches abound, set not your heart upon them," This is applicable to sensual satisfactions, as well as to temporal goods and spiritual consolations.

From this we learn that not only temporal goods and bodily pleasures hinder us on the road to God, but spiritual delight and consolations also, if we attach ourselves to them or seek them; for these things are hindrances on the way of the cross of Christ, the Bridegroom. He, therefore, that will go onwards must not only not stop to gather flowers, but must also have the courage and resolution to say as follows:

"I will fear no wild beasts and I will go over the mighty and the frontiers."

Here we have the three enemies of the soul which make war against it, and make its way full of difficulties. The wild beasts are the world; the mighty, the devil; and the frontiers are the flesh.

The world is the wild beasts, because in the beginning of the heavenly journey the imagination pictures the world to the soul as wild beasts, threatening and fierce, principally in three ways. The first is, we must forfeit the world's favor, lose friends, credit, reputation, and property; the second is not less cruel: we must suffer the perpetual deprivation of all the comforts and pleasures of the world; and the third is still worse: evil tongues will rise against us, mock us, and speak of us with contempt. This strikes some persons so vividly that it becomes most difficult for them, I do not say to persevere, but even to enter on this road at all.

But there are generous souls who have to encounter wild beasts of a more interior and spiritual nature — trials, temptations, tribulations, and afflictions of diverse kinds, through which they must pass. This is what God sends to those whom He is raising upwards to high perfection, proving them and trying them as gold in the fire; as David says: "Many are the tribulations of the just; and out of all these our Lord will deliver them." But the truly enamored soul, preferring the Beloved above all things, and relying on His love and favor, finds no difficulty in saying:

"I will fear no wild beats" "and pass over the mighty and the frontiers."

Evil spirits, the second enemy of the soul, are called the mighty, because they strive with all their might to seize on the passes of the spiritual road; and because the temptations they suggest are harder to overcome, and the craft they employ more difficult to detect, than all the seductions of the world and the flesh; and because, also, they strengthen their own position by the help of the world and the flesh in order to fight vigorously against the soul. Hence the Psalmist calls them mighty, saying: "The mighty have sought after my soul." The prophet Job also speaks of their might: "There is no power upon the earth that may be compared with him who was made to fear no man."

There is no human power that can be compared with the power of the devil, and therefore the divine power alone can overcome him, and the divine light alone can penetrate his devices. No soul therefore can overcome his might without prayer, or detect his illusions without humility and mortification. Hence the exhortation of St. Paul to the faithful: "Put on the armor of God, that you may stand against the deceits of the devil: for our wrestling is not against flesh and blood." Blood here is the world, and the armor of God is prayer and the cross of Christ, wherein consist the humility and mortification of which I have spoken.

The soul says also that it will cross the frontiers: these are the natural resistance and rebellion of the flesh against the spirit, for, as St. Paul says, the "flesh lusts against the spirit," and sets itself as a frontier against the soul on its spiritual road. This frontier the soul must cross, surmounting difficulties, and trampling underfoot all sensual appetites and all natural affections with great courage and resolution of spirit: for while they remain in the soul, the spirit will be by them hindered from advancing to the true life and spiritual delight. This is set clearly before us by St. Paul, saying: "If by the spirit you mortify the deeds of the flesh, you shall live." This, then, is the process which the soul in this stanza says it becomes it to observe on the way to seek the Beloved: which briefly is a firm resolution not to stoop to gather flowers by the way; courage not to fear the wild beasts, and strength to pass by the mighty and the frontiers; intent solely on going over the mountains and the strands of the virtues, in the way just explained.

Stanza IV

O groves and thickets
Planted by the hand of the Beloved;
O verdant meads
Enameled with flowers,
Tell me, has He passed by you?

The disposition requisite for entering on the spiritual journey, abstinence from joys and pleasure, being now described; and the courage also with which to overcome temptations and trials, wherein consists the practice of self-knowledge, which is the first step of the soul to the knowledge of God. Now, in this stanza the soul begins to advance through consideration and knowledge of creatures to the knowledge of the Beloved their Creator. For the consideration of the creature, after the practice of self-knowledge, is the first in order on the spiritual road to the knowledge of God, Whose grandeur and magnificence they declare, as the Apostle says: "For His invisible things from the creation of the world are seen, being understood by these things that are made." It is as if he said, "The invisible things of God are made known to the soul by created things, visible and invisible."

The soul, then, in this stanza addresses itself to creatures inquiring after the Beloved. And we observe, as St. Augustine says, that the inquiry made of creatures is a meditation on the Creator, for which they furnish the matter. Thus, in this stanza the soul meditates on the elements and the rest of the lower creation; on the heavens, and on the rest of created and material things which God has made therein; also on the heavenly Spirits, saying:

"O groves and thickets."

The groves are the elements, earth, water, air, and fire. As the most pleasant groves are studded with plants and shrubs, so the elements are thick with creatures, and here are called thickets because of the number and variety of creatures in each. The earth contains innumerable varieties of animals and plants, the water of fish, the air of birds, and fire concurs with all in animating and sustaining them. Each kind of animal lives in its proper element, placed and planted there, as in its own grove and soil where it is born and nourished; and, in truth, God so ordered it when He made them; He commanded the earth to bring forth herbs and animals; the waters and the sea, fish; and the air He gave as a habitation to birds. The soul, therefore, considering that this is the effect of His commandment, cries out,

"Planted by the hand of the Beloved."

That which the soul considers now is this: the hand of God the Beloved only could have created and nurtured all these varieties and wonderful things. The soul says deliberately, "by the hand of the Beloved," because God does many things by the hands of others, as of angels and men; but the work of creation has never been, and never is, the work of any other hand than His own. Thus the soul, considering the creation, is profoundly stirred up to love God the Beloved for it beholds all things to be the work of His hands, and goes on to say:

"O verdant meads."

These are the heavens; for the things which He has created in the heavens are of incorruptible freshness, which neither perish nor wither with time, where the just are refreshed as in the green pastures. The present consideration includes all the varieties of the stars in their beauty, and the other works in the heavens.

The Church also applies the term "verdure" to heavenly things; for while praying to God for the departing soul, it addresses it as follows: "May Christ, the Son of the living God, give you a place in the ever-pleasant verdure of His paradise." The soul also says that this verdant mead is

"Enameled with flowers."

The flowers are the angels and the holy souls who adorn and beautify that place, as costly and fine enamel on a vase of pure gold.

"Tell me, has He passed by you?"

This inquiry is the consideration of the creature just spoken of, and is in effect: Tell me, what perfections has He created in you?

Stanza V: Answer of the Creatures

A thousand graces diffusing
He passed through the groves in haste,
And merely regarding them
As He passed,
Clothed them with His beauty.

This is the answer of the creatures to the soul which, according to St. Augustine, in the same place, is the testimony which they furnish to the majesty and perfections of God, for which it asked in its meditation on created things. The meaning of this stanza is, in substance, as follows: God created all things with great ease and rapidity, and left in them some tokens of Himself, not only by creating them out of nothing, but also by endowing them with innumerable graces and qualities, making them beautiful in admirable order and unceasing mutual dependence. All this He wrought in wisdom, by which He created them, which is the Word, His only begotten Son. Then the soul says;

"A thousand graces diffusing."

These graces are the innumerable multitude of His creatures. The term "thousand," which the soul makes use of, denotes not their number, but the impossibility of numbering them. They are called grace because of the qualities with which He has endowed them. He is said to diffuse them because He fills the whole world with them.

"He passed through the groves in haste."

To pass through the groves is to create the elements; here called groves, through which He is said to pass, diffusing a thousand graces, because He adorned them with creatures which are all beautiful. Moreover, He diffused among them a thousand graces, giving the power of generation and self-conservation. He is said to pass through, because the creatures are, as it were, traces of the passage of God, revealing His majesty, power, and wisdom, and His other divine attributes. He is said to pass in haste, because the creatures are the least of the works of God: He made them, as it were, in passing. His greatest works, wherein He is most visible and at rest, are the incarnation of the Word and the mysteries of the Christian faith, in comparison with which all His other works were works wrought in passing and in haste.

"And thereby regarding them As He passed, Clothed them with His beauty."

The son of God is, in the words of St. Paul, "the brightness of His glory and the figure of His substance." God saw all things only in the face of His Son. This was to give them their natural being, bestowing upon them many graces and natural gifts, making them perfect, as it is written in the book of Genesis: "God saw all the things that He had made: and they were very good." To see all things very good was to make them very good in the Word, His Son. He not only gave them their being and their natural graces when He beheld them, but He also clothed them with beauty in the face of His Son, communicating to them a supernatural being when He made man, and exalted him to the beauty of God, and, by consequence, all creatures in him, because He united Himself to the nature of them all in man. For this cause the Son of God Himself said, "And I, if I be lifted up from the earth will draw all things to Myself." And thus in this exaltation of the incarnation of His Son, and the glory of His resurrection according to the flesh, the Father not only made all things beautiful in part, but also, we may well say, clothed them wholly with beauty and dignity.

Note

But beyond all this — speaking now of contemplation as it affects the soul and makes an impression on it — in the vivid contemplation and knowledge of created things the soul beholds such a multiplicity of graces, powers, and beauty with which God has endowed them, that they seem to it to be clothed with admirable beauty and supernatural virtue derived from the infinite supernatural beauty of the face of God, whose beholding of them clothed the heavens and the earth with beauty and joy; as it is written: "You open Your hand and fill with blessing every living creature." Hence the soul wounded with love of that beauty of the Beloved which it traces in created things, and anxious to behold that beauty which is the source of this visible beauty, sings as in the following stanza:

Stanza VI: the Bride

Oh! who can heal me?
Give me perfectly Yourself,
Send me no more
A messenger
Who cannot tell me what I wish.

Aa created things furnish to the soul traces of the Beloved, and exhibit the impress of His beauty and magnificence, the love of the soul increases, and consequently the pain of His absence: for the greater the soul's knowledge of God the greater its desire to see Him, and its pain when it cannot; and as it sees there is no remedy for this pain except in the presence and vision of the Beloved, distrustful of every other remedy, it prays in this stanza for the fruition of His presence, saying: "Entertain me no more with any knowledge or communications or impressions of Your grandeur, for these do but increase my longing and the pain of Your absence; Your presence alone can satisfy my will and desire." The will cannot be satisfied with anything less than the vision of God, and therefore the soul prays that He may be pleased to give Himself to it in truth, in perfect love.

"O! who can heal me?"

That is, there is nothing in all the delights of the world, nothing in the satisfaction of the senses, nothing in the sweet taste of the spirit that can heal or content me, and therefore it adds:

"Give me at once Yourself."

No soul that really loves can be satisfied or content short of the fruition of God. For everything else, as I have just said, not only does not satisfy the soul, but rather increases the hunger and thirst of seeing Him as He us. Thus every glimpse of the Beloved, every knowledge and impression or communication from Him — these are the messengers suggestive of Him — increase and quicken the soul's desire after Him, as crumbs of food in hunger stimulate the appetite. The soul, therefore, mourning over the misery of being entertained by matters of so little moment, cries out:

"Give me perfectly Yourself."

Now all our knowledge of God in this life, however great it may be, is not a perfectly true knowledge of Him, because it is partial and incomplete; but to know Him essentially is true knowledge, and that is it which the soul prays for here, not satisfied with any other kind. Hence it says:

"Send me no more a messenger."

That is, grant that I may no longer know You in this imperfect way by the messengers of knowledge and impressions, which are so distant from that which my soul desires; for these messengers, as You well know, O my Bridegroom, do but increase the pain of Your absence. They renew the wound which You have inflicted by the knowledge of You which they convey, and they seem to delay Your coming. Henceforth send me no more of these inadequate communications, for if I have been hitherto satisfied with them, it was owing to the slightness of my knowledge and of my love: now that my love has become great, I cannot satisfy myself with them; therefore, give me at once Yourself.

This, more clearly expressed, is as follows: "O Lord my Bridegroom, Who gave me Yourself partially before, give me Yourself wholly now. You who showed glimpses of Yourself before, show Yourself clearly now. You who communicated Yourself hitherto by the instrumentality of messengers — it was as if You mocked me — give Yourself by Yourself now. Sometimes when You visited me You gave me the pearl of Your possession, and, when I began to examine it, lo, it was gone, for You had hidden it Yourself: it was like a mockery. Give me then Yourself in truth, Your whole self, that I may have You wholly to myself wholly, and send me no messengers again."

"Who cannot tell me what I wish."

"I wish for You wholly, and Your messengers neither know You wholly, nor can they speak of You wholly, for there is nothing in earth or heaven that can furnish that knowledge to the soul which it longs for. They cannot tell me, therefore, what I wish. Instead, then, of these messengers, be You the messenger and the message."

Stanza VII

All they who serve are telling me
Of Your unnumbered graces;
And all wound me more and more,
And something leaves me dying,
I know not what, of which they are darkly speaking.

The soul describes itself in the foregoing stanza as wounded, or sick with love of the Bridegroom, because of the knowledge of Him which the irrational creation supplies, and in the present, as wounded with love because of the other and higher knowledge which it derives from the rational creation, nobler than the former; that is, angels and men. This is not all, for the soul says also that it is dying of love, because of that marvelous immensity not wholly but partially revealed to it through the rational creation. This it calls "I know not what," because it cannot be described, and because it is such that the soul dies of it.

It seems, from this, that there are three kinds of pain in the soul's love of the Beloved, corresponding to the three kinds of knowledge that can be had of Him. The first is called a wound; not deep, but slight, like a wound which heals quickly, because it comes from its knowledge of the creatures, which are the lowest works of God. This wounding of the soul, called also sickness, is thus spoken of by the bride in the Canticle: "I adjure you, O daughters of Jerusalem, if you find my Beloved, that you tell Him that I languish with love." The daughters of Jerusalem are the creatures.

The second is called a sore which enters deeper than a wound into the soul, and is, therefore, of longer continuance, because it is as a wound festering, on account of which the soul feels that it is really dying of love. This sore is the effect of the knowledge of the works of God, the incarnation of the Word, and the mysteries of the faith. These being the greatest works of God, and involving a greater love than those of creation, produce a greater effect of love in the soul. If the first kind of pain is as a wound, this must be like a festering, continuous sore. Of this speaks the Bridegroom, addressing Himself to the bride, saying: "You have wounded My heart, My sister, My bride; you have wounded My heart with one of your eyes, and with one hair of your neck." The eye signifies faith in the incarnation of the Bridegroom, and the one hair is the love of the same.

The third kind of pain is like dying; it is as if the whole soul were festering because of its wound. It is dying a living death until love, having slain it, shall make it live the life of love, transforming it in love. This dying of love is affected by a single touch of the knowledge of the Divinity; it is the "I know not what," of which the creatures, as in the stanza is said, are speaking indistinctly. This touch is not continuous nor great, — for then soul and body would part — but soon over, and thus the soul is dying of love, and dying the more when it sees that it cannot die of love. This is called impatient love, which is spoken of in the book of Genesis, where the Scripture says that Rachel's love of children was so great that she said to Jacob her husband, "Give me children, otherwise I shall die." And the prophet Job said, "Who will grant that . . . He that has begun the same would cut me off."

These two-fold pains of love — that is, the wound and the dying — are in the stanza said to be merely the rational creation. The wound, when it speaks of the unnumbered graces of the Beloved in the mysteries and wisdom of God taught by the faith. The dying, when it is said that the rational creation speaks indistinctly. This is a sense and knowledge of the Divinity sometimes revealed when the soul hears God spoken of. Therefore it says:

"All they who serve."

That is, the rational creation, angels and men; for these alone are they who serve God, understanding by that word intelligent service; that is to say, all they who serve God. Some serve Him by contemplation and fruition in heaven — these are the angels; others by loving and longing for Him on earth — these are men. And because the soul learns to know God more distinctly through the rational creation, whether by considering its superiority over the rest of creation, or by what it teaches us of God — the angels interiorly by secret inspirations, and men exteriorly by the truths of Scripture — it says:

"Telling me of Your unnumbered graces."

That is, they speak of the wonders of Your grace and mercy in the Incarnation, and in the truths of the faith which they show forth and are ever telling more distinctly; for the more they say, the more do they reveal Your graces.

"And all wound me more and more."

The more the angels inspire me, the more men teach me, the more do I love You; and thus all wound me more and more with love.

"And something leaves me dying, I know not what, of which they are darkly speaking."

It is as if it said: "But beside the wound which the creatures inflict when they tell me of Your unnumbered graces, there is yet something which remains to be told, one thing unknown to be uttered, a most clear trace of the footsteps of God revealed to the soul, which it should follow, a most profound knowledge of God, which is ineffable, and therefore spoken of as `I know not what.'" If that which I comprehend inflicts the wound and festering sore of love, that which I cannot comprehend but yet feel profoundly, kills me.

This happens occasionally to souls advanced, whom God favors in what they hear, or see, or understand — and sometimes without these or other means —

with a certain profound knowledge, in which they feel or apprehend the greatness and majesty of God. In this state they think so highly of God as to see clearly that they know Him not, and in their perception of His greatness they recognize that not to comprehend Him is the highest comprehension. And thus, one of the greatest favors of God, bestowed transiently on the soul in this life, is to enable it to see so distinctly, and to feel so profoundly, that it clearly understands it cannot comprehend Him at all. These souls are herein, in some degree, like the saints in heaven, where they who know Him most perfectly perceive most clearly that He is infinitely incomprehensible, for those who have the less clear vision, do not perceive so distinctly as the others, how greatly He transcends their vision. This is clear to none who have not had experience of it. But the experienced soul, comprehending that there is something further of which it is profoundly sensible, calls it, "I know not what." As that cannot be understood, so neither can it be described, though it is felt, as I have said. Hence the soul says that the creatures speak indistinctly, because they cannot distinctly utter that which they would say: it is the speech of infants, who cannot explain distinctly or speak intelligibly that which they would convey to others.

The other creatures, also, are in some measure a revelation to the soul in this way, but not of an order so high, whenever it is the good pleasure of God to manifest to it their spiritual sense and significance; they are seemingly on the point of making us understand the perfections of God, and cannot compass it; it is as if one were about to explain a matter and the explanation is not given; and thus they stammer "I know not what." The soul continues to complain, and addresses its own life, saying, in the stanza that follows:

Stanza VIII

But how you persevere, O life!
Not living where you live;
The arrows bring death
Which you receive
From your conceptions of the Beloved.

The soul, perceiving itself to be dying of love, as it has just said, and yet not dying so as to have the free enjoyment of its love, complains of the continuance of its bodily life, by which the spiritual life is delayed. Here the soul addresses itself to the life it is living upon earth, magnifying the sorrows of it. The meaning of the stanza therefore is as follows: "O life of my soul, how can you persevere in this life of the flesh, seeing that it is your death and the privation of the true spiritual life in God, in Whom you live in substance, love, and desire, more truly than in the body? And if this were not reason enough to depart, and free yourself from the body of this death, so as to live and enjoy the life of God, how can you still remain in a body so frail? Besides, these wounds of love made by the Beloved in the revelation of His majesty are by themselves alone sufficient to put an end to your life, for they are very deep; and thus all your feelings towards Him, and all you know of Him, are so many touches and wounds of love that kill,

"But how you persevere, O life! Not living where you live."

We must keep in mind, for the better understanding of this, that the soul lives there where it loves, rather than in the body which it animates. The soul does not live by the body, but, on the contrary, gives it life, and lives by love in that which it loves. For beside this life of love which it lives in God Who loves it, the soul has its radical and natural life in God, like all created things, according to the saying of St. Paul: "In Him we live, and move, and are;" that is, our life, motion, and being is in God. St. John also says that all that was made was life in God: "That which was made, in Him was life."

When the soul sees that its natural life is in God through the being He has given it, and its spiritual life also because of the love it bears Him, it breaks forth into lamentations, complaining that so frail a life in a mortal body should have the power to hinder it from the fruition of the true, real, and delicious life, which it lives in God by nature and by love. Earnestly, therefore, does the soul insist upon this: it tells us that it suffers between two contradictions — its natural life in the body, and its spiritual life in God; contrary the one to the other, because of their mutual repugnance. The soul living this double life is of necessity in great pain; for the painful life hinders the delicious, so that the natural life is as death, seeing that it deprives the soul of its spiritual life, wherein is its whole being and life by nature, and all its operations and feelings by love. The soul, therefore, to depict more vividly the hardships of this fragile life, says:

"The arrows bring death which you receive."

That is to say: "Besides, how can you continue in the body, seeing that the touches of love — these are the arrows — with which the Beloved pierces your heart, are alone sufficient to deprive you of life?" These touches of love make the soul and heart so fruitful of the knowledge and love of God, that they may well be called conceptions of God, as in the words that follow:

"From your conceptions of the Beloved."

That is, of the majesty, beauty, wisdom, grace, and power, which you know to be His.

Note

As the hart wounded with a poisoned arrow cannot be easy and at rest, but seeks relief on all sides, plunging into the waters here and again there, while the poison spreads notwithstanding all attempts at relief, till it reaches the heart, and occasions death; so the soul, pierced by the arrow of love, never ceases from seeking to alleviate its pains. Not only does it not succeed, but its pains increase, let it think, and say, and do what it may; and knowing this, and that there is no other remedy but the resignation of itself into the hands of Him Who wounded it, that He may relieve it, and effectually slay it through the violence of its love; it turns towards the Bridegroom, Who is the cause of all, and says:

Stanza IX

Why, after wounding
This heart, have You not healed it?
And why, after stealing it,
Have You thus abandoned it,
And not carried away the stolen prey?

Here the soul returns to the Beloved, still complaining of its pain; for that impatient love which the soul now exhibits admits of no rest or cessation from pain; so it sets forth its griefs in all manner of ways until it finds relief. The soul seeing itself wounded and lonely, and as no one can heal it but the Beloved Who has wounded it, asks why He, having wounded its heart with that love which the knowledge of Him brings, does not heal it in the vision of His presence; and why He thus abandons the heart which He has stolen through the love Which inflames it, after having deprived the soul of all power over it. The soul has now no power over its heart — for he who loves has none — because it is surrendered to the Beloved, and yet He has not taken it to Himself in the pure and perfect transformation of love in glory.

"Why, after wounding this heart, have You not healed it?"

The enamored soul is complaining not because it is wounded, for the deeper the wound the greater the joy, but because, being wounded, it is not healed by being wounded to death. The wounds of love are so deliciously sweet, that if they do not kill, they cannot satisfy the soul. They are so sweet that it desires to die of them, and hence it is that it says, "Why, after wounding this heart, have You not healed it?" That is, "Why have You struck it so sharply as to wound it so deeply, and yet not healed it by killing it utterly with love? As You are the cause of its pain in the affliction of love, be You also the cause of its health by a death from love; so the heart, wounded by the pain of Your absence, shall be healed in the delight and glory of Your Sweet presence." Therefore it goes on:

"And why, after stealing it, have You thus abandoned it?"

Stealing is nothing else but the act of a robber in dispossessing the owner of his goods, and possessing them himself. Here the soul complains to the Beloved that He has robbed it of its heart lovingly, and taken it out of its power and possession, and then abandoned it, without taking it into His own power and possession as the thief does with the goods he steals, carrying them away with him. He who is in love is said to have lost his heart, or to have it stolen by the object of his love;

because it is no longer in his own possession, but in the power of the object of his love, and so his heart is not his own, but the property of the person he loves.

This consideration will enable the soul to determine whether it loves God simply or not. If it loves Him it will have no heart for itself, nor for its own pleasure or profit, but for the honor, glory, and pleasure of God; because the more the heart is occupied with self, the less is it occupied with God. Whether God has really stolen the heart, the soul may ascertain by either of these two signs: Is it anxiously seeking after God? and has it no pleasure in anything but in Him, as the soul here says? The reason of this is that the heart cannot rest in peace without the possession of something; and when its affections are once placed, it has neither the possession of itself nor of anything else; neither does it perfectly possess what it loves. In this state its weariness is in proportion to its loss, until it shall enter into possession and be satisfied; for until then the soul is as an empty vessel waiting to be filled, as a hungry man eager for food, as a sick man sighing for health, and as a man suspended in the air.

"And not carried away the stolen prey?"

"Why do You not carry away the heart which Your love has stolen, to fill it, to heal it, and to satiate it giving it perfect rest in Yourself?"

The loving soul, for the sake of greater conformity with the Beloved, cannot cease to desire the recompense and reward of its love for the sake of which it serves the Beloved, otherwise it could not be true love, for the recompense of love is nothing else, and the soul seeks nothing else, but greater love, until it reaches the perfection of love; for the sole reward of love is love, as we learn from the prophet Job, who, speaking of his own distress, which is that of the soul now referred to, says: "As a servant longs for the shade, as the hireling looks for the end of his work; so I also have had empty months, and have numbered to myself wearisome nights. If I sleep, I say, When shall I arise? and again, I shall look for the evening, and shall be filled with sorrows even till darkness."

Thus, then, the soul on fire with the love of God longs for the perfection and consummation of its love, that it may be completely refreshed. As the servant wearied by the heat of the day longs for the cooling shade, and as the hireling looks for the end of his work, so the soul for the end of its own. Observe, Job does not say that the hireling looks for the end of his labor, but only for the end of his work. He teaches us that the soul which loves looks not for the end of its labor, but for the end of its work; because its work is to love, and it is the end of this work, which is love, that it hopes for, namely, the perfect love of God. Until it attains to this, the words of Job will be always true of it — its months will be empty, and its nights wearisome and tedious. It is clear, then, that the soul which loves God seeks and looks for no other reward of its services than to love God perfectly.

Note

The soul, having reached this degree of love, resembles a sick man exceedingly wearied, whose appetite is gone, and to whom his food is loathsome, and all things annoyance and trouble. Amidst all things that present themselves to his thoughts, or feelings, or sight, his only wish and desire is health; and everything that does not contribute to it is weariness and oppressive. The soul, therefore, in pain because of its love of God, has three peculiarities. Under all circumstances, and in all affairs, the thought of its health — that is, the Beloved — is ever present to it; and though it is obliged to attend to them because it cannot help it, its heart is ever with Him. The second peculiarity, namely, a loss of pleasure in everything, arises from the first. The third also, a consequence of the second, is that all things become wearisome, and all affairs full of vexation and annoyance.

The reason is that the palate of the will having touched and tasted of the food of the love of God, the will instantly, under all circumstances, regardless of every other consideration, seeks the fruition of the Beloved. It is with the soul now as it was with Mary Magdalene, when in her burning love she sought Him in the garden. She, thinking Him to be the gardener, spoke to Him without further reflection, saying: "If you have taken Him hence, tell me where you have laid Him, and I will take Him away." The soul is under the influence of a like anxiety to find Him in all things, and not finding Him immediately, as it desires — but rather the very reverse — not only has no pleasure in them, but is even tormented by them, and sometimes exceedingly so: for such souls suffer greatly in their intercourse with men and in the transactions of the world, because these things hinder rather than help them in their search.

The bride in the Canticle shows us that she had these three peculiarities when seeking the Bridegroom. "I sought Him and found Him not; the keepers that go about the city found me, they struck me and wounded me: the keepers of the walls took away my cloak." The keepers that go about the city are the affairs of this world, which, when they "find" a soul seeking after God, inflict upon it much pain, and grief, and loathing; for the soul not only does not find in them what it seeks, but rather a hindrance. They who keep the wall of contemplation, that the soul may not enter — that is, evil spirits and worldly affairs — take away the cloak of peace and the quiet of loving contemplation. All this inflicts infinite vexation on the soul enamored of God; and while it remains on earth without the vision of God, there is no relief, great or small, from these afflictions, and the soul therefore continues to complain to the Beloved, saying:

Stanza X

Quench my troubles,
For no one else can soothe them;
And let my eyes behold You,
For You are their light,
And I will keep them for You alone.

Here the soul continues to beseech the Beloved to put an end to its anxieties and distress — none other than He can do so — and that in such a way that its eyes may behold Him; for He alone is the light by which they see, and there is none other but He on whom it will look.

"Quench my troubles."

The desire of love has this property, that everything said or done which does not become that which the will loves, wearies and annoys it, and makes it peevish when it sees itself disappointed in its desires. This and its weary longing after the vision of God is here called "troubles." These troubles nothing can remove except the possession of the Beloved; hence the soul prays Him to quench them with His presence, to cool their feverishness, as the cooling water him who is wearied by the heat. The soul makes use of the expression "quench," to denote its sufferings from the fire of love.

"For no one else can soothe them."

The soul, in order to move and persuade the Beloved to grant its petition, says, "As none other but You can satisfy my needs, You quench my troubles." Remember here that God is then close at hand, to comfort the soul and to satisfy its wants, when it has and seeks no satisfaction or comfort out of Him. The soul that finds no pleasure out of God cannot be long unvisited by the Beloved.

"And let my eyes behold You."

Let me see You face to face with the eyes of the soul,

"For you are their light."

God is the supernatural light of the soul, without which it abides in darkness. And now, in the excess of its affection, it calls Him the light of its eyes, as an earthly lover, to express his affection, calls the object of his love the light of his eyes. The soul says in effect in the foregoing terms, "Since my eyes have no other light, either of nature or of love, but You, let them behold You, Who in every way are their light." David was regretting this light when he said in his trouble, "The light of my eyes, and the same is not with me;" and Tobit, when he said, "What

manner of joy shall be to me who sit in darkness, and see not the light of heaven?"
He was longing for the clear vision of God; for the light of heaven is the Son of
God; as St. John says in the Revelation: "And the city needs not sun, nor moon
to shine in it; for the glory of God has illuminated it, and the Lamb is the lamp
thereof."

"And I will keep them for You alone."

The soul seeks to constrain the Bridegroom to let it see the light of its eyes, not
only because it would be in darkness without it, but also because it will not look
upon anything but on Him. For as that soul is justly deprived of this divine light
if it fixes the eyes of the will on any other light, proceeding from anything that is
not God, for then its vision is confined to that object; so also the soul, by a certain
fitness, deserves the divine light, if it shuts its eyes against all objects whatever, to
open them only for the vision of God.

Note

But the loving Bridegroom of souls cannot bear to see them suffer long in the
isolation of which I am speaking, for, as He says by the mouth of Zachariah, "He
that shall touch you, touches the apple of My eye;" especially when their
sufferings, as those of this soul, proceed from their love for Him. Therefore does
He speak through Isaiah, "It shall be before they call, I will hear; as they are yet
speaking, I will hear." And the wise man says that the soul that seeks Him as
treasure shall find Him. God grants a certain spiritual presence of Himself to the
fervent prayers of the loving soul which seeks Him more earnestly than treasure,
seeing that it has abandoned all things, and even itself, for His sake.

In that presence He shows certain profound glimpses of His divinity and
beauty, whereby He still increases the soul's anxious desire to behold Him. For as
men throw water on the coals of the forge to cause intenser heat, so our Lord in
His dealings with certain souls, in the intermission of their love, makes some
revelations of His majesty, to quicken their fervor, and to prepare them more and
more for those graces which He will give them afterwards. Thus the soul, in that
obscure presence of God, beholding and feeling the supreme good and beauty
hidden there, is dying in desire of the vision, saying in the stanza that follows:

Stanza XI

Reveal Your presence,
And let the vision and Your beauty kill me.
Behold the malady
Of love is incurable
Except in Your presence and before Your face.

The soul, anxious to be possessed by God, Who is so great, Whose love has wounded and stolen its heart, and unable to suffer more, beseeches Him directly, in this stanza, to reveal His beauty — that is, the divine Essence — and to slay it in that vision, separating it from the body, in which it can neither see nor possess Him as it desires. And further, setting before Him the distress and sorrow of heart, in which it continues, suffering it because of its love, and unable to find any other remedy than the glorious vision of the divine essence, cries out: "Reveal Your presence."

To understand this clearly we must remember that there are three ways in which God is present in the soul. The first is His presence in essence, not in holy souls only, but in wretched and sinful souls as well, and also in all created things; for it is by this presence that He gives life and being, and were it once withdrawn all things would return to nothing. This presence never fails in the soul.

The second is His presence by grace, whereby He dwells in the soul, pleased and satisfied with it. This presence is not in all souls; for those who fall into mortal sin lose it, and no soul can know in a natural way whether it has it or not. The third is His presence by spiritual affection. God is wont to show His presence in many devout souls in diverse ways, in refreshment, joy, and gladness; yet this, like the others, is all secret, for He does not show Himself as He is, because the condition of our mortal life does not admit of it. Thus this prayer of the soul may be understood of any one of them.

"Reveal Your presence."

Inasmuch as it is certain that God is ever present in the soul, at least in the first way, the soul does not say, "Be present"; but, "Reveal and manifest Your hidden presence, whether natural, spiritual, or affective, in such a way that I may behold You in Your divine essence and beauty." The soul prays Him that as He by His essential presence gives it its natural being, and perfects it by His presence of grace, so also He would glorify it by the manifestation of His glory. But as the soul is now loving God with fervent affections, the presence, for the revelation of which it prays the Beloved to manifest, is to be understood chiefly of the affective presence of the Beloved. Such is the nature of this presence that the soul felt there was an infinite being hidden there, out of which God communicated to it certain obscure visions of His own divine beauty. Such was the effect of these visions that the soul longed and fainted away with the desire of that which is hidden in that presence.

This is in harmony with the experience of David, when he said: "My soul longs and faints for the courts of our Lord." The soul now faints with desire of being absorbed in the Sovereign Good which it feels to be present and hidden; for though it is hidden, the soul is most profoundly conscious of the good and delight which are there. The soul is therefore attracted to this good with more violence than matter is to its center, and is unable to contain itself, by reason of the force of this attraction, from saying:

"Reveal Your presence."

Moses, on Mount Sinai in the presence of God, saw such glimpses of the majesty and beauty of His hidden Divinity, that, unable to endure it, he prayed twice for the vision of His glory saying: "Whereas You have said: I know you by name, and you have found grace in my sight. If, therefore, I have found grace in Your sight, show me Your face, that I may know You and may find grace before Your eyes;" that is, the grace which he longed for — to attain to the perfect love of the glory of God. The answer of our Lord was: "You can not see My face, for man shall not see Me and live." It is as if God had said: "Moses, your prayer is difficult to grant; the beauty of My face, and the joy in seeing Me is so great, as to be more than your soul can bear in a mortal body that is so weak." The soul accordingly, conscious of this truth, either because of the answer made to Moses or also because of that which I spoke of before, namely, the feeling that there is something still in the presence of God here which it could not see in its beauty in the life it is now living, because, as I said before, it faints when it sees but a glimpse of it. Hence it comes that it anticipates the answer that may be given to it, as it was to Moses, and says:

"Let the vision and Your beauty kill me."

That is, "Since the vision of You and Your beauty is so full of delight that I cannot endure, but must die in the act of beholding them, let the vision and Your beauty kill me."

Two visions are said to be fatal to man, because he cannot bear them and live. One, that of the basilisk, at the sight of which men are said to die at once. The other is the vision of God; but there is a great difference between them. The former kills by poison, the other with infinite health and bliss. It is, therefore, nothing strange for the soul to desire to die by beholding the beauty of God in order to enjoy Him for ever. If the soul had but one single glimpse of the majesty and beauty of God, not only would it desire to die once in order to see Him for ever, as it desires now, but would most joyfully undergo a thousand most bitter deaths to see Him even for a moment, and having seen Him would suffer as many deaths again to see Him for another moment.

It is necessary to observe for the better explanation of this line, that the soul is now speaking conditionally, when it prays that the vision and beauty may slay it; it assumes that the vision must be preceded by death, for if it were possible before death, the soul would not pray for death, because the desire of death is a natural imperfection. The soul, therefore, takes it for granted that this corruptible life cannot coexist with the incorruptible life of God, and says:

"Let the vision and Your beauty kill me."

St. Paul teaches this doctrine to the Corinthians when he says: "We would not be spoiled, but overclothed, that that which is mortal may be swallowed up of life," That is, "we would not be divested of the flesh, but invested with glory." But reflecting that he could not live in glory and in a mortal body at the same time, he says to the Philippians: "having a desire to be dissolved and to be with Christ."

Here arises this question, Why did the people of Israel of old dread and avoid the vision of God, that they might not die, as it appears they did from the words of Manoah to his wife, "We shall die because we have seen God," when the soul desires to die of that vision? To this question two answers may be given.

In those days men could not see God, though dying in the state of grace, because Christ had not come. It was therefore more profitable for them to live in the flesh, increasing in merit, and enjoying their natural life, than to be in Limbo, incapable of meriting, suffering in the darkness and in the spiritual absence of God. They therefore considered it a great grace and blessing to live long upon earth.

The second answer is founded on considerations drawn from the love of God. They in those days, not being so confirmed in love, nor so near to God by love, were afraid of the vision: but, now, under the law of grace, when, on the death of the body, the soul may behold God, it is more profitable to live but a short time, and then to die in order to see Him. And even if the vision were withheld, the soul that really loves God will not be afraid to die at the sight of Him; for true love accepts with perfect resignation, and in the same spirit, and even with joy, whatever comes to it from the hands of the Beloved, whether prosperity or adversity — yes, and even chastisements such as He shall be pleased to send, for, as St. John says, "perfect charity casts out fear."

Thus, then, there is no bitterness in death to the soul that loves, when it brings with it all the sweetness and delights of love; there is no sadness in the remembrance of it when it opens the door to all joy; nor can it be painful and oppressive, when it is the end of all unhappiness and sorrow, and the beginning of all good. Yes, the soul looks upon it as a friend and its bride, and exults in the recollection of it as the day of espousals; it yearns for the day and hour of death more than the kings of the earth for principalities and kingdoms.

It was of this kind of death that the wise man said, "O death, your judgment is good to the needy man." If it is good to the needy man, though it does not supply his wants, but on the contrary deprives him even of what he has, how much more good will it be to the soul in need of love and which is crying for more, when it will not only not rob it of the love it has already, but will be the occasion of that fullness of love which it yearns for, and is the supply of all its necessities. It is not without reason, then, that the soul ventures to say:

"Let the vision and Your beauty kill me."

The soul knows well that in the instant of that vision it will be itself absorbed and transformed into that beauty, and be made beautiful like it, enriched, and abounding in beauty as that beauty itself. This is why David said, "Precious in the sight of the Lord is the death of His saints," but that could not be if they did not become partakers of His glory, for there is nothing precious in the eyes of God except that which He is Himself, and therefore, the soul, when it loves, fears not death, but rather desires it. But the sinner is always afraid to die, because he suspects that death will deprive him of all good, and inflict upon him all evil; for in the words of David, "the death of the wicked is very evil," and therefore, as the wise man says, the very thought of it is bitter: "O death, how bitter is your memory to a man that has peace in his riches!" The wicked love this life greatly, and the next but little, and are therefore afraid of death; but the soul that loves God lives more in the next life than in this, because it lives rather where it loves than where it dwells, and therefore esteeming but lightly its present bodily life, cries out: "Let the vision and Your beauty kill me."

"Behold, the malady of love is incurable, except in Your presence and before Your face."

The reason why the malady of love admits of no other remedy than the presence and countenance of the Beloved is that the malady of love differs from every other sickness, and therefore requires a different remedy. In other diseases, according to sound philosophy, contraries are cured by contraries; but love is not cured but by that which is in harmony with itself. The reason is that the health of the soul consists in the love of God; and so when that love is not perfect, its health is not perfect, and the soul is therefore sick, for sickness is nothing else but a failure of health. Thus, that soul which loves not at all is dead; but when it loves a little, however little that may be, it is then alive, though exceedingly weak and sick because it loves God so little. But the more its love increases, the greater will be its health, and when its love is perfect, then, too, its health also is perfect. Love is not perfect until the lovers become so on an equality as to be mutually transformed into one another; then love is wholly perfect.

And because the soul is now conscious of a certain adumbration of love, which is the malady of which it here speaks, yearning to be made like to Him of whom it is a shadow, that is the Bridegroom, the Word, the Son of God, Who, as St. Paul says, is the "splendor of His glory, and the figure of His substance;" and because it is into this figure it desires to be transformed by love, cries out, "Behold, the malady of love is incurable except in Your presence, and in the light of Your Countenance." The love that is imperfect is rightly called a malady, because as a sick man is enfeebled and cannot work, so the soul that is weak in love is also enfeebled and cannot practice heroic virtue.

Another explanation of these words is this: he who feels this malady of love — that is, a failure of it — has an evidence in himself that he has some love, because he ascertains what is deficient in him by that which he possesses. But he who is not conscious of this malady has evidence therein that he has no love at all, or that he has already attained to perfect love.

Note

The soul now conscious of a vehement longing after God, like a stone rushing to its center, and like wax which has begun to receive the impression of the seal which it cannot perfectly represent, and knowing, moreover, that it is like a picture lightly sketched, crying for the artist to finish his work, and having its faith so clear as to trace most distinctly certain divine glimpses of the majesty of God, knows not what else to do but to turn inward to that faith — as involving and veiling the face and beauty of the Beloved — from which it has received those impressions and pledges of love, and which it thus addresses:

Stanza XII

O crystal well!
O that on Your silvered surface
You would mirror forth at once
Those desired eyes
Which are outlined in my heart.

The soul vehemently desiring to be united to the Bridegroom, and seeing that there is no help or succor in created things, turns towards the faith, as to that which gives it the most vivid vision of the Beloved, and adopts it as the means to that end. And, indeed, there is no other way of attaining to true union, to the spiritual betrothal of God, according to the words of Hosea: "I will betrothe you to Me in faith." In this fervent desire it cries out in the words of this stanza, which are in effect this: "O faith of Christ, my Bridegroom! Oh that you would manifest clearly those truths concerning the Beloved, secretly and obscurely infused — for faith is, as theologians say, an obscure habit — so that your informal and obscure communications may be in a moment clear; Oh that you would withdraw yourself formally and completely from these truths — for faith is a veil over the truths of God — and reveal them perfectly in glory." Accordingly it says:

"O crystal well!"

Faith is called crystal for two reasons: because it is of Christ the Bridegroom; because it has the property of crystal, pure in its truths, a limpid well clear of error, and of natural forms. It is a well because the waters of all spiritual goodness flow from it into the soul. Christ our Lord, speaking to the woman of Samaria, calls faith a well, saying, "The water that I will give him shall become in him a well of water springing up into life everlasting." This water is the Spirit which they who believe shall receive by faith in Him. "Now this He said of the Spirit which they who believed in Him should receive."

"Oh that on your silvered surface."

The articles and definitions of the faith are called silvered surfaces. In order to understand these words and those that follow, we must know that faith is compared to silver because of the propositions it teaches us, the truth and substance it involves being compared to gold. This very substance which we now believe, hidden behind the silver veil of faith, we shall clearly behold and enjoy hereafter; the gold of faith shall be made manifest. Hence the Psalmist, speaking of this, says: "If you sleep amidst the lots, the wings of the dove are laid over with silver, and the hinder parts of the back in the paleness of gold." That means if we shall keep the eyes of the understanding from regarding the things of heaven and of earth — this the Psalmist calls sleeping in the midst — we shall be firm in the faith, here called dove, the wings of which are the truths laid over with silver, because in this life the faith puts these truths before us obscurely beneath a veil. This is the reason why the soul calls them silvered surface. But when faith shall have been consummated in the clear vision of God, then the substance of faith, the silver veil removed, will shine as gold.

As the faith gives and communicates to us God Himself, but hidden beneath the silver of faith, yet it reveals Him none the less. So if a man gives us a vessel made of gold, but covered with silver, he gives us in reality a vessel of gold, though the gold is covered over. Thus, when the bride in the Canticle was longing for the fruition of God, He promised it to her so far as the state of this life admitted of it, saying: "We will make you chains of gold inlaid with silver." He thus promised to give Himself to her under the veil of faith. Hence the soul addresses the faith, saying: "Oh that on your silvered surface" — the definitions of faith — "in which you hide" the gold of the divine rays — which are the desired eyes, — instantly adding:

"You would mirror forth at once those desired eyes!"

By the eyes are understood, as I have said, the rays and truths of God, which are set before us hidden and informal in the definitions of the faith. Thus the words say in substance: "Oh that you would formally and explicitly reveal to me those hidden truths which You teach implicitly and obscurely in the definitions of the faith; according to my earnest desire." Those truths are called eyes, because of the special presence of the Beloved, of which the soul is conscious, believing Him to be perpetually regarding it; and so it says:

"Which are outlined in my heart."

The soul here says that these truths are outlined in the heart — that is, in the understanding and the will. It is through the understanding that these truths are infused into the soul by faith. They are said to be outlined because the knowledge of them is not perfect. As a sketch is not a perfect picture, so the knowledge that comes by faith is not a perfect understanding. The truths, therefore, infused into the soul by faith are as it were in outline, and when the clear vision shall be granted, then they will be as a perfect and finished picture, according to the words of the Apostle: "When that shall come which is perfect, that shall be made void which is in part." "That which is perfect" is the clear vision, and "that which is in part" is the knowledge that comes by faith.

Besides this outline which comes by faith, there is another by love in the soul that loves — that is, in the will — in which the face of the Beloved is so deeply and vividly pictured, when the union of love occurs, that it may be truly said the Beloved lives in the loving soul, and the loving soul in the Beloved. Love produces such a resemblance by the transformation of those who love that one may be said to be the other, and both but one. The reason is, that in the union and transformation of love one gives himself up to the other as his possession, and each resigns, abandons, and exchanges himself for the other, and both become but one in the transformation wrought by love.

This is the meaning of St. Paul when he said, "I live, now, not I, but Christ lives in me." In that He says, "I live, now, not I," his meaning is, that though he lived, yet the life he lived was not his own, because he was transformed in Christ: that his life was divine rather than human; and for that reason, he said it was not he that lived, but Christ Who lived in him. We may therefore say, according to this likeness of transformation, that his life and the life of Christ were one by the union of love. This will be perfect in heaven in the divine life of all those who shall merit the beatific vision; for, transformed in God, they will live the life of God and not their own, since the life of God will be theirs. Then they will say in truth. "We live, but not we ourselves, for God lives in us."

Now, this may take place in this life, as in the case of St. Paul, but not perfectly and completely, though the soul should attain to such a transformation of love as shall be spiritual marriage, which is the highest state it can reach in this life; because all this is but an outline of love compared with the perfect image of transformation in glory. Yet, when this outline of transformation is attained in this life, it is a grand blessing, because the Beloved is so greatly pleased therewith. He desires, therefore, that the bride should have Him thus delineated in her soul, and says to her, "Put Me as a seal upon your heart, as a seal upon your arm." The heart here signifies the soul, wherein God in this life dwells as an impression of the seal of faith, and the arm is the resolute will, where He is as the impressed token of love.

Such is the state of the soul at that time. I speak but little of it, not willing to leave it altogether untouched, though no language can describe it.

The very substance of soul and body seems to be dried up by thirst after this living well of God, for the thirst resembles that of David when he cried out, "As the hart longs for the fountains of waters, so my soul longs for You, O God. My soul has thirsted after the strong living God; when shall I come and appear before the face of God?" So oppressive is this thirst to the soul, that it counts it as nothing to break through the camp of the Philistines, like the valiant men of David, to fill its pitcher with "water out of the cisterns of Bethlehem," which is Christ. The trials of this world, the rage of the devil, and the pains of hell are nothing to pass through, in order to plunge into this fathomless fountain of love.

To this we may apply those words in the Canticle: "Love is strong as death, jealousy is hard as hell." It is incredible how vehement are the longings and sufferings of the soul when it sees itself on the point of testing this good, and at the same time sees it withheld; for the nearer the object desired, the greater the pangs of its denial: "Before I eat," says Job, "I sigh, and as it were overflowing waters so my roaring" and hunger for food. God is meant here by food; for in proportion to the soul's longing for food, and its knowledge of God, is the pain it suffers now.

Note

The source of the grievous sufferings of the soul at this time is the consciousness of its own emptiness of God — while it is drawing nearer and nearer to Him — and also, the thick darkness with the spiritual fire, which dry and purify it, that, its purification ended, it may be united with God. For when God sends not forth a ray of supernatural light into the soul, He is to it intolerable darkness when He is even near to it in spirit, for the supernatural light by its very brightness obscures the mere natural light. David referred to this when he said: "Cloud and mist round about Him . . . a fire shall go before Him." And again: "He put darkness His covert; His tabernacle is round about Him, darksome waters in the clouds of the air. Because of the brightness in His sight the clouds passed, hail and coals of fire." The soul that approaches God feels Him to be all this more and more the further it advances, until He shall cause it to enter within His divine brightness through the transformation of love. But the comfort and consolations of God are, by His infinite goodness, proportional to the darkness and emptiness of the soul, as it is written, "As the darkness thereof, so also the light thereof." And because He humbles souls and wearies them, while He is exalting them and making them glorious, He sends into the soul, in the midst of its weariness, certain divine rays from Himself, in such gloriousness and strength of love as to stir it up from its very depths, and to change its whole natural condition. Thus, the soul, in great fear and natural awe, addresses the Beloved in the first words of the following stanza, the remainder of which is His answer:

Stanza XIII

Turn them away, O my Beloved!
I am on the Wing.
The Bridegroom
Return, My Dove!
The wounded hart
Looms on the hill
In the air of your flight and is refreshed.

Explanation

Amid those fervent affections of love, such as the soul has shown in the preceding stanzas, the Beloved is wont to visit His bride, tenderly, lovingly, and with great strength of love; for ordinarily the graces and visits of God are great in proportion to the greatness of those fervors and longings of love which have gone before. And, as the soul has so anxiously longed for the divine eyes — as in the foregoing stanza — the Beloved reveals to it some glimpses of His majesty and Godhead, according to its desires. These divine rays strike the soul so profoundly and so vividly that it is rapt into an ecstasy which in the beginning is attended with great suffering and natural fear. Hence the soul, unable to bear the ecstasies in a body so frail, cries out, "Turn away your eyes from me."

"Turn them away, O my Beloved!"

That is, "Your divine eyes, for they make me fly away out of myself to the heights of contemplation, and my natural force cannot bear it." This the soul says because it thinks it has escaped from the burden of the flesh, which was the object of its desires; it therefore prays the Beloved to turn away His eyes; that is, not to show them in the body where it cannot bear and enjoy them as it would, but to show them to it in its flight from the body. The Bridegroom at once denies the request and hinders the flight, saying, "Return, My Dove! for the communications I make to you now are not those of the state of glory wherein you desire to be; but return to Me, for I am He Whom you, wounded with love, are seeking, and I, too, as the hart, wounded with your love, begin to show Myself to you on the heights of contemplation, and am refreshed and delighted by the love which your contemplation involves." The soul then says to the Bridegroom:

"Turn them away, O my Beloved!"

The soul, because of its intense longing after the divine eyes — that is, the Godhead — receives interiorly from the Beloved such communications and knowledge of God as compel it to cry out, "Turn them away, O my Beloved!" For such is the wretchedness of our mortal nature, that we cannot bear — even when it is offered to us — but at the cost of our life, that which is the very life of the soul, and the object of its earnest desires, namely, the knowledge of the Beloved. Thus the soul is compelled to say, with regard to the eyes so earnestly, so anxiously sought for, and in so many ways — when they become visible — "Turn them away."

So great, at times, is the suffering of the soul during these ecstatic visitations — and there is no other pain which so wrenches the very bones, and which so oppresses our natural forces — that, were it not for the special interference of God, death would ensue. And, in truth, such is it to the soul, the subject of these visitations, for it feels as if it were released from the body and a stranger to the flesh. Such graces cannot be perfectly received in the body, because the spirit of man is lifted up to the communion of the Spirit of God, Who visits the soul, and must therefore of necessity be in some measure a stranger to the body. Hence it is that the flesh has to suffer, and consequently the soul in it, by reason of their union in one person. The great agony of the soul, therefore, in these visitations, and the great fear that overwhelms it when God deals with it in the supernatural way, force it to cry out, "Turn them away, O my Beloved!"

But it is not to be supposed, however, that the soul really wishes Him to turn away His eyes; for this is nothing else but the expression of natural awe, as I said before. Yes, rather, cost they what they may, the soul would not willingly miss these visitations and favors of the Beloved; for though nature may suffer, the spirit flies to this supernatural recollection in order to enjoy the spirit of the Beloved, the object of its prayers and desires. The soul is unwilling to receive these visitations in the body, when it cannot have the perfect fruition of them, and only in a slight degree and in pain; but it covets them in the flight of the disembodied spirit when it can enjoy them freely. Hence it says, "Turn them away, my Beloved" — that is, Do not visit me in the flesh.

"I am on the wing."

It is as if it said, "I am taking my flight out of the body, that You may show them when I shall have left it; they being the cause of my flight out of the body." For the better understanding of the nature of this flight we should consider that which I said just now. In this visitation of the divine Spirit the spirit of the soul is with great violence borne upwards into communion with the divine, the body is abandoned, all its acts and senses are suspended, because they are absorbed in God. Thus the Apostle, St. Paul, speaking of his own ecstasy, says, "Whether in the body or out of the body, I cannot tell." But we are not to suppose that the soul abandons the body, and that the natural life is destroyed, but only that its actions have then ceased.

This is the reason why the body remains insensible in raptures and ecstasies, and unconscious of the most painful inflictions. These are not like the swoons and faintings of the natural life, which cease when pain begins. They who have not arrived at perfection are liable to these visitations, for they happen to those who are walking in the way of proficients. They who are already perfect receive these visitations in peace and in the sweetness of love: ecstasies cease, for they were only graces to prepare them for this greater grace.

This is a fitting place for discussing the difference between raptures, ecstasies, other elevations and subtle flights of the spirit, to which spiritual persons are liable; but, as I intend to do nothing more than explain briefly this canticle, as I undertook in the prologue, I leave the subject for those who are better qualified than I am. I do this the more readily, because our mother, the blessed Teresa of Jesus, has written admirably on this matter, whose writings I hope in God to see published soon. The flight of the soul in this place, then, is to be understood of ecstasy, and elevation of spirit in God. The Beloved immediately says:

"Return, My Dove."

The soul was joyfully quitting the body in its spiritual flight, thinking that its natural life was over, and that it was about to enter into the everlasting fruition of the Bridegroom, and remain with Him without a veil between them. He, however, restrains it in its flight, saying:

"Return, My Dove."

It is as if He said, "O My Dove, in your high and rapid flight of contemplation, in the love with which you are inflamed, in the simplicity of your regard" — these are three characteristics of the dove — "return from that flight in which you aim at the true fruition of Myself — the time is not yet come for knowledge so high — return, and submit yourself to that lower degree of it which I communicate in this your rapture."

"The wounded hart."

The Bridegroom likens Himself to a hart, for by the hart here He means Himself. The hart by nature climbs up to high places, and when wounded hastens to seek relief in the cooling waters. If he hears his consort moan and sees that she is wounded, he runs to her at once, comforts, and caresses her. So the Bridegroom now; for, seeing the bride wounded with His love, He, too, hearing her moaning, is wounded Himself with her love; for with lovers the wound of one is the wound of the other, and they have the same feelings in common. The Bridegroom, therefore, says in effect: "Return, my bride, to Me; for as you are wounded with the love of Me, I too, like the hart, am wounded by love for you. I am like the hart, looming on the top of the hill." Therefore He says:

"Looms on the hill."

That is, "on the heights of contemplation, to which you have ascended in your flight." Contemplation is a lofty eminence where God, in this life, begins to communicate Himself to the soul, and to show Himself, but not distinctly. Hence it is said, "Looms on the hill," because He does not appear clearly. However profound the knowledge of Himself which God may grant to the soul in this life, it is, after all, but an indistinct vision. We now come to the third property of the hart, the subject of the line that follows:

"In the air of your flight, and is refreshed."

The flight is contemplation in the ecstasy spoken of before, and the air is the spirit of love produced in the soul by this flight of contemplation, and this love produced by the flight is here with great propriety called "air," for the Holy Spirit also is likened to air in the Sacred Writings, because He is the breath of the Father and the Son. And so as He is there the air of the flight — that is, that He proceeds by the will from the contemplation and wisdom of the Father and the Son, and is breathed — so here the love of the soul is called air by the Bridegroom, because it proceeds from the contemplation of God and the knowledge of Him which at this time is possessed by the soul.

We must observe here that the Bridegroom does not say that He comes at the flight, but at the air of the flight, because properly speaking God does not communicate Himself to the soul because of that flight, which is, as I have said, the knowledge it has of God, but because of the love which is the fruit of that knowledge. For as love is the union of the Father and the Son, so is it also of God and the soul.

Hence it is that notwithstanding the most profound knowledge of God, and contemplation itself, together with the knowledge of all mysteries, the soul without love is worth nothing, and can do nothing, as the Apostle says, towards its union with God. In another place he says, "Have charity, which is the bond of perfection." This charity then and love of the soul make the Bridegroom run to drink of the fountain of the Bride's love, as the cooling waters attract the thirsty and the wounded hart, to be refreshed therein.

"And is refreshed."

As the air cools and refreshes him who is wearied with the heat, so the air of love refreshes and comforts him who burns with the fire of love. The fire of love has this property, the air which cools and refreshes it is an increase of the fire itself. To him who loves, love is a flame that burns with the desire of burning more and more, like the flame of material fire. The consummation of this desire of burning more and more, with the love of the bride, which is the air of her flight, is here called refreshment. The Bridegroom says in substance, "I burn more and more because of the ardor of your flight, for love kindles love."

God does not establish His grace and love in the soul but in proportion to the good will of that soul's love. He, therefore, that truly loves God must strive that his love fail not; for so, if we may thus speak, will he move God to show him greater love, and to take greater delight in his soul. In order to attain to such a degree of love, he must practice those things of which the Apostle speaks, saying: "Charity is patient, is benign: charity envies not, deals not perversely; is not puffed up, is not ambitious, seeks not her own, is not provoked to anger, thinks not evil, rejoices not upon iniquity, but rejoices with the truth; bears all things, believes all things, hopes all things, endures all things."

Note

When the dove — that is the soul — was flying on the gale of love over the waters of the deluge of the weariness and longing of its love, "not finding where her foot might rest," the compassionate father Noah, in this last flight, put forth the hand of his mercy, caught her, and brought her into the ark of his charity and love. That took place when the Bridegroom, as in the stanza now explained, said, "Return, My Dove." In the shelter within the ark, the soul, finding all it desired, and more than it can ever express, begins to sing the praises of the Beloved, celebrating the magnificence which it feels and enjoys in that union, saying:

Stanza XIV: The Bride

My Beloved is the mountains,
The solitary wooded valleys,
The strange islands,
The roaring torrents,
The whisper of the amorous gales;

Before I begin to explain these stanzas, I must observe, in order that they and those which follow may be better understood, that this spiritual flight signifies a certain high estate and union of love, to which, after many spiritual exercises, God is wont to elevate the soul: it is called the spiritual betrothal of the Word, the Son of God. In the beginning, when this occurs the first time, God reveals to it great things of Himself, makes it beautiful in majesty and grandeur, adorns it with graces and gifts, and endows it with honor, and with the knowledge of Himself, as a bride is adorned on the day of her betrothal. On this happy day the soul not only ceases from its anxieties and loving complaints, but is, moreover, adorned with all grace, entering into a state of peace and delight, and of the sweetness of love, as it appears from these stanzas, in which it does nothing else but recount and praise the magnificence of the Beloved, which it recognizes in Him, and enjoys in the union of the betrothal.

In the stanzas that follow, the soul speaks no more of its anxieties and sufferings, as before, but of the sweet and peaceful intercourse of love with the Beloved; for now all its troubles are over. These two stanzas, which I am about to explain, contain all that God is wont at this time to bestow upon the soul; but we are not to suppose that all souls, thus far advanced, receive all that is here described, either in the same way or in the same degree of knowledge and of consciousness. Some souls receive more, others less; some in one way, some in another; and yet all may be in the state of spiritual betrothal. But in this stanza the highest possible is spoken of, because that embraces all.

Explanation

As in the ark of Noah there were many chambers for the different kinds of animals, as the Sacred Writings tell us, and "all food that may be eaten," so the soul, in its flight to the divine ark of the bosom of God, sees therein not only the many mansions of which our Lord speaks, but also all the food, that is, all the magnificence in which the soul may rejoice, and which are here referred to by the common terms of these stanzas. These are substantially as follows:

In this divine union the soul has a vision and foretaste of abundant and inestimable riches, and finds there all the repose and refreshment it desired; it attains to the secrets of God, and to a strange knowledge of Him, which is the food of those who know Him most; it is conscious of the awful power of God beyond all other power and might, tastes of the wonderful sweetness and delight of the Spirit, finds its true rest and divine light, drinks deeply of the wisdom of God, which shines forth in the harmony of the creatures and works of God; it feels itself filled with all good, emptied, and delivered from all evil, and, above all, rejoices consciously in the inestimable banquet of love which confirms it in love. This is the substance of these two stanzas.

The bride here says that her Beloved in Himself and to her is all the objects she enumerates; for in the ecstatic communications of God the soul feels and understands the truth of the saying of St. Francis: "God is mine and all things are mine." And because God is all, and the soul, and the good of all, the communication in this ecstasy is explained by the consideration that the goodness of the creatures referred to in these stanzas is a reflection of His goodness, as will appear from every line thereof. All that is here set forth is in God eminently in an infinite way, or rather, every one of these grandeurs is God, and all of them together are God. Inasmuch as the soul is one with God, it feels all things to be God according to the words of St. John: "What was made, in Him was life."

But we are not to understand this consciousness of the soul as if it saw the creatures in God as we see material objects in the light, but that it feels all things to be God in this fruition of Him; neither are we to imagine that the soul sees God essentially and clearly because it has so deep a sense of Him; for this is only a strong and abundant communication from Him, a glimmering light of what He is in Himself, by which the soul discerns this goodness of all things, as I proceed to explain.

"My Beloved is the mountains."

Mountains are high fertile, extensive, beautiful, lovely, flowery, and odorous. These mountains my Beloved is to me.

"The solitary wooded valleys."

Solitary valleys are tranquil, pleasant, cooling, shady, abounding in sweet waters, and by the variety of trees growing in them, and by the melody of the birds that frequent them, enliven and delight the senses; their solitude and silence procure us a refreshing rest. These valleys my Beloved is to me.

"The strange islands."

Strange islands are girt by the sea; they are also, because of the sea, distant and unknown to the commerce of men. They produce things very different from those with which we are conversant, in strange ways, and with qualities hitherto unknown, so as to surprise those who behold them, and fill them with wonder. Thus, then, by reason of the great and marvelous wonders, and the strange things that come to our knowledge, far beyond the common notions of men, which the soul beholds in God, it calls Him the strange islands. We say of a man that he is strange for one of two reasons: either because he withdraws himself from the society of his fellows, or because he is singular or distinguished in his life and conduct. For these two reasons together God is called strange by the soul. He is not only all that is strange in undiscovered islands, but His ways, judgments, and works are also strange, new, and marvelous to men.

It is nothing wonderful that God should be strange to men who have never seen Him, seeing that He is also strange to the holy angels and the souls who see Him; for they neither can nor shall ever see Him perfectly. Yes, even to the day of the last judgment they will see in Him so much that is new in His deep judgments, in His acts of mercy and justice, as to excite their wonder more and more. Thus God is the strange islands not to men only, but to the angels also; only to Himself is He neither strange nor new.

"The roaring torrents."

Torrents have three properties. 1. They overflow all that is in their course. 2. They fill all hollows. 3. They overpower all other sounds by their own. And hence the soul, feeling most sweetly that these three properties belong to God, says, "My Beloved is the roaring torrents."

As to the first property of which the soul is conscious, it feels itself to be so overwhelmed with the torrent of the Spirit of God, and so violently overpowered by it, that all the waters in the world seem to it to have surrounded it, and to have drowned all its former actions and passions. Though all this is violent, yet there is nothing painful in it, for these rivers are rivers of peace, as it is written, God, speaking through Isaiah, saying, "I will decline upon her, as it were, a flood of peace, and as a torrent overflowing glory." That is, "I will bring upon the soul, as it were, a river of peace, and a torrent overflowing with glory." Thus this divine overflowing, like roaring torrents, fills the soul with peace and glory. The second property the soul feels is that this divine water is now filling the vessels of its humility and the emptiness of its desires, as it is written: "He has exalted the humble, and filled the hungry with good." The third property of which the soul is now conscious in the roaring torrents of the Beloved is a spiritual sound and voice overpowering all other sounds and voices in the world. The explanation of this will take a little time.

This voice, or this murmuring sound of the waters, is an overflowing so abundant as to fill the soul with good, and a power so mighty seizing upon it as to seem not only the sound of many waters, but a most loud roaring of thunder. But the voice is a spiritual voice, unattended by material sounds or the pain and torment of them, but rather with majesty, power, might, delight, and glory: it is, as it were, a voice, an infinite interior sound which endows the soul with power and might. The Apostles heard in spirit this voice when the Holy Spirit descended upon them in the sound "as of a mighty wind," as we read in the Acts of the Apostles. In order to manifest this spiritual voice, interiorly spoken, the sound was heard exteriorly, as of a rushing wind, by all those who were in Jerusalem. This exterior manifestation reveals what the Apostles interiorly received, namely, fullness of power and might.

So also when our Lord Jesus prayed to the Father because of His distress and the rage of His enemies, He heard an interior voice from heaven, comforting Him in His Sacred Humanity. The sound, solemn and grave, was heard exteriorly by the Jews, some of whom said that it thundered: others said, "An angel has spoken to Him." The voice outwardly heard was the outward sign and expression of that strength and power which Christ then inwardly received in His human nature. We are not to suppose that the soul does not hear in spirit the spiritual voice because it is also outwardly heard. The spiritual voice is the effect on the soul of the audible voice, as material sounds strike the ear, and impress the meaning of it on the mind. This we learn from David when he said, "He will give to His voice the voice of strength;" this strength is the interior voice. He will give to His voice — that is, the outward voice, audibly heard — the voice of strength which is felt within. God is an infinite voice, and communicating Himself thus to the soul produces the effect of an infinite voice.

This voice was heard by St. John, saying in the Revelation, "I heard a voice from heaven as the voice of many waters, and as the voice of great thunder." And, lest it should be supposed that a voice so strong was distressing and harsh, he adds immediately, "The voice which I heard was as the voice of harpers harping on their harps." Ezekiel says that this sound as of many waters was "as it were the sound of the High God," profoundly and sweetly communicated in it. This voice is infinite, because, as I have said, it is God Who communicates Himself, speaking in the soul; but He adapts Himself to each soul, uttering the voice of strength according to its capacity, in majesty and joy. And so the bride sings in the Canticle: "Let Your voice sound in my ears, for Your voice is sweet."

"The whisper of the amorous gales."

Two things are to be considered here — gales and whisper. The amorous gales are the virtues and graces of the Beloved, which, because of its union with the Bridegroom, play around the soul, and, most lovingly sent forth, touch it in their own substance. The whisper of the gales is a most sublime and sweet knowledge of God and of His attributes, which overflows into the understanding from the contact of the attributes of God with the substance of the soul. This is the highest delight of which the soul is capable in this life.

That we may understand this the better, we must keep in mind that as in a gale two things are observable — the touch of it, and the whisper or sound — so there are two things observable also in the communications of the Bridegroom — the sense of delight, and the understanding of it. As the touch of the air is felt in the sense of touch, and the whisper of it heard in the ear, so also the contact of the perfections of the Beloved is felt and enjoyed in the touch of the soul — that is, in the substance thereof, through the instrumentality of the will; and the knowledge of the attributes of God felt in the hearing of the soul — that is, in the understanding.

The gale is said to blow amorously when it strikes deliciously, satisfying his desire who is longing for the refreshing which it ministers; for it then revives and soothes the sense of touch, and while the sense of touch is thus soothed, that of hearing also rejoices and delights in the sound and whisper of the gale more than the touch in the contact of the air, because the sense of hearing is more spiritual, or, to speak with greater correctness, is more nearly connected with the spiritual than is that of touch, and the delight thereof is more spiritual than is that of the touch. So also, inasmuch as this touch of God greatly satisfies and comforts the substance of the soul, sweetly fulfilling its longing to be received into union; this union, or touch, is called amorous gales, because, as I said before, the perfections of the Beloved are by it communicated to the soul lovingly and sweetly, and through it the whisper of knowledge to the understanding. It is called whisper, because, as the whisper of the air penetrates subtly into the organ of hearing, so this most subtle and delicate knowledge enters with marvelous sweetness and delight into the inmost substance of the soul, which is the highest of all delights.

The reason is that substantial knowledge is now communicated intelligibly, and stripped of all accidents and images, to the understanding, which philosophers call passive or passible, because inactive without any natural efforts of its own during this communication. This is the highest delight of the soul, because it is in the understanding, which is the seat of fruition, as theologians teach, and fruition is the vision of God. Some theologians think, inasmuch as this whisper signifies the substantial intelligence, that our father Elijah had a vision of God in the delicate whisper of the air, which he heard on the mount at the mouth of the cave. The Holy Scripture calls it "the whistling of a gentle wind," because knowledge is begotten in the understanding by the subtle and delicate communication of the Spirit. The soul calls it here the whisper of the amorous gales, because it flows into the understanding from the loving communication of the perfections of the Beloved. This is why it is called the whisper of the amorous gales.

This divine whisper which enters in by the ear of the soul is not only substantial knowledge, but a manifestation also of the truths of the Divinity, and a revelation of the secret mysteries thereof. For in general, in the Holy Scriptures, every communication of God said to enter in by the ear is a manifestation of pure truths to the understanding, or a revelation of the secrets of God. These are revelations on purely spiritual visions, and are communicated directly to the soul without the intervention of the senses, and thus, what God communicates through the spiritual ear is most profound and most certain. When St. Paul would express the greatness of the revelations made to him, he did not say, "I saw or I perceived secret words," but "I heard secret words which it is not granted to man to utter." It is thought that St. Paul also saw God, as our father Elijah, in the whisper of a gentle air. For as "faith comes by hearing" — so the Apostle teaches — that is, by the hearing of the material ear, so also that which the faith teaches, the intelligible truth, comes by spiritual hearing.

The prophet Job, speaking to God, when He revealed Himself to him, teaches the same doctrine, saying, "With the hearing of the ear I have heard You, but now my eye sees You." It is clear, from this, that to hear with the ear of the soul is to see with the eye of the passive understanding. He does not say, "I heard with the hearing of my ears," but "with the hearing of my ear"; nor, "with the seeing of my eyes," but "with the eye of my understanding"; the hearing of the soul is, therefore, the vision of the understanding.

Still, we are not to think that what the soul perceives, though pure truth, can be the perfect and clear fruition of Heaven. For though it is free from accidents, as I said before, it is dim and not clear, because it is contemplation, which in this life, as St. Dionysius says, "is a ray of darkness," and thus we may say that it is a ray and an image of fruition, because it is in the understanding, which is the seat of fruition. This substantial truth, called here a whisper, is the "eyes desired" which the Beloved showed to the bride, who, unable to bear the vision, cried, "Turn them away, O my Beloved."

There is a passage in the book of Job which greatly confirms what I have said of rapture and betrothal, and, because I consider it to be much to the purpose, I will give it here, though it may delay us a little, and explain those portions of it which belong to my subject. The explanation shall be short, and when I shall have made it, I shall go on to explain the other stanza. The passage is as follows: "To me there was spoken a secret word," said Eliphaz the Themanite, "and, as it were, my ear by stealth received the veins of its whisper. In the horror of a vision by night, when deep sleep is wont to hold men, fear held me and trembling, and all my bones were made sore afraid: and when the spirit passed before me the hair of my flesh stood upright. There stood one whose countenance I knew not, an image before my eyes, and I heard the voice, as it were, of a gentle wind."

This passage contains almost all I said about rapture in the thirteenth stanza, where the bride says: "Turn them away, O my Beloved." The "word spoken in secret" to Eliphaz is that secret communication which by reason of its greatness the soul was not able to endure, and, therefore, cried out: "Turn them away, O my Beloved." Eliphaz says that his "ear as it were by stealth received the veins of its whisper." By that is meant the pure substance which the understanding receives, for the "veins" here denote the interior substance. The whisper is that communication and touch of the virtues whereby the said substance is communicated to the understanding. It is called a whisper because of its great gentleness. And the soul calls it the amorous gales because it is lovingly communicated. It is said to be received as it were by stealth, for as that which is stolen is alienated, so this secret is alien to man, speaking in the order of nature, because that which he received does not appertain to him naturally, and thus it was not lawful for him to receive it; neither was it lawful for St. Paul to repeat what he heard. For this reason the prophet says twice, "My secret to myself, my secret to myself."

When Eliphaz speaks of the horror of the vision by night, and of the fear and trembling that seized upon him, he refers to the awe and dread that comes upon the soul naturally in rapture, because in its natural strength it is unable, as I said before, to endure the communication of the Spirit of God. The prophet gives us to understand that, as when sleep is about to fall upon men, a certain vision which they call a nightmare is wont to oppress and terrify them in the interval between sleeping and waking, which is the moment of the approach of sleep, so in the spiritual passage between the sleep of natural ignorance and the waking of the supernatural understanding, which is the beginning of an ecstasy or rapture, the spiritual vision then revealed makes the soul fear and tremble.

"All my bones were affrighted"; that is, were shaken and disturbed. By this he meant a certain dislocation of the bones which takes place when the soul falls into an ecstasy. This is clearly expressed by Daniel when he saw the angel, saying, "O my lord, at the sight of you my joints are loosed." "When the spirit passed before me" — that is, "When my spirit was made to transcend the ways and limitations of nature in ecstasies and raptures" — "the hair of my flesh stood upright"; that is, "my body was chilled, and the flesh contracted, like that of a dead man."

"There stood One" — that is God, Who reveals Himself after this manner — "Whose countenance knew not": in these communications or visions, however high they may be, the soul neither knows nor beholds the face and being of God. "An image before my eyes"; that is, the knowledge of the secret words was most deep, as it were the image and face of God; but still this is not the essential vision of God. "I heard the voice, as it were, of a gentle wind"; this is the whisper of the amorous gales — that is, of the Beloved of the soul.

But it is not to be supposed that these visits of God are always attended by such terrors and distress of nature: that happens to them only who are entering the state of illumination and perfection, and in this kind of communication; for in others they come with great sweetness.

Stanza XV

The tranquil night
At the approaches of the dawn,
The silent music,
The murmuring solitude,
The supper which revives, and enkindles love.

"The Tranquil Night."

In this spiritual sleep in the bosom of the Beloved the soul is in possession and fruition of all the calm, repose, and quiet of a peaceful night, and receives at the same time in God a certain dim, unfathomable divine intelligence. This is the reason why it says that the Beloved is to it the tranquil night.

"At the approaches of the dawn."

This tranquil night is not like a night of darkness, but rather like the night when the sunrise is drawing nigh. This tranquillity and repose in God is not all darkness to the soul, as the dark night is, but rather tranquillity and repose in the divine light and in a new knowledge of God, whereby the mind, most sweetly tranquil, is raised to a divine light.

This divine light is here very appropriately called the approaches of the dawn, that is, the twilight; for as the twilight of the morn disperses the darkness of the night and reveals the light of day, so the mind, tranquil and reposing in God, is raised up from the darkness of natural knowledge to the morning light of the supernatural knowledge of God; not clear, indeed, as I have said, but dim, like the night at the approaches of the dawn. For as it is then neither wholly night nor wholly day, but, as they say, twilight, so this solitude and divine repose is neither perfectly illumined by the divine light nor yet perfectly alien from it.

In this tranquillity the understanding is lifted up in a strange way above its natural comprehension to the divine light: it is like a man who, after a profound sleep, opens his eyes to unexpected light. This knowledge is referred to by David when he says, "I have watched, and am become as the lonely sparrow on the housetop"; that is, "I opened the eyes of my understanding and was raised up above all natural comprehension, lonely, without them, on the housetop, lifted up above all earthly considerations." He says that he was "become as the lonely sparrow," because in this kind of contemplation, the spirit has the properties of the sparrow. These are five in number:

i. It frequents in general high places; and the spirit, in this state, rises to the highest contemplation.

ii. It is ever turning its face in the direction of the wind, and the spirit turns its affections thither whence comes the spirit of love, which is God.

iii. It is in general solitary, abstaining from the companionship of others, and flying away when any approach it: so the spirit, in contemplation, is far away from all worldly thoughts, lonely in its avoidance of them; neither does it consent to anything except to this solitude in God.

iv. It sings most sweetly, and so also does the spirit at this time sing to God; for the praises which it offers up proceed from the sweetest love, most pleasing to itself, and most precious in the sight of God.

v. It is of no definite color; so also is the perfect spirit, which in this ecstasy is not only without any tinge of sensual affection or self-love, but also without any particular consideration of the things of heaven or earth; neither can it give any account whatever of them, because it has entered into the abyss of the knowledge of God.

"The silent music."

In this silence and tranquillity of the night, and in this knowledge of the divine light, the soul discerns a marvelous arrangement and disposition of God's wisdom in the diversities of His creatures and operations. All these, and each one of them, have a certain correspondence with God, whereby each, by a voice peculiar to itself, proclaims what there is in itself of God, so as to form a concert of sublimest melody, transcending all the harmonies of the world. This is the silent music, because it is knowledge tranquil and calm, without audible voice; and thus the sweetness of music and the repose of silence are enjoyed in it. The soul says that the Beloved is silent music, because this harmony of spiritual music is in Him understood and felt. He is not this only, He is also —

"The murmuring solitude."

This is almost the same as the silent music. For though the music is inaudible to the senses and the natural powers, it is a solitude most full of sound to the spiritual powers. These powers being in solitude, emptied of all forms and natural apprehensions, may well receive in spirit, like a resounding voice, the spiritual impression of the majesty of God in Himself and in His creatures; as it happened to St. John, who heard in spirit as it were "the voice of harpers harping on their harps." St. John heard this in spirit: it was not material harps that he heard, but a certain knowledge that he had of the praises of the blessed, which every one of them, each in his own degree of glory, is continually singing before God. It is as it were music. For as every one of the saints had the gifts of God in a different way, so every one of them sings His praises in a different way, and yet all harmonize in one concert of love, as in music.

In the same way, in this tranquil contemplation, the soul beholds all creatures, not only the highest, but the lowest also, each one according to the gift of God to it, sending forth the voice of its witness to what God is. It beholds each one magnifying Him in its own way, and possessing Him according to its particular capacity; and thus all these voices together unite in one strain in praise of God's greatness, wisdom, and marvelous knowledge. This is the meaning of those words of the Holy Spirit in the Book of Wisdom: "The Spirit of our Lord has replenished the whole world, and that which contains all things has the knowledge of the voice." "The voice" is the murmuring solitude, which the soul is said to know, namely, the witness which all things bear to God. Inasmuch as the soul hears this music only in solitude and in estrangement from all outward things, it calls it silent music and murmuring solitude. These are the Beloved.

"The supper which revives, and enkindles love."

Lovers find recreation, satisfaction, and love in feasts. And because the Beloved in this sweet communication produces these three effects in the soul, He is here said to be the supper that revives, and enkindles love. In Holy Scripture supper signifies the divine vision, for as supper is the conclusion of the day's labors, and the beginning of the night's repose, so the soul in this tranquil knowledge is made to feel that its trials are over, the possession of good begun, and its love of God increased. Hence, then, the Beloved is to the soul the supper that revives, in being the end of its trials, and that enkindles love, in being the beginning of the fruition of all good.

That we may see more clearly how the Bridegroom is the supper of the soul, we must refer to those words of the Beloved in the Revelation: "Behold, I stand at the door and knock. If any man shall hear My voice, and open to Me the gate, I will enter into him, and will sup with him, and he with Me." It is evident from these words that He brings the supper with Him, which is nothing else but His own sweetness and delights, wherein He rejoices Himself, and which He, uniting Himself to the soul, communicates to it, making it a partaker of His joy: for this is the meaning of "I will sup with him, and he with Me." These words describe the effect of the divine union of the soul with God, wherein it shares the very goods of God Himself, Who communicates them graciously and abundantly to it. Thus the Beloved is Himself the supper which revives, and enkindles love, refreshing the soul with His abundance, and enkindling its love in His graciousness.

But before I proceed to explain the stanzas which follow, I must observe that, in the state of betrothal, wherein the soul enjoys this tranquillity, and wherein it receives all that it can receive in this life, we are not to suppose its tranquillity to be perfect, but that the higher part of it is tranquil; for the sensual part, except in the state of spiritual marriage, never loses all its imperfect habits, and its powers are never wholly subdued, as I shall show hereafter. What the soul receives now is all that it can receive in the state of betrothal, for in that of the marriage the blessings are greater. Though the bride-soul has great joy in these visits of the Beloved in the state of betrothal, still it has to suffer from His absence, to endure trouble and afflictions in the lower part, and at the hands of the devil. But all this ceases in the state of spiritual marriage.

Note

The bride now in possession of the virtues in their perfection, whereby she is ordinarily rejoicing in peace when the Beloved visits her, is now and then in the fruition of the fragrance and sweetness of those virtues in the highest degree, because the Beloved touches them within her, just as the sweetness and beauty of the lilies and other flowers when in their bloom are perceived when we handle them. For in many of these visits the soul discerns within itself all its virtues which God has given it; He shedding light upon them. The soul now, with marvelous joy and sweetness of love, binds them together and presents them to the Beloved as a nosegay of beautiful flowers, and the Beloved in accepting them — for He truly accepts them then — accepts thereby a great service. All this takes place within the soul, feeling that the Beloved is within it as on His own couch, for the soul presents itself with the virtues which is the greatest service it can render Him, and thus this is one of the greatest joys which in its interior conversation with God the soul is wont to receive in presents of this kind made to the Beloved.

The devil, beholding this prosperity of the soul, and in his great malice envying all the good he sees in it, now uses all his power, and has recourse to all his devices, in order to thwart it, if possible, even in the slightest degree. He thinks it of more consequence to keep back the soul, even for an instant, from this abundance, bliss, and delight, than to make others fall into many and mortal sins. Other souls have little or nothing to lose, while this soul has much, having gained many and great treasures; for the loss of one grain of refined gold is greater than the loss of many of the baser metals.

The devil here has recourse to the sensual appetites, though now they can give him generally but little or no help because they are mortified, and because he cannot turn them to any great account in distracting the imagination. Sometimes he stirs up many movements in the sensitive part of the soul, and causes other vexations, spiritual as well as sensual, from which the soul is unable to deliver itself until our Lord shall send His angel, as it is written, "The angel of the Lord shall put in himself about them that fear Him, and shall deliver them;" and so establish peace, both in the spiritual and sensitive parts of the soul. With a view to show forth this truth, and to ask this favor, the soul, apprehensive by experience of the craft which the devil makes use of to thwart this good, addressing itself to the angels, whose function it is to succor it at this time by putting the evil spirits to flight, speaks as in the following stanza:

Stanza XVI

Catch us the foxes,
For our vineyard has flourished;
While of roses
We make a nosegay,
And let no one appear on the hill.

The soul, anxious that this interior delight of love, which is the flowers of the vineyard, should not be interrupted, either by envious and malicious devils, or the raging desires of sensuality, or the various comings and goings of the imagination, or any other consciousness or presence of created things, calls upon the angels to seize and hinder all these from interrupting its practice of interior love, in the joy and sweetness of which the soul and the Son of God communicate and delight in the virtues and graces.

"Catch us the foxes, for our vineyard has flourished."

The vineyard is the plantation in this holy soul of all the virtues which minister to it the wine of sweet taste. The vineyard of the soul is then flourishing when it is united in will to the Bridegroom, and delights itself in Him in all the virtues. Sometimes, as I have just said, the memory and the fancy are assailed by various forms and imaginings, and diverse motions and desires trouble the sensual part. The great variety and diversity of these made David say, when he felt the inconvenience and the trouble of them as he was drinking of the sweet wine of the spirit, thirsting greatly after God: "For You my soul has thirsted, for You my flesh, O how many ways."

Here the soul calls the whole troop of desires and stirrings of sense, foxes, because of the great resemblance between them at this time. As foxes pretend to be asleep that they may pounce upon their prey when it comes in their way, so all the desires and powers of sense in the soul are asleep until the flowers of virtue grow, flourish, and bloom. Then the desires and powers of sense awake to resist the Spirit and domineer. "The flesh lusts against the spirit," and as the inclination of it is towards the sensual desires, it is disgusted as soon as it tastes of the Spirit, and herein the desires prove extremely troublesome to spiritual sweetness.

"Catch us the foxes."

The evil spirits now molest the soul in two ways. They vehemently excite the desires, and employ them with other imaginations to assail the peaceful and flourishing kingdom of the soul. Then — and this is much worse — when they do not succeed in stirring up the desires, they assail the soul with bodily pains and noises in order to distract it. And, what is still more serious, they fight with spiritual horror and dread, and sometimes with fearful torments, which, at this time, if God permits them, they can most effectually bring about, for inasmuch as the soul is now spiritually detached, so as to perform its spiritual exercises, the devil being himself a spirit presents himself before it with great ease.

At other times the evil spirit assails the soul with other horrors, before it begins to have the fruition of the sweet flowers, when God is beginning to draw it forth out of the house of sense that it may enter on the interior exercises in the garden of the Bridegroom, for he knows well that once entered into this state of recollection it is there so protected that, notwithstanding all he can do, he cannot hurt it. Very often, too, when the devil goes forth to meet the soul, the soul becomes quickly recollected in the secret depths of its interior, where it finds great sweetness and protection; then those terrors of Satan are so far off that they not only produce no fear, but are even the occasion of peace and joy. The bride, in the Canticle, speaks of these terrors, saying, "My soul troubled me for the chariots of Aminadab." Aminadab is the evil spirit, and his chariots are his assaults upon the soul, which he makes with great violence, noise, and confusion.

The bride also says what the soul says here, namely: "Catch us the little foxes that destroy the vineyards; for our vineyard has flourished." She does not say, "Catch me" but "Catch us," because she is speaking of herself and the Beloved; for they are one, and enjoy the flourishing of the vineyard together.

The reason why the vineyard is said to be flourishing and not bearing fruit is this: the soul in this life has the fruition of virtues, however perfect they may be, only in their flower, because the fruit of them is reserved for the life to come.

"While of roses we make a nosegay."

Now, at this time, while the soul is rejoicing in the flourishing of the vineyard, and delighting itself in the bosom of the Beloved, all its virtues are perfect, exhibiting themselves to the soul, and sending forth great sweetness and delight. The soul feels them to be in itself and in God so as to seem to be one vineyard most flourishing and pleasing belonging to both, wherein they feed and delight. Then the soul binds all its virtues together, makes acts of love in each of them separately, and in all together, and then offers them all to the Beloved, with great tenderness of love and sweetness, and in this the Beloved helps it, for without His help and favor it cannot make this union and oblation of virtue to the Beloved. Hence it says, "We make a nosegay" — that is "the Beloved and myself."

This union of the virtues is called a nosegay; for as a nosegay is cone-like in form, and a cone is strong, containing and embracing many pieces firmly joined together, so this cone-like nosegay of the virtues which the soul makes for the Beloved is the uniform perfection of the soul which firmly and solidly contains and embraces many perfections, great virtues, and rich endowments; for all the perfections and virtues of the soul unite together to form but one. And while this perfection is being accomplished, and when accomplished, offered to the Beloved on the part of the soul, it becomes necessary to catch the foxes that they may not hinder this mutual interior communication. The soul prays not only that this nosegay may be carefully made, but also adds, "And let no one appear on the hill."

This divine interior exercise requires solitude and detachment from all things, whether in the lower part of the soul, which is that of sense, or in the higher, which is the rational. These two divisions comprise all the faculties and senses of man, and are here called the hill; because all our natural notions and desires being in them, as quarry on a hill, the devil lies in wait among these notions and desires, in order that he may injure the soul.

"And let no one appear on the hill."

That is, let no representation or image of any object whatever, appertaining to any of these faculties or senses, appear in the presence of the soul and the Bridegroom: in other words, let the spiritual powers of the soul, memory, understanding, and will, be divested of all notions, particular inclinations, or considerations whatsoever; and let all the senses and faculties of the body, interior as well as exterior, the imagination, the fancy, the sight and hearing, and the rest, be divested of all occasions of distractions, of all forms, images, and representations, and of all other natural operations.

The soul speaks in this way because it is necessary for the perfect fruition of this communication of God, that all the senses and powers, both interior and exterior, should be disencumbered and emptied of their proper objects and operations; for the more active they are, the greater will be the hindrance which they will occasion. The soul having attained to a certain interior union of love, the spiritual faculties of it are no longer active, and still less those of the body; for now that the union of love is actually wrought in love, the faculties of the soul cease from their exertions, because now that the goal is reached all employment of means is at an end. What the soul at this time has to do is to wait lovingly upon God, and this waiting is love in a continuation of unitive love. Let no one, therefore, appear on the hill, but the will only waiting on the Beloved in the offering up of self and of all the virtues in the way described.

Note

For the clearer understanding of the following stanza, we must keep in mind that the absence of the Beloved, from which the soul suffers in the state of spiritual betrothal, is an exceedingly great affliction, and at times greater than all other trials whatever. The reason is this: the love of the soul for God is now so vehement and deep that the pain of His absence is vehement and deep also. This pain is increased also by the annoyance which comes from intercourse with creatures, which is very great; for the soul, under the pressure of its quickened desire of union with God, finds all other conversation most painful and difficult to endure. It is like a stone in its flight to the place whither it is rapidly tending; every obstacle it meets with occasions a violent shock. And as the soul has tasted of the sweetness of the Beloved's visits, which are more desirable than gold and all that is beautiful, it therefore dreads even a momentary absence, and addresses itself as follows to aridities, and to the Spirit of the Bridegroom: —

Stanza XVII

O killing north wind, cease!
Come, south wind, that awakens love!
Blow through my garden,
And let its odors flow,
And the Beloved shall feed among the flowers.

Beside the causes mentioned in the foregoing stanza, spiritual dryness also hinders the fruition of this interior sweetness of which I have been speaking, and afraid of it the soul had recourse to two expedients, to which it refers in the present stanza. The first is to shut the door against it by unceasing prayer and devotion. The second, to invoke the Holy Spirit; it is He Who drives away dryness from the soul, maintains and increases its love of the Bridegroom — that He may establish in it the practice of virtue, and all this to the end that the Son of God, its Bridegroom, may rejoice and delight in it more and more, for its only aim is to please the Beloved.

"Killing north wind, cease."

The north wind is exceedingly cold; it dries up and parches flowers and plants, and at the least, when it blows, causes them to draw in and shrink. So, dryness of spirit and the sensible absence of the Beloved, because they produce the same effect on the soul, exhausting the sweetness and fragrance of virtue, are here called the killing north wind; for all the virtues and affective devotions of the soul are then dead. Hence the soul addresses itself to it, saying, "Killing north wind, cease." These words mean that the soul applies itself to spiritual exercise, in order to escape aridity. But the communications of God are now so interior that by no exertion of its faculties can the soul attain to them if the Spirit of the Bridegroom do not cause these movements of love. The soul, therefore, addresses Him, saying:

"Come, south wind, that awakens love."

The south wind is another wind commonly called the south-west wind. It is soft, and brings rain; it makes the grass and plants grow, flowers to blossom and scatter their perfume abroad; in short, it is the very opposite in its effects of the north wind. By it is meant here the Holy Spirit, Who awakens love; for when this divine Breath breathes on the soul, it so inflames and refreshes it, so quickens the will, and stirs up the desires, which were before low and asleep as to the love of God, that we may well say of it that it quickens the love between Him and the soul. The prayer of the soul to the Holy Spirit is thus expressed, "Blow through my garden."

This garden is the soul itself. For as the soul said of itself before, that it was a flourishing vineyard, because the flowers of virtue which are in it give forth the wine of sweetness, so here it says of itself that it is a garden, because the flowers of perfection and the virtues are planted in it, flourish, and grow.

Observe, too, that the expression is "blow through my garden," not blow in it. There is a great difference between God's breathing into the soul and through it. To breathe into the soul is to infuse into it graces, gifts, and virtues; to breathe through it is, on the part of God, to touch and move its virtues and perfections now possessed, renewing them and stirring them in such a way that they send forth their marvelous fragrance and sweetness. Thus aromatic spices, when shaken or touched, give forth the abundant odors which are not otherwise so distinctly perceived. The soul is not always in the conscious fruition of its acquired and infused virtues, because, in this life, they are like flowers in seed, or in bud, or like aromatic spices covered over, the perfume of which is not perceived till they are exposed and shaken.

But God sometimes is so merciful to the bride-soul, as — the Holy Spirit breathing meanwhile through the flourishing garden — to open these buds of virtue and expose the aromatic herbs of the soul's gifts, perfections, and riches, to manifest to it its interior treasures and to reveal to it all its beauty. It is then marvelous to behold, and sweet to feel, the abundance of the gifts now revealed in the soul, and the beauty of the flowers of virtue now flourishing in it. No language can describe the fragrance which every one of them diffuses, each according to its kind. This state of the soul is referred to in the words, "Let its odors flow."

So abundant are these odors at times, that the soul seems enveloped in delight and bathed in inestimable bliss. Not only is it conscious itself of them, but they even overflow it, so that those who know how to discern these things can perceive them. The soul in this state seems to them as a delectable garden, full of the joys and riches of God. This is observable in holy souls, not only when the flowers open, but almost always; for they have a certain air of grandeur and dignity which inspires the beholders with awe and reverence, because of the supernatural effects of their close and familiar conversation with God. We have an illustration of this in the life of Moses, the sight of whose face the people could not bear, by reason of the glory that rested upon it — the effect of his speaking to God face to face.

While the Holy Spirit is breathing through the garden — this is His visitation of the soul — the Bridegroom Son of God communicates Himself to it in a profound way, enamored of it. It is for this that He sends the Holy Spirit before Him — as He sent the Apostles — to make ready the chamber of the soul His bride, comforting it with delight, setting its garden in order, opening its flowers, revealing its gifts, and adorning it with the tapestry of graces. The bride-soul longs for this with all its might, and therefore bids the north wind not to blow, and invokes the south wind to blow through the garden, because she gains much here at once.

The bride now gains the fruition of all her virtues in their sweetest exercise. She gains the fruition of her Beloved in them, because it is through them that He converses with her in most intimate love, and grants her favors greater than any of the past. She gains, too, that her Beloved delights more in her because of the actual exercise of virtue, which is what pleases her most, namely, that her Beloved should be pleased with her. She gains also the permanent continuance of the sweet fragrance which remains in the soul while the Bridegroom is present, and the bride entertains Him with the sweetness of her virtues, as it is written: "While the King was at His repose," that is, in the soul, "my spikenard sent forth its odor." The spikenard is the soul, which from the flowers of its virtues sends forth sweet odors to the Beloved, Who dwells within it in the union of love.

It is therefore very much to be desired that every soul should pray the Holy Spirit to blow through its garden, that the divine odors of God may flow. And as this is so necessary, so blissful and profitable to the soul, the bride desires it, and prays for it, in the words of the Canticle, saying, "Arise, north wind, and come, south wind; blow through my garden, and let the aromatic spices thereof flow." The soul prays for this, not because of the delight and bliss consequent upon it, but because of the delight it ministers to the Beloved, and because it prepares the way and announces the presence of the Son of God, Who comes to rejoice in it. Hence the soul adds:

"And my Beloved shall feed among the flowers."

The delight which the Son of God finds now in the soul is described as pasture. This word expresses most forcibly the truth, because pasture not only gladdens, but also sustains. Thus the Son of God delights in the soul, in the delights thereof, and is sustained in them — that is, He abides within it as in a place which pleases Him exceedingly, because the place itself really delights in Him. This, I believe, is the meaning of those words recorded in the proverbs of Solomon: "My delights were to be with the children of men;" that is, when they delight to be with Me, Who am the Son of God.

Observe, here, that it is not said that the Beloved shall feed on the flowers, but that He shall feed among the flowers. For, as the communications of the Beloved are in the soul itself, through the adornment of the virtues, it follows that what He feeds on is the soul which He transformed into Himself, now that it is prepared and adorned with these flowers of virtues, graces, and perfections, which are the things whereby, and among which, He feeds. These, by the power of the Holy Spirit, are sending forth in the soul the odors of sweetness to the Son of God, that He may feed there the more in the love thereof; for this is the love of the Bridegroom, to be united to the soul amid the fragrance of the flowers.

The bride in the Canticle has observed this, for she had experience of it, saying: "My Beloved is gone down into His garden, to the bed of aromatic spices, to feed in the gardens, and to gather lilies. I to my Beloved, and my Beloved to me, Who feeds among the lilies." That is, "Who feeds and delights in my soul, which is His garden, among the lilies of my virtues, perfections, and graces."

Note

In the state of spiritual espousals the soul contemplating its great riches and excellence, but unable to enter into the possession and fruition of them as it desires, because it is still in the flesh, often suffers exceedingly, and then more particularly when its knowledge of them becomes more profound. It then sees itself in the body, like a prince in prison, subject to all misery, whose authority is disregarded, whose territories and wealth are confiscated, and who of his former substance receives but a miserable dole. How greatly he suffers anyone may see, especially when his household is no longer obedient, and his slaves and servants, forgetting all respect, plunder him of the scanty provisions of his table. Thus is it with the soul in the body, for when God mercifully admits it to a foretaste of the good things which He has prepared for it, the wicked servants of desire in the sensual part, now a slave of disorderly motions, now other rebellious movements, rise up against it in order to rob it of its good.

The soul feels itself as if it were in the land of enemies, tyrannized over by the stranger, like the dead among the dead. Its feelings are those which the prophet Baruch gave vent to when he described the misery of Jacob's captivity: "How happens it, O Israel, that you are in your enemies' land? You have grown old in a strange country, you are defiled with the dead: you are counted with them that go down into hell." This misery of the soul, in the captivity of the body, is thus spoken of by Jeremiah, saying: "Is Israel a bondman or a home-born slave? Why then is he become a prey? The lions have roared upon him, and have made a noise." The lions are the desires and the rebellious motions of the tyrant king of sensuality. In order to express the trouble which this tyrant occasions, and the desire of the soul to see this kingdom of sensuality with all its hosts destroyed, or wholly subject to the spirit, the soul lifting up its eyes to the Bridegroom, as to one who can effect it, speaks against those rebellious motions in the words of the next stanza.

Stanza XVIII

O nymphs of Judea!
While amid the flowers and the rose-trees
The amber sends forth its perfume,
Tarry in the suburbs,
And touch not our thresholds.

It is the bride that speaks; for seeing herself, as to the higher part of the soul, adorned with the rich endowments of her Beloved, and seeing Him delighting in her, she desires to preserve herself in security, and in the continued fruition of them. Seeing also that hindrances will arise, as in fact they do, from the sensual part of the soul, which will disturb so great a good, she bids the operations and motions of the soul's lower nature to cease, in the senses and faculties of it, and sensuality not to overstep its boundaries to trouble and disquiet the higher and spiritual portion of the soul: not to hinder even for a moment the sweetness she enjoys. The motions of the lower part, and their powers, if they show themselves during the enjoyment of the spirit, are so much more troublesome and disturbing, the more active they are.

"O nymphs of Judea."

The lower, that is the sensual part of the soul, is called Judea. It is called Judea because it is weak, and carnal, and blind, like the Jewish people. All the imaginations, fancies, motions, and inclinations of the lower part of the soul are called nymphs, for as nymphs with their beauty and attractions entice men to love them, so the operations and motions of sensuality softly and earnestly strive to entice the will from the rational part, in order to withdraw it from that which is interior, and to fix it on that which is exterior, to which they are prone themselves. They also strive to influence the understanding to join with them in their low views, and to bring down reason to the level of sense by the attractions of the latter. The soul, therefore, says in effect: "O sensual operations and motions."

"While amid the flowers and the rose-trees."

The flowers, as I have said, are the virtues of the soul, and the rose-trees are its powers, memory, understanding, and will, which produce and nurture the flowers of divine conceptions, acts of love and the virtues, while the amber sends forth its perfume in the virtues and powers of the soul.

"The amber sends forth its perfume."

The amber is the divine spirit of the Bridegroom Who dwells in the soul. To send forth the perfume among the flowers and the rose-trees, is to diffuse and communicate Himself most sweetly in the powers and virtues of the soul, thereby filling it with the perfume of divine sweetness. Meanwhile, then, when the Divine Spirit is filling my soul with spiritual sweetness,

"Tarry in the suburbs."

In the suburbs of Judea, which is the inferior or sensual part of the soul. The suburbs are the interior senses, namely, memory, fancy, and imagination, where forms and images of things collect, by the help of which sensuality stirs up concupiscence and desires. These forms are the nymphs, and while they are quiet and tranquil the desires are also asleep. They enter into the suburbs of the interior senses by the gates of the outward senses, of sight, hearing, smell, etc. We can thus give the name of suburbs to all the powers and interior or exterior senses of the sensual part of the soul, because they are outside the walls of the city.

That part of the soul which may be called the city is that which is most interior, the rational part, which is capable of conversation with God, the operations of which are contrary to those of sensuality. But there is a natural intercourse between those who dwell in the suburbs of the sensual part — that is, the nymphs — and those who dwell in the higher part, which is the city itself; and, therefore, what takes place in the lower part is ordinarily felt in the higher, and consequently compels attention to itself and disturbs the spiritual operation which is conversant with God. Hence the soul bids the nymphs tarry in the suburbs — that is, to remain at rest in the exterior and interior senses of the sensual part,

"And touch not our thresholds."

Let not even your first movements touch the higher part, for the first movements of the soul are the entrance and thresholds of it. When the first movements have passed into the reason, they have crossed the threshold, but when they remain as first movements only they are then said merely to touch the threshold, or to cry at the gate, which is the case when reason and sense contend over an unreasonable act. The soul here not only bids these not to touch it, but also charges all considerations whatever which do not minister to its repose and the good it enjoys to keep far away.

Note

The soul in this state is become so great an enemy of the lower part, and its operations, that it would have God communicate nothing to it when He communicates with the higher. If He will communicate with the lower, it must be in a slight degree, or the soul, because of its natural weakness, will be unable to endure it without fainting, and consequently the spirit cannot rejoice in peace, because it is then troubled. "For," as the wise man says, "the body that is corrupted burdens the soul." And as the soul longs for the highest and noblest conversation with God, which is impossible in the company of the sensual part, it begs of God to deal with it without the intervention of the senses. That sublime vision of St. Paul in the third heaven, wherein, he says, he saw God, but yet knew not whether he was in the body or out of the body, must have been, be it what it may, independent of the body: for if the body had any share in it, he must have known it, and the vision could not have been what it was, seeing that he "heard secret words which it is not lawful for a man to speak." The soul, therefore, knowing well that graces so great cannot be received in a vessel so mean, and longing to receive them out of the body, — or at least without it, addresses the Bridegroom in the words that follow:

Stanza XIX

Hide yourself, O my Beloved!
Turn Your face to the mountains,
Do not speak,
But regard the companions
Of her who is traveling amidst strange islands.

Here the bride presents four petitions to the Bridegroom. She prays that He would be pleased to converse with her most interiorly in the secret chamber of the soul. The second, that He would invest and inform her faculties with the glory and excellence of His Divinity. The third, that He would converse with her so profoundly as to surpass all knowledge and expression, and in such a way that the exterior and sensual part may not perceive it. The fourth, that He would love the many virtues and graces which He has implanted in her, adorned with which she is ascending upwards to God in the highest knowledge of the Divinity, and in transports of love most strange and singular, surpassing those of ordinary experience.

"Hide Yourself, O my Beloved!"

"O my Bridegroom, most beloved, hide Yourself in the inmost depths of my soul, communicating Yourself to it in secret, and manifesting Your hidden wonders which no mortal eyes may see.

"Turn Your face to the mountains."

The face of God is His divinity. The mountains are the powers of the soul, memory, understanding, and will. Thus the meaning of these words is: Enlighten my understanding with Your Divinity, and give it the divine intelligence, fill my will with divine love, and my memory with divine possession of glory. The bride here prays for all that may be prayed for; for she is not content with that knowledge of God once granted to Moses — the knowledge of Him by His works — for she prays to see the face of God, which is the essential communication of His Divinity to the soul, without any intervening medium, by a certain knowledge thereof in the Divinity. This is something beyond sense, and divested of accidents, inasmuch as it is the contact of pure substances — that is, of the soul and the Divinity.

"Do not speak."

That is, do not speak as before, when Your conversation with me was known to the outward senses, for it was once such as to be comprehended by them; it was not so profound but they could fathom it. Now let Your conversation with me be so deep and so substantial, and so interior, as to be above the reach of the senses; for the substance of the spirit is incommunicable to sense, and the communication made through the senses, especially in this life, cannot be purely spiritual, because the senses are not capable of it. The soul, therefore, longing for that substantial and essential communication of God, of which sense cannot be cognizant, prays the Bridegroom not to speak: that is to say, let the deep secret of the spiritual union be such as to escape the notice of the senses, like the secret which St. Paul heard, and which it is not lawful for a man to speak.

"But regard the companions."

The regard of God is love and grace. The companions here are the many virtues of the soul, its gifts, perfections, and other spiritual graces with which God has endowed it; pledges, tokens, and presents of its betrothal. Thus the meaning of the words seems to be this: "Turn Your face to the interior of my soul, O my Beloved; be enamored of the treasures which You have laid up there, so that, enamored of them, You may hide Yourself among them and there dwell; for in truth, though they are Yours, they are mine also, because You have given them."

"Of her who travels amidst strange islands."

That is, "Of my soul tending towards You through strange knowledge of You, by strange ways" — strange to sense and to the ordinary perceptions of nature. It is as if the bride said, by way of constraining Him to yield: "Seeing that my soul is tending towards You through knowledge which is spiritual, strange, unknown to sense, also communicate Yourself to it so interiorly and so profoundly that the senses may not observe it."

Note

IN order to the attainment of a state of perfection so high as this of the spiritual marriage, the soul that aims at it must not only be purified and cleansed from all the imperfections, rebellions, and imperfect habits of the inferior part, which is now — the old man being put away — subject and obedient to the higher, but it must also have great courage and most exalted love for so strong and close an embrace of God. For in this state the soul not only attains to exceeding pureness and beauty, but also acquires a terrible strength by reason of that strict and close bond which in this union binds it to God. The soul, therefore, in order to reach this state must have purity, strength, and adequate love. The Holy Spirit, the author of this spiritual union, desirous that the soul should attain thus far in order to merit it, addresses Himself to the Father and the Son, saying: "Our sister is little, and has no breasts. What shall we do to our sister in the day when she is to be spoken to? If she is a wall, let us build upon it bulwarks of silver; if she is a door, let us join it together with boards of cedar."

The "bulwarks of silver" are the strong heroic virtues comprised in the faith, which is signified by silver, and these heroic virtues are those of the spiritual marriage, which are built upon the soul, signified by the wall, relying on the strength of which, the peaceful Bridegroom reposes undisturbed by any infirmities. The "boards of cedar" are the affections and accessories of this deep love which is signified by the cedar-tree, and this is the love of the spiritual marriage. In order "to join it together," that is, to adorn the bride, it is necessary she should be the door for the Bridegroom to enter through, keeping the door of the will open in a perfect and true consent of love, which is the consent of the betrothal given previous to the spiritual marriage. The breasts of the bride are also this perfect love which she must have in order to appear in the presence of Christ her Bridegroom for the perfection of such a state.

It is written in the Canticle that the bride in her longing for this presence immediately replied, saying: "I am a wall: and my breasts are as a tower" — that is, "My soul is strong, and my love most deep" — that He may not fail her on that ground. The bride, too, had expressed as much in the preceding stanzas, out of the fullness of her longing for the perfect union and transformation, and particularly in the last, wherein she set before the Bridegroom all the virtues, graces, and good dispositions with which she was adorned by Him, and that with the object of making Him the prisoner of her love.

Now the Bridegroom, to bring this matter to a close, replies in the two stanzas that follow, which describe Him as perfectly purifying the soul, strengthening and disposing it, both as to its sensual and spiritual part, for this state, and charging all resistance and rebellion, both of the flesh and of the devil, to cease, saying:

Stanzas XX, XXI: the Bridegroom

Light-winged birds,
Lions, fawns, bounding does,
Mountains, valleys, strands,
Waters, winds, heat,
And the terrors that keep watch by night;
By the soft lyres
And the siren strains, I adjure you,
Let your fury cease,
And touch not the wall,
That the bride may sleep in greater security.

Here the Son of God, the Bridegroom, leads the bride into the enjoyment of peace and tranquillity in the conformity of her lower to her higher nature, purging away all her imperfections, subjecting the natural powers of the soul to reason, and mortifying all her desires, as it is expressed in these two stanzas, the meaning of which is as follows. In the first place the Bridegroom adjures and commands all vain distractions of the fancy and imagination from henceforth to cease, and controls the irascible and concupiscible faculties which were previously the sources of so much affliction. He brings, so far as it is possible in this life, the three powers of memory, understanding, and will to the perfection of their objects, and then adjures and commands the four passions of the soul, joy, hope, grief, and fear, to be still, and bids them from henceforth be moderate and calm.

All these passions and faculties are comprehended under the expressions employed in the first stanza, the operations of which, full of trouble, the Bridegroom subdues by that great sweetness, joy, and courage which the bride enjoys in the spiritual surrender of Himself to her which God makes at this time; under the influence of which, because God transforms the soul effectually in Himself, all the faculties, desires, and movements of the soul lose their natural imperfection and become divine.

"Light-winged birds."

These are the distractions of the imagination, light and rapid in their flight from one subject to another. When the will is tranquilly enjoying the sweet conversation of the Beloved, these distractions produce weariness, and in their swift flight quench its joy. The Bridegroom adjures them by the soft lyres. That is, now that the sweetness of the soul is so abundant and so continuous that they cannot interfere with it, as they did before when it had not reached this state, He adjures them, and bids them cease from their disquieting violence. The same explanation is to be given of the rest of the stanza.

"Lions, fawns, bounding does."

By the lions is meant the raging violence of the irascible faculty, which in its acts is bold and daring as a lion. The "fawns and bounding does" are the concupiscible faculty — that is, the power of desire, the qualities of which are two, timidity and rashness. Timidity betrays itself when things do not turn out according to our wishes, for then the mind retires within itself discouraged, and in this respect the soul resembles the fawns. For as fawns have the concupiscible faculty stronger than many other animals, so are they more retiring and more timid. Rashness betrays itself when we have our own way, for the mind is then neither retiring nor timid, but desires boldly, and gratifies all its inclinations. This quality of rashness is compared to the does, who so eagerly seek what they desire that they not only run, but even leap after it; hence they are described as bounding does.

Thus the Bridegroom, in adjuring the lions, restrains the violence and controls the fury of rage; in adjuring the fawns, He strengthens the concupiscible faculty against timidity and irresolution; and in adjuring the does He satisfies and subdues the desires which were restless before, leaping, like deer, from one object to another, to satisfy that concupiscence which is now satisfied by the soft lyres, the sweetness of which it enjoys, and by the siren strains, in the delight of which it revels.

But the Bridegroom does not adjure anger and concupiscence themselves, because these passions never cease from the soul — but their vexations and disorderly acts, signified by the "lions, fawns, and bounding does," for it is necessary that these disorderly acts should cease in this state.

"Mountains, valleys, strands."

These are the vicious and disorderly actions of the three faculties of the soul — memory, understanding, and will. These actions are disorderly and vicious when they are in extremes, or, if not in extreme, tending to one extreme or other. Thus the mountains signify those actions which are vicious in excess, mountains being high; the valleys, being low, signify those which are vicious in the extreme of defect. Strands, which are neither high nor low, but, inasmuch as they are not perfectly level, tend to one extreme or other, signify those acts of the three powers of the soul which depart slightly in either direction from the true mean and equality of justice. These actions, though not disorderly in the extreme, as they would be if they amounted to mortal sin, are nevertheless disorderly in part, tending towards venial sin or imperfection, however slight that tendency may be, in the understanding, memory, and will. He adjures also all these actions which depart from the true mean, and bids them cease before the soft lyres and the siren strains, which so effectually charm the powers of the soul as to occupy them completely in their true and proper functions, so that they avoid not only all extremes, but also the slightest tendency to them.

"Waters, winds, heat, and the terrors that keep watch by night."

These are the affections of the four passions, grief, hope, joy, and fear. The waters are the affections of grief which afflict the soul, for they rush into it like water. "Save me, O God," says the Psalmist, "for the waters have come in even to my soul." The winds are the affections of hope, for they rush forth like wind, desiring what which is not present but hoped for, as the Psalmist says: "I opened my mouth and drew breath: because I longed for Your commandments." That is, "I opened the mouth of my hope, and drew in the wind of desire, because I hoped and longed for Your commandments." Heat is the affections of joy which, like fire, inflame the heart, as it is written: "My heart waxed hot within me; and in my meditation a fire shall burn"; that is, "while I meditate I shall have joy."

The "terrors that keep watch by night" are the affections of fear, which in spiritual persons who have not attained to the state of spiritual marriage are usually exceedingly strong. They come sometimes from God when He is going to bestow certain great graces upon souls, as I said before; He is wont then to fill the mind with dread, to make the flesh tremble and the senses numb, because nature is not made strong and perfect and prepared for these graces. They come also at times from the evil spirit, who, out of envy and malignity, when he sees a soul sweetly recollected in God, labors to disturb its tranquillity by exciting horror and dread, in order to destroy so great a blessing, and sometimes utters his threats, as it were in the interior of the soul. But when he finds that he cannot penetrate within the soul, because it is so recollected, and so united with God, he strives at least in the province of sense to produce exterior distractions and inconstancy, sensible pains and horrors, if perchance he may in this way disturb the soul in the bridal chamber.

These are called terrors of the night, because they are the work of evil spirits, and because Satan labors, by the help thereof, to involve the soul in darkness, and to obscure the divine light wherein it rejoices. These terrors are called watchers, because they awaken the soul and rouse it from its sweet interior slumber, and also because Satan, their author, is ever on the watch to produce them. These terrors strike the soul of persons who are already spiritual, passively, and come either from God or the evil spirit. I do not refer to temporal or natural terrors, because spiritual men are not subject to these, as they are to those of which I am speaking.

The Beloved adjures the affections of these four passions, compels them to cease and to be at rest, because He supplies the bride now with force, and courage, and satisfaction, by the soft lyres of His sweetness and the siren strains of His delight, so that not only they shall not domineer over the soul, but shall not occasion it any distaste whatever. Such is the grandeur and stability of the soul in this state, that, although formerly the waters of grief overwhelmed it, because of its own or other men's sins — which is what spiritual persons most feel — the consideration of them now excites neither pain nor annoyance; even the sensible feeling of compassion no longer exists, though the effects of it continue in perfection. The weaknesses of its virtues are no longer in the soul, for they are now constant, strong, and perfect. As the angels perfectly appreciate all sorrowful things without the sense of pain, and perform acts of mercy without the sentiment of pity, so the soul in this transformation of love. God, however, dispenses sometimes, on certain occasions, with the soul in this matter, allowing it to feel and suffer, that it may become more fervent in love, and grow in merit, or for some other reasons, as He dispensed with His Virgin Mother, St. Paul, and others. This, however, is not the ordinary condition of this state.

Neither do the desires of hope afflict the soul now, because, satisfied in its union with God, so far as it is possible in this life, it has nothing of this world to hope for, and nothing spiritual to desire, seeing that it feels itself to be full of the riches of God, though it may grow in charity, and thus, whether living or dying, it is conformed to the will of God, saying with the sense and spirit, "Your will be done," free from the violence of inclination and desires; and accordingly even its longing for the beatific vision is without pain.

The affections of joy, also, which were wont to move the soul with more or less vehemence, are not sensibly diminished; neither does their abundance occasion any surprise. The joy of the soul is now so abundant that it is like the sea, which is not diminished by the rivers that flow out of it, nor increased by those that empty themselves into it; for the soul is now that fountain of which our Lord said that it is "springing up into life everlasting."

I have said that the soul receives nothing new or unusual in this state of transformation; it seems to lose all accidental joy, which is not withheld even from the glorified. That is, accidental joys and sweetness are indeed no strangers to this soul; indeed, those which it ordinarily has cannot be numbered; yet, for all this, as to the substantial communication of the spirit, there is no increase of joy, for that which may occur anew the soul possesses already, and thus what the soul has already within itself is greater than anything that comes anew. Hence, then, whenever any subject of joy and gladness, whether exterior or spiritually interior, presents itself to the soul, the soul immediately starts rejoicing in the riches it possesses already within itself, and the joy it has in them is far greater than any which these new accessions minister, because, in a certain sense, God is become its possession, Who, though He delights in all things, yet in nothing so much as in Himself, seeing that He has all good eminently in Himself. Thus all accessions of joy serve to remind the soul that its real joy is in its interior possessions, rather than in these accidental causes, because, as I have said, the former are greater than the latter.

It is very natural for the soul, even when a particular matter gives it pleasure, that, possessing another of greater worth and gladness, it should remember it at once and take its pleasure in it. The accidental character of these spiritual accessions, and the new impressions they make on the soul, may be said to be as nothing in comparison with that substantial source which it has within itself: for the soul which has attained to the perfect transformation, and is full-grown, grows no more in this state by means of these spiritual accessions, as those souls do who have not yet advanced so far. It is a marvelous thing that the soul, while it receives no accessions of delight, should still seem to do so and also to have been in possession of them. The reason is that it is always tasting them anew, because they are ever renewed; and thus it seems to be continually the recipient of new accessions, while it has no need of them whatever.

But if we speak of that light of glory which in this, the soul's embrace, God sometimes produces within it, and which is a certain spiritual communion wherein He causes it to behold and enjoy at the same time the abyss of delight and riches which He has laid up within it, there is no language to express any degree of it. As the sun when it shines upon the sea illumines its great depths, and reveals the pearls, and gold, and precious stones therein, so the divine sun of the Bridegroom, turning towards the bride, reveals in a way the riches of her soul, so that even the angels behold her with amazement and say: "Who is she that comes forth as the morning rising, fair as the moon, bright as the sun, terrible as the army of a camp set in array." This illumination adds nothing to the grandeur of the soul, notwithstanding its greatness, because it merely reveals that which the soul already possessed in order that it might rejoice in it.

Finally, the terrors that keep watch by night do not come close to her, because of her pureness, courage, and confident trust in God; the evil spirits cannot shroud her in darkness, nor alarm her with terrors, nor disturb her with their violent assaults. Thus nothing can approach her, nothing can molest her, for she has escaped from all created things and entered into God, to the fruition of perfect peace, sweetness, and delight, so far as that is possible in this life. It is to this state that the words of Solomon are applicable: "A secure mind is as it were a continual feast." As in a feast we have the savor of all meat, and the sweetness of all music, so in this feast, which the bride keeps in the bosom of her Beloved, the soul rejoices in all delight, and has the taste of all sweetness. All that I have said, and all that may be said, on this subject, will always fall short of that which passes in the soul which has attained to this blessed state. For when it shall have attained to the peace of God, "which," in the words of the Apostle, "surpasses all understanding," no description of its state is possible.

"By the soft lyres and the siren strains I adjure you."

The soft lyres are the sweetness which the Bridegroom communicates to the soul in this state, and by which He makes all its troubles to cease. As the music of lyres fills the soul with sweetness and delight, carries it rapturously out of itself, so that it forgets all its weariness and grief, so in like manner this sweetness so absorbs the soul that nothing painful can reach it. The Bridegroom says, in substance: "By that sweetness which I give you, let all your bitterness cease." The siren strains are the ordinary joys of the soul. These are called siren strains because, as it is said, the music of the sirens is so sweet and delicious that he who hears it is so rapt and so carried out of himself that he forgets everything. In the same way the soul is so absorbed in, and refreshed by, the delight of this union that it becomes, as it were, charmed against all the vexations and troubles that may assail it; it is to these the next words of the stanza refer:

"Let your fury cease."

This is the troubles and anxieties which flow from unruly acts and affections. As anger is a certain violence which disturbs peace, overlapping its bounds, so also all these affections in their motions transgress the bounds of the peace and tranquillity of the soul, disturbing it whenever they touch it. Hence the Bridegroom says:

"And touch not the wall."

The wall is the territory of peace and the fortress of virtue and perfections, which are the defenses and protection of the soul. The soul is the garden wherein the Beloved feeds among the flowers, defended and guarded for Him alone. Hence it is called in the Canticle "a garden enclosed." The Bridegroom bids all disorderly emotions not to touch the territory and wall of His garden.

"That the bride may sleep in greater security." That is, that she is delighting herself with more sweetness in the tranquillity and sweetness she has in the Beloved. That is to say, that now no door is shut against the soul, and that it is in its power to abandon itself whenever it wills to this sweet sleep of love, according to the words of the Bridegroom in the Canticle, "I adjure you, O daughters of Jerusalem, by the roes and the harts of the fields, that you raise not up nor make the beloved to awake till herself will."

Note

The Bridegroom was so anxious to rescue His bride from the power of the flesh and the devil and to set her free, that, having done so, He rejoices over her like the good shepherd who, having found the sheep that was lost, laid it upon his shoulders rejoicing; like the woman who, having found the money she had lost, after lighting a candle and sweeping the house, called "together her friends and neighbors, saying, Rejoice with me." So this loving Shepherd and Bridegroom of souls shows a marvelous joy and delight when He beholds a soul gained to perfection lying on His shoulders, and by His hands held fast in the longed-for embrace and union. He is not alone in His joy, for He makes the angels and the souls of the blessed partakers of His glory, saying, as in the Canticle, "Go forth, you daughters of Zion, and see king Solomon in the diadem with which his mother crowned him in the day of his betrothal, and in the day of the joy of his heart." He calls the soul His crown, His bride, and the joy of His heart: He carries it in His arms, and as a bridegroom leads it into His bridal chamber, as we shall see in the following stanza:

Stanza XXII

The bride has entered
The pleasant and desirable garden,
And there reposes to her heart's content;
Her neck reclining
On the sweet arms of the Beloved.

The bride having done what she could in order that the foxes may be caught, the north wind cease, the nymphs, hindrances to the desired joy of the state of spiritual marriage, forgo their troublesome importunities, and having also invoked and obtained the favorable wind of the Holy Spirit, which is the right disposition and means for the perfection of this state, it remains for me now to speak of it in the stanza in which the Bridegroom calls the soul His bride, and speaks of two things: 1. He says that the soul, having gone forth victoriously, has entered the delectable state of spiritual marriage, which they had both so earnestly desired. 2. He enumerates the properties of that state, into the fruition of which the soul has entered, namely, perfect repose, and the resting of the neck on the arms of the Beloved.

"The bride has entered."

For the better understanding of the arrangement of these stanzas, and of the way by which the soul advances till it reaches the state of spiritual marriage, which is the very highest, and of which, by the grace of God, I am now about to treat, we must keep in mind that the soul, before it enters it, must be tried in tribulations, in sharp mortifications, and in meditation on spiritual things. This is the subject of this canticle till we come to the fifth stanza, beginning with the words, "A thousand graces diffusing." Then the soul enters on the contemplative life, passing through those ways and straits of love which are described in the course of the canticle, till we come to the thirteenth, beginning with "Turn them away, O my Beloved!" This is the moment of the spiritual betrothal; and then the soul advances by the unitive way, the recipient of many and very great communications, jewels and gifts from the Bridegroom as to one betrothed, and grows into perfect love, as appears from the stanzas which follow that beginning with "Turn them away, O my Beloved!" (the moment of betrothal), to the present, beginning with the words:

"The bride has entered."

The spiritual marriage of the soul and the Son of God now remains to be accomplished. This is, beyond all comparison, a far higher state than that of betrothal, because it is a complete transformation into the Beloved; whereby they surrender each to the other the entire possession of themselves in the perfect union of love, wherein the soul becomes divine, and, by participation, God, so far as it is in this life. I believe that no soul ever attains to this state without being confirmed in grace, for the faithfulness of both is confirmed; that of God being confirmed in the soul. Hence it follows, that this is the very highest state possible in this life. As by natural marriage there are "two in one flesh," so also in the spiritual marriage between God and the soul there are two natures in one spirit and love, as we learn from St. Paul, who made use of the same metaphor, saying, "He that cleaves to the Lord is one spirit." So, when the light of a star, or of a candle, is united to that of the sun, the light is not that of the star, nor of the candle, but of the sun itself, which absorbs all other light in its own.

It is of this state that the Bridegroom is now speaking, saying, "The bride has entered"; that is, out of all temporal and natural things, out of all spiritual affections, ways, and methods, having left on one side, and forgotten, all temptations, trials, sorrows, anxieties and cares, transformed in this embrace.

"The pleasant and desirable garden."

That is, the soul is transformed in God, Who is here called the pleasant garden because of the delicious and sweet repose which the soul finds in Him. But the soul does not enter the garden of perfect transformation, the glory and the joy of the spiritual marriage, without passing first through the spiritual betrothal, the mutual faithful love of the betrothed. When the soul has lived for some time as the bride of the Son, in perfect and sweet love, God calls it and leads it into His flourishing garden for the celebration of the spiritual marriage. Then the two natures are so united, what is divine is so communicated to what is human, that, without undergoing any essential change, each seems to be God — yet not perfectly so in this life, though still in a manner which can neither be described nor conceived.

We learn this truth very clearly from the Bridegroom Himself in the Canticle, where He invites the soul, now His bride, to enter this state, saying: "I am come into my garden, O My sister, My bride: I have gathered My myrrh with My aromatic spices." He calls the soul His sister, His bride, for it is such in love by that surrender which it has made of itself before He had called it to the state of spiritual marriage, when, as He says, He gathered His myrrh with His aromatic spices; that is, the fruits of flowers now ripe and made ready for the soul, which are the delights and grandeurs communicated to it by Himself in this state, that is Himself, and for which He is the pleasant and desirable garden.

The whole aim and desire of the soul and of God, in all this, is the accomplishment and perfection of this state, and the soul is therefore never weary till it reaches it; because it finds there a much greater abundance and fullness in God, a more secure and lasting peace, and a sweetness incomparably more perfect than in the spiritual betrothal, seeing that it reposes between the arms of such a Bridegroom, Whose spiritual embraces are so real that it, through them, lives the life of God. Now is fulfilled what St. Paul referred to when he said: "I live; now not I, but Christ lives in me." And now that the soul lives a life so happy and so glorious as this life of God, consider what a sweet life it must be — a life where God sees nothing displeasing, and where the soul finds nothing irksome, but rather the glory and delight of God in the very substance of itself, now transformed in Him.

"And there reposes to her heart's content; her neck reclining on the sweet arms of the Beloved."

The neck is the soul's strength, by means of which its union with the Beloved is wrought; for the soul could not endure so close an embrace if it had not been very strong. And as the soul has labored in this strength, practiced virtue, overcome vice, it is fitting that it should rest there from its labors, "her neck reclining on the sweet arms of the Beloved."

This reclining of the neck on the arms of God is the union of the soul's strength, or, rather, of the soul's weakness, with the strength of God, in Whom our weakness, resting and transformed, puts on the strength of God Himself. The state of spiritual matrimony is therefore most fitly designated by the reclining of the neck on the sweet arms of the Beloved; seeing that God is the strength and sweetness of the soul, Who guards and defends it from all evil and gives it to taste of all good.

Hence the bride in the Canticle, longing for this state, says to the Bridegroom: "Who shall give to me You my brother, sucking the breast of my mother, that I may find You without, and kiss You, and now no man may despise me." By addressing Him as her Brother she shows the equality between them in the betrothal of love, before she entered the state of spiritual marriage. "Sucking the breast of my mother" signifies the drying up of the passions and desires, which are the breasts and milk of our mother Eve in our flesh, which are a bar to this state. The "finding Him without" is to find Him in detachment from all things and from self when the bride is in solitude, spiritually detached, which takes place when all the desires are quenched. "And kiss You" — that is, be united with the Bridegroom, alone with Him alone.

This is the union of the nature of the soul, in solitude, cleansed from all impurity, natural, temporal, and spiritual, with the Bridegroom alone, with His nature, by love only — that of love which is the only love of the spiritual marriage, wherein the soul, as it were, kisses God when none despises it nor makes it afraid. For in this state the soul is no longer molested, either by the devil, or the flesh, or the world, or the desires, seeing that here is fulfilled what is written in the Canticle: "Winter is now past, the rain is over and gone. The flowers have appeared in our land."

Note

When the soul has been raised to the high state of spiritual marriage, the Bridegroom reveals to it, as His faithful consort, His own marvelous secrets most readily and most frequently, for he who truly and sincerely loves hides nothing from the object of his affections. The chief matter of His communications are the sweet mysteries of His incarnation, the ways and means of redemption, which is one of the highest works of God, and so is to the soul one of the sweetest. Though He communicates many other mysteries, He speaks in the following stanza of His incarnation only, as being the chief; and thus addresses the soul in the words that follow:

Stanza XXIII

Beneath the apple-tree
There were you betrothed;
There I gave you My hand,
And you were redeemed
Where your mother was corrupted.

The Bridegroom tells the soul of the wondrous way of its redemption and betrothal to Himself, by referring to the way in which the human race was lost. As it was by the forbidden tree of paradise that our nature was corrupted in Adam and lost, so it was by the tree of the Cross that it was redeemed and restored. The Bridegroom there stretched forth the hand of His grace and mercy, in His death and passion, "making void the law of commandments" which original sin had placed between us and God.

"Beneath the apple-tree,"

That is the wood of the Cross, where the Son of God was conqueror, and where He betrothed our human nature to Himself, and, by consequence, every soul of man. There, on the Cross, He gave us grace and pledges of His love.

"There were you betrothed, there I gave you My hand."

"Help and grace, lifting you up out of your base and miserable condition to be My companion and My bride."

"And you were redeemed where your mother was corrupted."

"Your mother, human nature, was corrupted in her first parents beneath the forbidden tree, and you were redeemed beneath the tree of the Cross. If your mother at that tree sentenced you to die, I from the Cross have given you life." It is thus that God reveals the order and dispositions of His wisdom: eliciting good from evil, and turning that which has its origin in evil to be an instrument of greater good. This stanza is nearly word for word what the Bridegroom in the Canticle says to the bride: "Under the apple-tree I raised you up: there your mother was corrupted; there she was deflowered that bare you."

It is not the betrothal of the Cross that I am speaking of now — that takes place, once for all, when God gives the first grace to the soul in baptism. I am speaking of the betrothal in the way of perfection, which is a progressive work. And though both are but one, yet there is a difference between them. The latter is effected in the way of the soul, and therefore slowly: the former in the way of God, and therefore at once.

The betrothal of which I am speaking is that of which God speaks Himself by the mouth of the prophet Ezekiel, saying: "You were cast out upon the face of the earth in the abjection of your soul, in the day that you were born. And passing by you, I saw that you were trodden under foot in your blood; and I said to you when you were in your blood: Live: I said to you, I say; in your blood live. Multiplied as the spring of the field have I made you; and you were multiplied and made great, and you went in, and came to the ornaments of woman; your breasts swelled and your hair budded: and you were naked and full of confusion. And I passed by you and saw you, and behold, your time, the time of lovers; and I spread My garment over you and covered your ignominy. And I swore to you; and I entered a covenant with you, says the Lord God; and you were made Mine. And I washed you with water, and made clean your blood from off you: and I anointed you with oil. And I clothed you with diverse colors, and shod you with hyacinth, and I girded you with silk and clothed you with fine garments. And I adorned you with ornaments, and put bracelets on your hands, and a chain about your neck. And I put a jewel upon your forehead and rings in your ears, and a crown of beauty on your head. And you were adorned with gold and silver, and were clothed with silk, and embroidered work, and many colors: you ate fine flour, and honey, and oil, and were made beautiful exceedingly, and advanced to be a queen. And your name went forth among the nations because of your beauty." These are the words of Ezekiel, and this is the state of that soul of which I am now speaking.

Note

After the mutual surrender to each other of the bride and the Beloved, comes their bed. Thereon the bride enters into the joy of Christ. Thus the present stanza refers to the bed, which is pure and chaste, and divine, and in which the bride is pure, divine, and chaste. The bed is nothing else but the Bridegroom Himself, the Word, the Son of God, in Whom, through the union of love, the bride reposes. This bed is said to be of flowers, for the Bridegroom is not only that, but, as He says Himself of Himself, "I am the flower of the field and the lily of the valleys." The soul reposes not only on the bed of flowers, but on that very flower which is the Son of God, and which contains in itself the divine odor, fragrance, grace, and beauty, as He says by the mouth of David, "With me is the beauty of the field." The soul, therefore, in the stanza that follows, celebrates the properties and beauties of its bed, saying:

Stanza XXIV: The Bride

Our bed is of flowers
By dens of lions encompassed,
Hung with purple,
Made in peace,
And crowned with a thousand shields of gold.

In two of the foregoing stanzas — the fourteenth and the fifteenth — the bride-soul celebrated the grace and magnificence of the Beloved, the Son of God. In the present stanza she not only pursues the same subject, but also sings of her high and blessed state, and her own security in it. She then proceeds to the virtues and rich gifts with which she is endowed and adorned in the chamber of the Bridegroom; for she says that she is in union with Him, and is strong in virtue. Next she says that she has attained to the perfection of love, and then that she enjoys perfect spiritual peace, endowed and adorned with gifts and graces, so far as it is possible to have them in this life. The first subject of the stanza is the joy which the bride feels in her union with the Beloved, saying:

"Our bed is of flowers."

I have already said that this bed of the soul is the bosom and love of the Son of God, full of flowers to the soul, which now united to God and reposing in Him, as His bride, shares the bosom and love of the Beloved. That is, the soul is admitted to a knowledge of the wisdom, secrets and graces, and gifts and powers of God, whereby it is made so beautiful, so rich, so abounding in delights that it seems to be lying on a bed of many-colored divine flowers, the touch of which makes it thrill with joy, and the odors of which refresh it.

This union of love with God is therefore most appropriately called a bed of flowers, and is so called by the bride in the Canticle, saying to the Beloved, "Our bed is of flowers." She speaks of it as ours, because the virtues and the love, one and the same, of the Beloved are common to both together, and the delight of both is one and the same; as it is written: "My delights were to be with the children of men." The bed is said to be of flowers, because in this state the virtues in the soul are perfect and heroic, which they could not be until the bed had flowered in perfect union with God.

"By dens of lions encompassed."

The dens of lions signify the virtues with which the soul is endowed in the state of union. The dens of lions are safe retreats, protected from all other animals, who, afraid of the boldness and strength of the lion within, are afraid not only to enter, but even to appear in sight. So each virtue of the soul in the state of perfection is like a den of lions where Christ dwells united to the soul in that virtue; and in every one of them as a strong lion. The soul also, united to Him in those very virtues, is as a strong lion, because it then partakes of the perfections of God.

Thus, then, the perfect soul is so defended, so strong in virtue, and in all virtues together, reposing on the flowery bed of its union with God, that the evil spirits are not only afraid to assault it, but even dare not appear before it; such is their dread of it, when they behold it strong, courageous, and mature in its perfect virtues, on the bed of the Beloved. The evil spirits fear a soul transformed in the union of love as much as they fear the Beloved Himself, and they dare not look upon it, for Satan is in great fear of that soul which has attained to perfection.

The soul's bed is encompassed by virtues: they are the dens, for when the soul has advanced to perfection, its virtues are so perfectly ordered, and so joined together and bound up one with another, each supporting the other, that no part of it is weak or exposed. Not only is Satan unable to penetrate within it, but even worldly things, whether great or little, fail to disturb or annoy it, or even move it; for being now free from all molestation of natural affections, and a stranger to the worry of temporal anxieties, it enjoys in security and peace the participation of God.

This is that for which the bride longed when she said, "Who shall give to me You my brother, sucking the breast of my mother, that I may find You without, and kiss You, and now no man may despise me?" The "kiss" here is the union of which I am speaking, whereby the soul, by love, becomes in a sense the equal of God. This is the object it desires when it says, "Who shall give to me You my brother?" That means and makes equality. "Sucking the breast of my mother"; that is, destroying all the imperfections and desires of nature which the soul inherits from its mother Eve. "That I may find You without"; that is, "be united to You alone, away from all things, in detachment of the will and desires." "And now no man may despise me"; that is, the world, the devil, and the flesh will not venture to assail it, for being free and purified, and also united to God, none of these can molest it. Thus, then, the soul is in the enjoyment now of habitual sweetness and tranquillity that never fail it.

But beside this habitual contentment and peace, the flowers of the virtues of this garden so open in the soul and diffuse their odors that it seems to be, and is, full of the delights of God. I say that the flowers open; because the soul, though filled with the virtues in perfection, is not always in the actual fruition of them, notwithstanding its habitual perception of the peace and tranquillity which they produce. We may say of these virtues that they are in this life like the budding flowers of a garden; they offer a most beautiful sight — opening under the inspirations of the Holy Spirit — and diffuse most marvelous perfumes in great variety.

Sometimes the soul will discern in itself the mountain flowers — the fullness, grandeur, and beauty of God — intermingled with the lilies of the valley — rest, refreshment, and defense; and again among them, the fragrant roses of the strange islands — the strange knowledge of God; and further, the perfume of the water lilies of the roaring torrents — the majesty of God filling the whole soul. And amid all this, it enjoys the exquisite fragrance of the jasmine, and the whisper of the amorous gales, the fruition of which is granted to the soul in the estate of union, and in the same way all the other virtues and graces, the calm knowledge, silent music, murmuring solitude, and the sweet supper of love; and the joy of all this is such as to make the soul say in truth, "Our bed is of flowers, by dens of lions encompassed." Blessed is that soul which in this life deserves at times to enjoy the perfume of these divine flowers.

"Hung with purple."

Purple in Holy Scripture means charity, and kings are clad in it, and for that reason the soul says that the bed of flowers is hung with purple, because all the virtues, riches, and blessings of it are sustained, flourish, and are delighted only in charity and love of the King of heaven; without that love the soul can never delight in the bed nor in the flowers thereof. All these virtues, therefore, are, in the soul, as if hung on the love of God, as on that which preserves them, and they are, as it were, bathed in love; for all and each of them always make the soul love God, and on all occasions and in all actions they advance in love to a greater love of God. That is what is meant by saying that the bed is hung with purple.

This is well expressed in the sacred Canticle: "King Solomon has made himself a litter of the wood of Lebanon; the pillars thereof he has made of silver, the seat of gold, the going up of purple; the midst he has paved with charity." The virtues and graces which God lays in the bed of the soul are signified by the wood of Lebanon: the pillars of silver and the seat of gold are love, for, as I have said, the virtues are maintained by love, and by the love of God and of the soul are ordered and bring forth fruit.

"Made in peace."

This is the fourth excellence of the bed, and depends on the third, of which I have just spoken. For the third is perfect charity, the property of which is, as the Apostle says, to cast out fear; hence the perfect peace of the soul, which is the fourth excellence of this bed. For the clearer understanding of this we must keep in mind that each virtue is in itself peaceful, gentle, and strong, and consequently, in the soul which possesses them, produces peace, gentleness, and fortitude. Now, as the bed is of flowers, formed of the flowers of virtues, all of which are peaceful, gentle, and strong, it follows that the bed is wrought in peace, and the soul is peaceful, gentle, and strong, which are three qualities unassailable by the world, Satan, and the flesh. The virtues preserve the soul in such peace and security that it seems to be wholly built up in peace. The fifth property of this bed of flowers is explained in the following words:

"Crowned with a thousand shields of gold."

The shields are the virtues and graces of the soul, which, though they are also the flowers, serve for its crown, and the reward of the toil by which they are acquired. They serve also, like strong shields, as a protection against the vices, which it overcame by the practice of them; and the bridal bed of flowers therefore — that is, the virtues, the crown and defense — is adorned with them by way of reward, and protected by them as with a shield. The shields are said to be of gold, to show the great worth of the virtues. The bride in the Canticle sets forth the same truth, saying: "Three score valiant men of the most valiant of Israel surround the little bed of Solomon, all holding swords; . . . every man's sword upon his thigh, because of fears in the night."

Thus in this stanza the bride speaks of a thousand shields, to express the variety of the virtues, gifts, and graces with which God has endowed the soul in this state. The Bridegroom also in the Canticle has employed the same expression, in order to show forth the innumerable virtues of the soul, saying: "Your neck is as the tower of David, which is built with bulwarks; a thousand shields hang upon it, all the armor of valiant men."

Note

The soul, having attained to perfection, is not satisfied with magnifying and extolling the excellencies of the Beloved, the Son of God, nor with recounting and giving thanks for the graces received at His hands and the joy into which it has entered, but recounts also the graces conferred on other souls. In this blessed union of love the soul is able to contemplate both its own and others' graces; thus praising Him and giving Him thanks for the many graces bestowed upon others, it sings as in the following stanza:

Stanza XXV

In Your footsteps
The young ones run Your way;
At the touch of the fire
And by the spiced wine,
The divine balsam flows.

Here the bride gives thanks to her Beloved for three graces which devout souls receive from Him, by which they encourage and excite themselves to love God more and more. She speaks of them here because she has had experience of them herself in this state of union. The first is sweetness, which He gives them, and which is so efficacious that it makes them run swiftly on the road of perfection.

The second is a visit of love, by which they are suddenly set on fire with love. The third is overflowing charity infused into them, with which He so inebriates them that they are as much excited by it as by the visit of love, to utter the praises of God, and to love Him with all sweetness.

"In Your footsteps."

These are the marks on the ground by which we trace the course of one we seek. The sweetness and knowledge of Himself which God communicates to the soul that seeks Him are the footsteps by which it traces and recognizes Him. Thus the soul says to the Word, the Bridegroom, "In Your footsteps" — "in the traces of Your sweetness which You diffuse, and the odors which You scatter."

"The young ones run Your way."

"Devout souls run with youthful vigor in the sweetness which Your footsteps communicate." They run in many ways and in various directions — each according to the spirit which God bestows and the vocation He has given — in the diversified forms of spiritual service on the road of everlasting life, which is evangelical perfection, where they meet the Beloved in the union of love, in spiritual detachment from all things.

This sweetness and impression of Himself which God leaves in the soul render it light and active in running after Him; for the soul then does little or nothing in its own strength towards running along this road, being rather attracted by the divine footsteps, so that it not only advances, but even runs, as I said before, in many ways. The bride in the Canticle, therefore, prays for the divine attraction, saying, "Draw me, we will run after You to the odor of Your ointments"; and David says, "I have run the way of Your commandments, when You dilated my heart."

"At the touch of the fire, and by the spiced wine, the divine balsam flows."

I said, while explaining the previous lines, that souls run in His footsteps in the way of exterior works. But the three lines I have just quoted refer to the interior acts of the will, when souls are under the influence of the other two graces, and interior visits of the Beloved. These are the touch of fire, and spiced wine; and the interior act of the will, which is the result of these visits, is the flowing of the divine balsam. The contact of the fire is that most delicate touch of the Beloved which the soul feels at times even when least expecting it, and which sets the heart on fire with love, as if a spark of fire had fallen upon it and made it burn. Then the will, in an instant, like one roused from sleep, burns with the fire of love, longs for God, praises Him and gives Him thanks, worships and honors Him, and prays to Him in the sweetness of love.

This is the flowing of the divine balsam, which obeys the touch of the fire that issues forth from the consuming love of God which that fire kindled; the divine balsam which comforts the soul and heals it with its odor and its substance.

The bride in the Canticle speaks of this divine touch, saying, "My Beloved put His hand through the opening, and my belly trembled at His touch." The touch of the Beloved is the touch of love, and His hand is the grace He bestows upon the soul, and the opening through which He puts His hand is the vocation and the perfection, at least the degree of perfection of the soul; for accordingly will His touch be heavier or lighter, in proportion to its spiritual state. The belly that trembled is the will, in which the touch is effected, and the trembling is the stirring up of the desires and affections to love, long for, and praise God, which is the flowing of the balsam from this touch.

"The spiced wine" is that exceedingly great grace which God sometimes bestows upon advanced souls, when the Holy Spirit inebriates them with the sweet, luscious, and strong wine of love. Hence it is here called spiced wine, for as such wine is prepared by fermentation with many and diverse aromatic and strengthening herbs; so this love, the gift of God to the perfect, is in the soul prepared and seasoned with the virtues already acquired. This love, seasoned with the precious spices, communicates to the soul such a strong, abundant inebriation when God visits it that it pours forth with great effect and force those acts of rapturous praise, love, and worship which I referred to before, and that with a marvelous longing to labor and to suffer for Him.

This sweet inebriation and grace, however, do not pass quickly away, like the touch of the fire, for they are of longer continuance. The fire touches and passes, but the effects abide often; and sometimes the spiced wine continues for a considerable time, and its effects also; this is the sweet love of the soul, and continues occasionally a day or two, sometimes even many days together, though not always in the same degree of intensity, because it is not in the power of the soul to control it. Sometimes the soul, without any effort of its own, is conscious of a most sweet interior inebriation, and of the divine love burning within, as David says, "My heart waxed hot within me, and in my meditation a fire shall burn."

The outpourings of this inebriation last sometimes as long as the inebriation itself. At other times there are no outpourings; and they are more or less intense when they occur, in proportion to the greater or less intensity of the inebriation itself. But the outpourings, or effects of the fire, generally last longer than the fire which caused them; indeed the fire leaves them behind in the soul, and they are more vehement than those which proceed from the inebriation, for sometimes this divine fire burns up and consumes the soul in love.

As I have mentioned fermented wine, it will be well to touch briefly upon the difference between it, when it is old, and new wine; the difference between old wine and new wine is the same, and will furnish a little instruction for spiritual men. New wine has not settled on the lees, and is therefore fermenting; we cannot ascertain its quality or worth before it has settled, and the fermentation has ceased, for until then there is great risk of its corruption. The taste of it is rough and sharp, and an immoderate draught of it intoxicates. Old wine has settled on the lees, and ferments no more like new wine; the quality of it is easily ascertained and it is now very safe from corruption, for all fermentation which might have proved pernicious has entirely ceased. Well-fermented wine is very rarely spoiled, the taste of it is pleasant, and its strength is in its own substance, not in the taste, and drinking it produces health and a sound constitution.

New lovers are compared to new wine; these are beginners in the service of God, because the fervor of their love manifests itself outwardly in the senses; because they have not settled on the lees of sense, frail and imperfect; and because they measure the strength of love by the sweetness of it, for it is sensible sweetness that ordinarily gives them their strength for good works, and it is by this they are influenced; we must, therefore, place no confidence in this love till the fermentation has subsided, with the coarse satisfaction of sense.

For as these fervors and sensible warmth may incline men to good and perfect love, and serve as an excellent means to it, when the lees of imperfections are cleared; so also is it very easy at first, when sensible sweetness is fresh, for the wine of love to fail, and the sweetness of the new to vanish. New lovers are always anxious, sensibly tormented by their love; it is necessary for them to put some restraint upon themselves, for if they are very active in the strength of this wine, their natural powers will be ruined with these anxieties and fatigues of the new wine, which is rough and sharp, and not made sweet in the perfect fermentation, which then takes place when the anxieties of love are over, as I shall show immediately.

The Wise Man employs the same illustration; saying, "A new friend is as new wine; it shall grow old, and you shall drink it with pleasure." Old lovers, therefore, who have been tried and proved in the service of the Bridegroom, are like old wine settled on the lees; they have no sensible emotions, nor outbursts of exterior zeal, but they taste the sweetness of the wine of love, now thoroughly fermented, not sweet to the senses as was that of the love of beginners, but rather settled within the soul in the substance and sweetness of the spirit, and in perfect good works. Such souls as these do not seek after sensible sweetness and fervors, neither do they wish for them, lest they should suffer from loathing and weariness; for he who gives the reins to his desires in matters of sense must of necessity suffer pain and loathing, both in mind and body.

Old lovers, therefore, free from that spiritual sweetness which has its roots in the senses, suffer neither in sense nor spirit from the anxieties of love, and thus scarcely ever prove faithless to God, because they have risen above that which might be an occasion of falling, namely, the flesh. These now drink of the wine of love, which is not only fermented and free from the lees, but spiced also with the aromatic herbs of perfect virtues, which will not allow it to corrupt, as may happen to new wine.

For this cause an old friend is of great price in the eyes of God: "Forsake not an old friend, for the new will not be like to him." It is through this wine of love, tried and spiced, that the divine Beloved produces in the soul that divine inebriation, under the influence of which it sends forth to God the sweet and delicious outpourings. The meaning of these three lines, therefore, is as follows: "At the touch of the fire, by which You stir up the soul, and by the spiced wine with which You do so lovingly inebriate it, the soul pours forth the acts and movements of love which are Your work within it."

Note

Such, then, is the state of the blessed soul in the bed of flowers, where all these blessings, and many more, are granted it. The seat of that bed is the Son of God, and the hangings of it are the charity and love of the Bridegroom Himself. The soul now may say, with the bride, "His left hand is under my head," and we may therefore say, in truth, that such a soul is clothed in God, and bathed in the Divinity, and that, not as it were on the surface, but in the interior spirit, and filled with the divine delights in the abundance of the spiritual waters of life; for it experiences that which David says of those who have drawn near to God: "They shall be inebriated with the plenty of Your house, and You shall make them drink of the torrent of Your pleasure, for with You is the fountain of life."

This fullness will be in the very being of the soul, seeing that its drink is nothing else but the torrent of delights, and that torrent the Holy Spirit, as it is written: "And he showed me a river of living water, clear as crystal, proceeding from the throne of God and the Lamb." This water, being the very love itself of God, flows into the soul, so that it drinks of the torrent of love, which is the spirit of the Bridegroom infused into the soul in union. Thence the soul in the overflowing of its love sings the following stanza:

Stanza XXVI

In the inner cellar
Of my Beloved have I drunk; and when I went forth
Over all the plain
I knew nothing,
And lost the flock I followed before.

Here the soul speaks of that sovereign grace of God in taking it to Himself into the house of His love, which is the union, or transformation of love in God. It describes two effects proceeding therefrom: forgetfulness of, and detachment from, all the things of this world, and the mortification of its tastes and desires.

"In the inner cellar."

In order to explain in any degree the meaning of this, I have need of the special help of the Holy Spirit to direct my hand and guide my pen. The cellar is the highest degree of love to which the soul may attain in this life, and is therefore said to be the inner. It follows from this that there are other cellars not so interior; that is, the degrees of love by which souls reach this, the last. These cellars are seven in number, and the soul has entered into them all when it has in perfection the seven gifts of the Holy Spirit, so far as it is possible for it. When the soul has the spirit of fear in perfection, it has in perfection also the spirit of love, inasmuch as this fear, the last of the seven gifts, is filial fear, and the perfect fear of a son proceeds from his perfect love of his father. Thus when the Holy Scripture speaks of one as having perfect charity, it says of him that he fears God. So the prophet Isaiah, announcing the perfections of Christ, says of Him, "The spirit of the fear of the Lord shall replenish him." Holy Simeon also is spoken of by the Evangelist as a "just man full of fear," and the same applies to many others.

Many souls reach and enter the first cellar, each according to the perfection of its love, but the last and inmost cellar is entered by few in this world, because therein is wrought the perfect union with God, the union of the spiritual marriage, of which the soul is now speaking. What God communicates to the soul in this intimate union is utterly ineffable, beyond the reach of all possible words — just as it is impossible to speak of God Himself so as to convey any idea of what He is — because it is God Himself who communicates Himself to the soul now in the marvelous bliss of its transformation. In this state God and the soul are united, as the window is with the light, or coal with the fire, or the light of the stars with that of the sun, yet, however, not so essentially and completely as it will be in the life

to come. The soul, therefore, to show what it received from the hands of God in
the cellar of wine, says nothing else, and I do not believe that anything could be
said but the words which follow:

"Of my Beloved have I drunk."

As a draught diffuses itself through all the members and veins of the body, so
this communication of God diffuses itself substantially in the whole soul, or
rather, the soul is transformed in God. In this transformation the soul drinks of
God in its very substance and its spiritual powers. In the understanding it drinks
wisdom and knowledge, in the will the sweetest love, in the memory refreshment
and delight in the thought and sense of its bliss. That the soul receives and drinks
delight in its very substance, appears from the words of the bride in the Canticle:
"My soul melted as He spoke" — that is, when the Bridegroom communicated
Himself to the soul.

That the understanding drinks wisdom is evident from the words of the bride
longing and praying for the kiss of union: "There You shall teach me, and I will
give you a cup of spiced wine." "You shall teach me wisdom and knowledge in
love, and I will give You a cup of spiced wine — that is, my love mingled with
Yours." The bride says that the will also drinks of love, saying: "He brought me
into the cellar of wine; He has ordered in me charity," — that is, "He gave me His
love, embracing me, to drink of love"; or, to speak more clearly, "He ordered in
me His charity, tempering His charity and to the purpose making it mine." This
is to give the soul to drink of the very love of its Beloved, which the Beloved
infuses into it.

There is a common saying that the will cannot love that of which the
understanding has no knowledge. This, however, is to be understood in the order
of nature, it being impossible, in a natural way, to love anything unless we first
know what it is we love. But in a supernatural way God can certainly infuse love
and increase it without infusing and increasing distinct knowledge, as is evident
from the texts already quoted. Yes, many spiritual persons have experience of this;
their love of God burns more and more, while their knowledge does not grow.
Men may know little and love much, and on the other hand, know much and
love but little.

In general, those spiritual persons whose knowledge of God is not very great are
usually very rich in all that belongs to the will, and infused faith suffices them for
this knowledge, by means of which God infuses and increases charity in them and
the acts thereof, which are to love Him more and more though knowledge is not
increased. Thus the will may drink of love while the understanding drinks in no
fresh knowledge. In the present instance, however, all the powers of the soul
together, because of the union in the inner cellar, drink of the Beloved.

As to the memory, it is clear that the soul drinks of the Beloved in it, because
it is enlightened with the light of the understanding in remembering the blessings
it possesses and enjoys in union with the Beloved.

"And when I went forth."

That is, after this grace: the divine draught having so deified the soul, exalted it, and inebriated it in God. Though the soul is always in the high estate of marriage ever since God has placed it there, nevertheless actual union in all its powers is not continuous, though the substantial union is. In this substantial union the powers of the soul are most frequently in union, and drink of His cellar, the understanding by knowledge, the will by love, etc. We are not, therefore, to suppose that the soul, when saying that it went out, has ceased from its substantial or essential union with God, but only from the union of its faculties, which is not, and cannot be, permanent in this life; it is from this union, then, it went forth when it wandered over all the plain — that is, through the whole breadth of the world.

"I knew nothing."

This draught of God's most deep wisdom makes the soul forget all the things of this world, and consider all its previous knowledge, and the knowledge of the whole world besides, as pure ignorance in comparison with this knowledge.

For a clearer understanding of this, we must remember that the most regular cause of the soul's ignoring the things of the world, when it has ascended to this high state, is that it is informed by a supernatural knowledge, in the presence of which all natural and worldly knowledge is ignorance rather than knowledge. For the soul in possession of this knowledge, which is most profound, learns from it that all other knowledge not included in this knowledge is not knowledge, but ignorance, and worthless. We have this truth in the words of the Apostle when he said that "the wisdom of this world is foolishness with God."

This is the reason why the soul says it knows nothing, now that it has drunk of the divine wisdom. The truth is that the wisdom of men and of the whole world is mere ignorance, and not deserving any attention, but it is a truth that can be learned only in that truth of the presence of God in the soul communicating to it His wisdom and making it strong by this draught of love that it may see it distinctly. This is taught us by Solomon, saying: "The vision that the man spoke, with whom God is, and who being strengthened by God abiding with him, said: I am the most foolish of men, and the wisdom of men is not with me."

When the soul is raised to this high wisdom of God, the wisdom of man is in its eyes the lowest ignorance: all natural science and the works of God, if accompanied by ignorance of Him, are as ignorance; for where He is not known, there nothing is known. "The deep things of God are foolishness to men." Thus the divinely wise and the worldly wise are fools in the estimation of each other; for the latter cannot understand the wisdom and science of God, nor the former those of the world, for the wisdom of the world is ignorance in comparison with the wisdom of God; and the wisdom of God is ignorance with respect to that of the world.

Moreover, this deification and elevation of the spirit in God, whereby the soul is, as it were, rapt and absorbed in love, one with God, suffer it not to dwell upon any worldly matter. The soul is now detached, not only from all outward things, but even from itself: it is, as it were, undone, assumed by, and dissolved in, love — that is, it passes out of itself into the Beloved. Thus the bride, in the Canticle, after speaking of her own transformation by love into the Beloved, expresses her state of ignorance by the words "I knew not." The soul is now, in a certain sense, like Adam in paradise, who knew no evil. It is so innocent that it sees no evil; neither does it consider anything to be amiss. It will hear much that is evil, and will see it with its eyes, and yet it shall not be able to understand it, because it has no evil habits whereby to judge of it. God has rooted out of it those imperfect habits and that ignorance resulting from the evil of sin, by the perfect habit of true wisdom. Thus, also, the soul knows nothing on this subject.

Such a soul will scarcely intermeddle with the affairs of others, because it forgets even its own; for the work of the Spirit of God in the soul in which He dwells is to incline it to ignore those things which do not concern it, especially such as do not minister to edification. The Spirit of God abides within the soul to withdraw it from outward things rather than to lead it among them; and thus the soul knows nothing as it knew it formerly. We are not, however, to suppose that it loses the habits of knowledge previously acquired, for those habits are improved by the more perfect habit of supernatural knowledge infused, though these habits are not so powerful as to necessitate knowledge through them, and yet there is no reason why they should not do so occasionally.

In this union of the divine wisdom, these habits are united with the higher wisdom of other knowledge, as a little light with another which is great; it is the great light that shines, overwhelming the less, yet the latter is not therefore lost, but rather perfected, though it is not the light which shines pre-eminently. Thus, I imagine, will it be in heaven; the acquired habits of knowledge in the just will not be destroyed, though they will be of no great importance there, seeing that the just will know more in the divine wisdom than by the habits acquired on earth.

But the particular notions and forms of things, acts of the imagination, and every other apprehension having form and figure are all lost and ignored in this absorbing love, and this for two reasons. First, the soul cannot actually attend to anything of the kind, because it is actually absorbed by this draught of love. Secondly, and this is the principal reason, its transformation in God so conforms it to His purity and simplicity — for there is no form or imaginary figure in Him — as to render it pure, cleansed and empty of all the forms and figures it entertained before, being now purified and enlightened in simple contemplation. All spots and stains in the glass become invisible when the sun shines upon it, but they appear again as soon as the light of the sun is withheld.

So is it with the soul; while the effects of this act of love continue, this ignorance continues also, so that it cannot observe anything in particular until these effects have ceased. Love has set the soul on fire and transmuted it into love, has annihilated it and destroyed it as to all that is not love, according to the words of David: "My heart has been inflamed, and my reins have been changed; and I am brought to nothing, and I knew not." The changing of the reins, because the heart is inflamed, is the changing of the soul, in all its desires and actions, in God, into a new manner of life, the utter undoing and annihilation of the old man, and therefore the prophet said that he was brought to nothing and knew not.

These are the two effects of drinking the wine of the cellar of God; not only is all previous knowledge brought to nothing and made to vanish, but the old life also with its imperfections is destroyed, and into the new man renewed; this is the second of the two effects described in the words that follow:

"And lost the flock I followed before."

Until the soul reaches the state of perfection, however spiritual it may be, there always remains a troop of desires, likings, and other imperfections, sometimes natural, sometimes spiritual, after which it runs, and which it tries to feed while following and satisfying them. With regard to the understanding, there are certain imperfections of the desire of knowledge. With regard to the will, certain likings and peculiar desires, at times in temporal things, as the wish to possess certain trifles, and attachment to some things more than to others, certain prejudices, considerations, and punctilios, with other vanities, still savoring of the world: and again in natural things, such as eating and drinking, the preference of one kind of food over another, and the choice of the best: at another time, in spiritual things, such as seeking for sweetness, and other follies of spiritual persons not yet perfect, too numerous to recount here. As to the memory, there are many inconsistencies, anxieties, unseemly reminiscences, which drag the soul captive after them.

The four passions of the soul also involve it in many useless hopes, joys, griefs, and fears, after which it runs. As to this flock, some men are more influenced by it than others; they run after and follow it, until they enter the inner cellar, where they lose it altogether, being then transformed in love. In that cellar the flock of imperfections is easily destroyed, as rust and mold on metal in the fire. Then the soul feels itself free from the pettiness of self-likings and the vanities after which it ran before, and may well say, "I have lost the flock which I followed before."

Note

God communicates Himself to the soul in this interior union with a love so intense that the love of a mother, who so tenderly caresses her child, the love of a brother, or the affection of a friend bear no likeness to it, for so great is the tenderness, and so deep is the love with which the Infinite Father comforts and exalts the humble and loving soul. O wonders worthy of all awe and reverence! He humbles Himself in reality before that soul that He may exalt it, as if He were its servant, and the soul His lord. He is as anxious to comfort it as if He were a slave, and the soul God. So great is the humility and tenderness of God. In this communion of love He renders in a certain way those services to the soul which He says in the Gospel He will perform for the elect in heaven. "Amen, I say to you, that He will gird Himself and make them sit down to meat, and passing will minister to them."

This very service He renders now to the soul, comforting and cherishing it, as a mother her child whom she nurtures in her bosom. And the soul recognizes herein the truth of the words of Isaiah, "You shall be carried at the breasts, and upon the knees they shall caress you." What must the feelings of the soul be amid these sovereign graces? How it will melt away in love, beholding the bosom of God opened for it with such overflowing love. When the soul perceives itself in the midst of these delights, it surrenders itself wholly to God, gives to Him the breasts of its own will and love, and under the influence thereof addresses the Beloved in the words of the bride in the Canticle, saying: "I to my Beloved, and His turning is towards me. Come, my Beloved, let us go forth into the field, let us abide in the villages. Let us rise early to the vineyards, let us see if the vineyard flourish, if the flowers are ready to bring forth fruits, if the pomegranates flourish; there will I give You my breasts" — that is, "I will employ all the joy and strength of my will in the service of Your love." This mutual surrender in this union of the soul and God is the subject of the stanza which follows:

Stanza XXVII

There He gave me His breasts,
There He taught me the science full of sweetness.
And there I gave to Him
Myself without reserve;
There I promised to be His bride.

Here the soul speaks of the two contracting parties in this spiritual betrothal, itself and God. In the inner cellar of love they both met together, God giving to the soul the breasts of His love freely, whereby He instructs it in His mysteries and wisdom, and the soul also actually surrendering itself, making no reservation whatever either in its own favor or in that of others, promising to be His for ever.

"There He gave me His breasts."

To give the breast to another is to love and cherish him and communicate one's secrets to him as a friend. The soul says here that God gave it His breasts — that is, He gave it His love and communicated His secrets to it. It is thus that God deals with the soul in this state, and more, too, as it appears from the words that follow:

"There He taught me the science full of sweetness."

This science is mystical theology, which is the secret science of God, and which spiritual men call contemplation. It is most full of sweetness because it is knowledge by love, love is the master of it, and it is love that renders it all so sweet. Inasmuch as this science and knowledge are communicated to the soul in that love with which God communicates Himself, it is sweet to the understanding, because knowledge belongs to it, and sweet to the will, because it comes by love which belongs to the will.

"There I gave to Him myself without reserve"

The soul in this sweet draught of God, surrenders itself wholly to Him most willingly and with great sweetness; it desires to be wholly His, and never to retain anything which is unbecoming His Majesty. God is the author of this union, and of the purity and perfection requisite for it; and as the transformation of the soul in Himself makes it His, He empties it of all that is alien to Himself. Thus it comes to pass that, not in will only, but in act as well, the whole soul is entirely given to God without any reserve whatever, as God has given Himself freely to it. The will of God and of the soul are both satisfied, each given up to the other, in mutual delight, so that neither fails the other in the faith and constancy of the betrothal; therefore the soul says:

"There I promised to be His bride."

As a bride does not give her love to another, and as all her thoughts and actions are directed to her bridegroom only, so the soul now has no affections of the will, no acts of the understanding, neither object nor occupation of any kind which it does not wholly refer to God, together with all its desires. The soul is, as it were, absorbed in God, and even its first movements have nothing in them — so far as it can comprehend them — which is at variance with the will of God. The first movements of an imperfect soul in general are, at least, inclined to evil, in the understanding, the memory, the will, the desires and imperfections; but those of the soul which has attained to the spiritual state of which I am speaking are ordinarily directed to God, because of the great help and courage it derives from Him, and its perfect conversion to goodness. This is set forth with great clearness by David, when he says: "Shall not my soul be subject to God? For from Him is my salvation. For He is my God and my Savior; He is my protector, I shall be moved no more." "He is my protector" means that the soul, being now received under the protection of God and united to Him, is no longer subject to any movements contrary to God.

It is quite clear from this that the soul which has attained the spiritual betrothal knows nothing else but the love of the Bridegroom and the delights thereof, because it has arrived at perfection, the form and substance of which is love, according to St. Paul. The more a soul loves, the more perfect it is in its love, and hence it follows that the soul which is already perfect is, if we may say so, all love, all its actions are love, all its energies and strength are occupied in love. It gives up all it has, like the wise merchant, for this treasure of love which it finds hidden in God, and which is so precious in His sight, and the Beloved cares for nothing else but love; the soul, therefore, anxious to please Him perfectly, occupies itself wholly in pure love for God, not only because love does so occupy it, but also because the love wherein it is united influences it towards love of God in and through all things. As the bee draws honey from all plants, and makes use of them only for that end, so the soul most easily draws the sweetness of love from all that happens to it; makes all things subserve it towards loving God, whether they are sweet or bitter; and being animated and protected by love, has no sense, feeling, or knowledge, because, as I have said, it knows nothing but love, and in all its occupations, its joy is its love of God. This is explained by the following stanza.

Note

I have said that God is pleased with nothing but love; but before I explain this, it will be as well to set forth the grounds on which the assertion rests. All our works, and all our labors, however grand they may be, are nothing in the sight of God, for we can give Him nothing, neither can we by them fulfill His desire, which is the growth of our soul. As to Himself He desires nothing of this, for He has need of nothing, and so, if He is pleased with anything it is with the growth of the soul; and as there is no way in which the soul can grow but in becoming in a manner equal to Him, for this reason He is only pleased with our love. It is the property of love to place him who loves on an equality with the object of his love. Hence the soul, because of its perfect love, is called the bride of the Son of God, which signifies equality with Him. In this equality and friendship all things are common, as the Bridegroom Himself said to His disciples: "I have called you friends, because all things, whatsoever I have heard of my Father, I have made known to you."

Stanza XXVIII

My soul is occupied,
And all my substance in His service;
Now I guard no flock,
Nor have I any other employment:
My sole occupation is love.

The soul, or rather the bride having given herself wholly to the Bridegroom without any reserve whatever, now recounts to the Beloved how she fulfills her task. "My soul and body," she says, "all my abilities and all my capacities, are occupied not with other matters, but with those pertaining to the service of the Bridegroom." She is therefore not seeking her own proper satisfaction, nor the gratification of her own inclinations, neither does she occupy herself in anything whatever which is alien to God; yes, even her communion with God Himself is nothing else but acts of love, inasmuch as she has changed her former mode of conversing with Him into loving.

"My soul is occupied."

This refers to the soul's surrender of itself to the Beloved in this union of love, wherein it devotes itself, with all its faculties, understanding, will, and memory, to His service. The understanding is occupied in considering what most tends to His service, in order that it might be accomplished; the will in loving all that is pleasing to God, and in desiring Him in all things; the memory in recalling what ministers to Him, and what may be more pleasing to Him.

"And all my substance in His service."

By substance here is meant all that relates to the sensual part of the soul, which includes the body, with all its powers, interior and exterior, together with all its natural capacities — that is, the four passions, the natural desires, and the whole substance of the soul, all of which is employed in the service of the Beloved, as well as the rational and spiritual part, as I explained in the previous section. As to the body, that is now ordered according to God in all its interior and exterior senses, all the acts of which are directed to God; the four passions of the soul are also under control in Him; for the soul's joy, hope, fear, and grief are conversant with God only; all its appetites, and all its anxieties also, are directed to Him only.

The whole substance of the soul is now so occupied with God, so intent upon Him, that its very first movements, even inadvertently, have God for their object and their end. The understanding, memory, and will tend directly to God; the affections, senses, desires and longings, hope and joy, the whole substance of the soul, rise instantly towards God, though the soul is making no conscious efforts in that direction. Such a soul is very often doing the work of God, intent upon Him and the things of God, without thinking or reflecting on what it is doing for Him. The constant and habitual practice of this has deprived it of all conscious reflection, and even of that fervor which it usually had when it began to act. The whole substance of the soul being thus occupied, what follows cannot be but true also.

"Now I guard no flock."

"I do not now go after my likings and desires; for having fixed them upon God, I no longer feed or guard them." The soul not only does not guard them now, but has no other occupation than to wait upon God.

"Nor have I any other employment."

Before the soul succeeded in effecting this gift and surrender of itself, and of all that belongs to it, to the Beloved, it was entangled in many unprofitable occupations, by which it sought to please itself and others, and it may be said that its occupations of this kind were as many as its habits of imperfection.

To these habits belong that of speaking, thinking, and the doing of things that are useless; and likewise, the not making use of these things according to the requirements of the soul's perfection; other desires also the soul may have, with which it ministers to the desires of others, to which may be referred display, compliments, flattery, human respect, aiming at being well thought of, and the giving pleasure to people, and other useless actions, by which it labored to content them, wasting its efforts herein, and finally all its strength. All this is over, says the soul here, for all its words, thoughts, and works are directed to God, and, conversant with Him, freed from their previous imperfections. It is as if it said: "I follow no longer either my own or other men's likings, neither do I occupy or entertain myself with useless pastimes, or the things of this world."

"My sole occupation is love."

"All my occupation now is the practice of the love of God, all the powers of soul and body, memory, understanding, and will, interior and exterior senses, the desires of spirit and of sense, all work in and by love. All I do is done in love; all I suffer, I suffer in the sweetness of love." This is the meaning of David when he said, "I will keep my strength to You."

When the soul has arrived at this state all the acts of its spiritual and sensual nature, whether active or passive, and of whatever kind they may be, always occasion an increase of love and delight in God: even the act of prayer and communion with God, which was once carried on by reflections and diverse other methods, is now wholly an act of love. So much so is this the case that the soul may always say, whether occupied with temporal or spiritual things, "My sole occupation is love." Happy life! happy state! and happy the soul which has attained to it! where all is the very substance of love, the joyous delights of the betrothal, when it may truly say to the Beloved with the bride in the Canticle,

"The new and the old, my Beloved, have I kept for You" "All that is bitter and painful I keep for Your sake, all that is sweet and pleasant I keep for You." The meaning of the words, for my purpose, is that the soul, in the state of spiritual betrothal, is for the most part living in the union of love — that is, the will is habitually waiting lovingly on God.

Note

In truth the soul is now lost to all things, and gained only to love, and the mind is no longer occupied with anything else. It is, therefore, deficient in what concerns the active life, and other exterior duties, that it may apply in earnest to the one thing which the Bridegroom has pronounced necessary; and that is waiting upon God, and the continuous practice of His love. So precious is this in the eyes of God that He rebuked Martha because she would withdraw Mary from His feet to occupy her actively in the service of our Lord. Martha thought that she was doing everything herself, and that Mary at the feet of Christ was doing nothing. But it was far otherwise: for there is nothing better or more necessary than love. Thus, in the Canticle, the Bridegroom protects the bride, adjuring the daughters of Jerusalem — that is, all created things — not to disturb her spiritual sleep of love, nor to waken her, nor to let her open her eyes to anything till she pleased. "I adjure you, O daughters of Jerusalem, that you do not stir up, nor awake my beloved till she please."

Observe, however, that if the soul has not reached the state of unitive love, it is necessary for it to make acts of love, as well in the active as in the contemplative life. But when it has reached it, it is not requisite it should occupy itself in other and exterior duties — unless they are matters of obligation — which might hinder, were it but for a moment, the life of love in God, though they may minister greatly to His service; because an instant of pure love is more precious in the eyes of God and the soul, and more profitable to the Church, than all other good works together, though it may seem as if nothing were done. Thus, Mary Magdalene, though her preaching was most edifying, and might have been still more so afterwards, out of the great desire she had to please God and benefit the Church, hid herself, nevertheless, in the desert thirty years, that she might surrender herself entirely to love; for she considered that she would gain more in that way, because an instant of pure love is so much more profitable and important to the Church.

When the soul, then, in any degree possesses the spirit of solitary love, we must not interfere with it. We should inflict a grievous wrong upon it, and upon the Church also, if we were to occupy it, were it only for a moment, in exterior or active duties, however important they might be. When God Himself adjures all not to waken it from its love, who shall venture to do so, and be blameless? In a word, it is for this love that we are all created. Let those men of zeal, who think by their preaching and exterior works to convert the world, consider that they would be much more edifying to the Church, and more pleasing to God — setting aside the good example they would give — if they would spend at least one half their time in prayer, even though they may have not attained to the state of unitive love. Certainly they would do more, and with less trouble, by one single good work than by a thousand: because of the merit of their prayer, and the spiritual strength it supplies. To act otherwise is to beat the air, to do little more than nothing, sometimes nothing and occasionally even mischief; for God may give up such persons to vanity, so that they may seem to have done something, when in reality their outward occupations bear no fruit; for it is quite certain that good works cannot be done but in the power of God. O how much might be written on this subject! this, however, is not the place for it.

I have said this to explain the stanza that follows, in which the soul replies to those who call in question its holy tranquillity, who will have it wholly occupied with outward duties, that its light may shine before the world: these persons have no conception of the fibers and the unseen root whence the sap is drawn, and which nourish the fruit.

Stanza XXIX

If then on the common land
I am no longer seen or found,
You will say that I am lost;
That, being enamored,
I lost myself; and yet was found.

The soul replies here to a tacit reproach. Worldly people are in the habit of censuring those who give themselves up in earnest to God, regarding them as extravagant, in their withdrawal from the world, and in their manner of life. They say also of them that they are useless for all matters of importance, and lost to everything the world prizes and respects! This reproach the soul meets in the best way; boldly and courageously despising it with everything else that the world can lay to its charge. Having attained to a living love of God, it makes little account of all this; and that is not all: it confesses it itself in this stanza, and boasts that it has committed that folly, and that it is lost to the world and to itself for the Beloved.

That which the soul is saying here, addressing itself to the world, is in substance this: "If you see me no longer occupied with the subjects that engrossed me once, with the other pastimes of the world, say and believe that I am lost to them, and a stranger to them, yes, that I am lost of my own choice, seeking my Beloved whom I so greatly love." But that they may see that the soul's loss is gain, and not consider it folly and delusion, it adds that its loss was gain, and that it therefore lost itself deliberately.

"If then on the common I am no longer seen or found."

The common is a public place where people assemble for recreation, and where shepherds feed their flocks. By the common here is meant the world in general, where men amuse themselves and feed the herd of their desires. The soul says to the worldly-minded: "If you see me no more where I used to be before I gave myself up wholly to God, look upon me as lost, and say so": the soul rejoices in that and would have men so speak of it.

"Say that I am lost."

He who loves is not ashamed before men of what he does for God, neither does he hide it through shame though the whole world should condemn it. He who shall be ashamed to confess the Son of God before men, neglecting to do His work, the Son of God also will be ashamed to acknowledge him before His Father.

"He that shall deny Me before men, I will also deny him before My Father Who is in heaven." The soul, therefore, in the courage of its love, glories in what ministers to the honor of the Beloved, in that it has done anything for Him and is lost to the things of the world.

But few spiritual persons arrive at this perfect courage and resolution in their conduct. For though some attempt to practice it, and some even think themselves proficient therein, they never entirely lose themselves on certain points connected with the world or self, so as to be perfectly detached for the sake of Christ, despising appearances and the opinion of the world. These can never answer, "Say that I am lost," because they are not lost to themselves, and are still ashamed to confess Christ before men through human respect; these do not therefore really live in Christ.

"That being enamored,"

That is, practicing virtues for the love of God,

"I lost myself; and yet was found."

The soul remembers well the words of the Bridegroom in the Gospel: "No man can serve two masters; for either he will hate the one and love the other," and therefore, in order not to lose God, loses all that is not God, that is, all created things, even itself, being lost to all things for the love of Him. He who truly loves makes a shipwreck of himself in all else that he may gain the more in the object of his love. Thus the soul says that it has lost itself — that is, deliberately, of set purpose.

This loss occurs in two ways. The soul loses itself, making no account whatever of itself, but of the Beloved, resigning itself freely into His hands without any selfish views, losing itself deliberately, and seeking nothing for itself. Secondly, it loses itself in all things, making no account of anything save that which concerns the Beloved. This is to lose oneself — that is, to be willing that others should have all things. Such is he that loves God; he seeks neither gain nor reward, but only to lose all, even himself, according to God's will; this is what such a one counts gain. This is real gain, for the Apostle says, "to die is gain" — that is, to die for Christ is my gain and profit spiritually. This is why the soul says that it "was found"; for he who does not know how to lose, does not find, but rather loses himself, as our Savior teaches us in the Gospel, saying, "He that will save his life shall lose it; and he that shall lose his life for My sake shall find it."

But if we wish to know the deeper spiritual meaning of this line, and its peculiar fitness here, it is as follows: When a soul has advanced so far on the spiritual road as to be lost to all the natural methods of communing with God; when it seeks Him no longer by meditation, images, impressions, nor by any other created ways, or representations of sense, but only by rising above them all, in the joyful communion with Him by faith and love, then it may be said to have found God of a truth, because it has truly lost itself as to all that is not God, and also as to its own self.

Note

The soul being thus gained, all its works are gain, for all its powers are exerted in the spiritual intercourse of most sweet interior love with the Beloved. The interior communications between God and the soul are now so delicious, so full of sweetness, that no mortal tongue can describe them, nor human understanding comprehend them. As a bride on the day of her betrothal attends to nothing but to the joyous festival of her love, and brings forth all her jewels and ornaments for the pleasure of the bridegroom, and as he too in the same way exhibits his own magnificence and riches for the pleasure of his bride, so is it in the spiritual betrothal where the soul feels that which the bride says in the Canticle, "I to my Beloved and my Beloved to me." The virtues and graces of the bride-soul, the grandeur and magnificence of the Bridegroom, the Son of God, come forth into the light, for the celebration of the bridal feast, communicating each to the other the goods and joys with the wine of sweet love in the Holy Spirit. The present stanza, addressed to the Bridegroom by the soul, has this for its subject.

Stanza XXX

Of emeralds, and of flowers
In the early morning gathered,
We will make the garlands,
Flowering in Your love,
And bound together with one hair of my head.

The bride now turns to the Bridegroom and addresses Him in the intercourse and comfort of love; the subject of the stanza being the solace and delight which the bride-soul and the Son of God find in the possession of the virtues and gifts of each other, and in the exercise thereof, both rejoicing in their mutual love. Thus the soul, addressing the Beloved, says that they will make garlands rich in graces and acquired virtues, obtained at the fitting and convenient season, beautiful and lovely in the love He bears the soul, and kept together by the love which it itself has for Him. This rejoicing in virtue is what is meant by making garlands, for the soul and God rejoice together in these virtues bound up as flowers in a garland, in the common love which each bears the other.

"Of emeralds, and of flowers."

The flowers are the virtues of the soul; the emeralds are the gifts it has received from God. Then of these flowers and emeralds

"In the early morning gathered."

That is, acquired in youth, which is the early morning of life. They are said to be gathered because the virtues which we acquire in youth are most pleasing to God; because youth is the season when our vices most resist the acquisition of them, and when our natural inclinations are most prone to lose them. Those virtues also are more perfect which we acquire in early youth. This time of our life is the early morning; for as the freshness of the spring morning is more agreeable than any other part of the day, so also are the virtues acquired in our youth more pleasing in the sight of God.

By the fresh morning we may understand those acts of love by which we acquire virtue, and which are more pleasing to God than the fresh morning is to the sons of men; good works also, wrought in the season of spiritual dryness and hardness; this is the freshness of the winter morning, and what we then do for God in dryness of spirit is most precious in His eyes. Then it is that we acquire virtues and graces abundantly; and what we then acquire with toil and labor is for the most part better, more perfect and lasting than what we acquire in comfort and spiritual sweetness; for virtue sends forth its roots in the season of dryness, toil, and trial: as it is written, "Virtue is made perfect in infirmity." It is with a view to show forth the excellence of these virtues, of which the garland is wrought for the Beloved, that the soul says of them that they have been gathered in the early morning; because it is these flowers alone, with the emeralds of virtue, the choice and perfect graces, and not the imperfect, which are pleasing to the Beloved, and so the bride says:

"We will make the garlands."

All the virtues and graces which the soul, and God in it, acquire are as a garland of diverse flowers with which the soul is marvelously adorned as with a vesture of rich embroidery. As material flowers are gathered, and then formed into a garland, so the spiritual flowers of virtues and graces are acquired and set in order in the soul: and when the acquisition is complete, the garland of perfection is complete also. The soul and the Bridegroom rejoice in it, both beautiful, adorned with the garland, as in the state of perfection.

These are the garlands which the soul says they will make. That is, it will wreathe itself with this variety of flowers, with the emeralds of virtues and perfect gifts, that it may present itself worthily before the face of the King, and be on an equality with Him, sitting as a queen on His right hand; for it has merited this by its beauty. Thus David says, addressing himself to Christ: "The queen stood on Your right hand in vestments of gold, girt with variety." That is, at His right hand, clad in perfect love, girt with the variety of graces and perfect virtues.

The soul does not say, "I will make garlands," nor "You will make them," but, "We will make them," not separately, but both together; because the soul cannot practice virtues alone, nor acquire them alone, without the help of God; neither does God alone create virtue in the soul without the soul's concurrence. Though it is true, as the Apostle says, that "every best gift, and every perfect gift, is from above, descending from the Father of lights," still they enter into no soul without that soul's concurrence and consent. Thus the bride in the Canticle says to the Bridegroom; "Draw me; we will run after you." Every inclination to good comes from God alone, as we learn here; but as to running, that is, good works, they proceed from God and the soul together, and it is therefore written, "We will run" — that is, both together, but not God nor the soul alone.

These words may also be fittingly applied to Christ and His Church, which, as His bride, says to Him, "We will make the garlands." In this application of the words the garlands are the holy souls born to Christ in the Church. Every such soul is by itself a garland adorned with the flowers of virtues and graces, and all of them together a garland for the head of Christ the Bridegroom.

We may also understand by these beautiful garlands the crowns formed by Christ and the Church, of which there are three kinds. The first is formed of the beauty and white flowers of the virgins, each one with her virginal crown, and forming altogether one crown for the head of the Bridegroom Christ. The second, of the brilliant flowers of the holy doctors, each with his crown of doctor, and all together forming one crown above that of the virgins on the head of Christ. The third is composed of the purple flowers of the martyrs, each with his own crown of martyrdom, and all united into one, perfecting that on the head of Christ. Adorned with these garlands He will be so beautiful, and so lovely to behold, that heaven itself will repeat the words of the bride in the Canticle, saying: "Go forth, you daughters of Zion, and see king Solomon in the diadem with which his mother crowned him in the day of his betrothal, and in the day of the joy of his heart." The soul then says we will make garlands.

"Flowering in Your love."

The flowering of good works and virtues is the grace and power which they derive from the love of God, without which they not only flower not, but even become dry, and worthless in the eyes of God, though they may be humanly perfect. But if He gives His grace and love they flourish in His love.

"And bound together with one hair of my head."

The hair is the will of the soul, and the love it bears the Beloved. This love performs the function of the thread that keeps the garland together. For as a thread binds the flowers of a garland, so loves knits together and sustains virtues in the soul. "Charity" — that is, love — says the Apostle, "is the bond of perfection." Love, in the same way, binds the virtues and supernatural gifts together, so that when love fails by our departure from God, all our virtue perishes also, just as the flowers drop from the garland when the thread that bound them together is broken. It is not enough for God's gift of virtues that He should love us, but we too must love Him in order to receive them, and preserve them.

The soul speaks of one hair, not of many, to show that the will by itself is fixed on God, detached from all other hairs; that is, from strange love. This points out the great price and worth of these garlands of virtues; for when love is single, firmly fixed on God, as here described, the virtues also are entire, perfect, and flowering in the love of God; for the love He bears the soul is beyond all price, and the soul also knows it well.

Were I to attempt a description of the beauty of that binding of the flowers and emeralds together, or of the strength and majesty which their harmonious arrangement furnishes to the soul, or the beauty and grace of its embroidered vesture, expressions and words would fail me; for if God says of the evil spirit, "His body is like molten shields, shut close up with scales pressing upon one another, one is joined to another, and not so much as any air can come between them"; if the evil spirit is so strong, clad in malice thus compacted together — for the scales that cover his body like molten shields are malice, and malice is in itself but weakness — what must be the strength of the soul that is clothed in virtues so compacted and united together that no impurity or imperfection can penetrate between them; each virtue severally adding strength to strength, beauty to beauty, wealth to wealth, and to majesty, dominion and grandeur?

What a marvelous vision will be that of the bride-soul, when it shall sit on the right hand of the Bridegroom-King, crowned with graces! "How beautiful are your steps in shoes, O prince's daughter!" The soul is called a prince's daughter because of the power it has; and if the beauty of the steps in shoes is great, what must be that of the whole vesture? Not only is the beauty of the soul crowned with admirable flowers, but its strength also, flowing from the harmonious order of the flowers, intertwined with the emeralds of its innumerable graces, is terrible: "Terrible as the army of a camp set in array." For, as these virtues and gifts of God refresh the soul with their spiritual perfume, so also, when united in it, do they, out of their substance, minister strength. Thus, in the Canticle, when the bride was weak, languishing with love — because she had not been able to bind together the flowers and the emeralds with the hair of her love — and anxious to strengthen herself by that union of them, cries out: "Stay me with flowers, compass me about with apples; because I languish with love." The flowers are the virtues, and the apples are the other graces.

Note

I believe I have now shown how the intertwining of the garlands and their lasting presence in the soul explain the divine union of love which now exists between the soul and God. The Bridegroom, as He says Himself, is the "flower of the field and the lily of the valleys," and the soul's love is the hair that unites to itself this flower of flowers. Love is the most precious of all things, because it is the "bond of perfection," as the Apostle says, and perfection is union with God. The soul is, as it were, a sheaf of garlands, for it is the subject of this glory, no longer what it was before, but the very perfect flower of flowers in the perfection and beauty of all; for the thread of love binds so closely God and the soul, and so unites them, that it transforms them and makes them one by love; so that, though in essence different, yet in glory and appearance the soul seems God and God the soul. Such is this marvelous union, baffling all description.

We may form some conception of it from the love of David and Jonathan, whose "soul was knit with the soul of David." If the love of one man for another can be thus strong, so as to knit two souls together, what must that love of God be which can knit the soul of man to God the Bridegroom? God Himself is here the suitor Who in the omnipotence of His unfathomable love absorbs the soul with greater violence and efficacy than a torrent of fire a single drop of the morning dew which resolves itself into air. The hair, therefore, which accomplishes such a union must, of necessity, be most strong and subtle, seeing that it penetrates and binds together so effectually the soul and God. In the present stanza the soul declares the qualities of this hair.

Stanza XXXI

By that one hair
You have observed fluttering on my neck,
And on my neck regarded,
You were captivated;
And wounded by one of my eyes.

There are three things mentioned here. The first is, that the love by which the virtues are bound together is nothing less than a strong love; for in truth it need be so in order to preserve them. The second is, that God is greatly taken by this hair of love, seeing it to be alone and strong. The third is, that God is deeply enamored of the soul, beholding the purity and integrity of its faith.

"By that one hair You have observed fluttering on my neck."

The neck signifies that strength in which, it is said, fluttered the hair of love, strong love, which bound the virtues together. It is not sufficient for the preservation of virtues that love be alone, it must be also strong so that no contrary vice may anywhere destroy the perfection of the garland; for the virtues so are bound up together in the soul by the hair, that if the thread is once broken, all the virtues are lost; for where one virtue is, all are, and where one fails, all fail also. The hair is said to flutter on the neck, because its love of God, without any hindrance whatever, flutters strongly and lightly in the strength of the soul.

As the air causes hair to wave and flutter on the neck, so the breath of the Holy Spirit stirs the strong love that it may fly upwards to God; for without this divine wind, which excites the powers of the soul to the practice of divine love, all the virtues the soul may possess become ineffectual and fruitless. The Beloved observed the hair fluttering on the neck — that is, He considered it with particular attention and regard; because strong love is a great attraction for the eyes of God.

"And on my neck regarded."

This shows us that God not only esteems this love, seeing it alone, but also loves it, seeing it strong; for to say that God regards is to say that He loves, and to say that He observes is to say that He esteems what He observes. The word "neck" is repeated in this line, because it, being strong, is the cause why God loves it so much. It is as if the soul said, "You have loved it, seeing it strong without weakness or fear, and without any other love, and flying upwards swiftly and fervently."

Until now God had not looked upon this hair so as to be captivated by it, because He had not seen it alone, separate from the others, withdrawn from other loves, feelings, and affections, which hindered it from fluttering alone on the neck of strength. Afterwards, however, when mortifications and trials, temptations and penance had detached it, and made it strong, so that nothing whatever could break it, then God beholds it, and is taken by it, and binds the flowers of the garlands with it; for it is now so strong that it can keep the virtues united together in the soul.

But what these temptations and trials are, how they come, and how far they reach, that the soul may attain to that strength of love in which God unites it to Himself, I have described in the "Dark Night," and in the explanation of the four stanzas which begin with the words, "O living flame of love!" The soul having passed through these trials has reached a degree of love so high that it has merited the divine union.

"You were captivated."

O joyful wonder! God captive to a hair. The reason of this capture so precious is that God was pleased to observe the fluttering of the hair on the soul's neck; for where God regards He loves. If He in His grace and mercy had not first looked upon us and loved us, as St. John says, and humbled Himself, He never could have been taken by the fluttering of the hair of our miserable love. His flight is not so low as that our love could lay hold of the divine bird, attract His attention, and fly so high with a strength worthy of His regard, if He had not first looked upon us. He, however, is taken by the fluttering of the hair; He makes it worthy and pleasing to Himself, and then is captivated by it. "You have seen it on my neck, You were captivated by it." This renders it credible that a bird which flies low may capture the royal eagle in its flight, if the eagle should fly so low and be taken by it willingly.

"And wounded by one of my eyes."

The eye is faith. The soul speaks of but one, and that this has wounded the Beloved. If the faith and trust of the soul in God were not one, without admixture of other considerations, God never could have been Wounded by love. Thus the eye that wounds, and the hair that binds, must be one. So strong is the love of the Bridegroom for the bride, because of her simple faith, that, if the hair of her love binds Him, the eye of her faith imprisons Him so closely as to wound Him through that most tender affection He bears her, which is to the bride a further progress in His love.

The Bridegroom Himself speaks in the Canticle of the hair and the eyes, saying to the bride, "You have wounded My heart, My sister, My bride; you have wounded My heart with one of your eyes, and with one hair of your neck." He says twice that His heart is wounded, that is, with the eye and the hair, and therefore the soul in this stanza speaks of them both, because they signify its union with God in the understanding and the will; for the understanding is subdued by faith, signified by the eye, and the will by love. Here the soul exults in this union, and gives thanks to the Bridegroom for it, it being His gift; accounting it a great matter that He has been pleased to requite its love, and to become captive to it. We may also observe here the joy, happiness, and delight of the soul with its prisoner, having been for a long time His prisoner, enamored of Him.

Note

Great is the power and courage of love, for God is its prisoner. Blessed is the soul that loves, for it has made a captive of God Who obeys its good pleasure. Such is the nature of love that it makes those who love do what is asked of them, and, on the other hand, without love the utmost efforts will be fruitless, but one hair will bind those that love. The soul, knowing this, and conscious of blessings beyond its merits, in being raised up to so high a degree of love, through the rich endowments of graces and virtues, attributes all to the Beloved, saying:

Stanza XXXII

When You regarded me,
Yours eyes imprinted in me Your grace:
For this You loved me again,
And thereby my eyes merited
To adore what in You they saw.

It is the nature of perfect love to seek or accept nothing for itself, to attribute nothing to itself, but to refer all to the Beloved. If this is true of earthly love, how much more so of the love of God, the reason of which is so constraining. In the two foregoing stanzas the bride seemed to attribute something to herself; for she said that she would make garlands with her Beloved, and bind them with a hair of her head; that is a great work, and of no slight importance and worth: afterwards she said that she exulted in having captivated Him by a hair, and wounded Him with one of her eyes. All this seems as if she attributed great merits to herself. Now, however, she explains her meaning, and removes the wrong impression with great care and fear, lest any merit should be attributed to herself, and therefore less to God than His due, and less also than she desired. She now refers all to Him, and at the same time gives Him thanks, saying that the cause of His being the captive of the hair of her love, and of His being wounded by the eye of her faith, was His mercy in looking lovingly upon her, thereby rendering her lovely and pleasing in His sight; and that the loveliness and worth she received from Him merited His love, and made her worthy to adore her Beloved, and to bring forth good works worthy of His love and favor.

"When You regarded me."

That is, with loving affection, for I have already said, that where God regards there He loves.

"Yours eyes imprinted in me Your grace."

The eyes of the Bridegroom signify here His merciful divinity, which, mercifully inclined to the soul, imprints or infuses in it the love and grace by which He makes it beautiful, and so elevates it that He makes it the partaker of His divinity. When the soul sees to what height of dignity God has raised it, it says:

"For this You loved me again."

To love again is to love much; it is more than simple love, it is a twofold love, and for two reasons. Here the soul explains the two motives of the Bridegroom's love; He not only loved it because captivated by the hair, but He loved it again, because He was wounded with one of its eyes. The reason why He loved it so deeply is that He would, when He looked upon it, give it the grace to please Him, endowing it with the hair of love, and animating with His charity the faith of the eye. And therefore the soul says:

"For this You loved me again."

To say that God shows favor to the soul is to say that He renders it worthy and capable of His love. It is therefore as if the soul said, "Having shown Your favor to me, worthy pledges of Your love, You have therefore loved me again"; that is, "You have given me grace upon grace"; or, in the words of St. John, "grace for grace"; grace for the grace He has given, that is more grace, for without grace we cannot merit His grace.

If we could clearly understand this truth, we must keep in mind that, as God loves nothing beside Himself, so loves He nothing more than Himself, because He loves all things with reference to Himself. Thus love is the final cause, and God loves nothing for what it is in itself. Consequently, when we say that God loves such a soul, we say, in effect, that He brings it in a manner to Himself, making it His equal, and thus it is He loves that soul in Himself with that very love with which He loves Himself. Every good work, therefore, of the soul in God is meritorious of God's love, because the soul in His favor, thus exalted, merits God Himself in every act.

"And thereby my eyes merited."

That is, "By the grace and favor which the eyes of Your compassion have wrought, when You looked upon me, rendering me pleasing in Your sight and worthy of Your regard."

"To adore what in You they saw."

That is: "The powers of my soul, O my Bridegroom, the eyes by which I can see You, although once fallen and miserable in the vileness of their mean occupations, have merited to look upon You." To look upon God is to do good works in His grace. Thus the powers of the soul merit in adoring because they adore in the grace of God, in which every act is meritorious. Enlightened and exalted by grace, they adored what in Him they saw, and what they saw not before, because of their blindness and meanness. What, then, have they now seen? The greatness of His power, His overflowing sweetness, infinite goodness, love, and compassion, innumerable benefits received at His hands, as well now when so near Him as before when far away. The eyes of the soul now merit to adore, and by adoring merit, for they are beautiful and pleasing to the Bridegroom. Before they were unworthy, not only to adore or behold Him, but even to look upon Him at all: great indeed is the stupidity and blindness of a soul without the grace of God.

It is a melancholy thing to see how far a soul departs from its duty when it is not enlightened by the love of God. For being bound to acknowledge these and other innumerable favors which it has every moment received at His hands, temporal as well as spiritual, and to worship and serve Him unceasingly with all its faculties, it not only does not do so, but is unworthy even to think of Him; nor does it make any account of Him whatever. Such is the misery of those who are living, or rather who are dead, in sin.

Note

For the better understanding of this and of what follows, we must keep in mind that the regard of God benefits the soul in four ways: it cleanses, adorns, enriches, and enlightens it, as the sun, when it shines, dries, warms, beautifies, and brightens the earth. When God has visited the soul in the three latter ways, whereby He renders it pleasing to Himself, He remembers its former uncleanness and sin no more: as it is written, "All the iniquities that he has wrought, I will not remember."

God having once done away with our sin and uncleanness, He will look upon them no more; nor will He withhold His mercy because of them, for He never punishes twice for the same sin, according to the words of the prophet: "There shall not rise a double affliction."

Still, though God forgets the sin He has once forgiven, we are not for that reason to forget it ourselves; for the Wise Man says, "Be not without fear about sin forgiven." There are three reasons for this. We should always remember our sin, that we may not presume, that we may have a subject of perpetual thanksgiving, and because it serves to give us more confidence that we shall receive greater favors; for if, when we were in sin, God showed Himself to us so merciful and forgiving, how much greater mercies may we not hope for when we are clean from sin, and in His love?

The soul, therefore, calling to mind all the mercies it has received, and seeing itself united to the Bridegroom in such dignity, rejoices greatly with joy, thanksgiving, and love. In this it is helped exceedingly by the recollection of its former condition, which was so mean and filthy that it not only did not deserve that God should look upon it, but was unworthy that He should even utter its name, as He says by the mouth of the prophet David: "Nor will I be mindful of their names by My lips." Thus the soul, seeing that there was, and that there can be, nothing in itself to attract the eyes of God, but that all comes from Him of pure grace and goodwill, attributes its misery to itself, and all the blessings it enjoys to the Beloved; and seeing further that because of these blessings it can merit now what it could not merit before, it becomes bold with God, and prays for the divine spiritual union, wherein its mercies are multiplied. This is the subject of the following stanza:

Stanza XXXIII

Despise me not,
For if I was swarthy once,
You can regard me now;
Since You have regarded me,
Grace and beauty have You given me.

The soul now is becoming bold, and respects itself, because of the gifts and endowments which the Beloved has bestowed upon it. It recognizes that these things, while itself is worthless and underserving, are at least means of merit, and consequently it ventures to say to the Beloved, "Do not disregard me now, or despise me"; for if before it deserved contempt because of the filthiness of its sin, and the meanness of its nature, now that He has once looked upon it, and thereby adorned it with grace and beauty, He may well look upon it a second time and increase its grace and beauty. That He has once done so, when the soul did not deserved it, and had no attractions for Him, is reason enough why He should do so again and again.

"Despise me not."

The soul does not say this because it desires in any way to be esteemed — for contempt and insult are of great price, and occasions of joy to the soul that truly loves God — but because it acknowledges that in itself it merits nothing else, were it not for the gifts and graces it has received from God, as it appears from the words that follow.

"For if I was swarthy once."

"If, before You graciously looked upon me You found me in my filthiness, black with imperfections and sins, and naturally mean and vile,"

"You can regard me now; since You have regarded me."

After once looking upon me, and taking away my swarthy complexion, defiled by sin and disagreeable to look upon, when You rendered me lovely for the first time, You may well look upon me now — that is, now I may be looked on and deserve to be regarded, and thereby to receive further favors at Your hands. For Your eyes, when they first looked upon me, not only took away my swarthy complexion, but rendered me also worthy of Your regard; for in Your look of love,
—

"Grace and beauty have You given me."

The two preceding lines are a commentary on the words of St. John, "grace for grace," for when God beholds a soul that is lovely in His eyes He is moved to bestow more grace upon it because He dwells well-pleased within it. Moses knew this, and prayed for further grace: he would, as it were, constrain God to grant it because he had already received so much "You have said: I know you by name, and you have found favor in My sight: if therefore I have found favor in Your sight, show me Your face, that I may know You, and may find grace before Yours eyes."

Now a soul which in the eyes of God is thus exalted in grace, honorable and lovely, is for that reason an object of His unutterable love. If He loved that soul before it was in a state of grace, for His own sake, He loves it now, when in a state of grace, not only for His own sake, but also for itself. Thus enamored of its beauty, through its affections and good works, now that it is never without them, He bestows upon it continually further grace and love, and the more honorable and exalted He renders that soul, the more is He captivated by it, and the greater His love for it.

God Himself sets this truth before us, saying to His people, by the mouth of the prophet, "since you became honorable in My eyes, and glorious, I have loved you." That is, "Since I have cast My eyes upon you, and thereby showed you favor, and made you glorious and honorable in My sight, you have merited other and further favors"; for to say that God loves, is to say that He multiplies His grace. The bride in the Canticle speaks to the same effect, saying, "I am black, but beautiful, O you daughters of Jerusalem." and the Church adds, saying, "Therefore has the King loved me, and brought me into His secret chamber." This is as much as saying: "O you souls who have no knowledge nor understanding of these favors, do not marvel that the heavenly King has shown such mercy to me as to plunge me in the depths of His love, for, though I am swarthy, He has so regarded me, after once looking upon me, that He could not be satisfied without betrothing me to Himself, and calling me into the inner chamber of His love."

Who can measure the greatness of the soul's exaltation when God is pleased with it? No language, no imagination is sufficient for this; for in truth God does this as God, to show that it is He who does it. The dealings of God with such a soul may in some degree be understood; but only in this way, namely, that He gives more to him who has more, and that His gifts are multiplied in proportion to the previous endowments of the soul. This is what He teaches us Himself in the Gospel, saying; "He that has to him shall be given, and he shall abound: but he that has not, from him shall be taken away even that which he has."

Thus the talent of that servant, not then in favor with his lord, was taken from him and given to another who had gained others, so that the latter might have all, together with the favor of his lord. God heaps the noblest and the greatest favors of His house, which is the Church militant as well as the Church triumphant, upon him who is most His friend, ordaining it thus for His greater honor and glory, as a great light absorbs many little lights. This is the spiritual sense of those words, already cited, the prophet Isaiah addressed to the people of Israel: "I am the Lord your God, the Holy One of Israel, your Savior: I have given Egypt for your atonement and Seba for you. I will give men for you, and people for your life."

Well may You then, O God, gaze upon and prize that soul which You regard, for You have made it precious by looking upon it, and given it graces which in Your sight are precious, and by which You are captivated. That soul, therefore, deserves that You should regard it not only once, but often, seeing that You have once looked upon it; for so is it written in the book of Esther by the Holy Spirit: "This honor is he worthy of, whom the king has a mind to honor."

Note

The gifts of love which the Bridegroom bestows on the soul in this state are inestimable; the praises and endearing expressions of divine love which pass so frequently between them are beyond all utterance. The soul is occupied in praising Him, and in giving Him thanks; and He in exalting, praising, and thanking the soul, as we see in the Canticle, where He thus speaks to the bride: "Behold, you are fair, O My love, behold, you are fair; your eyes are as those of doves." The bride replies: "Behold, you are fair, my Beloved, and comely." These, and other like expressions, are addressed by them each to the other.

In the previous stanza the soul despised itself, and said it was swarthy and unclean, praising Him for His beauty and grace, Who, by looking upon the soul, rendered it gracious and beautiful. He, Whose way it is to exalt the humble, fixing His eyes upon the soul, as He was entreated to do, praises it in the following stanza. He does not call it swarthy, as the soul calls itself, but He addresses it as His white dove, praising it for its good dispositions, those of a dove and a turtle-dove.

Stanza XXXIV: The Bridegroom

The little white dove
Has returned to the ark with the bough;
And now the turtle-dove
Its desired mate
On the green banks has found.

It is the Bridegroom Himself who now speaks. He celebrates the purity of the soul in its present state, the rich rewards it has gained, in having prepared itself, and labored to come to Him. He also speaks of its blessedness in having found the Bridegroom in this union, and of the fulfillment of all its desires, the delight and joy it has in Him now that all the trials of life and time are over.

"The little white dove."

He calls the soul, on account of its whiteness and purity — effects of the grace it has received at the hands of God — a dove, "the little white dove," for this is the term He applies to it in the Canticle, to mark its simplicity, its natural gentleness, and its loving contemplation. The dove is not only simple, and gentle without gall, but its eyes are also clear, full of love. The Bridegroom, therefore, to point out in it this character or loving contemplation, wherein it looks upon God, says of it that its eyes are those of a dove: "Your eyes are dove's eyes."

"Has returned to the ark with the bough."

Here the Bridegroom compares the soul to the dove of Noah's ark, the going and returning of which is a figure of what befalls the soul. For as the dove went forth from the ark, and returned because it found no rest for its feet on account of the waters of the deluge, until the time when it returned with the olive branch in its mouth — a sign of the mercy of God in drying the waters which had covered the earth — so the soul went forth at its creation out of the ark of God's omnipotence, and having traversed the deluge of its sins and imperfections, and finding no rest for its desires, flew and returned on the air of the longings of its love to the ark of its Creator's bosom; but it only effected an entrance when God had dried the waters of its imperfections. Then it returned with the olive branch, that is, the victory over all things by His merciful compassion, to this blessed and perfect recollection in the bosom of the Beloved, not only triumphant over all its enemies, but also rewarded for its merits; for both the one and the other are symbolized by the olive bough. Thus the dove-soul returns to the ark of God not only white and pure as it went forth when He created it, but with the olive branch of reward and peace obtained by the conquest of itself.

"And now the turtle dove its desired mate on the green banks has found."

The Bridegroom calls the soul the turtle-dove, because when it is seeking after the Beloved it is like the turtle-dove when it cannot find its desired mate. It is said of the turtle-dove, when it cannot find its mate, that it will not sits on the green boughs, nor drink of the cool refreshing waters, nor retire to the shade, nor mingle with companions; but when it finds its mate then it does all this.

Such, too, is the condition of the soul, and necessarily, if it is to attain to union with the Bridegroom. The soul's love and anxiety must be such that it cannot rest on the green boughs of any joy, nor drink of the waters of this world's honor and glory, nor recreate itself with any temporal consolation, nor shelter itself in the shade of created help and protection: it must repose nowhere, it must avoid the society of all its inclinations, mourn in its loneliness, until it shall find the Bridegroom to its perfect contentment.

And because the soul, before it attained to this estate, sought the Beloved in great love, and was satisfied with nothing short of Him, the Bridegroom here speaks of the end of its labors, and the fulfillment of its desires, saying: "Now the turtle-dove its desired mate on the green banks has found." That is: Now the bride-soul sits on the green bough, rejoicing in her Beloved, drinks of the clear waters of the highest contemplation and of the wisdom of God; is refreshed by the consolations it finds in Him, and is also sheltered under the shadow of His favor and protection, which she had so earnestly desired. There is she deliciously and divinely comforted, refreshed and nourished, as she says in the, Canticle: "I sat down under His shadow Whom I desired, and His fruit was sweet to my palate."

Note

The Bridegroom proceeds to speak of the satisfaction which He derives from the happiness which the bride has found in that solitude wherein she desired to live — a stable peace and unchangeable good. For when the bride is confirmed in the tranquillity of her soul and solitary love of the Bridegroom, she reposes so sweetly in the love of God, and God also in her, that she requires no other means or masters to guide her in the way of God; for God Himself is now her light and guide, fulfilling in her what He promised by the mouth of Hosea, saying: "I will lead her into the wilderness, and I will speak to her heart." That is, it is in solitude that He communicates Himself, and unites Himself, to the soul, for to speak to the heart is to satisfy the heart, and no heart can be satisfied with less than God. And so the Bridegroom Says:

Stanza XXXV

In solitude she lived,
And in solitude built her nest;
And in solitude, alone
Has the Beloved guided her,
In solitude also wounded with love.

In this stanza the Bridegroom is doing two things: one is, He is praising the solitude in which the soul once lived, for it was the means whereby it found the Beloved, and rejoiced in Him, away from all its former anxieties and troubles. For, as the soul abode in solitude, abandoning all created help and consolation, in order to obtain the fellowship and union of the Beloved, it deserved thereby possession of the peace of solitude in the Beloved, in Whom it reposes alone, undisturbed by any anxieties.

The second is this: the Bridegroom is saying that, inasmuch as the soul has desired to be alone, far away, for His sake, from all created things, He has been enamored of it because of its loneliness, has taken care of it, held it in His arms, fed it with all good things, and guided it to the deep things of God. He does not merely say that He is now the soul's guide, but that He is its only guide, without any intermediate help, either of angels or of men, either of forms or of figures; for the soul in this solitude has attained to true liberty of spirit, and is wholly detached from all subordinate means.

"In solitude she lived."

The turtle-dove, that is, the soul, lived in solitude before she found the Beloved in this state of union; for the soul that longs after God derives no consolation from any other companionship, — yes, until it finds Him everything does but increase its solitude.

"And in solitude built her nest."

The previous solitude of the soul was its voluntary privation of all the comforts of this world, for the sake of the Bridegroom — as in the instance of the turtledove — its striving after perfection, and acquiring that perfect solitude wherein it attains to union with the Word, and in consequence to complete refreshment and repose. This is what is meant by "nest"; and the words of the stanza may be thus explained: "In that solitude, wherein the bride formerly lived, tried by afflictions and troubles, because she was not perfect, there, in that solitude, has she found refreshment and rest, because she has found perfect rest in God." This, too, is the spiritual sense of these words of the Psalmist: "The sparrow has found herself a house, and the turtle a nest for herself, where she may lay her young ones; that is, a sure stay in God, in Whom all the desires and powers of the soul are satisfied."

"And in solitude."

In the solitude of perfect detachment from all things, wherein it lives alone with God — there He guides it, moves it, and elevates it to divine things. He guides the understanding in the perception of divine things, because it is now detached from all strange and contrary knowledge, and is alone. He moves the will freely to love Himself, because it is now alone, disencumbered from all other affections. He fills the memory with divine knowledge, because that also is now alone, emptied of all imaginations and fancies. For the instant the soul clears and empties its faculties of all earthly objects, and from attachments to higher things, keeping them in solitude, God immediately fills them with the invisible and divine; it being God Himself Who guides it in this solitude. St. Paul says of the perfect, that they "are led by the Spirit of God," and that is the same as saying "In solitude has He guided her."

"Alone has the Beloved guided her."

That is, the Beloved not only guides the soul in its solitude, but it is He alone Who works in it directly and immediately. It is of the nature of the soul's union with God in the spiritual marriage that God works directly, and communicates Himself immediately, not by the ministry of angels or by the help of natural capacities. For the exterior and interior senses, all created things, and even the soul itself, contribute very little towards the reception of those great supernatural favors which God bestows in this state; indeed, inasmuch as they do not fall within the cognizance of natural efforts, ability and application, God effects them alone.

The reason is, that He finds the soul alone in its solitude, and therefore will not give it another companion, nor will He entrust His work to any other than Himself.

There is a certain fitness in this; for the soul having abandoned all things, and passed through all the ordinary means, rising above them to God, God Himself becomes the guide, and the way to Himself. The soul in solitude, detached from all things, having now ascended above all things, nothing now can profit or help it to ascend higher except the Bridegroom Word Himself, Who, because enamored of the bride, will Himself alone bestow these graces on the soul. And so He says:

"In solitude also wounded with love."

That is, the love of the bride; for the Bridegroom not only loves greatly the solitude of the soul, but is also wounded with love of her, because the soul would abide in solitude and detachment, on account of its being itself wounded with love of Him. He will not, therefore, leave it alone; for being wounded with love because of the soul's solitude on His account, and seeing that nothing else can satisfy it, He comes Himself to be alone its guide, drawing it to, and absorbing it in, Himself. But He would not have done so if He had not found it in this spiritual solitude.

Note

It is a strange characteristic of persons in love that they take a much greater pleasure in their loneliness than in the company of others. For if they meet together in the presence of others with whom they need have no intercourse, and from whom they have nothing to conceal, and if those others neither address them nor interfere with them, yet the very fact of their presence is sufficient to rob the lovers of all pleasure in their meeting. The cause of this lies in the fact that love is the union of two persons, who will not communicate with each other if they are not alone. And now the soul, having reached the summit of perfection, and liberty of spirit in God, all the resistance and contradictions of the flesh being subdued, has no other occupation or employment than indulgence in the joys of its intimate love of the Bridegroom. It is written of holy Tobit, after the trials of his life were over, that God restored his sight, and that "the rest of his life was in joy." So is it with the perfect soul, it rejoices in the blessings that surround it.

The prophet Isaiah says of the soul which, having been tried in the works of perfection has arrived at the goal desired: "Your light shall arise up in darkness, and your darkness shall be as the noonday. And the Lord will give you rest always, and will fill your soul with brightness, and deliver your bones, and you shall be as a watered garden and as a fountain of water whose waters shall not fail. And the deserts of the world shall be built in you: you shall raise up the foundations of generation and generation; and you shall be called the builder of the hedges, turning the paths into rest. If you turn away your foot from the Sabbath, from doing your will in My holy day, and call the Sabbath delicate, and the Holy of our Lord glorious, and glorify Him while you do not your own ways, and your will be not found, to speak a word: then shall you be delighted in the Lord, and I will lift you up above the heights of the earth, and will feed you with the inheritance of Jacob your father," Who is God Himself. The soul, therefore, has nothing else to do now but to rejoice in the delights of this pasture, and one thing only to desire — the perfect fruition of it in everlasting life. Thus, in the next and the following stanzas it implores the Beloved to admit it into this beatific pasture in the clear vision of God, and says:

Stanza XXXVI: The Bride

Let us rejoice, O my Beloved,
Let us go forth to see ourselves in Your beauty,
To the mountain and the hill,
Where the pure water flows:
Let us enter into the heart of the thicket.

The perfect union of love between itself and God being now effected, the soul longs to occupy itself with those things that belong to love. It is the soul which is now speaking, making three petitions to the Beloved. In the first place, it asks for the joy and sweetness of love, saying, "Let us rejoice." In the second place, it prays to be made like Him, saying, "Let us go forth to see ourselves in Your beauty." In the third place, it begs to be admitted to the knowledge of His secrets, saying, "Let us enter into the heart of the thicket."

"Let us rejoice, O my Beloved."

That is, in the sweetness of our love; not only in that sweetness of ordinary union, but also in that which flows from active and affective love, whether in the will by an act of affection, or outwardly in good works which tend to the service of the Beloved. For love, as I have said, where it is firmly rooted, ever runs after those joys and delights which are the acts of exterior and interior love. All this the soul does that it may be made like to the Beloved.

"Let us go forth to see ourselves in Your beauty."

"Let us so act, that, by the practice of this love, we may come to see ourselves in Your beauty in everlasting life." That is: "Let me be so transformed in Your beauty, that, being alike in beauty, we may see ourselves both in Your beauty; having Your beauty, so that, one beholding the other, each may see his own beauty in the other, the beauty of both being Yours only, and mine absorbed in it. And thus I shall see You in Your beauty, and myself in Your beauty, and You shall see me in Your beauty; and I shall see myself in You in Your beauty, and You Yourself in me in Your beauty; so shall I seem to be Yourself in Your beauty, and You myself in Your beauty; my beauty shall be Yours, Yours shall be mine, and I shall be You in it, and You myself in Your own beauty; for Your beauty will be my beauty, and so we shall see, each the other, in Your beauty."

This is the adoption of the sons of God, who may truly say what the Son Himself says to the Eternal Father: "All My things are Yours, and Yours are Mine," He by essence, being the Son of God by nature, we by participation, being sons by adoption. This He says not for Himself only, Who is the Head, but for the whole mystical body, which is the Church. For the Church will share in the very beauty of the Bridegroom in the day of her triumph, when she shall see God face to face. And this is the vision which the soul prays that the Bridegroom and itself may go in His beauty to see.

"To the mountain and the hill."

That is, to the morning and essential knowledge of God, which is knowledge in the Divine Word, Who, because He is so high, is here signified by "the mountain." Thus Isaiah says, calling upon men to know the Son of God: "Come, and let us go up to the mountain of our Lord"; and before: "In the last days the mountain of the house of the Lord shall be prepared."

"And to the hill."

That is, to the evening knowledge of God, to the knowledge of Him in His creatures, in His works, and in His marvelous laws. This is signified by the expression "hill," because it is a kind of knowledge lower than the other. The soul prays for both when it says "to the mountain and the hill."

When the soul says, "Let us go forth to see ourselves in Your beauty to the mountain," its meaning is, "Transform me, and make me like the beauty of the Divine Wisdom, the Word, the Son of God." When it says "to the hill," the meaning is, "Instruct me in the beauty of this lower knowledge, which is manifest in Your creatures and mysterious works." This also is the beauty of the Son of God, with which the soul desires to shine.

But the soul cannot see itself in the beauty of God if it is not transformed in His wisdom, wherein all things are seen and possessed, whether in heaven or in earth. It was to this mountain and to this hill the bride longed to come when she said, "I will go to the mountain of myrrh, and to the hill of frankincense." The mountain of myrrh is the clear vision of God, and the hill of frankincense the knowledge of Him in His works, for the myrrh on the mountain is of a higher order than the incense on the hill.

"Where the pure water flows."

This is the wisdom and knowledge of God, which cleanse the understanding, and detach it from all accidents and fancies, and which clear it of the mist of ignorance. The soul is ever influenced by this desire of perfectly and clearly understanding the divine verities, and the more it loves the more it desires to penetrate them, and hence the third petition which it makes:

"Let us enter into the heart of the thicket;"

Into the depths of God's marvelous works and profound judgments. Such is their multitude and variety, that they may be called a thicket. They are so full of wisdom and mystery, that we may not only call them a thicket, but we may even apply to them the words of David: "The mountain of God is a rich mountain, a mountain curdled as cheese, a rich mountain." The thicket of the wisdom and knowledge of God is so deep, and so immense, that the soul, however much it knows of it, can always penetrate further within it, because it is so immense and so incomprehensible. "O the depth," cries out the Apostle, "of the riches of the wisdom and of the knowledge of God! How incomprehensible are His judgments, and how unsearchable His ways!"

But the soul longs to enter this thicket and incomprehensibility of His judgments, for it is moved by that longing for a deeper knowledge of them. That knowledge is an inestimable delight, transcending all understanding. David, speaking of the sweetness of them, says: "The judgments of our Lord are true, justified in themselves, to be desired above gold and many precious stones, and sweeter than honey and the honey-comb. For Your servant keeps them." The soul therefore earnestly longs to be engulfed in His judgments, and to have a deeper knowledge of them, and for that end would esteem it a joy and great consolation to endure all sufferings and afflictions in the world, and whatever else might help it to that end, however hard and painful it might be; it would gladly pass through the agonies of death to enter deeper into God.

Hence, also, the thicket, which the soul desires to enter, may be fittingly understood as signifying the great and many trials and tribulations which the soul longs for, because suffering is most sweet and most profitable to it, inasmuch as it is the way by which it enters more and more into the thicket of the delicious wisdom of God. The most pure suffering leads to the most pure and the deepest knowledge, and consequently to the purest and highest joy, for that is the issue of the deepest knowledge. Thus, the soul, not satisfied with ordinary suffering, says, "Let us enter into the heart of the thicket," even the anguish of death, that I may see God.

Job, desiring to suffer that he might see God, thus speaks "Who will grant that my request may come, and that God may give me what I look for? And that He that has begun may destroy me, that He may let loose His hand and cut me off? And that this may be my comfort, that afflicting me with sorrow, He spare not." O that men would understand how impossible it is to enter the thicket, the manifold riches of the wisdom of God, without entering into the thicket of manifold suffering making it the desire and consolation of the soul; and how that the soul which really longs for the divine wisdom longs first of all for the sufferings of the Cross, that it may enter in.

For this cause it was that St. Paul admonished the Ephesians not to faint in their tribulations, but to take courage: "That being rooted and founded in charity, you may be able to comprehend with all the saints what is the breadth, and length, and height, and depth; to know also the charity of Christ, which surpasses all knowledge, that you may be filled to all the fullness of God." The gate by which we enter into the riches of the knowledge of God is the Cross; and that gate is narrow. They who desire to enter in that way are few, while those who desire the joys that come by it are many.

Note

One of the principal reasons why the soul desires to be released and to be with Christ is that it may see Him face to face, and penetrate to the depths of His ways and the eternal mysteries of His incarnation, which is not the least part of its blessedness; for in the Gospel of St. John He, addressing the Father, said: "Now this is eternal life: that they may know You, the only true God, and Jesus Christ Whom You have sent." As the first act of a person who has taken a long journey is to see and converse with him whom he was in search of, so the first thing which the soul desires, when it has attained to the beatific vision, is to know and enjoy the deep secrets and mysteries of the incarnation and the ancient ways of God depending on them. Thus the soul, having said that it longed to see itself in the beauty of God, sings as in the following stanza:

Stanza XXXVII

We shall go at once
To the deep caverns of the rock
Which are all secret;
There we shall enter in,
And taste of the new wine of the pomegranate.

One of the reasons which most influence the soul to desire to enter into the "thicket" of the wisdom of God, and to have a more intimate knowledge of the beauty of the divine wisdom, is, as I have said, that it may unite the understanding with God in the knowledge of the mysteries of the Incarnation, as of all His works the highest and most full of sweetness, and the most delicious knowledge. And here the bride therefore says, that after she has entered in within the divine wisdom — that is, the spiritual marriage, which is now and will be in glory, seeing God face to face — her soul united with the divine wisdom, the Son of God, she will then understand the deep mysteries of God and Man, which are the highest wisdom hidden in God. They, that is, the bride and the Bridegroom, will enter in — the soul engulfed and absorbed — and both together will have the fruition of the joy which springs from the knowledge of mysteries, and attributes and power of God which are revealed in those mysteries, such as His justice, His mercy, wisdom, power, and love.

"We shall go at once to the deep caverns of the rock."

"This rock is Christ," as we learn from St. Paul. The deep caverns of the rock are the deep mysteries of the wisdom of God in Christ, in the hypostatical union of the human nature with the Divine Word, and in the correspondence with it of the union of man with God, and in the agreement of God's justice and mercy in the salvation of mankind, in the manifestation of His judgments. And because His judgments are so high and so deep, they are here fittingly called "deep caverns"; deep because of the depth of His mysteries, and caverns because of the depth of His wisdom in them. For as caverns are deep, with many windings, so each mystery of Christ is of deepest wisdom, and has many windings of His secret judgments of predestination and foreknowledge with respect to men.

Notwithstanding the marvelous mysteries which holy doctors have discovered, and holy souls have understood in this life, many more remain behind. There are in Christ great depths to be fathomed, for He is a rich mine, with many recesses full of treasures, and however deeply we may descend we shall never reach the end, for in every recess new veins of new treasures abound in all directions: "In Whom," according to the Apostle, "are hid all the treasures of wisdom and knowledge." But the soul cannot reach these hidden treasures unless it first passes through the thicket of interior and exterior suffering: for even such knowledge of the mysteries of Christ as is possible in this life cannot be had without great sufferings, and without many intellectual and moral gifts, and without previous spiritual exercises; for all these gifts are far inferior to this knowledge of the mysteries of Christ, being only a preparation for it.

Thus God said to Moses, when he asked to see His glory, "Man shall not see Me and live." God, however, said that He would show him all that could be revealed in this life; and so He set Moses "in a hole of the rock," which is Christ, where he might see His "back parts"; that is, He made him understand the mysteries of the Sacred Humanity.

The soul longs to enter in earnest into these caverns of Christ, that it may be absorbed, transformed, and inebriated in the love and knowledge of His mysteries, hiding itself in the bosom of the Beloved. It is into these caverns that He invites the bride, in the Canticle, to enter, saying: "Arise, My love, My beautiful one, and come; My dove in the clefts of the rock, in the hollow places of the wall." These clefts of the rock are the caverns of which we are here speaking, and to which the bride refers, saying:

"And there we shall enter in."

That is, in the knowledge of the divine mysteries. The bride does not say "I will enter" alone, which seems the most fitting — seeing that the Bridegroom has no need to enter in again — but "we will enter," that is, the Bridegroom and the bride, to show that this is not the work of the bride, but of the Bridegroom with her. Moreover, inasmuch as God and the soul are now united in the state of spiritual marriage, the soul does nothing of itself without God. To say "we will enter," is as much as to say, "there shall we transform ourselves" — that is, "I shall be transformed in You through the love of Your divine and sweet judgments": for in the knowledge of the predestination of the just and in the foresight of the wicked, wherein the Father prevented the just in the benedictions of His sweetness in Jesus Christ His Son, the soul is transformed in a most exalted and perfect way in the love of God according to this knowledge, giving thanks to the Father, and loving Him again and again with great sweetness and delight, for the sake of Jesus Christ His Son. This the soul does in union with Christ and together with Him. The delight flowing from this act of praise is ineffably sweet, and the soul speaks of it in the words that follow:

"And taste of the new wine of the pomegranates."

The pomegranates here are the mysteries of Christ and the judgments of the wisdom of God; His power and attributes, the knowledge of which we have from these mysteries; and they are infinite. For as pomegranates have many grains in their round orb, so in each one of the attributes and judgments and power of God is a multitude of admirable arrangements and marvelous works contained within the sphere of power and mystery, appertaining to those works. Consider the round form of the pomegranate; for each pomegranate signifies some one power and attribute of God, which power or attribute is God Himself, symbolized here by the circular figure, which has neither beginning not end. It was in the contemplation of the judgments and mysteries of the wisdom of God, which are infinite, that the bride said, "His belly is of ivory set with sapphires." The sapphires are the mysteries and judgments of the divine Wisdom, which is here signified by the "belly" — the sapphire being a precious stone of the color of the heavens when clear and serene.

The wine of the pomegranates which the bride says that she and the Bridegroom will taste is the fruition and joy of the love of God which overflows the soul in the understanding and knowledge of His mysteries. For as the many grains of the pomegranate pressed together give forth but one wine, so all the marvels and magnificence of God, infused into the soul, issue in but one fruition and joy of love, which is the drink of the Holy Spirit, and which the soul offers at once to God the Word, its Bridegroom, with great tenderness of love.

This divine drink the bride promised to the Bridegroom if He would lead her into this deep knowledge: "There You shall teach me," says the bride, "and I will give You a cup of spiced wine, and new wine of my pomegranates." The soul calls them "my pomegranates," though they are God's Who had given them to it, and the soul offers them to God as if they were its own, saying, "We will taste of the wine of the pomegranates"; for when He states it He gives it to the soul to taste, and when the soul tastes it, the soul gives it back to Him, and thus it is that both taste it together.

Note

In the two previous stanzas the bride sung of those good things which the Bridegroom is to give her in everlasting bliss, namely, her transformation in the beauty of created and uncreated wisdom, and also in the beauty of the union of the Word with flesh, wherein she shall behold His face as well as His back. Accordingly two things are set before us in the following stanza. The first is the way in which the soul tastes of the divine wine of the pomegranates; the second is the soul's putting before the Bridegroom the glory of its predestination. And though these two things are spoken of separately, one after the other, they are both involved in the one essential glory of the soul.

Stanza XXXVIII

There you will show me
That which my soul desired;
And there You will give at once,
O You, my life,
That which You gave me the other day.

The reason why the soul longed to enter the caverns was that it might attain to the consummation of the love of God, the object of its continual desires; that is, that it might love God with the pureness and perfection with which He has loved it, so that it might thereby requite His love. Hence in the present stanza the bride says to the Bridegroom that He will there show her what she had always aimed at in all her actions, namely, that He would show her how to love Him perfectly, as He has loved her. And, secondly, that He will give her that essential glory for which He has predestined her from the day of His eternity.

"There You will show me That which my soul desired."

That which the soul aims at is equality in love with God, the object of its natural and supernatural desire. He who loves cannot be satisfied if he does not feel that he loves as much as he is loved. And when the soul sees that in the transformation in God, such as is possible in this life, notwithstanding the immensity of its love, it cannot equal the perfection of that love with which God loves it, it desires the clear transformation of glory in which it shall equal the perfection of love with which it is itself beloved of God; it desires, I say, the clear transformation of glory in which it shall equal His love.

For though in this high state, which the soul reaches on earth, there is a real union of the will, yet it cannot reach that perfection and strength of love which it will possess in the union of glory; seeing that then, according to the Apostle, the soul will know God as it is known of Him: "Then I shall know even as I am known." That is, "I shall then love God even as I am loved by Him." For as the understanding of the soul will then be the understanding of God, and its will the will of God, so its love will also be His love. Though in heaven the will of the soul is not destroyed, it is so intimately united with the power of the will of God, Who loves it, that it loves Him as strongly and as perfectly as it is loved of Him; both wills being united in one sole will and one sole love of God.

Thus the soul loves God with the will and strength of God Himself, being made one with that very strength of love with which itself is loved of God. This strength is of the Holy Spirit, in Whom the soul is there transformed. He is given to the soul to strengthen its love; ministering to it, and supplying in it, because of its transformation in glory, that which is defective in it. In the perfect transformation, also, of the state of spiritual marriage, such as is possible on earth, in which the soul is all clothed in grace, the soul loves in a certain way in the Holy Spirit, Who is given to it in that transformation.

We are to observe here that the bride does not say, "There will You give me Your love," though that is true — for that means only that God will love her — but that He will there show her how she is to love Him with that perfection at which she aims, because there in giving her His love He will at the same time show her how to love Him as He loves her. For God not only teaches the soul to love Himself purely, with a disinterested love, as He has loved us, but He also enables it to love Him with that strength with which He loves the soul, transforming it in His love, wherein He bestows upon it His own power, so that it may love Him. It is as if He put an instrument in its hand, taught it the use thereof, and played upon it together with the soul. This is showing the soul how it is to love, and at the same time endowing it with the capacity of loving.

The soul is not satisfied until it reaches this point, neither would it be satisfied even in heaven, unless it felt, as St. Thomas teaches, that it loved God as much as it is loved of Him. And as I said of the state of spiritual marriage of which I am speaking, there is now at this time, though it cannot be that perfect love in glory, a certain vivid vision and likeness of that perfection, which is wholly indescribable.

"And there You will give me at once, O You my life, that which You gave me the other day."

What He will give is the essential glory which consists in the vision of God. Before proceeding further it is requisite to solve a question which arises here, namely, Why is it, seeing that essential glory consists in the vision of God, and not in loving Him, the soul says that its longing is for His love, and not for the essential glory? Why is it that the soul begins the stanza with referring to His love, and then introduces the subject of the essential glory afterwards, as if it were something of less importance?

There are two reasons for this. The first is this: As the whole aim of the soul is love, the seat of which is in the will, the property of which is to give and not to receive — the property of the understanding, the subject of essential glory, being to receive and not to give — to the soul inebriated with love the first consideration is not the essential glory which God will bestow upon it, but the entire surrender of itself to Him in true love, without any regard to its own advantage.

The second reason is that the second object is included in the first, and has been taken for granted in the previous stanzas, it being impossible to attain to the perfect love of God without the perfect vision of Him. The question is solved by the first reason, for the soul renders to God by love that which is His due, but with the understanding it receives from Him and does not give.

I now resume the explanation of the stanza, and inquire what day is meant by the "other day," and what is it that God then gave the soul, and what that is which it prays to receive afterwards in glory? By "other day" is meant the day of the eternity of God, which is other than the day of time. In that day of eternity God predestined the soul to glory, and determined the degree of glory which He would give it and freely gave from the beginning before He created it. This now, in a manner, so truly belongs to the soul that no event or accident, high or low, can ever take it away, for the soul will enjoy for ever that for which God had predestined it from all eternity.

This is that which He gave it "the other day"; that which the soul longs now to possess visibly in glory. And what is that which He gave it? That what "eye has not seen nor ear has heard, neither has it ascended into the heart of man." "The eye has not seen," says Isaiah, "O God, beside You, what things You have prepared for them that expect You." The soul has no word to describe it, so it says "what." It is in truth the vision of God, and as there is no expression by which we can explain what it is to see God, the soul says only "that which You gave me."

But that I may not leave the subject without saying something further concerning it, I will repeat what Christ has said of it in the Revelation of St. John, in many terms, phrases, and comparisons, because a single word once uttered cannot describe it, for there is much still unsaid, notwithstanding all that Christ has spoken at seven different times. "To him that overcomes," says He, "I will give to eat of the tree of life, which is in the paradise of My God." But as this does not perfectly describe it, He says again: "Be faithful to death; and I will give you the crown of life."

This also is insufficient, and so He speaks again more obscurely, but explaining it more: "To him that overcomes I will give the hidden manna, and will give him a white counter, and on the counter a new name written which no man knows but he that receives it." And as even this is still insufficient, the Son of God speaks of great power and joy, saying: "He that shall overcome and keep My works to the end, I will give him power over the nations: and he shall rule them with a rod of iron, and as a vessel of the potter they shall be broken: as I also have received of My Father. And I will give him the morning star." Not satisfied with these words, He adds: "He that shall overcome shall thus be vested in white garments, and I will not put his name out of the book of life, and I will confess his name before My Father."

Still, all this falls short. He speaks of it in words of unutterable majesty and grandeur: "He that shall overcome I will make Him a pillar in the temple of My God, and he shall go out no more; and I will write upon him the name of My God, and the name of the city of My God, the new Jerusalem which descends out of heaven from My God, and My new name." The seventh time He says: "He that shall overcome I will give to him to sit with Me in My throne: as I also have overcome, and sat with My Father in His throne. He that has an ear let him hear what the Spirit says to the Churches."

These are the words of the Son of God; all of which tend to describe that which was given to the soul. The words correspond most accurately with it, but still they do not explain it, because it involves infinite good. The noblest expressions befit it, but none of them reach it, no, not all together.

Let us now see whether David has said anything of it. In one of the Psalms he says, "O how great is the multitude of your sweetness, O Lord, which You have hidden for them that fear You." In another place he calls it a "torrent of pleasure," saying, "You shall make them drink of the torrent of Your pleasure." And as he did not consider this enough, he says again, "You have prevented him with blessings of sweetness." The expression that rightly fits this "that" of the soul, namely, its predestined bliss, cannot be found. Let us, therefore, rest satisfied with what the soul has used in reference to it, and explain the words as follows:

"That which You gave me."

That is, "That weight of glory to which You predestined me, O my Bridegroom, in the day of Your eternity, when it was Your good pleasure to decree my creation, You will then give me in my day of my betrothal and of my nuptials, in my day of the joy of my heart, when, released from the burden of the flesh, led into the deep caverns of Your bridal chamber and gloriously transformed in You, we drink the wine of the sweet pomegranates."

Note

But inasmuch as the soul, in the state of spiritual marriage, of which I am now speaking, cannot but know something of this "that," seeing that because of its transformation in God something of it must be experienced by it, it will not omit to say something on the subject, the pledges and signs of which it is conscious of in itself, as it is written: "Who can withhold the words He has conceived?" Hence in the following stanza the soul says something of the fruition which it shall have in the beatific vision, explaining so far as it is possible the nature and the manner of it.

Stanza XXXIX

The breathing of the air,
The song of the sweet nightingale,
The grove and its beauty
In the serene night,
With the flame that consumes, and gives no pain.

The soul refers here, under five different expressions, to that which the Bridegroom is to give it in the beatific transformation. 1. The aspiration of the Holy Spirit of God after it, and its own aspiration after God. 2. Joyous praise of God in the fruition of Him. 3. The knowledge of creatures and the order of them. 4. The pure and clear contemplation of the divine essence. 5. Perfect transformation in the infinite love of God.

"The breathing of the air."

This is a certain faculty which God will there give the soul in the communication of the Holy Spirit, Who, like one breathing, raises the soul by His divine aspiration, informs it, strengthens it, so that it too may breathe in God with the same aspiration of love which the Father breathes with the Son, and the Son with the Father, which is the Holy Spirit Himself, Who is breathed into the soul in the Father and the Son in that transformation so as to unite it to Himself; for the transformation will not be true and perfect if the soul is not transformed in the Three Persons of the Most Holy Trinity in a clear manifest degree. This breathing of the Holy Spirit in the soul, whereby God transforms it in Himself, is to the soul a joy so deep, so exquisite, and so grand that no mortal tongue can describe it, no human understanding, as such, conceive it in any degree; for even that which passes in the soul with respect to the communication which takes place in its transformation wrought in this life cannot be described, because the soul united with God and transformed in Him breathes in God that very divine aspiration which God breathes Himself in the soul when it is transformed in Him.

In the transformation which takes place in this life, this breathing of God in the soul, and of the soul in God, is of most frequent occurrence, and the source of the most exquisite delight of love to the soul, but not however in the clear and manifest degree which it will have in the life to come. This, in my opinion, is what St. Paul referred to when he said: "Because you are sons, God has sent the Spirit of His Son into your hearts, crying Abba, Father." The blessed in the life to come, and the perfect in this, thus experience it.

Nor is it to be thought possible that the soul should be capable of so great a thing as that it should breathe in God as God in it, in the way of participation. For granting that God has bestowed upon it so great a favor as to unite it to the most Holy Trinity, whereby it becomes like God, and God by participation, is it altogether incredible that it should exercise the faculties of its understanding, perform its acts of knowledge and of love, or, to speak more accurately, should have it all done in the Holy Trinity together with It, as the Holy Trinity itself? This, however, takes place by communication and participation, God Himself effecting it in the soul, for this is "to be transformed in the Three Persons" in power, wisdom, and love, and herein it is that the soul becomes like God, Who, that it might come to this, created it to His own image and likeness.

How this can be so cannot be explained in any other way than by showing how the Son of God has raised us to so high a state, and merited for us the "power to be made the sons of God." He prayed to the Father, saying: "Father, I will that where I am they also whom You have given Me may be with Me, that they may see My glory which You have given Me." That is, "that they may do by participation in Us what I do naturally, namely, breathe the Holy Spirit." He says also: "Not for them only do I pray, but for them also who through their word shall believe in Me; that they all may be one, as You, Father, in Me, and I in You, that they also may be one in Us: that the world may believe that You have sent Me. And the glory which You have given Me, I have given to them: that they may be one as We also are one. I in them and You in Me, that they may be made perfect in one, and the world may know that You have sent Me, and have loved them as You have also loved Me," — that is, in bestowing upon them that love which He bestows upon the Son, though not naturally as upon Him, but in the way I speak of, in the union and transformation of love.

We are not to suppose from this that our Lord prayed that the saints might become one in essence and nature, as the Father and the Son are; but that they might become one in the union of love as the Father and the Son are one in the oneness of love. Souls have by participation that very God which the Son has by nature, and are therefore really gods by participation like unto God and of His society.

St. Peter speaks of this as follows: "Grace to you and peace be accomplished in the knowledge of God, and Christ Jesus our Lord; as all things of His divine power, which pertain to life and godliness, are given us by the knowledge of Him Who has called us by His own proper glory and virtue, by Whom He has given us most great and precious promises: that by these you may be made partakers of the divine nature." Thus far St. Peter, who clearly teaches that the soul will be a partaker of God Himself, and will do, together with Him, the work of the Most Holy Trinity, because of the substantial union between the soul and God. And though this union is perfect only in the life to come, yet even in this, in the state of perfection, which the soul is said now to have attained, some anticipation of its sweetness is given it, in the way I am speaking of, though in a manner wholly ineffable.

O souls created for this and called to this, what are you doing? What are your occupations? Your aim is meanness, and your enjoyments misery. Oh, wretched blindness of the children of Adam, blind to so great a light, and deaf to so clear a voice; you do not see that, while seeking after greatness and glory, you are miserable and contemptible, ignorant, and unworthy of blessings so great. I now proceed to the second expression which the soul has made use of to describe that which He gave it.

"The song of the sweet nightingale."

Out of this "breathing of the air" comes the sweet voice of the Beloved addressing Himself to the soul, in which the soul sends forth its own sweet song of joy to Him. Both are meant by the song of the nightingale. As the song of the nightingale is heard in the spring of the year, when the cold, and rain, and changes of winter are past, filling the ear with melody, and the mind with joy; so, in the true intercourse and transformation of love, which takes place in this life, the bride, now protected and delivered from all trials and changes of the world, detached, and free from the imperfections, sufferings, and darkness both of mind and body, becomes conscious of a new spring in liberty, largeness, and joy of spirit, in which she hears the sweet voice of the Bridegroom, Who is her sweet nightingale, renewing and refreshing the very substance of her soul, now prepared for the journey of everlasting life.

That voice is sweet to her ears, and calls her sweetly, as it is written: "Arise, make haste, My love, My dove, My beautiful one, and come. For winter is now past, the rain is over and gone. The flowers have appeared in our land, the time of pruning is come: the voice of the turtle is heard in our land." When the bride hears the voice of the Bridegroom in her inmost soul, she feels that her troubles are over and her prosperity begun. In the refreshing comfort and sweet sense of this voice she, too, like the nightingale, sends forth a new song of rejoicing to God, in unison with Him Who now moves her to do so.

It is for this that the Beloved sings, that the bride in unison with Him may sing to God; this is the aim and desire of the Bridegroom, that the soul should sing with the spirit joyously to God; and this is what He asks of the bride in the Canticle: "Arise, my love, my beautiful one, and come; my dove in the clefts of the rock, in the hollow places of the wall, show me your face, let your voice sound in my ears."

The ears of God signify the desire He has that the soul should sing in perfect joy. And that this song may be perfect, the Bridegroom bids the soul to send it forth, and to let it sound in the clefts of the rock, that is, in the transformation which is the fruit of the mysteries of Christ, of which I spoke just now. And because in this union of the soul with God, the soul sings to Him together with Him, in the way I spoke of when I was speaking of love, the song of praise is most perfect and pleasing to God; for the acts of the soul, in the state of perfection, are most perfect; and thus the song of its rejoicing is sweet to God as well as to itself.

"Your voice is sweet," says the Bridegroom, "not only to you, but also to Me, for as we are one, your voice is also in unison and one with Mine." This is the Canticle which the soul sings in the transformation which takes place in this life, about which no exaggeration is possible. But as this song is not so perfect as the new song in the life of glory, the soul, having a foretaste of that by what it feels on earth, shadows forth by the grandeur of this the magnificence of that in glory, which is beyond all comparison nobler, and calls it to mind and says that what its portion there will be is the song of the sweet nightingale.

"The grove and its beauty."

This is the third thing which the Bridegroom is to give the soul. The grove, because it contains many plants and animals, signifies God as the Creator and Giver of life to all creatures, which have their being and origin from Him, reveal Him and make Him known as the Creator. The beauty of the grove, which the soul prays for, is not only the grace, wisdom, and loveliness which flow from God over all created things, whether in heaven or on earth, but also the beauty of the mutual harmony and wise arrangement of the inferior creation, and the higher also, and of the mutual relations of both. The knowledge of this gives the soul great joy and delight. The fourth request is:

"In the serene night."

That is, contemplation, in which the soul desires to behold the grove. It is called night, because contemplation is dim; and that is the reason why it is also called mystical theology — that is, the secret or hidden wisdom of God, where, without the sound of words, or the intervention of any bodily or spiritual sense, as it were in silence and in repose, in the darkness of sense and nature, God teaches the soul — and the soul knows not how — in a most secret and hidden way.

Some spiritual writers call this "understanding without understanding," because it does not take place in what philosophers call the active understanding which is conversant with the forms, fancies, and apprehensions of the physical faculties, but in the understanding as it is possible and passive, which without receiving such forms receives passively only the substantial knowledge of them free from all imagery. This occurs without effort or exertion on its part, and for this reason contemplation is called night, in which the soul through the channel of its transformation learns in this life that it already possesses, in a supreme degree, this divine grove, together with its beauty.

Still, however clear may be its knowledge, it is dark night in comparison with that of the blessed, for which the soul prays. Hence, while it prays for the clear contemplation, that is, the fruition of the grove, and its beauty; with the other objects here enumerated, it says, let it be in the night now serene; that is, in the clear beatific contemplation: let the night of dim contemplation cease here below, and change into the clear contemplation of the serene vision of God above. Thus the serene night is the clear and unclouded contemplation of the face of God. It was to this night of contemplation that David referred when he said, "Night shall be my light in my pleasures"; that is, when I shall have my delight in the essential vision of God, the night of contemplation will have dawned in the day and light of my understanding.

"With the flame that consumes, and gives no pain."

This flame is the love of the Holy Spirit. "Consumes" means absolute perfection. Therefore, when the soul says that the Beloved will give it all that is mentioned in this stanza, and that they will be its possession in love absolute and perfect, all of them and itself with them in perfect love, and that without pain, its purpose is to show forth the utter perfection of love. Love, to be perfect, must have these two properties: it must consume and transform the soul in God; the burning and transformation wrought in the soul by the flame must give no pain. But this can be only in the state of the blessed, where the flame is sweet love, for in this transformation of the soul therein there is a blessed agreement and contentment on both sides, and no change to a greater or less degree gives pain, as before, when the soul had attained to the state of perfect love.

But the soul having attained to this state abides in its love of God, a love so like His and so sweet, God being, as Moses says, a consuming fire — "the Lord your God is a consuming fire" — that it perfects and renews it. But this transformation is not like that which is wrought in this life, which though most perfect and in love consummate was still in some measure consuming the soul and wearing it away. It was like fire in burning coals, for though the coals may be transformed into fire, and made like it, and ceased from seething, and smoke no longer arises from them as before they were wholly transformed into fire, still, though they have become perfect fire, the fire consumes them and reduces them to ashes.

So is it with the soul which in this life is transformed by perfect love: for though it is wholly conformed, yet it still suffers, in some measure, both pain and loss. Pain, on account of the beatific transformation which is still wanting; loss, through the weakness and corruption of the flesh coming in contact with love so strong and so deep; for everything that is grand hurts and pains our natural infirmity, as it is written, "The corruptible body is a load upon the soul." But in the life of bliss there will be neither loss nor pain, though the sense of the soul will be most acute, and its love without measure, for God will give power to the former and strength to the latter, perfecting the understanding in His wisdom and the will in His love.

As, in the foregoing stanzas, and in the one which follows, the bride prays for the boundless knowledge of God, for which she requires the strongest and the deepest love that she may love Him in proportion to the grandeur of His communications, she prays now that all these things may be bestowed upon her in love consummated, perfect, and strong.

Stanza XL

None saw it;
Neither did Aminadab appear
The siege was intermitted,
And the cavalry dismounted
At the sight of the waters.

The bride perceiving that the desire of her will is now detached from all things, cleaving to God with most fervent love; that the sensual part of the soul, with all its powers, faculties, and desires, is now conformed to the spirit; that all rebellion is quelled forever; that Satan is overcome and driven far away in the varied contest of the spiritual struggle; that her soul is united and transformed in the rich abundance of the heavenly gifts; and that she herself is now prepared, strong and apparelled, "leaning upon her Beloved," to go up "by the desert" of death; full of joy to the glorious throne of her espousals, — she is longing for the end, and puts before the eyes of her Bridegroom, in order to influence Him the more, all that is mentioned in the present stanza, these five considerations:

The first is that the soul is detached from all things and a stranger to them. The second is that the devil is overcome and put to flight. The third is that the passions are subdued, and the natural desires mortified. The fourth and the fifth are that the sensual and lower nature of the soul is changed and purified, and so conformed to the spiritual, as not only not to hinder spiritual blessings, but is, on the contrary, prepared for them, for it is even a partaker already, according to its capacity, of those which have been bestowed upon it.

"None saw it."

That is, my soul is so detached, so denuded, so lonely, so estranged from all created things, in heaven and earth; it has become so recollected in You, that nothing whatever can come within sight of that most intimate joy which I have in You. That is, there is nothing whatever that can cause me pleasure with its sweetness, or disgust with its vileness; for my soul is so far removed from all such things, absorbed in such profound delight in You, that nothing can behold me. This is not all, for:

"Neither did Aminadab appear."

Aminadab, in the Holy Writings, signifies the devil; that is the enemy of the soul, in a spiritual sense, who is ever fighting against it, and disturbing it with his innumerable artillery, that it may not enter into the fortress and secret place of interior recollection with the Bridegroom. There, the soul is so protected, so strong, so triumphant in virtue which it then practices, so defended by God's right hand, that the devil not only dares not approach it, but runs away from it in great fear, and does not venture to appear. The practice of virtue, and the state of perfection to which the soul has come, is a victory over Satan, and causes him such terror that he cannot present himself before it. Thus Aminadab did not appear with any right to keep the soul away from the object of its desire.

"The siege was intermitted."

By the siege is meant the passions and desires, which, when not overcome and mortified, surround the soul and fight against it on all sides. Hence the term "siege" is applied to them. This siege is "intermitted" — that is, the passions are subject to reason and the desires mortified. Under these circumstances the soul entreats the Beloved to communicate to it those graces for which it has prayed, for now the siege is no hindrance. Until the four passions of the soul are ordered in reason according to God, and until the desires are mortified and purified, the soul is incapable of seeing God.

"The cavalry dismounted at the sight of the waters."

The waters are the spiritual joys and blessings which the soul now enjoys interiorly with God. The cavalry is the bodily senses of the sensual part, interior as well as exterior, for they carry with them the phantasms and figures of their objects. They dismount now at the sight of the waters, because the sensual and lower part of the soul in the state of spiritual marriage is purified, and in a certain way spiritualized, so that the soul with its powers of sense and natural forces becomes so recollected as to participate and rejoice, in their way, in the spiritual grandeurs which God communicates to it in the spirit within. To this the Psalmist referred when he said, "My heart and my flesh have rejoiced in the living God."

It is to be observed that the cavalry did not dismount to taste of the waters, but only at the sight of them, because the sensual part of the soul, with its powers, is incapable of tasting substantially and properly the spiritual blessings, not merely in this life, but also in the life to come. Still, because of a certain overflowing of the spirit, they are sensibly refreshed and delighted, and this delight attracts them — that is, the senses with their bodily powers — towards that interior recollection where the soul is drinking the waters of the spiritual benedictions. This condition of the senses is rather a dismounting at the sight of the waters than a dismounting for the purpose of seeing or tasting them. The soul says of them that they dismounted, not that they went, or did anything else, and the meaning is that in the communication of the sensual with the spiritual part of the soul, when the spiritual waters become its drink, the natural operations subside and merge into spiritual recollection.

All these perfections and dispositions of the soul the bride sets forth before her Beloved, the Son of God, longing at the same time to be translated by Him out of the spiritual marriage, to which God has been pleased to advance her in the Church militant, to the glorious marriage of the Church triumphant. To that end

may He bring of His mercy all those who call upon the most sweet name of Jesus, the Bridegroom of faithful souls, to Whom be all honor and glory, together with the Father and the Holy Spirit,
IN SÆCULA SÆCULORUM.

Twenty Poems by St. John of the Cross

Table of Contents

His Heart an Open Wound
Stanzas Applied Spiritually to Christ and the Soul.

A lone young shepherd lived in pain
withdrawn from pleasure and contentment,
his thoughts fixed on a shepherd-girl
his heart an open wound with love.

He weeps, but not from the wound of love,
there is no pain in such affliction,
even though the heart is pierced;
he weeps in knowing he's been forgotten.

That one thought: his shining one
has forgotten him, is such great pain
that he bows to brutal handling in a foreign land,
his heart an open wound with love.

The shepherd says: I pity the one
who draws herself back from my love,
and does not seek the joy of my presence
though my heart is an open wound with love for her.

After a long time he climbed a tree,
and spread his shining arms,
and hung by them, and died,
his heart an open wound with love.

Trinity

Romance on the Gospel Text Regarding the Blessed Trinity.

In the beginning the Word
was; he lived in God
and possessed in him
his infinite happiness.
That same Word was God,
who is the Beginning;
he was in the beginning
and had no beginning.
He was himself the Beginning
and therefore had no beginning!
The Word is called Son;
he was born of the Beginning
who had always conceived him,
and was always conceiving him,
giving of his substance always,
yet always possessing it.
And thus the glory of the Son
was the Father's glory,
and the Father possessed
all his glory in the Son.
As the lover in the beloved
each lived in the other,
and the Love that unites them
is one with them,
their equal, excellent as
the One and the Other:
Three Persons, and one Beloved
among all three.
One love in them all
makes of them one Lover,
and the Lover is the Beloved
in whom each one lives.
For the being that the three possess
each of them possesses,

and each of them loves
him who bears this being.
Each one is this being,
which alone unites them,
binding them deeply,
one beyond words.
Thus it is a boundless
Love that unites them,
for the three have one love
which is their essence;
and the more love is one
the more it is love.

Within the Trinity
On the Communication among the Three Persons.

In that immense love
proceeding from the two
the Father spoke words
of great affection to the Son,
words of such profound delight
that no one understood them;
they were meant for the Son,
and he alone rejoiced in them.
What he heard
was this:
"My Son, only your
company contents me,
and when something pleases me
I love that thing in you;
whoever resembles you most
satisfies me most,
and whoever is like you in nothing
will find nothing in me.
I am pleased with you alone,
O life of my life!
You are the light of my light,
you are my wisdom,
the image of my substance
in whom I am well pleased.
My Son, I will give myself
to him who loves you
and I will love him
with the same love I have for you,
because he has loved
you whom I love so."

By the Waters of Babylon
A Romance on the Psal

By the rivers
of Babylon
I sat down weeping,
there on the ground.
And remembering you,
0 Zion, whom I loved,
in that sweet memory
I wept even more.
I took off my feast-day clothes
and put on my working ones;
I hung on the green willows
all the joy I had in song,
putting it aside for that
which I hoped for in you.
There love wounded me
and took away my heart.
I begged love to kill me
since it had so wounded me;
I threw myself in its fire
knowing it burned,
excusing now the young bird
that would die in the fire.
I was dying in myself,
breathing in you alone.
I died within myself for you
and for you I revived,
because the memory of you
gave life and took it away.
The strangers among whom
I was captive rejoiced;
they asked me to sing
what I sang in Zion:
Sing us a song from Zion,
let's hear how it sounds.
I said: How can I sing,
in a strange land where I weep
for Zion, sing of the happiness

that I had there?
I would be forgetting her
if I rejoiced in a strange land.
May the tongue I speak with
cling to my palate if I forget you
in this land where I am.
Zion, by the green branches
Babylon holds out to me,
may my right hand be forgotten
(that I so loved when home in you)
if I do not remember you,
my greatest joy,
or celebrate one feast-day,
or feast at all without you.
O Daughter of Babylon,
miserable and wretched!
Blessed is he
in whom I have trusted,
for he will punish you
as you have me;
and he will gather his little ones
and me, who wept because of
you,
at the rock who is Christ
for whom I abandoned you.

Song of the Soul That Rejoices in Knowing God Through Faith.

For I know well the spring that flows and runs,
although it is night.
That eternal spring is hidden, for I know well where it has its rise,
although it is night.

I do not know its origin, nor has it one,
but I know that every origin has come from it,
although it is night.

I know that nothing else is so beautiful,
and that the heavens and the earth drink there,
although it is night.

I know well that it is bottomless
and no one is able to cross it,
although it is night.

Its clarity is never darkened,
and I know that every light has
come from it,
although it is night.

The Dark Night

Songs of the Soul That Rejoices in Having Reached the High State of Perfection, Which Is Union with God, by the Path of Spiritual Negation.

One dark night,
fired with love's urgent longings
- ah, the sheer grace! -
I went out unseen,
my house being now all stilled.

In darkness, and secure,
by the secret ladder, disguised,
ah, the sheer grace! -
in darkness and concealment,
my house being now all stilled.

On that glad night
in secret, for no one saw me,
nor did I look at anything
with no other light or guide
than the one that burned in my heart.

This guided me
more surely than the light of noon
to where he was awaiting me
- him I knew so well -
there in a place where no one appeared.

O guiding night!
O night more lovely than the dawn!
O night that has united
the Lover with his beloved,
transforming the beloved in her Lover.

Upon my flowering breast,

which I kept wholly for him alone,
there he lay sleeping,
and I caressing him
there in a breeze from the fanning cedars.

When the breeze blew from the turret,
as I parted his hair,
it wounded my neck
with its gentle hand,
suspending all my senses.

I abandoned and forgot myself,
laying my face on my Beloved;
all things ceased; I went out from myself,
leaving my cares
forgotten among the lilies.

The Living Flame Of Love

Songs of the Soul in the Intimate Communication of Loving Union with God.

O living flame of love
that tenderly wounds my soul
in its deepest center! Since
now you are not oppressive,
now consummate! if it be your will:
tear through the veil of this sweet encounter!

O sweet cautery,
O delightful wound!
O gentle hand! O delicate touch
that tastes of eternal life
and pays every debt!
In killing you changed death to life.

O lamps of fire!
in whose splendors
the deep caverns of feeling,
once obscure and blind,
now give forth, so rarely, so exquisitely,
both warmth and light to their Beloved.

How gently and lovingly
you wake in my heart,
where in secret you dwell alone;
and in your sweet breathing,
filled with good and glory,
how tenderly you swell my heart with love.

Stanzas Concerning an Ecstasy Experienced in High Contemplation

I entered into unknowing,
and there I remained unknowing
transcending all knowledge.

I entered into unknowing,
yet when I saw myself there,
without knowing where I was,
I understood great things;
I will not say what I felt
for I remained in unknowing
transcending all knowledge.

That perfect knowledge
was of peace and holiness
held at no remove
in profound solitude;
it was something so secret
that I was left stammering,
transcending all knowledge.

I was so 'whelmed,
so absorbed and withdrawn,
that my senses were left
deprived of all their sensing,
and my spirit was given
an understanding while not understanding,
transcending all knowledge.

He who truly arrives there
cuts free from himself;
all that he knew before
now seems worthless,
and his knowledge so soars

that he is left in unknowing
transcending all knowledge.

The higher he ascends
the less he understands,
because the cloud is dark
which lit up the night;
whoever knows this
remains always in unknowing
transcending all knowledge.

This knowledge in unknowing
is so overwhelming
that wise men disputing
can never overthrow it,
for their knowledge does not reach
to the understanding of not understanding,
transcending all knowledge.

And this supreme knowledge
is so exalted
that no power of man or learning
can grasp it;
he who masters himself
will, with knowledge in
unknowing,
always be transcending.

And if you should want to hear:
this highest knowledge lies
in the loftiest sense
of the essence of God;
this is a work of his mercy,
to leave one without
understanding,
transcending all knowledge.

Stanzas of the Soul That Suffers with Longing to See God.

I live, but not in myself,
and I have such hope
that I die because I do not die.

I no longer live within myself
and I cannot live without God,
for having neither him nor myself
what will life be?
It will be a thousand deaths,
longing for my true life
and dying because I do not die.

This life that I live
is no life at all,
and so I die continually
until I live with you;
hear me, my God:
I do not desire this life,
I am dying because I do not die.

When I am away from you
what life can I have
except to endure
the bitterest death known?
I pity myself,
for I go on and on living,
dying because I do not die.

A fish that leaves the water
has this relief:
the dying it endures
ends at last in death.
What death can equal my pitiable life?

For the longer I live, the more drawn out is my dying.

When I try to find relief
seeing you in the Sacrament,
I find this greater sorrow:
I cannot enjoy you wholly.
All things are affliction
since I do not see you as I desire,
and I die because I do not die.

And if I rejoice, Lord,
in the hope of seeing you,
yet seeing I can lose you
doubles my sorrow.
Living in such fear
and hoping as I hope,
I die because I do not die.

Lift me from this death,
my God, and give me life;
do not hold me bound
with these bonds so strong;
see how I long to see you;
my wretchedness is so complete
that I die because I do not die.

I will cry out for death
and mourn my living
while I am held here
for my sins.
O my God, when will it be
that I can truly say:
now I live because I do not die?

Stanzas Given a Spiritual Meaning.

I went out seeking love,
and with unfaltering hope
I flew so high, so high,
that I overtook the prey.

That I might take the prey
of this adventuring in God
I had to fly so high
that I was lost from sight;
and though in this adventure
I faltered in my flight,
yet love had already flown so high
that I took the prey.

When I ascended higher
my vision was dazzled,
and the most difficult conquest
came about in darkness;
but since I was seeking love
the leap I made was blind and dark,
and I rose so high, so high,
that I took the prey.

The higher I ascended
in this seeking so lofty
the lower and more subdued
and abased I became.
I said: No one can overtake it!
And sank, ah, so low,
that I was so high, so high,
that I took the prey.

In a wonderful way
my one flight surpassed a
thousand,

for the hope of heaven
attains as much as it hopes for;
this seeking is my only hope,
and in hoping, I made no mistake,
because I flew so high, so high,
that I took the prey.

Stanzas Applied Spiritually to Christ and the Soul

A lone young shepherd lived in pain
withdrawn from pleasure and contentment,
his thoughts fixed on a
shepherd-girl
his heart an open wound with love.

He weeps, but not from the wound of love,
there is no pain in such affliction,
even though the heart is pierced;
he weeps in knowing he's been forgotten.

That one thought: his shining one
has forgotten him, is such great pain
that he bows to brutal handling in a foreign land,
his heart an open wound with love.

The shepherd says: I pity the one
who draws herself back from my love,
and does not seek the joy of my presence,
though my heart is an open wound with love for her.

After a long time he climbed a tree,
and spread his shining arms,
and hung by them, and died,

On the Communication Among the Three Persons.

In that immense love
proceeding from the two
the Father spoke words
of great affection to the Son,
words of such profound delight
that no one understood them;
they were meant for the Son,
and he alone rejoiced in them.

What he heard
was this:
"My Son, only your
company contents me,
and when something pleases me
I love that thing in you;
whoever resembles you most
satisfies me most,
and whoever is like you in nothing
will find nothing in me.
I am pleased with you alone,
O life of my life!
You are the light of my light,
you are my wisdom,
the image of my substance
in whom I am well pleased.
My Son, I will give myself
to him who loves you
and I will love him
with the same love I have for you,
because he has loved
you whom I love so."

On creation.

"My Son, I wish to give you
a bride who will love you.
Because of you she will deserve
to share our company,
and eat at our table,
the same bread I eat,
that she may know the good
I have in such a Son;
and rejoice with me
in your grace and fullness."
"I am very grateful,"
the Son answered;
"I will show my brightness
to the bride you give me,
so that by it she may see
how great my Father is,
and how I have received
my being from your being.
I will hold her in my arms
and she will burn with your love,
and with eternal delight
she will exalt your goodness."
"Let it be done, then," said the Father,
for your love has deserved it.
And by these words
the world was created,
a palace for the bride
made with great wisdom
and divided into rooms,
one above, the other below.
The lower was furnished
with infinite variety,
while the higher was made
beautiful
with marvelous jewels,
that the bride might know
the Bridegroom she had.
The orders of angels
were placed in the higher,
but humanity was given
the lower place,
for it was, in its being,
a lesser thing.

And though beings and places
were divided in this way,
yet all form one,
who is called the bride;
for love of the same Bridegroom
made one bride of them.
Those higher ones possessed
the Bridegroom in gladness;
the lower in hope, founded
on the faith that he infused in them,
telling them that one day
he would exalt them,
and that he would lift them
up from their lowness
so that no one
could mock it any more;
for he would make himself
wholly like them,
and he would come to them
and dwell with them;
and God would be man
and man would be God,
and he would walk with them
and eat and drink with them;
and he himself would be
with them continually
until the consummation
of this world,
when, joined, they would rejoice
in eternal song;
for he was the Head
of this bride of his
to whom all the members
of the just would be joined,
who form the body of the bride.
He would take her
tenderly in his arms
and there give her his love;
and when they were thus one,
he would lift her to the Father
where God's very joy
would be her joy.
For as the Father and the Son

and he who proceeds from them
live in one another,
so it would be with the bride;
for, taken wholly into God,
she will live the life of God.
By this bright hope
which came to them from above,
their wearying labors
were lightened;
but the drawn-out waiting
and their growing desire
to rejoice with their Bridegroom
wore on them continually.
So, with prayers
and sighs and suffering,
with tears and moanings
they asked night and day
that now he would determine
to grant them his company.
Some said: "If only
this joy would come in my time!"
Others: "Come, Lord,
send him whom you will send!"
And others: "Oh, if only these heavens
would break, and with my own eyes
I could see him descending;
then I would stop my crying out."
"Oh, clouds, rain down from your height,
earth needs you,
and let the earth open,
which has borne us thorns;
let it bring forth that flower
that would be its flowering."
Others said: "What gladness
for him who is living then,
who will be able to see God
with his own eyes,
and touch him with his hand
and walk with him
and enjoy the mysteries
which he will then ordain."
In these and other prayers
a long time had passed;

but in the later years
their fervor swelled and grew
when the aged Simeon
burned with longing,
and begged God that he
might see this day.
And so the Holy Spirit
answering the good old man
gave him his word
that he would not see death
until he saw Life
descending from the heights,
until he took God himself
into his own hands
and holding him in his arms,
pressed him to himself.

The Incarnation
Now that the time had come
when it would be good
to ransom the bride
serving under the hard yoke
of that law
which Moses had given her,
the Father, with tender love,
spoke in this way:
"Now you see, Son, that your bride
was made in your image,
and so far as she is like you
she will suit you well;
yet she is different, in her flesh,
which your simple being does not have.
In perfect love
this law holds:
that the lover become
like the one he loves;
for the greater their likeness
the greater their delight.
Surely your bride's delight
would greatly increase
were she to see you like her,
in her own flesh."
"My will is yours,"

the Son replied,
"and my glory is
that your will be mine.
This is fitting, Father,
what you, the Most High, say;
for in this way
your goodness will be more
evident,
your great power will be seen
and your justice and wisdom.
I will go and tell the world,
spreading the word
of your beauty and sweetness
and of your sovereignty.
I will go seek my bride
and take upon myself
her weariness and labors
in which she suffers so;
and that she may have life,
I will die for her,
and lifting her out of that deep,
I will restore her to you."
Then he called
the archangel Gabriel
and sent him to
the virgin Mary,
at whose consent
the mystery was wrought,
in whom the Trinity
clothed the Word with flesh.
and though Three work this,
it is wrought in the One;
and the Word lived incarnate
in the womb of Mary.
And he who had only a Father
now had a Mother too,
but she was not like others
who conceive by man.
From her own flesh
he received his flesh,
so he is called
Son of God and of man.

The Birth
When the time had come
for him to be born,
he went forth like the
bridegroom
from his bridal chamber,
embracing his bride,
holding her in his arms,
whom the gracious Mother
laid in a manger
among some animals
that were there at that time.
Men sang songs
and angels melodies
celebrating the marriage
of Two such as these.
But God there in the manger
cried and moaned;
and these tears were jewels
the bride brought to the
wedding.
The Mother gazed in sheer wonder
on such an exchange:
in God, man's weeping,
and in man, gladness,
to the one and the other
things usually so strange.
Finis

A Gloss (With Spiritual Meaning)

Without support yet with support,
living without light, in darkness,
I am wholly being consumed. 1. My soul is disentangled
from every created thing
and lifted above itself
in a life of gladness
supported only in God.
So now it can be said
that I most value this:
My soul now sees itself
without support yet with support.

And though I suffer darknesses
in this mortal life,
that is not so hard a thing;
for even if I have no light
I have the life of heaven.
For the blinder love is
the more it gives such life,
holding the soul surrendered,
living without light in darkness.

After I have known it
love works so in me
that whether things go well or badly
love turns them to one sweetness
transforming the soul in itself.
And so in its delighting flame
which I am feeling within me,
swiftly, with nothing spared,
I am wholly being consumed.

A Gloss
Not for all of beauty
will I ever lose myself,

but for I-don't-know-what
which is so gladly gained.

Delight in the world's good things
at the very most
can only tire the appetite
and spoil the palate;
and so, not for all of sweetness
will I ever lose myself,
but for I-don't-know-what
which is so gladly found.

The generous heart
never delays with easy things
but eagerly goes on
to things more difficult.
Nothing satisfies it,
and its faith ascends so high
that it tastes I-don't-know-what
which is so gladly found.

He who is sick with love,
whom God himself has touched,
finds his tastes so changed
that they fall away
like a fevered man's
who loathes any food he sees
and desires I-don't know-what
which is so gladly found.

Do not wonder
that the taste should be left like this,
for the cause of this sickness
differs from all others;
and so he is withdrawn
from all creatures,
and tastes I-don't-know-what
which is so gladly found.

For when once the will
is touched by God himself,
it cannot find contentment
except in the Divinity;

but since his Beauty is open
to faith alone, the will
tastes him in I-don't-know-what
which is so gladly found.

Tell me, then, would you pity
a person so in love,
who takes no delight
in all creation;
alone, mind empty of form and figure,
finding no support or foothold,
he tastes there I-don't-know-what
which is so gladly found.

Do not think that he who lives
the so-precious inner life
finds joy and gladness
in the sweetness of the earth;
but there beyond all beauty
and what is and will be and was,
he tastes I-don't-know-what
which is so gladly found.

Whoever seeks to advance
takes much more care
in what he has yet to gain
than in what he has already gained;
and so I will always tend
toward greater heights;
beyond all things, to I-don't-know- what
which is so gladly found.

I will never lose myself
for that which the senses
can take in here,
nor for all the mind can hold,
no matter how lofty,
nor for grace or beauty,
but only for I-don't-know-what
which is so gladly found.

Christmas Refrain
The Virgin, weighed

with the Word of God,
comes down the road:
if only you'll shelter her.

The Sum of Perfection
Forgetfulness of created things,
remembrance of the Creator,
attention turned toward inward things,
and loving the Beloved.

Full of Hope I Climbed the Day

Full of hope I climbed the day
while hunting the game of love,
and soared so high, high above
that at last caught my prey.

In order to seize the game
— the divine love in the sky —
I had to fly so high, high
I floated unseen and became
lost in that dangerous day;
and so my flight fell short of
height — yet so high was my love
that I at last caught my prey.

Dazzled and stunned by light
as I rose nearer the sun,
my greatest conquest was won
in the very black of night.
Yet since love opened my way
I leapt dark, blindly above
and was so high, near my love,
that at last I caught my prey.

In this most exalted quest
the higher I began to soar
the lower I felt — more sore
and broken and depressed.
I said: None can seize the prey!
and groveled so low, so low
that high, higher did I go,
and at last I caught my prey.

By strange reckoning I saw
a thousand flights in one flight;
for hope of heavenly light

is achieved by hoping now.
I hoped only for this way
and was right to wait for love,
and climbed so high, high above
that at last I caught my prey.

I Came into the Unknown

I came into the unknown
and stayed there unknowing
rising beyond all science.

I did not know the door
but when I found the way,
unknowing where I was,
I learned enormous things,
but what I felt I cannot say,
for I remained unknowing,
rising beyond all science.

It was the perfect realm
of holiness and peace.
In deepest solitude
I found the narrow way:
a secret giving such release
that I was stunned and stammering,
rising beyond all science.

I was so far inside,
so dazed and far away
my senses were released
from feelings of my own.
My mind had found a surer way:
a knowledge of unknowing,
rising beyond all science.

And he who does arrive
collapses as in sleep,
for all he knew before
now seems a lowly thing,
and so his knowledge grows so deep
that he remains unknowing,
rising beyond all science.

The higher he ascends
the darker is the wood;
it is the shadowy cloud
that clarified the night,
and so the one who understood
remains always unknowing,
rising beyond all science.

This knowledge by unknowing
is such a soaring force
that scholars argue long
but never leave the ground.
Their knowledge always fails the source:
to understand unknowing,
rising beyond all science.

This knowledge is supreme
crossing a blazing height;
though formal reason tries
it crumbles in the dark,
but one who would control the night
by knowledge of unknowing
will rise beyond all science.

And if you wish to hear:
the highest science leads
to an ecstatic feeling
of the most holy Being;
and from his mercy comes his deed:
to let us stay unknowing,
rising beyond all science.

I Live Yet Do Not Live in Me

I live yet do not live in me,
am waiting as my life goes by,
and die because I do not die.

No longer do I live in me,
and without God I cannot live;
to him or me I cannot give
my self, so what can living be?
A thousand deaths my agony
waiting as my life goes by,
dying because I do not die.

This life I live alone I view
as robbery of life, and so
it is a constant death — with no
way out until I live with you.
God, hear me, what I say is true:
I do not want this life of mine,
and die because I do not die.

Being so removed from you I say
what kind of life can I have here
but death so ugly and severe
and worse than any form of pain?
I pity me — and yet my fate
is that I must keep up this lie,
and die because I do not die.

The fish taken out of the sea
is not without a consolation:
his dying is of brief duration
and ultimately brings relief.
Yet what convulsive death can be
as bad as my pathetic life?
The more I live the more I die.

When I begin to feel relief
on seeing you in the sacrament,
I sink in deeper discontent,
deprived of your sweet company.
Now everything compels my grief:
I want — yet can't — see you nearby,
and die because I do not die.

Although I find my pleasure, Sir,
in hope of someday seeing you,
I see that I can lose you too,
which makes my pain doubly severe,
and so I live in darkest fear,
and hope, wait as life goes by,
dying because I do not die.

Deliver me from death, my God,
and give me life; now you have wound
a rope about me; harshly bound
I ask you to release the cord.
See how I die to see you, Lord,
and I am shattered where I lie,
dying because I do not die.

My death will trigger tears in me,
and I shall mourn my life: a day
annihilated by the way
I fail and sin relentlessly.
O Father God, when will it be
that I can say without a lie:
I live because I do not die?

Love's Living Flame

(Songs that the soul sings in her intimate union with God, her beloved
Bridegroom.)
O Love's living flame,
Tenderly you wound
My soul's deepest center!
Since you no longer evade me,
Will you, please, at last conclude:
Rend the veil of this sweet encounter!

O cautery so tender!
O pampered wound!
O soft hand! O touch so delicately strange,
Tasting of eternal life
And canceling all debts!
Killing, death into life you change!

O lamps of fiery lure,
In whose shining transparence
The deep cavern of the senses,
Blind and obscure,
Warmth and light, with strange flares,
Gives with the lover's caresses!

How tame and loving
Your memory rises in my breast,
Where secretly only you live,
And in your fragrant breathing,
Full of goodness and grace,
How delicately in love you make me feel!

The Fountain

How well I know that flowing spring
in black of night.

The eternal fountain is unseen.
How well I know where she has been
in black of night.

I do not know her origin.
None. Yet in her all things begin
in black of night.

I know that nothing is so fair
and earth and firmament drink there
in black of night.

I know that none can wade inside
to find her bright bottomless tide
in black of night.

Her shining never has a blur;
I know that all light comes from her
in black of night.

I know her streams converge and swell
and nourish people, skies and hell
in black of night.

The stream whose birth is in this source
I know has a gigantic force
in black of night.

The stream from but these two proceeds
yet neither one, I know, precedes
in black of night.

The eternal fountain is unseen
in living bread that gives us being
in black of night.

She calls on all mankind to start
to drink her water, though in dark,
for black is night.

O living fountain that I crave,
in bread of life I see her flame in black of night.

The Sum of Perfection

Creation forgotten,
Creator only known,
Attention turned inward
In love with the Beloved alone.

Without a Place and With a Place

Without a place and with a place
to rest — living darkly with no ray
of light — I burn my self away.

My soul — no longer bound — is free
from the creations of the world;
above itself it rises hurled
into a life of ecstasy,
leaning only on God. The world
will therefore clarify at last
what I esteem of highest grace:
my soul revealing it can rest
without a place and with a place.

Although I suffer a dark night
in mortal life, I also know
my agony is slight, for though
I am in darkness without light,
a clear heavenly life I know;
for love gives power to my life,
however black and blind my day,
to yield my soul, and free of strife
to rest — living darkly with no ray.

Love can perform a wondrous labor
which I have learned internally,
and all the good or bad in me
takes on a penetrating savor,
changing my soul so it can be
consumed in a delicious flame.
I feel it in me as a ray;
and quickly killing every trace
of light — I burn my self away.

On the Communion of the Three Persons (from Romance on the Gospel)

Out of the vast love
born of them both,
the Father spoke to the Son
with words of celebration,

with words of such full delight
that none can know;
only the Son, only he took joy,
since they were breathed in his ear alone.

But here is what
can be understood:
— "Nothing, my Son, pleases me,
but your company.

"If something is sweet,
through you alone do I taste it.
The more of you I see in its reflection,
the wider my smile;

"What is unlike you,
has nothing of me.
In you alone is my delight,
life of my life!

"You are the fire of my fire,
my knowing;
the form of my substance,
in you am I well pleased.

"Whoever gives his love to you, my Son,
to him I give myself,
and him I fill

with the love I feel for you
just for making you beloved,
my Beloved."

A Spiritual Canticle of the Soul and the Bridegroom Christ

The Bride
Where have You hidden Yourself,
And abandoned me in my groaning, O my Beloved?
You have fled like the hart,
Having wounded me.
I ran after You, crying; but You were gone.

O shepherds, you who go
Through the sheepcots up the hill,
If you shall see Him
Whom I love the most,
Tell Him I languish, suffer, and die.

In search of my Love
I will go over mountains and strands;
I will gather no flowers,
I will fear no wild beasts;
And pass by the mighty and the frontiers.

O groves and thickets
Planted by the hand of the Beloved;
O verdant meads
Enameled with flowers,
Tell me, has He passed by you?

Answer of the Creatures
A thousand graces diffusing
He passed through the groves in haste,
And merely regarding them
As He passed
Clothed them with His beauty.

The Bride
Oh! who can heal me?

Give me at once Yourself,
Send me no more
A messenger
Who cannot tell me what I wish.

All they who serve are telling me
Of Your unnumbered graces;
And all wound me more and more,
And something leaves me dying,
I know not what, of which they are darkly speaking.

But how you persevere, O life,
Not living where you live;
The arrows bring death
Which you receive
From your conceptions of the Beloved.

Why, after wounding
This heart, have You not healed it?
And why, after stealing it,
Have You thus abandoned it,
And not carried away the stolen prey?

Quench my troubles,
For no one else can soothe them;
And let my eyes behold You,
For You are their light,
And I will keep them for You alone.

Reveal Your presence,
And let the vision and Your beauty kill me,
Behold the malady
Of love is incurable
Except in Your presence and before Your face.

O crystal well!
Oh that on Your silvered surface
You would mirror forth at once
Those eyes desired
Which are outlined in my heart!

Turn them away, O my Beloved!
I am on the wing:

The Bridegroom
Return, My Dove!
The wounded hart
Looms on the hill
In the air of your flight and is refreshed.

My Beloved is the mountains,
The solitary wooded valleys,
The strange islands,
The roaring torrents,
The whisper of the amorous gales;

The tranquil night
At the approaches of the dawn,
The silent music,
The murmuring solitude,
The supper which revives, and enkindles love.

Catch us the foxes,
For our vineyard has flourished;
While of roses
We make a nosegay,
And let no one appear on the hill.

O killing north wind, cease!
Come, south wind, that awakens love!
Blow through my garden,
And let its odors flow,
And the Beloved shall feed among the flowers.

O nymphs of Judea!
While amid the flowers and the rose-trees
The amber sends forth its perfume,
Tarry in the suburbs,
And touch not our thresholds.

Hide yourself, O my Beloved!
Turn Your face to the mountains,
Do not speak,
But regard the companions
Of her who is traveling amidst strange islands.

The Bridegroom
Light-winged birds,
Lions, fawns, bounding does,
Mountains, valleys, strands,
Waters, winds, heat,
And the terrors that keep watch by night;

By the soft lyres
And the siren strains, I adjure you,
Let your fury cease,
And touch not the wall,
That the bride may sleep in greater security.

The bride has entered
The pleasant and desirable garden,
And there reposes to her heart's content;
Her neck reclining
On the sweet arms of the Beloved.

Beneath the apple-tree
There were you betrothed;
There I gave you My hand,
And you were redeemed
Where your mother was corrupted.

The Bride
Our bed is of flowers
By dens of lions encompassed,
Hung with purple,
Made in peace,
And crowned with a thousand shields of gold.

In Your footsteps
The young ones run Your way;
At the touch of the fire
And by the spiced wine,
The divine balsam flows.

In the inner cellar
Of my Beloved have I drunk; and when I went forth
Over all the plain

I knew nothing,
And lost the flock I followed before.

There He gave me His breasts,
There He taught me the science full of sweetness.
And there I gave to Him
Myself without reserve;
There I promised to be His bride.

My soul is occupied,
And all my substance in His service;
Now I guard no flock,
Nor have I any other employment:
My sole occupation is love.

If, then, on the common land
I am no longer seen or found,
You will say that I am lost;
That, being enamored,
I lost myself; and yet was found.

Of emeralds, and of flowers
In the early morning gathered,
We will make the garlands,
Flowering in Your love,
And bound together with one hair of my head.

By that one hair
You have observed fluttering on my neck,
And on my neck regarded,
You were captivated;
And wounded by one of my eyes.

When You regarded me,
Your eyes imprinted in me Your grace:
For this You loved me again,
And thereby my eyes merited
To adore what in You they saw

Despise me not,
For if I was swarthy once
You can regard me now;
Since You have regarded me,

Grace and beauty have You given me.

The Bridegroom
The little white dove
Has returned to the ark with the bough;
And now the turtle-dove
Its desired mate
On the green banks has found.

In solitude she lived,
And in solitude built her nest;
And in solitude, alone
Has the Beloved guided her,
In solitude also wounded with love.

The Bride
Let us rejoice, O my Beloved!
Let us go forth to see ourselves in Your beauty,
To the mountain and the hill,
Where the pure water flows:
Let us enter into the heart of the thicket.

We shall go at once
To the deep caverns of the rock
Which are all secret,
There we shall enter in
And taste of the new wine of the pomegranate.

There you will show me
That which my soul desired;
And there You will give at once,
O You, my life!
That which You gave me the other day.

The breathing of the air,
The song of the sweet nightingale,
The grove and its beauty
In the serene night,
With the flame that consumes, and gives no pains.

None saw it;
Neither did Aminadab appear
The siege was intermitted,

And the cavalry dismounted
At the sight of the waters.